MW00783122

WHAT OTHERS ARE SAYING

I liked the study so much that I plan to teach it once a year to my congregation.
—Rev. Pete Giacalone, Senior Pastor, Rainbow Temple Assembly of God, McKeesport, PA

Knowledge is power! This study will equip the believer to survive the spiritual warfare they will encounter when a decision is made to follow a Christ-centered lifestyle.
—Oleen Eagle, Former President, Cornerstone TeleVision Network

Finally, a book that brings spiritual concepts down to a practical level. I used this study in my midweek Bible class and found it to be insightful, thought provoking, and extremely relevant—a real treat for every child of God.
—Rev. Dennis K. Campbell, Senior Pastor, Praise Assembly of God Church, North Versailles, PA

This study will help equip Christians to obtain victory in their battle with the powers of darkness in these last days!
—James F. Fitzgerald, President of WatchWORD Productions, the creator of the WatchWORD Bible

This course ought to be required for every Christian—especially new believers.
—Katie Burt, City Coordinator, Pittsburgh Prayer Network; Pa. State Coordinator, National Day of Prayer

Being a new believer, it helped me understand more about the Bible and the ongoing invisible war around us.
—Jim White, President of JBW & Associates, Spartanburg, SC

This study influenced me significantly and expanded my acceptance and understanding of spiritual warfare. The power of this course is the consistent and persistent use of Scripture as its foundation. This study provides a depth of information that brings the reality of spiritual warfare within the grasp of everyone.
—Michael Hurka, Controller, Green Key Books, Holiday, FL

This is basic training every Christian must have!! Having taken the course, I can tell you that the information presented in the DVD and workbook is priceless. Rest assured, you will get more than your money's worth with this study. **—Gary**

It helped me to see truth and gave me the tools to help me through tough times. **—Paul**

It opened my eyes to see how I can live victoriously in a world so saturated with the enemy's power and has enabled me to deal with life's situations with God's empowerment. **—Mary Anne**

This study does an excellent job of exposing the spiritual enemies we face and how to combat them with spiritual weapons. **—Kim**

This book gave me the tools needed to see clearly with my heart what my human eyes could not see. **—Lisa**

ABOUT THE AUTHOR

David Skeba

This DVD series and workbook are the result of more than 30 years of research and seeking God by David Skeba. His collective experience in seminary, as pastor, on-air Bible teacher, author, and former VP of Programming for a national Christian television ministry has uniquely prepared him to speak and write on the subject of spiritual warfare.

David and his wife, Mary Anne, have been married for 28 years. An avid student of the Bible, he continues to search for effective ways to communicate God's Word in simple, practical ways. His prayer is that through this study, you will discover the defensive and offensive weaponry God has provided and become empowered by God to Win the Invisible War.

For more information about David Skeba, visit www.DiscoverMinistries.com.

IN MEMORY AND DEDICATION

This book is dedicated to Professor Walter H. Beuttler D.D. (1904-1974) whose ministry I had the privilege of experiencing at Northeast Bible Institute near Philadelphia, PA. His teachings on satan, Job, and The Lord's Prayer are the foundation of this study on spiritual warfare. In fact, this book would not have been written if it were not for the impact of these teachings on my life. I want to thank his daughter Norma, and her husband Glenn, for giving me permission to incorporate his teachings into this workbook.

Walter H. Beuttler

If ever a person knew God's heart and was able to reveal it to His people, this man did. He cultivated an intimate relationship with Christ in a way few people ever have. He paid whatever price God demanded of him to have the anointing of the Presence of God when he taught and ministered. The Holy Spirit revealed to him gem after gem of spiritual truth to share with the Body of Christ—many times being awakened in the middle of the night. He left an impeccable legacy of how to live a godly life, and that it is possible for a human being to have an intimate walk with a holy God.

His death was a tremendous loss to the Body of Christ. He is sorely missed, even today, by those who knew and loved him. Through these teachings you, too, will be indirectly touched by this genuine man of God. May the Holy Spirit continue to anoint the basic truths He gave to this spiritual giant in the Faith.

SPECIAL ACKNOWLEDGMENTS

Special thanks to **Bishop Joseph L. Garlington, Sr., Ph. D.,** a precious gift to the Body of Christ, who took time out of his extremely busy schedule to support me by critiquing the content of this study, providing wisdom and valuable insights, and writing the Foreword.

Original Art Direction:	Done by my wonderful and talented wife, Mary Anne
Illustration of Roman Soldier:	Courtesy of Munn Art Studios. Used by permission.
The "hell scene" in Lesson 13:	Excerpt taken from the video, M10.28, produced by Lockhorn Limited. Used by permission.
	Videos may be obtained at www.M1028.com.
Roman Sword in Lesson 15:	Courtesy of ArmsofValor.com. Used by permission.
The Picture in Lesson 16: *"Genesis 3:15 The Promise Fulfilled"*	By James Robert Kessler (www.JimKessler.com) Used by permission.

THE ARMOR OF GOD

WINNING THE INVISIBLE WAR

by David Skeba

© Copyright 2006–by Discover Ministries

All rights reserved. This book is protected by the copyright laws of the United States of America. This book may not be copied or reprinted for commercial gain or profit. The use of short quotations or occasional page copying for personal or group study is permitted and encouraged. Permission will be granted upon request. Unless otherwise identified, Scripture quotations marked scriptures are taken from the New International Version (NIV). Scripture taken from the HOLY BIBLE: NEW INTERNATIONAL VERSION®. NIV®. Copyright © 1973, 1978, 1984 by International Bible Society. Used by permission of The Zondervan Corporation. Please note that Destiny Image's publishing style capitalizes certain pronouns in Scripture that refer to the Father, Son, and Holy Spirit, and may differ from some publishers' styles. Take note that the name satan and related names are not capitalized. We choose not to acknowledge him, even to the point of violating grammatical rules.

Scripture taken from the HOLY BIBLE: NEW INTERNATIONAL VERSION®. NIV®. Copyright © 1973, 1978, 1984 by International Bible Society. Used by permission of The Zondervan Corporation.

The "NIV" and "New International Version" trademarks are registered in the United States Patent and Trademark Office by International Bible Society.

Scripture quotations marked (**NIrV**) are Scripture taken from the HOLY BIBLE: NEW INTERNATIONAL READER'S VERSION®. NIrV®. Copyright © 1995, 1996, 1998 by International Bible Society. Used by permission of The Zondervan Corporation. The "NIrV" and "New International Reader's Version" trademarks are registered in the United States Patent and Trademark Office by International Bible Society.

Scripture quotations marked (**NLT**) are taken from the *Holy Bible*, New Living Translation, copyright © 1996. Used by permission of Tyndale House Publishers, Inc., Wheaton, Illinois 60189. All rights reserved.

Scripture quotations marked (**TLB**) are taken from the *Holy Bible*, The Living Bible Translation, copyright © 1971. Used by permission of Tyndale House Publishers, Inc., Wheaton, Illinois 60189. All rights reserved.

Scripture quotations marked (**NASB**) are taken from the NEW AMERICAN STANDARD BIBLE ®, copyright © The Lockman foundation 1960, 1962, 1963, 1968, 1971, 1972, 1973, 1975, 1977, 1995. Used by permission.

Scriptures quotations marked (**KJV**) are taken from the King James Version of the Bible.

Scripture quotations marked (**GNT**) are from the Good News Translation in Today's English Version – Second Edition © 1992 by American Bible Society. Used by Permission.

Scripture quotations marked (**NKJV**) are taken from the New King James Version. Copyright © 1979, 1980, 1982 by Thomas Nelson, Inc. Used by permission. All rights reserved.

Scripture quotations marked (**Phillips**) are taken from the New Testament in Modern English, translated by J. B. Phillips. Copyright © 1958, 1959, 1960, and 1972 by The Macmillan Company, and © 1983 by Harper Collins Publishers Ltd. All rights reserved. Reprinted by permission of HarperCollins Publishers Ltd.

Included in this work are excerpts from *Vine's Complete Expository Dictionary of Old and New Testament Words*. Used by permission of Thomas Nelson, Inc.

Zoom of New York City on the open of the videos courtesy of the NASA/Goddard Space Flight Center Scientific Visualization Studio. Used by Permission.

DESTINY IMAGE® PUBLISHERS, INC.

P.O. Box 310, Shippensburg, PA 17257-0310

"Speaking to the Purposes of God for this Generation and for the Generations to Come."

This book and all other Destiny Image, Revival Press, Mercy Place, Fresh Bread, Destiny Image Fiction, and Treasure House books are available at Christian bookstores and distributors worldwide.

For a U.S. bookstore nearest you, call **1-800-722-6774.**

For more information on foreign distributors, call **717-532-3040.**

Or reach us on the Internet: **www.destinyimage.com**

ISBN 10: 0-7684-3112-3   ISBN 13: 978-0-7684-3112-4

For Worldwide Distribution, Printed in the U.S.A.

2 3 4 5 6 7 8 9 10 11 / 17 16 15 14 13

TABLE OF CONTENTS

THE BREASTPLATE OF RIGHTEOUSNESS (continued)

THE HELMET OF SALVATION

SHOES FOR COMBAT

THE SHIELD OF FAITH

THE SWORD OF THE SPIRIT

PRAYER AND PRAISE

FOREWORD

When I read C.S. Lewis' second book in his space trilogy, I was genuinely intrigued by the gripping way he described the "warfare" a friend encountered during his journey to meet with Ransom, Lewis' main character. When Ransom asked his friend, "You got through the barrage without any damage?" I immediately recognized Lewis as one who had a deep understanding of the reality of spiritual warfare. This awareness by Lewis proves that true intellectuality and true spirituality are not mutually exclusive values, nor are they opposed to one another. In fact, in another classic work dealing with spiritual warfare, Lewis, speaking through one of the characters in the book, asserts that either ignoring these matters or giving entirely too much attention to them is our downfall.

The truth is this: spiritual warfare is real; it is not a byproduct of first century superstition nor is it an expression of twenty-first century religious fanaticism. In fact, it is an integral part of the normal Christian experience. Sadly, many Christians, on the one hand, live their entire lives unable to achieve the victorious Christian life they know is their inheritance—through ignorance. While on the other hand, other believers insist that their struggles are simply part of an emotional or psychological impotence.

Jesus said very simply, "You shall know the truth, and the truth will set you free." Let me paraphrase Jesus' words this way: "You shall know the truth, and *the truth you know,* will set you free." The Scriptures are filled with truths, however, the Church is filled with people who themselves are void of these same truths that can set them free. The Apostle Paul warned the Corinthians that satan had "schemes" and that the apostles were not ignorant of those schemes. He is reminding us that there is a satanic intelligence that is utterly opposed to our victory and eventual downfall.

Throughout the history of Christianity, in times of great need, God raised up teachers who were willing to press through where others were reluctant to go. These teachers found paradigms for failure and victory, and through their persistence and passion they discovered "a way through" for others. The Scriptures are filled with stories of battles, large and small, of warfare that requires strategy, planning, and great movement, and every victory was achieved by an understanding that "the battle is the Lord's."

When Elisha encouraged his fearful disciple with the words, "Do not fear, for those who are with us are more than those who are with them," he was alluding to the invisible combatants that are arrayed against us in the diabolical purposes of the evil one, but more appropriately, it is the sovereign affirmation of the promise of victory to every believer, that we are on the winning side.

There is a war; it is often invisible, but it is winnable and more believers are winning than ever in kingdom history. David Skeba has taken great pains to make available not just a "Survivor's Manual" but in actuality a "Manual for Victory." I had the joy of sitting with him for hours providing feedback as he conscientiously approached this project with a real desire to see believers set free. I commend his work to those in search of greater levels of victory.

Bishop Joseph L. Garlington, Sr., Ph. D.

Senior Pastor
Covenant Church of Pittsburgh

Presiding Bishop
Reconciliation Ministries International

INTRODUCTION

Thank you for choosing this study on spiritual warfare, and for the opportunity to present these eye-opening, life-changing truths to you. The purpose of this study is to give a true picture of the world we live in from God's perspective, gain a greater understanding of ourselves, reveal our enemies and their strategies, and gain insight into the weapons God has provided so we can overcome all of our spiritual adversaries. It is designed to be a spiritual survival guide to living victoriously on planet earth, the realm of satan's domain. These lessons are based on the spiritual armor God has provided in **Ephesians 6:10-18.**

Now please reflect for a moment on the day you were born. You "landed" on planet earth and began the process of discovering life's meaning and finding your place in this world. You became totally dependent upon a family to nurture you so you could receive the proper love, development, and instruction in truth for this formative stage of your life. Little did you know that from the moment you were conceived, you would live forever.

As you grew up, you needed major questions answered:

◆**Who am I?**　　◆**Where did I come from?**　　◆**What did I inherit from my ancestors?**
◆**Why am I here?**　　◆**Will my life's assignment make a contribution to mankind?**
◆**What sense can I make of this world?**　　◆ **Why is there evil in our world?**
◆**What worldview should I adopt and base my life upon?**
◆**Is my future predetermined, or can my choices determine my future?**　　◆**Where am I going?**

Biblical truths will be provided in this study to help you answer these important questions of life.

We all have developed our own perceptions of what the world is like, but are they accurate? Or do we believe things that aren't true? We view our perspectives through "tinted glasses" formed by our training and experience. However, I'm sure we all sense that something is not right with this world that God originally created *"good."*

The Bible is the **only** book on Earth that gives us a true and accurate picture of the world we live in. It also tells us all we need to know to successfully live our lives as we interact with the spirit world around us. The Bible is the **only** book that reveals satan's empire of evil, his tactics, and the nature of the spiritual warfare in which we find ourselves. In fact, every author of the New Testament affirms the reality of satan. And many of the passages in the New Testament that refer to satan, demons, and the world, come from the very lips of Jesus Himself! What greater authority can we have than He? *The Armor of God* contains over 1000 Scripture references to support its information.

The Bible says we share this planet with evil spiritual powers. So how do we go about dealing with forces we cannot see? How can we be safe from them? This study will bring awareness of all your spiritual enemies and how to deal with them so you can victoriously finish your journey on earth and live with God forever.

There is a school of thought that believes people who see the world clearly are sadder but wiser. This will be true of this study. The truths presented will greatly impact many of us who view our world in an innocent and naïve way. However, this study is intended to build your confidence, trust, and focus on Jesus Christ and His victory on the cross—not on the devil and his evil forces.

Some people mistakenly believe that if they don't bother the devil, the devil won't bother them, or that somehow he will leave them alone because they are Christians or because they are within the four walls of their churches. Others believe that satan and his forces are in hell and have no influence on the earth. And many believe that he doesn't even exist. You may have a great concern about thinking or talking excessively about the devil. Allow me to allay your fears. Whenever we study something new, there is a period of concentrated time on the topic. When that period is over, the concentration ceases and that which has been truly learned will instinctively be applied and lived out. So don't be uncomfortable learning about your adversaries. God wants and expects you to know these truths. This information is critical to understand, for it will save your life. God said, *"...my people are destroyed from lack of knowledge."* **(Hosea 4:6).**

There is a mighty spiritual war raging all around us. As the nations of Europe were drawn into WWI and WWII against their wills, likewise we are also drawn into this invisible war. You see, we are caught in the middle of satan's war against God's kingdom and we have the most to lose in this war. God will always be God. Satan's future doom is sealed, but the outcome of our lives is still being determined. We have become his targets. We are the prize. The battle is for our very souls! We either win big or lose big. Victory means heaven! Defeat means hell! It is imperative that we educate ourselves so that we triumph in the end.

Before engaging an enemy in combat, our armed service personnel enter boot camp and receive basic training and conditioning to prepare them for war. They are instructed to know their enemy—how they think, their tactics and operational procedures, and their weaponry. Ignorance in these areas could mean defeat or death. How much more is this true when dealing with our spiritual foes where greater eternal consequences are at stake?

The Armor of God will help you to develop the ability to win this conflict by equipping you with Bible-based information on how to recognize and overcome the world, the flesh, and the devil. You will learn how satan thinks, his tactics (over 30 are given), his targets, his motives and goals, and his weaponry. More importantly, you will learn of the defensive and offensive weaponry that God has provided so you can safely and victoriously overcome not only these invisible, powerful, and formidable foes, but also the enemy within us, our sinful nature, by the power of the Holy Spirit. This is basic training every Christian must have!

Expect to encounter opposition. There are truths contained in this study that satan, the enemy of your soul, does not want you to know. Therefore, you must determine not to allow him to rob you of them by keeping you from completing this study and from applying its truths. Don't be fearful, God is with you.

Some of the information you are about to study, you may already know. Some will be a revelation of new truth. Some may challenge your beliefs. Please be open to new concepts that may be contrary to what you already believe or have already been taught. Be willing to change and unlearn them if necessary. As with any teaching, accept only those things that have a Scriptural basis and to that which the Holy Spirit bears witness. You can have the confidence that God *"...will teach you all things and...guide you into all truth."* **(John 14:25; 16:13).** If you happen to disagree with something, the important thing is that after prayerfully considering all the Scriptures related to the topic, you finally decide on a position. God will speak to you through this study. These lessons will challenge your life, so be prepared to be honest with yourself and with God. If you then embrace these truths, they will radically change the way you think and act.

Finally, our struggle with evil forces cannot be successful apart from a vibrant relationship with Jesus Christ—the **only** Victor over satan—and also involvement with, and accountability to, other members of the Body of Christ. We are in this war together and we desperately need each other. We cannot survive living in isolation. In fact, that's what the devil wants. We are then most vulnerable. We also must know who we are in Christ in order to walk confidently in that knowledge and authority.

My prayer for you is: "Heavenly Father, I ask that through this study You will draw this person or group closer to You and help them to grasp this material. Open their eyes to their enemies and give them awareness and discernment. May it help them to walk in the victory that Your Son purchased on the cross. Give them the power to be triumphant over all their enemies—their sinful nature, the devil, and the world. Through the marvelous truths of Your Word, impact and transform their life and circumstances. Amen."

So without further delay let's put on the "glasses" of God's Word so that we can clearly and accurately view the world as He sees it. Then, walking in Christ's victory and power, use the spiritual weaponry He has provided to successfully engage this invisible war and prepare yourself for the perilous days ahead.

HOW TO USE THIS STUDY

Y ou are about to embark on a study that has the potential of bringing you closer to God, and of radically changing your thinking and behavior. To best accomplish this, it is important to approach these lessons with the guidelines given below. This study is designed to be used for individual use, for groups, and for Sunday school or midweek services. Recommendations for each follow.

I liken this study to a lake. You can skim its surface by doing the very minimum of watching the videos and reading each lesson's summary and the three appendices. This will give you an adequate overview of the message of the book. Or, you can descend as deep as you want to go by reading each page, highlighting truths that impact you, making your own notes, looking up Scripture references, and asking the Holy Spirit to enlighten you as you further contemplate the material. As with anything, you will only get out of this study what you put into it.

Actually, this workbook is designed to become more valuable to you **after** you complete the study. Whenever you encounter spiritual warfare, use it often as a reference book to gain a better perspective, awareness, and insight into your situation; to discern the tactic being used against you; and how God would direct you to respond in order to achieve victory.

In order for *The Armor of God* to have the greatest impact, I recommend the following approach:

1. First, decide on whether you will be using the workbook or the Lesson Handouts—or a combination of both. Lesson Handouts are a condensed version of each session and average five pages. They come with a table of contents that matches its own page numbering sequence. All that is needed is a 3-ring binder with a front plastic see-through sleeve to insert a picture of the cover. You can order Lesson Handouts from our website: www.TheArmorofGod.org.

2. If you are using the workbook, review the *Table of Contents* to get an overview of the study and what awaits you. Then be sure to read the *Introduction* and the remainder of this section, *How to Use this Study*.

3. Do only one lesson at a time in succession because each lesson builds upon the preceding one.

4. Some of the 16 lessons (2, 9, 12, 13, 14, 15, and 16) are broken down into two or three parts (that we'll call **sessions**) for a total of 24 weeks to complete the study (or three 8-week periods). It could also fit into two, 13-week terms totaling 26 weeks, allowing two extra sessions for flex or for **exams** (actually there are four quarterly exams which can be combined into two if need be or taken after Lessons 5, 10, 13, and 16; they can be obtained from www.TheArmorofGod.org). Allow the Holy Spirit to guide your pace.

5. **Home groups** should allow two hours for each session using the video and 1½ hours without it. Allot extra time if a devotional period is to be included before the session. **Individual users** will tend to go through the lessons more quickly because they don't have the discussion time that groups have.

6. A checkmark ☑ indicates important instructions. Please don't skip over them. Read them carefully.

7. Generally, words in bold typeface and in parentheses **(in bold typeface)** direct you to check the index under that name for more information on the topic.

8. The symbol **Q:** indicates a question that can be used for group discussion.

9. All Scripture references and verses are taken from the New International Version (NIV) of the Bible unless otherwise indicated. Symbols for other versions can be found on the copyright page (p. iv).

10. Following each lesson is a section called **Study Questions and Application** (SQ&A). It contains questions that either enlarge on a topic or ask you to evaluate areas of your life in relation to the material you just covered. A **Summary** concludes each lesson recapping the material and provides the answers to the blanks.

11. There are three **Appendices** that contain very important information. I will refer you to each of them at specific points in the lessons. **Appendix A** gives an overview of the occult—satan's religious systems. **Appendix B** deals with Counterfeit Christian Religions. **Appendix C** covers Christian Denominations That Hold False Essential Beliefs. You will not want to miss these insights. Finally, there is an **Index and Summary of satan's Tactics,** and a **Topical** and **Scripture Index.**

12. **DVDs** are available as a companion to this workbook. Sixteen 25 minute videos give an overview of each of the 16 lessons. They are a great add-on feature to the study that helps reinforce the material. A sample video clip can be viewed on my website. There is much more content that has been added to the workbook that is <u>not</u> on the video; however, all of the content on the video is contained in the workbook. The gray **vertical lines** with the DVD symbol to the left of the paragraphs denote what is on the video. Sections without this symbol contain the supplemental material. If you do not have the videos, don't be concerned. The videos are not needed in order to use this workbook successfully—just disregard the video references.

Note: DVDs or workbooks can be purchased separately from our website: www.TheArmorofGod.org.

A. After watching the video, pick up again at the checkmark ☑ where you left off and begin reading the material from the start to reinforce what you just learned. As you do, fill in the blank lines. The **answers are found in the Summary** at the end of each lesson. For your convenience, the word is underlined and numbered with the same number or letter as it appears in your lesson. I do <u>not</u> recommend using the video to obtain answers to the blank spaces because searching for the answer tends to become the focus and you will miss the truths I want to share with you. Also, due to the new material that was added, you'll be distracted by trying to keep up with where you are in the workbook.

13. **General Recommendations for Groups and Leaders:** There is no Leader's Guide for this study. Don't panic! Keep in mind that you don't have the pressure to teach or do extra time consuming research. Let the material do the work for you. Please refrain from paraphrasing the contents to the group. Instead, read it aloud word for word and allow it to speak for itself. Otherwise, you run the risk of not giving or misstating what the author intended. Simply oversee the proceedings, guide the discussion, and ensure all the material is covered within your time frame. Just follow these steps to get started:

A. **Preparation Before the First Meeting:**

(1) **Select a Leader:** One leader is the ideal. If your situation makes it difficult for one person to be the leader, perhaps certain capable members of the group can take turns leading. This distributes the workload so that all the responsibility doesn't fall on one person.

(2) **Select a Start and End Date:** Select a starting date common to all. Then determine the date of the final session of the study so the group knows in advance how long it will last. Look ahead on the calendar to see which days will conflict with holidays, vacations, etc., that may extend the study. Will you still meet that week? Plan accordingly. Be upfront with your group about the time commitment for the study. Two hours should be allotted for each session.

(3) **Workbooks:** Determine the number of workbooks you will need and get them into each member's hands at least <u>one</u> <u>week</u> <u>before</u> the first meeting. Tell them to read over everything up to the first page of Lesson 1 for the **Non-preparation Model** listed below. If the **Preparation Model** is chosen, also include Lesson 1 and pass along the other instructions given in this model.

(4) **Choose a Model:** Select one of the following models in conducting your study. Be sure all members agree to it before the first meeting. If you can't, then discuss it at the first meeting.

   • **Preparation Model:** As the name suggests, <u>all</u> members of the group pledge to study the lesson (without the video) **before** coming together. Then when you meet, begin each lesson by reading the first section, "Before starting the video." Next follow the directions for viewing the video designated by ☑. Review the video recommendations mentioned in point 12. After watching the video, begin at the first page of the lesson and, taking it a section at a time, encourage discussion of the material. Members should have already filled in the blank spaces. Ensure they have the correct word. Read whatever portions need to be emphasized. Ensure the material is covered thoroughly. Be led by the Holy Spirit. Complete each lesson by doing the Study Questions and Application and the Summary. Assign unfinished material as homework.

- **Non-preparation Model:** Due to busy schedules, members of the group come together each time without doing any prior studying. Begin each lesson by reading the first section, **Before Starting the Video**. Next, follow the directions about viewing the video (see point 12). After watching the video, pick up again on the first page at the checkmark ☑ where you left off and begin taking turns reading a section to reinforce what you just learned. Stop to answer questions and encourage comments. Provide answers to the blank lines from the Summary to save time. Assign Scripture references to members of the group, and when all have located them, begin reading them in order. Complete each lesson by doing the Study Questions and Application (SQ&A) and reading the Summary. Assign unfinished material as homework.

- **Sunday school or Midweek Service Model:** First decide whether each member of the class will have their own workbook (besides the instructor), or whether you will use our condensed **Lesson Handouts** instead. You can order them from our website: www.TheArmorofGod.org. Secondly, decide whether or not you will use the DVDs in your presentation. Each of the 16 videos is approximately 25 minutes. The study can be taught over two 13-week periods totaling 26-weeks, or in three 8-week sessions totaling 24 weeks. At the minimum, you can have a 16 week study by condensing the 16 lessons to fit the length of your class—preferably that lasts one hour.

(5) **Create an Effective Learning Environment:** Do this by producing the best seating arrangement to accommodate writing in a workbook and viewing videos. If videos are used, is the monitor large and high enough for all to see? Is there glare on the screen? Is the lighting right for viewing? Also, is the room temperature comfortable for all? Provide name tags, if desirable and extra pens or pencils. This all needs to be set up and tested **beforehand.**

(6) **Get Acquainted with the Material and the Video:** What are the main points that Lesson 1 is trying to convey? Prayerfully decide what points, if any, should be emphasized to meet specific needs of the group. Plan your approach. Also diligently pray for each member of your group—for the study, for wisdom, and for God's anointing. Do this for each lesson.

B. **At the First Meeting:** Introduce each member. If most have not done so yet, read together the **Introduction** and **How to Use This Study** up through point 12. Encourage them to look over the Table of Contents to get a feel as to what the study will cover. Allow more time for the first meeting.

(1) **Pacing:** Find the balance between thoroughly covering the material within your allotted time and the comments, questions, and needs of your group. Encourage discussion but avoid getting bogged down unnecessarily. Pace yourself so you ensure completion of the lesson. Keep things moving without rushing. Follow the Spirit's leading. Try not to exceed the two hour time commitment.

(2) **Answering Questions:** Try your best to answer any questions. For questions that fall outside the scope of the lesson, try looking up a key word contained in their question in the **Topical Index** to see if the study will address it later. If so, you won't have to take unnecessary time to deal with it during class. Wait until that section of the study if you can. If you don't know the answer, use the upcoming week to check the Topical Index to locate the answer, or try to get an answer from your pastor to present at the next session. If all else fails, e-mail us and we will be glad to try to provide answers to questions that you cannot handle (info@DiscoverMinistries.com).

EPHESIANS 6:10-18

...Be strong in the Lord and in his mighty power. [11]Put on the full armor of God so that you can take your stand against the devil's schemes. [12]For our struggle is not against flesh and blood, but against the rulers, against the authorities, against the powers of this dark world and against the spiritual forces of evil in the heavenly realms. [13]Therefore put on the full armor of God, so that when the day of evil comes, you may be able to stand your ground, and after you have done everything, to stand. [14]Stand firm then, with the belt of truth buckled around your waist, with the breastplate of righteousness in place, [15]and with your feet fitted with the readiness that comes from the gospel of peace. [16]In addition to all this, take up the shield of faith, with which you can extinguish all the flaming arrows of the evil one. [17]Take the helmet of salvation and the sword of the Spirit, which is the word of God. [18]And pray in the Spirit on all occasions with all kinds of prayers and requests...

Lesson 1
THE BELT OF TRUTH: Who Rules The World?

☑ Before starting the DVD:

Hopefully, you have already read the **Introduction** and **How To Use This Study.** If you have not done so, please read them now before beginning this lesson. The latter gives you options of how either single users or groups can approach and conduct this study. It also provides you with important information about the videos and the meaning of the symbols used throughout. Furthermore, a review of the **Table of Contents** will also give you an overall perspective of what to expect from the course.

The world is becoming an ever increasingly different and perilous place. We are approaching the beginning of the end times that the Bible foretells. As sinful deeds are increasingly committed, they unleash more demonic power into our nation and our world forcing God to lift His hand of protection. Therefore, it should behoove every one of us to learn how to defend ourselves in this invisible war and to prepare for the inevitable judgment of God.

God selected the analogy of the pieces of armor the Roman soldier wore in battle to describe the spiritual counterpart in the warfare of the believer. The belt (the *cingulim* or apron) was thought to be the first piece of armor the Roman soldier put on as he prepared for combat. We begin by gathering intelligence for this war with the Belt of Truth, which covers the next five lessons. The Belt represents the first step in preparation for spiritual warfare. **This involves a continual learning of biblical truth to counteract deception, and developing the proper attitudes for battle.**

Without a true picture of the way things really are, we are unable to have the proper perspective to convince ourselves that a war even exists, let alone be persuaded to engage in it and know how to fight it with the proper weapons. In this lesson, we will be looking at our world from God's perspective, and we'll discover it is not what it appears to be. Then I want to make you aware of our first enemy, satan, and his origin.

† **Ephesians 6:13-14**—*Stand firm then, with the belt of truth buckled around your waist.*

☑ **If you are using the DVD:** Before proceeding further in this workbook, I have a few introductory remarks to share with you about this series. Begin by viewing the **Introduction** on the DVD (3 min.). Then watch **Lesson 1** for an overview of this lesson (25 min.). Shortly into the video on Lesson 1, I will lead you in a prayer for God to make these truths real to you.

☑ When you're through, pick up again at this point. As you go through the material, fill in the blanks from the Summary at the end of this lesson.

HOW GOD SEES OUR WORLD

I'm sure you sense that there is something radically wrong with this world we live in although you may not be able to explain it. For example, **Q:** why is there evil, pain, suffering, injustice, and death in our world? Also, have you ever noticed that in the secular world apart from the church, the Body of Christ, there is almost complete silence about the God of the Bible? Sadly, His name is mainly used in cursing—especially in America. **Q:** Also, why is it that there is no worship given to His name, no seeking of His face, or knowledge of Him and His ways outside of His church? In light of Him being Creator and God, does this not seem strange to you?

> † **Ephesians 6:11-12** (TLB)—*Put on all of God's armor so that you will be able to stand safe against all strategies and tricks of Satan. For we are not fighting against people made of flesh and blood, but against persons without bodies; the evil rulers of the unseen world, those mighty satanic beings and great evil princes of darkness who rule this world and against huge numbers of wicked spirits in the spirit world.*

Who Actually Rules The World?

1. <u>M_____</u> has limited rule over the world system. However, mankind has the God-given authority to rule in these ways:

   A. As a steward over God's creation—the fish of the sea, the birds of the air and creatures on land—and the production of food **(Genesis 1:26-28; 2:15, 19-20).**

   B. The man is to love and rule his family **(Ephesians 5:22-6:4; 1 Corinthians 11:3, 8-9).**

   C. God has ordained human government to deter evil and restrain the devil by establishing moral laws to protect the rights of its citizens, keep order, bring justice, imprison offenders, and administer capital punishment **(Romans 13:1-6; Genesis 9:5-6).** However, most law enforcement officials are largely unaware that much of the evil they confront is caused by satanic spirits and that they are really fighting against demonic powers.

   D. To rule over citizens through political offices, but only as God sovereignly bestows upon one a period of rulership (i.e. **Daniel 2:21; 5:18-21; Isaiah 44:24, 28; 45:1-4; Judges 3:12-14; 2 Kings 19:20, 23-28).**

   > † **Daniel 4:17**—…*the Most High is sovereign over the kingdoms of men and gives them to anyone he wishes and sets over them the lowliest of men.*

   > † **Proverbs 21:1** (NLT)—*The king's heart is like a stream of water directed by the LORD; he turns it wherever he pleases.*

▶**CONSIDER THIS:** Aside from a sovereign selection by God, some leaders also come to power (and are removed) because God answered the prayers of His people. Prayer can change corrupt existing conditions. God can also arrange that an evil ruler comes to power as an act of judgment on that nation—giving the people what they deserve **(Zechariah 11:16).** However, I don't believe that every time a person rules over others that we can say it is God's will. Rulers can also come to power without God's involvement by the choice of the people (vote), by human appointment, by succession, by conspiring and scheming, and some by sheer brutal force. In addition, demonic spirits can bring a ruler to office and empower him **(Revelation 13:1-5)**. But when in office, a person can choose to rule using God's laws and principles, which brings God's blessings. Or he or she can rule out of their own self-interests which then opens the door for demonic power to work through that person and oppress the people **(Proverbs 29:2)**.

2. J_____ said that He does not rule the world system, but God ultimately has everything under His sovereign control.

   † **John 18:36**—*Jesus said: "My kingdom is not of this world...my kingdom is from another place."*

   A. Jesus referred to satan as the ruling *"p_____ of this world."* **(John 14:30; 12:31; 16:11)**

   † **Matthew 6:10**—Jesus taught us to pray *"...your kingdom come..."*

▶**CONSIDER THIS:** Why would Jesus instruct us to pray for His kingdom to come if it were already here? Jesus also taught us to include in our prayers, *"...deliver us from the evil one"* **(Matthew 6:13).**

   † **Luke 4:5-7**—*The devil led him* [Jesus] *up to a high place and showed him in an instant all the kingdoms of the world. 6. And he said to him, "I will give you all their authority and splendor, for it has been given to me, and I can give it to anyone I want to. 7. So if you worship me, it will all be yours."*

   † **Revelation 11:15**—*The seventh angel sounded his trumpet, and there were loud voices in heaven, which said: "The kingdom of the world has become the kingdom of our Lord and of his Christ, and he will reign for ever and ever."*

▶**CONSIDER THIS:** Christ's visible kingdom on earth has not yet occurred—it is still future. There would be no need to state that the kingdoms of this world have become our Lord's if they were already His and submitted to His rule! However, until that time, Jesus said His kingdom (the church) is being established within the hearts of people who enthrone Him as ruler over their lives **(Luke 17:20-21)**. The Body of Christ (His church) is composed of all truly *"born-again"* believers from every Christian denomination worldwide. Jesus said that the Church is in the world but distinct from it (see illustration), and that we should invade this system to rescue souls and influence its culture. For a Christian, this world is not our home, but we are responsible to do much more than "just pass through."

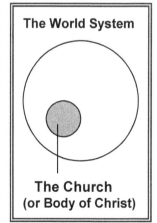

The World System

The Church (or Body of Christ)

   † **John 17:14-18** (NLT)—Jesus prayed, *15. "I'm not asking you to take them out of the world, but to keep them safe from the evil one. 16. They are not part of this world any more than I am...18. As you sent me into the world, I am sending them into the world."*

✝ **Colossians 1:13,16** (NLT)—*13. For he has rescued us from the one who rules in the kingdom of darkness, and he has brought us into the Kingdom of his dear Son.*

3. The Bible clearly states that satan rules the world system.

✝ **1 John 5:19**—*"...the whole world is under the control of the evil one."*

✝ **Matthew 12:24-28**—Jesus said satan has a kingdom: *26. "...How then can his kingdom stand?"*

✝ **Daniel 10:10-14, 20**—These verses seem to indicate that at least one top-ranked demonic spirit rules over each nation (in this case, *"the prince of the kingdom of Persia"* and *"the prince of Greece"*). They presumably are appointed by satan. These verses also infer that the human ruler(s) of that nation are secretly empowered by them.

✝ **2 Corinthians 4:4**—Satan is referred to as the *"god of this world"* (or age).

SATAN'S ORIGIN

Where did this person come from? What kind of person is he?

1. His original name was "L_____" **Isaiah 14:12** (KJV).

   A. His name means L_____ B_____. (Or *"morning star"* in some translations. He reflected God's glorious light—not his own).

2. He was "C_____" **Ezekiel 28:13,15**—a spirit personality without a physical body in the angelic class and does not possess divine attributes (also see **Psalm 148:2, 5-6**). He has:

   A. Intellect—*"he knows that his time is short"* (**Revelation 12:12**);—*"full of wisdom"* (**Ezekiel 28:12**).

   B. Emotion—he has wrath or *"fury"* (**Revelation 12:12,17**).

   C. Will—*"I will"* He was created with "free will" (**Isaiah 14:13-14**). Also see **2 Timothy 2:26**.

▶ **CONSIDER THIS:** These three components (intellect, emotion, and will) together with the "breath of life," make up the essence of a person—with or without a physical body. Just because we cannot physically see something does not mean it does not exist. For example, we continually inhale oxygen and exhale carbon dioxide, and can be killed from overexposure to carbon monoxide. These and other gases we cannot see or detect with our five senses. Radio and television frequencies are all around us, but only when we have the proper instrument to tune them in can we know that they are there. We cannot see the wind but can observe its effects. Why then should it be hard for us to believe in an invisible spirit world? Under normal circumstances, we cannot see God, angels, satan, or demons with our natural eyes, but nonetheless they do exist **(Luke 24:39).** We can discern them in our spirit, and some of our senses can detect their presence.

   D. He possesses the faculties of <u>speech</u>, <u>hearing</u>, <u>sight</u>, and has limited <u>power</u>.

3. He was a "C_____"—always keep in mind that he is no more than an angel **(Ezekiel 28:14)**.

4. He was "P_____" (sinless). God did not create him evil.

   † **Ezekiel 28:12,15**—*You were the model of perfection...blameless in your ways...*

5. He was the F_____ to S____—never to be pardoned by God.

   † **Ezekiel 28:15-17**—*...till wickedness was found in you. Through your widespread trade you were filled with violence, and you sinned... Your heart became proud on account of your beauty, and you corrupted your wisdom because of your splendor.*

   Note: Pride was the root cause of lucifer's downfall (see **1 Timothy 3:6; Proverbs 16:18**).

   † **1 John 3:8**—*He who does what is sinful is of the devil, because the devil has been sinning from the beginning.*

📖 DEFINITION—SIN (Iniquity)

The Old Testament uses the Hebrew word '*avel* or '*awla* meaning **unrighteousness** and it "refers to behavior contrary to God's character and against which He must respond."[1] The disease of leprosy also gives us a graphic picture of sin.

The New Testament uses the Greek word *hamartanō* which means "a missing of the mark."[2] This was a sporting term used when someone shot at a target and missed. They would in effect say, "You sinned." Also, in **2 Thessalonians 2:6-8,** the apostle Paul refers to *"the mystery of iniquity"* (KJV) or *"the secret power of lawlessness"* (NIV) that continues to work in our world as an enslaving, progressive evil. The apostle John also called sin *"lawlessness"* **(1 John 3:4).** Finally, there is the term "original sin" which refers to Adam genetically passing sin down to all of his descendants and indicates how sin entered our world **(Romans 5:12).**

The above definitions help us fix our definition for sin as: **"Behavior opposite to that of the character of God"**—a difference as vast as light is from darkness. Sin is character and it begins when self-will rebels against God, dethroning Him from reigning on the throne of one's heart, thereby making oneself God. This is what this high ranking defector, lucifer, did. He birthed sin and set it in motion as a law and principle. He "missed the mark" or purpose for which he was created by God. A created being is designed to be in subjection to his Creator. When one strays from this proper order, it is sin.

A. Let us review **Isaiah 14:13** and **14** (KJV) and learn how lucifer's self-deification manifested itself as rebellion against God as he aspired for:

   (1) Self-aggrandizement—*"I will ascend into heaven"*
   (2) Power—*"I will exalt my throne"*
   (3) Position—*"I will sit also in the mount"*
   (4) Supremacy—*"I will ascend above the heights"*
   (5) Equality with God—*"I will be like the most high"*

6. He F_____ from H_____—losing his position and becoming satan, the adversary.

 † **Luke 10:18**—Jesus said, *"I saw Satan fall like lightning from heaven."*
 Note: Jesus was there when it happened.

 † **Isaiah 14:12**—God said, *"How you have fallen from heaven, O morning star, son of the dawn* [Lucifer KJV]*! You have been cast down to the earth, you who once laid low the nations!"*

 † **Ezekiel 28:16-17**—God said, *"So I threw you to the earth."*

▶**CONSIDER THIS:** Though we don't know this for sure, it is quite possible that lucifer's original assignment (before he fell) was over our earth prior to the creation of Adam and Eve (see **Ezekiel 28:13; Luke 4:5-6**).

7. He U_____ R_____ over the earth (world system/social order).

 † **Genesis 1:26-28; 2:16-3:24**—This took place in the Garden of Eden.

 † **Luke 4:5-6** (GNT)—*Then the devil took him* [Jesus] *up and showed him in a second all the kingdoms of the world. 6. "I will give you all this power, and all this wealth," the devil told him. "It was all handed over to me and I can give it to anyone I choose."*

▶**CONSIDER THIS:** Who gave the devil this authority over the kingdoms of the world in verse six? Was it God, or Adam and Eve? Some hold the view that God had given lucifer the domain of the earth prior to his fall, which he then subsequently lost control of when he sinned, but regained it through Adam's rebellion in the Garden of Eden.

📖 **DEFINITION—USURP**

It means an illegal seizure of authority. Lucifer, who now became satan, obviously had his downfall prior to the creation of man and woman on earth. God created Adam and Eve in His image and likeness and designed that they would populate the earth, subdue it, and have dominion or rule over every living thing. God tested them by commanding them not to eat the fruit of the Tree of the Knowledge of Good and Evil. Satan beguiled them through the serpent. Adam and Eve disobeyed, ate the fruit, and in so doing handed over ruling control of the social order to satan—authority that God did not intend the devil to have. Through sin's enslavement, mankind now also became a captive of satan—a prisoner of war if you will **(2 Timothy 2:25-26)**.

▶**CONSIDER THIS:** Did lucifer's fall and subsequent usurping control over the earth take God by surprise? No!! God, being omniscient (all-knowing), foreknew this would happen. The moment God created angels and humanity with the power to choose whom they would serve, rebellion and evil became a possibility in the universe. The angels' decision to exalt themselves and not serve God was the beginning of sin and evil. **Q:** "Is God ultimately responsible for all the evil, injustices, pain, and misery that are so much a part of our world?" NO! They are the result of rejecting God's rule over our lives—a disaster we bring on ourselves and on others. "Free will," as we call it, is a sacred gift God has given to us all. God chose not to create automatons to worship and serve Him, but rather that His creation would freely choose to love and serve Him.

8. He was <u>D_____</u> by Christ 2000 years ago on the cross.

    A. Christ challenged satan's right to rule when He came down to earth.

        † **1 John 3:8b**—*...the reason the Son of God appeared was to destroy the devil's work.*

        † **Hebrews 2:14-15**—*Since the children have flesh and blood, he [Jesus] too shared in their humanity so that by his death he might destroy him who holds the power of death—that is, the devil—15. and free those who all their lives were held in slavery by their fear of death.*

▶**CONSIDER THIS:** Even though Christ defeated satan on the cross, His victory is not automatically passed down to all human beings. We have to take possession of Christ's victory and apply it to our lives by receiving Him as Lord and Savior. Have you done that? To which kingdom do you belong? And remember, although satan is a defeated foe, he can still defeat you after your conversion if you disobey God.

    B. When Jesus obtained victory over satan by His death on the cross and resurrection, He recaptured the rule over the social order that was usurped from Adam. But one might ask, "Why would Jesus have to die on the cross to defeat someone He created?" In God's wisdom and plan, satan is allowed to temporarily continue his rule over the world system (with limitations) until a future date when Christ literally returns to earth to rule the nations.

    C. Meanwhile during this church age, the Holy Spirit continues to proclaim Christ's victory through us. Those who respond will be rescued out of satan's kingdom of darkness and brought into the Kingdom of God which is now being established in the hearts of people **(Luke 17:20-21).**

    D. Attempts have been made to explain the existence of evil in our world. Some have misinterpreted God's decision to allow the devil and evil to continue as God being limited in His power with wickedness beyond His control (see **Finite godism** in index). Others explain evil as an ongoing, necessary coexistence of opposites (i.e. yin and yang), while most pantheists explain evil as an illusion because if all is god, how can evil be a part of god? (See **Pantheism** in index.)

    E. I agree that it is difficult to reconcile belief in a loving God who is perfect in every way with the injustices we see happening in our world. **DANGER ZONE!** We must be extremely careful to not find fault with God here. We must not place God in the role of defendant, with us as judge and jury—and satan as the prosecutor. If we do, our faith in God risks being permanently damaged and we could fall into the hands of the enemy of our soul. We must trust God and not accuse Him of what we might perceive to be imperfections in His character. We should also recognize that the source of evil lies within the hearts of men and that evil is personified by satan and his demons. We must trust God's character and what the Bible tells us about these matters.

    ☑ This ends the video content for Lesson 1.
    ☑ Continue on in this workbook for additional material **not** on the video.

DEMONIC SPIRITS

📖 DEFINITION—DEMON

In the New Testament the main Greek word for demon was *daimōn* which means "a knowing one." It "signified, among pagan Greeks, an inferior deity; whether good or bad. In the New Testament it denotes an evil spirit."[3] There is only one devil but many demons that follow and serve him. We battle against these fallen supernatural angelic beings.

1. Where did these demons come from? When lucifer defected, it seems that he was influential in persuading an indeterminable number of angels to side with him in his rebellion and hatred against God. They, like him, became "fallen angels." (Note: **Revelation 12:3-4** may be a reference to this, but it may also be interpreted as a future event). Nonetheless, the Bible states that they are with us on this earth **(Revelation 12:7-9; 9:14-16; Matthew 12:24; 25:41),** and they do the bidding of their master satan. They are not disembodied spirits of human beings.

2. The same fallen angels that fell from heaven with satan are still alive today. In fact, they will never die and just "go away," but will be cast into a future lake of fire. Until then, they are active in our world inflicting evil. Some fallen angels have been imprisoned **(2 Peter 2:4-5; Jude 1:6; 1 Peter 3:18-20).**

3. These once godly angels that sinned with satan also took on a character opposite of God's. The Bible tells us about some types of these spirits and what they are like:

   A. Evil spirits—a general term for them all **(Luke 8:2)**

   B. Unclean spirits—**Zechariah 13:2; Acts 5:16; Revelation 16:13-14**

   C. Lying spirits—**1 Kings 22:19-24**

   D. Spirits of fear—**2 Timothy 1:7**

   E. Spirits that torment—**1 Samuel 16:14-15**

   F. Seducing spirits—**1 Timothy 4:1**

   G. Spirits of divination—**Acts 16:16** (i.e. seeking supernatural knowledge apart from the true God)

   H. Spirits of error—**1 John 4:6** (i.e. doctrinal error see Lesson 15)

   I. Spirits of infirmity—**Luke 13:11; Mark 9:25**

   J. Spirits of prostitution—**Hosea 4:12; 5:4**

   K. Familiar spirits—**1 Samuel 28:7-8; Deuteronomy 18:9-12** (Also see index)

   L. Perverse spirits—**Isaiah 19:14**

4. What are some further aspects about satan and these "fallen angels" ¿

A. They are still persons with individual personalities who can se speak the various languages of mankind.

B. They retained all of the limited intelligence, power, and ur possessed before their fall, but now use them for evil.

† **Acts 10:38b**—[Jesus] *...went around doing good and healing au who were under the power of the devil...*

† **Acts 26:18**—*...turn them...from the power of Satan unto God...*

† **Job 1:12** (NASB)—God said to satan regarding Job: *"...all that he has is in your power..."*—he has the power to strategize and execute the plan he devised against Job.

C. They can recognize a person, observe their actions, hear their words, and differentiate between those who are God's servants and those who are not **(Acts 19:15; Mark 1:34).**

D. Satan has limited power over the elements of nature. In the case of Job, he caused the *"fire of God"* (possibly lightning) to burn up his sheep and servants **(Job 1:16;** also see **Revelation 13:13).** He also exercised his power to use wind as a destructive force— killing Job's children **(Job 1:19).**

E. To some degree, satan still temporarily retains the power to take life **(Hebrews 2:14).**

F. He and his demons have the ability to inflict physical sickness and disease. A *"spirit of infirmity"* may be the cause of mysterious or chronic types of illnesses. **(Job 2:7; Luke 13: 11-13; Matthew 12:22).**

G. He also has the power to heal or simulate healing **(Revelation 13:3,12,14).**

H. He has the power to seemingly give "life" to an inanimate object **(Revelation 13:15; Exodus 7:10-12).**

I. He and his fallen angels have the ability to inhabit the body of a human or animal (see **Demon possession** in the index).

J. He can cause some plagues, like frogs, to come upon a land **(Exodus 8:6-7).**

K. He and his demons can perform miracles and deceitful wonders through a human being **(2 Thessalonians 2:9-10; Revelation 13:13-14; 16:13-14).**

L. They have power to deceive, influence, and use people to carry out their evil intentions. **(Job 1:13-15; Acts 19:16).**

M. Demonic spirits oppress us—weighing down people with heavy burdens—physically, mentally, and spiritually by the wicked use of their power **(Acts 10:38).**

Wars among nations can be instigated by satan and his troops who are the unseen, unsuspected personalities energizing the rulers of nations to engage in battle **(Revelation 20:7-9).**

O. Satan can inspire rulers in their lust for position and power and then give them their power, position, and authority to rule over people to carry out his agenda **(Revelation 13:2,5,7).**

P. Demons are spiritual foes of unimaginable superhuman might especially when they team up and concentrate their power.

Q. Demons travel swiftly but are not omnipresent (everywhere at the same time). For example, it is doubtful that an evil spirit can attack Eric in St. Louis and Kathy in Pittsburgh at the same time **(Job 2:2; 1 Peter 5:8).** It is very likely that there is no geographical area on this planet where a human can flee that demons don't also have access. The sheer numbers of them and the speed in which they can travel in the spirit realm can network information and make it seem like they are everywhere.

R. Some, if not all, seem to have the capability to have sexual intercourse with human beings **(Genesis 6:1-4).** Also see: **Demonic spirits, human sexuality** in the index.

S. Although they are invisible spirit beings, demons can manifest themselves to our physical senses. Furthermore, we can recognize their activity like we can see the effects of the invisible wind.

T. They are highly organized and carry out their leader's assignments.

U. There are different degrees of wickedness among demons—just as they vary in power, rank, and authority **(Matthew 12:43-45).**

V. God has set general boundaries for what they can and cannot do. It seems that they can only oppress and enslave a person to the degree that person (or their parents) sins and invites them. We only need to read the crime statistics to see the extent of evil powers at work in our world through human beings.

▶**CONSIDER THIS:** There occur strange and inexplicable physiological, psychological, and circumstantial phenomena that may be manifestations of demonic power. We must use caution and not be quick to attribute these phenomena to dark forces. Some may be a trick or illusion, or have a natural explanation. Careful investigation and analysis must be made, and pray for discernment. For example, the source of physical and emotional problems could be physiological like a chemical or nutritional imbalance, etc. Circumstantial happenings, like one's car engine catching on fire, could be the result of failing to heed warning signs or do proper maintenance. However, if after we have thoroughly exhausted all possibilities and there is still no natural explanation for its source, then it may be of demonic origin.

The following examples are suspect: mysterious and chronic types of illnesses, abnormal depression, oppression, and fears; UFOs and claims of extra-terrestrial life; some crop circles (note: currently, most occur in the vicinity of Stonehenge in England); some incidences in the "Bermuda triangle" (the Atlantic Ocean between Bermuda, Miami, and San Juan, Puerto Rico); stigmatic wounds that ooze blood or other liquids; and spontaneous human combustion.

STUDY QUESTIONS AND APPLICATION

This section contains questions that either enlarge on a topic or ask you to evaluate areas of your life in relation to the material you just covered. Occasionally, you will be asked to evaluate yourself using a scale to see where you are on a given topic. Though you may feel that you fluctuate depending on the day or week, try to choose a number that represents your average. Then write the current month and year below the number you select on the scale so you can compare your growth (or lack of) should you answer the question again at a future time.

1. On the scale below indicate how you presently view satan and demonic forces. Consider "0" as a balanced view.

       You Look for   **You Ignore the Devil**
       the Devil   **as Though He Doesn't**
    "Behind Every Bush"   **Exist**

         5   4   3   2   1   0   1   2   3   4   5

    Note: A research pole taken by George Barna in 2004 showed what Americans believe about satan.[4]

    •   Three out of five adults (60%) say that the devil, or satan, is not a living being but is a symbol of evil, compared to 58% in 2001.

    •   50% of born again Christians deny satan's existence compared with 45% in 2001.

    •   Slightly more than seven out of ten Catholics (73%) say the devil is non-existent and only a symbol of evil.

2. Referring to question 1 above, identify at least one thing you could do to move yourself closer to the center. Then begin doing it.

3. How convinced are you that satan rules this world system?

    ☐ Strongly convinced   ☐ Somewhat convinced   ☐ Not convinced

4. God has designed three things to restrain sin and evil in a society. Read these Scriptures and name them:

    A. **Romans 2:14-15:** _____

    B. **Romans 13:1-5:** _____

    C. **2 Thessalonians 2:6-10:** _____

Note: Sin and evil will overrun a nation if these three fail to be the restraining influence God intended them to be: if we don't heed our conscience, if civil government lacks the will to enact Godly laws and enforce them, and if the church is complacent and her voice silent.

5. What are your honest thoughts about the following statements?

    A. **Q:** Why do you think God created the angels and mankind with free will when He knew they would make wrong choices?

    B. Jesus said, *"All power is given to me in heaven and earth."* **(Matthew 28:18).**

    Q: Why do you think God permits satan to continue usurping control over the kingdoms of this world (with all of its pain, suffering, injustices, and death) after Christ defeated him on the cross? **Q:** Why do you suppose God didn't stop it then before it got this far? (See **Revelation 11:15; 12:7-10; 19:6, 11-16; 1 Corinthians 15:24-25).**

6. Choose the one correct answer to this question regarding satan and his demons. (The answer is at the end of the Summary).

    ☐ A. They are stronger than mankind and almost as powerful as God.

    ☐ B. They are spirit personalities who now use the attributes they were created with for evil.

    ☐ C. Though fallen, they are still classified in the angelic category.

    ☐ D. All of the above

    ☐ E. Only B and C

    ☐ F. Only A and B

SUMMARY

This lesson began the explanation, and the putting on, of the full armor God has provided for us in this invisible war. The Holy Spirit directed the apostle Paul to use the analogy of the pieces of armor the Roman soldier wore in battle to describe the spiritual counterpart in the warfare of the believer. The belt (the *cingulim* or apron) was thought to be the first piece of armor the Roman soldier put on as he prepared for combat. It was the first step in his transition from relaxation to readiness for battle. It is said that the collective jangling sound made by the apron when the soldiers marched helped to strike fear into the enemy.

Its equivalent, the Belt of Truth, represents the first step in preparation for spiritual warfare. This involves acquiring knowledge of biblical truth and having the proper attitudes for battle. This truth gives us the proper perspective of the world around us, from God's viewpoint, and helps us engage this war with His weapons and methods enabling us to be victorious.

I'm sure you sense that there is something radically wrong with this world we live in although you may not be able to explain it. Why is there evil, pain, suffering, and injustice in our world? Why do bad things happen to good people? Why is it that in the secular world apart from the church, the Body of Christ, there is almost complete silence about the God of the Bible—except primarily in cursing? Why is it that there is also no worship given to His name, no seeking of His face, or knowledge of Him and His ways outside of the church? In light of Him being Creator and God, does this not seem rather strange to you?

The Bible reveals that **1.** <u>mankind</u> really doesn't rule this world system but has the God-given authority to rule in some limited ways: as a steward over God's creation, over his family, and human government to restrain evil. **2.** <u>Jesus</u> said that He doesn't rule it—but ultimately He has all things under His sovereign control. However, the Bible clearly states that satan is *"the god of this world."* Jesus referred to satan as the ruling **2A.** *"<u>prince</u> of this world."*

Until Christ's visible kingdom on earth arrives, Jesus said His kingdom (the Church or the Body of Christ) is being established within the hearts of people. It is made up of all truly *"born again"* believers from every Christian denomination worldwide. Jesus said that the church is in the world but distinct from it, and that we should invade this system to rescue souls and influence its culture.

We learned who satan is, where he came from, and what he is like. His original name was **1.** "<u>lucifer</u>" meaning **1A.** <u>light</u> <u>bearer</u>. He was **2.** "<u>created</u>" a **3.** "<u>cherub</u>" in the angelic class with the power of free will. He was also created **4.** "<u>perfect</u>" and given person-like qualities such as intelligence, emotion, and choice along with the faculties of speech, hearing, sight, and limited power. We're not dealing here with a metaphor or principle of evil, or a "personified symbol of sin," or an "impersonal force," or a "mythological figure." Neither is this a product of superstition from the Middle Ages. We're dealing with a real spiritual being living today in the 21st century who is bent on evil and destruction!

At some point in his life prior to the creation of Adam and Eve, lucifer desired to *"...be like the most high"* **(Isaiah 14:14)**—the foolish, self-delusive quest to become equal with God. Through his rebellion he became the **5.** <u>first</u> to <u>sin</u> which is "behavior opposite to that of the character of God." He **6.** <u>fell</u> from <u>heaven</u> and was expelled from his heavenly position and cast down to earth. Later, when Adam and Eve were created, satan (lucifer's new name meaning "adversary") was present to deceive them into disobeying God.

The dominion over the social order that God intended for man to have was now relinquished to satan. In this way, satan **7.** <u>usurped</u> <u>rule</u> over the earth (world system/social order). The angels that rebelled with him, now known as demons, serve their master satan here on earth. Six thousand years after Adam's fall, satan and his fellow angels are still, as Dr. Hal Lindsey says, "alive and well on planet earth"—seeking whom they may devour. But God was not taken by surprise. He foreknew the disaster would occur because the moment God gave His creation free will, the possibility of evil and rebellion came into being.

When Adam sinned, God began a godly genealogical line that 4,000 years later He would use to insert His sinless Son, Jesus Christ, into this hostile world through the virgin birth. Jesus would defeat satan by His perfect life, His death on the cross, and His resurrection from the dead. satan is **8.** <u>defeated</u>!! After Christ's resurrection, He shook the gates of hell and showed them that He now had possession of the keys of hell and of death **(Revelation 1:17-18).** He recaptured the rule over the social order that was usurped from Adam. Now during the church age, the Holy Spirit is establishing Christ's kingdom in people's hearts.

Satan is permitted to continue to rule the world system until a future day when *"the kingdoms of this world will become the Kingdoms of our Lord and of His Christ."* At that time, Jesus will return and set up a 1,000 year reign on earth in Jerusalem from where He will rule the world. This victory Christ got over satan is not automatically credited to everyone, but is made available to all who choose to enthrone Christ in their lives.

The difference between the way life is and the way things ought to be is very tragic and disappointing. How did our world go from God pronouncing His creation *"very good"* **(Genesis 1:31)** to the evil that infects our planet? The presence of evil, pain, suffering, injustice, and death in our world can cause one to draw several conclusions: Either believe (1) God does not exist; (2) God exists but is a mixture of good and evil; (3) everything that happens is God's will so "whatever will be will be"; or (4) God is limited in His attributes and has lost control of a rebellious planet. Any one of these beliefs can cause someone to want to have nothing to do with God.

A fifth conclusion is that the God of the Bible is a God of love and has no flaws or limitations in His nature. He enters emotionally into our failures and sufferings; He interacts personally in the affairs of humanity around our free will; He sent His only Son to die for our sins in order to rescue us and bring us into a right relationship with Him; and He is directing history toward a purposeful goal. God is sovereign and is completely in control at all times.

Undoubtedly, satan and his fallen angels are responsible for much of the suffering, pain, and evil in our world. Mankind also inflicts the same on his fellow man and himself from his sinful nature through bad choices. This in turn forces God to remove his restraining hand of protection and mete out His judgment. It remains a great mystery how our just, omnipotent God continues to allow sin, suffering, and these created evil beings to rebel and express their malevolent deeds. But we trust Him!!

The answer to SQ&A [#]6 is **E** (Satan is <u>not</u> almost as powerful as God).

Lesson 2
THE BELT OF TRUTH:
The Imprint of Satan's Character
Is Upon the Entire World System

☑ Before starting the DVD:

In developing what it takes to win this invisible war, we continue our intelligence gathering by putting on the Belt of Truth. Now that we have established who rules the world system, this lesson will define the Bible's meaning of *"world,"* identify its parts, and get a true picture of the world as God views it (especially of its religious and philosophical systems). Due to the quantity of information in this lesson, I have divided it into two sessions. The Summary will begin session two which also requires reading Appendix A. Now pray that God will reveal these awesome, life-changing truths to you.

HOW GOD SEES OUR WORLD (continued)

📖 DEFINITION—WORLD

The Holy Spirit used three Greek words in the New Testament that were translated "world" according to *Vine's Expository Dictionary of New Testament Words:*[1]

1. *Oikoumenē*: the inhabited earth.

2. *Aiōn*: an age or period of time.

3. *Kosmos*: its primary meaning is "order or arrangement" the entire cosmos (or physical world) which God created and pronounced "very good" **(Genesis 1:31)**. It also carries the meaning of "'the present condition of human affairs,' in alienation from and opposition to God."

Therefore, an accurate definition of the Bible's meaning of "world" (*kosmos*) that God forbids us to be a part of is this:

The entire social, economic, and political order, ever since the fall of Adam and Eve, consisting of the daily interaction of mankind, where generally self-seeking interests are the law of life and the God of the Bible is excluded. Its system tends to attract and appeal to man's sinful nature, competing with God for the possession of our hearts, and whose pursuits in life are indifferent and in opposition to both the will and glory of God.

We will enlarge on the **Components of the World System** at the end of this lesson.

> ☑ **DVD Users:** Watch Lesson 2 for an overview before proceeding further (26 min.).
> ☑ When you're through, pick up again at this point. Fill in the blanks from the Summary.

1. The world's ~~&~~ God (ruler) is satan (**Ephesians 6:12; 2:2**).

    † **2 Corinthians 4:4** (Phillips)—*The god of this world has blinded the minds of those who do not believe, and prevents the light of the glorious gospel of Christ, the image of God, from shining on them.*

    † **1 John 5:19**—*...the whole world is under the control of the evil one.*

2. The world's Kingdoms are controlled by satan. (**Luke 4:5-7; Daniel 10:10-14, 20).**

3. The world's Character is evil.

    † **Galatians 1:4** (KJV)—The Lord Jesus Christ: *Who gave himself for our sins, that He might deliver us from this present evil world...*

►**CONSIDER THIS:** If God is a God of love, then why did He allow evil and suffering to enter our world? If God has the power to stop evil, then why does He allow it to continue? We will attempt to answer these questions as the lessons progress.

4. The world's Spiritual Condition is darkness and blindness—people dead in their relationship to their Creator, and seeking to meet their spiritual needs apart from the true God.

    † **John 1:5, 10-11**—*The light shines in the darkness, but the darkness has not understood it. 10. He* [Jesus] *was in the world, and the world was made through him, the world did not recognize him. 11. He came to that which was his own, but his own did not receive him.*

    † **1 John 2:15-16** (NASB)—*16. For all that is in the world, the lust of the flesh, and the lust of the eyes, and the boastful pride of life, is not from the Father...*

    † **James 4:4** (GNT)—*...whoever wants to be the world's friend makes himself God's enemy.*

    † **Ephesians 2:2**—The devil is at work in those who are disobedient to God.

    † **John 15:17-25**—The world has a hatred for the true God and those who serve Him.

    † **John 12:46**—Jesus said: *"I have come into the world as a light, so that no one who believes in me should stay in darkness."*

    † **John 14:17; 17:25**—Jesus said: *"...the Spirit of Truth. The world cannot accept him, because it neither sees him nor knows him...25. Righteous Father, though the world does not know you ...I have made you known to them, and will continue to..."*

    † Other Related Scriptures: **John 3:19-21, 8:12; Matthew 5:14; Acts 17:16-23; Exodus 5:1-2.**

5. The world's __Wisdom__ (philosophies and worldviews) excludes the true God resulting in ignorance about Him. (We will enlarge on this in the next session.)

   † **1 Corinthians 1:20-21**—*Where is the wise man? Where is the scholar? Where is the philosopher of this age? Has not God made foolish the wisdom of the world? 21. For since in the wisdom of God the world through its wisdom did not know him.*
   (Also see **1 Corinthians 3:18-20**).

   † **John 18:37**—Jesus said, *"...I came to bring truth to the world. All who love the truth recognize that what I say is true."*

   † **Revelation 12:9** (TLB)—*...Satan, the one deceiving the whole world...*

   A. The entire world: Every person, every nation and every culture since Adam has been deceived and led astray by satan—even to the most brilliant minds this world has ever known! Think of it!

   B. The world's philosophies and worldviews compete against the Biblical worldview for the minds and hearts of humanity. They form the basis of one's belief system and actions. For example, if one adopts a worldview that believes a human life ends at death and has no eternal significance, then the tendency will be to view life with little or no value. It is then an easy step to join those who accept abortion, infanticide, and euthanasia.

   C. Christians especially have to guard against the danger of embracing beliefs that are contrary to Scripture. Instead of living by a true Biblical worldview, many of us have unwittingly taken some truths from Scripture, some beliefs from our public school education, some from our culture, some from our parents, etc., and this hodgepodge has formed and become our unique worldview. Our perceptions of reality must become aligned with the Word of God's truth about reality.

▶**CONSIDER THIS:** All the knowledge and wisdom acquired in Egypt's institutes of learning were not adequate to equip and prepare Moses for the work to which God had called him. He spent 40 years "unlearning" many of the things he was taught of the world's ways as he entered into God's "schools" to learn faith, obedience, and His ways. Notwithstanding, God also utilizes that which we have learned from the world's academics to prepare us for His work **(Acts 7:22)**.

6. The world's __Religions__ (and __Prophets__) draw people away from worshiping the true God to a false deity. Demonic power is the deceptive force behind all false gods and religions.

   † **1 Corinthians 10:19-21**—*Do I mean then that a sacrifice offered to an idol is anything, or that an idol is anything? 20. No, but the sacrifices of pagans are offered to demons, not to God, and I do not want you to be participants with demons. 21. You cannot drink the cup of the Lord and the cup of demons too; you cannot have a part in both the Lord's table and the table of demons.*

   † **Psalm 106:34-38**—*37. They [Israel] sacrificed their sons and their daughters to demons... 38. whom they sacrificed to the idols of Canaan, and the land was desecrated with their blood.*

✝ **Psalm 96:5**—*For all the gods of the nations are idols* ("*daimonia*" in the Septuagint translation), *but the Lord made the heavens.*

✝ Also read these related Scriptures: **Deuteronomy 32:16-17; Leviticus 17:7; 2 Chronicles 11:15; Revelation 9:20.**

✝ **Romans 1:19-25** (GNT)—*23. ...instead of worshipping the immortal God, they worship images made to look like mortal man or birds or animals or reptiles...25. they worship what God has created instead of the Creator himself...*

✝ **1 John 4:1-6** (NLT)—*...do not believe everyone who claims to speak by the Spirit. You must test them to see if the spirit they have comes from God. For there are many false prophets in the world. 2. This is the way to find out if they have the Spirit of God: If a prophet acknowledges that Jesus Christ became a human being, that person has the Spirit of God. 3. If a prophet does not acknowledge Jesus, that person is not from God. Such a person has the spirit of the Antichrist... 5. These people belong to this world, so they speak from the world's viewpoint, and the world listens to them. 6....That is how we know if someone has the Spirit of truth or the spirit of deception.*

✝ **Matthew 7:15-20**—Jesus said: *"Watch out for false prophets...by their fruit you will recognize them."*

▶**CONSIDER THIS:** Since Adam and Eve relinquished control of the world to the devil, there have come into being many erroneous religions and literally millions of false gods to whom people have committed themselves. While most have been inspired by satan and his demons, some can be attributed to man alone. The Tower of Babel **(Genesis 11:1)** typifies the essence of all human religion: man's rebellious attempt to search for God in his own way and by his own efforts. Christianity, on the other hand, is God's search for man, the only religion whose founder is not in his tomb.

Dr. Norman Geisler, co-founder of Southern Evangelical Seminary, has skillfully given us a simple breakdown of the seven major religious worldviews, which I have adapted for this study. This overview will be dealt with in the next session. (For further information about groups that claim to be Christian, please refer to **Marks of a Counterfeit Christian Religion** in Lesson 15.)

7. The world's DURATION is only temporary—it will pass away shortly.

✝ **1 John 2:17**—*The world and its desires pass away, but the man who does the will of God lives forever.*

8. The world's children will be dealt with in Lesson 3.

SATAN'S FUTURE

1. "C_____ O____ of H_____" in the Tribulation period—**Revelation 12:7-9.**

2. "B_____ P____" for 1,000 years—**Revelation 20:1-3.**

3. "L_____ of F_____" the second death—**Revelation 20:10.**

►**CONSIDER THIS:** The Lake of Fire was prepared
However, the Lake of Fire will also be a place for those ⊦
rebellion against God. If one shares satan's objectives
unspeakable horror of living with these hideous spiri'
find themselves in hell no longer remain in a s⊦
mankind has been promised an escape from God's ⌐

CHRIST'S FUTURE REIGN

1. Christ will one day reign on the earth for 1,000 years (also refe⌐
   of Christ). It coincides with satan's imprisonment in the botto⌐
   influence of the devil and his fallen angels is removed from the earth, th⌐
   a different world—one in which Christ truly reigns and reflects His influenc⌐

NOW	MILLENNIAL REIGN OF CHRIS⌐
• One cannot find the true knowledge of God outside the Church of Jesus Christ.	• **Isaiah 11:9b:** *...for the earth will be full of the knowledge of the Lord as the waters cover the sea.* (See also **Jeremiah 31:33-34.**)
• Violence in the animal kingdom	• **Isaiah 11:6-9a:** *The wolf will live with the lamb, the leopard will lie down with the goat, the calf and the lion and the yearling together; and a little child will lead them. 7. The cow will feed with the bear, their young will lie down together, and the lion will eat straw like the ox. 8. The infant will play near the hole of the cobra, and the young child put his hand into the viper's nest. 9. They will neither harm nor destroy on all my holy mountain...*
• False gods and religions	• **Jeremiah 3:17:** (NLT) *In that day Jerusalem will be known as The Throne of the Lord. All nations will come there to honor the Lord.*
	• **Zechariah 8:22:** *And many peoples and powerful nations will come to Jerusalem to seek the Lord Almighty and to entreat Him.*
• Wars and lust for power	• **Isaiah 2:4:** *He will judge between the nations and will settle disputes for many peoples. They will beat their swords into plowshares and their spears into pruning hooks. Nation will not take up sword against nation, nor will they train for war anymore.*

►**CONSIDER THIS:** Read **Revelation 20:7-10; 16:13-14.** Then notice the effect which the loosing of satan will have upon the inhabitants of the earth that have just lived under Christ's 1,000 year reign—beside the fact that God was influencing it as well **(Zechariah 14:2).**

the DVD content for Lesson 2.

on in this workbook for material **not** on the DVD.

COMPONENTS OF THE WORLD SYSTEM

...duction—Prior to the Fall, God intended that Adam and Eve and their descendents would ...an orderly infrastructure within which to live. The institutions in this structure comprise the ...s of human life to which God calls and gifts us in order to meet the needs of the whole ...mmunity. However, due to Adam and Eve's rebellion against God and the subsequent illegal take-over by satan, these institutions have come under the devil's control and have become corrupted by self-centered interests. What has emerged is what the Scriptures refer to as the *"world"*—or satan's kingdom—the sphere in which he operates. God's kingdom here on earth operates within this corrupt world system, and God uses it to further His kingdom. Each kingdom has its own set of principles by which it operates.

1. The following chart is an attempt to dissect the present world infrastructure to bring clarity to what we are identifying as the "world system" (note that it does <u>not</u> include God's creation of nature—animal, vegetable, and mineral).

2. When people in influential positions within these institutions operate by God's laws and principles, the Kingdom of God is advanced within the kingdom of satan. When those who shape societies' values operate by fallen man's self-centered values, then satan uses it to advance his kingdom. Actually, one can discern which kingdom is ruling in any given area of life by the character emanating from it (God's or satan's)—whether it be a person, family, business, government, religion, geographical area, etc.

3. The chart is a breakdown of the components of the "world system" that the Bible makes reference to. These cultural shapers of values aren't evil in themselves. They become evil when sin becomes the spirit that permeates and motivates their operation. For this reason, it is imperative that Christians become involved and affect their culture with Godly influence. Jesus calls His Church to be *"light"* and *"salt"* (to retard corruption) in the world in which it resides. The Holy Spirit has given us the authority and power to invade satan's kingdom and to bring Christ's rule to its institutions. However, only when Christ returns will satan's kingdom be totally overthrown.

4. We now conclude this first session by learning about the institutions that comprise the world system, which shape our values and make our world go around. But first a word about Session 2 in which we will enlarge on two of these institutions, Religion and Education (worldviews).

It will be on the battlefield of the school classroom that our republic will stand or fall. Since the early 1960s, with the aid of our Supreme Court, America's public school system has systematically eradicated every trace of its Christian heritage and has in the process removed from our children the acknowledgment of God and the Holy Scriptures that provided the moral compass of right from wrong. It is now more acceptable to bring condoms to school than Bibles. Get involved in what is happening in the classroom. Read the textbooks, attend meetings, and be familiar with all aspects of your child's learning process. As Abraham Lincoln once said, "The philosophy of the classroom of one generation will be the philosophy of government in the next."

INSTITUTIONS OF THE WORLD SYSTEM

These institutions are listed in the likely biblical order of importance and are contrasted with how it probably is in the United States of America. Study the chart below. Keep in mind our definition of *"world."* Then write in how you are influencing each area for God. If you're not, seek God for what He would have you to do! (Note: You may need to return to this chart after you have read the next session.)

CULTURAL SHAPERS OF VALUES (for good or evil) Below is the likely biblical order of importance	USA's Order	How Can You Influence These Areas For God's Kingdom?
1. Religion (the Church): **Exodus 20:3-6; Matt. 22:36-40** (Exists to represent the God of the Bible, evangelize, disciple, restrain evil, and influence the world. The church is in the world but operates within a Biblical worldview—see bottom of page 3)	**5.**	For example: witnessing and proclaiming the Gospel; maintaining your relationship with God, serving your church, etc.
2. The Family Unit (Society): **Matt. 19:4-6; Eph. 5:21-33** Consists of the marriage of 1 man and 1 woman. Exists to populate the earth; love, nurture, and teach their children.	**4.**	For example: cultivating marriage; raising Godly kids, TV viewing vs. family time; influencing the workplace, etc.
A. Educational/Academic System (Worldviews) • Primary schooling (K-4) • Secondary (5-12) • Post-graduate (college)	**2.**	For example: being involved in your school
3. Civil Government: **Romans 13:1-7; Genesis 9:6** A. Political Systems: (America's are **bolded**) • *Theocracy*—rule by God (i.e. Israel under the Mosaic law prior to their kings) • *Monarchy*—rule by one (i.e. Saddam Hussein in Iraq; Emperor worship in Japan) • *Oligarchy*—rule by a few elite (The USSR) • *Democracy*—rule by majority • *Republic*—**rule by law** (U.S.A.*) **Executive Branch** (law enforcement body) **Legislative Branch** (law making body) **Judicial Branch** (legal body) • *Anarchy*—rule by none (a temporary stage) * Though founded as a republic, there is good reason to believe it now to be an oligarchy.	**1.**	For example: pray, vote, support a candidate, run for office, etc.
B. Economic Systems: (The Business Sector including Technology & Commercial Industry): • **Free Enterprise (called Capitalism)** • Fascism (private ownership with gov't control) • Socialism (government owns the property and controls the production)		
4. The Communications Media (via TV / radio / internet / print publications / music) • Arts and Entertainment Industry • The News	**3.**	For example: complaint letters, boycott products, be salt & light, influence it for good.

☑ **Note: I strongly recommend that the remainder of this lesson (including Appendix A)
be treated as a separate session.** This is the lengthiest of all the sessions because I felt
compelled to include this critically important information to equip you with an accurate perspective
of the world system you live in—its religious systems, worldviews, and philosophies. Please don't
skip over any of them. If you can't handle all of it now, stay at it until you finish. It will shed
invaluable light on any erroneous philosophies you may believe, occult involvement you may have
had, and current problems you may be experiencing, or prevent you from exposing yourself to
demonic powers in the future. Session 2 begins by summarizing the first part of this lesson.

Session 2
SUMMARY

In the last session, we continued to "put on" the Belt of Truth. The Bible has enlightening things to say about
the world we find ourselves in. Behind its superficial veneer of respectability, prosperity, success, and
achievement, lies a kingdom ruled by satan. The Bible refers to it as the *"world"* system, and satan's wicked
character is manifested throughout. An accurate definition of the Bible's meaning of *"world"* is this: "The
entire, social, economic, and political order, ever since the fall of Adam and Eve, consisting of the daily
interaction of mankind, where generally self-seeking interests are the law of life and the God of the Bible is
excluded. Its system tends to attract and appeal to man's sinful nature, competing with God for the possession
of our hearts, and whose pursuits in life are indifferent and in opposition to both the will and glory of God."

We discovered these aspects about our world: Its **1.** god is satan. The world's **2.** kingdoms are controlled
by him through sinful human beings who, for the most part, unwittingly become puppets in the devil's
hand. We learned from the book of Daniel that there is even a Scriptural basis for powerful, high ranking
demonic spirits who control nations and empower its leaders. The world's **3.** character is evil and its
4. spiritual condition is darkness and blindness—its subjects being dead in their relationship to the true
God. The world's **5.** wisdom (philosophies and worldviews) that mankind creates through rationalization
and unbelief excludes the true God and results in ignorance of Him.

Its **6.** religions (and prophets) draw people away from worshiping the true God to a false deity. The Bible
states that demonic power is the deceptive force behind false gods and religions. Satan continues to
deceive the inhabitants of the earth. He keeps them blinded to the truth and tries to eradicate any
knowledge about the true God. Satan attempts to get his subjects to worship and serve anyone or anything
else other than the God of the Bible. He does this by his false religions and prophets through which he
steals their love, worship, and dedication that rightfully belong to God. However, the world's
7. duration is only temporary—it will shortly pass away.

Further evidence of the absence of God's rule over the present world system is seen in stark contrast to
Christ's future 1,000 year reign in Jerusalem when He returns again to earth. We also learned of satan's
future. When Christ returns, satan and his demons will be **1.** cast out of heaven, and Christ will bind them
in the **2.** bottomless pit concurrent with His 1,000 year reign *"to keep him from deceiving the nations
anymore."* **(Revelation 20:3).** With his evil influence removed from the earth, the character of Christ's
rule becomes clearly visible: The knowledge of God is plentiful; there is peace both among mankind and
the animal kingdom; all nations will come to worship the one and only King; and wars will cease.

However, when after the one thousand years are over and satan is let loose from his prison, how quickly
deception, war, and blindness once again return with him to the world. If Christ were truly ruling the world
system today, His character would emanate forth just as it will during His future millennial reign. Christ
will eventually seal the doom of satan and his demons by casting them into **3.** the Lake of Fire for eternity.

RELIGIONS OF THE WORLD SYSTEM

Introduction—All religions view God in one of seven different ways. Dr. Norman Geisler, President of Southern Evangelical Seminary, has skillfully condensed all the various concepts of God into seven major categories he calls religious worldviews. The following material has been adapted from his insightful books, *False Gods of Our Time* and *Worlds Apart: A Handbook on Worldviews* (visit www.normgeisler.com—used by permission). Please refer to the following chart for a categorization of the major religions under these **Seven Views of God.** This knowledge is essential because from a biblical standpoint, only one can be correct. **Q:** Which view do you hold to?

1. **Monotheism**—This view of God believes that there is one personal, infinite, eternal, unchangeable, absolutely perfect, and limitless God. He exists within and beyond His creation, the universe, and sustains it and acts within it in a supernatural way. Monotheism is the belief that God is only one person and is held by both orthodox Jews and Islam (**unitarian** monotheism). Most Christians believe the Bible teaches one God existing in three persons (**trinitarian** monotheism)—not **tritheism,** a belief in three separate gods.

   Note: **Judaism** and **Christianity** have the same God of the Bible with the exception that Judaism does not recognize the New Testament nor that Jesus Christ is the Son of God. **Islam's** God, Allah, is **not** the God of the Bible, but is based on their inspired writings, the Koran. Islam originally was a polytheistic religion and Allah was one of its gods (a moon god, thus their crescent symbol). However, one cannot have a relationship with Allah like one can with the God of the Bible. Let's enlarge a bit more on the core beliefs of these three religions:

   A. **The World**—Creation was brought into existence by God out of nothing that preexisted.

   B. **Man**— Created by God in His likeness, man has a mortal body and an immortal soul and whose deeds will be rewarded or punished in the afterlife.

   Both <u>Judaism</u> and <u>Christianity</u> believe in original sin—that Adam and Eve, after falling into sin, genetically passed down their sinful nature to their descendents. <u>Islam</u> denies original sin and teaches that man is born inherently good.

   C. **Salvation** – **Rabbinic Judaism**—They believe they escape God's judgment by obeying the Law of Moses (and other traditions), but without a blood sacrifice.

   Christianity: By grace alone through faith alone in Christ alone through His blood that He shed for us on the cross. Jesus himself said, *"I am the way, and the truth, and the life. No one comes to the Father except through Me."* **(John 14:6).**

   Islam: By obeying the Five (5) Pillars that consist of good works to merit salvation that outweigh one's bad deeds. Also, only through dying while engaged in <u>jihad</u> (holy war) will one be assured of going to Paradise. Allah requires you shed your blood for him. Christianity's God shed His blood for us.

   Author's note: Someone once said that it is very possible that more blood has been shed over religious disagreements than for any other reason. How ironic. Satan stirs up wars in the name of religion by making people believe, for example, that their religion is divinely commissioned to conquer the world. Islam and Shintoism (Japan in WWII) are two prime examples.

2. **Deism**—This view of God is monotheistic with one major exception. God exists in and beyond the universe, but he does <u>not</u> supernaturally intervene in the world or interact with mankind. It's like God created the world, set things in motion, and then left it to operate by its own natural laws—never to interrupt it with supernatural events like miracles. This belief was prevalent in the 16th-19th centuries. Its effects are still with us today.

3. **Pantheism**—This concept of God believes that one infinite God exists within the universe, and can be personal or impersonal. The universe just doesn't contain God—it is God. In fact, everything that exists is part of God. However, views differ as to *how* God and the world are to be identified. Pantheism is an ancient belief, prevalent in Hinduism (see **Reincarnation**), that is having a widespread resurgence today especially in the West. Closely related is <u>monism,</u> which is the belief that everything in the cosmos is united together as one. Many view this unifying element as a universal divine energy that permeates all things. To others it's not divine. Scores of names have been given to this unknown impersonal force. The Hindus call it *prana* (universal energy). It is called *ch'i* by the Chinese, *ki* by the Japanese, and *mana* (life force) by the Polynesians. This energy is also known as universal consciousness; cosmic Mind; universal intelligence; bioenergy; a psychic force; animal magnetism (universal fluid); orgone; psychotronic energy; psi-energy; odic force; the kundalini, etc. This energy is believed to reside within the human body as an untapped source of psychic power. Through meditation and other occult practices, this power can allegedly be cultivated, channeled, controlled, redirected, and released to others. See **Parapsychology, Meditation, New Age Medicine, Fatalism, and Luck.** This is another clever lie designed by the devil. This belief not only distorts the truth of God's omnipresence, but it allows for demons to disguise themselves as "energy forces."

4. **Panentheism**—This view of God holds to one personal, imperfect, finite, changing God who cooperates with the world in order to achieve greater perfection in his nature. He is bipolar—God's body (the universe) is the actual pole and his mind (what is beyond the universe) is his potential pole. This bipolar notion of God depicts him as both finite and infinite, relative and absolute, dependent and independent, in the process of changing and becoming and yet immutable. Very few religious groups hold to this view.

5. **Finite Godism**—This concept of God believes that there is one personal, imperfect, and finite God who exists in and outside of His creation. But He is viewed as being limited in his nature and power especially by those who can't reconcile the existence of evil and suffering in the world with a loving omnipotent God. Not many religious groups hold to this view—but people do.

6. **Polytheism**—This view of God believes that there is more than one God in the universe—but not beyond it. Generally, these gods or goddesses had a beginning but do not have an end. They are personal—influencing events and acting in people's lives. They are finite—limited in their attributes and are changing—made in the image of man. They rule over distinct areas in the universe but do not have equal power or rule. They determine man's destiny and history. Some religions, like Hinduism, have both polytheistic and pantheistic aspects (i.e. henotheism).

7. **Atheism**—This view believes that God does not exist. God is just the invention of man. **G-O-D** Incredibly, there is even such a thing as religious atheism like one form of Buddhism. **Agnosticism GOD?**—Related to atheism, it holds that no one can know for sure if God exists.

The following is a summary of these views which also explains the chart:

One either believes in some kind of God or one does <u>not</u> (**7. atheism**). If there is a God, then one either believes in <u>many</u> Gods (**6. polytheism**), or else in just <u>one</u> God. If *one God*, then one either believes that this God is <u>finite</u>—limited in his attributes (**5. finite godism;** or **4. panentheism**), or that this God is <u>infinite</u>—unlimited in his attributes. If *infinite*, then one either believes that God is everything and everything is God (**3. pantheism**), or that this God is <u>personal</u> and exists both in and beyond the universe (**monotheism**). If infinite, personal, and distinct from His creation, then one either believes this God does <u>not</u> <u>interact</u> supernaturally with His creation (**2. deism**), or that (**1.**) <u>He</u> <u>does</u>. If He does interact, then He exists as either one person (unitarian monotheism) or He is three persons in one (trinitarian monotheism).

I have attempted to categorize false religions under these seven views of God. Keep in mind that it doesn't matter to satan which god you believe in (or even if you don't) as long as you are not serving the true God. The devil receives one's worship regardless of the false religion. Here are the current top 12 world religions; 11 rival Christianity for the hearts of people. Think of it! Out of six billion people on this earth, two-thirds serve other gods or are atheists.

1. Christianity (2 Billion) **2**. Islam (1.2 Billion) **3**. Hinduism (785 Million) **4**. Buddhism (360 Million) **5**. Judaism (17 Million) **6**. Sikhism (16 Million) **7**. Baha'i (5 Million) **8**. Confucianism (5 Million) **9**. Jainism (4 Million) **10**. Shintoism (3 Million) **11**. Wicca (700,000) **12**. Zoroastrianism (200,000).
Source: www. christianity.about.com (under "world religions")

WORLDVIEWS OF THE WORLD SYSTEM

1. A worldview is a belief system derived from how we interpret facts and perceive reality and is formed by our view of God. The rest of this session consists of learning about today's **Dominant Worldviews,** and **Philosophies of the World System. Q:** What is your worldview? Does it align with the Bible's? The next exercise will test you to see if it does.

2. After presenting an overview of the worldviews and philosophies and how they influence our public schools and universities, this session will then close with an **Overview of the Occult.** The chart on the last page acts both as an overview and as a table of contents for **Appendix A** which enlarges on each topic of the occult and is located at the end of Lesson 16. Learning this vital information can reveal any occult involvement you may have had in the past (but weren't aware of) and problems you may be experiencing as a result. It will also equip you with knowledge that can prevent you from exposing yourself to demonic powers in the future.

☑ After studying the Seven Views of God chart, proceed to #3—**Compare Your Worldview With the Bible's.**

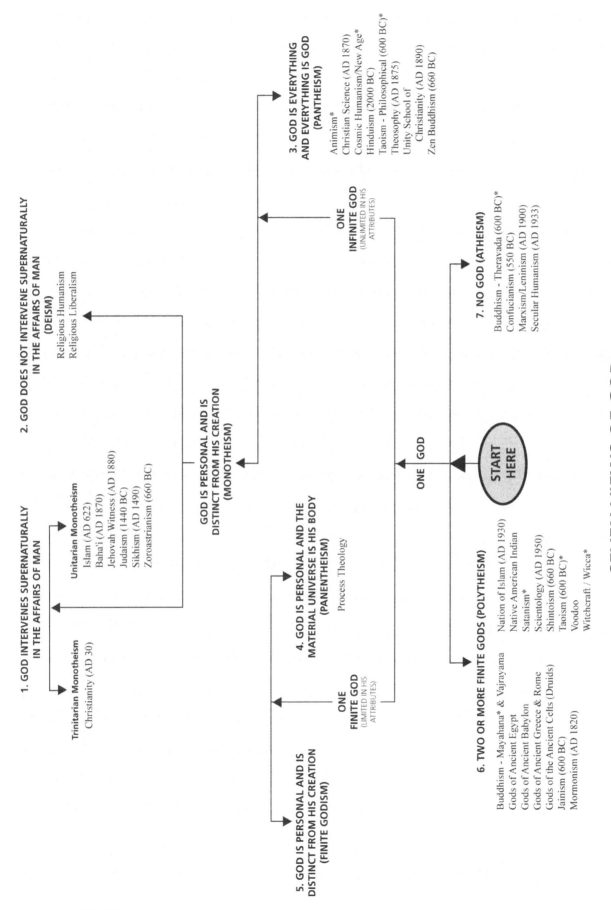

SEVEN VIEWS OF GOD

Adapted from *False Gods of Our Time*, www.normgeisler.com
Specific religions put in by David Skeba, www.discoverministries.com
Dates indicate approximate date of origin
*Other Variations Exist

1. GOD INTERVENES SUPERNATURALLY IN THE AFFAIRS OF MAN

Trinitarian Monotheism
Christianity (AD 30)

Unitarian Monotheism
Islam (AD 622)
Baha'i (AD 1870)
Jehovah Witness (AD 1880)
Judaism (1440 BC)
Sikhism (AD 1490)
Zoroastrianism (660 BC)

2. GOD DOES NOT INTERVENE SUPERNATURALLY IN THE AFFAIRS OF MAN (DEISM)
Religious Humanism
Religious Liberalism

GOD IS PERSONAL AND IS DISTINCT FROM HIS CREATION (MONOTHEISM)

3. GOD IS EVERYTHING AND EVERYTHING IS GOD (PANTHEISM)
Animism*
Christian Science (AD 1870)
Cosmic Humanism/New Age* (2000 BC)
Hinduism (2000 BC)
Taoism - Philosophical (600 BC)*
Theosophy (AD 1875)
Unity School of Christianity (AD 1890)
Zen Buddhism (660 BC)

ONE INFINITE GOD (UNLIMITED IN HIS ATTRIBUTES)

7. NO GOD (ATHEISM)
Buddhism - Theravada (600 BC)*
Confucianism (550 BC)
Marxism/Leninism (AD 1900)
Secular Humanism (AD 1933)

ONE GOD

START HERE

4. GOD IS PERSONAL AND THE MATERIAL UNIVERSE IS HIS BODY (PANENTHEISM)
Process Theology

5. GOD IS PERSONAL AND IS DISTINCT FROM HIS CREATION (FINITE GODISM)

ONE FINITE GOD (LIMITED IN HIS ATTRIBUTES)

6. TWO OR MORE FINITE GODS (POLYTHEISM)
Buddhism - Mayahana* & Vajrayama
Gods of Ancient Egypt
Gods of Ancient Babylon
Gods of Ancient Greece & Rome
Gods of the Ancient Celts (Druids)
Jainism (600 BC)
Mormonism (AD 1820)
Nation of Islam (AD 1930)
Native American Indian
Satanism*
Scientology (AD 1950)
Shintoism (660 BC)
Taoism (600 BC)*
Voodoo
Witchcraft / Wicca*

COMPARE YOUR WORLD VIEW WITH THE BIBLE'S

How does your world view compare to the Biblical Christian world view? Select only one answer, A – E, for each category (see below for answers). Please don't look at the next chart until you have first taken this quiz. The Barna Group cited statistics showing just 9% of all born again adults and just 7% of Protestants possess a Biblical worldview and that only 51% of our country's Protestant pastors have one [2] (see below *). When finished, learn about the other dominant world views that rival Christianity given on the next chart.

	A	B	C	D	E
1. View of God (Theology)	☐ One God exists in 3 persons	☐ There is more than one God	☐ God fills everything and all is God	☐ There is no God	☐ One cannot know
2. View of Reality and Truth (Philosophy)	☐ Only matter exists, not spirit, soul or afterlife, and is known by reason alone	☐ Matter is an illusion; everything is spiritual and known by mysticism	☐ Both matter and spirit exist and is known by reason and revelation: truth is absolute	☐ Truth is relative and defined by one's community and is not known through reason	☐ One cannot know
3. Origin of Life (Biology)	☐ Life arrived from life beyond the earth	☐ An infinite God created with intelligent design	☐ Through evolution by random natural processes	☐ The universe created itself	☐ One cannot know
4. Nature of Man (Psychology)	☐ Humans are inherently good and self-perfectible	☐ Humans are divine	☐ Humans are programmed by their environment which makes them good or evil	☐ Man made in the image of God with free will, but through rebellion has a sinful nature	☐ One cannot know
5. Moral Values (Ethics)	☐ Right and wrong are determined by what has been made legal	☐ Right and wrong are based on and determined by the situation	☐ One determines their own standards for right and wrong	☐ Whatever advances the cause of government is good – if not, it's bad	☐ An unchangeable universal standard of right and wrong
6. View of Religion, Family and Government (Sociology)	☐ Belief in freedom of religion, the traditional family, and government to protect, bring justice, and restrain evil	☐ Belief that religious institutions inhibit progress; the non-traditional family, and expanded government	☐ Belief that religion, family, and rival governments should be abolished	☐ Belief that religions should join together; the traditional family, limited government	☐ I hold to another view
7. Code of Rules (Laws & Rights)	☐ Laws and rights are made only to benefit and advance the government	☐ Laws and rights are based only on natural law	☐ Laws and rights are man-made and man-given	☐ Laws based on the Bible and natural law; rights come from God	☐ Each person makes laws and rights for himself
8. View of Government (Politics)	☐ Rule by a few elite	☐ Rule by majority	☐ Rule by God and law	☐ Rule by one person	☐ A one world political unity of all nations
9. Economic System	☐ Private ownership with government control	☐ Government owns the property and controls production	☐ A system based on the American dollar	☐ Common ownership of goods that are equally distributed	☐ Private ownership and stewardship of property
10. View of History	☐ Everything is predetermined - "Whatever will be, will be"	☐ God acts in history with man's free will and directs it toward a purposeful goal	☐ Nothing guides history but random chance	☐ Collectively our deeds determine the future through reincarnation	☐ I hold to another view

ANSWERS: 1A, 2C, 3B, 4D, 5E, 6A, 7D, 8C, 9E, 10B

* For more information on the Barna Group study or to see how they define a Biblical world view, please see their website listed in the Source Notes.

© www.DiscoverMinistries.com

DOMINANT WORLD VIEWS THAT RIVAL CHRISTIANITY IN THE WEST *

	Biblical Christianity	Secular Humanism	Cosmic Humanism (New Age Movement)	Marxism – Leninism	Islam
Authoritative Sources	The Bible	Humanist Manifestos I, II, 2000	Writings of Spangler, Ferguson, Chopra, etc.	Communist Manifesto and Writings of Marx, Engels, Lenin	Qur'an (Koran) and The Hadith (tradition)
1. View of God (Theology)	Trinitarian Monotheism (One God in 3 persons; Incarnation of the Son)	Atheism (No gods exist)	Pantheism (Everything is God)	Atheism (No gods exist)	Unitarian Monotheism (Allah only – no personal relationship)
2. View of Reality and Truth (Philosophy)	Supernaturalism Both physical & spiritual exist (Thru reason & revelation)	Naturalism (Thru reason alone) (Only the natural / material exists – no soul, spirit, etc)	Non-naturalism All is spiritual / divine (Through mysticism)	Dialectical Materialism All is matter; conflict brings progress (Thru reason alone)	Supernaturalism Both physical & spiritual exist (Thru reason & revelation)
3. Origin of Life (Biology)	Creation (Intelligent design)	Evolution (Darwinian)	Evolution (Cosmic)	Evolution (Punctuated)	Creation (Intelligent design)
4. Nature of Man (Psychology)	Made in the image of God with free will ; inherited a sinful nature; is redeemable	Humans are inherently good and perfectible (Self-realization)	Humans are Divine (God-realization)	Behaviorism – Man is only matter and is programmed by his environment	Man is born a Muslim and is inherently good, and must work for salvation
5. Moral Values (Ethics)	Moral absolutes (From God's nature; revealed in creation and the Bible)	Moral Relativism (Humans decide what is right and wrong)	Moral Relativism (Through the Law of Karma and reincarnation; good & evil are one)	Proletariat Morality (Only what advances the cause of Communism is morally good; if not it's evil)	Moral Absolutes (Based on the Qur'an (Koran) and The Hadith)
6. View of Religion, Family and Government (Sociology)	Belief in the Church, the traditional family, and government (to protect, bring justice, & restrain evil)	Religious institutions inhibit progress; non-traditional family; expanded government	Non-traditional (NT) religion; NT family; and NT government. (Eliminate hindrances to evolution)	Abolition of religion, family and government (Including private property and class distinctions)	Islamic control of religion, family, and government
7. Code of Rules (Laws & Rights)	Based on Biblical and natural law; Rights come from God	Man-made Law Rights come from human government	Self-Law and Karma Rights come from the Divine Self	Proletariat Law (Only Laws that advance the working class are moral) Rights come from Government.	Shari'a law – based on the Qur'an, Hadith (tradition), and Ijima' (consensus); Rights come from Allah
8. View of Government (Politics)	Rule of law (Freedom, justice, and order under God)	World Government (Oligarchy–rule by a few elite)	New Age Order (Evolving toward the spiritual and political unity of all nations)	World Government {Socialism leading to Communism (No government)}	Jihad leading to Islamic states worldwide
9. Economic System	Free enterprise (Stewardship of private property)	Some hold to socialism and some to capitalism	Higher consciousness leads to higher income (Some advocate Enlightened Communism)	Socialism leading to Communism	Free market Controlled by Islamic law
10. View of History	God directs history toward a purposeful goal; Belief in a resurrection	Historical Evolution (Guided by nature and humanity)	Evolutionary Godhood One must realize one is god Belief in reincarnation	Historical Materialism (The dialectic drives history toward Communism)	Global Islam Belief in a resurrection

* Adapted from *Understanding the Times* video series. This is **must viewing** for all. For more information visit www.summit.org.

PHILOSOPHIES OF THE WORLD SYSTEM

Introduction—Every day throughout the earth, each of us is living out our worldview and is contributing to what happens in our world. A worldview is a belief system that attempts to make sense of life and is derived from how we interpret facts and perceive reality—like a pair of glasses through which we view the world. It drives all that we think, say, and do. Our view of the world really begins with our view of God which determines the rest of our beliefs and the way we live our lives. Jesus taught us that we can know the true nature of something by its fruit **(Matthew 7:15-20).** For example, a tree bears fruit by the nourishment it draws from its root system. Similarly, we draw our beliefs from what we have been taught (whether true or false). This underscores the critical importance of receiving correct information and forming an accurate belief system. After all, there's nothing worse than believing a lie. Some of us have thought through our worldview. Others have not stopped to consider one, but they still live by one. Many times we use it as an excuse or a license to live our lives the way we want to, without God, especially when many other people also adhere to it. Non-biblical worldviews constantly bombard us from the media and, without thinking, we can easily imbibe parts of them into our Christian worldview.

Just how influential can a belief be? Take **reincarnation** and **evolution** for example. These two related theories have had more of a devastating effect on humanity over the last 150 years than practically anything else. False philosophies and worldviews take root in a culture and lead it away from the true God. If we Christians are to present the Gospel effectively, we must understand the major philosophies of our day in order to meet people where they are (see Dominant Worldviews chart). We should also be wise and be able to discern the direction that subversive groups are taking our country. Then we must pray and get involved in the political process so we can preserve the Judeo-Christian worldview and freedom to proclaim the Gospel—or live under someone else's worldview.

Below are some additional philosophies that reflect *"the wisdom of the world."* Be acquainted with them. They are not fully developed worldviews, but they negatively impact our culture in a huge way. Keep in mind that our social ills are the result of cause and effect. Some are the result of a deliberate unconventional war being waged by those who hold a different worldview than you do.

1. **Postmodernism**—This is one of the latest, major anti-biblical philosophies. It is a belief system that resulted from disillusionment with the outcomes of modernism (which is basically the worldview of Secular Humanism), which reduced everything to materialism and rationalism and left man's inner being untouched. It came not from disagreement (a rational rejection), but from experiencing life under modernism's philosophy and finding it deficient to meet the inner needs of their lives. It was determined that there is nothing more to life than to live for the passion of the moment, and that no one is better than another.[3]

   Postmodernists rejected the main philosophy of the Modern era, namely: (1) there is a real world (2) there is truth (3) reason is objective and (4) language can be used to describe reality. Instead, they have concluded: (1) there is no real world out there; (2) truth is relative and is defined by your culture, group, or personal preference—no absolute truth exists; (3) standards of rationality are relative too, and determined by one's community; therefore, there is no such concept as something being reasonable or unreasonable because it is derived from objective reasoning. Instead, rhetoric is elevated above reason. People are persuaded to accept their point of view, not through intellectual reasoning, but by packaging their version of truth in storyline, imagery, and metaphor that appeal to their emotions.

Postmodernists also believe that (4) language can have various meanings—not just one broad, collectively held definition. The meaning of a word is determined by one's group. They seek not to understand the author's meaning and intent of a story, etc., but rather their own interpretation determines what is meant. (5) Anything that leads someone to categorize something better than another is looked upon as an attempt to elevate oneself and put another down—like that which is true or false, real or unreal, right or wrong, rational or irrational, etc. (6) They reject the idea that there is just one worldview that's right for everyone. Instead, worldviews held by each group are all held equally true. No one is excluded—except those who are intolerant of another's idea.[4]

The *Oxford Dictionary* defines philosophy as "The use of <u>argument</u> and <u>reason</u> in order to establish the <u>truth</u> about <u>reality</u>." (underlines are mine) Gradually during the modern era, <u>reality</u>, <u>truth</u>, and even <u>reason</u> came under attack and were one by one thrown onto the trash heap of history by many people. Tragically, the definition of philosophy today has been reduced to an ***argument*** by postmodernists. So if all opinions are equally valid, then no one is permitted to elevate their point of view above another. It is a philosophy of those who are crying out for an answer for the fulfillment of one's inner being which only Christ can satisfy. However, in its quest, the concept and nature of absolute truth has been replaced with one's relative personal preferences—a disaster in the making. Though not a full fledged worldview, it is a philosophy that especially affects the arts and literature. Postmodernism, together with Secular Humanism and Marxism, are being taught to our children in our universities, colleges, and public schools and are leading them away from the true God.[5]

2. **Marxism-Leninism**—Even though this worldview is represented in the chart, I am giving it a brief summary because of its significance of being a notorious killing machine in our world, and its uncanny ability to repackage its worldview and infiltrate a society and even some churches. In brief, a Marxist (Communist) worldview holds that all of man's problems are the direct result of the rise of economic classes seeking to oppress and exploit the other for its own economic advantage. In their view, a free market system (like "capitalism") is the main offender because it breeds exploitation of the proletariat (non-property working class) by the bourgeoisie (property owners), which leads to crime, social unrest, greed, and inequality. This is the main reason Marxists hate America and why they have infiltrated us to destroy us from within. Another reason for the aggression is because America permits freedom of religion (Marxists are atheists).

For the Marxist, a peaceful society is possible only when capitalism is replaced by socialism (an economic system run by the ruling government class). Socialism, in their view, is the next predetermined evolutionary step (the dialectic) in the transition from capitalism to communism (i.e. historically from slavery → feudalism → capitalism → socialism → communism). Capitalism, they believe, is historically destined to pass off the scene like feudalism. They feel it is their duty to hasten the inevitable day when the oppressed workers of the world will rise up and overthrow their oppressors and replace Capitalism with a more "humane" system—Communism. Communism promises a utopia of permanent peace and liberation from oppression, exploitation, unemployment, and poverty which is ironically what life is like now whenever and wherever they rule. Wherever socialism has been practiced in the world, it has miserably failed its people in every way.

There are differences of opinion among Marxist leaders as to the proper approach in attacking a capitalistic society like America. One group advocates a gradual approach (social-democratic Marxism). The early strategy for America was summed up by the late Dr. Fred Schwarz: "External encirclement plus internal demoralization leads to progressive surrender."[6] A second believes that a violent overthrow by the working class is the best solution. Note that this method has been used by satan to murder over 100 million people during the last century alone and may have been one of the main reasons satan brought it into being. A third, a "humanistic" version better known as "liberation theology," has successfully been used to infiltrate some Christian churches, colleges, and seminaries (especially in the areas of sociology and economics). It was also used to exploit the injustices of black and feminist groups.

Emerging in the 1960s, liberation theology was the Marxist strategy of deceptively repackaging their worldview by blending it with Christian doctrine especially within the Roman Catholic Church in Latin America. They did this in order to gain entrance into the religious Latin American countries that would have otherwise rejected it. The Marxists themselves exploited the legitimate needs of Latin America's poverty-stricken people through this approach in order to take control of their governments and to instill hatred for America and other capitalistic countries.

In dealing with the Church, they sought to reinterpret the basic doctrines of the Bible with an emphasis on the poor and social injustices. For example, Jesus was viewed as a liberator of the poor and oppressed—rather than as the Son of God who died for our sins on the cross. They redefined the church's mission to be the ushering in of a classless society ("God's kingdom") free of oppression and injustice through liberation of the exploited—instead of winning souls. "Sin" was redefined as a social and economic injustice rather than the condition of the human heart. Violence was sin if committed by an oppressor, but condoned if committed by the oppressed in their struggle to free themselves from their oppressors. Church—beware of insidious doctrines like this!! Be watchful and informed!

The Marxist-Leninist worldview is very much active in the world. They change their strategies to fit the conditions. Marxists work for groups with legitimate social grievances in order to come to power over them. They are masters of deception and of demoralizing and destabilizing a country. Today, Marxists are implementing a fourth approach—that of undermining America's traditional moral values and changing its culture-shaping institutions. Old values must be replaced with new ones (theirs). They have used the subversive power of rock music as a successful weapon toward this end (see **"Do what thou wilt"**). Also, our colleges and universities are infiltrated with those who teach a Marxist worldview to our children.

In 1920, Roger Baldwin, a Communist sympathizer, founded the American Civil Liberties Union (ACLU) whose purpose was to attack America's Constitution, national sovereignty, and its Judeo-Christian moral and religious foundation using our own court system (see Lesson 4).[7] Also, many of our judicial and congressional leaders lean toward socialism. The strategy of using drugs as a weapon against our young people has also been successfully implemented to weaken and demoralize our country. America is under attack—not with guns and bombs, but subversively from within. Be informed! Be discerning! In conclusion, I believe if there ever was a good example of satan's character emanating from an organization, it would be Marxism-Leninism (Communism). For information or teaching materials on worldviews, visit www.summit.org.

3. **Reincarnation**—Originating from Hinduism, it is their solution to the problem of evil and what takes place in the afterlife. They share this belief (with variations) with followers of other Eastern religious traditions such as Sikhism, Buddhism, and Jainism. This belief rivals Christianity's teaching of heaven and hell. Instead, it teaches that one can "atone" for their "sins" through a cycle of birth, life, and rebirth until one eventually achieves perfection and godhood. When a person dies, their soul "transmigrates" into another body here on earth. This body can be human (male or female), animal, fish, or insect. In Hinduism, ultimately over countless reincarnations everyone will unite with God (Brahman). Some believe in progressive transmigration—the belief that once one attains the human stage, one cannot come back into a lesser form of life.

Since Hinduism does not believe in a personal God, a non-personal "law" of karma determines the circumstances and type of body one will receive when one is "reborn." It teaches that the prosperity or suffering that one is experiencing in their present life is the result of the good or evil they did in previous lives. The law of karma states that every thought, word, and action produced by a human being has a ripple effect that travels throughout the universe affecting everything it comes in contact with. These consequences or fruit's of one's actions (good or bad) eventually return to the doer in another lifetime. "Salvation" is thus earned by a person's actions. It is taught that there are things one can do to rise above the influence of karma such as practicing Transcendental Meditation. However, they are unable to tell us how we got here the first time with no previous actions to determine our karma.

This teaching is the main reason Hindus do not have humanitarian outreaches. They believe that the suffering person is working out their bad karma and should not be helped because they are getting what they deserve. Furthermore, they believe that interfering with that person's karma will adversely affect their own. This is also why they practice vegetarianism and will not kill other living things.

Reincarnation is an insidious, deceptive, wicked, and lethal lie. Satan has cleverly twisted the Bible truths of the "born again" Christian experience **(John 3:3)** and the resurrection of our bodies—into the belief of reincarnation. He has perverted the law of "sowing and reaping" **(Galatians 6:7)** and the meting out of rewards and punishments by the true God *"according to their works"* **(Revelation 20:12)**—into the law of karma. By so doing, he calculatingly undermines the authority of the Scriptures, and circumvents Christ's work on the cross by doing away with the need of a Savior to atone for one's sins. Through this teaching, satan also deceptively alleviates one's concern for death and judgment—giving a person a false view of the afterlife. He leads them to believe that death will only advance their evolution to godhood thereby repudiating a place of eternal punishment. In addition, reincarnation's beliefs support and justify other anti-biblical positions such as abortion (i.e. its okay to destroy the fetal tissue prior to the entry of a reincarnated person at some point near birth), and homosexuality (i.e. in our past and future lives, we will live in bodies of the opposite sex). Reincarnation is a prevalent belief in the New Age Movement and in other branches of the occult.

4. **Evolution**—In 1859, Charles Darwin published "The Origin of Species" which gave an alternative view (theory) for the origin of life. Originating from the naturalistic philosophy of the day (that only matter exists), Darwin rejected outright the prevailing belief that the God of the Bible made all things *"after his kind,"* with intelligent design, by speaking it into existence.

According to his theory, about 15 billion years ago there was a sing
happened by chance (without design) that started the natural process
has been referred to as the "Big Bang" theory. Since that event, suppo⸱
have evolved into living things and into higher forms of life through ⸱
"the survival of the fittest." This evolutionary process is slowly ⸱
ultimately producing a perfect specimen of humanity. This impersonal fo⸱
for the origin of everything instead of the true God.

Oddly enough, the theory of evolution gained acceptance through our court deci⸱⸱ ⸱nd has been cleverly disguised as a science. According to Dr. D. James Kennedy, "It's the only politically protected scientific theory that has ever existed." He also stated that since Darwin's view was published, many anti-Christian "isms" have been based upon this theory (which has been blindly accepted as fact). These include: Humanism, Freudianism, Marxism-Leninism (Communism), Nazism, and Fascism.[8] It has been freely taught in our public schools and colleges for decades, and has imbedded itself in the mainstream community. It has even paved the way for the widespread acceptance of psychic phenomenon through the belief that mankind has undergone a major leap in his evolutionary progression.

Like no other device, evolution has been used as a tool to destroy the faith of multitudes in the existence of the true God and the Bible. I believe evolution was ingeniously designed by demons to neutralize the central truths of the Gospel. You see, if evolution is true, then humanity is not created with unique purpose in the image of God. So if mankind is believed to come from "primordial soup," then it is easy to form other false beliefs like the devaluing of human life itself. This is sadly expressed in so many ways in our world today. If evolution is believed, then there also can be no sin, no hell, no heaven, no God, and no need for what Jesus did for us on the cross. When you think of it, it's absolutely incredible how the devil has energized this notion to the point that it is so universally accepted as truth! It is a graphic example of his ability to blind and deceive mankind! The evidence is on the side of creation, and when put under scientific scrutiny, every major pillar of evolution has collapsed. We must take a stand for the real truth and proclaim it! Variations of evolution also exist (like cosmic and punctuated evolution).

5. **Fatalism**—This and various related beliefs revolve around how much **free will** humans have, if any. On the extreme end, fatalism is an ancient belief that all events and choices are foreordained by a power called **fate,** which cannot be altered or prevented by anything a human being can do. According to this view, all we really can do is to accept our lot in life since our destiny has been decreed and is moving us toward a predetermined goal, and is beyond our control to change. Unlike **reincarnation** where allegedly one's future is determined by one's deeds in a previous life, fatalism teaches that humans do not have free will and that one's life is totally predestined by some capricious force "out there." For example, instead of believing that the reason one's house burned down was the direct result of natural causes or choices (like arson or carelessness), the fatalist believes that it was foreordained to happen before they were ever born and nothing they could have done could have prevented it. People express it today by saying things like, "Whatever will be, will be." Or, "If it was meant to be, it will happen." Or, "It was a 'twist of fate'."

Historically, fate has been viewed as either being an irrational force—governed by random chance—or having intelligence. It can be impersonal or personal; a natural force or a deity. Some

...ious deities were the ancient Greek's Moerae, or Fates, who consisted of the three daughters of Zeus/Night—Clotho, Lachesis, and Atropos. They supposedly arrived at one's birth and together overshadowed that person's entire life and determined their luck and unalterable destiny. The Roman Fates were the Parcae—Nona, Decuma, and Morta. Many religious systems have had similar counterparts. Variations of fatalism are the foundation of some occult practices such as astrology. There are religions like Islam that have some of its elements as well.

Fatalism obviously produces a very negative outlook on life—one of despair and hopelessness. If any variation of fatalism is true, it could naturally lead one to conclude that life is meaningless—that nothing is worth living for or dying for. It fosters a non-caring attitude that says, "It doesn't matter *what* I do because my efforts won't make any difference anyhow. So why should I bother to fight evil and injustice or help others with social problems?" Some people use this philosophy as a way to cope with disappointment; or to explain why bad things happen; or to enable them to accept things that they cannot change. It can also become a means of excusing ourselves for our shortcomings because if all our actions are caused by forces beyond our control, then how can we be held accountable for our actions? It is a destructive philosophy—a lie straight from the pit of hell!

6. **Luck**—is the name given to the belief in an unknown force that brings good fortune or adversity indiscriminately by chance. It should be differentiated from the law of averages, other mathematical probabilities, or things that just occur randomly due to cause and effect. Some popular sayings are: "Maybe their luck will rub off on me;" "I was lucky to meet him;" "I am lucky to be alive;" "Lady Luck was with me;" or as a parting gesture, "Good luck!" In any case, luck is viewed as a type of deity or force—a higher power that we place our faith in and commit our lives to. Think about it! Though we mean well, should we call upon some deity by wishing someone "luck?" Instead, is it not better to invoke God's blessings on them by saying "God bless you" or "God be with you"?

Some mix in <u>superstition</u> with luck whereby a person believes that the outcome of certain future events can be influenced for good by some action they perform. Therefore, good luck may depend on carrying or wearing an object—like a rabbit's foot or charm (see **Amulet, Talisman**); or it may depend upon the words that they say; or performing little rituals before important events like making the sign of the cross (i.e. crossing their fingers), or knocking on wood, etc. Some may try to improve their luck by what they think (i.e. positive thinking)—optimistically having faith that good things will happen to them as they get negative emotions under control. Some believe in a lucky or unlucky number, day, color, stones, stars, etc., and are careful to not do anything to "jinx" their luck. In reality, one's thinking becomes magical.

But how does one know whether a good or bad event has happened by chance or by design? Is it perceived as being arbitrarily sent by a universal, impersonal, natural force with no purpose? Or sent by a person or a spirit being with deliberate intent? The Bible says, *"Whatever is good and perfect comes to us from God above…"* (**James 1:17** NLT). Jesus said that His Father *"…gives his sunlight to both the evil and the good, and he sends rain on the just and on the unjust, too."* (**Matthew 5:45** NLT). Whatever good we receive in this life is graciously and undeservedly given to us from the God of the Bible, and not from a mysterious force. Let's give rightful credit to whom credit is due! Also, satan can bring favorable things our way to keep us believing in something other than the true God.

Adverse things can come into our lives from harvesting bad words and actions that we have planted. The true God can cause adversity to try to get our attention so we serve Him, or He may be sending His discipline or judgment. Demonic spirits can also be the cause. Our positive or negative outlook on life may affect the good or bad fortune we encounter. The bottom line is this: Believing in luck and chance is as much idolatry as believing in some pagan idol. It is but another attempt by satan to divert us from acknowledging or placing our faith in the true God. How big is the God of the Bible? He is all-powerful, all-knowing, flawless, and He *"fills heaven and earth."* It is only our view of Him that limits His abilities in our lives. **Q:** How big is your God?

7. **Hedonism**—is the devoted pursuit of pleasure and happiness which is considered the highest good one can do. This lifestyle can lead one to adopt an ethical standard of right and wrong that believes that the rightness of an action is determined by evaluating the pleasures and pains that it will produce. Accordingly, then, whatever causes pleasure is right. "If it feels good, do it." This self-indulging philosophy centers mainly on achieving the complete gratification of all sensual desires as one lives for the pleasure of the moment (asceticism is at the opposite end of the pole). There are other variations of hedonism like those who adhere to the tenets of Utilitarianism, which judges the rightness of an action from whatever makes everyone the happiest. But the Bible teaches that right and wrong are absolute values based on the nature of God and His Word. And feelings are not a reliable guide to determining morality.

God wants us to enjoy life to its fullest—as long as we put Him first in our lives and derive our fulfillment and satisfaction from our relationship with Him. God made us so that we would obtain true happiness by doing His will and loving, helping, and serving others. However, our natural instinct is to pursue pleasure—the gratification of the cravings of our sinful nature through the five senses of our body. Ironically, self-pleasure contains within it the seeds of discontent and misery. King Solomon of the Old Testament learned this firsthand when he gave himself over to the pursuit of pleasure. He described his experience in the second chapter of the Book of Ecclesiastes. He said he did not restrain himself from any pleasure or the accumulation of possessions. His conclusion was that it was all so empty and meaningless; however, that which did bring fulfillment and meaning to his life was to *"...fear God and obey his commands..."* **(1 Sam. 12:13-14).** *The Westminster Larger Catechism* summarizes God's Word regarding man's existence by this statement: "Man's chief and highest end is to glorify God, and fully to enjoy Him forever."

8. **"Do what thou wilt"**—Satanist, Aleister Crowley, is credited with originating the philosophy, "Do what thou wilt shall be the whole of the law" (see **Judges 17:6**). Many rock bands and musicians have been used to promote this evil philosophy to our children. Some rock stars even claim to have received their words and music from something outside of themselves. The Bible tells us that angels have musical ability **(Job 38:4,7).** Since the mid-1960s, our youth have been especially targeted for demoralization and have been under severe, relentless attack from this media and from the drug industry. They are defenseless to deal with the agenda rock music has for them. Rock music is a major shaper of values of our youth as its lyrics promote sex, drugs, alcohol, the occult, satanism, rape, violence, rebellion, suicide, murder, and other self-destructive behaviors—all in the name of free speech. These lyrics become a philosophy to our young people. All of the devil's forces—satanists, Marxists/Communists, occultists, etc.,—have been using rock music to recruit our youth and to impact them with their subversive messages. It has intentionally widened the generation gap by driving a wedge between them and their parents. Far from being just the cultural

trend, the use of rock music as a weapon of war is a deliberate strategy to corrupt our youth in order to demoralize our culture. Parents, you must prepare and equip your kids so they are able to successfully deal with this evil assault against them. If you don't, who will?

WHAT IS BEING TAUGHT IN OUR PUBLIC SCHOOLS AND UNIVERSITIES?

1. Education in early America was started by the Puritans for the express purpose of teaching the Bible. Their goal was to pass on their Christian heritage to the next generation by producing Christian moral character, knowledge, and wisdom in their children. However, philosophical changes which had been developing converged in the mid 1800s. As a result of the Renaissance (A.D. 1400-1600) and the Enlightenment (A.D. 1600-1800), the philosophies of rationalism, naturalism, and humanism from the ancient Greeks were revived in Europe. They greatly influenced the thinking of that day and quickly spread to America. Rationalism is the belief that truth can only be discovered by reason and the sciences (not revelation). Naturalism is the belief that everything is made up of only physical matter. And Humanism is the belief that man is supreme. These three beliefs convinced many to reject that the spiritual and the supernatural exist (or can't be known). Thus God became irrelevant and His existence was denied.

2. In the 1840s, a naïve Protestant Church in America agreed to place the education of their children in the hands of the Government—assuming that the curriculum would be rooted in biblical principles. The Catholic Church, however, wisely retained control of their schools. A new generation of educators had been trained in the early 1900s to be shapers of society rather than molders of character. Gradually the school system relinquished by Protestants fell into the hands of John Dewey and the Secular Humanists and the Marxists who embraced those three major tenets in #1 above. They began to teach their atheistic, materialistic worldviews, until in 1962, the true God, His Bible, and prayer were removed from the public school system by order of the Supreme Court. The 1960's liberal educrats used our public schools for social experimentation and behavior modification instead of for learning. Consequently, the content and approach to public education in America changed to fit the new socialist agenda. In the latter part of the 1900s, postmodern thinking and New Age practices have joined these others and are also being taught to our children today. These liberal worldviews have firmly entrenched themselves in all levels of American education. America has begun to enter the post-Christian era.

3. Is it any wonder our public schools are: teaching moral relativism; forcing early sex education and promoting the same-sex agenda; fostering anti-family sentiments; eradicating all traces of Judeo-Christian values; omitting or revising American history; portraying our nation as a discriminatory and oppressive society, thereby instilling hatred and distrust of America and capitalism through "social justice" classes, etc.; dumbing down the curriculum; and emphasizing multiculturalism. A wedge has been driven between the younger and older generation in order to instill in our children their worldviews. These ideologies are being inculcated into our children and, in turn, they enter society and infect it with these views. We've long been under attack in this area and many are ignorant of what is really happening. Pray for discernment.

4. Vulnerable and defenseless, our children enter our nation's public school system—many without the benefit of guidance from parents who are unaware of the true nature of what is being taught to them. "The reality is this," writes Chuck Edwards of Summit Ministries, "if a child goes through twelve years of government-funded public education and four years of a state-supported college with no other educational influences from parents, church, or other counter-

balancing sources, chances are good he or she will graduate as a liberal with a Secular Humanist outlook on life. If this same twenty-two year old goes on to three years of graduate school, he or she will more than likely become a leftist liberal (Marxist). And by the time this student completes a year or two of post-graduate training, he or she will be a full-fledged radical leftist liberal…"[9] (For information or teaching materials on worldviews visit www.summit.org).

5. Since our schools have become a breeding ground for every type of anti-Christian worldview, ask God if you should take advantage of the options of either home schooling or sending your children to a Christian school. Regardless, become actively involved in the content of your child's education and ask God how you can bring a Christian influence to your school system. Remember, it will be only a matter of time (if it hasn't already occurred—the outcome of the 2008 elections being any indication), before the subversive forces within the USA cause the tipping point that marks the beginning of the end of the greatest nation the world has ever seen.

THE OCCULT

Introduction—Throughout history, most nations were steeped in the worship of false gods which impacted their culture. Satan and his demons have a stranglehold on people through superstition and fear. The devil is a hard taskmaster and requires 100% ownership of his subjects. All kinds of abhorrent and detestable practices were used in the name of worship. These people were coerced into attempting to appease these gods to win their favor. However, there is another aspect to satan's religious system that is not as easily categorized as the religions on our Seven Views of God chart. It is called the "occult," meaning "secret" (see next chart for overview). Occult practices are energized by demonic power and are usually incorporated into one's religious expression. Within the occult's aura of mystery and secrecy, satan lures mankind with the attractive bait of becoming god-like—obtaining supernatural knowledge and power over others. When one opens the door to the occult, oppression and enslavement result. One can only be set free by the power of the Holy Spirit. There is no such thing as "harmless involvement" in any aspect of the occult. Just one exposure is all it can take to give the devil a foothold in your life resulting in **demonization.**

Caution! These areas are extremely dangerous. God forbids us to dabble in any occult practice or false religion. For our protection, He warns us of the eternal consequences of rejecting Him.

1. Read these Scriptural references and write in God's reaction toward someone involved in an area of satan's religious system. When finished, go to #2 on the next page.

   A. **Leviticus 19:31** _____

   B. **Judges 2:11-12** _____

   C. **Judges 2:14-15** _____

   D. **Deuteronomy 18:9-12** _____

   E. **Leviticus 20:6** _____

   F. **2 Kings 1:2-4** _____

   G. **Revelation 21:8** _____

OVERVIEW OF THE OCCULT

2. Below is an overview of satan's religious systems known as the "occult." These elements cover the three areas that devotees of false religions and the occult attempt to do to their false gods: 1. **Appease** them, 2. **Inquire** of them, and 3. **Invoke** them to do something. **Below is an overview of Appendix A where each point is enlarged upon** (located in the back of this workbook). Please don't skip over this section. This information can be vital to you.

Lesson 3

THE BELT OF TRUTH: Mankind Reflects One of Two Fathers

☑ Before starting the DVD:

Today, we continue to put on the Belt of Truth by learning more about the true nature of the world around us. We also continue to lay a foundation for this study. As you will notice, the first seven points on the list below are a recap from the last two lessons. The eighth point, "Its children," will be the basis of this lesson and will wrap up the overview of what the Bible has to say about our world. In this lesson, we will learn more about both God's character and satan's character and what sin is. Also a brief treatment of demonization, demon possession, and the casting out of demons will be given. Ask the Holy Spirit, who guides us into all truth, to reveal this great truth to you as you proceed with this study.

☑ **DVD Users:** Watch Lesson 3 (27 min.). When you're through, pick up again at this point.

HOW GOD SEES OUR WORLD (continued)

1. Its <u>god</u> (ruler) is satan.
2. Its <u>kingdoms</u> are controlled by satan.
3. Its <u>character</u> is evil.
4. Its <u>spiritual</u> <u>condition</u> is darkness and blindness.
5. Its <u>wisdom</u> omits the true God.
6. Its <u>religions</u> and <u>prophets</u> steal people away from the true God.
7. Its <u>duration</u> is temporary.
8. Its C͟h͟i͟l͟d͟r͟e͟n͟ .

   † **Matthew 13:38** (KJV)—Referring to the Parable of the Sower, Jesus said: *"The field is the world; the good seed are the children of the kingdom; but the tares are the children of the wicked one."*

A. Jesus divided the world into T͟w͟o͟ C͟l͟a͟s͟s͟e͟s͟ of people.

   † **1 John 3:10,12**—*This is how we know who the children of God are and who the children of the devil are: Anyone who does not do what is right is not a child of God; neither is anyone who does not love his brother. **12.** Do not be like Cain, who belonged to the evil one and murdered his brother.*

   † **John 8:44**—Jesus said: *"You belong to your father, the devil, and you want to carry out your father's desire. He was a murderer from the beginning, not holding to the truth, for there is no truth in him. When he lies, he speaks his native language, for he is a liar and the father of lies."*

   † **Genesis 3:15**—God said to the serpent (satan) in the Garden of Eden: *"And I will put enmity...between your offspring and hers* [Eve's].

D

st as children reflect their parents, God's character and the devil's
rough people's actions. We have a choice as to which character we
everyone's God (Creator and Judge), but not everyone's Father. It
erience to enable us to consistently portray God's character and
y connected to Jesus **(John 15:1-6),** and allow the Spirit to have
character will be produced in us **(Galatians 5:22-25).**

engaging in this invisible war, it is imperative that we know our enemy, and even
more critical, to better know our Heavenly Father. Let us now compare their character.
(This lesson's Summary will present an enlargement of this rich truth. Lesson 7 will shed
even more light).

GOD'S CHARACTER	SATAN'S CHARACTER (sin)
1. Love	1. Hatred / Maliciousness
2. Faithful	2. Deserter / Betrayer / Backstabber
3. Truth	3. Lie / Deceive / Distort
4. Humble	4. Proud
5. Saves	5. Condemns / Dooms
6. Guides	6. Entraps / Leads Astray
7. Forgives / Reconciles	7. Accuses / Revengeful
8. Liberates / Delivers	8. Enslaves / Binds
9. Compassion	9. Merciless
10. Pure	10. Perverted / Defiled / Unclean
11. Submissive	11. Rebellious
12. Defend / Exalt	12. Slander / Defames / Blasphemes
13. Gentle	13. Violent / Destructive
14. Meets Needs (provider)	14. Makes Destitute
15. Magnanimous Giver	15. Greedy / Covetous / Envy
16. Burden Bearer / Remover	16. Burden Giver (oppresses)
17. Righteous / Justice / Fairness	17. Thief / Injustice / Unfairness
18. Self-control	18. Unrestraint / Excess / Wasteful

GOD (The Giver of)	SATAN (The Giver of)
19. Peace / Unity / Tranquility	19. Discord / Strife / Division
20. Joy	20. Misery / Despair
21. Confidence / Courage	21. Fear / Terror / Intimidation
22. Hope	22. Discouragement / Depression
23. Comfort	23. Torment / Affliction
24. Happiness / Blessings	24. Vexation / Harassment / Trouble

▶**CONSIDER THIS:** All these wicked, sinful character traits are character opposite of God's. They were in existence before God created Adam and Eve—first occurring in lucifer (satan) and his fallen angels at the time of their rebellion against God. When we sin by allowing satan's character to be expressed in our actions, it originates from our sinful nature rather than being caused by a demon.

This evil character comes into existence when a free moral being (angel or human) decides to reject God's laws and His will from ruling over their life, and they enthrone self-rule in God's place. The Bible tells us that *"sin is lawlessness"* **(1 John 3:4).** This declaration of independence from God says, "My laws are higher than Your laws for my life. I will not allow You to reign over me." From this initial sin proceeds the rest of this dark character that plagues us all today. It really all comes down to this: Will we live reflecting God's character? Or will we "live like the devil" and "miss the mark" for the reason God created us?

> ☑ This ends the DVD content for Lesson 3.
> ☑ Continue on in this workbook for additional material **not** on the DVD.

DEMON POSSESSION AND DEMONIZATION

1. The true biblical accounts of people in Jesus' day who had demons living inside their bodies provide us with an incredible insight into the true nature and personalities of evil spirits. In fact, observing those who are possessed furnishes us with the main opportunity to see the evil actions of these invisible spirits for who they really are. Note that these spirits are not, as some believe, the souls of deceased human beings trying to gain access into one's body.

2. Although the actual words, **"demon possession,"** do not occur in the Bible, the term has been used extensively within the church to denote one or more evil spirits who enter and reside in a human body and control the person. But in recent times, scholars are frequently suggesting that a more accurate word to use is **"demonize"**—a general term for a progressive range of demonic control and influence that includes possession. New Testament translations also use the phrases *"have a spirit,"* or *"demon,"* or *"an unclean spirit,"* to describe the condition that we have traditionally called "possessed." However, a distinction needs to be made between when a demon inhabits a body and when he influences or attacks a person from outside their body. Let's provide working definitions for these two familiar terms for clarification purposes.

Demon Possession

📖 **DEFINITION—DEMON POSSESSION**

"Demonize" comes from the Greek word *daimonizomai*. The word signifies "to be possessed of a demon, to act under the control of a demon."[1] For clarity let the following be our working definition of the term demon possession: **It is when one or more evil spirits, after gaining initial access, enter and leave a physical body at will in order to inhabit, control, express, and gratify themselves through the one being indwelt.** When a person becomes demon possessed, his personality is overridden by the new personality of the demon(s) while in that state and becomes a different person. Other manifestations are also present as given in the list below. Demon possession should not be mistaken for some types of personality disorders and mental illnesses traceable to natural causes—although in some cases that is exactly what the cause is.

One may wonder why evil spirits seek to inhabit a body—as if they lost something when they fell. Regardless, do not be fearful that they can inhabit your body at will (we'll soon cover whether a Christian can be possessed). An opening must be given to them. Some of the ways they can gain access is through persistently committing a particular sin, involvement with occult practices, victimization, and from something our parents did. However, regardless of how bad a person is bound by satan, they can still choose to leave his bondage as God is present to deal with that person.

Facts About Demon Possession

Be aware of the following aspects regarding evil spirits and demon possession which still occur today. Note the destructive way their father, the devil, treats his children. (I encourage you to look up the Scripture references. However, it may not be feasible to do so in a group setting due to time constraints. An individual study of the Scripture references at a later time will prove invaluable.)

1. More than one evil spirit can live inside a human body **(Mark 5:9,13; Luke 8:2).**

2. There can be a chief spokesperson for multiple evil spirits inside a person **(Mark 5:8-12).**

3. Evil spirits can have meaningful names which they can be expected to disclose by an authoritative command **(Mark 5:9).**

4. Evil spirits can audibly cry out as well as converse with human beings—even in different languages. Their own individual voice can be heard by other bystanders **(Mark 5:7-12; 9:26; Luke 4:33-35; Acts 8:7; 19:15).**

5. They have intellectual capabilities of thought and reasoning and can try to persuade someone into choosing a course of action **(Mark 5:9-12).**

6. Evil spirits know human beings by name and can differentiate between those who are effective servants of God and those who are not **(Acts 19:13-15).**

7. Demons can possess, or reside in, animals **(Luke 8:33),** and attach themselves to and accompany inanimate objects like religious figurines.

8. They can compel someone to live in unnatural places such as *"in the tombs"* or in *"solitary places"* **(Luke 8:27, 29).**

9. They can be the cause of unnatural indecent exposure, stripping one of all that one has **(Luke 8:27).**

10. Some evil spirits (perhaps all) exhibit a violent behavior with a malicious intent to destroy **(Matthew 8:28, 32; Mark 5:5; 9:18-22).**

11. Evil spirits can exhibit superhuman strength and knowledge through the human beings they possess **(Mark 5:3-4; Luke 8:29; Acts 16:16; 19:16).**

12. Human beings can be demon possessed from an adult to a child (probably due to something their parents did—perhaps even from the womb) **Mark 7:25-26; 9:17,21.**

13. Evil spirits can be the cause of physical illness and mental disorders beyond any possible cure apart from the casting out of the demon causing it **(Matthew 17:15,18; Mark 5:15; 9:20; 9:17,25; Luke 7:21; 8:2-3; Acts 8:7).** However, not every illness or mental problem is caused by them nor should be attributed to them **(Matthew 4:23-24; 10:8; 12:22; Mark 1:32-34; 6:13; 16:17-18; Luke 4:40-41; 6:18-19; 9:1-2).**

14. Evil spirits fear their future time of torment and judgment **(Matthew 8:29).** They also fear existing regions of the underworld such as the Abyss **(Luke 8:31).**

15. Evil spirits believe and acknowledge the deity of Jesus Christ—that He is the Son of God. They must bow before Him in recognition of His name and His authority **(Mark 3:11; 5:6-8; Luke 4:33-34; James 2:19).**

16. Faith in the authority and power of the name of Jesus Christ, together with fasting and prayer, can cast out evil spirits that possess human beings with total deliverance. It is done by the Holy Spirit's power through a human vessel—whether it be Jesus, the apostles, or a believer today **(Matthew 10:1; 12:28; 17:18-21; Mark 7:29-30; 9:23,24,28,29; 16:17; Luke 4:36; 6:18-19; 8:34-35; Acts 8:5-8; 19:11-12).** (See section on **Driving Out Evil Spirits**).

17. Those who have had evil spirits driven out from living inside their bodies can be possessed again if they fall away from serving Christ **(Matthew 12:43-45).**

18. A person can also experience intermittent possession of an evil spirit like some psychic healers or spiritualistic mediums who conduct séances where demons who impersonate the deceased through the medium come and go as they are conjured up.

19. There are varying degrees of wickedness between evil spirits just as they vary in power and authority **(Matthew 12:45).**

20. The evil spirits within the person can exhibit strong abhorrence toward the things of the God of the Bible. For example, they cringe at the sight of religious symbols (i.e. the cross) or the mention of the name of Jesus Christ or His sacrificial blood. The person himself has a difficult time saying the name of Jesus Christ.

CAN A CHRISTIAN BECOME DEMON POSSESSED?

1. There is a controversy in the Body of Christ over whether a true *"born again"* Christian having the Holy Spirit residing in them can have an evil spirit living within their body too. **Q:** So can a Christian be demon possessed? My personal belief is that a true Christian can **not** be possessed by an evil spirit as we have defined it above. When one is truly *"born again,"* one becomes a *"new creation"* **(2 Corinthians 5:17).** It is inconceivable to me that the Holy Spirit

and an evil spirit could live together in the same body and co-control the person. However, new believers may need to undergo deliverance which may involve this, as well as Christians who backslide to the point where they grieve the Holy Spirit and He is forced to leave them.

2. Yet, much of the respected deliverance ministry of the late Derek Prince claimed to deal with casting demons out of Christians. Other prominent ministers believe a Christian can be possessed in their body and/or soul, but not their spirit (like floors of a house). Some others would counter that God and demons already co-exist because the Holy Spirit is omnipresent. Somehow I think that is different. In the final analysis, I must admit that I cannot be dogmatic in this area.

3. **Q:** Are the physical ailments and mental disorders that a Christian suffers almost always caused by demons within them that need to be "cast out?" Some Christian groups hold to this belief. Granted, there is a Scriptural basis for demons causing illness as a result of demon possession (the illness leaves when the demon is cast out). However, we **cannot** make the general assumption that most illnesses and mental disorders that a Christian (or unbeliever) experiences are due to an evil spirit causing the infirmity—let alone be the result of demon possession.

   A. Much of human sickness and disease are caused by other things like: unhealthy foods and substances that we ingest into our bodies or expose them to; abusing our body; emotional sins such as anger and unforgiveness which in turn affect the body; and the natural aging process of death working in us—to name a few. Discernment is needed here **(1 Corinthians 12:10).**

   B. The Bible makes a distinction between natural illness and those who are demon possessed **(Matthew 4:24; 8:16).** Of course, evil spirits can cause illness in a Christian's life without "possessing" them—as in the case of Job **(Job 2:7),** and the apostle Paul **(2 Corinthians 12:7).** In such cases, it is either permitted by God or brought on by ourselves. In any case, we indeed need to confront the sickness through prayer—standing firm in the healing Christ purchased for us on the cross. But I don't believe we should view the sickness as caused by a demon residing **within** us who needs to be "cast out." In the final analysis, I think we would find that most of our illnesses are **not** of demonic origin at all.

4. It is difficult to comment more about demon possession in the unbeliever, especially the conditions that have to be present for one to enter. The Bible gives us a basic understanding—and that is all.

Demonization

📖 DEFINITION—DEMONIZATION

Again we refer to the Greek word *daimonizomai*. For the sake of clarity, let us define demonization as: **When an evil spirit attacks, influences, or controls a person from outside their body without inhabiting it.** I believe this is mainly what a Christian encounters. The unbeliever is a prey to both this and possession. These attacks are directed to our body, soul, and spirit.

1. When a person is "demonized," it can take the form of pressure to sin; harassment; mental obsessions; physical pain or illness; emotional depression and instability; and spiritual oppression. If something becomes habitual or obsessive beyond our control, it is very possible that the source is demonic involvement.

2. Demonization can come as a result of: (1) the devil's retaliation for effective ministry which damages his kingdom (some, I believe, are on the devil's "hit list"); (2) wrong choices we make to sin which invite the enemy and give him a foothold in our lives; (3) opposition to try to prevent us from entering God's will or when spiritual breakthrough is just ahead; (4) God's permission for the devil to afflict one of His children to test them or to work out the image of Christ in their life; (5) victimization; and (6) exposure to the occult. Like demon possession, usually when the evil spirit(s) departs, the problems stop, too. Note that those in the medical and psychological professions who do not believe in the supernatural will attribute possession and demonization to natural causes. (See **"Recapturing lost territory: five steps to"** in index.)

DRIVING OUT EVIL SPIRITS

📖 DEFINITION—CASTING OUT Evil Spirits

The Greek word the Holy Spirit used was *ekballō* meaning "to drive out." Due to Christ's redemptive work, an evil spirit possessing a person can be driven out! However, this should only be resorted to after all other possible natural and spiritual explanations have been explored. In addition, it should only be attempted by mature Spirit-filled believers who have unwavering faith in Christ's victory on the cross and have received careful instruction in dealing with these situations. Sadly, the practice of this essential type of deliverance ministry has been generally neglected by the church. This avoidance is due to its unpleasant and time-consuming nature, fear, and a lack of proper training. There are those who discount it altogether because they either believe the devil doesn't exist, or he's bound somewhere, or that this type of deliverance was meant just for the early church.

1. On what basis can evil spirits be driven out of demon-possessed people?

   A. On the basis of satan's irreversible defeat through the death and resurrection of Jesus Christ whereby He stripped demonic rulers of their power, and sealed satan's doom.

   † **Hebrews 2:14-15**—*...that by his* [Christ's] *death he might destroy...the devil—15. and free those who all their lives were held in slavery...*

   † **Colossians 2:15**—*And having disarmed the powers and authorities, he* [Jesus] *made a public spectacle of them, triumphing over them by the cross.*

   B. On the basis of the power and authority given to Christ's disciples **(Matthew 10:1),** and later to all believers through the Baptism of the Holy Spirit.

   † **Mark 16:17**—Jesus said to His disciples: *"And these signs will accompany those who believe: in my name they will drive out demons..."*

   C. On the basis that it is an integral part of Christ's great commission and part of the proclamation of liberty to those who are bound as satan's captives **(Luke 4:18).**

2. What does it mean to cast out devils *"in my name?"*

   A. It means to have the power of attorney—a delegated right to act in Christ's place as though He Himself were doing so.

† **Luke 9:1**—*When Jesus had called the Twelve together, he gave them power and authority to drive out all demons and to cure diseases...*

Note: The *"power"* Jesus gave them had to do with the dynamic of expulsion, whereas the *"authority"* had to do with the <u>right</u> to use that power. It is possible to have authority without the faith and power **(Mark 9:18, 28-29)**. This power and authority extends over *"all demons"*—none excluded.

3. How are evil spirits driven out?

A. It is done by a *"miracle"* accomplished by the supernatural power of God **(Mark 9:38,39)**.

B. They are driven out by *"the finger of God"* **(Luke 11:20)** meaning by God Himself working through human instrumentality through the power of the Holy Spirit to *"bind the strong man"* (the devil) and set his captives free **(Matthew 12:28-29)**.

C. It is done *"with a word."* Jesus cast out spirits with an authoritative command **(Matt 8:16)**.

D. They are driven out by addressing spirits by name and commanding them in an unhesitating manner with assurance and authority **(Mark 9:25)**.

E. They are driven out by *"prayer and fasting."* Certain kinds of spirits can only be dislodged in this manner—probably due to their power and tenacity **(Matthew 17:21)**.

F. Evil spirits, and satan himself, are subject to the believer through the name of Jesus Christ.

† **Luke 10:17,19**—[They] *returned with joy and said, "Lord, even the demons submit to us in your name." He* [Jesus] *replied, "...I have given you authority to trample on snakes and scorpions, and to overcome all the power of the enemy; nothing will harm you..."*

Note: The practice of casting out evil spirits is not contingent on affiliation with any particular denominational group. It might even be forbidden by some in the mistaken belief that whenever ministries lie outside the circle of their particular group, they are necessarily wrong and must be disapproved **(Mark 9:38-40)**.

4. What things are involved with a person in recovery?

A. Depression, lack of self-esteem, and guilt (the deep scars that are probably left over from possession) will be exploited by the enemy to try to negate the deliverance.

B. They will need a period of rebuilding their spiritual lives to keep their deliverance through concentrated time in the Bible, prayer, and exposure to Christian influences and fellowship.

5. There is a difference between driving out evil spirits and **exorcism.**

📖 DEFINITION—EXORCISM

The Greek word is *exorkistēs* and it denotes one who attempts to drive out demons by incantations and the use of magical formulas. The Bible does not condone exorcism because its effectiveness rests in the words and magical rituals themselves and not in the powerful sacrifice of Jesus Christ, or in the model He gave us on how we should drive them out. Note that this term is used interchangeably for the real thing, but biblically it should not be.

A. **Acts 19:13** is the only biblical reference regarding exorcism. The seven sons of Skeva, professional exorcists, tried to imitate those who had divine credentials by employing a ritualistic invocation of the name of Jesus over a man demon possessed. Instead, the man jumped on them and beat them and drove them out of the house naked and bleeding.

Note: The casting out of evil spirits must be done by those in whom the Holy Spirit dwells and whose faith is anchored in Christ's victory of the devil on the cross. One can be letter perfect in the ritual but lack the power and relationship with Christ.

STUDY QUESTIONS AND APPLICATION

1. Compare the character traits under the headings, "God's Character" and "satan's Character" that were given earlier in this lesson. How much of God's character do you exhibit? How much do you reflect satan's character?

2. Referring to question [#]1 above, what steps can you immediately take to reflect more of God's character in your life?

3. Read the following story and answer the questions at the end. The answers follow:

   Imagine finding yourself alone in a warm and comfortable place surrounded by water. You hear a constant rhythmic pounding, but you can't figure out what it is or where it's coming from. You get accustomed to it. You feel very secure and protected in this cozy place.

   Weeks later, you hear muffled voices outside but can't make out what is being said. "Who are those people?" you ask yourself. Soon you begin to feel an intermittent pressure on your head. The pressure comes and goes for hours, and by now you have quite a headache. "How strange!" you think, "This has never happened before." You wonder what it is.

   Unexpectedly, you begin to experience a new sensation like you are falling. You notice that the water that surrounded you is gone. "How could it have vanished so quickly?" Now for the first time you begin to feel very insecure. Your environment is no longer warm and comfortable. Now you feel like you are being squeezed at irregular intervals. That pounding sound has stopped. You don't like what's happening.

   Your head begins to be cold, and gradually so is the rest of you. You open your eyes to see where you are and wow, there is such brightness. Now you sense an unfamiliar new feeling—as if you are being lifted up. A strange sensation is occurring in your mouth. Suddenly, you feel the need to take a deep breath of air. You cough. Then you let out a big cry!

   A. Name that warm and comfortable environment you were in? _____

   B. What had just happened to you when you let out that big cry? _____

ANSWERS to #3:

A. Your mother's womb

B. You were just born—born into satan's kingdom, that is, if the devil through an abortionist didn't kill you first. Certainly, one would think that the womb, of all places, would be a very safe and secure place; however, not even it is exempt from satan's destructive reach. And once out of your mother's womb, be thankful she didn't dispose of you in the dumpster, etc., like some do, or that your life wasn't taken in some other way. Then there's the tragic possibility you could have been born with an alcohol or drug dependency from your mother during pregnancy, or with mental or physical defects, or with an incurable sexually transmitted disease.

Welcome to planet earth! That's just the way it is here. You did not ask to be born, but here you are. God has a plan for your life—an assignment just for you **(Jeremiah 29:11)**. He has placed within you unique giftings to benefit mankind and bring glory to Himself. You are uniquely created! There has not ever been, and there will never be, another you!

4. But wait. There's more. Not only have you entered satan's domain, but it may shock you to know you were born with the following strikes against you due to our first parents, Adam and Eve. It is critical to have an awareness of what these are to help us in this invisible war. Read these Scriptures and write what God's Word says you inherited from Adam's sin. Then thank God Christ came to reverse these and deliver us from them. (Recommended for groups: First assign Scriptures to members of your group. When everyone has located them, then take turns reading the verses.)

Romans 5:19; 7:18-25 _____

John 8:34; Romans 6:6 _____

2 Timothy 2:26 _____

John 8:42-44 _____

Romans 5:10; Colossians 1:21 _____

John 3:36; Ephesians 2:3 _____

Romans 5:12; 6:23; Matthew 26:24 _____

5. In your daily interactions, ask the Holy Spirit to teach you to use the powerful weapon of discernment in order to ascertain whether something is of God or of satan. Be alert and learn to recognize the type of character (God's or satan's) that emanates from a person, a group, a business, entertainment, a situation, etc. Whenever you see the wicked character of satan, then realize that the sinful nature is in control and evil spirits are given the liberty to work—avoid them! Whenever you see Christ's character portrayed, further check out their fruit and track record. Beware of any deception because the devil likes to masquerade behind godliness.

6. What are your personal beliefs regarding the following questions? After you're through, compare your answers with the following Scriptures: **Psalm 139:13-16; Jeremiah 1:4-5; Luke 1:13-15, 36, 39-44; Zechariah 12:1; Psalm 51:5.** (See what I believe to be the correct answers at end of this SQ&A section below.)

A. What is the origin of our being (i.e. soul, spirit, personhood) prior to inhabiting our body in our mother's womb? (Check one).

    1. ☐ From being created at the moment the sperm impregnates the egg at conception

    2. ☐ From a previous life   3. ☐ From being created by God before the world began

    4. ☐ Other:_____

B. When does a person's life begin on earth?

    1. ☐ At conception 2. ☐ Sometime during the 9 months of gestation 3. ☐ Delivery at birth

C. At what point does one become a person?

    1. ☐ Prior to conception 2. ☐ At conception 3. ☐ Sometime during the 9 months of gestation

    4. ☐ Delivery at birth 5. ☐ Sometime after birth

D. At what point does God hold a person responsible for their sins?

    1. ☐ At conception   2. ☐ Sometime during the 9 months of gestation

    3. ☐ Delivery at birth 4. ☐ After the "age of accountability" (when the child knows right from wrong)

E. When an aborted or miscarried baby dies, where do you think the baby goes, to heaven or to hell? _____

F. Where do you think a child who is born goes (heaven or hell) if he or she dies before "the age of accountability?" _____

G. If it is true that satan promotes abortion and tries to keep all people from reaching heaven, then give your opinion as to why it is that he allows millions of aborted babies to presumably go to heaven (the majority of which probably would not have gone there if they were not aborted and lived out their lives)?

Did you know? Contraceptives (i.e. condoms) prevent conception, but chemicals (i.e. the birth control pill, a shot, the patch, IUD) are actually abortifacients which, once the sperm impregnates the egg, prevent implantation and kill life that has already been conceived. Stem cell harvesting through cloning and embryonic *in vitro* fertilization creates life and then destroys the life of the embryo by removing the stem cells.

7. At times God can use demonic spirits to accomplish His objectives in a person's life. How did God employ the instrumentality of evil spirits in the lives of:

A. Abimelech in **Judges 9:1-5, 22-24, 52-57?** _____

_____

B. King Ahab in **2 Chronicles 18: 3-8, 18-22, 33-34?** _____

_____

C. Backslidden Christians in **1 Corinthians 5:1-5; 1 Timothy 1:20?** _____

_____

D. The apostle Paul in **2 Corinthians 12:7-10?** _____

E. The unrepentant in **Revelation 9:1-15?** _____

Answers to SQ&A [#]6:   **A.**—1;   **B.**—1;   **C.**—2;   **D.**—4;   **E.**—Heaven;   **F.**—Heaven;

SUMMARY

We have armed ourselves with more truth (as the belt denotes). We completed an overview of our world from God's perspective by finishing up the eighth point—its **8. children.** Jesus divided up the whole world into **8A** two classes (or families): children of God and children of the devil. Children reflect their parents so we have a choice as to which character we will visibly express through our actions.

We learned that God is everyone's God but not everyone's Heavenly Father. To become a child of God requires a *"born-again"* experience. One of the things we receive from Christ's atoning work on the cross is adoption into God's family (more will be said about this in Lesson 8). As we stay connected to Jesus in a vital relationship, He enables us to live a life that consistently reflects His character.

Before engaging in this invisible war, we emphasized the importance of knowing our enemy. We will now enlarge on contrasting God's character with that of satan's and his demons to get a close-up look at our adversary and also get to know our Heavenly Father better. This comparison will also enable us to see the spectrum of sin and gain insight into how each father treats their children. **Note: This summary is lengthy because I want to be sure you get the full impact of the points that I am trying to make about God's and satan's character traits.**

1. God is unconditional LOVE and seeks our highest good **(1 John 4:8-16).** Satan has intense HATRED and malice for everyone—without cause. Being *"...a murderer from the beginning"* **(John 8:44),** he and his cohorts are the active force behind the taking of life because they have utter contempt for the sacredness of life. They were the moving force that stirred up hatred for the

Jews resulting in the German death camps of WWII as well as in the killing of the Bethlehem area, during Jesus' day, as ordered by Herod. An evil spirit moved Saul to God's anointed **(1 Samuel 19:6, 9-12)**. They are also the instigators behind those w. genocide and ethnic cleansing. In contrast, God's hatred is based on a righteous abhorre and evil. And Jesus came that through His death on the cross, *"He might destroy him wh. .iad the power of death, that is, the devil"* **(Hebrews 2:14)**.

2. God is FAITHFUL—especially to His own **(2 Thessalonians 3:3; Lamentations 3:23; Revelation 19:11)**. Though everyone else fails us, God will be faithful to us and will *"never leave us or forsake us."* Satan is unfaithful to his own and is a DESERTER. He may work in your behalf—and even take care of you for a time—but only to further his plans. However, as soon as you become useless to him, he will discard you like he did Judas Iscariot. He used Judas to betray Jesus with a kiss and then he turned around and betrayed Judas—moving him to commit suicide through the remorse Judas felt. He is the ultimate back-stabber. However, there is one area that we can trust the devil. We can count on him to be exactly what he is in his evil character.

3. God and His Word are absolute TRUTH. The Holy Spirit *"guides us into all truth"* **(John 16:13)**. One of the reasons Jesus came to earth was to proclaim truth **(John 14:6; 18:37)**. But Jesus had this to say about the devil, *"there is no truth in him...he is a liar and the father of it."* **(John 8:44)**. He also is a DECEIVER—the ultimate master of the art of deception—and he has been doing so practically undetected since the fall of Adam and Eve: *"...Satan which deceived the whole world."* **(Revelation 12:9)**. He skillfully disguises falsehood with truth. He masquerades—passing himself off for what he is not—by wearing, so to speak, a mask or costume as a concealment of his true identity and purpose. He can make things look like the work of an angry God, when in reality, he was the one behind it. He deludes people into giving their lives for religious causes like crashing commercial airliners into buildings and suicide bombings in public places. He accomplishes his purposes through lies and deception.

4. In Jesus, God is HUMBLE **(John 13:14-16)** in that He laid aside His attributes and came to earth to live among us, sitting where we sit, and dying a cruel death for us on the cross. Though God fills heaven and earth and is exalted in the highest, He is "small" enough to live within us. But satan is PROUD **(Ezekiel 28:17)**. Pride is the deification of self which casts off the throne rights of the Creator over one's life. Lucifer said *"...I will exalt my throne above the stars of God...I will be like the most high"* **(Isaiah 14:13-14)**. His prideful lust for the power and position of almighty God—along with the delusion that he could attain it, brought his downfall. But the capabilities and power he was created with were retained after his fall so that now here is a being with superhuman power with selfishness as his driving motivation.

5. God SAVES **(John 3:17)**. Jesus came to rescue us from sin, the devil, and eternal hell at the cost of His own life. Satan CONDEMNS—he tries to ensure our doom and destruction by every possible means **(Job 1:8-11)**.

6. The Holy Spirit GUIDES us in the way we should go and has our best interests in mind **(Isaiah 30:21; 58:11; Psalm 48:14)**. The devil leads us astray from that which is best for us in order to ENTRAP us **(1 Timothy 3:7)**. We must walk very carefully in life to avoid his pitfalls. He and his cohorts have used their corrupted superhuman wisdom and knowledge to invent snares and traps for us—as only their evil minds can contrive. They will tempt, lure, and seduce us in order to destroy us.

7. God FORGIVES us as we meet His conditions of repentance and forgiveness of others **(Matthew 6:14-15; 18:21-35).** All sin can be forgiven by God except for knowingly attributing the works of the Holy Spirit to the devil and harboring unforgiveness. God's heart always reaches out in reconciliation **(2 Corinthians 5:19).** But in contrast, satan is full of revenge and is called *"the accuser of the brethren"* **(Revelation 12:10).** He ACCUSES us before God day and night (whether it be true or false), to try to move God to test His children.

8. God LIBERATES. His heart is always bent toward setting people free and making them whole **(Luke 4:17-18).** Satan ENSLAVES **(2 Timothy 2:26).** The devil took pleasure in crippling a dear Jewish woman in Jesus' day. She was bowed over and could not stand erect. Jesus said that satan had bound her for 18 years with a spirit of infirmity. Christ liberated the woman from her prison **(Luke 13:11-16).** The enemy also delights in getting us addicted to the invisible chains of drugs, alcohol, and other substance abuses, or to illicit sex and other addictive, destructive behaviors. He also binds people through forced labor like black slavery, or through the coercion of forced prostitution like the millions of children who are forced into the international sex trafficking industry worldwide each year. Satan wants us bound so we can't be free.

9. God exudes COMPASSION. His heart is touched with our pain, sorrow, and needs **(Matthew 9:36; 14:14).** He delights to show undeserved mercy. Satan is devoid of any compassion. This horrible creature is UNMERCIFUL. He *"walks about seeking whom he may devour"* **(1 Peter 5:8).** We see how satan delighted to overwhelm Job with grief and sorrow through successive tragedies to crush him in order that Job might curse God **(Job 1:14-20).** He has the same goal for our lives. He will try to drive you to the brink of despair and insanity.

10. God is PURE and HOLY. There is no evil in His nature. Satan and his demons are depraved. They delight in defiling that which is pure and holy. These PERVERTED beings DEFILE and CORRUPT the things of God and invert them for evil **(Acts 13:10; Mark 11:15-17).** They call good, evil; and evil, good. They loathe those who uphold retaining one's virginity until marriage, while trying to seduce our youth to give up theirs. Satanists mock the Roman Catholic mass by mixing blood and urine in the communion cup, displaying upside-down crosses, saying the Lord's Prayer backwards, and having sex with an unclothed woman on the "communion table" as a "living altar." Jesus called them *"unclean spirits"* and they are vulgar, depraved, and obscene.

11. Jesus is SUBMISSIVE to His Father's will—even to coming to this evil world and experiencing death on a cross for us **(Philippians 2:5-9).** He said His very sustenance was to do His Father's will—no matter the cost **(John 4:34). Ephesians 2:2** states that *"the prince of the power of the air is the spirit that now works in the children of disobedience."* Satan is REBELLIOUS and ever seeks to convince others to join him in his rebellion against God.

12. God DEFENDS us and will fight for us **(Joshua 23:10).** God builds us up in the faith and in confidence **(Acts 20:32).** He EXALTS us when we cooperate with Him. Satan tries to defame our character with SLANDER which pulls us down and destroys our reputation. He stirs people to be false witnesses. In fact, his very name, *"devil,"* means "slanderer." He BLASPHEMES God.

13. God can be very GENTLE with us—especially when we are beaten down and crushed **(Isaiah 42:3; 2 Corinthians 10:1a).** His touch can take the form of a whisper, an encouraging sign, a tender moment. Satan and his demons are VIOLENT and DESTRUCTIVE. In Jesus' day, a father's only child was possessed by an evil spirit. This spirit enjoyed hurting the boy, throwing him to the ground, and causing him to have severe convulsions with foaming at the mouth and gnashing of his teeth. The evil spirit also was the cause of his inability to speak or hear. The spirit would often throw him into the fire or water to kill him. Jesus cast this wicked spirit out of the boy **(Mark 9:17-27)**. This spirit (and many others like him) are still living today and are the cause of many of humanity's afflictions. God said to satan regarding Job, *"...you move me against him to destroy him without cause"* **(Job 2:3)**. They also inspire wars between nations. Jesus said the enemy has come to *"kill, steal and destroy"* **(John 10:10)**.

14. Our Heavenly Father loves to MEET OUR NEEDS and make us as complete a person as possible **(John 14:13; Philippians 1:6; 4:19)**. One of His names, Jehovah-Jireh, means "God will provide." He is the ultimate provider. No one could give us more expert care than He. But satan MAKES DESTITUTE. His purpose is to strip us of all that we have, leaving us barren and empty.

15. MAGNANIMOUS giving is so much a part of God's nature **(1 Timothy 6:17)**. His ultimate expression of extravagant giving was the gift of His Son as our substitute for judgment so we could be His child and live with Him forever in heaven **(John 3:16; 2 Corinthians 8:9)**. Satan is GREEDY and COVETOUS because of his selfishness. As lucifer, he covets God's power and has an insatiable appetite for that which is not rightfully his. He comes as a thief to rob us of our most precious possessions.

16. God loves to be a BURDEN-BEARER—to remove the loads we carry that are designed to weigh us down and crush us. Jesus said, *"Come to me, all you who are weary and burdened, and I will give you rest"* **(Matt. 11:28)**. Satan is a BURDEN-GIVER. He oppresses mankind spiritually, mentally, and emotionally and tries to heap troubles and weights upon us **(Job 1:12-19)**. For example, Jesus said this of the devil's children, the Pharisees: *"They tie up heavy loads and put them on men's shoulders, but they themselves are not willing to lift a finger to move them"* **(Matthew 23:4)**.

17. God is a God of RIGHTEOUS justice and fairness **(Psalm 89:14; 97:1-2)**. Satan is a THIEF and is behind injustice and unfairness **(John 10:10)**. **18.** God's character is SELF-CONTROL. Satan's is UNRESTRAINT. **19.** God is the GIVER OF PEACE and tranquility **(John 14:27)** and is the author of unity. Satan is the GIVER OF DISCORD and strife. He tries to bring division. **20.** God is the GIVER OF JOY that isn't dependent on circumstances **(Galatians 5:22; Romans 14:17)**. Satan is the GIVER OF MISERY and depression and can cause some health-related illnesses. He is the kind of insidious person that would inspire someone to kidnap a five-year-old child, then sexually molest and asphyxiate her thereby inflicting the greatest heartbreak to her parents. He would like to make our lives so miserable that we would pray to die.

21. God is the GIVER OF CONFIDENCE and courage **(Deuteronomy 31:6)**. Satan is the GIVER OF FEAR. He would have you live in unnatural fear and be controlled by it. **22.** God is the GIVER OF HOPE **(Romans 15:13; Hebrews 6:19)**. Satan is the GIVER OF DISCOURAGEMENT and despair. **23.** God is the GIVER OF COMFORT **(John 14:16, 26; 2 Corinthians 1:3-4)**. Satan is the GIVER OF TORMENT and affliction. He and his demons get great delight in inflicting unimaginable pain on people as well as using instruments of torture to satisfy their sadistic nature. **24.** God is the GIVER OF HAPPINESS, fulfillment, and the source of all our blessings. Satan is the GIVER OF VEXATION as he tries to aggravate, harass, and bring trouble our way **(Acts 5:16)**. We get this very sobering insight into how evil and wicked these spirits are by examining the biblical accounts of the character and behavior of evil spirits who possessed certain people in Jesus' day.

Although the actual words, "demon possession," do not occur in the Bible, the term has been used extensively within the church to denote one or more evil spirits who enter and reside in a human body and control the person. For the sake of clarity, we defined **"demon possession"** as: "When one or more evil spirits, after gaining initial access, enter and leave a physical body at will in order to inhabit, control, express, and gratify themselves through the one being indwelt." We are not to be fearful that they can inhabit our body at will. An opening must be given to them. Some of the ways they can gain access is through us persistently committing a particular sin, getting involved with occult practices, through victimization, and at birth from something our parents did. Thank God demons can be driven out of a person on the basis of satan's irreversible defeat through the death and resurrection of Jesus Christ whereby He stripped the demonic rulers of their power and sealed their doom. There is controversy in the Body of Christ over whether a true *"born again"* Christian can be demon possessed. The author's position is a qualified "no."

Another way demons attack us is by **"demonization."** This is our definition: "when an evil spirit attacks, influences, or controls a person from <u>outside</u> their body without inhabiting it." When a person is "demonized," it can take the form of pressure to sin; harassment; mental obsessions; physical pain or illness; emotional depression and instability; and spiritual oppression. Demonization can come as a result of: (1) the devil's retaliation for effective ministry which damages his kingdom; (2) wrong choices we make to sin that invite the enemy and give him a foothold in our lives; (3) opposition to try to prevent us from entering God's will or when spiritual breakthrough is just around the corner; (4) God's permission for the devil to afflict one of His children to test them or to work out the image of Christ in their life; and (5) victimization and exposure to the occult. Like demon possession, usually when the evil spirit(s) departs, the problems stop, too. I believe demonization is mainly what a Christian encounters. The unbeliever is a prey to both this and possession.

Evil spirit(s) possessing a person can be driven out through Christ's victory on the cross. However, there are Christians who believe that the casting out of spirits was only for the early Church and not applicable today. Do we tell those possessed by demons that we are sorry we cannot help them because Christ's atonement is limited to deliver them? Do we really believe that during the history of the church age, God treats one part of His church differently than He does another—giving His power and gifts to some while depriving others of the same?

Think of it! Satan and his demons are still roaming our world today trying to satisfy their depraved and evil desires which can never be satisfied. Do not underestimate their wickedness or take them lightly. Their goal is to try to bring about the damnation of every possible soul by every possible means. The only place of safety is in Christ. He is the only One that has defeated them.

Evil character (that is opposite of God's character) comes into existence when a free moral being (angel or human) decides to reject God from ruling their life and enthrones self-rule instead. From this initial *"sin of lawlessness"* proceeds the rest of this dark character that the Bible calls *"sin."*

Tragically, everyone born into this world is born a sinner having inherited a sinful nature from Adam; however, satan's sinful character was in existence before Adam was created. Worse yet, we are born not only enslaved to sin but also captives of satan and are his children because we act like him and serve him. This all sounds absolutely incredible, but God's Word teaches us that it is absolutely and positively true. **Who is your father? Whose character do you reflect?**

Lesson 4

THE BELT OF TRUTH: Satan's War Against God's Kingdom

☑ Before starting the DVD:

A fallen superhuman angelic being has made a declaration of war. Satan's motive for this war is his envy and extreme hatred for the God of the Bible. This animosity and abhorrence of God is also shared by the other fallen angels who ever seek to involve all mankind in their rebellion against Him. Their contempt for God is unquenchable and it extends to all that God loves and all that belongs to Him—especially God's people. We, the Church, are standing in his way. Therefore, the position we find ourselves in once we become God's child is this: We are caught between two warring parties and have become the target of the devil's hatred. So then warfare is automatically chosen for us. Just like the nations that were forced to enter World Wars I and II against their wills, so it is not an option for us. In this lesson, you will learn more about your enemy—the specific ways satan wages his warfare against God and against you and me as well! In later lessons, we'll cover the weapons and power God has provided for us to be victorious in this invisible war. Yet it remains a great mystery how our just and omnipotent God allows these created evil beings to continue to rebel and express their malevolent deeds. But we trust Him completely!

☑ **DVD Users:** Watch Lesson 4 for an overview before proceeding further (25 min.).
☑ When you're through, pick up again at this point. Fill in the blanks from the Summary.

MANIFESTATIONS OF SATAN'S WARFARE AGAINST GOD

▶ **CONSIDER THIS:** Satan will fiercely contest any threat to the interests of his kingdom.

† **Revelation 12:7-9**—*And there was war in heaven. Michael and his angels fought against the dragon, and the dragon and his angels fought back.* **8.** *But he was not strong enough...* **9.** *The great dragon was hurled down—that ancient serpent called the devil, or Satan, who leads the whole world astray...*

The following are some of the ways that satan used to try to prevent the fulfillment and arrival of God's Deliverer, Jesus Christ, from invading his kingdom through *"the seed of the woman"* (the godly lineage promised by God in **Genesis 3:15),** and so thwart God's plan of redemption.

† **Genesis 4:8, 25; 1 John 3:12**—By inciting Cain to kill his brother Abel (God provided Seth).

† **Genesis 6:1-8**—By trying to corrupt the human race, which resulted in God's decision to destroy the world with a flood and to preserve the godly lineage through Noah's son, Shem.

† **Exodus 1:15-16, 22**—By using Pharaoh to issue a decree to kill all the male children born to the Israelites.

† **2 Chronicles 22:10-12**—By instigating Queen Athaliah to destroy the only children left in the Davidic line.

† **Esther 3:1-15**—By using a prominent man whose pride was wounded (Haman), to obtain permission from King Ahasuerus of Media-Persia to massacre the entire Jewish race in a day.

† **Matthew 2:7-18; Revelation 12:4**—Satan even used King Herod to try to kill Jesus, the promised *"seed"* Himself, when He arrived on planet earth!!

Here are some of the main ways satan wages war against God's kingdom:

1. He O_____ the angels in their work for God—such as bringing answers to prayer.

    † **Daniel 10:12-13, 20**—*Then* [the angel] *continued, "Do not be afraid, Daniel. Since the first day that you set your mind to gain understanding and to humble yourself before your God, your words were heard, and I have come in response to them. 13. But the prince of the Persian kingdom resisted me twenty-one days. Then Michael, one of the chief princes, came to help me, because I was detained there with the king of Persia..." 20. So he said, "Do you know why I have come to you? Soon I will return to fight against the prince of Persia, and when I go, the prince of Greece will come."*

▶ **CONSIDER THIS:** One reason for experiencing a delay in receiving answered prayer could be due to demonic opposition in the heavenlies, which needs to be "prayed through" by us here on earth.

   A. Satan has a highly O_____ kingdom for efficient warfare—a hierarchy of fallen angels each appointed specific responsibilities, including rulers assigned over each nation. They can also set up headquarters in certain geographical locales, presumably by satan's appointment. Demons also establish, control, and preserve violent gangs, the Mafia, drug cartels, etc.

    † **Revelation 2:13**—*I know where you live* [Pergamum]—*where Satan has his throne. Yet you remain true to my name. You did not renounce your faith in me, even in the days of Antipas, my faithful witness, who was put to death in your city—where Satan lives.*

    † **Revelation 18:2**—*With a mighty voice he shouted: "Fallen! Fallen is Babylon the Great! She has become a home for demons and a haunt for every evil spirit..."*

▶ **CONSIDER THIS:** There are cities, regions, and places throughout the world that have significantly more demonic activity than others, and where one can sense a strong demonic presence. Why only certain areas? It is because demonic spirits are active in a community to the degree that its people sin and give them that authority. And once they have that permission, repossessing it will take a great spiritual struggle through repentance and travailing prayer. Each of us must realize that our actions contribute to the spiritual climate of our communities. Some areas are strongholds of pornography, sexual perversions, organized crime, witchcraft, occult activities, gambling, etc. There seems to be less demonic activity in places where people have not allowed evil spirits to gain a foothold. If one contrasts the countries that incorporate Christian principles with those that do not, it appears that there is greater demonic control of all aspects of its national life. This is attested to by missionaries where God has sent them to bring His truth.

B. The meanings of the Greek words used in **Ephesians 6:12** below for *"principalities,"* *"powers"*, and *"rulers,"* collectively denote aspects of a ranking, authoritative power structure.

    † **Ephesians 6:12** (KJV)—*"For we wrestle not against flesh and blood, but against principalities, against powers, against the rulers of the darkness of this world, against spiritual wickedness in high places."*

C. Note that Satan's base of operations is **not** from hell or from some other confined area:

    † **Job 1:6-7** (NLT)—*"Where have you come from?" the Lord asked Satan. And Satan answered the Lord, "I have been going back and forth across the earth, watching everything that's going on."*

2. He is the source of P_____ against those who represent the true God as he works to prevent them from damaging his kingdom.

    † **Revelation 12:13** (KJV)—*"And when the dragon [Satan] saw that he was cast unto the earth, he persecuted the woman which brought forth the man child"*

    † **Revelation 2:10** (NLT)—Jesus said, *"Don't be afraid of what you are about to suffer. The Devil will throw some of you into prison and put you to the test. You will be persecuted for 'ten days.' Remain faithful even when facing death, and I will give you the crown of life."*

►**CONSIDER THIS:** Can there be a correlation between the amount of damage done to the kingdom of satan by yielded, obedient servants, and the types of physical and spiritual attacks they and their loved ones suffer? Or the kind of deaths they die? **Q:** Could this be a reason why bad things happen to godly people who are truly effective, shining lights for Christ?

📖 **DEFINITION—PERSECUTE**

The Greek word used in the New Testament is *diōkō*. It means "to put to flight, drive away...to pursue."[1]

A. Persecution is a result of a craving for acquiring, maintaining, or expanding power over others. It is a consciously planned, malicious effort against those "standing in the way"— especially people with non-mainstream beliefs and practices. Though the source of and reasons for the persecution of a person or group vary, the motives and methods used are much the same. The reasons can be due to race, class, ethnic origin, and over both religious and non-religious issues. The source can be from man or from evil spirits.

B. The source of persecution of Old and New Testament believers is normally fueled by demonic spirits who work through believers as well as non-believers. Demons can also attack the targeted person one on one. When the enemy senses his turf is being threatened, he will pursue that person or group in order to drive them out by force. Here are some examples:

(1) Many of the Old Testament prophets were killed by God's own people to whom He had sent them with His special messages.

    † **Hebrews 11:35-37** (NLT)—*...But others trusted God and were tortured, preferring to die rather than turn from God and be free. They placed their hope in the resurrection to a better life. 36. Some were mocked, and their backs were cut open with whips. Others were chained in dungeons. 37. Some died by stoning, and some were sawed in half; others were killed with the sword.*

(2) Most of Jesus' 12 apostles died violent martyrs' deaths. Peter and Andrew were crucified; Thomas was said to have been speared to death; James (the less) was stoned and clubbed to death; Paul was beheaded **(Acts 22:4; 26:11; Galatians 1:13, 23);** John is said to be the only apostle to die peacefully; although at one point he was boiled in oil and exiled. The Christian worldview will **always** clash with satan's religious worldviews.

(3) The early Christians were severely persecuted by Rome. In the Roman Coliseum, God's people were made sport of and severely tortured to force them to renounce their faith in Christ because, among other things, they refused to acknowledge the emperor as god. Many lives were lost. Christians have been cruelly tortured for their faith throughout this entire church age—even up to this present day. God forewarns us in His Word that our allegiance to Him will produce suffering, but we can count on Him to be right by our side—faithfully helping us to endure. Great will be our reward in the afterlife!

> † **John 15:20**—Jesus said, *"...The servant is not greater than his lord. If they have persecuted me, they will also persecute you..."*

> † **Matthew 28:20**—Jesus said, *"...And be sure of this: I am with you always, even to the end of the age."*

C. Any persecution against the Body of Christ is in reality directed to Christ.

> † **Acts 9:4-5** (NASB)—*and he fell to the ground and heard a voice saying to him, "Saul, Saul, why are you persecuting Me?" **5.** And he said, "Who are You, Lord?" And He said, "I am Jesus whom you are persecuting..."*

D. The Jewish race has always been a target of satan's hatred **(Revelation 12:13).** He hates the Jews for giving us Jesus, the Bible, and the Church. God has promised a future day of blessing for the nation of Israel that is tied to the second coming of Christ. Satan will continue to persecute the Jews to try and prevent this prophetic fulfillment. In the 1940s, satan used Adolph Hitler in his attempt to exterminate them, but God intervened and caused Israel to become a bona-fide nation—the first time in 2500 years. Today we see that hatred and desire for genocide of the Jews being expressed through the Arab nations.

Note: In the SQ&A we will learn of a five-step pattern of persecution that was used on most groups dating back to the early church.

E. The enemy also uses persecution to cause a person to quit serving Christ **(Matthew 13:5, 20-21).**

3. He R_____ human efforts to further the Gospel by exerting force as an adversary in opposing our work for God—attempting to stop every advancement of God's kingdom.

> † **Zechariah 3:1** (KJV)—*And he showed me Joshua the high priest standing before the angel of the Lord, and Satan standing at his right side to resist him.*

† **Revelation 20:7-9**—Satan and his demons have the ability to inspire and energize people in authority—*"to gather them to battle"* (KJV) against those who stand for the principles of the true God.

† **1 Corinthians 16:9**—The apostle Paul said: *"because a great door for effective work has opened to me, and there are many who oppose me."*

A. When God attempts to birth something in satan's domain, the enemy is there to try to oppose and devour it—sometimes successfully.

† **Revelation 12:4** (NASB)—*And the dragon* [satan] *stood before the woman who was about to give birth, so that when she gave birth he might devour her child.*

B. Our adversary will attempt to ruin the labors of a servant of God as in the case of the apostle Paul who founded the Thessalonian church.

† **1 Thessalonians 3:5**—*For this reason, when I could stand it no longer, I sent Timothy to find out about your faith. I was afraid that in some way the tempter might have tempted you and our efforts might have been useless.*

C. What are some of the other ways the devil uses people to resist the work God has called us to do? Here are some tactics encountered by Ezra and Nehemiah as they attempted to rebuild the temple and city of Jerusalem:

(1) The enemy tries to deceptively join our group so as to work from within **(Ezra 4:1-2)**.

(2) The enemy attempts to discourage us, intimidate us with fear, and frustrate the plan of God **(Ezra 4:4-5; Nehemiah 6:9-10)**.

(3) The enemy attempts to exert outside pressure such as moving upon those in higher positions who have the authority to withhold finances or stop God's work **(Ezra 4:6-24)**.

(4) He tries to insult, mock, and ridicule us in the hope we will give up **(Nehemiah 2:17-20; 4:1-5)**.

(5) The enemy devises schemes that we might disobey God's Word in order to discredit us and our work in the eyes of others **(Nehemiah 6:10-14)**.

▶**CONSIDER THIS:** We can expect to encounter demonic attack especially during these times: when God is preparing us for the call He has placed on our hearts; when we are attempting to make spiritual advances in our lives; when we are invading and inflicting damage to satan's kingdom; and when we are exposing the devil and his agenda. Those with divinely accredited ministries must prepare themselves for opposition. We must keep pressing on and be faithful to God's assignment and to His call upon our lives. God will give us victory and breakthroughs in due time. Pat Robertson, founder of the Christian Broadcasting Network, has said that doing the will of God "...is like walking into the teeth of a blizzard. The wind and snow make walking quite difficult, but it cannot stop you. Only *you* can stop you! You must keep walking."[2] Determine that you will work through the enemy's opposition and intimidation and not allow it to stop you.

D. When all other ways fail, the enemy will attempt to put away the one causing him problems.

> † **Acts 9:22-23** (TLB)—*Saul's preaching became more and more powerful, and the Jews in Damascus couldn't refute his proofs that Jesus was indeed the Messiah.* ***23.*** *After a while the Jewish leaders decided to kill him.* (Also read **Acts 14:1-7, 19-20.**)

4. He H_____, or interferes with, the spreading and dissemination of the truth. How?

A. By preventing the journey of a servant of God to prevent the spiritual nurturing of God's people.

> † **1 Thessalonians 2:18**—*For we wanted to come to you—certainly I, Paul, did, again and again—but Satan stopped us.*

B. He hinders by moving on offended parties who then dissuade others from putting faith in Christ.

> † **Acts 13:7-10**—*...The proconsul, an intelligent man, sent for Barnabas and Saul because he wanted to hear the word of God.* ***8.*** *But Elymas the sorcerer...opposed them and tried to turn the proconsul from the faith.* ***9.*** *Then Saul, who was also called Paul, filled with the Holy Spirit, looked straight at Elymas and said,* ***10.*** *"You are a child of the devil and an enemy of everything that is right! You are full of all kinds of deceit and trickery..."*

> † **Acts 14:1, 2**—*At Iconium Paul and Barnabas went as usual into the Jewish synagogue. There they spoke so effectively that a great number of Jews and Gentiles believed.* ***2.*** *But the Jews who refused to believe stirred up the Gentiles and poisoned their minds against the brothers.*

▶**CONSIDER THIS:** A head-on collision is inevitable when we seek to advance the Gospel into areas entrenched by demonic powers, especially on the mission field. This may help explain why false religions seem to prosper and grow without any opposition.

5. He secretly and subtly plants his children among God's children to I_____ God's church, masquerading among them, in order to cause harm from within and decrease its effectiveness.

> † **Matthew 13:24-30, 38-39**—In the parable of the wheat and tares Jesus said: ***38.*** *"...the tares are the children of the wicked one.* ***39.*** *The enemy that sowed them is the devil..."*

6. He A_____ the veracity and credibility of God's Word, the Bible, the only book that reveals the truth about satan, his tactics, and the true God and His ways—so that the truth will not be made known to the inhabitants of planet earth.

A. His attack on the Bible involves outlawing it, discrediting it, taking it out of context, mixing it with half-truths, adding to it, detracting from it, and substituting it for some other "sacred writing." (See **Revelation 22:18-19; Galatians 1:6-9; 1 Timothy 4:1.**)

B. He works to remove Bible reading, the displaying of the Ten Commandments, prayer made to the God of the Bible, and references to Christmas and Easter from America's public schools, etc. Today, we see him using the clever twisting of the erroneous concept of "separation of church and state" in his effort to drive out and eradicate every teaching and mention of God from all influences of public life and education.

7. He fiendishly delights to C_____ and <u>defile</u> that which is pure, sacred, and consecrated to God. **(Luke 11:24-26.)** Here are some of the ways he does this:

   A. He corrupts by immoral, unethical, and perverse practices that occur in a place separated to the true God **(Matthew 21:12-13).**

   B. By desecrating the "House of the Lord" **(Jer. 7:30-31; Ezek. 23:38-39; 2 Kings 23:4-7).**

   C. By enticing people (especially God's children) to sin and to turn their backs on God, thereby inflicting pain in the heart of God and provoking Him to anger **(Genesis 6:11-12,** then verses **6** and **7; 2 Kings 17:9-23; Ezekiel 16:1-21; Hosea 4:12;5:4; Revelation 2:14).**

   D. He corrupts by encouraging the intermarriage of a believer with an unbeliever which can affect a godly offspring **(Ezra 9:1-2).**

   E. He defiles by attacking the sacredness of virginity and the institution of marriage, enticing us to commit fornication, adultery, and other things that lead to divorce and the breakup of the home.

8. He B_____ God and tries to get mankind to do the same.

   † **Revelation 13:4-6**—Acting under the dragon's (Satan's) influence, the beast (antichrist) *5....was given a mouth to utter proud words and blasphemies...6. to blaspheme God, and to slander His name, and His dwelling place and those who live in heaven.*

📖 DEFINITION—BLASPHEMY

Words or conduct that defame the honor, reputation, and holiness of God or His sacred things.

   A. It is amazing how satan has turned the holy name of God and of Jesus into profanity. I believe he and his cohorts influence humanity to use His name in this way countless times a day—especially in America. Why is His holy name chosen over so many others?

   B. The entertainment industry is also guilty of defaming God's character and reputation with its cruel and degrading portrayal of Christ in their productions as a womanizer, fathering children out of wedlock, and as a homosexual.

   C. Note that *"blasphemy against the Holy Spirit"* (and unforgiveness) are the only sins that the Bible says will not be forgiven by God. The former is knowingly, consciously, and willfully attributing the works of the Holy Spirit to satan and/or demonic power **(Matthew 12:24-32).** Note that some Bible scholars also believe it can extend to one's deliberate and repeated rejection of the offer of salvation by the Spirit in full awareness of His attempt to woo and convict them.

9. He uses the "things of the world" to R_____ God and compete with Him for the possession of our hearts so God is displaced as the center of our lives. (We will enlarge more on this in Lesson 10).

   A. They become competing "seeds" in our hearts that choke out the things of God.

> † **Mark 4:18-19** (NLT)—*The thorny ground represents those who hear and accept the Good News, 19. but all too quickly the message is crowded out by the cares of this life, the lure of wealth, and the desire for nice things, so no crop is produced.*

10. He R_____ God of the worship, love, and obedience that should rightly go to Him by trying to divert a person's allegiance to something else—thereby unwittingly giving to satan what belongs to God. (Also see **1 Kings 12:25-33; 13:33-34.**)

> † **Romans 1:23,25** (GNT)—*instead of worshipping the immortal God, they worship images made to look like mortal man or birds or animals or reptiles...25. They exchange the truth about God for a lie; they worship and serve what God has created instead of the Creator himself...*

   A. Satan has done an incredible job in capturing the majority of the hearts and minds of mankind so that they will serve other gods rather than the God of the Bible. His goal is to cause us to believe in anything but the true God. We see an example of this in the picture on the right. This is one of Hinduism's many deities, Hanuman, the monkey god, whose shrines are worshiped throughout India.

   B. Satan craves worship and receives it when a person chooses not to worship and serve the God of the Bible.

> † **Matthew 4:9**—Satan said to Jesus: *"All this will I give you...if you will bow down and worship me."*

> † **Deuteronomy 32:16-17**—*They made him jealous with their foreign gods and angered him with their detestable idols. 17. They sacrificed to demons, which are not God...*

   (1) We are told in the Bible that the worship of a man (controlled by the devil) by nearly all of earth's population is to come upon the scene in *"the last days"* {known as *"the Beast"* **(Revelations 13:1 ff)**; *"man of sin"* **(1 Thessalonians 2:3)**, or *"Antichrist"* **(1 John 2:18)**}.

✝ **2 Thessalonians 2:4**—*He* [the antichrist] *will oppose and will exalt himself over everything that is called God or is worshiped, so that he sets himself up in God's temple, proclaiming himself to be God.* (Also see **Revelation 13:4,8.**)

11. He H_____ and blinds the truth of God's Word from mankind—deceiving us into believing things that are not true, thereby causing us to trust our *"darkness"* to be what we believe is the real *"light"* **(Matthew 6:22-23).**

  A. Satan and his minions know the truth: that there is a supreme God; that Jesus is the Son of God; and that there is a literal heaven, hell, and a Lake of Fire. But they won't tell you! They are determined to do all they can to prevent everyone from hearing this truth.

    ✝ **Luke 4:41**—*Moreover, demons came out of many people, shouting, "You are the Son of God!" But he* [Jesus] *rebuked them and would not allow them to speak, because they knew he was the Christ.*

    ✝ **James 2:19**—*You believe that there is one God. Good! Even the demons believe that—and shudder.*

    ✝ **2 Corinthians 4:4** (Phillips)—*The god of this world has blinded the minds of those who do not believe, and prevents the light of the glorious gospel of Christ, the image of God, from shining on them.*

    ✝ **Acts 26:9-20**—Jesus said to Saul, the persecutor, at his Damascus Road conversion: *18. "I am sending you to open their eyes and turn them from darkness to light, and from the power of Satan to God, so that they may receive forgiveness of sins..."*

    ✝ **Mark 4:15**—Jesus said: *"Some people are like seed along the path, where the word is sown. As soon as they hear it, Satan comes and takes away the word that was sown in them."*

  B. He tries to blind us by believing in "the letter of the law" and traditions that are false. (Also see **Matthew 23:1-3, 16-24.**)

    ✝ **Luke 13:13-17** (NLT)—*14. But the leader in charge of the synagogue was indignant that Jesus had healed her on the Sabbath day. "There are six days of the week for working," he said to the crowd. "Come on those days to be healed, not on the Sabbath."*

  Note: At times God allows the truth to be hidden from people—like those who are wise in their own conceit **(Luke 10:21; John 9:39),** but **never** from a sincere seeker of truth.

12. Satan targets people (especially followers of Christ) to devour and D_____ in order that he might cause as many as he can to go to the Lake of Fire with him.

    ✝ **1 Peter 5:8** (GNT)—*Be alert, be on watch! Your enemy, the Devil, roams around like a roaring lion, looking for someone to devour.*

  A. A lion roars after he kills his prey to announce his triumph and intimidate nearby animals. This Scripture implies that he boastfully roars in the face of God each time he has isolated, attacked, and victoriously conquered someone—especially if it is one of God's children. He also wants us to be intimidated and demoralized when we see the many wasted lives and those who die without Christ.

B. Demonic forces are constantly active and never sleep. We are being relentlessly pursued by a ferocious enemy who has the ability to observe the things we do and say and whose main goal is to separate us from God and keep us out of heaven. Satan tailors his deceptive strategies to fit each people group (i.e. his approach to the people of India differs from how he attacks Americans). There is safety—only in the arms of Jesus who conquered him.

C. This world is a dangerous place. If the enemy doesn't kill you by an abortionist before you come out of your mother's womb, then perhaps awaiting you in your very home is violence, turmoil, rejection, and child molestation or abuse. And if you try to flee and run away from problems at home, the pornographers, sexual predators, drug dealers, thieves, and gangs are waiting for you on the streets. When you are in school, the enemy is there to inflict deep hurts through the words of your fellow classmates, and to provide curriculum that will lead you away from the true God. He exploits your adolescent needs, vulnerabilities, and naiveté through harmful music, peer pressure—hooking you at an early age on tobacco, alcohol, drugs, and illicit premarital sex—luring you into looking in all the wrong places to meet your basic need to be loved and accepted. If you marry, your marriage may turn out to be abusive and a living hell ending tragically in the awful pain of divorce. You may even at some point become a victim of crime, or contract a debilitating disease. God never intended the world to be like this!! Free will has made it possible.

▶**CONSIDER THIS:** We desperately need to have God's protection lest we end up becoming one of hell's statistics. God has provided all the security to His children that they need and promises His people that *"...no weapon forged against you will prevail."* **(Isaiah 54:17).** However, if one chooses not to serve God, in reality, one is making a choice to serve satan. And God normally does not protect a child of the devil.

> ☑ This ends the DVD content for Lesson 4.
> ☑ Continue on in this workbook for additional material **not** on the DVD.

13. He I_____ God—making it difficult to distinguish the real from the counterfeit.

> † **2 Corinthians 11:13-15**—*For such men are false apostles, deceitful workmen, masquerading as apostles of Christ. 14. And no wonder, for Satan himself masquerades as an angel of light. 15. It is not surprising, then, if his servants masquerade as servants of righteousness. Their end will be what their actions deserve.*

A. This can be illustrated by the story of a young boy who, while walking through a heavily wooded area one day, found some bags full of money. Excitedly, he quickly hid them in a hole at the base of a tree and covered them with brush. Reaching into his pocket, he just happened to have a piece of white twine. He tied it around the trunk of the tree at eye level so he could find it later. Then he ran home to tell the good news to his father. When they returned, as he and his dad approached the wooded area, to their utter amazement someone had tied white twine around every tree making it almost impossible to find the real tree.

B. Satan is called an *"angel of light"* because he passes himself off for what he is not by wearing, so to speak, a mask or costume as a concealment of his true identity and purpose. Through deception he makes people unaware of his subtle activity; therefore, they are susceptible to his influence and available as his instrument without them knowing it. Satan must camouflage himself and his tactics or else we would flee from him.

† **Matthew 7:15-16** (NLT)—Jesus taught: *"Beware of false prophets who come disguised as harmless sheep, but are really wolves that will tear you apart. 16. You can detect them by the way they act, just as you can identify a tree by its fruit."*

C. Satan also has his *"apostles"* (lit. "sent forth ones"); *"servants"* (*"ministers"* KJV); and *"false prophets."* They deceptively masquerade as the clergy of Christ claiming to be Christian, or they don the religious garb of an outright false religion. These people are recruited and raised up by him to seal the doom of multitudes by perverting the gospel **(see Galatians 1:6-7)**.

D. Satan uses different methods to adapt himself to the opportunity at hand, the pattern of the culture, and even the nature of a religious system. His goal is to deceive people so that they follow his counterfeit—convincing them that they are following the truth and the true God.

►**CONSIDER THIS:** "If the devil is real, then God must be." (Fr. Karl Patzelt); And if God is real, the devil must be.

E. The following examples are some of the deceptive ways satan imitates God and His ways.

(Note: due to time constraints, it may not be feasible to look up these Scriptures when in a group).

TOPIC	TRUTH	SATAN'S IMITATION
1. The Old Testament Levitical priesthood, ceremonies, and its blood sacrifices including worship, prayer and fasting	**Hebrews 9:18-22** **Matthew 6:5-18**	**2 Thessalonians 2:4.** False religions also have these elements. See **How They Appease Their Gods** in Appendix A.
2. The New Testament Church and its leadership: apostles, prophets, evangelists, pastors, and teachers	**Ephesians 4:11-12**	**2 Corinthians 11:13-15; Matthew 7:15-16; 24:4,11; Acts 20:28-31; 1 John 2:18-19; 2 John 1:7; Titus 1:10-11**
3. Doctrinal beliefs	**Ephesians 4:11-16**	**Galatians 1:6-9; 2 Corinthians 11:2-4; 1 Timothy 4:1-5; 1 John 4:1-3.**
4. The Trinity	**Matthew 3:16-17**	**Revelation 16:13** Some false religions also have this.
5. The incarnation of Jesus Christ through the virgin birth, and His resurrection from the dead	**Luke 1:26-35**	Some false religions preceding Christ's birth had gods who came to earth in human form (some by a virgin birth), and suffered, died, and were reborn.

TOPIC	TRUTH	SATAN'S IMITATION
6. God's people	1 John 3:10-12 John 13:34-35 Galatians 5:22-24	Matthew 7:16-20; 12:33-35; 13:24-30; Galatians 5:19-21
7. Demonstrations of power	Acts 2:22,43; John 14:11-12	Exodus 7:10-12; 19-22; 8:5-7; Acts 8:9-11; Matthew 24:23-25; 2 Thessalonians 2:9-10; Revelation 13:3, 13-15; 16:14 Also see **Psychokinesis, Magician,** and **Healing, in the Occult** in index
8. Spiritual gifts—prophetic utterances, dreams, and visions	1 Corinthians 12:4-7; 10-11; 14:1-40	1 Kings 18:27-29; Jeremiah 23:13 Also see **Clairvoyance, Dreams, Telepathy, Oracles, Xenoglossy**

STUDY QUESTIONS AND APPLICATION

1. On a scale from 1 to 10, to what degree do you truly believe that you are personally caught between two warring entities—satan and God? Write the current month and year below the number.

**I Do Not
Believe It At All**   **I Am Totally
Convinced**

```
0    1    2    3    4    5    6    7    8    9    10
```

Note: If you scored under 7, ask the Holy Spirit to make this truth more real to you.

2. Review these 13 manifestations of Satan's warfare against God. Then identify those affecting:

Your Life?_____

Your Family? _____

Your Church? _____

3. On the scale below, to what degree do you know with certainty that you are under the umbrella of God's protection against these wicked demonic spirits? Write the current month and year below the number.

**I Don't Believe
I Have Any
Protection**   **I Feel Fully
Secure In Christ**

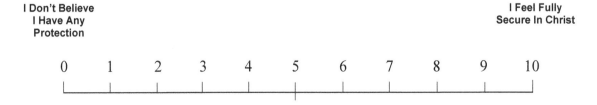

```
0    1    2    3    4    5    6    7    8    9    10
```

Note: If you scored under 7, ask the Holy Spirit to make this truth more real to you. We will deal with this topic further in the next lesson.

4. If you are a child of God, then God has provided protection for you from the devil who prowls about seeking whom he may devour. Read each of the following scriptures and name the type of protection God has made available to you.

    A. **1 Corinthians 6:19; Romans 8:11** _____

    B. **Job 1:10** _____

    C. **Job 1:11-12; 2:4-6** _____

    D. **Hebrews 1:14; Psalm 91:9-12; 2 Kings 6:15-17** _____

    E. **John 10:28-29** _____

    F. **Ephesians 6:11-12** _____

5. In their book, *The Extermination of Christianity—A Tyranny of Consensus*, Paul and Robert Schenck wrote about a five-step pattern used on most groups especially since the first century. Recently it was evident in the persecution of the Jews by the Nazis, and of Christians by the Communists. It is a real eye-opener as to what is happening to Christianity and religious freedom in America today. (Visit their website: www.faithandaction.org.)

    A. Here is a summary of their five (5) progressive steps that lead to outright persecution:

        (1) **Identifying and stereotyping the group or individual**

            The powers in control identify groups or individuals in society that are in opposition and a threat to their ideology. Then they target them. Their negative stereotyping mixes an element of truth with lies. Their portrayal of the group becomes exaggerated and distorted. For instance, they may be painted as being uneducated, intolerant, undesirable, sub-human, evil, or extremist. This stereotype profoundly influences the societies' formation of attitudes toward the targeted group or individual. They are pre-judged on wrong information which results in mistrust, suspicion, and hostility.

        (2) **Marginalization**

            The powers in control begin to push the group or individual out of the mainstream to the margins of society where they become isolated. In America today, these "powers" include the media (TV, entertainment industry), educators, and the government—especially the judicial system. These are just some of the players in America's ongoing civil war against traditional Christian values. The group or individual then becomes an easy target for ridicule, scorn, and harassment. They are banned from prominent positions of employment in society (i.e. teachers, judges, lawyers, etc.).

        (3) **Vilification**

            In this stage, the group or individual is characterized as wicked, subversive, and dangerous to society. The propaganda paves the way for the group to become scapegoats for the cause of certain social problems. Indifference is created in the psyche of society so when the time comes for the group to be harmed, the general population isn't sympathetic to help them. At the time of the writing of their book (1993), the Schencks believed that we in America were in this stage and moving into the next.

(4) Criminalization

In this stage, legislation is passed imposing legal restrictions upon the group and eventually their activities are criminalized.

(5) Outright persecution

This stage includes: intimidation; denial of civil and constitutional rights; false accusations; arrests; detentions; fines; seizure of property; imprisonment in jails, mental hospitals, or forced labor camps; torture; and death. The triumph of one worldview over another has taken place in that nation. The subversion of that culture is successfully completed as the targeted group is driven underground or eradicated.

One of the main legal persecutors of Christians and Jews in America is the American Civil Liberties Union (ACLU). Founded in 1920 by Roger Baldwin, an agnostic, socialist, and Communist sympathizer, his worldview and ideology still permeate the ACLU today.[3] From its inception, the ACLU's objective was to promote the ideals of Socialism and Communism and mold America to fit its atheistic agenda.[4] Notably, the same repressive spirit against religion that drives Communism is evident in the ACLU and its cohorts. News talk show host, Bill O'Reilly, has called the ACLU "the most dangerous organization in America."[5]

The ACLU (and its allies on the Left) have continued to implement the strategy of "internal demoralization" of America, which was an integral part of Communism's battle plan for the conquest of the U.S.A. This tactic is having more success and is causing more damage to the United States than anything else that has been attempted. They accomplish this by using our own judicial system against us. Since 1920, the ACLU has been waging a largely uncontested war in the courtroom against America's core values, its Constitution, and its national sovereignty—all in the name of "rights" and "liberty" and until recently, has won by default.[6] It is especially using the promotion of the false interpretation of "separation of church and state" to subvert and erode our religious and moral foundation of Judeo-Christian values. These social engineers build on legal precedents to turn the tide in their favor.[7] They have gone to any length to circumvent our political process and have even overturned the will of the people in an election by using the judicial system to override their vote. The ACLU has played a major role in shaping our culture into what it has degenerated to today.

They conduct their war through a campaign of fear, legal intimidation, and disinformation by exhausting the will and resources of those who oppose them, and by bullying public officials in order to coerce them to cave in to their agenda.[8] They relentlessly attack our moral infrastructure by supporting legislation and filing lawsuits that weaken marriage and the family, undermine parental authority, and harm children. They help organizations that share their values to muscle their way into our public school systems and indoctrinate our children with their worldview. They have consistently sided with those who advocate legalized abortion, gay rights issues, the unlimited distribution of pornography, the sexual exploitation of children by alleged pedophiles and pedophilic organizations (like NAMBLA), the redefinition of marriage and the family, prisoner rights, infanticide, and euthanasia.[9]

One of their main goals is to eradicate every trace of Judeo-Christian religious faith and values and their expression from all areas of influence in American public life (including Christmas); and to silence the voice of Christian churches and ministries by criminalizing their religious free speech and activities through moral issues and forcing them to violate their core beliefs.[10] The ACLU is also attempting to circumvent and override our Constitution by misinterpreting it, rewriting it, and advocate the use of selective international law and the United Nations to help interpret it and resolve our domestic issues.[11]

Though many Americans don't realize it, we are in another civil war where a battle is raging over whose value system and worldview will be reflected in the laws we will live by. The ACLU and its allies are out to impose their socialistic values on us all. Whether America will remain a Judeo-Christian nation hangs in the balance. The ACLU's agenda will lead us to a secularized state with social anarchy and totalitarianism, which will bring the collapse of our great country and pave the way for the emergence of the anti-christ. The ACLU promotes so many destructive things to our society that it is evident that it is being used by satan because it bears the character of the evil one. For more resources and ways that you can combat the ACLU and preserve our liberties, contact Alliance Defense Fund (www.acluvsamerica.com); and American Center for Law and Justice (www.aclj.org).

6. Read the following Bible references regarding persecution, and briefly list each aspect.

   A. What type of attitude should we have toward persecution?

     (1) **1 John 3:13** _____

     (2) **John 15:18-25; Mark 10:28-30** _____

     (3) **John 3:19-20; 7:7** _____

     (4) **2 Timothy 3:12** _____

     (5) **Matthew 5:10-12; Luke 6:22-23** _____

     (6) **Acts 9:3-5** _____

     (7) **Galatians 6:12** _____

     (8) **Acts 13:50; Ephesians 6:12** _____

     (9) **Deuteronomy 30:7** _____

   B. What are we instructed to do when being persecuted?

     (1) **Matthew 5:44-45** _____

     (2) **Romans 12:14** _____

     (3) **Luke 23:33-34** _____

     (4) **Matthew 10:23** _____

     (5) **1 Corinthians 4:12** _____

     (6) **Luke 21:12-15** _____

SUMMARY

More reasons were given to convince us of the necessity for putting on the protective armor God has provided in order to effectively fight this invisible war. We also continued to arm ourselves with truth by putting on the Belt of Truth as we gained another insight about satan—his adversarial role. In fact, his very name, *"satan,"* means adversary. Motivated by an intense hatred of God, satan and his highly organized dark forces have unleashed a full scale assault against God's kingdom, namely, upon God Himself, His angels, and His people on earth.

Who would ever have thought when we were born on this planet that we would find ourselves in such a hostile environment and caught between two warring parties? Warfare is automatically chosen for us. Since satan already holds captive his own children in the unbelieving world, he focuses his attention on God's children who become special targets and objects of his hatred.

Satan will fiercely contest any threat to the interests of his kingdom. The following are manifestations of his warfare against God and us. Satan and his fallen angels: **1.** oppose the good angels in their work for God such as in bringing answers to prayer. He has a highly **1A.** organized kingdom for efficient warfare and can set up headquarters in certain geographical locales. Certain areas have significantly more demonic activity than others.

They are the source of **2.** persecution against those who serve and represent the true God as satan tries to stop or prevent damage from occurring to his kingdom. Realize that adversity is a normal part of our Christian walk and does not necessarily indicate that we are out of God's will. This also helps shed light on why bad things happen to good people. We discussed ways they **3.** resist and **4.** hinder servants of the true God as they labor establishing His kingdom and penetrating satan's kingdom of darkness. Those with a divinely accredited ministry must be prepared for opposition, and must keep pressing on with God's assignment without quitting. God will give us victory and breakthroughs in due time.

The devil also secretly and subtly plants his own children among God's people to **5.** infiltrate and masquerade among them in order to destroy their effectiveness and cause damage from within. They relentlessly **6.** attack the veracity and credibility of the Bible because it is the only revelation that exposes satan and his tactics and reveals the true God and His ways. They attempt to discredit it, add to it, subtract from it, mix it with half-truths, and take it out of context in order to keep people from the truth. They also try to shut down effective individual and corporate prayer to the true God.

They fiendishly delight to **7.** corrupt and defile that which is pure and holy; they **8.** blaspheme God and try to get mankind to do the same; they use "the things of the world" to **9.** rival God and compete with Him for the possession of our hearts in order to try to displace Him as the center of our lives. They **10.** rob God of mankind's worship, love, and obedience that should rightly go to Him—unwittingly giving to satan what rightfully belongs to God. Satan and his forces purposefully **11.** hide and blind people to that which they know to be the truth so as to ensure humanity's eternal destruction.

We are being relentlessly pursued by a ferocious enemy who has the ability to watch everything we do and say, and whose only goal is to keep us apart from God and out of heaven. They search for and target people (especially followers of Christ) to try to devour and **12.** destroy them. Satan tailors his strategies to fit each people group. We are only safe in the arms of Jesus who conquered him. Finally, they **13.** imitate God by making it difficult to distinguish the real from the counterfeit. This is planet earth, the sphere of satan's domain, where He *"prowls around like a roaring lion looking for someone to devour."* We critically need to put on God's protection and fight this invisible war in God's way.

Lesson 5
THE BELT OF TRUTH: Attitudes for Battle

> ☑ Before starting the DVD:

In this session we will complete our study on clothing ourselves with the Belt of Truth. The belt was thought to be the first piece of armor the Roman soldier put on as he prepared for combat. It was the first step in his transition from relaxation to readiness for battle. It was like putting on his "game face"—a **militant attitude** toward his enemy. In further developing the ability to win this invisible war, the objective of this lesson is to teach about the attitudes God wants us to have as we engage in this warfare. The Holy Spirit inspired the apostle Paul to use these pieces of armor the Roman soldier wore in combat as an analogy to describe their spiritual counterpart used in the spiritual warfare of the believer. The 1st Qtr. Exam can be taken after this lesson—obtainable from our website.

The Belt of Truth speaks to us primarily of two things:

1. The Christian warrior must continually acquire a thorough knowledge of biblical truth and maintain a firm belief in it. This will give us the necessary insight, the strength of confidence, and the skill to fight in this invisible war.

   Note: The enemy successfully works by keeping us in ignorance. Putting on the Belt of Truth counteracts this.

2. The proper attitudes one should have prior to, and while engaging in this combat.

> ☑ **DVD Users:** Watch Lesson 5 for an overview before proceeding further (26 min.).
> ☑ When you're through, pick up again at this point. Fill in the blanks from the Summary.

ATTITUDES IN PREPARATION FOR BATTLE

1. Develop the attitude of A_lertness_ .

   † **1 Peter 5:8** (GNT)—*Be alert, be on watch! Your enemy, the Devil, roams around like a roaring lion, looking for someone to devour.*

📖 DEFINITION—BE ALERT

The Greek word used in **1 Peter 5:8** is *nēphō* and is translated *"alert"* in the GNT; *"sober"* in the KJV; and *"self-controlled"* in the NIV. It "signified to be free from the influence of intoxicants."[1]

A lion bides his time waiting for a vulnerable moment when he can catch his victim off guard. It is critical to have our spiritual and mental faculties function unimpaired by intoxication with other interests. We must not allow things to consume our attention, dull our senses, or weigh us down with the cares of this life so as to <u>prevent</u> us from seeing the dangers—just as we are instructed to do in anticipation of Christ's return **(Luke 21:34).** This attitude will help us to be continually alert to the devil's schemes—especially *"when the day of evil comes"* **(Ephesians 6:13)**. This *"day of evil"* refers to a subtle planned attack implemented when we are most vulnerable and off guard.

2. Develop the attitude of <u>Watchfulness</u> **(1 Peter 5:8** GNT**)**.

📖 **DEFINITION—BE ON WATCH**

The Greek word the Holy Spirit used in **1 Peter 5:8** is *grēgoreō*. It is translated *"vigilant"* in the KJV. It means to be on guard, to "be watchful."[2]

> † **Matthew 10:16**—Jesus said, *"I am sending you out like sheep among wolves..."*

We must be on guard against this determined adversary with his immense resources of cunning and might. Being cautious and alert will enable us to discern the strategies, traps, and pitfalls that he sets for us so we will not be outwitted by him **(1 Corinthians 2:11)**. See also **Matthew 13:25; 26:38-41.** However, being watchful does **not** mean living our lives in paranoia (like the birds and animals seem to be whenever they eat or drink) as though the devil is constantly stalking us.

3. Develop the attitude that will consistently <u>Submit</u> to God's rule, for then you will be in a position to resist the enemy.

> † **James 4:7**—*Submit yourselves, then, to God. Resist the devil, and he will flee from you.*

📖 **DEFINITION—SUBMIT**

The Greek word the Holy Spirit used in **James 4:7** is *hupotassō*. It is "...primarily a military term, one 'to rank under'...be in subjection..."[3] It's like falling under authority in the chain of command. We must be totally submissive to God's Word and His will in our lives. We cannot have authority over anything (in this case the devil) until we come under God's authority.

A. We must walk in obedience if we expect God to work on our behalf **(Joshua 7:6-12)**.

4. Develop the attitude that it will be a <u>Lifelong</u> battle.

A. That you will have to "<u>Wrestle</u>": Accept the fact that the conflict will be very strenuous at times as you struggle against the spiritual forces of evil. The word implies that one must undergo "spiritual conditioning" in order to be in shape for this invisible war.

> † **Ephesians 6:12** (KJV)—*For we wrestle not against flesh and blood, but against principalities, against powers, against the rulers of the darkness of this world, against spiritual wickedness in high places.*

B. That you will have to <u>Oppose</u>: You must view this as a long term war and make the decision that you will confront these wicked spirits and that you will stand firm, holding your ground—resisting them to the bitter end with steadfast, unyielding opposition. You must take a firm stand in the beginning if you expect to have one at the end. This can only be done in the power and authority of, and with faith in our Commander in Chief, Jesus Christ.

> † **Ephesians 6:13**—*Therefore put on the full armor of God, so that when the day of evil comes, you may be able to stand your ground, and after you have done everything, to stand.*

C. That you will need to "RESIST_____"

† **1 Peter 5:9** (GNT)—*Be firm in your faith and resist him...*

† **James 4:7**—*Resist the devil, and he will flee from you.*

(1) Resist by your <u>faith</u>. In order to successfully oppose and resist the devil, you must be fully persuaded, beyond a shadow of a doubt, that the Bible is God's inerrant revelation of Himself to mankind—to the point that you commit yourself totally to Him and order your life according to His precepts. You must be so convinced that Christ is alive today and that He defeated satan and sin on the cross. Your relationship with Christ must be so real that you would give your life rather than renounce Him. This matter is so critical because much of what is involved in this battle is centered on how well you know your God and His truth so you do not build your life on lies.

(2) Resist by your <u>obedience</u>. By ordering your life upon the Bible, you can confidently resist with unyielding firmness in any attack of the enemy. Your acts of obedience proclaim your submission to God and reinforce within you (and to the enemy) your commitment to His Lordship. This generates a corresponding response from God— He will come on the scene to empower you and rout your adversaries.

(3) Resist by your <u>perseverance</u>. A key to victory is to go the distance when trusting in God's Word and character. Continue to press on through the opposition or infirmity until you cannot go any farther. Never retreat or give up the ground on which you have already made progress. This is one way breakthroughs occur.

(4) Resist by your <u>declaration</u>. Address the forces of darkness by declaring out loud what God's Word says about your situation, who you are in Christ (your position and authority), and the specific stand you are taking in the matter. Verbally denying them permission to work in your life is the kind of unwavering faith and persistence that causes the enemy to flee.

(5) Resist by your <u>prayer</u> and <u>intercession</u>.

Q: What are some ways that you have resisted in your experience?

▶**CONSIDER THIS:** Our culture has led us to believe that life consists of the pursuit of pleasure and materialism. For the Christian, however, life is actually a battlefield—not a playground. The attitude we have toward these two views will determine our goals and lifestyle. Fighting is something that may not come naturally to us, or may not be something with which we are comfortable. Unfortunately, we have no choice in the matter.

In this warfare, we **cannot** be unresponsive, retreat, or hide from the enemy. God wants us to stand firm in His power and Christ's victory, confronting and opposing our adversary through faith, obedience, declaration, and prayer. The Holy Spirit will teach us and help us to become spiritual warriors. Also, God does not intend for us to always focus our energies fighting satan directly. Our humility, obedience to His Word, and sanctification are some of the weapons that will indirectly fight spiritual forces of evil in our lives and nation. Our Father will then take care of demonic forces for us.

5. Develop the attitude that you will determine to
K̲n̲o̲w̲ your enemy's T̲a̲c̲t̲i̲c̲s̲ .

† **2 Corinthians 2:11**—*...in order that Satan might not outwit us. For we are not unaware of his schemes.*

📖 **DEFINITION—SCHEMES**

The Greek word used by the Holy Spirit in this verse is *noēma*, translated "devices" in the KJV meaning "that which is thought out."[4] In **Ephesians 6:11,** the word translated in the NIV for the devil's *"schemes" ("wiles"* in the KJV) is *methodia* which denotes "craft, deceit" or "a cunning device..."[5] From it we get our word method.

A. These evil spirits can devise plans by thinking out moves in advance, much like in a chess game, with calculated goals. They use the most evil, cunning, and crafty methods to deceive, entrap, enslave, and finally destroy their victim. These wicked plans are formed with devious intrigue and executed with consummate skill. They exercise great patience in their attacks on us, and if one method fails, they will seek to use another. They will also adapt their strategies to fit the culture of a society.

B. Immediately following the surprise 9/11 terrorist attack on the World Trade Center in New York City, among the first questions we had to ask ourselves were: Who is this enemy? What was their motive? What is their worldview? What are their tactics? How could we begin to fight a war without being armed with this information? Our conflict with the devil is much the same. The same questions need to be asked. We must know those things about our spiritual enemies through what the Holy Spirit has revealed, through the Scriptures, and through our experiences and those of others.

▶**CONSIDER THIS:** Ignorance of satan's strategies is deadly. Not only will it make us ineffective but can also bring about certain defeat. **Q:** How many of his tactics do you know and daily keep in mind? It is impossible to deal with an enemy that we know little or nothing about. It is important to be well informed in order to discern his intentions and thwart his purposes. In Lesson 9 we will begin the first of over 30 of his tactics.

6. Develop the attitude of P̲r̲o̲p̲e̲r̲ R̲e̲s̲p̲e̲c̲t̲ for your enemy.

† **Jude 1:9** (Phillips)—*But I would remind you that even the archangel Michael when he was contending with the devil in the dispute over the body of Moses did not dare to condemn him with mockery. He simply said, the Lord rebuke you!*

In reference to Michael the Archangel, other translations of **Jude 1:9** read:

† *"...did not dare to accuse even Satan, or jeer at him..."* (TLB)

✝ *"...Michael did not dare condemn the devil with insulting words..."* (GNT)

Also see **Zechariah 3:2** and **2 Peter 2:11.**

▶ **CONSIDER THIS:** No matter how intensely we would want to react in anger and outrage at the havoc and destruction wrought by these wicked spirits on people, when verbally addressing the devil and evil spirits, we must stay within the paradigm that Jesus and the Archangel Michael set before us in the Scriptures. Whatever we see our Lord and His angels doing in the Bible, we should do. What we **do see** them doing is quoting Scripture. And, except in the cases when Jesus cast demons out of people (rebuking them with authoritative commands), they restrained themselves and left all rebuking, judgment, and vengeance up to almighty God.

Nowhere in Scripture do we read of Christ (or His angels) verbally taunting evil powers; jeering at them; ridiculing them; challenging them in a mocking, sarcastic, insulting way; or arguing with them. Nor did they rebuke evil spirits in a scolding, berating, or abusive manner. They neither underestimated nor overestimated these adversaries. Their confidence was in God and not in themselves.

Wisdom would have us follow this model, have proper respect, and do not be timid but exercise the authority Christ has given us. Never fear the devil more than you fear God!

7. Develop the attitude that you have a H~u~man Responsibility.

✝ **Ephesians 6:11**—*Put on the full armor of God, so that you can take your stand against the devil's schemes.*

A. God has also commanded us to *"put off"* and to *"put on"* certain things—putting sin to death in our lives. He will not do it for us. God expects us to do it by an act of our will in obedience. When we do, He shows himself strong on our behalf by empowering us.

✝ **Ephesians 4:22-24**—*You were taught, with regard to your former way of life, to put off your old self, which is being corrupted by its deceitful desires;* **23.** *to be made new in the attitude of your minds;* **24.** *and to put on the new self, created to be like God in true righteousness and holiness.* (See also verses **25-32.**)

✝ **1 Peter 4:1**—*Therefore, since Christ suffered in his body, arm yourselves also with the same attitude, because he who has suffered in his body is done with sin.*

✝ Also see **Colossians 3:8-10; Philippians 2:5-8.**

▶ **CONSIDER THIS:** Nothing in the storehouse of human resources, neither our strength nor our intelligence, is adequate for this warfare. That is why God has supplied the various pieces of defensive and offensive armor for us to use. If we neglect this provision, it will cause us certain defeat—with eternal consequences. It is a comforting thought that we do not have to be concerned about having to put these pieces of armor on all by ourselves. God will help us put them on. Putting on this armor maintains the work God has done in and for us and helps us to keep our part of the New Testament. We will enlarge on this in Lessons 7 and 8.

8. Develop the attitude that you are <u>secure</u> in <u>Christ</u>.

    † **John 10:27-29**—*My sheep listen to my voice; I know them, and they follow me.* ***28.*** *I give them eternal life, and they shall never perish; no one can snatch them out of my hand.* ***29.*** *My Father, who has given them to me, is greater than all; no one can snatch them out of my Father's hand.*

This is the security that God has given to us:

A. The Holy Spirit <u>Lives In</u> you.

    † **1 Corinthians 6:19**—*Do you not know that your body is a temple of the Holy Spirit, who is in you, whom you have received from God?*
    (Also see **Romans 8:11.**)

►**CONSIDER THIS**: For the Holy Spirit to live in us, we have to receive Christ into our hearts and give Him control of our lives—having a *"born again"* experience. When this occurs, we are adopted into His family and become His sons or daughters. Therefore, the confidence of our security rests upon our new relationship with our Heavenly Father and our position in Christ due to His work on the cross. By faith you must believe what God's Word says about who you are in Christ, and openly declare and appropriate your position as a child of God.

B. A "<u>Hedge</u>" of <u>Protection</u> is around about you.

    † **Job 1:9-10**—*"Does Job fear God for nothing?" Satan replied.* ***10.*** *"Have you not put a hedge around him and his household and everything he has?..."*

(1) Our protective hedge is the "blood of Christ." This term figuratively refers to His sacrifice on Calvary that defeated satan and his dark forces. If you have become God's child and have appropriated what Christ's blood accomplished for you, then like being protected under an umbrella, you are under the protection of His blood covering.

(2) Another aspect of this protection is the gift of "salvation" which Christ secured by His work on the cross. It is a removal from danger into a place of safety and protection. Dr. Michael Youssef wrote, "Once we are marked with the blood we cannot be touched—by God's judgment or by the devil. Because the blood says, 'Pass over, do not harm.' No power in hell can get past that blood, because it is a seal established on the authority of God and God's Word."[6]

    † **Exodus 12:13** (NLT)—God said, *"When I see the blood, I will pass over you. This plague of death will not touch you..."*

(3) As a child of God, like Israel, you also have a **wall of fire** around you—the assurance of God's personal presence. There is nothing that can pass through this fiery wall but that which has to go through Him first.

† **Zechariah 2:5** (NASB)—*"For I," declares the Lord, "will be a wall of fire around her* (Israel)*, and I will be the glory in her midst."*

† **2 Thessalonians 3:3** (NASB)—*But the Lord is faithful, and He will strengthen and protect you from the evil one.*

† **John 17:15-16**—Jesus said to His Father: *"My prayer is not that you take them out of the world but that you protect them from the evil one."*

† **Psalm 125:2** (NLT)—*Just as the mountains surround and protect Jerusalem, so the Lord surrounds and protects his people, both now and forever.*

C. Satan must obtain <u>Permission</u> from God in order to touch one of His children. God also sets limits as to what He allows the devil to do—if anything.

† **Job 1:11-12**—Satan said, *"But stretch out your hand and strike everything he has, and he will surely curse you to your face." **12.** The Lord said to Satan, "Very well, then, everything he has is in your hands, but on the man himself do not lay a finger." Then Satan went out from the presence of the Lord.* (Also see **Job 2:3-6.**)

† **Luke 22:31-32**—Jesus said to Peter: *"Simon, Simon, behold, Satan has demanded permission to sift you like wheat; **32.** but I have prayed for you, that your faith may not fail..."*

(1) As we stay under the umbrella of God's protection, satanic forces cannot touch us without God's permission; unless, of course, we step out from beneath it through our disobedience. We can confidently say to our adversaries—both spiritual and human, "The only way that you can touch me is if my Heavenly Father permits you to penetrate the covering of Christ's protective blood over my life."

D. God commissions <u>Guardian Angels</u> to watch over you and fight for you.

† **Hebrews 1:14**—*Are not all angels ministering spirits sent to serve those who will inherit salvation?* (Also see **Matthew 18:10.**)

† **Psalms 91:9-15** (NASB)—*For you have made the Lord, my refuge, Even the Most High, your dwelling place. **10.** No evil will befall you, Nor will any plague come near your tent. **11.** For He will give His angels charge concerning you, To guard you in all your ways. **12.** They will bear you up in their hands, Lest you strike your foot against a stone. **13.** ...the young lion and the serpent you will trample down. **14.** "Because he has loved Me, therefore I will deliver him; I will set him securely on high, because he has known My name. **15.** He will call upon Me, and I will answer him; I will be with him in trouble; I will rescue him, and honor him."*

✝ **2 Kings 6:15-17** (NLT)—*When the servant of the man of God got up early the next morning and went outside, there were troops, horses, and chariots everywhere. "Alas, my lord, what shall we do now?" he cried out to Elisha. **16.** "Don't be afraid!" Elisha told him. "For there are more on our side than on theirs!" **17.** Then Elisha prayed, "O Lord, open his eyes and let him see!" The Lord opened his servant's eyes, and when he looked up, he saw that the hillside around Elisha was filled with horses and chariots of fire.*

▶ **CONSIDER THIS:** God has given His children security and protection, but we must stay "under" His protection. However, you can be your own worst enemy. Due to free will you can make a decision to step outside the hedge or umbrella of His protection through disobedience and bring all hell upon yourself. You can even decide to quit serving God and so to speak "jump out" of His secure hand—a place where no one else can touch you. You can also continually sin and grieve the Holy Spirit, Who lives in you, to the point where you can cause Him to leave you.

I believe the following statement is biblically true and comforting: **God is involved in everything that affects your life as a child of God—even if you bring it on yourself.** What I mean is that the things that happen to us are either: sent by Him, permitted by Him, or used by Him **(Romans 8:28).** What I mean by "bring it on yourself" is the law of planting and harvesting **(Galatians 6:7-8)** whereby we reap the consequences of our actions and give the devil a foothold. By putting sin to death in our lives, Christ will hold us secure so that the devil cannot assault us in order to sever our vital union with Him.

✝ **1 John 5:18** (NLT)—*We know that those who have become part of God's family do not make a practice of sinning, for God's Son holds them securely, and the evil one cannot get his hands on them.*

9. Develop the attitude that sin, satan, and death have already been D_____ by Christ through His sacrificial blood on the cross.

✝ **1 John 4:4**—*You, dear children, are from God and have overcome them, because the one who is in you is greater than the one who is in the world.*

✝ **Ephesians 6:10**—*Finally, be strong in the Lord and in his mighty power.*

✝ **Luke 10:17-20**—*The seventy-two returned with joy and said, "Lord, even the demons submit to us in your name." **18.** He replied... **19.** "I have given you authority to trample on snakes and scorpions and to overcome all the power of the enemy; nothing will harm you. **20.** However, do not rejoice that the spirits submit to you, but rejoice that your names are written in heaven."*

✝ **Colossians 2:15** (Phillips)—*And then* [on the cross] *having drawn the sting of all the powers and authorities ranged against us, he* [Jesus] *exposed them, shattered, empty, and defeated, in his own triumphant victory.*

▶ **CONSIDER THIS:** The fact is that the war is already won. On the cross, Christ victoriously disarmed the powers of darkness of their right to rule humanity that they had usurped from Adam, and recovered it back for mankind. Jesus has already given to His church both His **power** (or ability—*dunamis*) via the outpouring of the Holy Spirit, and His **authority** (*exousia*)—the legal right to use His power to continue what He began, which is destroying the works of the devil in people's lives. These evil forces must be challenged.

† **Matthew 28:18-19** (NASB)—Jesus said, *"All authority has been given to Me in heaven and on earth. 19. Go therefore and make disciples of all the nations...and lo, I am with you always, even to the end of the age."*

A. God has designed for us to live a life of victory through Christ. The devil would have you believe that he is so powerful that he would cause you to cower in fear of him thinking it is useless to even try to combat him. Nothing could be further from the truth. **Satan's defeat is not future, it already happened on the cross!** The key to victory is knowing that you are a child of God, and using the authority and power that Christ has already given to you.

B. For example, law enforcement officers are given the power and authority (the legal right to use this power) by the city and state to enforce its laws. If they don't use them, crime will continue unrestrained. Envision Mary Anne, a policewoman, directing traffic at an intersection and she encounters a tractor-trailer speeding toward her. Now she within herself does not have the power or authority to command the truck to stop. But she merely has to stretch out her hand (exercising her power and authority) and signal "STOP," and the truck driver must respond because he recognizes the power and authority behind her uniform and badge.

C. Similarly, Christians are given the power (the Holy Spirit) and authority (the legal right to use this power) by Jesus Christ over satan and his kingdom of darkness. If we don't use them, sin and demonic activity will continue unrestrained. Now Mary Anne, a Christian, does not have the power or authority within herself to command demons to obey her. But when she issues a command to demonic powers in the name of Jesus (exercising her God-given power and authority), the demons must obey because they recognize the power and authority behind the name of Jesus and her position in Christ.

D. Although satan is now a defeated foe, he tenaciously holds his ground until we exercise our God-given authority over him. But there is a difference between having been given authority and power, and using it. Often Christians allow a defeated enemy to steal the victory in their lives that was won for them on the cross because they do not walk in that power and authority.

† **Matthew 8:29**—The evil spirits said to Jesus: *"What do you want with us, Son of God?" they shouted. "Have you come here to torture us before the appointed time?"*

† **Romans 8:37-39** (TLB)—*No, despite all these things, overwhelming victory is ours through Christ, who loved us. 38. And I am convinced that nothing can ever separate us from his love. Death can't, and life can't. The angels can't, and the demons can't. Our fears for today, our worries about tomorrow, and even the powers of hell can't keep God's love away. 39. Whether we are high above the sky or in the deepest ocean, nothing in all creation will ever be able to separate us from the love of God that is revealed in Christ Jesus our Lord.*

E. By faith, we must affirm the truth of Christ's victory and boldly exercise His authority and power to change our circumstances. God expects us to use the awesome power released by the death and resurrection of Jesus to stand up to these wicked spirits—putting them to flight. We are to trample upon them, not them on us!

✝ **Ephesians 1:18-23**—*I pray also that the eyes of your heart may be enlightened in order that you may know the hope to which he has called you, the riches of his glorious inheritance in the saints, **19.** and his incomparably great power for us who believe. That power is like the working of his mighty strength, **20.** which he exerted in Christ when he raised him from the dead and seated him at his right hand in the heavenly realms, **21.** far above all rule and authority, power and dominion, and every title that can be given, not only in the present age but also in the one to come. **22.** And God placed all things under his feet and appointed him to be head over everything for the church, **23.** which is his body, the fullness of him who fills everything in every way.*

F. It is beyond our understanding why God allows satan to continue to operate 2000 years after Christ defeated him on the cross. The following Scripture reveals that God has a gradual, far reaching plan, and we are to simply trust Him because He knows and directs the future.

✝ **1 Corinthians 15:20-26** (NASB)—*But now Christ has been raised from the dead, the first fruits of those who are asleep. **21.** For since by a man came death, by a man also came the resurrection of the dead. **22.** For as in Adam all die, so also in Christ all shall be made alive. **23.** But each in his own order: Christ the first fruits, after that those who are Christ's at His coming, **24.** then comes the end, when He delivers up the kingdom to the God and Father, when He has abolished all rule and all authority and power. **25.** For He must reign until He has put all His enemies under His feet. **26.** The last enemy that will be abolished is death.*

> ☑ This ends the DVD content for Lesson 5.
> ☑ Continue on with the Study Questions and Application and the Summary.

STUDY QUESTIONS AND APPLICATION

1. Read the following Scriptures that reveal the results of Christ's defeat of satan by His death and resurrection. Then fill in the blanks with the specific ways Christ triumphed over him.

   A. **Colossians 2:15** _____

   B. **Matthew 28:18; 1 Peter 3:22** _____

   C. **Luke 10:18-20** _____

   D. **1 John 3:7-8**_____ (i.e. He undoes the devil's work in lives.)

   E. **Hebrews 2:14-15** _____

   F. **Matthew 25:41; Revelation 20:10** _____

2. How would you rate your overall attitude toward spiritual warfare?

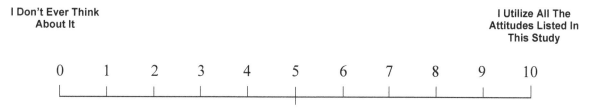

Note: If you scored under 7, what steps can you take to better your attitude?

3. Which three of the nine attitudes do you need to improve on the most, and what can you do to begin the process to change it?

_____ —How to begin? _____

_____ —How to begin? _____

_____ —How to begin? _____

4. Ask the Holy Spirit to reveal to you any way that you may have stepped outside of God's umbrella of protection. (Note: We will be covering **How to Recapture Territory Lost to the Enemy** in Lesson 12.)

5. **Questions to ponder:** "Why does God allow evil to continue in our world?" **Q:** "If most of mankind will die without faith in Christ and go to an eternal hell, then why does God permit human history to continue?" **Q:** "How much does the difference between the way life is with sin and the way it ought to be without it, trouble me?" **Then ask yourself:** "What is my view of God?" **Q:** "Can He, or can He not, control evil?" **Q:** "Is He limited or unlimited in His attributes?" **Q:** "Is He perfect or imperfect in His nature?" **Q:** "Do I harbor any ill feeling toward God due to this?" **Q:** "Is any of my faith and confidence in God shaken over this?"

6. On the scale below, to what degree do you believe in Christ's authority and victory over the devil as it relates to your life? Write the current month and year below the number.

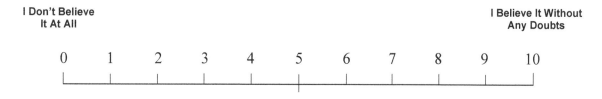

Note: If you scored under 7, ask the Holy Spirit to make this truth more real to you. Try to identify that which hinders your faith in this truth.

SUMMARY

In this session we concluded our study on clothing ourselves with the Belt of Truth. The belt was considered to be the first piece of armor the Roman soldier put on as he prepared for combat. It was the first step in his transition from relaxation to readiness for battle. It was like putting on his "game face"—a **militant attitude** toward his enemy. The Holy Spirit inspired the apostle Paul to use this analogy of these pieces of armor the Roman soldier wore in combat to describe its spiritual counterpart used in the spiritual warfare of the believer.

The Belt of Truth speaks to us primarily of two things: (1) the Christian warrior must continually acquire a thorough knowledge of biblical truth and maintain a firm belief in it in order to fight with confidence and skill in this invisible war, and (2) there are proper attitudes one should have prior to, and while engaging in this warfare. The main objective of this lesson was to explore the biblical attitudes for battle.

These attitudes from God's Word which must be developed for battle are: **1.** alertness and **2.** watchfulness which will prevent us from consuming our attention, dulling our senses, or weighing ourselves down with the cares of this life so as to hinder us from seeing the dangers; consistently **3.** submit to God's rule in our lives as His children so we are in a position to resist the enemy; the attitude that this will be a **4.** lifelong battle that, at times, will involve strenuous exertion. In this invisible war, we will have to **4A.** wrestle, **4B.** oppose (standing firm, and holding our ground), and **4C.** resist (by our faith, obedience, perseverance, declaration, and prayer and intercession). Develop the attitude that determines to **5.** know your enemy's tactics, and have **6.** proper respect for him by following the example Christ and the angels modeled for us. Also, develop the attitude that you have a **7.** human responsibility to *"put off"* and *"put on"* certain things including the armor, and that God will not do it for you.

Develop the attitude that you are **8.** secure in Christ and that you must stay "under" His protection without straying outside the boundaries of His security. This security includes: the Holy Spirit who **8A.** lives in you; God places a **8B.** "hedge" of protection around you—the blood of Christ; satan needs to obtain **8C.** permission from God in order to touch you; and God commissions **8D.** guardian angels to watch over you and fight for you. This leads us to believe this truth: **God is involved in everything that affects your life as a child of God—even if you bring it on yourself. They are either sent by Him, permitted by Him, or used by Him.**

Finally, take on the attitude that satan has been **9.** defeated by Jesus Christ by His death on the cross and His triumphant resurrection. He disarmed these wicked principalities and powers and overcame all the power of the enemy. As children of God, Christ has given us the authority to use His name and the power of the Holy Spirit. Although satan is now a defeated foe, he will tenaciously hold his ground until we exercise our God-given authority over him. He and his demonic spirits must submit to the power and authority of the name of Jesus Christ. We Christians often allow a defeated enemy to steal the victory in our lives that Christ won for us on the cross because we do not walk in that power and authority. God expects us to use the awesome power released by the death and resurrection of Jesus to stand up against these wicked spirits—putting them to flight. We are to trample upon them, not them on us!

Lesson 6

INTRODUCTION TO THE
BREASTPLATE OF RIGHTEOUSNESS: The Trinity of Man

☑ Before starting the DVD:

Many times we are not adequately educated in the critical issues of life before they occur. For example, wouldn't you have really welcomed a course that prepared you for the dos and don'ts of marriage and raising children? Or what about a study on the proper things to feed your body—instead of some of those courses you had to take that have not proved beneficial in everyday life?

This study as a whole, and especially what we are about to embark on, is more critical to know than practically any other information available. In developing the ability to win this invisible war, this is basic "Bible 101" that we should have been taught by our teenage years. But for some, this may be the first opportunity you have had to learn about it. But, better late than never! Start today by asking the Lord to help you incorporate these truths into your daily life.

We now leave the Belt of Truth and move on to the Breastplate of Righteousness. In Roman times, the breastplate was made from overlapping strips of iron secured by leather straps, which made it extremely strong, yet flexible. In order to comprehend the deeper spiritual meanings behind this piece of armor, we will lay a foundation as we did for the Belt of Truth. This will be the goal of Lessons 6 and 7. In Lesson 8 we will begin to define the breastplate.

God created our being in a threefold composition of *"spirit, soul, and body."* In this lesson, we will identify the components of our soul and spirit and learn about their functions <u>prior</u> to Adam's fall and discover more about the inner workings of ourselves. The Bible isn't consistently clear in its distinction between the *"spirit,"* *"soul,"* and *"heart."* For clarity and for illustration purposes, I have carefully attempted to categorize each without taking Scripture out of context or drawing an incorrect conclusion.

☑ **DVD Users:** Watch Lesson 6 for an overview before proceeding further (26 min.).
☑ When you're through, pick up again at this point. Fill in the blanks from the Summary.

OVERVIEW OF THE TRINITY OF MAN

This overview is intended to depict God's awesome design and creation of Adam and Eve prior to their fall into sin. It is also intended to enable us to be knowledgeable about how God created us. The Bible states that God made us *"spirit, soul and body"* and that we are *"...fearfully and wonderfully made..."* **(Psalm 139:14).** Now, let's learn about them!

✝ **1 Thessalonians 5:23b**—*May your whole spirit, soul and body be kept blameless at the coming of our Lord Jesus Christ.*

OVERVIEW OF THE TRINITY OF MAN (continued)

1. Our **BODY** is W_____ (or earth)—consciousness.

📖 **DEFINITION—BODY**

Sōma is the Greek word used. It is the "house" we live in—our earth suit as it were. It interacts with the tangible physical world around us via our five senses: hearing, sight, smell, touch, and taste. It is not the real "you" but houses and expresses the real "you." Our body carries out the dictates of our spirit and soul. It was made from the "dust of the earth" (**Genesis 2:7; 3:19**). Having done a chemical analysis of the human body, science confirms that it is composed of the same elements as found in the soil. And the blood contains its life (**Leviticus 17:11**).

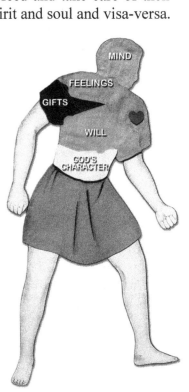

† **Genesis 1:26**—*Then God said, "Let us make man in our image, in our likeness, and let them rule..."*

A. *"Image"* in **1:26** means "a representation of the deity"[1]

B. *"Likeness"* in **1:26** indicates that God created man in His likeness—a trinity of spiritual, character, and physical likeness.

   (1) Man's physical form is made after the spiritual form of God (**Numbers 12:8; Exodus 33:18-23; Revelation 5:1-7; Matthew 18:10**).

   Note: God expected Adam and Eve (and us) to properly feed and take care of their bodies. Also, the condition of the body will affect one's spirit and soul and visa-versa. (See **Matthew 26:41**.)

2. Our **SOUL** is S_____—consciousness.

📖 **DEFINITION—SOUL**

Psuchē is the Greek word used. It means breath or to breathe. It is the part of us that expresses our personality—who we truly are as a person. Our soul should be a servant to our spirit. The soul has no latent power in itself to know or to do superhuman things. It is depicted by the picture on the right.

† **Genesis 2:7** (KJV)—*And the Lord God formed man of the dust of the ground, and breathed into his nostrils the breath of life; and man became a living soul.*

Note: The Hebrew word for the breath of *"life"* (*chayim*) literally means the breath of *"lives"* possibly referring to the creation of two lives—the soul and the spirit.

A.   What are the components of our soul?

(1) Our I_____—It has the ability to think, comprehend, reason, and plan. It can project into the future through imagination, and reflect on the past through memory. It may also include our subconscious. Our attitudes and motives (why we do what we do) may also be formed here.

(2) Our F_____ (emotions)—They were originally designed to be dependent upon the intellect and the will and to flow from them and reflect them. Emotions can be a powerful influencer of the will. The part of us that loves with tender affection (Greek *phileō*) is in the soul and is designated by the heart on our illustration. Moods probably reside here too. Develop the ability to recognize a feeling or mood as it is occurring. We must be in control of our emotions and not allow them to dominate us.

(3) Our W_____—It is the most important component of our soul. Like the angels, we were created with "free will." God has given us this incredible gift—the ability to make our own decisions. He will respect our choices—even those that are wrong. Our will acts like a door where our thoughts and actions pass through. The decisions we make today determine what we, and our circumstances, will be tomorrow—whether good or bad. Our will cannot afford to choose wrong as it could lead us to death. We may not have the choice of being born (or in other matters of life), but we **do** have the ability to choose where we will spend eternity.

▶ **CONSIDER THIS:** We believe the God of the Bible has no limits to His attributes—that He is all-powerful (omnipotent), all-knowing (omniscient), and present everywhere (omnipresent). However, by creating us with "free will," God has chosen to limit Himself to some extent when dealing with mankind. This could be a reason why He didn't prevent sin from occurring, why He doesn't exercise His power over things like sometimes we think He should, or why He doesn't force Himself on us but simply knocks on the door of our hearts for permission to enter.

(4) The C_____ likeness and image of God.

(a) We were also made in God's moral likeness—Adam and Eve were created in God's character likeness without sin. The white colored area in the last illustration depicts this.

(5) Our T_____ and personality. It is the unique blend of characteristics and charisma that distinguishes our individuality. There never has been, nor will there ever be, another you on this planet!

Note: I recommend that you check out some of the personality tests to learn more about yourself and how to respect and work with other people's temperament types. Some are available at www.keirsey.com; www.onlinedisc.com. Also, keep in mind that the psychologists (and the realm of psychology) deal with the soul, whereas Christian pastors and counselors deal with both spirit and soul.

(6) Our G_____ and talents. Are you aware of the gifts God has created you with, or has bestowed upon you for the purpose of ministry, to benefit mankind? (See **1 Timothy 4:14; 2 Timothy 1:6.**) **Q:** Are you operating in your giftings?

▶**CONSIDER THIS:** God gave us an illustration in nature of the peach that depicts mankind's three-part being. The outer part we eat represents our body. The inner stone corresponds to our soul. Inside the stone is a seed, which portrays our spirit.

3. Our **SPIRIT** is G_____-consciousness.

📖 **DEFINITION—SPIRIT**

Pneuma is the Greek word used in the New Testament.

In addition to **1 Thessalonians 5:23, Hebrews 4:12** also tells us that our soul and spirit are separate entities. This latter Scripture states that the Word of God as a sharp sword *"...penetrates even to dividing soul* (psuchē) *and spirit* (pneuma) *...it judges the thoughts and attitudes of the heart* (kardia)."

Note: The Bible figuratively uses the word *"heart"* to generally describe various aspects of our soul and spirit—both in a good and a bad sense (see **Luke 6:45**). And it sometimes refers to our inner man as the control center. The heart in our illustration refers to our love in the soul. Interestingly, all three words, *"soul," "spirit,"* and *"heart"* are mentioned in **Hebrews 4:12.**

A. Spiritual likeness—Adam and Eve were created in the image of God as spiritual beings **(John 4:24; Zechariah 12:1).**

B. It is the main part of us that interacts with the spirit world—God, angels, and evil spirits. It can also detect the disposition of the spirit of another fellow human being. We are more than just physical beings attuned to the physical world—we are also spiritual beings affected by the spirit world around us.

C. Scripture implies that our spirit is located in the midst of our body (see **Daniel 7:15** KJV; **John 7:37-39; Luke 24:32**).

D. What are the components of our spirit?

(1) The part that D_____—our sixth sense.

(a) Our C_____—a built-in moral compass that points us to God's "true north" moral standards—distinguishing and warning us between right and wrong. Since Adam's fall, this is the most likely place where the Holy Spirit convicts us of sin.

† **Romans 2:14-15** (NLT)—*Even when Gentiles, who do not have God's written law, instinctively follow what the law says, they show that in their hearts they know right from wrong. 15. They demonstrate that God's law is written within them, for their own consciences either accuse them or tell them they are doing what is right.* Also see **Romans 1:19-21.**

   (b) Our I_____—a quick insight, or hunch, known through instinct and perception, rather than through learning, acquiring facts, or by rationalization. Become more aware of your intuitive gut feelings.

(2) The part where we receive R_____ knowledge about God and where we hear His "voice" speaking to us.

† **1 Corinthians 2:10,14**—*...God has revealed it to us by His Spirit.*

† **John 6:63**—Jesus said, *"The words I have spoken to you are spirit and they are life."*

Note: The Word of God is directed to our spirit by the Holy Spirit to nourish and give it life.

† **1 Corinthians 12:8-11**—The Holy Spirit imparts to us the nine Gifts of the Spirit—gifts of revelation, power, and inspiration (see also **Mark 2:8**).

† **Romans 8:16** (NLT)—*For His Holy Spirit speaks to us deep in our hearts and tells us that we are God's children.*

† **Colossians 3:15**—*Let the peace of Christ rule in your hearts...* (i.e. like an umpire to settle disputes and give clear direction).

(3) The part that F_____ (communes) with God's Spirit.

   (a) Adam and Eve were created with their spirits alive in their relationship with God.

     Note: Since Adam's Fall, our spirit is born in a state where it is dead in its relationship with God. Only the new birth can make our relationship alive to God again. In light of this, we can clearly see that if someone is dead in their relationship to God, it's foolish for that person to think he or she can rely on church membership, good works, etc., alone to make them right with God.

   (b) Prayer and worship originate and ascend to God as a fragrance from our spirit. **1 Corinthians 14:14** says *"...my spirit prays..."*

† **Romans 8:26-27**—The Holy Spirit births intercession in our spirit to the Father.

† **John 4:24** (KJV)—Jesus said, *"God is a Spirit; and they that worship Him must worship Him in spirit and in truth."*

▶**CONSIDER THIS:** It is my personal opinion that music generally stirs our soul while Christian music should inspire our spirit in order to usher us into the presence of God. But not all Christian music is conducive to evoking true worship because some just elate our soul rather than minister to our spirit.

(c) God created a place in our spirit that can only be satisfied by His presence, which in turn satisfies the whole man. Attempting to satisfy it with anything else will only prove to be temporary, empty, and futile. Our spirit is specifically designed to hunger and thirst for God and His presence.

† **Psalm 42:1-2** (NLT)—*As the deer pants for streams of water, so I long for you, O God. 2. I thirst for God, the living God...* (Also see **Psalm 63:1-2**).

(d) Contentment and fulfillment is also dependent upon accepting God's purpose and implementing His assignments in our lives.

† **John 4:31-34**—*"My food," said Jesus, "is to do the will of him who sent me and to finish his work."*

(e) Our spirit needs to be fed with its own kind of food, God's life, for it to be nourished and to grow. Are you feeding or starving your spiritual life?

† **John 4:13-15**—Jesus said, *"...whoever drinks the water I give him will never thirst."*

† **John 6:35**—Then Jesus declared, *"I am the bread of life. He who comes to me will never go hungry, and he who believes in me will never be thirsty."*

† **John 7:37-39** (NLT)—*On the last day, the climax of the festival, Jesus stood and shouted to the crowds, "If you are thirsty, come to me! 38. If you believe in me, come and drink! For the Scriptures declare that rivers of living water will flow out from within." 39. (When he said "living water," he was speaking of the Spirit, who would be given to everyone believing in him...)*

† **Deuteronomy 8:3**—*...Man does not live on bread alone but on every word that comes from the mouth of the Lord.*

† **Romans 7:22**—*For in my inner being I delight in God's law.*

(f) The presence of God can create a burning-type sensation within our spirit.

† **Luke 24:32**—*They asked each other, "Were not our hearts burning within us while he [Jesus] talked with us on the road and opened the Scriptures to us?"*

† **Jeremiah 20:9**—The prophet Jeremiah said, *"...his word is in my heart like a fire, a fire shut up in my bones."*

(g) Our spirit can be so full of God's presence that it is possible for our physical body to radiate its glory.

† **Exodus 34:29-35** (NLT)—*29. When Moses came down the mountain carrying the stone tablets inscribed with the terms of the covenant, he wasn't aware that his face glowed because he had spoken to the Lord face to face.* (Also see **Matthew 17:1,2** and **Acts 6:15.**)

(4) The <u>fruit of the Spirit</u> (being the character of God), originates within our spirit by the Holy Spirit and is expressed through our soul.

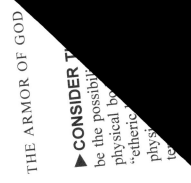

† **Galatians 5:22-23** (NASB)—*...the fruit of the Spirit* *goodness, faithfulness, 23. gentleness, self-control...* (S

(a) Another type of love exists within our spirit th in our soul. The Bible calls it *agapē* love (desc is God's unconditional, self-sacrificing love th also the primary characteristic that distinguish leading fruit of the Spirit in **Galatians 5:22.**

Note: Since Adam's fall, a third type of love ex centered, erotic kind of love in our sinful nature tl

(b) The fruit of *"joy"* in our spirit is designed to be constant and does not fluctuate with circumstances like its unstable counterpart does in our soul **(Acts 5:41; Heb. 12:2).**

† **1 Peter 3:3-4** (NLT)—*Don't be concerned about the outward beauty that depends on fancy hairstyles, expensive jewelry, or beautiful clothes. 4. You should be known for the beauty that comes from within, the unfading beauty of a gentle and quiet spirit, which is so precious to God.*

(5) The part of us that exercises <u>faith</u> seems to also come from our spirit.

† **Romans 10:10** (NASB)—*for with the heart a person believes...and with the mouth he confesses...*

▶**CONSIDER THIS:** God created us with specific needs in our trinity. Like our body, there are needs and appetites in our soul and spirit that cry out for fulfillment. We should be aware of them, and know how to properly satisfy them—according to the Word. Be very careful not to look in the wrong places or to the wrong people for the fulfillment of these needs. Our <u>seven main needs</u> are:

- For God's presence and spiritual fulfillment
- For provision of basic physical needs to live: food, water, clothing, and shelter
- To live in freedom

- To love; and be loved and accepted
- To fulfill your purpose and to make a difference in this world
- To be valued, appreciated, and respected
- To be secure and protected

While living on this earth, there are <u>eight key relationships</u> that God instructs us to give quality time and attention. They are **1.** God **(Mark 12:30); 2.** our spouse **(Ephesians 5:22-25, 31); 3.** our children **(Ephesians 6:4); 4.** our *"neighbor"* **(Mark 12:31); 5.** our parents **(Ephesians 6:1-3); 6.** the devil **(1 Peter 5:8); 7.** the planet **(Genesis 1:26; 2:15);** and very importantly, **8.** to know ourselves **(1 Thessalonians 5:23).**

It has been said that there are <u>four different views of ourselves</u>: (1) the person we think we are, (2) the person others think we are, (3) the person we think others think we are, and (4) the person we really are.

In summarizing God's Word regarding <u>the purpose of man's existence</u>, the *Westminster Larger Catechism* states: "Man's chief and highest end is to glorify God, and fully to enjoy him forever."

HIS: Science tells us that we are bioelectric, biomagnetic beings. Could there ...ty that our being emanates a type of electromagnetic field of energy around our ...dy that is visible in the spirit realm? In the occult, this is known as one's "aura," ...body," etc. Allegedly, one's aura changes color to match one's mental, emotional, and ...cal states. This is analogous to the mood ring that changes colors according to one's ...mperature, or like the infrared camera that photographs thermal energy radiating from an object. Actually, the paintings of halos around the heads of saints were considered to be part of this aura. Today, there are those who claim to be able to photograph the aura of plants and humans (i.e. electrophotography). Though we should never get involved in or trust what is promoted in the occult, I only offer this thought to you that the possibility of something like this might exist and could be a way the spirit world can "read" our disposition (but not our thoughts).

THE STAGES OF OUR LIFE

1. Tragically, Adam and Eve did not remain in their innocent state; therefore, our lives now consist of three (3) stages as a result of their fall:

   A. From our <u>B</u>_____ (conception) to the <u>D</u>_____ of our body.

   B. From the <u>death</u> of our body to the <u>R</u>_____ of our body. Our spirit and soul will go to either heaven or hell.

   C. From the <u>resurrection</u> of our body through a <u>N</u>_____ <u>E</u>_____ existence in either heaven or in the lake of fire.

      (1) The fall caused us all to be born with a unique blend of the temporal and the eternal. At death, our spirit and soul leave our body as we "give up the ghost" **(John 19:30; Acts 7:59; Luke 16:19-31; Luke 9:28-32; James 2:26;** and **Genesis 25:8).** Death will not touch our soul and spirit as they both continue to exist forever and one day be reunited with our resurrected body **(Luke 20:35-36).**

      (2) In the afterlife, we will still retain certain capabilities. We will take with us: our sense of hearing, sight, smell, feeling, and taste; our character; our intellectual processes such as thought, comprehension, reason, and memory; our emotions; our will; and, to some degree, our relationships **(Luke 16:19-31).**

2. Are you beginning to get the picture of the extremely high stakes in this invisible war? It's either eternal life or death! God calls us to choose life!

3. In the next lesson, we will learn about the results of Adam and Eve's fall into sin, and how it impacted their spirit, soul, and body—and us as well.

> ☑ This ends the DVD content for Lesson 6.
> ☑ Continue on with the Study Questions and Application and the Summary.

STUDY QUESTIONS AND APPLICATION

1. You have ☐ intellect, ☐ emotion, and ☐ will. Number them (1-3) from strongest to the weakest in your life. Then reflect on how these influence the way your will makes decisions.

2. Answer **True** or **False** to the following questions (circle one), according to your beliefs about God creating angels and mankind with "free will." The answers are found at the end of the Summary.

   A. **T** or **F** The Bible teaches that God created Adam, Eve, and their descendents with "free will"—the ability to make our own choices and be held accountable for them.

   B. **T** or **F** Before the *"foundation of the world,"* God has preprogrammed everyone's decisions (good and bad) and everything has a predetermined outcome that cannot be changed.

   C. **T** or **F** When God created humans with free will, He made it possible for evil to come into existence and for angels and humanity to come under judgment.

   D. **T** or **F** God allows us to make decisions apart from His will. This does not make Him in any way less perfect or limited in His attributes.

   E. **T** or **F** As God viewed the history of man through His foreknowledge prior to the creation of the world, He arbitrarily decided that certain people would go to heaven and the rest would go to hell based on His decision alone.

   F. **T** or **F** God is sovereign, has everything under control, and is directing history toward His ultimate purpose in spite of the free will of fallen angels and mankind.

   G. **T** or **F** As God viewed the history of man through His foreknowledge prior to the creation of the world, God foreknew the final outcomes of all decisions that would ever be made and those who would eventually choose to accept His provision of salvation. These are the *"elect"* He predestined to go to heaven.

   H. **T** or **F** God has designed that even if we experience events that we cannot control, we still have the freedom to choose how we will react toward them.

   I. **T** or **F** Our prayers can change the mind of God and alter some of His plans.

3. The Bible teaches us about various aspects of our conscience. Study the following Scriptures and write in those aspects. (If possible, use the NIV translation.)

   A. **Romans 2:14-15** _____

   B. In **Acts 24:16,** we are to conduct ourselves before God and man with a _____ conscience.

   C. Our conscience can be: (enter one word)

   (1) _____ **1 Corinthians 8:12**   (3) _____ **Titus 1:15**

   (2) _____ **1 Timothy 4:2**   (4) _____ **Hebrews 9:14**

SUMMARY

To fully comprehend what the breastplate of righteousness symbolizes, we laid a foundation by learning more about ourselves and the way God created us. When God made Adam and Eve, He created them in His image and likeness—a spiritual likeness (spirit), a moral or character likeness (soul), and a physical likeness (body). These three parts comprise the trinity of man (as illustrated in nature by the peach) and they operate as one unit. In this lesson, we attempted to identify the components of our soul and spirit and their functions **prior** to Adam's fall.

Our BODY is **1.** <u>world</u> (or earth)-consciousness. It is essentially the house we live in. It's your earth suit, made from the soil that expresses the real "you." Through its five senses it interacts with the physical world around us. Scripture uses soul and spirit (and heart) interchangeably and, for the most part, does not make a consistent distinction between them. However, we know these internal components exist because they can be identified. For clarity and for illustration purposes, we have carefully attempted to categorize each without taking the Scriptures out of context or drawing an incorrect conclusion. Our SOUL is **2.** <u>self</u>-consciousness. The components of our soul are our **2A(1)** <u>intellect</u>, our **2A(2)** <u>feelings</u> (emotions), our **2A(3)** <u>will</u>, the **2A(4)** <u>character</u> likeness and image of God; our **2A(5)** <u>temperament</u> and personality; and our **2A(6)** <u>gifts</u> and talents. Our soul is the part of us that truly expresses who we are as a person.

Our SPIRIT is **3.** <u>God</u>-consciousness. It is the part of us that interacts with the spirit world—God, angels, evil spirits, as well as detects the disposition of the spirit of another fellow human being. The Bible teaches that the soul (*psuchē*) is a distinct, separate entity from the spirit (*pneuma*). The components of our spirit are: the part that **3D(1)** <u>discerns</u> (our sixth sense) which is comprised of our **3D(1)(a)** <u>conscience</u> and our **3D(1)(b)** <u>intuition</u>. Our spirit is also the place where we receive **3D(2)** <u>revelation</u> knowledge about God; and the part that **3D(3)** <u>fellowships</u> (communes) with God's Spirit—where we pray and worship Him and maintain our spiritual life. The fruit of the Spirit also originates here and has a different kind of love (*agapē*) than in our soul (*phileō*). The fruit of the Spirit and the part of us that exercises faith also seems to reside here. We are more a spirit being than we are a physical being.

God designed that once a person is conceived, that person will live forever. Tragically, Adam and Eve did not remain in their innocent state; therefore, the fall caused us all to be born with a unique blend of the temporal and the eternal. Our lives now consist of three (3) stages: from **1A.** <u>birth</u> (conception) to the <u>death</u> of our body; from the death of our body to the **1B.** <u>resurrection</u> of our body; and from the resurrection of our body through a **1C.** <u>never</u> <u>ending</u> existence in either heaven, or in the lake of fire. Death will not touch our soul and spirit as they both continue to exist forever and one day be reunited with our resurrected body. In the afterlife, we will still retain certain capabilities that resided in our soul and spirit on earth. We will take with us: our sense of hearing, sight, smell, feeling, and taste; our character; our intellectual processes such as thought, comprehension, reason, and memory; our emotions; our will; and, to some degree, our relationships. Are you beginning to get the picture of the extremely high stakes in this invisible war? It's either eternal life or death! God has called us to choose life!

Answers to SQ&A [#]3: **A.** T; **B.** F; **C.** T; **D.** T; **E.** F; **F.** T; **G.** T (see **Romans 8:29-30; Ephesians 1:5,11; 2 Peter 1:10-11**); **H.** T.; **I.** T

Lesson 7

INTRODUCTION TO THE BREASTPLATE OF RIGHTEOUSNESS:
The Effect of Adam's Fall on Us

☑ Before starting the DVD:

In the last lesson, we identified the components of our soul and spirit and learned about their functions **prior** to Adam and Eve's fall into sin. This lesson picks up at that point and shows the effect that Adam's fall had on us all, as his descendents, and God's plan to reestablish the broken relationship. We will learn about God's covenants with mankind and the specific responsibilities of each party, and what happens to us when we are *"born again."* We will also begin to understand the relationship between the breastplate and our sinful nature. This will conclude our introduction to the Breastplate of Righteousness. The video will first summarize last week's material before getting into this lesson. Pray that the Holy Spirit will help you to comprehend the important information being presented here.

☑ **DVD Users:** Watch Lesson 7 for an overview before proceeding further (27 min.).
☑ When you're through, pick up again at this point. Fill in the blanks from the Summary.

THE RESULTS OF "THE FALL" OF ADAM AND EVE INTO SIN AND GOD'S PLAN TO RESTORE THE RELATIONSHIP

1. They were created S_____ (**Genesis 1:31; 2:25**).

2. They had F_____ with God.

3. God gave them the T_____! (**Genesis 2:16-17**).

4. D_____ was their choice (**Genesis 3:6,7**).
   These consequences followed:

   A. They lost their innocence, covering, and fellowship with God.

   B. They D_____ God's right to rule over their lives and instead enthroned their own self-will—thus transferring the control of their lives from God to themselves. In reality, they made themselves their own god. This happened, in part, because their spirit failed to maintain God's rule over their soul and body, and consequently lost dominion over them.

Figure 7-1

C. They took on a D_____ N_____. No longer would they exclusively reflect God's character likeness. Adam and Eve now took on a sinful nature and would mostly reflect satan's character—though still retaining some ability to portray God's character (see Figure 7-1). However, they did not become totally depraved like the fallen angels. Even though they sinned, God's Word declares that fallen man is still made in the image of God **(Genesis 9:6; 1 Corinthians 11:7)**. Adam and Eve became children of the devil **(1 John 3:10)**, captives of him **(2 Timothy 2:26)**, and slaves to sin **(John 8:34)**. See Lesson 3. We enter the world the same way!

▶ **CONSIDER THIS:** Adam and Eve's first impulse was to cover their nakedness with fig leaves. Common to us all is the deep-seated fear within that if others knew us as we really are, they wouldn't like us or would reject us. This fear of exposure becomes the powerful motivator that causes us to hide our true selves, putting on a front to cover our sins and our sense of inferiority, insecurities, imperfections, and/or inadequacies, and it dictates the way we present ourselves to others. "What will others think?" becomes more important than "What will God think?" Satan delights in exploiting this fear which drives people into harmful, self-destructive behaviors.

D. They R_____ the rule and dominion that God intended for them to have over the earth. Satan seized the "scepter" dropped by Adam.

E. They allowed sin to enter the world both in principle and character. The *"mystery of iniquity"* has been at work ever since **(2 Thessalonians 2:7** KJV**)**. This spirit of disobedience to God permeates our world and is energized by the devil who seeks to persuade and involve all mankind to join him in his rebellion against the God of the Bible.

† **Ephesians 2:2**—*...in which you used to live when you followed the ways of this world and of the ruler of the kingdom of the air, the spirit who is now at work in those who are disobedient.*

F. Adam broke covenant with God **(Hosea 6:7),** and became His *"enemy"* **(Romans 5:10).**

5. A threefold D_____ resulted. (See **Ezekiel 18:20; Genesis 2:17; 3:19**).

A. Spiritual death—separation from fellowship with God; their spirit became dead in its relationship to God causing darkness and blindness to come over their soul and spirit.

B. Physical death—sickness, disease, pain, and suffering now entered the human race. When Adam's body dies 930 years later, his soul and spirit will continue to have conscious existence forever.

C. The Second death—now in their sinful state, Adam and Eve must obey God's remedy to restore their relationship with God, or they will die in this tragic condition. If they don't accept God's remedy for sin while on the earth, then at the Great White Throne Judgment they will be sentenced to a conscious existence in the lake of fire for eternity **(Revelation 20:11-15).**

6. The law of "A_____ H___ K_____" (KJV) continues to be in effect.

† **Genesis 1:12, 21**—God designed that the plant and animal kingdom would reproduce their offspring by this law—including mankind. (Also see **Acts 17:26**).

   ✝ **Romans 5:12, 19**—*Therefore, just as sin entered the world through one man, and death through sin, and in this way death came to all men, because all sinned... **19.** through the disobedience of the one man the many were made sinners...*

A. The terrible consequences of our first parent's disobedience have been passed down to us through this law. In effect, Adam, as the head of the human race, made a horrendous choice that would affect all of us who descend from him.

▶**CONSIDER THIS:** No descendant from Adam could ever rescue and save his fellow man from the consequences of sin and bring them into a right standing with God. We are unable to because Adam's sinful nature is passed down genetically and spiritually to each of us— apparently through our father. This is why the doctrine of the virgin birth of Christ is so critical and foundational to Christianity. God's remedial plan was to insert His sinless Son into the human race in order to save all those who believe in Him. Jesus' conception was the result of the Holy Spirit and a human mother who gave Him His earthly body. This bypassed Joseph, Mary's husband, and prevented Adam's sinful nature from being a factor. However, after Christ, all of the children Mary had with Joseph were born with sinful natures.

7. **God's Remedy For Sin**—God designed the plan of S_____ in order to restore the broken fellowship with man caused by sin. It involved the shedding of the blood of an innocent victim as well as a covenant (or testament) requiring both God's part and man's part to make it work.

   ✝ **Luke 19:10**—Jesus said, *"For the Son of Man came to seek and to save what was lost."*

A. **God's Part of the Old Testament**—The substitute God provided for humanity was an innocent animal that would die for that person, and sometimes even by the hand of that person. The animal's blood covered, or *"atoned"* for that person's sins—thereby satisfying God's justice. **Q:** What gave these sacrifices their power? It was that they typified and pointed ahead to the coming of Christ, the Lamb of God, and the various aspects of His substitutionary death on the cross. This was planned before the creation of the world (see **1 Peter 1:18-20).**

   ✝ **Genesis 3:7,15,21**—God killed the first animal sacrifice to clothe Adam and Eve and cover their sin. He promised that *"the seed of the woman"* (Christ) would one day arrive to take away all sin.

   ✝ **Genesis 15:1-6**—With Abraham, "justification by faith" was taken to a higher level.

   ✝ **Genesis 22:1-14**—Abraham offering Isaac foreshadowed God the Father offering His Son—both occurring on the very same site, Mt. Moriah in Jerusalem.

   ✝ **Exodus 12:1-13; 14:15-31; 1 Corinthians 10:1-2**—Israel was saved from Egypt (a type of the world) and Pharaoh (a type of satan) through the killing of the Passover Lamb (a type of Christ), and was separated from Egypt (a type of the world) through the passing into the waters of the Red Sea (a type of water baptism). Their destination was the land of Canaan (a type of Heaven).

   ✝ **Leviticus 1:1-5**—When the Mosaic Law was instituted, repetitious animal sacrifices were required to be offered until the death of Christ. (Also see **Luke 16:16, 17; Galatians 3:19.**)

(1) In the Old Testament God's great plan of substitution consisted of four basic principles:

(a) By faith and obedience, people confessed their sins and transferred them onto designated innocent animals.

(b) God's judgment fell upon the substitutes as their life's blood was shed and their bodies burned in the fire.

(c) God accepted the death of the innocent animals as payment for sin in place of the lives of the people, allowing them to escape His judgment.

(d) In turn, the life and innocence of the substitutes were transferred to the sinners who received them by faith. God justified them—treating them just as if they never committed those sins.

B. **Man's Part of the Old Testament**

(1) It consisted of adhering to the four basic principles of substitution listed above and separating themselves from sin, through obedience, to maintain relationship with God.

(2) However, numerous times in the Old Testament, God gave the specific command to *"cut off"* a person from the community of believers if they rebelled and committed any number of specific transgressions. See **Exodus 31:14; Leviticus 17:10-14; Numbers 15:30-31; Jeremiah 34:18-20.** This set the precedent for the New Testament **(Matthew 18:15-20; 1 Corinthians 5:9-13; 2 Thessalonians 3:6).**

(a) Failing to circumcise was one of these sins in the Old Testament. It was instituted by God in a covenant with Abraham and his male descendants **(Genesis 17:9-14),** and later made part of the Mosaic Law **(Leviticus 12:3).** It was an outward sign of an inner work already done in Abraham's heart some 15 years earlier when his faith in God's promise justified him and made him righteous in God's sight. It also distinguished him and his offspring from all other peoples as a sign of separation to God. See **Romans 2:28-29; 4:9-12.**

C. **God's Part of the New Testament**—Christ came to restore the broken fellowship between God and man that was lost in the Garden of Eden. All the aspects of these animal sacrifices pointed to His substitutionary death on the cross. So when He died and rose from the dead, there was no longer any need for animal sacrifices **(Hebrews 10:4).** Jesus became the one and only sacrifice for sin—from Adam to the last person that will ever be born on this earth. Through the death of His Son, God completed the provision for forgiveness of sins. The principles of God's plan of substitution in the Old Testament remained the same for the New Testament under Christ. We will enlarge more on God's part in Lesson 8, but two main aspects of God's part of salvation are:

(1) *"Justification"*—For the legal record, Christ declares a sinner to be righteous in His "heavenly court," as though he or she had never sinned.

(2) *"Sanctification"*—God separates the believer to Himself for sacred use.

D. **Man's Part of the New Testament.**

(1) **Repent** of our sins—decide to change direction **(Luke 13:3)**—and identify with Christ by being baptized in water **(Acts 2:38; Mark 16:16; Matthew 28:19; Romans 6:3-5).**

Note: Water baptism is an outward expression of an inner work done in our hearts. If you have never been baptized in water since you gave your life to Christ, be obedient to God's Word and quickly do so. It is not an option. This public confession is a declaration to your community of your identification with, and commitment to, Christ. It also sends a message to demonic forces. Your walk with the Lord will be greatly strengthened. However, the rite in and of itself does not forgive sins. Only Christ's sacrifice can do that.

(2) **Believe** God's Word that His Son, Jesus Christ, died in our place as our sin bearer and was raised to life again **(Romans 10:9-10; John 6:29)**; faith will be demonstrated by our actions **(James 2:17-24)**; then **invite** Jesus into our heart and **receive** Him as Lord of our life—becoming *"born again"* **(John 1:12; 3:3).** Forgiveness of sins cannot be earned. Many people believe that somehow at the end of their lives their good deeds will outweigh their bad and they'll be allowed to enter heaven. It does not work that way.

(a) **Sanctification** is our human responsibility to separate ourselves to God for sacred use and separate ourselves from sin. It involves the principle of "walking worthy," cultivating and maintaining the wonderful work God has and is doing in our lives **(1 Thessalonians 4:3; Hebrews 12:14; Colossians 1:10; Ephesians 4:1).**

Note: Up to now, we have laid a foundation to explain the Breastplate of Righteousness. As we enter this area of sanctification, we are very close to understanding its meaning and function. More will be said about this in the next point as well as in Lesson 8. We will now enlarge on point D (2) above to show what occurs when we experience the new birth.

8. **What Happens To Us When We Become "B_____ A_____?"**

† **John 3:3-7**—...*Jesus declared, "I tell you the truth, no one can see the Kingdom of God unless he is born again."*

A. We receive Christ by choosing to step off the throne of our self-will and enthroning Christ and His rule in our heart—relinquishing the control we have over our lives to Him. In the final analysis, the evidence of whether one is *"saved"* or not is determined by whether one keeps Him in that position for the duration of their lives.

B. The Holy Spirit literally comes into our spirit. (This is illustrated by the dove in our spirit in Figure 7-2.)

(1) God now takes up residence within us **(2 Peter 1:4).** Like in the Old Testament, our bodies become a temple or sanctuary in which the Holy Spirit dwells—a treasure in our houses of clay. What an honor and a privilege!! Think of it!

(2) We become a *"new man"* **(Ephesians 4:22-24; Colossians 3:10).**

(3) God's creative power makes us a *"new creation"* (**2 Corinthians 5:17**).

(4) God's *"seed"* or life is implanted in us. He gives us the desire to resist sin and the ability to live a life that overcomes it so we don't continue to live a lifestyle of habitual sinning. This is the litmus test of our born-again experience. However, this Divine life must be protected and cultivated so that sin is not permitted to take root, grow, and choke out His life in us.

Figure 7-2

† **1 John 3:9** (TLB)—*The person who has been born into God's family does not make a practice of sinning because now God's life is in him; so he can't keep on sinning, for this new life has been born into him and controls him—he has been born again.*

(5) The greatest power in the universe, the Holy Spirit, is now residing within you! Therefore, *"I can do all things through Christ Who strengthens me"* (**Philippians 4:13** KJV). You also have the very best Counselor, who is only a prayer away. Learn to listen to His "voice" as He communicates His thoughts and wisdom to you. (One SQ&A will give you ways God does this at the end of this lesson.)

C. Blindness and darkness now begin to leave us and we gradually begin to "see."

D. Our spirit that was dead in its relationship to God now comes alive in fellowship with God, and asserts its rightful authority to rule over our soul and body that was lost in the fall.

▶**CONSIDER THIS:** God uses the born-again experience to bring us back to what Adam's state was before he fell—namely, having God's will enthroned as the center of our lives and reflecting His character. Pictured in Figure 7-2 is what an overcoming, born-again believer's soul and spirit is to look like. Note that the characteristics in the sinful nature are not growing but are being put to death.

E. All the treasures Christ purchased on the cross are put to our "account" as a gift.

F. We now, out of obedience and gratitude, walk in a manner worthy of His high calling (**1 Thessalonians 2:12; Ephesians 4:1**). Just as God has separated us to Himself for holy use, so we are commanded to separate ourselves to God for holy service. This is the life of ***"sanctification."***

† **Colossians 1:10**—*...in order that you may live a life worthy of the Lord and may please him in every way: bearing fruit in every good work, growing in the knowledge of God...*

(1) This involves living a life of separation from sin and the world system. It is our turn to be *"crucified"*—to bring death to that which displeases God. This will involve

warfare between the Godly and evil character within us. Just as Jesus experienced His own Gethsemane, we are called to follow in His footsteps as God takes each of us to our own Gethsemane—a place of crushing and death to our self-life.

Note: It is this life-long process of sanctification that is represented by the putting on of the Breastplate of Righteousness.

† **Hebrews 12:14**—*...without holiness* (sanctification) *no one will see the Lord.*

† **1 Peter 1:14-15**—*As obedient children, do not conform to the evil desires you had when you lived in ignorance.* **15.** *But just as he who called you is holy, so be holy in all you do;*

† **Hebrews 10:14**—*...by one sacrifice he has made perfect forever those who are being made holy.*

(2) Be assured that sanctification has nothing to do with earning our way into heaven by performing good works. Rather, it cultivates and maintains the life of our born-again experience—the gift of salvation that we have already received from Christ by faith. These *"good works"* are faithful acts of obedience to God as our part of the New Testament (that will be rewarded) rather than acts of merit to earn God's favor for salvation. It ensures that we don't allow ourselves to break covenant and be *"cut off"* from all that God has for us due to rebellion and habitual sin. The only "works" we do for our salvation is *"believe"* **(John 6:28-29),** and *"work out"* our walk with Christ **(Philippians 2:12).**

† **Titus 3:5,8** (KJV)—*Not by works of righteousness which we have done, but according to his mercy he saved us...* **8.** *This is a faithful saying, and these things I will that thou affirm constantly, that they which have believed in God might be careful to maintain good works...*

† **Ephesians 2:8-10**—*For it is by grace you have been saved, through faith—and this not from yourselves, it is the gift of God—* **9.** *not by works, so that no one can boast.* **10.** *For we are God's workmanship, created in Christ Jesus to do good works, which God prepared in advance for us to do.*

† **Hebrews 10:26-29** (NLT)—*Dear friends, if we deliberately continue sinning after we have received a full knowledge of the truth, there is no other sacrifice that will cover these sins.* **27.** *There will be nothing to look forward to but the terrible expectation of God's judgment...* **29.** *Think how much more terrible the punishment will be for those who have trampled on the Son of God and have treated the blood of the covenant as if it were common and unholy. Such people have insulted and enraged the Holy Spirit...*

(3) Everything in life needs nurturing and care. How much more our salvation? We must protect and guard this wonderful treasure and not allow sin to once again take control and cause us to disqualify ourselves, losing what God has done in and for us.

† **1 Corinthians 9:24-27** (NKJV)—The apostle Paul said: **27.** *"But I discipline my body and bring it into subjection, lest, when I have preached to others, I myself should become disqualified."*

Also see **Colossians 2:18; 2 John 1:8; Revelation 3:11.**

(4) Portraying God's character should become the main goal in our lives. To the degree we obey God and put our fallen nature to death, satan's character will be seen less and less. As we live out our Christian walk, we are to move from the rule of the *"old man"* (our sinful nature) to the rule of the *"new man"* (our reborn spirit). This can only be done with God's help. Figure 7-3 attempts to depict this process of sanctification.

(5) Prior to our new birth we were ruled by our self-life in our soul. When we invited Christ into our heart, His life (*zoe*) came into our spirit but it didn't do away with our self-life. It is in the soul where God does His main work, and it resists change. Our spirit must bring our soul under its control and make it obey God's Word.

AN OVERVIEW OF OUR CHRISTIAN LIFE

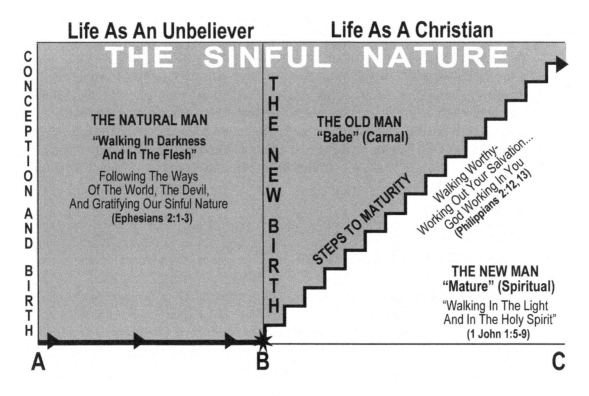

Figure 7-3

▶ **CONSIDER THIS:** The chart in Figure 7-3 illustrates an overview of the life of one who has experienced the new birth and is living out their Christian walk. It begins with our natural conception and birth (point **A**), and continues to the time in our lives when we make the decision to receive Christ and turn our lives over to Him (point **B**). When we experience "the new birth," the Holy Spirit comes into our spirit and establishes a beachhead, as it were, from which to help us conquer the land of darkness and evil especially within our soul. (Note: A beachhead is an area captured on a hostile shore from which to further advance into enemy territory.) We begin our Christian lives as *"babes"* in Christ **(1 Corinthians 3:1-2; 1 Peter 2:2-3),** and should continue to grow into spiritual maturity as we cooperate with God's working in us **(Philippians 2:13).** We become a *"spiritual"* person when our spirit communes regularly with God and makes the rest of our being obey His Word. We must be patient with new believers.

(6) Through the power of the Holy Spirit, we must invade the enemy within—squeezing out the darkness, deception, and bondage and allowing the light, truth, and *"fruit of the Spirit"* to increase in our lives—for Christ must increase and we must decrease **(John 3:30)**. In short, we must *"...die daily"* **(1 Corinthians 15:31)**. This is the *"sanctification"* process of walking worthy—putting to death the *"old man"* and putting on the *"new man."*

    (a) This corresponds to the Old Testament covenant of circumcision that was used as a type to indicate separation from sin (cut away in our hearts) and justification by faith.

† **Colossians 2:11-12**—*In him* (Christ) *you were also circumcised, in the putting off of the sinful nature, not with a circumcision done by the hands of men but with the circumcision done by Christ...*

(7) The steps in Figure 7-3 represent an idealized picture of what God desires our Christian life to be through *"sanctification."* The amount of darkness depicted would vary with each person depending on their obedience to the unfolding light of truth God gives them—along with other factors. These steps represent new inroads to our spiritual lives that are successfully achieved through faith, obedience, and persevering through the opposition. Spirit-filled living is pushing out the *"old man"* and replacing it with the *"new man."*

(8) One has to pass God-given tests and/or conquer something to break through to a new level. Demonic power will oppose us, but let us keep our focus on the advancement and not on the struggle. Many times the resulting blessing is in direct proportion with the severity of the attack.

(9) God holds us accountable for the light (truth) that He gives us. As we conscientiously seek, trust, and obey God; confess and repent of our sins; and allow the fruit of Christ's character to emanate from us, we have the assurance that should death occur at any time past point **B** (in Figure 7-3), we will go to be with the Lord.

    (a) However, what will happen to us if there is little or no fruit produced in our lives after all the years of effort that God has spent trying to cultivate the image of Christ in us? I don't know about you, but I wouldn't want to have to stand before our Lord one day and try to explain why and risk the consequences.

† **John 15:1 2,5,16** (NLT)—Jesus said, *"I am the true vine, and my Father is the gardener. 2. He cuts off every branch that doesn't produce fruit, and he prunes the branches that do bear fruit so they will produce even more... 5. Yes, I am the vine; you are the branches. Those who remain in me, and I in them, will produce much fruit. For apart from me you can do nothing... 16. I chose you. I appointed you to go and produce fruit that will last..."*

    (b) There are also many benefits that we can receive from God's hand when we walk in righteousness. Let us not rob ourselves of them. (Read **Psalm 34:15; 66:18; 34:17; 84:11; James 5:16; Matthew 5:8.**)

(10) Now let's turn our attention to the main problem area that causes the need for sanctification—that being our sinful nature which is rooted in self-seeking interests. This **enemy within** will ever be with us throughout our entire earthly lives.

9. Scriptural Terms for Our Sinful Nature—the Enemy Within:

A. The "O_____ M_____" (**Ephesians 4:22** KJV) (or the *"old self"* NIV)

B. The "W_____ of the F_____" (**Galatians 5:19** KJV)

C. The "L_____ of the F_____" (**Galatians 5:16** KJV)

📖 **DEFINITION—LUST**

It is a strong desire, craving, or appetite—especially to do something wrong that compels us to sin against God and His Word. The word is mainly associated with sexually related things, which it should not be because it can refer to any sin. With few exceptions, it has a negative connotation in the Bible.

D. The "N_____ M_____" (**1 Corinthians 2:14** KJV)—being totally dominated by the sinful nature, especially before we are born again.

E. The F_____ N_____—a common term used to describe the sinful nature.

F. S_____ C_____ is the personification of sin (**John 8:44**).

Note: For a contrast of the *"new man"* (God's character) and the *"old man"* (satan's character), revisit the comparative list in Lesson 3 and see the one at the end of this lesson.

G. "C_____"—when a believer is being governed by their sinful nature instead of by the Holy Spirit. See **1 Corinthians 3:1-4** (KJV); **Romans 8:7**.

H. "H_____"—Note that the Bible also uses this word in a good sense (as in **Luke 6:45**). Some see the heart as referring to both our spirit and soul together.

† **Jeremiah 17:9** (KJV)—*The heart is deceitful above all things, and desperately wicked: who can know it?*

† **Genesis 8:21** (NASB)—God said, *"...the intent of man's heart is evil from his youth..."*

† **Mark 7:21-23**—Jesus said, *"For from within, out of men's hearts, come evil thoughts, sexual immorality, theft, murder, adultery,* **22.** *greed, malice, deceit, lewdness, envy, slander, arrogance and folly.* **23.** *All these evils come from inside and make a man 'unclean.'"*

(1) What are the definitions of some of these words in **Mark 7**—especially those used in the KJV? (Words in parenthesis are the Greek word from which our word was translated.)

(a) *"Sexual immorality"*—it includes adultery (***moicheia***) and fornication (***porneia***). Note: This is covered more in Lesson 9 under **Sexual Impurity.** See index.

(b) *"Greed"* (***pleonexia***); *"covetousness"* (KJV)—a selfish "desire to have more...to have what belongs to others..."[1] An offshoot of this is elevating ourselves by putting another down at their expense.

(c) *"Lewdness"* (***aselgeia***); *"lasciviousness"* (KJV)—excessive lewd, sensual, indecent conduct done in shameless unrestraint.

(d) *"Folly"* (*aphrosunē*); *"foolishness"* (KJV)—a lack of good sense or judgment resulting from not being guided by God's wisdom or moral principles, but by the blindness of one's self-will—leading to bad decisions and ruinous consequences. Also see **1 Corinthians 1:18,21,23; 2:14**.

► **CONSIDER THIS:** As we raise our children, we are forced to deal with their soul. If we want to get a good picture of our self-life (soul), we can see it clearly portrayed in the selfish, rebellious behavior of a child. Parents are to oversee their child's soulish behavior through loving, corrective discipline to drive out the *"folly"* that is bound in their hearts **(Proverbs 22:15)**. Also see **Proverbs 13:24; 23:13-14; 29:15,17**. A big "thank you" is due to parents who raised their children scripturally and have dealt strongly with their souls. These children are better off later because it helps them to avoid having to deal with some of it as they grow older! In like manner, God also deals with His children's soulish behavior **(Hebrews 12:5-11)**.

† **Galatians 5:19-21**—*The acts of the sinful nature are obvious: sexual immorality, impurity and debauchery; 20. idolatry and witchcraft; hatred, discord, jealousy, fits of rage, selfish ambition, dissensions, factions 21. and envy; drunkenness, orgies, and the like. I warn you, as I did before, that those who live like this will not inherit the kingdom of God.*

(2) What are the definitions of some of the words above—especially those used in the KJV?

(a) *"Debauchery"* (*aselgeia*); *"lasciviousness"* (KJV)—same as *"lewdness"* in H (1) (c)

(b) *"Witchcraft"* (*pharmakia*)—see index.

(c) *"Discord"* (*eris*); *"variance"* (KJV)—strife, contention, quarreling

(d) *"Dissensions"* (*dichostasia*); *"seditions"* (KJV)—to separate oneself; to be divisive

(e) *"Factions"* (*hairesis*); *"heresies"* (KJV)—"a self-willed opinion which is substituted for...truth, and leads to division and the formation of sects..."[2] It is generally done with the expectation of personal advantage.

(f) *"Orgies"* (*kōmos*); *"revellings"* (KJV)—boisterous, excessive partying involving drunkenness. It is synonymous with *"lasciviousness"* in H (1) (c) above.

† **1 Corinthians 6:9-11**—*Do you not know that the wicked will not inherit the kingdom of God? Do not be deceived: Neither the sexually immoral nor idolaters nor adulterers nor male prostitutes nor homosexual offenders 10. nor thieves nor the greedy nor drunkards nor slanderers nor swindlers will inherit the kingdom of God. 11. And that is what some of you were. But you were washed, you were sanctified, you were justified in the name of the Lord Jesus Christ and by the Spirit of our God.*

† **Romans 1:29-32**—*They have become filled with every kind of wickedness, evil, greed and depravity. They are full of envy, murder, strife, deceit and malice. They are gossips, 30. slanderers, God-haters, insolent, arrogant and boastful; they invent ways of doing evil; they disobey their parents; 31. they are senseless, faithless, heartless, ruthless. 32. Although they know God's righteous decree that those who do such things deserve death, they not only continue to do these very things but also approve of those who practice them.*

...t are the definitions of some of these words—especially those used in the KJV?

(a) *"Envy"* (***phthonos***)—"the feeling of displeasure produced by witnessing or hearing of the advantage or prosperity of others... *'envy'* desires to deprive another of what he has, *'jealousy'* desires to have the same or same sort of thing for itself."[3] Examples of their destructive works are Joseph's brother's selling him to merchant traders **(Acts 7:9);** the chief priest's envy of Jesus resulted in delivering Him up to death **(Mark 15:10);** and jealousy moved the Jews in Thessalonica to riot and stop the spread of the Gospel **(Acts 17:5). James 3:14,15** says envy is *"of the devil."*

(b) *"Gossips"* (***psithuristēs***)—*"whisperers"* (KJV)—to defame and damage another's reputation by false charges or misrepresentations done secretly or underhandedly

(c) *"Slanderers"* (***katalalos***)—*"backbiters"* (KJV)—the same as (b) above but done openly in an overt way

▶**CONSIDER THIS:** When you see the wicked character of satan in the actions of people, then realize that the sinful nature is in control and evil spirits are given the liberty to work. Be alert, pray for discernment, and learn to recognize the type of character that is emanating from a person or a situation.

† **Luke 6:43-45**—Jesus said: *"No good tree bears bad fruit, nor does a bad tree bear good fruit.* ***44.*** *Each tree is recognized by its own fruit. People do not pick figs from thornbushes or grapes from briers.* ***45.*** *The good man brings good things out of the good stored up in his heart, and the evil man brings evil things out of the evil stored up in his heart. For out of the overflow of his heart his mouth speaks."*

Figure 7-4

Figure 7-5

☑ This ends the DVD content for Lesson 7. Continue on with the SQ&A.

STUDY QUESTIONS AND APPLICATION

1. This comprehensive list identifies the sins in our fallen nature that are equivalent to satan's character. They cry out for control and gratification causing us to "miss the mark" for that which God created us, and indicate a life lived apart from God. Since they will prevent us from entering heaven, God calls us to put them to death. This character is contrasted with the *"fruit of the Spirit"* as well as with Truth, Sexual Purity, and Freedom (this chart corresponds with Figures 7-4 and 7-5). Make note of the ones you are challenged by the most, and choose not to allow them to be expressed in your life.

The Evil Character in Our Sinful Nature

Sins Contrary to Love

Hatred (of others and God)
Self-abasement & abuse
Resentment & Bitterness
Uncontrolled Anger / Fits of Rage
Mercilessness
Unforgiveness
Revenge and Retaliation
Murder
Cruelty & Violence
Maliciousness
Wickedness
Destruction
Oppression
Burden-giver

Sins Contrary to Meekness & Humility

Pride
Arrogance
Haughtiness
Selfish Ambition
Boasting
Rebellion
Elevating Ourselves Above Others
Self-Righteousness
Foolishness
Self-Aggrandizement
Self-Centeredness

Sins Contrary to Joy, Peace, & Unity

Strife
Quarrelling
Contentions
Discord
Dissension
Divisions
Factions
Heresies
Excessive Mourning
Self-Pity

Sins Contrary to Self-Control

Excesses & Addictions like:

Drunkenness/Alcoholism & Other Chemical Dependencies
Gluttony/Eating Disorders
Lasciviousness (Lewdness)
Unrestrained indulgence
Gambling
Compulsive Behavior
Slothfulness

Sins Contrary to Faith & Patience

Unbelief
Abnormal Anxiety
Worry or Fear
Hopelessness
Impatience

Sins Contrary to Truth

Lying
Dishonesty/Cheating
Hypocrisy
Deceit
Seduction
False Accuser/Witness
Slander & Blasphemy
Gossiper (*"whisperer"*)
Injustice
To Discredit
Judgmental
Entrapment
Perversion

Sins Contrary to Kindness & Goodness

Greed
Covetousness
Jealousy
Envy
Theft
Swindle
Extortion
Craving for Power
The Pursuit of Riches and Status Symbols
(*"Pride of Life"*)

Sins Contrary to (Sexual) Purity

Fornication
Adultery
Homosexuality
Incest & Rape
Bestiality
Uncleanness & Defilement
Prostitution
Pornography
Sado-Masochism/Fetishes and Other Sexual Perversions
Orgies
Corruption of Pure & Holy
Profanity

Sins Contrary to Faithfulness

Unfaithfulness
Idolatry
Covenant Breakers
Adultery
Betrayal
Desertion

Sins Contrary to Freedom

Control
Domination
Possessiveness
Manipulation
Intimidation
Exploitation
Belittling
Rejection
Enslavement/Addic
Sorcery (*"witchcraft"*
Other Occult Involver
Divination

STUDY QUESTIONS AND APPLICATION (continued)

2. Now that you have become a child of God, do you know who you are in Christ? Discover many of them by looking up the following Scriptures and writing in your awesome heritage.

John 1:12,13; Romans 8:16	2 Corinthians 5:17
Ephesians 1:4-5	2 Corinthians 5:21
John 10:11-16	2 Corinthians 5:18-20
John 15:1-8	2 Corinthians 11:2; Revelation 19:7
John 15:13-15	Ephesians 2:10
Romans 8:1-2	Ephesians 3:12; Hebrews 10:19-22
Romans 8:17	Philippians 1:6; Romans 8:28
Romans 8:37; Philippians 4:13	Philippians 3:20; Ephesians 2:6
Romans 8:38-39	Colossians 3:3-4
1 Corinthians 3:16; 6:19-20	1 Peter 2:5,9; Revelation 1:6; 5:10
1 Corinthians 12:12,27	1 John 5:18
2 Corinthians 1:21,22	Matthew 5:13-14

3. If the Holy Spirit resides within our spirit once we invite Him in, then we should be able to communicate with Him, and He with us. Actually, we feel or sense things in two places—in our emotions (soul) and the Holy Spirit's impressions in our spirit. What are some of the ways the Spirit "talks" to us? Write them in below.

A. **Romans 8:16** _____

B. **Romans 5:5** _____

C. **Colossians 3:15** _____

D. **John 14:26** _____

E. **Mark 2:8; 1 Corinthians 12:7-11** _____

F. **Acts 20:22-23** _____

4. What priority does sanctification have in your life? What can you do to give it more of a priority?

☐ A. It is my top priority—I'm conscientiously trying my very best
☐ B. Medium priority—I give it an average effort but I need to make it my top priority
☐ C. Low priority—I've been sloppy and inconsistent in my effort
☐ D. No priority—I don't put any effort into it at all

5. If you were to sketch your own personal diagram of Figure 7-3, how would the "steps" look?

SUMMARY

This lesson concluded our introduction to the Breastplate of Righ
better understanding of the meaning of the breastplate, and the
armor. We saw the destructive consequences that came upon th
and Eve's "fall" into sin, and how God designed a plan to resto.

Our first parents were created **1.** <u>sinless</u> and had intimate, uninterrupted 2.
They were created with the power to make their own decisions and not as robots.
see if they would obey and serve Him as the number one priority in their lives so He ga,
3. <u>test</u>! Tragically, Adam and Eve failed and **4.** <u>disobedience</u> resulted. Consequently, they
their innocence, covering, and fellowship with God. They **4B.** <u>dethroned</u> God from ruling their
lives, and enthroned their own self-will in God's place—thereby deifying themselves. In doing
so, they allowed sin to enter the world both in principle and character. They also took on a
4C. <u>dual</u> <u>nature</u>. Now, instead of exclusively portraying God's character, they had a sinful nature
that was more reflective of satan than of God in their lives. Though not totally depraved as satan
and his fallen angels became when they rebelled, Adam and Eve still retained some ability to
portray God's character.

They **4D.** <u>relinquished</u> the rule and dominion that God intended them to have over the earth to
satan. And though God never intended sickness and suffering, these also came directly into the
human race as a result of Adam's fall. Sin introduced disease, infirmity, and brokenness into our
world. Adam broke covenant with God and became an *"enemy"* **(Romans 5:10)**. A threefold
5. <u>death</u> or separation also resulted—spiritual death, physical death, and the Second Death in the
lake of fire. The law of **6.** "<u>after</u> <u>his</u> <u>kind</u>" used to create the world continued to pass on these
consequences to all of Adam's descendants—wreaking havoc and misfortune to countless
billions of people. A sin-diseased couple propagated a sin-diseased race. In effect, Adam, as the
head of our race, made a horrible choice for us all—a choice that brought consequences we and
our children must now live with.

But God devised a plan that would meet the requirement of His character for justice and yet, in
love, would save Adam, Eve, and the whole human race from His judgment. This plan centered
around the principle of **7.** <u>substitution</u>—the shedding of the blood of an innocent victim in order
that the sinner might be forgiven and restored to fellowship with God. God's plan in the Old
Testament involved the killing of innocent animals as man's substitute which pointed toward
Christ's great sacrificial work on the cross as the Lamb of God. God used the virgin birth to
insert His sinless Son into our race to save us. The principles of salvation established in the Old
Testament are also being used in the New Testament.

The word "testament" means a covenant or contract. Both the Old and New covenants were
conditional upon each party keeping their respective parts. We covered both God's part and
mankind's part in the Old and New Testaments. To summarize man's part in the New Testament:
we are to repent of our sins; believe God's plan of salvation and receive Jesus Christ as Lord of
our life. What happens to us when we become **8.** *"<u>born</u> <u>again</u>?"* We step down off the throne of
our self-will and enthrone Christ and His rule—giving up the control we have over our lives. In
the final analysis, the evidence of whether one is *"saved"* or not is determined by whether one
keeps Him in that position for the duration of their lives.

OF GOD

Spirit literally comes into our spirit and takes up residence within us, and our bodies a temple or sanctuary in which God dwells!! We become a *"new man"* and a *"new"* as God's *"seed"* or life is implanted in us giving us the desire to resist sin, and the to live a life overcoming it so we don't continue a lifestyle of habitually sinning. The dness and darkness now begin to leave us and we gradually begin to "see." Our spirit which as dead in its relationship to God now comes alive in fellowship with God, and asserts its rightful authority to rule over our soul and body. All the treasures Christ purchased on the cross are also put to our "account" as a gift.

And just as God separated us to Himself for holy use, we are now to separate ourselves from sin and evil for holy service to God. Out of obedience and gratitude, we now walk in a manner worthy of His high calling—a life of *"sanctification"*—cultivating and maintaining the wonderful work God has and is doing in our lives. These "good works" are acts of obedience to maintain the life of our born-again experience rather than acts of merit to earn God's favor for salvation. It's our human responsibility to move from the rule of the *"old man"* (our sinful nature) to the rule of the *"new man"* (our reborn spirit).

When we experience "the new birth," the Holy Spirit comes into our spirit and establishes a beachhead, as it were, from which to help us invade and conquer the land of darkness and evil within. Through the power of the Holy Spirit, we must put to death the evil character of our sinful nature—squeezing out the darkness, deception, and bondage and allowing the light, truth, and *"fruit of the Spirit"* to increase in our lives. These progressive steps represent new inroads in to our spiritual lives that are successfully achieved through faith, obedience, conflict, and struggle.

We begin our Christian lives as *"babes"* in Christ, and must continue to grow into spiritual maturity as God produces the *"fruit of the Spirit"* in our lives. This life-long process of sanctification on our part is what putting on the Breastplate of Righteousness is mostly all about. This should not be confused with God's part of *"justification"* where He declares us righteous by imputing Christ's righteousness to our account. If we fail to keep our part of the New Covenant by not sanctifying ourselves and bearing godly fruit (i.e. allowing sin to habitually rule) we risk disqualifying ourselves from entering heaven.

The main reason for the need for sanctification is due to our sinful nature which is rooted in "self-seeking interests." There are eight interchangeable Scriptural terms for our sinful nature. It is called: the **9A.** *"old man"*; the **9B.** *"works of the flesh"*; the **9C.** *"lusts of the flesh"*; the **9D.** *"natural man"*; the **9E.** fallen nature; **9F.** satan's character; being **9G.** *"carnal,"* and in some sense, the **9H.** *"heart."* For a contrast of the *"new man"* (God's character) and the *"old man"* (satan's character), revisit the comparative list in Lesson 3.

Lesson 8
THE BREASTPLATE OF RIGHTEOUSNESS:
Putting Our Sinful Nature to Death

☑ Before starting the DVD:

Having completed the introductory material for this piece of armor, this lesson will now give you a better understanding of what the Bible means to *"put on"* the Breastplate of Righteousness. We will learn the "whys" and "hows" of putting our sinful nature to death. But first, the video will recap the results of Adam's fall. This will set up God's plan of salvation—specifically an enlargement of His part of the New Testament that we briefly discussed last session. We'll also summarize man's part. I refer you to my book, *Treasures from the Cross*, for an in-depth look at what Jesus purchased for you on the cross (www.discoverministries.com).

☑ **DVD Users:** Watch Lesson 8 for an overview before proceeding further (27 min.).
☑ When you're through, pick up again at this point. Fill in the blanks from the Summary.

GOD'S PART OF THE NEW TESTAMENT

God sent His Son to invade planet earth, the sphere of satan's kingdom of darkness. He did this to rescue mankind through the substitutionary death and resurrection of Christ—regaining all for mankind that was usurped from Adam. As Dr. J. Dwight Pentecost put it, Christ "came that He might wrest from satan the scepter which satan had taken from Adam."[1] He also established a beachhead in this hostile territory in order to penetrate satan's kingdom with light and undo the works of the devil—by birthing His Church to continue His work through the power of the Holy Spirit. Through Christ's death and resurrection, God replaced the Old Testament with the New Testament. Keep in mind that a *"testament"* is usually a conditional agreement, or covenant, with both parties having specific responsibilities to fulfill. The following are some of the key elements that God provided to fulfill His part of the new covenant:

1. R_____ means to recover ownership by buying back one who is enslaved **(Matthew 20:28; Revelation 5:9; 1 Corinthians 6:19-20).** Now that fallen man had become children of satan, God had to recover ownership. He purchased us back at a costly price. He did this in order to save and remove us from danger and into His protection.

2. S_____ means the innocent dying in place of the guilty. Christ took our judgment for sin **(Isaiah 53:4,6; 2 Corinthians 5:21; 1 Peter 1:18-20).**

3. P_____ means to appease God's wrath. Because Jesus received His Father's wrath and judgment for our sins while on the cross, His sacrifice appeased the anger and justice of God toward us. Sin lost its power to provoke His wrath. Mercy and forgiveness can now be extended to us **(1 John 4:10; Colossians 1:20; Exodus 12:13; 1 Timothy 1:13-14).**

4. R_____ means to bring peace by reestablishing friendship **(Romans 5:10; 2 Corinthians 5:18-19).** Christ's death brought God and man, who were out of fellowship with each other, back together again.

5. I_____ means to put to one's account **(Romans 4:22-25; Philippians 3:9).**

   A. When we receive Christ into our hearts, God the Father imputes the righteousness of Christ's sinless life to our spiritual "bank account." Our standing of righteousness is not any greater today than it was the day we became *"born again"* because God only does it as a "one time transaction." There is no accumulation of "good works" we can do to earn a right standing or add to Christ's work. The "good works" we do in Christ's name will only be rewarded. The imputation of Christ's righteousness to us is part of the meaning of the Breastplate of Righteousness.

6. J_____ means to declare one righteous **(Titus 3:5-7).** This is a legal standing we receive in God's court of law. God, the Judge, looks upon us as if we never sinned. In exchange for our faith in Christ, God wipes out the sin debt we owe Him. God chose something we all could give Him—our faith.

7. S_____ means to separate for holy use **(Hebrews 10:10-14).** This is an act of God whereby He separates us to Himself to become His sacred "property" for use in His service **(1 Corinthians 6:19-20).**

8. A_____ means to "place as a son" **(Galatians 4:3-7).**

📖 DEFINITION—ADOPTION

It "signifies the place and condition of a son given to one to whom it does not naturally belong." [2]

We were born a child of the devil because of the fall. Satan became our father because we now acted like him and he held us under his power because of sin. But when we receive Christ, we are transferred into God's family and He becomes our Father and gives us the honor and dignity of becoming His child. We then sever the relationship that we had with our old father. Along with this new position, God also gives us all the rights to His inheritance as well as the privileges of sonship. Remember, God is everyone's God (creatively), but not everyone's Father (redemptively). See Lesson 3.

MAN'S PART OF THE NEW TESTAMENT

God's Holy Spirit lovingly confronts us by wooing and convicting our hearts so that we will serve Him (many of us will never change until someone confronts us). Sometimes He uses difficult circumstances to bring us to the end of ourselves. Through an act of our will, we must respond to Him by humbling ourselves and doing the following:

1. R_____ of sin in a conversion experience (and throughout our Christian walk). It is a change of mind, heart, and will—turning 180° in the opposite direction to do God's will **(Luke 13:3; Acts 2:37-38; 1 John 1:9; Ezekiel 33:14-16; Proverbs 28:13).**

2. B_____ God's Word that Jesus Christ died as our substitute for sin on the cross and was raised to life again, and R_____ His Son into our spirit as our Savior from sin and judgment—making Him Lord of our life—becoming *"born again"* or regenerated **(John 1:12; 3:3; Titus 3:5).** We also receive all the spiritual treasures that Jesus purchased for us on the cross.

▶ **CONSIDER THIS:** Regeneration, or the impartation of God's life and divine nature, does not occur in our soul at the same time it occurs in our spirit. Our spirit is the part of us that is regenerated or *"born again."* Throughout our earthly life our soul needs to be continually renewed and brought into submission to God's will. Likewise, it is necessary for our body to now become an obedient servant to our spirit to do God's will.

3. S_____ is the human responsibility we have to separate ourselves to God for sacred use and to separate ourselves from sin and evil by putting it to death. God desires that every "room" in our "house," every area of our lives, come under His control. It also includes the principle of "walking worthy"—cultivating and maintaining the wonderful work God is doing in our lives **(1 Thessalonians 4:3; Hebrews 12:14; Colossians 1:10).** This was covered thoroughly in Lesson 7. No longer are we the center of our world because now Christ is.

   A. In summary, when our spirit was *"born again,"* we **were saved** from God's judgment, the penalty of sin; our soul is now **being saved** progressively from the power of sin through sanctification; and our body **shall be saved** from death, the result of sin, at the resurrection when it is transformed into a glorified body. When one is truly born again, there is nothing one can do to become more of a child of God than one already is.

▶ **CONSIDER THIS:** Herein is good news for those of you who have suffered physical misfortune where life seems to have robbed you. Look at it this way. All of our bodies are temporal and will soon die. However, the invisible part of us, our inner man (our spirit and soul), will live forever. It is this spiritual part that you can develop by cultivating a relationship with God. As you develop this relationship, the beauty of Christ's character can radiate from your life in such a way that God will use you to build His kingdom in your sphere of influence. Be encouraged! Turn your misfortune into a blessing. Don't allow your physical disabilities to keep you depressed and regretful and hold you back from making an impact with your life. Serve God from right where you are. Also, keep the future in mind—one day the Bible says that you will have a perfect, glorified body for eternity!

WHY PUT OUR SINFUL NATURE TO DEATH?

1. We are C_____ to by God—it is part of the sanctification process.

   † **Colossians 3:5-6**—*Put to death, therefore, whatever belongs to your earthly nature: sexual immorality, impurity, lust, evil desires and greed, which is idolatry. **6.** Because of these, the wrath of God is coming.*

▶ **CONSIDER THIS:** Keep in mind that we are referring now, not to the devil, but to our sinful nature—the enemy within us. Like the cartoon character, Pogo, once said, "We have met the enemy and he is us." Let us understand right from the very beginning that our sinful nature is not our friend and it does not have our best interests in mind. Lest you have any doubt, notice the latent power it has to drive us to indulge in actions that inflict harm upon us and make fools of ourselves. The strange, ironic thing is that it is part of our being. It's like carrying around an enemy within which is *"deceitful above all things and desperately wicked"* **(Jeremiah 17:9** KJV**).** It cannot be trusted to direct our lives.

Naturally, we don't expect a thought or feeling from within us to be something that will harm and lead us astray. But our sinful nature, with its arrogant pride, leads us into addictive, self-destructive behavior. In short, it wants to be in control of our lives and take the place of God's rule. Pride is the deification of self and it will lead us to our downfall (see **2 Chronicles 26:11-21; Proverbs 16:18**). The only option we have is to "kill" our fallen character before "it kills" us.

Nature itself teaches us the principle that life comes through death. A bird hunts a worm. A fish gulps down another fish. A leopard stalks a zebra. "Life and death are the law of field, stream, and jungle...The principle that nothing lives unless something else dies extends beyond nature to our daily walk with God. Interests of the flesh [sinful nature] must succumb to the interests of the Spirit, or else the interests of the Spirit will succumb to the interests of the flesh. In the jungles and fields and streams of our own heart, something must always die so that something else can live."[3]

2. Our sinful nature is an E_____ to us because:

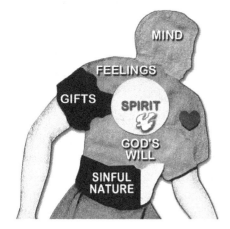

A. It's an E_____ of G____.

† **Romans 8:7-8**—*...the sinful mind is hostile to God. It does not submit to God's law, nor can it do so.* **8.** *Those controlled by the sinful nature cannot please God.*

† **Romans 5:10**—*...we were God's enemies...*

B. It W_____ against our spirit where the Holy Spirit resides (more will be said of this battlefield in Lesson 9).

† **Galatians 5:17**—*For the sinful nature desires what is contrary to the Spirit, and the Spirit what is contrary to the sinful nature. They are in conflict with each other, so that you do not do what you want.*

† **1 Peter 2:11**—*...sinful desires, which war against your soul.*

† **Romans 7:15-25**—*I do not understand what I do. For what I want to do I do not do, but what I hate I do.* **16.** *And if I do what I do not want to do, I agree that the law is good.* **17.** *As it is, it is no longer I myself who do it, but it is sin living in me.* **18.** *I know that nothing good lives in me, that is, in my sinful nature. For I have the desire to do what is good, but I cannot carry it out.* **19.** *For what I do is not the good I want to do; no, the evil I do not want to do—this I keep on doing.* **20.** *Now if I do what I do not want to do, it is no longer I who do it, but it is sin living in me that does it.* **21.** *So I find this law at work: When I want to do good, evil is right there with me.* **22.** *For in my inner being I delight in God's law;* **23.** *but I see another law at work in the members of my body, waging war against the law of my mind and making me a prisoner of the law of sin at work within my members.* **24.** *What a wretched man I am! Who will rescue me from this body of death?* **25.** *Thanks be to God—through Jesus Christ our Lord! So then, I myself in my mind am a slave to God's law, but in the sinful nature a slave to the law of sin.*

C. Our sinful nature R_____ us of G_____.

(1) Our *"natural man"* thinks spiritual things are foolishness.

† **1 Corinthians 2:14** (KJV)—*But the natural man receiveth not the things of the Spirit of God: for they are foolishness unto him: neither can he know them, because they are spiritually discerned.*

† **1 Corinthians 1:18-23**—*For the message of the cross is foolishness to those who are perishing, but to us who are being saved it is the power of God...*

(2) Our fallen nature promotes unbelief and is an enemy to our faith in God.

† **Hebrews 3:12-19**—*See to it, brothers, that none of you has a sinful, unbelieving heart that turns away from the living God...* **19.** *So we see that they* [Israel] *were not able to enter* [the Promised Land], *because of their unbelief.*

† **2 Corinthians 5:7** (KJV)—*For we walk by faith, not by sight.*

(3) Our sinful nature hides from God and the light of His Truth **(Genesis 3:8-10).**

† **John 3:19-21**—Jesus said: *"This is the verdict: Light has come into the world, but men loved darkness instead of light because their deeds were evil.* **20.** *Everyone who does evil hates the light, and will not come into the light for fear that his deeds will be exposed."*

(4) Our carnal nature resists the Lordship of Christ over it and opposes any spiritual advancement we make in Him.

† **2 Chronicles 36:14-16**—*Furthermore, all the leaders of the priests and the people became more and more unfaithful, following all the detestable practices of the nations and defiling the temple of the Lord, which he had consecrated in Jerusalem.* **15.** *The Lord, the God of their fathers, sent word to them through his messengers again and again, because he had pity on his people and on his dwelling place.* **16.** *But they mocked God's messengers, despised his words and scoffed at his prophets until the wrath of the Lord was aroused against his people and there was no remedy.*

† **Luke 13:34** (NLT)—Jesus said, *"O Jerusalem, Jerusalem, the city that kills the prophets and stones God's messengers! How often I have wanted to gather your children together as a hen protects her chicks beneath her wings, but you wouldn't let me."*

(a) It also tries to dissuade us from taking up our cross by insisting on self-preservation and avoiding self-denial and the hardships promised to those who follow Christ.

(5) Our *"old man"* is prone to worship God's creation rather than He who created it **(Romans 1:25,32).**

D. Our sinful nature E_____ and R_____ our lives.

  † **John 8:34**—*Jesus replied, "I tell you the truth, everyone who sins is a slave to sin."*

  † **Romans 6:6,12**—*...that we should no longer be slaves to sin...* **12.** *Therefore do not let sin reign in your mortal body so that you obey its evil desires.* (Also see **Proverbs 5:22.**)

  † **Genesis 4:7**—God said to Cain: *"If you do what is right, will you not be accepted? But if you do not do what is right, sin is crouching at your door; it desires to have you, but you must master it."* (Note that God Himself could not change Cain's mind—sin's pull was that strong!)

  † **Titus 3:3**—*At one time we too were foolish, disobedient, deceived and enslaved by all kinds of passions and pleasures. We lived in malice and envy, being hated and hating one another.*

  † **Romans 8:9**—*You, however, are controlled not by the sinful nature but by the Spirit, if the Spirit of God lives in you. And if anyone does not have the Spirit of Christ, he does not belong to Christ.*

  (1) Notice under the guise of "having a good time" or "wanting to be a part of the crowd," how the sinful nature drives us to harm our bodies through the use of alcohol, tobacco, drugs and the like (risking probable addiction), and often causing us to make fools of ourselves while under their influence. These self destructive, sado-masochistic tendencies will prompt us to do things that will imprison us both behaviorally and physically—like dragging around a ball and chain.

  (2) The sinful nature tries to deceive us by persuading us that somehow a sinful act is "good." It says: "How can something that feels so good be so wrong?" "If it feels good, do it!" "Let your senses be your guide." And foolishly, at times, we listen and obey!!

  (3) Thank God for His mercy so that it is possible to return to our right mind, but often through much pain (see **2 Chronicles 33:1-16**).

E. Our sinful nature gives the D_____ a F_____ in our lives and nation.

  † **Ephesians 4:26-27**—*...Do not let the sun go down while you are still angry,* **27.** *and do not give the devil a foothold.*

▶**CONSIDER THIS:** A *"foothold"* is also like a beachhead. It is an opportunity given to, and seized by, the enemy from which he can make further advancement into other areas (it is also like a "foot in the door" or a "toehold" for mountain climbers). Sin opens the door and gives the devil a legal right to enter. We must close and lock these doors to our sinful nature, and give the devil no room just as the sinless Jesus did **(John 14:30)**. Practicing sin is what keeps us a captive of the devil and under his control. He can only get authority over us as we give it to him. Our choices either aid the forces of evil or they repel them. Now that we are *"born-again"*, if we allow a sin to take control within us, we can actually invite demonic activity into our lives (see **Demonization**). On a national scale, leaders who neglect to carry out their God-given responsibilities in His way, give a foothold for the rulers of darkness to enter who will plague and weaken a country.

F. Our sinful nature brings S_____ D_____ and separation from God.

> † **Galatians 5:19-21**—*The acts of the sinful nature are obvious: sexual immorality, impurity and debauchery; **20.** idolatry and witchcraft; hatred, discord, jealousy, fits of rage, selfish ambition, dissensions, factions **21.** and envy; drunkenness, orgies, and the like. I warn you, as I did before, that those who live like this will not inherit the kingdom of God.*

> † **Romans 8:1** (NKJV)—*There is therefore now no condemnation to those who are in Christ Jesus, who do not walk according to the flesh, but according to the Spirit.*

> † **Romans 8:13**—*For if you live according to the sinful nature, you will die; but if by the Spirit you put to death the misdeeds of the body, you will live.*

> † Also read **1 Corinthians 6:9-11**.

HOW TO PUT OUR SINFUL NATURE TO DEATH

We cannot peaceably coexist with our sinful nature. Neither can we call for a cease-fire, nor retreat from it. We must face it head on each time and deal with it God's way. This is accomplished in both positive and negative ways as outlined below. Foremost, we should take a positive approach, which we will cover in our last point. These biblical prohibitions will release us into victorious living. It is impossible to do these things in our own strength, but only by the grace and power of the Holy Spirit. God exhorts us to do the following:

1. We are to "P_____ O_____" the character of our sinful nature, and *"put on"* God's character.

> † **Ephesians 4:22-24**—*...with regard to your former way of life...put off your old self, which is being corrupted by its deceitful desires... **24.** and put on the new self, created to be like God in true righteousness and holiness.*

> † **Romans 13:14**—*...clothe yourselves with the Lord Jesus Christ...*

A. We do this by taking the step to obey the Word of God. As we do, the power of the Holy Spirit is activated by our obedience, and He enables us to do His will. So *"throw off"* (NLT); *"lay aside"* (NASB); and *"get rid of"* (GNT) the character of your sinful nature whenever it raises its ugly head.

▶ **CONSIDER THIS:** Just as we are to *"put off"* and put to death self and pride (which is at the core of our sinful nature), so positively we are to clothe ourselves by putting on the *"new man,"* the *"fruit of the Spirit"* **(Galatians 5:22-25)** which reflect God's character. As we separate ourselves to God to allow more of His nature to emanate from our lives, He will use us as beacons of light in a very dark world. It all begins with putting on this Breastplate of Righteousness.

2. We are to ruthlessly "P_____ to D_____" the sinful character within us—especially the root of self in our soul that the character of our sinful nature stems from.

† **Colossians 3:5-10**—*Put to death, therefore, whatever belongs to your earthly nature: sexual immorality, impurity, lust, evil desires and greed, which is idolatry.* **6.** *Because of these, the wrath of God is coming.* **7.** *You used to walk in these ways, in the life you once lived.* **8.** *But now you must rid yourselves of all such things as these: anger, rage, malice, slander, and filthy language from your lips.* **9.** *Do not lie to each other, since you have taken off your old self with its practices* **10.** *and have put on the new self, which is being renewed in knowledge in the image of its Creator.*

† **Romans 6:6-11** (NLT)—**7.** *For when we died with Christ we were set free from the power of sin.* **8.** *And since we died with Christ, we know we will also share his new life.*

A. No amount of man-made remedies like education, culture, rehabilitation, or incarceration, can reform the sinful nature of man. Death is the only cure for the life, power, exercise, and activity of self-will, self-love, self-sufficiency, self-reliance, and self-preservation. Selfishness is the root that must be dug up and destroyed. Its destruction will allow God's life to emerge.

† **John 12:24** (NASB)—Jesus taught: *"...unless a grain of wheat falls into the earth and dies, it remains alone; but if it dies, it bears much fruit."*

B. We are to ruthlessly stamp out the evil character in our fallen nature just as God wanted Israel to annihilate the evil nations in the Promised Land, showing no mercy.

† **Deuteronomy 7:1-6**—**2.** *...you must destroy them totally. Make no treaty with them, and show them no mercy...* **6.** *For you are a people holy to the Lord your God. The Lord your God has chosen you...to be his people, his treasured possession.*

† **Galatians 5:24**—*Those who belong to Christ Jesus have crucified the sinful nature with its passions and desires.*

† **Galatians 2:20** (NLT)—*I have been crucified with Christ. I myself no longer live, but Christ lives in me. So I live my life in this earthly body by trusting in the Son of God, who loved me...*

▶**CONSIDER THIS:** The enemy within us is like a cancer that will eventually kill us! The only way to overcome it is to kill it before it kills us. Christ was crucified for our sins. His part is finished. All of our past sins have been crucified with Jesus. Now we are to take up our cross and follow the example Christ modeled for us. It is our turn to crucify the sinful character within us and confess and deal with future sins. Through His Holy Spirit, God will enable us to be the executioner and kill the sinful nature by our own hand, and keep it in a state of crucifixion.

3. We are to "A_____" from entertaining and pursuing sinful desires.

† **1 Peter 2:11**—*...abstain from sinful desires, which war against your soul.*

† **1 Thessalonians 5:22** (KJV)—*Abstain from all appearance of evil.*

Note: Restrain yourself from engaging in sinful practices by making decisions of obedience to God through an act of your will with the help of the Holy Spirit. You have the power to choose. You must be in control. Flee when sin lures you, and escape the trap that is deliberately set to destroy you **(Acts 15:19-20; 1 Timothy 6:9-11; 2 Timothy 2:22; Genesis 39:11-12).**

4. We are to S_____ I____ so as not to allow any sin to grow and become dominant.

   † **Romans 6:12** (NLT)—*Do not let sin control the way you live; do not give into its lustful desires.*

   † **Romans 13:14**—*...do not think about how to gratify the desires of the sinful nature.*

▶**CONSIDER THIS:** Sinful cravings do not go away by temporarily gratifying them. A law of nature is if you feed something it will grow. If you deprive it of nourishment, death will result. Never nurture any sinful desire and allow it to grow to where it will rule and control you. Destroy its supply line through feeding your spirit and you will be victorious. If you fill your spirit with God, you prevent a vacancy for sinful things to enter in. Keep in mind that it is easier to pull out weeds in their infant stage than when, through neglect, they are allowed to grow bigger.

5. We are to "D_____" its desire to act independently of God and rob us of God's best.

   † **Matthew 16:24**—Jesus said: *"...If anyone would come after me, he must deny himself and take up his cross and follow me."* (**Luke 9:23** adds *"...take up his cross daily..."*).

   † **2 Corinthians 5:15**—*And he died for all, that those who live should no longer live for themselves but for him who died for them and was raised again.*

   A. Jesus commanded us to deny our sinful nature its desire for growth and control. We are also to follow the example Jesus set for us in denying our will to act independently of God's will for our lives. Denying ourselves of material "things" is not necessary unless those material things contribute to the awakening of our sinful nature and interfere with God's will and putting Him first. Nor does it mean to practice asceticism. However, we may sometimes be required to deny ourselves of certain relationships that hinder our walk with God and rob us of His best by severing them (see **Matthew 10:37-38**).

   B. We are also commanded to take up our cross and follow Christ. The cross is formed when God's will crosses our will and we submit to God's will—no matter what it costs us. However, sickness for example, is normally not a cross because it's not something you can choose to "pick up." This death to self will bring life to our spirit.

6. We are to "L_____" our life in order to find God's life and plan.

   † **Matthew 16:25-26**—*Jesus said to His disciples, "For whoever wants to save his life* [psuchē] *will lose it, but whoever loses his life* [psuchē] *for me will find it. 26. What good will it be for a man if he gains the whole world, yet forfeits his soul? Or what can a man give in exchange for his soul?"*

   A. The Greek word used for *"life"* and *"soul"* in verses **25** and **26** is the word *psuchē*—the soul realm where our sinful nature resides. This process is not attractive to the self-preservation aspect of our soul.

B. Seeking to find our sense of fulfillment and worth in positions, possessions, pleasures, or accomplishments is much like the pursuit of a mirage. If and when we "catch" them, they are not at all what we perceived them to be and they will slip through our fingers like sand. Many times, instead of fulfillment there will be a greater sense of emptiness. Pursuing the temporal rather than the eternal will never produce lasting satisfaction in our lives.

▶**CONSIDER THIS:** Our world is filled with paradoxes. Here are some of them: "to save our life we must lose it" and "to live we must die;" "to be strong, we must be weak" (**2 Corinthians 12:10**); "to be great, we must serve" (**Matthew 20:26**); we must "bless them that curse us" (**Matthew 5:44**); and *the race is not to the swift nor the battle to the strong"* (**Ecclesiastes 9:11**).

7. We are to "H_____" our self-centered life and sinful character.

   † **John 12:25-26**—*Jesus replied, "...The man who loves his life* [psuchē] *will lose it, while the man who hates his life* [psuchē] *in this world will keep it for eternal life. 26. Whoever serves me must follow me; and where I am, my servant also will be..."*

   A. Once again the Greek word used for soul, *psuchē*, is translated "life." Jesus tells us to hate our self-centered soul life and our sinful nature for what it is—satan's character and the enemy it is to God and ourselves. **Romans 12:9** (KJV) says: *"...Abhor that which is evil..."* Let this attitude motivate us to put our sins to death so that God's life and spiritual fruit can spring forth. Keep in mind that hatred of our sinful nature will not produce love for God, but love for God will produce hate for our sinful nature.

   ☑ This ends the DVD content for Lesson 8.
   ☑ Continue on in this workbook for additional material **not** on the DVD.

8. We are called to "Walk in the Spirit."

   † **Galatians 5:16**—*...live by the Spirit* [walk in the Spirit—KJV] *and you will not gratify the desires of the sinful nature.*

   A. To *"Walk in the Spirit"* means a moment-by-moment steadfast determination to please God by pursuing Him and obeying His ways. It is putting God first when confronted with a choice between acting in the flesh or in the Spirit. This is the most positive approach.

   † **1 John 3:9**—*No one who is born of God will continue to sin, because God's seed remains in him...*

   B. Focus on your relationship with Christ and let your love for Him be the driving force behind the decisions you make. Think about Christ's love for you as He agonized and died on the cross. Nothing demonstrates God's hatred of sin more than the cross.

   Q: How can we entertain sinful thoughts when it was sin that nailed Him to the cross? Our heart must say: "I love Christ much too much to hurt Him by committing this sin."

C. Bishop Joseph L. Garlington, Senior Pastor of Covenant Church of Pittsburgh stated, "This positive lifestyle really boils down to this: when you say 'YES!' in obedience to the Holy Spirit and His Word, at the same time you say a resounding 'NO!' to your sinful nature. Therefore, walking in the Spirit naturally negates walking in the flesh. When you choose God's way in a situation, you have just chosen against the fallen nature to have its way. If you make the decision to tell the truth all the time, you won't lie."

D. Your pursuit of sanctification is accomplished by regularly presenting your members as *"instruments of righteousness,"* and giving the Holy Spirit your consent to rule over your flesh.

† **Romans 6:13-23**—*Do not offer the parts of your body to sin, as instruments of wickedness, but rather offer yourselves to God, as those who have been brought from death to life; and offer the parts of your body to him as instruments of righteousness. 14. For sin shall not be your master, because you are not under law, but under grace... 19. I put this in human terms because you are weak in your natural selves. Just as you used to offer the parts of your body in slavery to impurity and to ever-increasing wickedness, so now offer them in slavery to righteousness leading to holiness.*

† **1 Corinthians 9:24-27**—*Do you not know that in a race all the runners run, but only one gets the prize? Run in such a way as to get the prize. 25. Everyone who competes in the games goes into strict training. They do it to get a crown that will not last; but we do it to get a crown that will last forever. 26. Therefore I do not run like a man running aimlessly; I do not fight like a man beating the air. 27. No, I beat my body and make it my slave so that after I have preached to others, I myself will not be disqualified for the prize.*

►**CONSIDER THIS:** To summarize, the Breastplate of Righteousness has two aspects. First, it is the imputation of Christ's righteousness to our spiritual "bank account" when we receive Him as Lord and Savior. Second, it is our part of the New Testament (*"sanctification"*) whereby we separate ourselves from sin for sacred service and put our sinful nature to death.

A practical application of sanctification can be illustrated by this example: You, a *"born again"* believer, enter a Christian bookstore where you often shop. But today, your financial resources are at a low. Passing by a display of musical CD's, your eyes land on one that you have longed to own. The battle within begins! Your sinful nature begins to assert itself and gives you reasons to justify stealing it. The *"old man"* says—"I really want that CD but I don't have the money to buy it. But no one is looking. They won't miss **one** CD—and it's only $15." So the enemy within you works on your will to give in to its craving. The *"new man"* is hearing the Spirit say, "Thou shall not steal." It is at this moment that your spirit must exercise its authority over your soul and say, "No! We are not going to steal. We're going to obey and please God." As your will is being pressured by both entities, putting on the Breastplate of Righteousness would entail the decision to obey and please God. The same would be true for any situation where a sin in our fallen nature demanded control. By the way, if you aren't aware of it, sadly this is a big problem in many Christian bookstores today.

STUDY QUESTIONS AND APPLICATION

1. God has a way of faithfully highlighting problem areas in our lives so that we have the opportunity to confront them and be delivered. God applies just the right amount of pressure to cause that which is really inside of us to surface. Currently, is the Holy Spirit pointing out any area in your life that He is requiring you to surrender to His control? Start by praying this prayer: "Father, I am willing to let you talk to me about any area of my life, and there is no 'room' that I will hide from you and prevent you from having control over. Please speak to my heart."

2. List a few examples of the ways you can "put on" the Breastplate of Righteousness in your daily living:

3. What distinction do you make between confession of sin and repentance of sin? Do you believe that it is necessary to obtain forgiveness of your sins through any human being?

4. There are different views within the Body of Christ as to whether a true "born again" child of God can do anything to disqualify himself from entering heaven. While we strongly believe in our security in Christ, we must be aware that this possibility exists due to free will. Our security in Christ should not be weakened by this, but instead should motivate us to always live in a manner pleasing to God. Read the following Scriptures to see what the Bible has to say about this concept.

Matthew 7:21-23	Galatians 5:19-25	Hebrews 6:4-6	Hebrews 10:26-31, 38-39	James 5:19-20
2 Peter 2:20-22	Jude 1:3-5, 24	Hebrews 3:12-19	John 15:1-5	Matthew 10:32-33
Revelation 2:7,11,17,26	Revelation 3:5, 12, 15-21; 21:7	Hebrews 12:14-15	2 Peter 3:17	Luke 14:34-35
Joshua 24:20	1 Chronicles 28:9	2 Chronicles 15:2	Isaiah 63:10	Ezekiel 18:24, 26-28
James 4:4	2 Corinthians 6:14-18	Romans 8:1,13	1 John 5:16-17	Numbers 15:30-31
1 Samuel 16:14; 28:15-16	Romans 14:12-23	1 Timothy 4:1	Ephesians 5:3-7	

SUM

God sent His Son to invade planet earth, the s
to rescue mankind, to regain all that was usur
with the New. We learned that a **testament** is
both parties having specific responsibilities to
alone. Whatever the case, God is the initiator c
essential to know what elements each party is
conditional covenant. When Adam and Eve fe
with mankind involved these key provisi
1. redemption, **2.** substitution, **3.** propitiation,
7. sanctification, and **8.** adoption. This was al
the cross and His glorious resurrection. God i
work by faith. When we do, all these treasures

THE ARMOR OF GOD

This lesson has given us a better
what the Bible means to *"pu*
First, it is the imputation c
Savior. Second, it is o
ourselves from sin f
according to the s
the body, you wi

Our part of the New Testament consists of: **1.**
life; **2.** believe God's Word that Jesus Christ died as our substitute for sin on the cross and was
raised to life again, and receive His Son into our spirit as our Savior from sin and judgment—
making Him Lord of our life—becoming *"born again"* or regenerated. Then **3.** sanctification is
the believer's responsibility to "walk worthy"—maintaining our salvation by separating
ourselves from sin and evil to God for His sacred use (see Lesson 7). This involves the life-long
process of putting our sinful nature to death.

God gives us the reasons WHY we must put our sinful nature to death: First, we are
1. commanded to by Him. God warns us that our sinful nature is an **2.** enemy to us for the
following reasons. Because it is an **2A.** enemy of God; it **2B.** wars against our spiritual lives; it
2C. robs us of God because it looks down upon the things of God as foolishness; it **2D.** enslaves
and rules our lives; it gives the **2E.** devil a foothold in our lives; and it will eventually bring
2F. spiritual death and separation from God. In reality, it's like carrying around an enemy within
us. We must destroy it before it destroys us.

God also tells us **HOW** to put our sinful nature to death. The Bible instructs us to **1.** "put off" its
evil character and *"put on"* God's character; to ruthlessly **2.** "put to death" the sinful character
within us—especially the root of self in our soul from which it stems—like the way God wanted
Israel to annihilate the evil nations in the Promised Land; to **3.** "abstain" from entertaining and
pursuing these sinful desires; to **4.** starve it so as not to allow any area to grow and become
dominant whereby it rules us; to **5.** "deny" its desire to act independently of God's will and rob
us of God's best; to **6.** "lose" it in order to find God's life and purpose; to **7.** "hate" it for what it
is—satan's character and the enemy it is to us and to God.

Lastly, we are called to **8.** *"walk in the spirit"* which means a moment-by-moment steadfast
determination to please God by pursuing Him and putting Him first when confronted with a
choice between acting in the flesh or in the Spirit. As we live out this lifestyle, each time we say
"YES!" in obedience to the Holy Spirit and His Word, we say a resounding "NO!" to our sinful
nature and deprive it of growth. Only by the grace and power of the Holy Spirit can we expect to
do these things.

...understanding of what the Breastplate of Righteousness is and ...

... on" this piece of armor. The Breastplate has two aspects to it.

... of Christ's righteousness to us when we receive Him as Lord and ...

... part of the New Testament (sanctification) whereby we separate ...

... sacred service and put our sinful nature to death. *"For if you live*

...nful nature you will die; but if by the Spirit you put to death the misdeeds of

...ll live..." **(Romans 8:13-14).**

Lesson 9
THE BREASTPLATE OF RIGHTEOUSNESS:
Our Sinful Nature vs. Our Spirit (Battlefield #1)

☑ Before starting the DVD: Just as the Roman soldier put on a breastplate to protect his physical heart and organs, so the child of God is to put on their breastplate to protect his or her spiritual heart and life. Today, it would be like a policeman or a soldier wearing a flak jacket in the line of duty. Keep in mind that much of this invisible war is fought within us. As Kathryn Kuhlman once said, "The greatest battles ever fought are fought in the human heart."[1]

† **Ephesians 6:14**—*Stand firm then...with the breastplate of righteousness in place.*

Every war has its battlefields. This lesson begins to identify the first of five spiritual battlefields on which the believer wages warfare. Battlefield #1 is our sinful nature vs. our spirit (new nature) where the Holy Spirit resides. In developing the ability to win this invisible war, we will also begin to learn some of the tactics satan uses against us (some 30 overall). Notice that on the video I number each of the tactics, but in this workbook I do not. So disregard the numbering. This lesson will take two sessions to complete. In session one, we will deal with the first **TACTIC: Let Self Reign,** which is a foundational strategy that will also be applied over the next few lessons. The second session will deal with **Maintaining Sexual Purity.** We will learn from two of King David's biggest mistakes in the area of temptation, his numbering of Israel and his affair with Bathsheba. Pray that God will give you special insight into this area.

☑ **DVD Users:** Watch Lesson 9 for an overview before proceeding further (25 min.).
☑ When you're through, pick up again at this point. Fill in the blanks from the Summary.

🔰 **TACTIC: Let Self Reign**—The enemy will try to tempt your will to allow an area of your sinful nature to take control so as to break your relationship with God and, in turn, hope to bring you under God's judgment. ◎ *Main Target*: Your Will.

Since satan cannot force us to do anything against our will, he will try to influence our will to disobey God. If we do, we open the door and give him permission to gain a foothold in an area of our life. Thus, WE put ourselves in a position that requires God to send His chastisement and judgment upon us! Read how satan was successful in bringing God's judgment upon His chosen people Israel in the Old Testament in **Jeremiah 32:29-32.**

THE SIX STAGES AND OUTCOMES OF TACTIC: LET SELF REIGN

1. The first stage of this tactic is T_____ **(James 1:13-14).**

- God <u>tests</u> us **(Deuteronomy 8:2-3).**

- Satan <u>tempts</u> us **(Matthew 4:3; James 1:13).**

📖 **DEFINITION—TEMPTATION**

The Greek word used is *peirasmos,* which signifies to test, to try or prove and is used in three ways:

1. Trials with a beneficial purpose and effect (intended to strengthen us)
   See **Deuteronomy 8:2; 13:1-3; 2 Chronicles 32:31, 1 Peter 1:6-7; 4:12-13.**
2. Trials designed to lead to wrongdoing
3. Men "trying" or challenging God **(Hebrews 3:8)**[2]

Only God can do [#]1 above. He will try our faith, test our obedience, and prove our character for His purposes and our spiritual benefit and growth. Satan on the other hand incites mankind to do [#]2 and [#]3. Man can do [#]3 without satan's incitement. Satan's design in temptation is to entice and allure us to disobey God (something God does not do). Keep in mind that satan does not have foreknowledge of how we will react to his temptation. He gambles on the probabilities and uses what has always been successful for him. Only God knows how we will respond. But He assures us that no trial will be more than we can bear and with each one He will provide a way of escape **(1 Corinthians 10:13).**

There are <u>three</u> <u>sources</u> of temptation: the **flesh,** the **world,** and the **devil.**

A. The F_____.

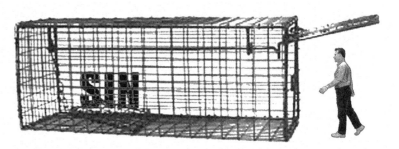

   † **James 1:14**—*...each one is tempted when, by his own evil desire, he is dragged away and enticed.*

📖 **DEFINITION—ENTICED**

The Greek word is *deleazō*. It carries the idea of being deceptively lured and baited like a hunted animal. Every temptation to sin is designed to entice us to rebel against God and live independently of Him.

   † **Mark 7:20-23**—Jesus taught: *"What comes out of a man is what makes him 'unclean.' 21. For from within, out of men's hearts, come evil thoughts, sexual immorality, theft, murder, adultery, 22. greed, malice, deceit, lewdness, envy, slander, arrogance and folly. 23. All these evils come from inside and make a man 'unclean.'"*

▶**CONSIDER THIS:** Our sinful nature is a separate, independent entity that has what looks to be the same characteristics and appetites as satan's. If the devil and all of his evil spirits ceased to exist at this moment, our sinful nature would still reflect satan's character. This is because whenever a person enthrones their self-will (whether angelic or human), they dethrone God's will from their lives and begin to reflect character opposite of God's, which is sin.

B. The W_____.

† **1 John 2:15-16**—*Do not love the world or anything in the world. If anyone loves the world, the love of the Father is not in him. 16. For everything in the world—the cravings of sinful man, the lust of his eyes and the boasting of what he has and does—comes not from the Father but from the world.*

Note: The sinful elements of the world system that appeal to our sinful nature serve as the enemy's bait in temptation.

C. The D_____.

† **Matthew 4:3**—*The tempter came to him* [Jesus] *and said, "If you are the Son of God, tell these stones to become bread."*

(1) From the spirit realm outside our body, the devil is able to stir up and stimulate our sinful nature by providing the right stimuli and conditions conducive for sinning.

(2) Since the devil can't force us to do something, he must work with something that influences our will so that we will choose to do it. Once we make the choice, sin becomes the master **(Romans 6:16).** To say "the devil made me do it" is both a false and inaccurate statement.

(3) Since the devil's rule over fallen mankind often goes unnoticed—he hides behind our sinful nature. His success depends on secrecy. Who would ever suspect the arson investigator would be the one who ignited the fires, as John Orr did in Southern California in the '70s and '80s? Satan has 6,000 years of experience in dealing with human weaknesses and behaviors, and knows what we are prone to fall for.

(4) We are more than physical beings attuned to the physical world—we are spiritual beings who interact, and are influenced by, the spirit world around us.

(5) The ability of demonic spirits to devise a trap presupposes their capability of observing and studying us. Most of what our enemy knows about us is revealed by our words and actions. They then strategize the best ways to lay traps for us in order to gain access into our lives; many times entering through doors we have opened by the choices we have made (see **Demonization** in index). The art of deception is to cleverly disguise the bait in such a way, making sin look so attractive and seductive, that it will lure our will to choose to take it and thereby cause us to believe that things are different than how they truly are and permissible for us to do. We are then manipulated to do something we would otherwise never do. Satan is the master of deceit.

† **Ephesians 6:11** (NLT)—*Put on all of God's armor so that you will be able to stand firm against all strategies and tricks of the Devil.*

▶**CONSIDER THIS:** Our spirits can be stirred to do something from the spirit world whether we are conscious of it or not (by the Holy Spirit, angelic beings, or demonic spirits). Satan uses available conditions to set his trap—seeking to get us to do what he wants us to do. Obviously, God often creates an atmosphere conducive to motivating us toward His interests. But in either case, we ultimately do the choosing. Yet God promises to be at work in us *giving you the desire to obey him and the power to do what pleases him"* **(Philippians 2:13** NLT**).** The examples that follow illustrate this truth by God, angels, and satan respectively.

  † **Ezra 1:1-5** (KJV)—*...the Lord stirred up the spirit of Cyrus, King of Persia, that he made a proclamation throughout all his kingdom....* [regarding Israel returning to their land from captivity].

  † **Haggai 1:14** (KJV)—*And the Lord stirred up the spirit of Zerubbabel...and the spirit of Joshua...and the spirit of all the remnant of the people; and they came and did work in the house of the Lord...*

  † **1 Chronicles 5:25-26**—At times circumstances appear to be the work of satan against God's children when in reality it is a sovereign act of God stirring up an enemy to bring discipline to His people.

  † Also see: **2 Peter 1:20-21; Jeremiah 51:11; 1 Samuel 10:26; Revelation 17:16-17; 1 Chronicles 12:18.**

  † **Matthew 2:13,14, 19-22**—The devil raised up King Herod to kill Jesus.

  † **Ephesians 2:2**—*...in which you used to live when you followed the ways of this world and of the ruler of the kingdom of the air, the spirit who is now at work in those who are disobedient.*

  † **Job 1:12,15,17**—Satan raised up marauders to attack Job's possessions.

DAVID'S NUMBERING OF ISRAEL'S MILITARY MIGHT
(1 Chronicles 21:1-27)

A. Let us use King David as an example of one who had experienced temptation and learn how the subsequent stages of this tactic played out in his life.

  (1) Satan's strategy was to harm the nation of Israel by gaining access through their leader—knowing that the consequences of one's deeds reach as far as their influence.

  † **1 Chronicles 21:1**—*Satan rose up against Israel and incited David to take a census of Israel.*

  (2) The origin of this idea to number Israel did not originate with David. Satan, in the spirit realm, was able to arouse this dormant, sinful desire that appealed to the selfish character of pride and self-glorification to try to move him from trust in God to trust in himself.

  (3) Though normally the taking of a census was not wrong in itself, the motive for taking this census was sinful because it was an issue of misplaced trust. David was tempted to trust in the strength and security of the size of his army for victory in battle rather than continuing to trust God and His promises as he normally did.

(4) Whenever a sinful thought comes into our minds, sometimes we carefully deliberate over it, and struggle with it, before making our decision. And sometimes we just impulsively open the door, throwing all caution to the wind. We are exhorted to judge each thought, discern its source, and then take it captive bringing it into subjection to God's Word by resisting it, starving it, and giving it a flat refusal on its very first encounter. The testimony of an ex-alcoholic is that when he was tempted to drink after his conversion to Christ, each time he would say: "Not today." With God's help, he hasn't had a drink now in over 40 years!

(5) Before acting, evaluate your decision to see if it will please God. Consider what the consequences of your decision will bring, and count the cost for the temporary gratification it will give you. Examine your motives for wanting to do it. Ask yourself, "Is it worth my losing the peace and presence of God over?" "Is it worth grieving the Holy Spirit, and giving the devil a foothold in my life?" "Is the fleeting moment of pleasure worth hurting loved ones and reaping a potential lifetime of haunting problems including losing your reputation and witness for Christ?" "Is it worth coming under the chastisement of God and stepping outside His umbrella of protection?" The obvious answer is—NO!!

✝ **Ephesians 4:27**—*...and do not give the devil a foothold.*

(6) In this first stage of temptation, our sinful nature asserts itself—pressuring our will to give in to its evil desires. The moment we stop fighting sin's advance, we will be brought under its control.

2. In the second stage of this tactic, our <u>W</u>   <u>C</u>   .

✝ **James 1:15a**—*Then, after desire has conceived, it gives birth to sin.*

A. To be tempted in itself, is not committing a sin. Giving into the sin and choosing to do it is!

B. In the example of David numbering Israel, he gave the order to take the census and wouldn't change his mind even when his closest associate advised him that he was making a wrong decision **(1 Chronicles 21:2-4).** Wisdom would have us listen to those around us—God might be speaking through them.

C. When your will is pressured to allow your sinful nature to have its way, it has two options:

(1) To listen and submit to your spirit, thereby obeying God's voice and rule in your life. If this is done, the devil's temptation attempt has failed. You have won this battle!

(2) Or you can listen and give into your sinful nature and its powerful desires, thereby giving your consent for evil to have its way in your life. This choice provokes a response from God, and sets in motion a future adverse harvest. You now step out from under God's protection.

✝ **Proverbs 25:28** (NLT)—*A person without self-control is as defenseless as a city with broken-down walls.*

D. In this stage, the sinful nature is **allowed** control. Our will is like a door. It can prevent or permit sin to pass through it. When we give into the temptation, we dethrone God's rule and enthrone our own will in that area of our life. We also open the door and invite both enemies (our sinful nature and satan) to seize control and we are on our way back to enslavement. It is our deliberate choice to disobey God's Word that makes us responsible for that sin and holds us accountable before God.

E. The sin begins to sprout like a seedling. As it is fed and nurtured, it takes deeper root (becomes habitual) and will try to invade other areas of our life.

F. **Q:** When does "conception" of sin officially become sin? **(James 1:15a)** Usually one would think it occurs when it manifests itself in an outward act. However, **Matthew 5:28** and **1 John 3:15** indicate more. It is when the imagined act is as satisfying to you as the actual act.

G. Once the life of that particular sin has been conceived, it gives birth to a manifestation of satan's character in our life. This will bring with it consequences.

H. Like a drop of water, one good or bad decision can set in motion waves of blessing or destructive consequences—not only in our lives, but also in those around us. It ripples out into our future and even on to our descendents!!

(See **Numbers 25:6-13; 1 Kings 15:28-30; 2 Kings 5:15-27; Exodus 20:5-6; 34:6-7; 2 Samuel 21:1-14**).

3. In the third stage, <u>D   </u> and <u>B   </u> set in.

    † **1 John 2:9-11—***11. But whoever hates his brother is in the darkness and walks around in the darkness; he does not know where he is going, because the darkness has blinded him.*

A. In this stage, we walk in darkness—unable to see things as they really are in areas of our life.

B. Our choice creates a "blind spot" in this particular area. This is the main reason why we can see another's failures when they can't see it in themselves. Spiritual blindness is possibly the worst "disease" one can have because it extends beyond the temporal into eternity.

C. Another dynamic is at work here. The addictive nature of sin begins to hold us in its grip making it very difficult to free ourselves of it in our own power. It is like being caught in an undertow or riptide in the ocean.

D. David was blinded and could not see that his decision was a wrong one as Joab his commander did **(1 Chronicles 21:5-6).**

4. In the fourth stage of this tactic, sin <u>B</u>_____ our <u>R</u>_____ (fellowship) with God.

> † **James 1:15b**—*...and sin, when it is full-grown, gives birth to death.*

📖 DEFINITION—DEATH

The Greek word *thanatos*, used here means separation. It is always used as the consequence of sin—whether it's the separation of man's relationship with God in this life **(Ephesians 2:1-6)**; the separation of the spirit (and soul) from the body **(James 2:26)**; or the eternal separation of man from God in hell and the lake of fire **(Revelation 20:13-15)**. From God's perspective, death does not mean nonexistence. As spiritual life is "conscious existence in communion with God," so spiritual "death" is "conscious existence in separation from God." This applies to this life and the afterlife—*"For the wages of sin is death"* **(Romans 6:23)**. Sin eats away Christ's abundant life in our spirit.

A. In this stage, sin causes an immediate breach in our fellowship with our Heavenly Father. A barrier is formed that, among other things, hinders our communion with God and could prevent Him from working on our behalf:

> † **Psalm 66:18** (KJV)—*If I regard iniquity in my heart, the Lord will not hear me.*

> † **Isaiah 59:2**—*But your iniquities have separated you from your God; your sins have hidden his face from you, so that he will not hear.*

> † **Ephesians 4:22-32**—Allowing sin control grieves the Holy Spirit within us, strengthens our sinful nature, and weakens our spiritual lives.

> † **Joshua 7:10-13**—God's sustaining power to overcome the enemy in battle was withdrawn from His people, Israel, until sin was dealt with and atoned for.

B. Our self-will tries to continue to keep us blinded and separated from God. If we don't deal with it, sin will move us toward the ultimate death—eternal separation from God.

C. We find ourselves in a dangerous, critical place. In the absence of God's satisfying presence, the natural tendency will be to search for a substitute for God's presence in the things of the world, which will only temporarily gratify our sinful nature.

D. The Holy Spirit will convict us and seek to bring us to a place of repentance and restoration through Christ's atonement. We have a choice to make. Will we harden our hearts and be rebellious or will we humble ourselves and submit to God? **Repentance will restore our broken fellowship with God.** Remember, God will forgive us of anything—no matter how bad—if we truly repent. (See **Matthew 12:31-32.**)

> † **1 John 1:9**—*If we confess our sins, he is faithful and just and will forgive us our sins and purify us from all unrighteousness.*

> † **Matthew 5:23-24**—Jesus said, *"Therefore, if you are offering your gift at the altar and there remember that your brother has something against you, 24. leave your gift there in front of the altar. First go and be reconciled to your brother; then come and offer your gift."*

E. In the example of David numbering Israel, when David finally came to his senses (awakening to the fact that he had sinned and asking for forgiveness), it was too late to avert the dreadful consequences of his sin. But it was just in time before his heart got hardened and unrepentant like his predecessor King Saul. Just as a disobedient decision got him into the mess, it would take an obedient decision to get him out of it (see **1 Chronicles 21:8,18**). So likewise, what we lose through disobedience must be regained by obedience.

> † **2 Timothy 2:25-26**—*...that God will grant them repentance leading them to a knowledge of the truth,* **26.** *and that they will come to their senses and escape from the trap of the devil, who has taken them captive to do his will.*

5. In the fifth stage of this tactic, we bring upon ourselves the loving C_____ of God.

A. In this stage, like a father disciplining his children, God tries to get our attention by providing correction in order to bring us to a place of repentance. This chastisement is motivated by God's great love for us as His child, and is also intended to discipline, correct, and train us so we won't make the wrong choice again. It is normally not vindictive punishment.

> † **Hebrews 12:5-14**—*And you have forgotten that word of encouragement that addresses you as sons: "My son, do not make light of the Lord's discipline, and do not lose heart when he rebukes you,* **6.** *because the Lord disciplines those he loves, and he punishes ["scourgeth"—KJV] everyone he accepts as a son."* **7.** *Endure hardship as discipline; God is treating you as sons. For what son is not disciplined by his father?* **8.** *If you are not disciplined (and everyone undergoes discipline), then you are illegitimate children and not true sons.* **9.** *Moreover, we have all had human fathers who disciplined us and we respected them for it. How much more should we submit to the Father of our spirits and live!* **10.** *Our fathers disciplined us for a little while as they thought best; but God disciplines us for our good, that we may share in his holiness.* **11.** *No discipline seems pleasant at the time, but painful. Later on, however, it produces a harvest of righteousness and peace for those who have been trained by it...* **14.** *without holiness* [sanctification] *no one will see the Lord.*

B. There are times when God will start out using gentle, loving ways to reach His child—especially those who are already crushed in spirit. He often, however, has to resort to using increasingly severer measures in His chastening when we do not respond quickly to His initial conviction. He will put as much pressure on His children as it takes to get them to turn back—even to the point of breaking them. Read **Leviticus 26:14-33** to get a picture of His progressive chastisement.

C. In the example of David numbering Israel, we see how severe the consequences can get. A plague sent from God killed 70,000 Israelites. Our sins not only have consequences for ourselves, but the death that our sins produce will likely affect others around us.

(1) David's sin was a reliance on his numerical military strength. God showed him that they could be taken in a moment **(1 Chronicles 21:9-17).** God was working to humble David's pride and work in the hearts of His people Israel.

(2) Through repentance and the shedding of the blood of innocent animals as atonement for his sin, David willingly paid the necessary price to be restored to fellowship with

his God. And because of his willingness to judge himself, he himself avoided satan's ultimate goal of bringing him under the judgment of God **(1 Chronicles 21:18-27).**

D. **WE** often bring unnecessary, self-inflicted hardships upon ourselves. **WE** place the rod into God's hand, and are solely responsible for it. It would be far better to simply obey Him!

> † **1 Corinthians 11:31-32**—*But if we judged ourselves, we would not come under judgment. 32. When we are judged by the Lord, we are being disciplined so that we will not be condemned with the world.*

E. Our Heavenly Father is the potter and we are the clay **(Isaiah 64:8; Jeremiah 18:6).** God wants to mold us into the image of His Son, and to mold clay one has to apply pressure and heat. So if we keep repeating a sin because we can't seem to get victory over the weakness, God will use this stage to work in us to root it out of our lives. There can even be times, as a last resort, when we might have to be handed over to satan for this so that our spirit may be saved (see **1 Corinthians 5:1, 5; 1 Timothy 1:19-20**). God wants us to be forever with Him in Heaven—not condemned with the world on Judgment Day.

> † **Psalm 119:67,71,75**—*Before I was afflicted I went astray, but now I obey your word. 71. It was good for me to be afflicted so that I might learn your decrees. 75. I know, O Lord, that your laws are righteous, and in faithfulness you have afflicted me.*

> † **Proverbs 20:30** (NLT)—*Physical punishment cleanses away evil; such discipline purifies the heart.*

> † **Hebrews 5:8** (NLT)—*So even though Jesus was God's Son, he learned obedience from the things he suffered.*

> † **1 Peter 4:1-2**—*Therefore, since Christ suffered in his body, arm yourselves also with the same attitude, because he who has suffered in his body is done with sin. 2. As a result, he does not live the rest of his earthly life for evil human desires, but rather for the will of God.*

> † **Philippians 1:6** (NLT)—*...God, who began the good work within you, will continue his work until it is finally finished...*

6. Finally, the last stage of **TACTIC**: **Let Self Reign** results in the J_____ of God—satan's ultimate goal.

A. Prior to the temptation, we kept ourselves under the umbrella of God's protection. Satan had no access to our lives. Then he tempted us to sin, hoping that we would step outside from under that safety zone so he could try to ultimately move us to this stage. When we sinned, he encouraged us to harden our hearts and resist the Holy Spirit's chastening throughout all these previous stages. God, over a long period of time, has tried using a range of measures, from gentle to severe, giving us many opportunities to repent. But repeatedly hardening our hearts and spurning His nurturing love, we rejected His rule in our lives. God has done all He can to get our attention, bring us to a place of submission, and restore the broken relationship. He knows we will never repent. In this stage, we leave God with no other alternative but to give us up to our own way and "turn us over to our sin" that we have preferred over Him. The result—eternal damnation! Believer, avoid this stage at all costs!! Don't ever allow satan to succeed with this tactic!

† **John 3:19-21**—Jesus said, *"This is the verdict: Light has come into the world, but men loved darkness instead of light because their deeds were evil. 20. Everyone who does evil hates the light, and will not come into the light for fear that his deeds will be exposed. 21. But whoever lives by the truth comes into the light, so that it may be seen plainly that what he has done has been done through God."*

† **Romans 1:24-32; Acts 7:42**—God will give us over to our sin to our own peril.

† **Psalm 81:11-12**—*But my people would not listen to me; Israel would not submit to me. 12. So I gave them over to their stubborn hearts to follow their own devices.* (See **Ezekiel 20:21-26**).

▶ **CONSIDER THIS:** David brought a punitive response from God upon his people that satan could never have done. The killing of those 70,000 Israelites illustrates this. What satan cannot do because God limits him, man can do on his own and yet unwittingly accomplish satan's purposes. This example demonstrates the intended outcome of the devil's **TACTIC: Let Self Reign,** and how it lets our self-will participate in its own ultimate destruction.

† **2 Thessalonians 2:9-12**—There can come a time when God will give us over to believe a lie due to our hardness of heart.

† **Proverbs 29:1**—*A man who remains stiff-necked after many rebukes will suddenly be destroyed without remedy.*

† **1 Samuel 16:14**—*Now the Spirit of the Lord had departed from Saul, and an evil spirit from the Lord tormented him.* If we ever force the Holy Spirit to depart from us, we leave ourselves wide open for demonic power.

† **1 Samuel 28:16; Isaiah 63:10**—There can even come a time when God leaves us and becomes our enemy.

† **Genesis 15:16**—God said: *"...for the sin of the Amorites has not yet reached its full measure."* Note: This verse seems to indicate that God gives a person or nation time and opportunity to repent. But when the appointed cut-off time arrives and there is still no response, they lose their opportunity and it becomes too late. And just like with Noah's ark, God will one day shut the door on any further opportunities and send His judgment **(Genesis 7:13-16).**

† **Genesis 6:5-13,17**—Satan was successful in using this tactic to bring the judgment of God via the great flood upon an entire generation who lived in Noah's day. Only eight people were spared!

B. The ultimate goal of satan is to bring God's judgment upon us as he already knows it is upon him. You can always trust the character of the devil—*"to kill, steal, and destroy"* **(John 10:10).** If the enemy is not successful in getting God's permission to assail His children as in the case of Job, he will try to tempt us to sin so we step outside God's hedge of protection and harden our hearts to God's corrective chastisement. **WE** then force God to send His final judgment upon us!!

▶ **CONSIDER THIS:** If an unbeliever rebels and resists the conviction of the Holy Spirit and God's Word long enough, eventually God gives them over to a *"reprobate mind"* **(Romans 1:28,** KJV **11:7-8).** *"Reprobate"* (*adokimos*) refers to a mind that has rejected God's rule and can no longer tell the difference between right and wrong. Likewise, a Christian who backslides into stage six disqualifies himself, and God can abandon him—giving him over to blindness and his depraved appetites.

☑ This ends our first session and the DVD content for Lesson 9. Continue on with the SQ&A.

STUDY QUESTIONS AND APPLICATION

1. Take a moment to examine your heart. Are you experiencing a time in your life where you can't sense God's presence, and/or it seems like He isn't there for you? Could it be that you have given into temptation and are in one of the stages of **TACTIC: Let Self Reign**? You may be under God's chastening hand. Ask the Holy Spirit for insight and if you have any unconfessed sins. (Refer to the sins on the chart in Lesson 7's SQ&A [#]1). Which stage on the chart below may you be in?

Six Stages of TACTIC: Let Self Reign

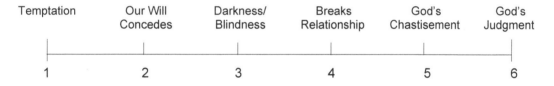

Temptation	Our Will Concedes	Darkness/ Blindness	Breaks Relationship	God's Chastisement	God's Judgment
1	2	3	4	5	6

A. If you have sinned, respond quickly to God's love for you by repenting so that the sweet fellowship with your Heavenly Father can be restored. Repentance enables us to begin anew.

B. Or, perhaps you are experiencing your Heavenly Father's hand as a Potter forming you, His clay. These trials are designed to mold His children into the image of Christ as well as to test and prove us in order for God's ultimate purposes to be accomplished for our good. These experiences are not necessarily chastisement for some sin we committed. Read the following Scriptures to discover more insight into God's molding and testing purposes:

• **James 1:2-4**   • **1 Peter 1:6-9**

• **1 Peter 4:12-16, 19**   • **John 15:1-2**

> ☑ When you are ready to begin this last session, continue on in this workbook for additional material about Battlefield #1 **not** on the DVD.
>
> ☑ I strongly suggest that the remainder of this lesson be done as a separate session.
>
> **Note:** For any number of reasons, you or your study group may choose not to proceed with the next session on maintaining sexual purity. Perhaps you don't believe it is a problem in your life, or you are not comfortable reading or discussing the topic, especially in your group. Let me encourage you not to skip over any part of this session. Leaders should know their people and tailor the study to their sensitivities, if necessary.
>
> Our culture is permeated with sexual material, which makes it nigh impossible for us to escape exposure to it. This material will help you to learn the ways satan so successfully uses it against us, to teach and warn your children, to help others in their struggle, or perhaps to equip yourself for something down the road. Pray and proceed as the Lord leads you.

Session 2
MAINTAINING SEXUAL PURITY

1. **The Gift of Sex**—God designed sex to be a wonderful gift to procreate the human race, and to bond one husband and one wife together in a loving marriage relationship. Often sex is looked upon as inherently impure but we need to remember that God created and designed it to be enjoyed. We were meant to have the greatest, penalty-free sex possible within this God-ordained boundary providing we don't commit sexual sin or conceive unwanted, unloved children.

   A. The Scriptures are very clear that having a sexual relationship outside of marriage is evil. God, knowing what is best for us and for the potential innocent child that might be conceived, has placed the prohibition of sex outside of marriage for our own good. Engaging in such self-destructive behavior will adversely affect other lives as well as hurt our relationship with God.

2. Satan uses sexual impurity to corrupt God's pure design for marriage; to destroy the family unit; to weaken the effectiveness of the church; and to ultimately subvert the nation.

♞ **TACTIC: Trap Them With Sexual Impurity**—The enemy will seduce you to choose to have sexual activity outside of marriage so as to bond your spirit with someone other than your spouse and Christ, so you walk in unfaithfulness and sin against your body, causing your holy temple to become an unclean vessel, and putting yourself at risk to contract a sexually transmitted disease—bringing you into a lose-lose situation. ◉ *Main Targets*: Your Body, Spouse, Family, and Church.

> † **1 Corinthians 6:13-20**—*...The body is not meant for sexual immorality, but for the Lord, and the Lord for the body... 15. Do you not know that your bodies are members of Christ himself? Shall I then take the members of Christ and unite them with a prostitute? Never! 16. Do you not know that he who unites himself with a prostitute is one with her in body? For it is said, "The two will become one flesh." 17. But he who unites himself with the Lord is one with him in spirit. 18. Flee from sexual immorality. All other sins a man commits are outside his body, but he who sins sexually sins against his own body. 19. Do you not know that your body is a temple of the Holy Spirit, who is in you, whom you have received from God? You are not your own; 20. you were bought at a price. Therefore honor God with your body.*

✝ **Acts 15:19,20, 28-29**—Abstaining from sexual impurity was one of the four main commands given by the church leaders to the early church.

✝ **1 Thessalonians 4:3-7**—*It is God's will...that you should avoid sexual immorality; **4.** that each of you should learn to control his own body in a way that is holy and honorable, **5.** not in passionate lust like the heathen, who do not know God...*

A. The enemy will lure a man by using a woman's dress, fragrance, body language, and words as bait. Many times she will use sex to make money or gain control over men, rather than to fulfill her emotional needs. Many a man has taken the bait, allowed their will to be worn down by her, and became entrapped with ruinous consequences. The devil knows what bait to use on us.

✝ **Proverbs 7:10-27** (NLT)—*The woman approached him, dressed seductively and sly of heart... **12.** She is often seen in the streets and markets, soliciting at every corner... **21.** So she seduced him with her pretty speech. With her flattery she enticed him. **22.** He followed her at once, like an ox going to the slaughter or like a trapped stag, **23.** awaiting the arrow that would pierce its heart. He was like a bird flying into a snare, little knowing it would cost him his life.*

✝ **Ecclesiastes 7:26** (NLT)—Solomon said:
I discovered that a seductive woman is more bitter than death. Her passion is a trap, and her soft hands will bind you. Those who please God will escape from her, but sinners will be caught in her snare.

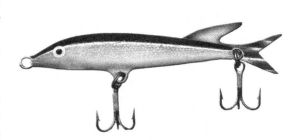

✝ **Proverbs 23:27-28** (NLT)—*A prostitute is a deep pit; an adulterous woman is treacherous. She hides and waits like a robber, looking for another victim...*

🐴 **TACTIC: Subvert Marriage and the Family**—Since God has designed marriage and the family to be the basic building block of a healthy society, the enemy will do all in his power to attack this institution to weaken it, pervert it, and cause its break-up, resulting in hurt, broken lives with children being vulnerable targets of destruction, and ultimately destroying the moral fabric of the nation. ◎ *Main Targets:* Marriage, the Family, and one's Nation.

B. Marriage and the family have many enemies. Some view them as the last obstruction to a new world where each individual is free of the restraint of tradition, morality, and responsibility. The sexual enemies include: adultery; fornication (i.e. premarital cohabitation); homosexuality and same-sex marriages; pornography; prostitution; incest; polygamy; etc. (see **Leviticus 20:10-21**).

Adultery

📖 **DEFINITION—ADULTERY**

The Greek word used in the New Testament is *moichos* which denotes one "who has unlawful [sexual] intercourse with the spouse of another."[3] Note: At the very heart of it is a betrayal of trust and misplaced affection—being unfaithful to the marriage vows made to one's spouse.

✝ **Exodus 20:14** (NLT)—*Do not commit adultery* (It is one of the Ten Commandments).

† **Matthew 5:31-32; 19:3-9; Mark 10:10-12**—Jesus defined its meaning.

† **Mark 7:20-23**—Jesus said adultery is evil and makes us unclean and polluted spiritually.

† **Hebrews 13:4** (NLT)—*Give honor to marriage, and remain faithful to one another in marriage. God will surely judge people who are immoral and those who commit adultery.*

† **Romans 7:1-3**—Marriage is a covenant that demands commitment to one man and one woman while each partner remains alive. The covenant ends when one dies and it frees the other to remarry. (Also see **1 Corinthians 7:39; 10-16**).

† **Matthew 5:27-30** (NLT)—Jesus taught: *28. "...anyone who even looks at a woman with lust in his eye has already committed adultery with her in his heart."* (Also see **Matt. 5:32**).

▶**CONSIDER THIS: Q:** When does an affair begin? Jesus taught not with the act itself but when we allow unfaithfulness within our sinful nature to sprout. We can form a strong emotional bond with that person in our heart. Our body and soul say, "I desire that person" but our spirit should say, "It is not God's will. Ask forgiveness and die to it." In order to win this battle, our spirit must overrule the fleshly appetites of our body and soul. And our love for God must win out over selfish desires. Furthermore Scripture exhorts us to meet our marriage partner's sexual needs. Depriving them of sexual intimacy, or failing to keep oneself attractive for each another, gives satan a dangerous opportunity to tempt them to look elsewhere to have their needs fulfilled **(1 Corinthians 7:3-5)**.

† **Proverbs 6:32-33**—*But the man who commits adultery is an utter fool, for he destroys his own soul. 33. Wounds and constant disgrace are his lot. His shame will never be erased.*

Fornication

📖 **DEFINITION—FORNICATION**

The Greek word used in the New Testament is *porneia* meaning "illicit sexual intercourse," and one who commits it is a fornicator (*pornos*).[4] At its very heart is a selfish gratification for pleasure, without commitment to the other person. It is like the indiscriminate mating done in the animal kingdom—a work of the flesh that "feels good"—giving a temporary "high." It is a perversion of God's original design for sex within the bonds of matrimony between one man and one woman. "Soul ties" develop through fornication as the two become one outside of marriage.

1. The sexual revolution is dealing a devastating blow to marriage and sex by undermining biblical commands about them. As a result, millions of people are now living together before marriage to test if their relationship will work out. This is perhaps the greatest enemy to marriage. After 30-years of observing the effects of cohabitation, studies show that in comparison to marriage: couples who live together have more conflict, instability, and less satisfaction with their relationships; they also have more insecurity with each other and with their children born into the illicit relationship; fathers are less likely to be involved with their children once the relationship ends; and it greatly increases the possibilities of a damaged or failed marriage. The divorce rate is currently 50 percent. These are just a few reasons for God's prohibition of fornication. Marriage is sacred and is the only safe place intended for a child to be raised with the secure, committed love of one father and one mother. Cohabitation is detrimental to everyone.

2. Satan tries to convince a young man that losing his virginity is manly but keeping it is weakness. He pressures a girl to lose her virginity to gain love and acceptance, and she is ridiculed if she doesn't.

3. Examples of other sexual perversions are: sado-masochistic practices (sexual pleasure derived from inflicting or receiving pain); homosexual behavior; child pornography; incest; rape, and bestiality (sex with animals—keep in mind that demons can possess animals). Also, those who fall prey to incest, rape, and other violent sexual abuse may encounter **Demonization**. Many of these victims enter the world of strip clubs, pornography, prostitution, and much worse.

(Please review the section in Appendix A, **Can Demons Influence Human Sexuality**? Look up "**Demonic spirits, and human sexuality**" in the index).

Homosexuality

📖 DEFINITION—HOMOSEXUALITY

It is the sexual desire for, and sexual activity with, another of the same sex. No scientific research will ever prove that there is a "gay gene" that predisposes one to be born with this sexual preference. We are all born with a sinful nature that contains the latent tendency toward all sin, including homosexuality. Homosexuals can and do change. It is a matter of choosing to pursue that change or stay in that lifestyle.

1. **The Institution of Marriage**—God's original design for humanity is marriage consisting of one man and one woman for life for the purpose of procreating our race **(Genesis 2:21-24; Matthew 19:3-9)** and producing godly offspring **(Malachi 2:14-16).** He wants this marriage relationship to be pure especially for the children who need the stability and role model of a father and the nurturing care of a mother. Any departure from the traditional family has severe detrimental effects on children and even their children after them. Adultery, fornication, and incest are just as evil as homosexual behavior and equally devastating to marriage and the family. God said that homosexual behavior is also *"detestable"* to Him **(Leviticus 18:22; 20:13).** It is a distortion of His original intent. Broken relationships with one parent or another can play a role in producing a homosexual bent in children as well as other forms of sexual impurity.

2. **Key to Survival**—From the beginning, the traditional family has been the building block of civilization. Whenever a people have violated the time-tested institution of marriage, they have not survived. History has shown that all great societies have crumbled when the traditional family is discarded in favor of rampant sexual immorality, which unleashed a self-destructive force upon the land **(Leviticus 18:26-28).** Countries that allow abortions, homosexual unions, etc., contribute to their declining population growth making them vulnerable to conquest.

3. **Origin of the Attack**—From a biblical perspective, this subversive attack on marriage and the family in our day originates from demonic forces. In America and other countries, the homosexual rights movement is one vehicle being used to subvert the family, the church, and the moral fabric of our nation. Radical homosexual activists use the legal system to gain unhindered access to schools and the like to propagate their lifestyle and indoctrinate our children—effectively bypassing parents and the church.

4. **What Is Legal Is Moral**—Behind the quest for legalization of same-sex marriages is the quest for giving this behavior legitimacy because people tend to believe that whatever is legal is morally acceptable. The eventual goal for many on the Left is to redefine marriage and

expand the traditional family to include other types of cohabiting situations—regardless of the sex, age, or the number of persons involved. This will then open the floodgate to other detestable practices forbidden by God like polygamy, marriage between blood relatives or to children, group marriages, and worse **(Leviticus 18:6-25)**. The legal fight to retain traditional marriage is critical for the survival of America. Leftist groups are replacing traditional values with their own via Congress and the courts.

5. **The Church Under Attack**—Sexual impurity is yet another front by which satan attacks and weakens the Church. Within the Church, the enemy uses this issue to bring impurity and division. Without, the radical homosexual agenda threatens the freedom of speech of those who believe homosexuality is a sin and who openly oppose it. Working through the judicial system, militant activists are using the same-sex marriage issue as a means in passing hate crime and anti-discrimination laws that will criminalize the Church's beliefs and activities and silence its voice. The same-sex marriage issue is being used to marginalize Christianity in society and ultimately bring upon it persecution. (See **"Persecution, 5-step pattern"** in index.)

6. **A Christian's Response**—We are to portray God's attitude toward homosexuals and other sexual offenders entrapped in these lifestyles. Hate the sin, but show love, sensitivity, and patience toward the person as we attempt to introduce them to Jesus. Gay and lesbian proponents must understand why Christians oppose their conduct: (1) The Bible says that God detests the behavior; (2) Historically, whenever same-sex marriages are allowed to flourish, a fatal blow is dealt to marriage, the traditional family, and in turn to that society; and (3) It results in a loss of religious freedom where the Church's voice is silenced and its beliefs and activities are criminalized by legislation.

THE ETERNAL CONSEQUENCES OF SEXUAL IMPURITY

1. If we don't repent, sexual impurity will disqualify us from entering heaven.

   † **1 Corinthians 6:9**—*Do you not know that the wicked will not inherit the kingdom of God? Do not be deceived: Neither the sexually immoral nor idolaters nor adulterers nor male prostitutes nor homosexual offenders.*

   † **Ephesians 5:3-6**—*But fornication and all uncleanness or covetousness, let it not even be named among you, as is fitting for saints... 5. For this you know, that no fornicator, unclean person, nor covetous man, who is an idolater, has any inheritance in the kingdom of Christ and God. 6. Let no one deceive you with empty words, for because of these things the wrath of God comes...*

   † **Revelation 21:8**—*"...the unbelieving, the vile, the murderers, the sexually immoral, those who practice magic arts, the idolaters and all liars—their place will be in the fiery lake of burning sulfur. This is the second death."*

▶**CONSIDER THIS:** Obviously, anything that encourages and feeds the desire to commit sexual impurity must be abstained from. Pornography is designed to be a fuel that feeds one's sexual fire, especially for men. Never feed a sinful desire—starve it, kill it—before it kills you. Don't let a spark become a blaze. Run from this trap to destroy you. Escape while you can. *"Flee from sexual immorality"* **(1 Corinthians 6:18)**. Note that this is the only time God permits us to retreat because He knows we men can't always make the right decision when confronted with pornography. But far from meaning defeat, victory can be attained through fleeing (abstaining).

† **Genesis 39:10-12**—*And though she* [Potiphar's wife] *spoke to Joseph day after day, he refused to go to bed with her or even be with her. 11. One day he went into the house to attend to his duties, and none of the household servants was inside. 12. She caught him by his cloak and said, "Come to bed with me!" But he left his cloak in her hand and ran out of the house.* (Also see **Judges 16:16-17; 2 Timothy 2:22.**)

🔪 **TACTIC: Wear Down Their Resistance**—Like constant dripping water on a rock, the enemy will persistently use a slow, wearing down process of our will until our resistance is overcome in order to get us to choose his agenda for our life. He also uses this tactic to subvert a nation. (See **Daniel 7:25**) ◎ *Main Target:* Your Will.

▶ **CONSIDER THIS:** For decades, little by little, the devil (through people) is changing the moral climate of America through a civil war of values—turning it away from our Judeo-Christian heritage.

THE EXAMPLE OF DAVID AND BATHSHEBA

Now let's learn how the stages of **TACTIC: Let Self Reign** played out again in another incident in the life of David in **2 Samuel 11:1** through **18:14**, as a trap was set for him to commit sexual impurity.

1. The Temptation stage:

    A. David had let down his guard and became idle **(11:1)**.

    B. A dormant, sinful desire was aroused through his eye gate: *"...he saw a woman bathing. The woman was very beautiful"* **(11:2)**.

    C. The struggle between right and wrong warred within him, but he pursued her further **(11:3)**.

2. David's Will Concedes to the sin:

    A. His covetousness prevailed as he rationalized and justified his decision—his choice is made: *"Then David sent messengers to get her. She came to him, and he slept with her."* **(11:4)**.

    B. The consequences began: *"I am pregnant."* **(11:5)**.

3. Sin causes Darkness and Blindness to set in:

    A. Self-preservation demands a cover up to "fix" the situation. David orchestrated a plan for Bathsheba's husband, Uriah (one of his bravest soldiers), to have sexual relations with her so that Uriah would think she had conceived his child **(11:6-13)**.

    B. The plan does not go as David had hoped, so he gave the order that indirectly caused Uriah's death: *"Put Uriah in the front line where the fighting is fiercest..."* **(11:14-26)**.

C. Then *"...she became his wife and bore him a son."* **(11:27).**

D. God in His love and mercy sent Nathan the prophet to confront David with his sins in order to dispel his blindness and bring him to a place of repentance. David's failure was that he *"despised the word of the Lord"* and elevated his own ways **(12:1-9).**

4. Sin <u>Breaks</u> his <u>Relationship</u> (fellowship) with God:

A. God was displeased **(2 Samuel 11:27b).**

B. It ruined his testimony for God—in his example to his people and his witness to the surrounding nations. *"...by doing this you have made the enemies of the Lord show utter contempt for the Lord."* **(12:14a).**

C. David came to his right mind too late but in time to repent and ask forgiveness. *"Then David said to Nathan, 'I have sinned against the Lord.' Nathan replied. 'The Lord has taken away your sin.'"* **(12:13)**. Hear David's repentant heart as you read **Psalm 51:1-19**.

5. The <u>Chastisement</u> of God came upon him (consequences also came into the lives of others):

A. *"...the son born to you will die."* **(12:14**; also see **12:10).**

B. *"...the sword will never depart from your house...Out of your own household I am going to bring calamity upon you. Before your very eyes I will take your wives and give them to one who is close to you, and he will lie with your wives in broad daylight. You did it in secret but I will do this thing in broad daylight before all Israel."* **(12:10-12; 16:21-23)**. Also see **Luke 12:2-3.**

▶ **CONSIDER THIS:** God will try to speak to us in a variety of ways: conviction, His Word, through another, etc. The tendency will be for us to hide and cover up our sin rather than deal with it. Once God has given us ample time to repent and we fail to judge ourselves, God in His love will allow our sin to be publicly exposed as part of the chastening process so that the shame perhaps will cause us to repent. Our eternal destiny is more important to Him than helping us to "save face." God expects His Church to adhere to the method by which we should administer discipline for believers who sin (see **Matthew 18:15-20**). The restoration of His erring child is the ultimate goal of this discipline. It also sends a message to everyone else that the church will not tolerate sin (as leaven) in its midst (see **1 Timothy 5:20**).

C. David's daughter Tamar, Absalom's sister, was raped by her brother Amnon who was then killed by Absalom. He usurped the kingship from his father David and was later killed—causing great heartache to David **(13:1** through **18:14).**

D. We can't dismiss the possibility that the sexual weaknesses of their son Solomon were passed on to him through his adulterous parents, while not absolving him of his responsibility, but which he could have overcome.

▶ **CONSIDER THIS:** If we quickly respond to God in repentance and obedience, God in His mercy and grace not only will forgive us and restore us to a close relationship with Him, but He can even make our legacy to read: *"I have found David son of Jesse a man after my own heart."* **(Acts 13:22).**

PORNOGRAPHY AND DRUG ADDICTION

1. The enemy uses two effective tactics in the pornography, alcohol, tobacco, and illegal drug industries. These tactics are also used to subvert a country by exploiting the legitimate grievances and social unrest of its citizens in order to topple its government (i.e. Marxism-Leninism). They are:

♞ TACTIC: Control and Enslave Them—The enemy will try to raise up and use people to find out the needs of a person or group, then inspire them to work to meet those needs with the intent of coming to power over that person or group in order to control and enslave them for profit or conquest. He also attempts to get us to sin more knowing that any character in our sinful nature is addictive and enslaving **(John 8:34).** ◎ *Main Targets*: Your Mind and Body.

2. Two other ways we use to control a person or group are through manipulation and intimidation. Manipulators use **guilt** in an effort to get the other person to do what they want. Intimidators use **coercion** to get their way. Both are effectively used in every phase of life—within the family, the workplace, and even in religion. Both are a work of the flesh.

♞ TACTIC: Get Them Addicted—The enemy will try to entice you to indulge in something that will give you a "high" for pleasure or as a means of escape from life's problems—knowing we will help him by finding reasons to justify its use. This often results in the chemical addiction of your body, which will enslave your entire trinity, and bring you under the control of evil forces. If you are a Christian, it further defiles the temple of the Holy Spirit, and he succeeds in making you a damaging, ineffective witness for Christ. ◎ *Main Targets:* Your Body, Mind, and Witness.

3. **Alcohol and Drugs**—Chemical dependency can cause us to lose everything we have. It is one of the most destructive weapons the devil uses. In 2003, addiction was the #1 public health issue in the United States.[5] These narcotics can put us into an altered state of consciousness. They also loosen inhibitions and impair our mind leaving us wide open to demonic power—many times without remembrance of the deeds we had done. How many crimes are being committed because someone has acted under the influence of alcohol or drugs? How many people are being killed in drug related automobile accidents? How many families are being torn apart as wives and children are terribly abused? Another drug is **nicotine**. Smoking kills more Americans each year than alcohol, cocaine, crack, heroin, homicide, suicide, fires, car accidents, and AIDS.[6] If you are a Christian addicted to tobacco products, pray, exert effort, and earnestly seek deliverance. The 12-step program is biblically based and is helpful in overcoming addictions. Visit www.CelebrateRecovery.com.

▶**CONSIDER THIS:** In very subtle ways believers can wrongly justify drinking alcoholic beverages. Take pain for example. I knew of a minister who was mightily used of God but due to physical and emotional pain, he began to use alcohol to get relief because pain medications weren't always effective. Gradually, addiction set in. One day, years later, he actually heard a voice say to him, "Now, I've got you!" He left the ministry and eventually died of alcohol-related causes.

    A. The illegal drug scourge that began in the mid-1960s came about deliberately as a weapon of the Cold War to weaken the United States (and other countries) by Red China and later by the Soviet Union. It was part of the Communist strategy at that time for the West.[7] The strategy was summed up by the late Dr. Fred Schwarz: "External encirclement plus internal demoralization leads to progressive surrender."[8]

4. **Behavioral/Psychological Addictions**—We also need to be aware of non-chemical dependency addictions such as cyclical obsessive/compulsive behavior that begins with a disturbed emotion, which causes self-destructive thinking leading to self-destructive ritual behavior and consequences. Examples of this type of addiction are gambling, workaholism, eating disorders, computer obsession, shopping, sexual addictions (i.e. pornography), etc. Our sinful nature, the enemy within, will enslave and destroy our lives if we allow it.

5. **Pornography**—The sexual revolution of the 1960s has opened a Pandora's Box, and one we will never get back into the proverbial "container." Since then, pornography has become increasingly more acceptable in our world. Consequently, pornography addiction has become an enormous, growing problem and tragically has invaded the church. As a result, we have exposed our precious children to sexual abuse and sexual predators—even to enslaving them through human sex trafficking. The adult entertainment industry is destructive to society because it devalues sex; dehumanizes women; promotes rape and violence; encourages child molestation; leaves families in ruins; provides false mindsets about sex, women, and children; and ensnares men in sexual addiction. Satan and his demonic forces are behind this insidious multibillion-dollar industry that is largely controlled by organized crime, and are the energizing force behind the scum of the earth who exploit and victimize innocent women and children. Where will it lead to? Sexual impurity will proliferate and eventually become one of the major sins of the future Tribulation period **(Revelation 9:20-21)**.

A. Driven by a voracious appetite for money, the sex industry is built on a vicious cycle of lies and deception. Business owners exploit and deceive the women who provide the titillation, the women exploit and deceive the men they perform for, and the men deceive themselves and their wives and family and keep the industry alive by their support.

B. The adult entertainment industry always seeks a victim. First, the person used in making porn; next the user; then the woman, child, or spouse who is victimized by the user. For example:

(1) Women are lured into the occupation by the money and to gain attention, but only to discover that they are manipulated and controlled by business owners, etc. who may physically abuse them (sometimes under the threat of death). According to Henry J. Rogers in his book, *The Silent War*, these women are kept trapped in a world where their only value is based on their body and their willingness to participate in degrading sexual practices in order to satisfy the lusts of men and make a profit for their boss. Outwardly, they portray an air of seduction, sexual fulfillment, and a deceptive smile as they exploit men's sexual weaknesses for money. But inwardly, most of them are full of the pain of abuse, mistrust, uncleanness, bondage, loneliness, hopelessness, and the hatred of men, as their lives are being destroyed from the inside out. Usually drugs and alcohol have to be used to cover up their revulsion of the activities demanded by their profession. And they may bathe often to try to cleanse themselves of the dirty feelings they carry within.[9]

(a) Many of these women were sexually molested as a child, which contributed to their entering the adult entertainment vocation. "As adults, these women now re-enact their childhood trauma by working in the sex industry…and are now…with people who will re-victimize them. They bond to the trauma that they experienced as children."[10] "Most women in the porn industry are trying to fill a void in their lives left vacant by their father."[11]—and many continually seek the approval of men that they have never received from their dads.

(2) Men who consume porn are lured into feeding their sexual cravings apart from God's way and insist on living in a fantasy world, not reality. They want to believe the girls are genuinely interested in them. The girls are—but mainly for their money! Many of these women have a deep-seated disgust for men that stems from either: their childhood where they may have been raped by a friend or neighbor; their father or brothers who may have had incestuous relationships with them; their bosses or pimps who continue to feed their hate by keeping them in bondage and revictimizing them; or their clientele who use them for selfish pleasure with no thought of their welfare or personhood. Men are seduced by the enemy into entering the brutal trap of sexual addiction.

C. Sexually oriented businesses also pollute their surrounding communities. Studies show that they spawn increased sexual assaults, crime, prostitution, and decreased property values.[12]

D. Sex was created by God to be wholesome and pure within the covenant of marriage, but satan and man have perverted it. In reality, pornography is intended to sexually arouse the viewer, reader, or listener to entice them to join satan's ranks of those who corrupt God's gift of love and sex. Why has satan done this? Pastor and author, Dr. Jack Hayford, offers this insight: "God has...given us this awesome power to create life and to do it at will. There is this one thing that has never been given over to satan—that he can't do, but you can, and that is he can't beget a human life. And he hates that creative gift in humankind. The primary reason why he assails us and lures and tempts mankind in the dimension of our sexuality is that he wants to pollute that image of God that we pass down to our children. Satan would like to establish a pattern of sexual impurity, beginning with you, and transmit it to your future generations."[13] What will you pass down to your children? Fathers, mothers, let it not be your sins and addictions! **(1 Kings 15:3)**

E. The following excerpts (in section E) are taken from the video, *A Drug Called Pornography*[14] (visit: www.harmfuleffectsofpornography.com): Pornography affects a man's body chemistry. "When we hear the word addiction, we usually associate it with a substance like alcohol or drugs. Yet pornography, even though it's not an ingestible substance like cocaine, seems to be used by many people in a compulsive drug-like way. In fact, many pornography addicts exhibit the same symptoms as drug addicts such as tolerance...dependence...and withdrawal..."

(1) Researchers tell us that neurotransmitters in our brain, such as endorphins, are responsible for all of our "highs" and mood-alterations. "Even when drugs are taken, it is these natural chemicals that are responsible for the high...Activities or events can also stimulate the release of these neurochemicals...creating the same high as cocaine...The pornography experience also triggers the release of powerful mood-altering neurotransmitters. The elements of addiction...that compel people to repeatedly engage in compulsive, pleasure-seeking activities are: arousal, relaxation, and fantasy."

(2) "Now of all the tools of addiction: drugs, gambling, sky diving, and television, sex addiction seems to combine these elements with more frequency and intensity than any other activity…and just as powerfully as the drug experience…. Another aspect of the pornography experience that adds to the addictive nature is the extreme emotional low, or shame, that directly follows the intense arousal. It is these two emotional extremes that create the addictive cycle…" The shame pulls him even farther into the addiction. The person becomes more and more isolated and alone. Their only relief is the addiction.

F. Dr. Victor B. Cline, a clinical psychologist and professor emeritus at the University of Utah and a specialist in the area of sexual addictions, stated that his research and experience showed that there are four stages that almost invariably occur to those who dabble in pornography:[15]

(1) **Addiction**—much like to alcohol or drugs regardless of the cost or consequences

(2) **Escalation**—After a while, it requires a rougher, more perverse type of material to achieve the same high, just like a drug addict needs larger doses to obtain the same initial effect.

(3) **Desensitization**—What was once thought inappropriate, repulsive, and immoral to the person eventually becomes acceptable and legitimate. The perception that "everybody does it" also plays a role. Pornography conditions men to explore sexual pleasure in areas they might not otherwise venture into. This smut trains us to view women and children as sex objects instead of as persons, who mainly exist to satisfy the sexual lust of men. It also falsely portrays women as always being turned-on sexually by whatever is done to them. These lies condition the user to the misinformation and desensitization process.

(4) **Acting Out**—The person now tends to act out their sexual fantasies on another that was viewed in the pornography. Reality and fantasy become blurred. This behavior also frequently grows into a sexual addiction. Driven now by lies and lust, men victimize women and children through sexual abuse and assault which would not have occurred if it were not for pornography. There is a strong connection between sexual abuse, sexual assault, and pornography. Two graphic examples are Ted Bundy, a serial rapist who killed 28 women, and Gary Bishop who murdered five young boys. Sex crimes and violent crimes increase dramatically wherever sexually oriented materials are available. Sexual abuse scars and ruins the lives of children who are plagued with low self-esteem believing the lie that they were at fault. Sexual addiction is not a victimless crime!!

G. Men use the fantasy world of porn for a sexual outlet for various reasons: as an escape from stress and boredom; to gain adventure and release; to boost male insecurities; to pursue the fulfillment of self-centered sexual fantasies; and as a weapon of retaliation against one's wife. Pornography destroys intimacy in marriage as it causes husbands to become dissatisfied with the sexual relationship with their wives. Their wives simply cannot compete. Porn presents a false view of sex and makes it devoid of love, relationship, and responsibility.

H. "What will the future hold for women who are raised in a society where they are dehumanized by a multi-billion dollar a year pornography industry that portrays them as sexually aroused by humiliation, exploitation, and molestation?"[16] What will it hold for our children? Pornography and the sex industry will not go away. If we don't rid it from our society, it will overtake and consume us! Will you allow the devil to "soften" your stand against pornography and eliminate you as an effective adversary against it in society?

▶**CONSIDER THIS: Believer, Beware!!** If you are involved with pornography, or are fanaticizing about sexual desires that the Bible condemns, you are opening yourself to demonic forces, giving them an invitation to wreak havoc in your life, your family, and your ministry. Is pornography the other woman in your marriage? Will you allow the devil to succeed in ruining all the work God has done in your life and family? *"I made a covenant with my eyes not to look lustfully at a girl"* **(Job 31:1).** Please read on.

SEXUAL IMPURITY—A LOSE-LOSE SITUATION

1. Allow me to continue to show you where the devil will take us if we persist on traveling down this road of sexual impurity. There are at least six (6) things that can occur when we have *just one* unlawful sexual encounter with another person—*and every one of them is harmful!!*

    A. **Contracting a Sexually Transmitted Disease (STD)**—One in five people in the U.S.A. has an STD with 19 million new infections each year (CDC, 2004). Scripture reveals that God has a built-in judgment and deterrent (like STDs) for violating His commands regarding sexual misconduct **(Roman 1:27; Proverbs 5:11-14)**. This indicates how serious the offense is to Him.

    B. **Pregnancy**—Children conceived out of wedlock tend to have less love and support from their parents. They may be aborted, abandoned, or raised mistreated and unwanted. The child's future life and their effect on society will bear the effects of this unloved environment.

    C. **Spousal and Family Victimization**—If married, satan will use your betrayal of trust to inflict emotional pain and rejection upon the one to whom you vowed your love and commitment. Wives of porn addicts experience betrayal, disgust, pain, and sorrow. For a married woman, sexual impurity is one of the deepest betrayals she can face as other partners are brought into the marriage relationship (through video images or in person), and she is robbed of what God intended to be hers. To make matters worse, you also run the risk of giving your spouse a STD! "In the wake of our perversion we leave a trail of tears from wives with scarred self-esteem and shattered dreams to sons who carry on our addiction into the next generation. And our daughters learn that the way to a man's heart is through seduction and sex. All because we surrendered to a lustful addiction..."[17] Think of it! You can enable the devil to successfully cause the death of your marriage; the breakup of your family; and your hurt, scarred children will become vulnerable to satanic attack. A man should be his family's protector, not their destroyer! We need look no farther than Judas Iscariot to see how detestable God views betrayal and unfaithfulness **(Matthew 26:24)**.

    D. **Betrayal of the Body of Christ**—**1 Corinthians 6:19** states that our body is the Temple of the Holy Spirit, who lives within us. Together we comprise the worldwide Body of Christ with whom we are one with each other. Pastor and author Dr. Jack Hayford stated: "Sex sin breeches trust with the whole Body of the church." When we walk in secret (or open) sexual impurity, we fail our brothers and sisters in the Lord and cause a spiritual disease and the leaven of sin to enter the church undetected. Our sin affects the overall level of godliness in the church. We also weaken the effectiveness of the Church because the godly character needed to do spiritual warfare is compromised. Our intensity in the battle against sexual impurity is weakened because of our tolerance and desensitization. A lust-filled Christian offers no threat to satan's kingdom. Then, when our sin is made known, we will disgrace God and injure unbelievers and believers for whom Christ died. "None of us have the right to breech this trust," Dr. Hayford says.[18] *"For none of us lives to himself alone and none of us dies to himself alone."* **(Romans 14:7)**

    E. **A Crippling Sense of Guilt and Condemnation**—Dr. Jack Hayford also stated that in his experience in pastoral counseling, he has observed that "sex sins produce a dimension of guilt in believers that is different from other sins. This guilt continues to occur long after they have been forgiven..."[19]

F. **We Bring Christ Into That Experience**—Jack Hayford goes on to say that when we give ourselves to another in sexual impurity, we force Jesus into that experience, too. He said, "In sexual immorality, a believer prostitutes the Body of Jesus."[20]

† **1 Corinthians 6:15-17**—*Do you not know that your bodies are members of Christ himself? Shall I then take the members of Christ and unite them with a prostitute? Never! 16. Do you not know that he who unites himself with a prostitute is one with her in body? For it is said, "The two will become one flesh." 17. But he who unites himself with the Lord is one with him in spirit.*

▶**CONSIDER THIS:** The Bible teaches that any sin brings forth death. Sexual impurity and addiction will eventually bring the death of your wife and children's love and trust; the death of your marriage; the death of your family; the death of your reputation, (resulting in shame and reproach for the rest of your life); the death of your job and career; the death of your witness for Christ (it is rare that one ever regains it); and possibly the death of your relationship with God culminating in *"the second death"* in the lake of fire. **With all that is at stake here, does it really make sense to bring upon yourself and your loved ones these horrific repercussions in exchange for a short-lived moment of selfish pleasure? Think about the consequences!** Admit to your problem if you have one, then confess your sin, repent, get help, and then begin the road to recovery. Sex addiction is a dark pit but one that God can help you climb out of. For help visit www.sexhelp.com. Don't lose all that you have to pornography or, for that matter, any sin. *"Do you not know that the wicked will not inherit the kingdom of God? Do not be deceived: Neither the sexually immoral..."* **(1 Corinthians 6:9).**

STUDY QUESTIONS AND APPLICATION

1. Which of these tactics are being used against you? If so, specifically how are you being attacked?

    ☐ Trap Them with Sexual Impurity   ☐ Control and Enslave Them

    ☐ Subvert Marriage and the Family   ☐ Get Them Addicted

    ☐ Wear Down Their Resistance

2. If you are (or have been) involved in sexual impurity, either by your choice or if done to you against your will, ask God to forgive you of each incident so that fellowship can be restored with your Heavenly Father. Then forgive that person and rededicate your body for sacred use. (See "Recapturing lost territory, five steps to" in index.) Repentance will enable you to begin anew. If you have committed sexual impurity and have not yet repented, can you identify which stage of **TACTIC: Let Self Reign** you are in on the chart below? I implore you to not continue to harden your heart and risk moving yourself into stage six. Get right with God today!

Six Stages of TACTIC: Let Self Reign

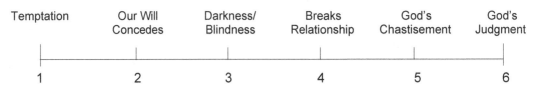

Temptation	Our Will Concedes	Darkness/ Blindness	Breaks Relationship	God's Chastisement	God's Judgment
1	2	3	4	5	6

3. Look up the following Scriptures that reveal shocking examples of spiritual darkness and blindness in stage 3. Notice the ways we humans can be so sure that what we believe is true, but in reality can be so wrong. We all have blind spots. The issue is not "if" we're blind, but "where." As you read through these examples, ask the Holy Spirit to reveal your blind areas.

John 1: 1-3, 10	Luke 23:33-34	Acts 8:1-3; 9:1-22; 26:9-18 Galatians 1:13,14,23; 1 Timothy 1:13-16	John 16:2-3	Matthew 7:3-5
Matthew 13:13-17	Matthew 15:1-14; 23:1-28 Luke 13:13-16; John 18:28-30	Psalm 10:2-11	Ezekiel 8:12; 9:9; Psalm 94:3-9	Micah 3:9-12

SUMMARY

Just as the Roman soldier put on the breastplate to protect his physical heart and organs, so the child of God is to put on the Breastplate of Righteousness to protect his or her spiritual heart and life. This lesson identified our first spiritual battlefield. It is the battle for control that rages between our sinful nature and our spirit. Satan knows that if he can get us to choose to allow any part of our sinful nature to take control it will break our relationship with God and, in turn, bring us under God's chastisement and hopefully His judgment. So he uses this strategy that we will call, **TACTIC: Let Self Reign**—the first of over 30 tactics. It can have up to six stages. To illustrate this tactic and to show its outcomes, we tracked two events in the life of King David: his numbering of Israel's military might and his affair with Bathsheba. These six stages are:

1. **Temptation**—Satan's design is to entice and allure us to disobey God. God tests us. Satan tempts us. He uses three sources of temptation. The **1A.** flesh (sinful nature); the **1B.** world (its elements are used as bait to appeal to our sinful nature), and the **1C.** devil, (who is able to use these things to stir up our sinful nature). We can be influenced to do something from the spirit world. In this stage, a part of our sinful nature is aroused and it pressures our will to give in and allow it to have control.

2. **Our will concedes**—The will now has two options: The first is to listen and submit to your spirit, thereby obeying the Holy Spirit's voice and rule in your life. If this is done the temptation attempt has failed. You have won this battle. Or you can listen to and give into your sinful nature and its powerful desire, thereby giving it permission to have its way. This choice brings a response from God, and sets in motion a future adverse harvest of consequences. We now step outside of God's hedge of protection. This sin produces a manifestation of satan's character in our life. In this stage, we allow the sinful nature to have control.

3. **Darkness and blindness set in**—A spiritual darkness comes over this area of our life and we walk in blindness to it—not being able to see things as they really are. This is the main reason why we can see another's failures when they can't see it in themselves. Spiritual blindness is possibly the worst "disease" we can have because its consequences extend beyond the temporal into eternity.

4. **It breaks our relationship with God**— Sin grieves the Holy Spirit within us and inflicts a blow to our spiritual life. Sin always brings forth death, which is separation from God's presence. We also block God's hand of blessing, as well as hinder the ability of our prayers from being heard and answered. If we are not careful, we will find ourselves in danger of trying to find a substitute for the satisfaction God's presence brought us—in the things of the world. The Holy Spirit will

convict us of the sin in order to bring us to a place of repentance so that our fellowship with Him will be restored. What was lost through disobedience must now be regained by obedience. The sooner we humble ourselves and respond, the better. But if we rebel and harden our hearts, we are responding just the way satan would want us to so he can move us onto the fifth and sixth stage.

5. It brings the <u>chastisement</u> of God—In this stage, our loving, faithful, Heavenly Father brings correction, not vindictive punishment. In effect, **WE** place the rod of discipline into His hand. **WE** force God to administer a range of loving and corrective measures designed to get our attention and bring us to a place of repentance (and/or to root the sin out of our lives). The discipline we receive as His children is many times self-inflicted—an experience we could have avoided if we would have judged ourselves and had not chosen to give into temptation. God will put as much pressure as it takes to get us to turn back—even if he has to break us. God wants us to be forever with Him in Heaven—not condemned with the world **(1 Corinthians 11:31-32).**

6. And finally the <u>judgment</u> of God—This is satan's ultimate goal. Prior to the temptation, he was not able to gain access to us due to God's protection and our obedience. So he creates a temptation hoping that we will step outside of that safety zone so he can move us toward this stage. When we gave in and sinned, he encouraged us throughout all these stages to harden our hearts and resist the Holy Spirit's chastening. A longsuffering God has tried using a range of measures, from gentle to severe over a long period of time, to bring us to a place of repentance and restoration. But repeatedly hardening our hearts and spurning His nurturing love, we rejected His rule in our lives. God has done all He can to get our attention to bring us to a place of submission and restore the broken relationship, and He knows we'll never repent. In this stage, we leave God with no other alternative but to give us up to our own way and "turn us over to our sin" that we have preferred over Him, and exercise His judgment upon us. The result—eternal damnation! Believer, avoid this stage at all costs!! Don't ever allow satan to succeed with this tactic!

The example of David and Bathsheba also illustrated the tactic above along with these strategies: The **TACTIC: Trap Them with Sexual Impurity** revealed satan's plan to corrupt God's pure design for marriage. Also, the enemy uses sexual impurity (like adultery and fornication) together with non-sexual adversaries in his **TACTIC: Subvert Marriage and the Family**. He knows that if he can weaken, pervert, and break it up, he will have destroyed God's design for the family as the basic building block of society, and in its wake cause broken, hurt lives and children as vulnerable targets of the enemy. In **TACTIC: Wear Down Their Resistance**, the enemy persistently tries a slow, wearing down process of our will until our resistance is overcome in order to get us to choose his agenda for our life. He also uses this to subvert a nation.

The devil also uses **TACTIC: Control and Enslave Them** so he can come to power over us. He also encourages us to manipulate and intimidate others to control them. This tactic is especially used in the pornography, alcohol, tobacco, and illegal drug industry, and is also used to subvert a country by exploiting the legitimate grievances and social unrest of its citizens in order to topple its government. **TACTIC: Get Them Addicted** works in tandem with it to get our bodies chemically dependent so we live in bondage, defiling our temple and bringing ourselves under the control of evil forces. The addictive nature of pornography affects a man's body chemistry, and along with alcohol, tobacco, and drug addiction, these weapons work extremely well for satan. They bring bitter self-inflicted consequences that are a lose-lose situation in our lives, in our families, and they weaken our effectiveness for Christ. As you can see, much of this invisible war is fought within us.

Lesson 10
THE BREASTPLATE OF RIGHTEOUSNESS:
The Things of the World vs. Our Love (Battlefield #2)

☑ Before starting the DVD:

In developing the ability to win this invisible war, we now explore the second battlefield we encounter. It is the battle for our love. Specifically, the devil uses the seductive things of the world system to bait and attract our love so as to compete with God for our hearts. To whom will you give this prized possession? Another aspect of the Breastplate of Righteousness is how it protects our spiritual heart—the seat of our affections. We will also learn tactics the enemy uses in this arena, and see how they were successfully used in the lives of King Solomon and Judas Iscariot. Keep in mind that there are three kinds of love: *Agapē* love in our spirit, and the two loves in our soul—*Phileō* in our emotions and *Eros* in our sinful nature (see Lesson 6). Pray for the Holy Spirit's illumination in this critical area. Again, please disregard the numbering of the tactics on the video. We will complete the study on the Breastplate in Lesson 12. The 2nd Qtr. Exam can be taken after this lesson.

☑ **DVD Users:** Watch Lesson 10 for an overview before proceeding further (26 min.).
☑ When you're through, pick up again at this point. Fill in the blanks from the Summary.

WHAT MAKES THE *"WORLD"* A FORBIDDEN PLACE?

† **1 John 2:15** (KJV)—*Love not the world, neither the things that are in the world. If any man love the world, the love of the Father is not in him.*

1. What are some reasons for God commanding us to *"Love not the world?"* What exactly is the *"world?"*

🐎 **TACTIC: Divert Their Love from God**—To divert your love and obedience that should rightfully go to God—to someone or something else via the things of this world, thereby displacing God as the center of your life.
◎ *Main Target*: Your Love and Affection.

A. Each day we live and work in the *"world."* It is our natural habitat. But we must remember that the world system is ruled by satan and has the imprint of his character upon it. Also, **Ephesians 2:1-2** teaches that following the ways of this world is the same thing as following satan, *"the ruler of the kingdom of the air."* Let's now review our definition of *"world."*

📖 DEFINITION—WORLD

The entire social, economic, and political order, ever since the fall of Adam and Eve, consisting of the daily interaction of humanity, where generally self-seeking interests are the law of life and the God of the Bible is excluded. Its system appeals to man's sinful nature, competing with God for the possession of our hearts, and whose pursuits in life are indifferent and in opposition to both the will and glory of God. **For an enlargement of what comprises the world system see Lesson 2.**

B. The world system is outwardly cultured, elegant, religious, and scientific, but within it is seething with political and commercial rivalries and ambitions. It is driven by demonically-inspired cravings for power and control. The world has a hatred for the true God and those who serve Him **(John 15:17-25).**

C. The entire unbelieving world has been blinded by satan, the false god of this world **(2 Corinthians 4:4)**. As part of satan's warfare against God, he works to divert the hearts of mankind from the things of God to the things of this world.

D. These things rival God and compete with Him for the possession of our hearts so as to displace Him as the center of our lives. When this occurs, we unwittingly give to satan what belongs to God in love, obedience, and worship through love of the world instead of love for God.

E. The believer's allegiance to God is tugged at from every direction. Now that we are *"born again,"* no idol should take God's place **(Exodus 20:3; 1 John 5:21)**. An idol is anything that becomes our main priority and receives more importance, love, and devotion than God does. It can be a person, possession, or vocation **(Ezekiel 14:3).**

F. The things of the world are active and vigorous in their appeal to the fallen aspects of our sinful nature. They have the potential to lead us away from God and His will for our lives.

G. The things of the world are also competing seeds in the soil of our hearts that choke out the seeds of God's Word—making them unfruitful **(Mark 4:18-19).**

H. Love for the world is incompatible and cannot co-exist with love for God. Once the love of the world takes the place of love for God, sinful tendencies and pursuits multiply until the believer is once again a part of the very world out of which he had been called **(2 Corinthians 6:14-18).**

† **James 4:4-6** (NLT)—*You adulterers! Don't you realize that friendship with this world makes you an enemy of God? I say it again, that if your aim is to enjoy this world, you can't be a friend of God. 5. What do you think the Scriptures mean when they say that the Holy Spirit, whom God has placed within us, jealously longs for us to be faithful? 6. He gives us more and more strength to stand against such evil desires...*

I. However, "love of the world" should not be understood as prohibiting the mere possession, appreciation, or the enjoyment of material things once God has His rightful first place in our heart **(Matthew 6:33; Ps. 37:4)**. These are gifts of *"...God, who richly provides us with everything for our enjoyment"* **(1 Timothy 6:17)**. There must be a balance. The prohibition is in the attachment for those things, which displace Him as the center of our lives and become the center themselves. It is one thing to possess something, but it is another thing to be possessed by them, for *"a man's life does not consist in the abundance of his possessions"* **(Luke 12:15).**

►**CONSIDER THIS:** The born-again child of God, who once belonged to satan's kingdom and was enslaved by the things of the world, is now a citizen of God's kingdom, the church—the world-wide Body of Christ **(Colossians 1:13).** For the believer, the world is an alien place—a bizarre, foreign land—incompatible with the things of God. Though we continue to live in this world system, we do so as *"foreigners and strangers"*—just as Jesus did when He visited it **(Hebrews 11:13-16; 1 Peter 2:11).**

> † **John 17:14-15** (GNT)—Jesus said, *"I gave them your message and the world hated them, because they do not belong to the world, just as I do not belong to the world. 15. I do not ask you to take them out of the world, but I do ask you to keep them safe from the Evil One."*

While we sojourn here, we are called to keep ourselves from being polluted by the world's behavior and philosophies **(James 1:27).** We are to be salt to the world to impede the spread of evil and corruption as well as shine as light in the midst of darkness so the true God can be seen **(Matthew 5:13-16).** Our mission is to rescue people from satan's kingdom, bringing them into God's kingdom through the new birth. It is also to influence and take back the areas that belong to satan and use them for God's purposes and glory (i.e. education, government, media, etc).

2. By which avenues does satan seek to ensnare our love and affection?

   A. The Bible states that the world makes its appeal to us in three ways:

> † **1 John 2:16**—*For everything in the world—the cravings of sinful man, the lust of his eyes and the boasting of what he has and does—comes not from the Father but from the world.*

> † **1 John 2:16** (KJV)—*For all that is in the world, the lust of the flesh, and the lust of the eyes, and the pride of life, is not of the Father, but is of the world.*

    (1) "The lust of the F_____"

      (a) Lust is an inordinate craving and desire for something forbidden by God. It is the hunger for the gratification of carnal appetites and sensual indulgences.

    (2) "The lust of the E_____"

      (a) It is the inordinate attraction to things forbidden by God coupled with a covetous desire for their possession—things which exert a powerful appeal to our sinful nature via sight.

    (3) "The P_____ of L_____"

      (a) The *"pride of life"* is the inordinate appeal to the latent desire to be like God, and is pursued through the acquisition of possessions, position, power, and status. Indications of its presence are: an exaggerated and unwarranted sense of self-importance; boasting and gloating over real or pretended virtues and achievements while disdaining others much better than ourselves; a selfish ambition for greatness and position and coveting status and status symbols; an addiction to the recognition and admiration of men; and a self-reliant, compulsive pursuit to "keep up with the Joneses."

† **Luke 16:15**—Jesus said: *"What is highly valued among men is detestable in God's sight."*

B. When God says *"love not the world,"* it is not that He is withholding something good from us but because they are harmful to us. When these things are present in our lives, they demand from us the love and obedience that is due to God alone. When left unchecked, they produce irreparable harm to our spiritual lives.

TACTIC: Peer Pressure—The enemy will attempt to exert peer pressure on you through close acquaintances—intimidating you to conform to the standards of this world system.
◎ *Main Target:* Our Will.

† **2 Corinthians 6:14-18**—*Do not be yoked together with unbelievers. For what do righteousness and wickedness have in common? Or what fellowship can light have with darkness? 15....What does a believer have in common with an unbeliever? 16. What agreement is there between the temple of God and idols? For we are the temple of the living God. As God has said: "I will live with them and walk among them, and I will be their God, and they will be my people."17. "Therefore come out from them and be separate, says the Lord. Touch no unclean thing, and I will receive you." 18. "I will be a Father to you, and you will be my sons and daughters, says the Lord Almighty."*

† **Judges 3:5-8**—Note the progression: toleration of evil leads to admiration which leads to conformity—*5. they "lived among;" 6. "they took;" they "served their gods;" 7. "they forgot the Lord."*

† **Romans 12:2** (Phillips)—*Don't let the world around you squeeze you into its own mold...*

Note: The devil's strategy to corrupt a society: Sinful practices seek public tolerance, then demand social acceptance, followed by the claim to special rights.

3. Our love is very special to God.

A. God is jealous for it and is not willing to share it with anyone **(Exodus 20:3-5; 34:14; James 4:5).**

B. To love God with all our being is the first and greatest commandment **(Matthew 22:36-40).** To be a true follower of Christ, there must be a willingness to give up any possession or relationship that competes for our allegiance to Him—even our own family.

† **Matthew 10:34-37** (NLT)—Jesus said: *37. "If you love your father or mother more than you love me, you are not worthy of being mine; or if you love your son or daughter more than me, you are not worthy of being mine."*

C. If our love for God diminishes, Jesus said we have *"fallen."* Love either grows or dies. Jesus said, *"For where your treasure is, there will your heart be also."* **(Matthew 6:21** KJV)

† **Revelation 2:4-5** (GNT)—Jesus said, *"But here is what I have against you: you do not love me now as you did at first. 5. Remember how far you have fallen! Turn from your sins and do what you did at first."*

D. Obedience is the proof that we love God **(John 14:23-24).**

WHAT IS LOVE FOR THE WORLD?

1. A love for things of the E_____ to the **neglect** of things that are A_____.

   † **Colossians 3:2** (KJV)—*Set your affection on things above, not on things of the earth.*

   † **2 Corinthians 4:18**—*So we fix our eyes not on what is seen, but on what is unseen. For what is seen is temporary, but what is unseen is eternal.*

2. A love for things that are T_____ to the **neglect** of things that are E_____.

   † **1 John 2:17**—*The world and its desires pass away, but the man who does the will of God lives forever.* (Contrast with **Genesis 25:29-34** and **Hebrews 12:16-17**.)

3. A love for things which are E_____ to the **neglect** of things that are I_____.

   † **1 Peter 3:3-4**—*Your beauty should not come from outward adornment, such as braided hair and the wearing of gold jewelry and fine clothes. 4. Instead, it should be that of your inner self, the unfading beauty of a gentle and quiet spirit, which is of great worth in God's sight.*

   † **1 Samuel 16:7**—*...The Lord does not look at the things man looks at. Man looks at the outward appearance, but the Lord looks at the heart.*

4. A love for things that are M_____ to the **neglect** of things that are S_____.

   † Read **Luke 12:15-21**.

   † **Matthew 16:26**—Jesus said, *"What good will it be for a man if he gains the whole world, yet forfeits his soul? Or what can a man give in exchange for his soul?"*

   † **1 Corinthians 7:31** (NLT)—*Those in frequent contact with the things of the world should make good use of them without becoming attached to them, for this world and all it contains will pass away.*

KING SOLOMON'S FALL

1. King Solomon, the son of King David and Bathsheba, ruled over Judah after his father David. This is the background, prior conditions, and the tactics used against Solomon that caused his downfall:

   A. God made him the wisest man who ever lived. **Q:** How could the wisest man on the face of the earth desert the true God and end up blinded and serving other gods? Let us see.

   † **1 Kings 3:5-13; 4:29-34**—Because Solomon asked in humility for God to give him understanding to rule His people, God appeared to him and gave him not only the gift of wisdom that he asked for, but blessed Him with what he didn't ask for—riches and honor.

B. Note the conditions surrounding Solomon's failure:

(1) Not while he was insecure, but after *"his kingdom was firmly established"* **(1 Kings 2:12)**

(2) Not during a time of conflict and danger, but in a time of peace and safety **(1 Kings 5:4)**

(3) Not during a time of need, but at a time of prosperity **(1 Kings 10:14-29)**

(4) Not when he was young and immature, but when he was older and experienced **(1 Kings 11:4)**

(5) Not before he had a relationship with God, but when he loved God **(1 Kings 3:3)**

(6) Not before God appeared to him, but after He appeared to him twice! **(1 Kings 11:9)**

▶**CONSIDER THIS:** Having prosperity and beauty can be unhealthy to our spiritual lives as they tend to lull us into an unwatchful, self-reliant state. Interestingly enough, according to Sir Alex Fraser Tyler, a Scottish jurist and historian, most great nations progress through eight stages—each lasting an average of 200 years. The third stage in this cycle is when liberty leads to abundance which leads to complacency, apathy, and eventually bondage **(Judges 3:8-15)**. When we're full, there is a danger of forgetting God as the source of our blessings, and thinking that they have come as a result of our own efforts. Actually, God has designed prosperity to work in a cycle: He blesses us so we, then, can bless others. The recipient then gives thanks and praise to God **(2 Corinthians 9:6-14)**. Selfishly hoarding our prosperity only brings us misery.

🐴 **TACTIC: Use Prosperity**—The enemy will visit you in times of spiritual and material prosperity with the hope of catching you with your guard down so as to make conditions right for you to choose to become self-reliant, so eventually you no longer remain dependent on God, thereby forgetting Him and His commandments. ◎ *Main Target:* Your Dependence on God; Pride; Selfishness.

† **Deuteronomy 8:6-20** (NLT)—*11....Beware that in your plenty you do not forget the Lord your God and disobey his commands, regulations, and laws. 12. For when you have become full and prosperous and have built fine homes to live in, 13. and when your flocks and herds have become very large and your silver and gold have multiplied along with everything else, 14. that is the time to be careful. Do not become proud at that time and forget the Lord your God, who rescued you from slavery in the land of Egypt... 17. He did it so you would never think that it was your own strength and energy that made you wealthy...*

† **Jeremiah 5:7** (NLT)—*I fed my people until they were fully satisfied. But they thanked me by committing adultery and lining up at the city's brothels.*

C. Solomon's failure originated in his disregard for God's word **(Deuteronomy 17:18-20)**. A valuable lesson to learn: knowing what to do is one thing, but to do it is quite another.

(1) Unscriptural Alliances—It began with the temptation to make a political marriage with the Egyptian Pharaoh's daughter—a marriage to an unbeliever **(1 Kings 3:1)**. He disobeyed God's command in **Deuteronomy 7:1-4:** *"for they will turn you away from following Me."*

(2) Unscriptural Resources—Then he gained possession of thousands of horses which brought him prestige and self-reliance—disobeying **Deuteronomy 17:14-16**. The result was he placed more trust and faith in himself when in battle than in the Lord.

(3) **Unscriptural Extravagance**—He made limitless expenditures for his own self-gratification and lived in opulent extravagance—disobeying **Deuteronomy 17:17b.**

(4) **Unscriptural Excess**—He gradually began to love many other foreign women. It was an easy move to take other heathen wives because he had already taken the first step by marrying Pharaoh's daughter. Eventually Solomon had 700 wives and 300 concubines (disobeying the warning in **Deuteronomy 17:17a**). This evil companionship turned away his heart after their gods.

† **1 Kings 11:1-4**—*King Solomon, however, loved many foreign women besides Pharaoh's daughter—Moabites, Ammonites, Edomites, Sidonians and Hittites. **2.** They were from nations about which the Lord had told the Israelites, "You must not intermarry with them, because they will surely turn your hearts after their gods." Nevertheless, Solomon held fast to them in love. **3.** He had seven hundred wives of royal birth and three hundred concubines, and his wives led him astray. **4.** As Solomon grew old, his wives turned his heart after other gods...* (Also read verses **5-13**).

▶ **CONSIDER THIS:** The moment a sinful temptation first comes to us, it must be repelled. We do this by first submitting to God, and then with His help, we resist it **(James 4:7)**. This first flat refusal brings strength and confidence for the next temptation. But if we give into it, it then becomes easier to take the second and third steps into sin, etc. The first refusal is critical!

🐴 **TACTIC: You're "Above the Law"**—The enemy will come to you during a time of God's special favor in your life to persuade you to think that you are "above" one of God's laws, and that somehow God will exempt and overlook your disobedience. ◎ *Main Targets:* Your Mind and Pride.

† **Numbers 32:23**—*...you may be sure that your sin will find you out.*

OUTCOMES OF THE TACTICS

What was the outcome of the **Tactic: Let Self Reign?**

1. **Temptation**—Solomon was demonically attacked during a time of peace and spiritual and material prosperity. With his guard down, conditions were right to become self-reliant. He was tempted to disobey God's word and make a political alliance with Pharaoh, king of Egypt—sealing it with the marriage to Pharaoh's daugh-ter, an unbeliever who worshiped false gods. His sinful nature was demanding control by bombarding his will. Solomon did not kill the desire but nurtured it. He was neither watchful nor cautious. Furthermore, he did not ask, "What does God's Word say about this?"

OD

cedes—His will gave consent and he chose to disobey God's Word and married . He further disobeyed God's Word in other areas: amassing to himself horses, silver etc.—allowing the enemy to invade other areas of his life and his earthly kingdom.

ness and blindness set in—These acts of disobedience opened the door to deception as began to do things he would never do in his right mind. Others saw how wrong he was but he couldn't see it. Solomon took more and more foreign wives who brought their gods with them. Gradually, before he knew it, the love he had for the Lord was diverted to his foreign wives and they further diverted his love to their gods whom he worshiped. In his blindness he built altars to the gods of his pagan wives that were used to sacrifice animals—and even the killing of human babies by fire to Chemosh, the god of Moab—among other detestable things.

4. **It breaks his relationship with God**—*"And the Lord was angry with Solomon, because his heart was turned from the Lord..."* **(1 Kings 11:9).**

5. **He brought the chastisement of God on himself**—Not only did he bring self-inflicted consequences from God upon himself but also on his children and his nation **(1 Kings 11:9-14, 23-26).** God tried to get his attention through severe measures, but Solomon, intoxicated with sexual pleasure and material possessions, hardened his heart. There is no record of his ever having repented.

6. **The judgment of God**—Did Solomon ever come to repentance and get right with God and make it to heaven? Perhaps the book of Ecclesiastes is an indication that he did. We will find out for sure in the next life, but today it should cause us all to be very alert and watchful.

▶**CONSIDER THIS:** The ultimate objectives of the devil were met by using a combination of these tactics, which produced tragic outcomes:

TACTIC: **Prosperity**—Catching Solomon with his guard down, the devil successfully tempted him to forget God and become self-reliant. Prosperity must be accompanied by humility. No matter how "big" we become, our task is to remain *"small in your own eyes"* **(1 Samuel 15:17; 1 Kings 3:7).**

TACTIC: **You're "Above the Law"**—The devil succeeded in convincing Solomon that God would exempt and overlook his disobedience. Even the king is not exempt from obeying the Word of God!

TACTIC: **Divert Their Love From God**—The devil was successful in diverting Solomon's love for God to his foreign wives and then to their gods—thereby displacing God as the center of his life—and in turn robbing God of Solomon's love and obedience.

TACTIC: **Let Self Reign**—Solomon took the devil's bait when tempted and chose to disobey God's Word and let his sinful nature take control in these areas. It plunged him into darkness and blindness—breaking his relationship with God which brought him under the chastisement and perhaps, the judgment of God.

JUDAS ISCARIOT'S FALL

1. Background

   A. Judas became a disciple of Jesus.

   B. Jesus' Father led Him to select Judas as one of His twelve apostles **(Luke 6:12-16).**

   C. The authority of the Holy Spirit to cast out devils and heal the sick was given to him (*"the twelve"*)—which he did like the other apostles **(Matthew 10:1-4).**

   D. Judas became treasurer of their group **(John 13:29).**

2. How was the **Tactic: Let Self Reign** used against Judas to cause his downfall?

   A. **Temptation**—He was enticed to steal money out of their treasury funds. The greed in his sinful nature was demanding control. Would he open the door of his will and give it access?

   B. **His will concedes**—His will succumbed to the temptation and allowed covetousness and greed to have its way. His love for God was being diverted to the love for money. He made a deliberate choice to steal the money for the first time.

   C. **Darkness and blindness set in**—Judas continued to steal in the very presence of Jesus!!

   † **John 12:3-6**—*Then Mary took about a pint of pure nard, an expensive perfume; she poured it on Jesus' feet and wiped his feet with her hair. And the house was filled with the fragrance of the perfume. 4. But one of his disciples, Judas Iscariot, who was later to betray him, objected, 5. "Why wasn't this perfume sold and the money given to the poor? It was worth a year's wages." 6. He did not say this because he cared about the poor but because he was a thief; as keeper of the money bag, he used to help himself to what was put into it.*

   (1) Satan got a foothold in Judas' life and proceeded to advance into other areas. The devil then planted the idea of betrayal into his mind. Notice that the idea had not originated with Judas and it was done prior to satan possessing him. Note also that the bait was thirty pieces of silver which appealed to his weakness of greed and love for money. His will conceded and it brought further darkness and blindness. The overpowering appetites of our fallen nature, if allowed control, could cause us (like Judas), to sell out the very Son of God! Finally, he chose to make a deal with the chief priests to betray Christ.

   † **John 13:2** (Phillips)—*By supper-time, the devil had already put the thought of betraying Jesus into the mind of Judas Iscariot...*

   D. **It broke his relationship with God.**—Things got so bad that satan actually **possessed** Judas right there at the last supper.

   † **John 13:27,30**—*As soon as Judas took the bread, Satan entered into him. "What you are about to do, do quickly," Jesus told him... 30. As soon as Judas had taken the bread, he went out. And it was night.*

(1) Judas was in such blindness that he led the chief priests and soldiers to where Jesus was in the Garden of Gethsemane and actually gave Jesus a kiss of betrayal—or, having been possessed by satan, was it the devil doing it through him?

E. **Then the chastisement and judgment of God**—Judas awoke and came to his senses too late.

✝ **Matthew 27:3-4**—*When Judas, who had betrayed him, saw that Jesus was condemned, he was seized with remorse and returned the thirty silver coins to the chief priests and the elders. 4. "I have sinned," he said, "for I have betrayed innocent blood." "What is that to us?" they replied. "That's your responsibility."*

(1) There is a point where our remorse alone can't rectify our deed. Judas had a form of repentance, but without faith. He may have believed his deed was unpardonable. So Judas returned the money to the chief priests, and lost that which he so coveted. The devil will always have us chase a deceptive mirage, to only lose it in the end.

✝ **Matthew 27:5-10**—*5. So Judas threw the money into the temple and left. Then he went away and hanged himself...*

(2) After having used him for a season, satan drove Judas to commit suicide—sealing his eternal fate in hell.

(3) Satan was successful in cultivating a misplaced affection in Judas' heart—diverting his love and obedience from God to money. In the end Judas brought on himself the judgment of God. Satan's warfare against God is ongoing and we are often caught in the middle.

✝ **1 Timothy 6:9-11** (NLT)—*But people who long to be rich fall into temptation and are trapped by many foolish and harmful desires that plunge them into ruin and destruction. 10. For the love of money is at the root of all kinds of evil. And some people, craving money, have wandered from the faith and pierced themselves with many sorrows.*

▶**CONSIDER THIS:** Judas Iscariot asked the chief priests, *"What will you give me if I hand Jesus over to you?"* **(Matthew 26:14** GNT**)**. It's been said that "everyone has a sell-out price." Judas sold out his Lord and his inheritance in the Kingdom of God for 30 pieces of silver (approximately $20). Examples of others who "sold out" are Esau, who sold his birthright for food **(Hebrews 12:16-17),** and Demas, who deserted Paul, leaving God's call into the ministry for the love of the world **(2 Timothy 4:10).**

Evangelist Steve Hill challenged those in his Cincinnati, Ohio Crusade: "What is your secret, spiritual sell-out price?" He said many times it remains a secret until the day of testing and crisis. Steve asks, "Is your faith for sale? What would someone have to give you to quit serving God and from following His call on your life? Is it sex, drugs, money, position, or someone hurting you?"[1] Whatever the devil is offering you, like Judas, you will lose it all in the end and weep bitter tears. Nothing comes close to what Christ has offered you: the price of His outpoured life so you can be forgiven, and the opportunity to become a child of God and inherit the inexplicable glories of the Kingdom of God. Keep your focus on Christ and don't sell out!

✝ **Galatians 6:14**—*... the cross of our Lord Jesus Christ, through which the world has been crucified to me, and I to the world.*

> ☑ This ends the DVD content for Lesson 10.
> ☑ Continue on with the Study Questions and Application and the Sun

STUDY QUESTIONS AND APPLICATION

1. Ask the Holy Spirit to reveal to you anyone or anything that you may love more than God

   (Note: When we choose to love and worship God as our Creator and Father, He receives one of th main blessings for which He created us. Free will must exist for this to occur.)

2. Do you find yourself loving the things of the world more than you love the things of God? Within each category below, identify the critical things you are neglecting that should be getting your prime attention.

   A. Eternal things vs. Transitory things: _____

   B. Internal things (our spirit) vs. External things: _____

   C. Spiritual things vs. Material things: _____

3. Is there any type of temptation you can identify that satan is currently using to lure you? Are you resisting, or has your will already conceded to it?

4. Ask the Holy Spirit to reveal if any of the following tactics are being used against you. If so, within each of these tactics, which of the six stages of **Let Self Reign** may you be in?

   ☐ A. Divert their love from God   ☐ C. Prosperity

   ☐ B. Peer pressure   ☐ D. You're "Above the Law"

5. We can be an invaluable help to each other by pointing out sins we see in each other's lives. Courageously give permission to a few select friends to tell you of any sins they might see in your life that you don't see. When you are confronted, do not be defensive or offended. See it as an expression of God's love through that friend and deal with it obediently through prayer and obedience to God. If you are one of those friends selected, do so with much love, prayer, wisdom, timing, and sensitivity.

6. Read **Acts 4:34–5:11.** Meditate on the way satan tempted Ananias and Sapphira. Describe what occurred to them in each of the six steps of **Tactic: Let Self Reign** and how they brought themselves under God's judgment. Then contrast them with the believers in **Hebrews 10:34.** What do you think it would take for a believer to get from the mindset of Ananias to the mindset of those in Hebrews 10:34?

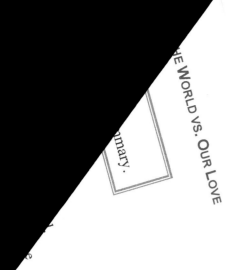

SUMMARY

… of Righteousness can protect our spiritual heart—the seat … field #2—the battle over who will get our love, God or … warfare against God, he uses the seductive things of the … in order to compete with God for its possession. He uses … **God** by trying to divert our love and obedience that … else via the things of the world in order to displace God … give this prized possession?

… natural habitat, God commands us to *"Love not the world"* and … it. It is not because He wishes to withhold something good from us, but … they rival God and compete with Him for the possession of our hearts. The evil characteristics in our sinful nature are awakened by the things of the world, and are used as the devil's bait in tempting us to disobey God's Word. However, we need to maintain a balanced view. *"Love not the world"* should not be understood as prohibiting the mere possession, appreciation, or the enjoyment of material things when God has first place in our lives. These are gifts of *"God, who richly provides us with everything for our enjoyment."* It is one thing to possess something but quite another to be possessed by something.

There are three ways satan uses the world to make its appeal to our fallen nature in attempting to ensnare our love: the lust of the **2A(1)** <u>flesh</u>, the lust of the **2A(2)** <u>eyes</u>, and the **2A(3)** <u>pride</u> of <u>life</u>. He uses the **TACTIC: Peer Pressure** to try to coerce us through close acquaintances to conform to the standards of this world. The devil will also use the **TACTIC: Use Prosperity**—visiting us in times of spiritual and material prosperity hoping to catch us with our guard down so as to make conditions ideal for us to choose to become self-reliant—forgetting God and His commands. Satan will even use the **TACTIC: You're "Above The Law"**—coming to us during a time of God's special favor in our life to try to convince us that somehow God will exempt and overlook our disobedience. He successfully used all these tactics on Solomon (including **TACTIC: Let Self Reign**), which precipitated his downfall.

Our love is very, very special to God and He is jealous for it. He is unwilling to share it with anything or anyone. Jesus said that to love God is the greatest commandment. Our love is measured by our obedience to God, and love either grows or dies. What exactly is love for the world? It is having a love for the things that are: of the **1.** <u>earth</u>, **2.** <u>transitory</u>, **3.** <u>external</u>, and **4.** <u>material</u>; to the **neglect** of things which are: **1.** <u>above</u>, **2.** <u>eternal</u>, **3.** <u>internal</u>, and **4.** <u>spiritual</u> respectively. These are like a gauge that indicates where our affections lie. God must always have first place in our hearts. Beware of those things satan uses to rob God through misplaced affection as he did with Judas Iscariot, who displaced God from the center of his life and brought himself under God's judgment. It is said that "everyone has a sell-out price." Nothing comes close to what Christ has offered us so let's keep our focus on Him and don't sell out!

The world has become an alien place for the *"born again"* believer—a bizarre, foreign land incompatible with the things of God. Though we must continue to live in this world system, we do so as *"foreigners and strangers"*—just as Jesus did when He visited it. This world is not our home. While we sojourn here, we are exhorted to keep ourselves *"...from being polluted by the world"* **(James 1:27).**

Lesson 11
THE HELMET OF SALVATION: Our Mind (Battlefield #3)

☑ Before starting the DVD: The first battlefield is between our sinful nature and our spirit. The second battlefield is the world system's attempt to get possession of our love. A third battlefield occurs in our mind, and it is in the heat of the conflict. In developing the ability to win this invisible war, we will learn how our mind was adversely affected by Adam's fall, and how it can be influenced by beings in the spirit realm. Also another tactic will be presented, and we will identify the types of blows that are delivered by the enemy to our minds. We will conclude this study on the Helmet in Lesson 12 by dealing with how to get victory in our thought life. Now to underscore the critical importance of the thoughts we entertain, I quote Frank Outlaw:

> Watch your thoughts; they become words.
> Watch your words; they become actions.
> Watch your actions; they become habits.
> Watch your habits; they become character.
> Watch your character; it becomes your (eternal) destiny.

☑ **DVD Users:** Watch Lesson 11 for an overview before proceeding further (26 min.).
☑ When you're through, pick up again at this point. Fill in the blanks from the Summary.

Our brain is part of our physical body, but our mind is in the realm of our soul which will continue to live after our body dies. Our conscience is in our spirit and is God's built-in moral law within us. Our mind is an awesome work of creation—no computer can compare to it. Just consider its capabilities (also see Lesson 6):

A. It understands and processes knowledge.

B. It has imagination.

C. It can reason.

D. It can plan with foresight.

E. It has a belief system.

F. It has memory recall.

G. It has attitudes.

H. It has motive.

HOW OUR MIND WAS AFFECTED BY "THE FALL"

1. Ever since Adam and Eve sinned in the garden, our fallen nature wars against what we know to be morally right (our conscience) and it tries to get the mind to think like it does and to live for self-centered interests. For example, the apostle Paul tells us of his personal struggle with this battlefield:

    † **Romans 7:22-25** (NLT)—*I love God's law with all my heart. **23.** But there is another law at work within me that is at war with my mind. This law wins the fight and makes me a slave to the sin that is still within me. **24.** Oh, what a miserable person I am! Who will free me from this life that is dominated by sin? **25.** Thank God! The answer is in Jesus Christ our Lord. So you see how it is: In my mind I really want to obey God's law, but because of my sinful nature I am a slave to sin.*

2. In addition, the fall adversely affected our minds in the following ways. When we were born:

    A. Our mind was in a somewhat D_____ state.

    † **Ephesians 4:17-18**—*So I tell you this, and insist on it in the Lord, that you must no longer live as the Gentiles do, in the futility of their thinking. **18.** They are darkened in their understanding and separated from the life of God because of the ignorance that is in them due to the hardening of their hearts.*

    † **John 12:46** (NLT)—*Jesus said: "I have come as a light to shine in this dark world, so that all who put their trust in me will no longer remain in the darkness."*

    † **Acts 26:17-18**—*The risen Christ said to Saul on the Damascus Road, "I am sending you **18.** to open their eyes and turn them from darkness to light, and from the power of Satan to God, so that they may receive forgiveness of sins…"*

    B. Our mind was in a B_____ state.

    † **2 Corinthians 4:3-4** (NLT)—*If the Good News we preach is veiled from anyone, it is a sign that they are perishing. **4.** Satan, the god of this evil world, has blinded the minds of those who don't believe, so they are unable to see the glorious light of the Good News that is shining upon them. They don't understand the message we preach…*

    † **2 Corinthians 3:14-16** (NLT)—*But the people's minds [the Jews] were hardened, and even to this day whenever the old covenant is being read, a veil covers their minds so they cannot understand the truth. And this veil can be removed only by believing in Christ. **15.** Yes, even today when they read Moses' writings, their hearts are covered with that veil, and they do not understand. **16.** But whenever anyone turns to the Lord, then the veil is taken away.*

    C. Our mind could not fully K_____ G_____ on its own.

    † **1 Corinthians 1:20-21** (NLT)—*So where does this leave the philosophers, the scholars, and the world's brilliant debaters? God has made them all look foolish and has shown their wisdom to be useless nonsense. **21.** Since God in his wisdom saw to it that the world would never find him through human wisdom, he has used our foolish preaching to save all who believe.*

▶**CONSIDER THIS:** An incredible irony exists. It is that we humans, through analytical thinking and reasoning, can comprehend the complexities of all the sciences insomuch as we can do unbelievable things like organ transplants and land people on the moon. However, when we apply this same faculty of reason to searching for the true God, His ways, and other spiritual matters, our unregenerate mind **cannot** be trusted. It will lead us to a wrong conclusion practically every time and keep us in ignorance about the truth. This is why someone can study all the wonders of nature and still not believe in the God who created them. Human reasoning and wisdom are no substitute for divine revelation, which must be accepted by faith—even if it defies logic.

(1) We know things in one of two places: in our mind or in our spirit. We receive revelation knowledge about the things of God in our spirit. Our mind receives it indirectly.

† **Ephesians 1:17-18**—*that God...may give you the Spirit of wisdom and revelation, so that you may know him better...that the eyes of your heart may be enlightened.*

† **Luke 24:45**—*Then [Jesus] opened their minds so they could understand the Scriptures.*

(2) The Holy Spirit within us will reveal the knowledge of God and His ways. God has His own school and has even provided His own personal Tutor!

† **John 7:15**—*The Jews were amazed and asked, "How did this man [Jesus] get such learning without having studied?"* (Also see **Matthew 13:54.**)

† **Acts 4:13**—*When they saw the courage of Peter and John and realized that they were unschooled, ordinary men, they were astonished and they took note that these men had been with Jesus.*

† **1 John 2:27** (NLT)—*But you have received the Holy Spirit, and he lives within you, so you don't need anyone to teach you what is true. For the Spirit teaches you all things, and what he teaches is true—it is not a lie. So continue in what he has taught you, and continue to live in Christ.*

† **John 16:13-15**—Jesus said, *"But when he, the Spirit of truth, comes, he will guide you into all truth... 15. ...the Spirit will take from what is mine and make it known to you."*

† **Proverbs 1:7**—*The fear of the Lord is the beginning of knowledge...*

D. Our mind H_____ us from P_____ God and receiving His best for our lives.

† **1 Corinthians 2:14**—*The man without the Spirit does not accept the things that come from the Spirit of God, for they are foolishness to him, and he cannot understand them, because they are spiritually discerned.*

(1) When our mind rationalizes spiritual things, we run the risk of it producing skepticism resulting in unbelief.

(2) Generally speaking, man's sin-tainted intelligence will lead him away from God. Knowledge abounds today like no other time in history and much of it is making our world a better place, but it's not leading us to knowledge of the true God.

(3) Our natural mind is hostile to the things of God.

† **Romans 8:5-7**—*Those who live according to the sinful nature have their minds set on what that nature desires; but those who live in accordance with the Spirit have their minds set on what the Spirit desires.* **6.** *The mind of sinful man is death, but the mind controlled by the Spirit is life and peace,* **7.** *because the sinful mind is hostile to God. It does not submit to God's law, nor can it do so.*

† **Colossians 1:21**—*Once you were alienated from God and were enemies in your minds because of your evil behavior.*

▶ **CONSIDER THIS:** We must continually bring our soul and body into subjection to our spirit, or they could cause us to miss a God moment. Take Peter for example. After fishing all night without success, Jesus told him to let down his nets **(Luke 5:4-9).** His body was saying, "I'm too tired." His emotions may have been saying, "I'm too frustrated" or "I'll risk embarrassment." His mind could have reasoned, "I know these waters, I've fished them all my life." But faith in Christ caused his spirit to obey. And a great catch of fish resulted that broke their nets and almost sunk their boats!

E. Our mind leads us A_____ from T_____.

† **Proverbs 16:25**—*There is a way that seems right to a man, but in the end it leads to death.*

† **Matthew 7:13-14**—Jesus said, *"Enter through the narrow gate. For wide is the gate and broad is the road that leads to destruction, and many enter through it.* **14.** *But small is the gate and narrow the road that leads to life, and only a few find it."*

† **Proverbs 3:5**—*Trust in the Lord with all your heart and lean not on your own understanding.*

† **2 Corinthians 11:3-4**—*But I am afraid that just as Eve was deceived by the serpent's cunning, your minds may somehow be led astray from your sincere and pure devotion to Christ...*

(1) Our minds are prone to accept error and deception. We are not to rely on our "unrenewed" mind to give us assurances concerning truth. It will lead us astray and cause us to believe in a lie. We can be sincere in our beliefs—but sincerely mistaken; however, our built-in conscience will try to guide us. This is why it is so important that the *"born-again"* believer have their mind saturated with God's Word so it can be *"renewed."* More will be said about this in Lesson 12.

† **Romans 12:2** (KJV)—*And be not conformed to this world: but be ye transformed by the renewing of your mind, that ye may prove what is that good, and acceptable, and perfect, will of God.*

† **Ephesians 4:22-23**—*You were taught to...put off your old self...* **23.** *...to be made new in the attitude of your minds.*

(2) Our concept of truth and the resulting philosophy we adopt will determine our actions and lifestyle. Thus, what we believe in is critical, for it will determine where we spend eternity when we leave our bodies at death.

3. What are the three sources from which we get our thoughts and ideas?

    A. From O____ own T_____ within us—gained from learning and experience.

    B. From other H_____ B_____—written or spoken.

    C. From the S_____ W_____ (God, angels, and evil spirits).

CAN OUR THOUGHTS BE KNOWN OR INFLUENCED BY SPIRIT BEINGS?

1. God is a spirit who is omnipresent and omniscient (all-knowing) and He is the **only one** who knows **all** that we think, say, and do. In fact, all of our words and thoughts—past, present, and future—are already fully known to Him. The Holy Spirit can also impress us with His thoughts.

    † **Ezekiel 11:5** (NLT)—*"...This is what the Lord says...I know every thought that comes into your minds..."* (Also see **Psalm 139:1-4.**)

2. Both righteous angels and fallen angels are neither omnipresent nor omniscient; therefore, they cannot know our thoughts. Neither do people who have died. However, this angelic class does have the following capabilities:

    A. The angelic realm has the ability to hear our conversations, and observe our actions and responses to everyday situations—thereby knowing our strengths and shortcomings. Fallen angels can catalog our weaknesses to later use against us.

    B. Since we too are spirit beings, there is a very good possibility that they can "read" the mood or disposition of our soul and spirit (but not our thoughts). For example, they probably can detect when we are sad or angry but don't know the thought that caused the emotion—unless they observed it by what we did or said.

▶**CONSIDER THIS:** In light of this, we should not be overly concerned about deciding what thoughts, etc. we should openly divulge. However, we should be aware and exercise care.

    C. Satan and demonic spirits can influence our thinking from the spirit world by offering suggestions and ideas to us—insomuch as we actually think them to be our own thoughts. However, we still have the power of choice to act upon them or not.

    † **John 13:2** (Phillips)—*By supper-time, the devil had already put the thought of betraying Jesus into the mind of Judas Iscariot...*

    † **Acts 5:3** (KJV)—*But Peter said, "Ananias, why hath Satan filled thine heart to lie to the Holy Ghost, and to keep back part of the price of the land?"* Note: Imagine receiving the subtle thought suggested to Ananias, "Keep back part of it for yourself."

    † **1 Chronicles 21:1**—The idea to take a census of Israel was given to David by satan.

    † **Matthew 16:21-23**—By satan's prompting, Peter rebuked Jesus to deter Him from the cross.

† **1 Kings 22:19-24**—*22. ...And the* [evil] *spirit replied, "I will go out and inspire all Ahab's prophets to speak lies."*

(1) Those in the occult, such as psychics, fortune-tellers, etc., unknowingly listen to demonic spirits as these spirits convey information to them about another person. The details they receive cannot be learned, known, or acquired in any other way. The occultist, in turn, tells their client who becomes amazed by the accuracy of the information and then believes and follows the advice given. That person has just been led astray to believe a lie.

(2) Many false religions and false doctrines in the church are originated by demonic spirits who convey them to humans who become the founders of these religions and promoters of these teachings. (Also see Lesson 15—**False Teachings and Doctrinal Errors.**)

† **1 Timothy 4:1-2**—*The Spirit clearly says that in later times some will abandon the faith and follow deceiving spirits and things taught by demons. 2. Such teachings come through hypocritical liars, whose consciences have been seared as with a hot iron.*

(3) The same is true about those who propagate false philosophies and worldviews inspired by demonic spirits who gain control and influence and lead a culture astray.

† **Isaiah 19:11-15** (NKJV)—*Pharaoh's wise counselors give foolish counsel... 13. They have also deluded Egypt... 14. a perverse spirit* [is] *in her midst; And they have caused Egypt to err...*

† **Isaiah 5:20** (NASB)—*Woe to those who call evil good, and good evil; Who substitute darkness for light and light for darkness; Who substitute bitter for sweet and sweet for bitter!*

(a) One example of this is **evolution**. I personally believe the theory of evolution originated in the mind of satan before he communicated it to man. The strategy is insidious: If evolution is true, then there was no creation of Adam and Eve in God's image and likeness, no fall of Adam and Eve, and no such thing as sin. If there is no sin, there is no need for the virgin birth to bring forth a savior to die to save mankind from eternal judgment. Evolution undercuts the very bedrock of the Christian faith and is designed by demons to neutralize the message of the Gospel. Dr. D. James Kennedy once said that "evolution is the basis for every anti-Christian 'ism' that has ever come down the pike since Darwin's time." This includes Marxism/Leninism (communism), Nazism, Fascism, and Humanism.[1] It is an attempt by satan to make mankind think that the human race is moving toward perfection by their efforts—apart from God and in the place of God.

(4) One can only wonder how much knowledge mankind has received from the spirit world about the sciences, technology, etc., which humanity thought was his own. Certainly, we have discovered a lot of it in and of ourselves. And God, out of His love, has given to mankind revelation knowledge in some of these areas based on the laws of the universe that He created. But has it all been given to man by God? Satan and fallen angels were created with great intelligence that became corrupted, and yet was retained when they rebelled and sinned **(Ezekiel 28:12,17)**. It would be interesting to know how much information, if any, has been passed along to mankind by evil spirits that has contributed to building up satan's kingdom here on earth.

(5) Here are some profound thoughts to consider from Dr. C.S. Lovett in his insightful book, *"Dealing With the Devil"*[2] (www.cslovettbooks.com):

(a) "...an idea strikes the mind...since it comes from within, you never suspect an OUTSIDER has anything to do with it. It appears to be your own idea, hence you are not suspicious. Therefore, you are inclined to entertain it. You let it linger in your imagination. Rejecting ideas that pop into the mind is a discipline." (Lovett, p. 56)

(b) "They arrive in our minds as though they were the truth." (Lovett, p. 55)

(c) "Since the ideas come from within us, we naturally view them AS OUR OWN...therefore Christians need the discipline of examining their thought-life and watching for satan's influences." (Lovett, p. 60)

(d) "The extent to which he can influence the thoughts of people, is the extent to which he can control them." (Lovett, p. 33)

(e) "Satan's control is by suggestion...by the power of suggestion...and in the hands of someone expert in human weakness, it is an awesome power...man is a suggestive being. He responds to suggestion." (Lovett, p. 54)

(f) "The power of suggestion is one of the greatest forces motivating people. Satan is a master at it. His knowledge of human weakness allows him to design suggestions like no other. They not only correspond to our weaknesses, but promise to satisfy your longing; hence they are almost irresistible until their source is recognized." (Lovett, p. 60)

(g) "Make a suggestion to a man which matches his passions and appeals to his weaknesses, do it at the right moment and he is likely to buy it every time." (Lovett, p. 54)

(h) "Man is free to respond to these suggestions or refuse them." (Lovett, pg. 124)

(i) "Satan controls the Christian by bombarding the thought-life with suggestions which appeal to SELF interest. SELF is the disguise for satanic activity in the Christian's mind." (Lovett, p. 124)

(j) "The only way to capture a man is to get him to think like you do. Ideas capture men, not weapons. Win a man's mind and you have him. Capture his thoughts and you control him. If you can find a way to get your ideas inside another so that he thinks like you do, you gain that man." (Lovett, p. 31)

(k) "Now most of God's suggestions...involve some denial or persecution of the flesh. It is easy to see why men would listen to satan's ideas quicker than God's...When you come right down to it, how many are interested in suggestions that squash the ego, deny the passions and overrule the instincts of the body?" (Lovett, p. 54)

D. As satanic spirits observe what we hear, they also have some ability to distract us from God's thoughts and words and even to *"snatch"* them away. This is especially true of unbelievers who hear the message of the gospel and don't understand it. Some of the ways these evil beings do this are by offering alternative thoughts and aiding our forgetfulness.

† **Matthew 13:18-19**—Jesus taught, *"Listen then to what the parable of the sower means: 19. When anyone hears the message about the kingdom and does not understand it, the evil one comes and snatches away what was sown in his heart. This is the seed sown along the path."*

† **Luke 8:11-12**—Jesus taught, *"This is the meaning of the parable: The seed is the word of God. 12. Those along the path are the ones who hear, and then the devil comes and takes away the word from their hearts, so that they can not believe and be saved."*

▶**CONSIDER THIS:** Can you remember the content of the last sermon you heard? Isn't it amazing how easily forgotten are the biblical messages we hear? Once we hear them, God holds us accountable for the light we have received. The condition of the soil of our hearts determines the success of the seed's growth. It takes effort to retain truth we have been taught. The devil is very concerned about the potential effects that God's Words will produce. This war is very personal, isn't it?

THE HELMET PROTECTS YOUR MIND FROM THE ENEMY'S BLOWS

1. Just as the helmet protected the physical head of the Roman soldier in battle, so putting on the Helmet of Salvation will protect our mind from the blows delivered by satanic forces.

🛡 **TACTIC: Mind Control**—The enemy will try to get control of your thought life by delivering blows to your mind. He will do this by offering his suggestions to influence you to think in the soulish realm and live for self-centered interests, causing you to doubt your *"born again"* experience and your security in Christ. ◎ *Main Target:* Your mind.

2. The enemy's blows will come to your mind in the form of:

   A. T_____ (see Lesson 9)

      (1) "Since the devil cannot touch our wills he must work with something to influence the will...A person's thought life so affects his will he is said to be the product of his thinking." (Lovett, p. 42)

   B. O_____—are abnormal, persistent thoughts that assault and haunt by relentlessly bombarding the mind. They are an attempt to overpower our will to coerce us to give in to them—and we often feel powerless to stop them. Their source could be the spirit world. We are not to live in bondage to inner voices.

      (1) Obsessive thoughts can be wide ranging—from compulsions of various kinds to thoughts of suicide, revenge, sexual impurity, and leaving your spouse and children.

      (2) One of the enemy's goals is to get you hooked with psychological addictions like cyclical obsessive/compulsive behavior that begins with a disturbed emotion, which causes self-destructive thinking leading to self-destructive ritual behavior and consequences.

(3) Some mental and emotional illnesses can be rooted in natural causes such as physically related disorders and nutritional deficiencies; however, it can also be a spiritual problem caused by demonic spirits. Prayer and discernment is needed here.

►**CONSIDER THIS:** Many times negative thoughts are actually planted through verbal abuse in our formative years and often in a marriage relationship. Whether originating from the sinful nature of a parent or one's spouse, or fueled by demonic forces, the impact is the same. These blows of verbal abuse include statements such as: "You're so stupid;" "You'll never amount to anything;" "You're a failure—you fail in everything you do;" "You're ugly—who would ever want you?;" "You're such a little coward—you make your daddy and I so ashamed—we wish we would never have had you." Or, they tear down any achievement that falls short of perfection.

These words and actions are capable of destroying one's self-esteem producing permanent emotional scars—whether spoken repeatedly or even once with authority. A person withdraws into their emotional wounds and becomes vulnerable to demonic attack in their mind. Victims who are deprived of attention, affection, and acceptance, often experience rejection. This can lead to fear of rejection in general. Self-rejection can also result where a person withdraws from close relationships to protect themselves against further hurt. Self-hate is another by-product. Rejection also lures one to get involved in sinful activities to fill their desperate need for love and acceptance. Personality disorders can also develop that have resentment, hatred, and rebellion at its root. Sadly, for many of us, childhood is something that we spend the rest of our lives trying to recover from.

The Bible has a word for this type of abuse—**a curse.** The Hebrew word *qālal* means "to curse by abusing or by belittling."[3] The Greek word *kakologeō* carries a similar meaning, "to speak evil."[4] When a person is used to inflict this type of verbal abuse, they are not walking in love but are acting like, or being used by, the devil. But the good news is that Christ is able to set you free from the corrosive effects of these words on your life! A thought cannot have any power over you unless you believe it. **Do not continue to believe a lie and do not let it debilitate you!**

> † **Ephesians 4:29** (NLT)—*Don't use foul or abusive language. Let everything you say be good and helpful, so that your words will be an encouragement to those who hear them.*

C. B_____ T_____, and D_____ about the character of God.

> † **Genesis 3:1, 4-5**—*Now the serpent was more crafty than any of the wild animals the Lord God had made. He said to the woman, "Did God really say, You must not eat from any tree in the garden'?" **4.** "You will not surely die," the serpent said to the woman. **5.** "For God knows that when you eat of it your eyes will be opened, and you will be like God, knowing good and evil."*

(1) Satan will try to convince you that God has imperfections in His character and can't be trusted in order to get you to quit serving Him. Give no place to those thoughts!

D. C_____ A_____ about the things of God: like skepticism, suspicions, cynicism, and distrust. Persuading us to live in an unhealthy negative state of mind is also part of the warfare.

E. Thoughts that you are not S_____ in Christ.

(1) Insecurities like doubts and fears that you won't make it to heaven.

† **1 John 5:11-13**—*And this is the testimony: God has given us eternal life, and this life is in his Son. **12.** He who has the Son has life; he who does not have the Son of God does not have life. **13**. I write these things to you who believe in the name of the Son of God so that you may know that you have eternal life.*

(2) Thoughts of <u>condemnation</u> that you have sinned too much and are beyond forgiveness. Or thoughts and feelings of guilt from former sinful deeds that haunt you from the past, but for which you have received forgiveness. Say aloud with faith in Christ's work on the cross for you, "That is no longer true of me. I have been justified and forgiven."

(3) Thoughts of <u>leaving God</u>—giving up your Christian walk to return to your former sinful lifestyle.

(4) Thoughts (and the fear) that you have committed the <u>unpardonable sin</u> which is knowingly attributing the workings of the Holy Spirit to the devil **(Matthew 12:22-32)**. This is rarely ever done by a Christian! We can quench **(1 Thessalonians 5:19)** and grieve Him **(Ephesians 4:30),** but these in themselves are not unpardonable.

(5) These types of thoughts will especially come to you when you go through dry spiritual times when you can't seem to sense God's presence. This may not be due to sin in your life. But God may be deliberately withholding "water" from you, like we do with some trees, to force you to dig deeper to find His presence so that when the season of strong winds comes, you won't be toppled over. Press into Him and trust Him.

(6) One practical aspect of what it means to put on the Helmet of Salvation is to <u>know your position in Christ</u> as a child of God so that you can't be talked out of it (refer to SQ&A [#]2 in Lesson 7). This means by faith believe what God says about you despite how you think or feel. Also, know and believe God's love for you and His desire to have you in His family, and all that He has done on the cross to atone for your sins and make you His child. This will prevent any demonic force from convincing you to the contrary. He has not brought you this far in your relationship with Him to abandon you or let you go as His valuable possession. Our faith is being assaulted here. More will be covered about faith in Lesson 14.

(7) We must be <u>secure in the knowledge of our salvation</u> in order to be successful in this invisible war. For the Christian, the Helmet of Salvation is his absolute confidence in the fact that he has been saved from the guilt and penalty of sin and is safe from condemnation **(Romans 8:1)**. Stand convinced of what you know to be true and don't allow a negative thought or comment to hurt you and cause you to believe in a lie. More aspects of the meaning of putting on the Helmet of Salvation and obtaining victory in your thought life will be covered in the next lesson.

(8) <u>Hope</u> is an essential part of our salvation experience. The apostle Paul also referred to the helmet as *"the hope of salvation"* **(1 Thessalonians 5:8** NASB**)** because of Christ's resurrection. *"This hope we have as an anchor of the soul, a hope both sure and steadfast..."* **(Hebrews 6:19** NASB**).** Keeping a positive attitude is extremely important. Allow nothing to detract from the hope God has given you in His Word so you remain very sure of your position and security in Christ. Always keep in mind that there is nowhere else, and no one else, to go to who will care for you like Jesus!

† **John 6:66-69**—*From this time many of his disciples turned back and no longer followed him.* **67.** *"You do not want to leave too, do you?" Jesus asked the Twelve.* **68.** *Simon Peter answered him, "Lord, to whom shall we go? You have the words of eternal life.* **69.** *We believe and know that you are the Holy One of God."*

† **Jeremiah 29:11**—*"For I know the plans I have for you," declares the Lord , "plans to prosper you and not to harm you, plans to give you hope and a future."*

> ☑ This ends the DVD content for Lesson 11.
> ☑ Continue on with the Study Questions and Application and the Summary.

STUDY QUESTIONS AND APPLICATION

1. How would you presently rate the assurance of your born-again experience and your security in Christ?

   ☐ Very strong   ☐ Above average   ☐ Average   ☐ Below average   ☐ Very weak

   A. If applicable, try to identify the two main causes that are hindering your assurance and security:

   (1)_____

   (2)_____

2. Is the **TACTIC: Mind Control** being used against you? Review the types of blows that can come to your mind and ask God for discernment to see whether your mind is being assaulted.

3. Reflect on your childhood and try to identify any verbal abuse that has caused you to believe in a lie. If you identify something, seek counsel by asking the Holy Spirit to lead you to someone qualified who can help you to be delivered and healed from its tentacles.

4. How can you tell the difference between the conviction of the Holy Spirit and condemnation from the devil?

SUMMARY

In this lesson, we learned about spiritual battlefield #3—the assault against our minds by our sinful nature and demonic spirits, and the protection God provided through the Helmet of Salvation. Our brain and mind are an awesome work of creation—no computer can compare to it. But the mind is part of our soul and is adversely affected by Adam's fall into sin. By nature we inherit from Adam a mind that: is in a somewhat **2A.** darkened state; is in a **2B.** blinded state; cannot fully **2C.** know God on its own; **2D.** hinders us from pursuing God; **2E.** leads us astray from truth. The thoughts we entertain and put into action today will eventually determine our eternal destiny.

There are three sources from where we get our thoughts and ideas: from **3A.** <u>our</u> own <u>thoughts</u> within us by learning and experience; from **3B.** other <u>human beings</u>; and perhaps to our surprise, our minds can be influenced by beings from the **3C.** <u>spirit world</u>. We know that God is a spirit and that He fills heaven and earth and is all-knowing. He is the **only** Being that knows **all** that we think, say, and do. By the Holy Spirit, He communicates thoughts and impressions in our spirits, especially to the believer. Both righteous angels and fallen angels are neither omnipresent nor omniscient; therefore, they cannot know our thoughts. Neither do people who have died. However, this angelic realm has these capabilities: They observe our actions and speech thereby knowing our strengths and weaknesses. Since we too are spirit beings, there is a very good possibility that they can "read" the mood or disposition of our soul and spirit—but not the thought that caused the emotion.

Satan and demonic spirits can influence our thinking by offering suggestions and ideas to us—insomuch as we actually think them to be our own. However, we still have the power of choice to act, or not act upon them. This transfer of information to human beings falls into at least three areas: (1) to deceive us and lead us away from God through fortune-tellers, psychics, etc. in the occult; false religions and false teachings in the church; or false philosophies and worldviews that influence the culture and lead it astray—such as evolution; (2) through the possibility of transferring some of their technological know-how in order to build up satan's kingdom here on earth; and (3) through tempting us to sin by suggesting a thought in our mind in order to hopefully bring us under God's judgment. Through the power of suggestion, these unsuspecting thoughts we receive can appear to be our very own ideas, but in reality are intended to appeal to our weaknesses and self-interests and impede and harm our walk with God. As we're caught in the middle of this invisible war, the devil and demonic spirits not only have the ability to blind us to the truth and plant their thoughts in our minds, but they also have some ability to prevent a seed thought that we've heard from God from taking root in our hearts. This is a very personal war, isn't it!

Just as the helmet protected the physical head of the Roman soldier in battle, putting on the Helmet of Salvation will protect your mind from the blows delivered by the enemy. Satan uses the **TACTIC: Mind Control** to try to get control of your thought life by delivering blows to your mind by offering his suggestions to influence you to think in the soulish realm and live for self-centered interests, causing you to doubt your *"born again"* experience and your security in Christ. Some of these blows come in the form of **2A.** <u>temptation</u>; **2B.** <u>obsessions</u>; **2C.** <u>blasphemous</u> <u>thoughts</u> and <u>doubts</u> about the character of God; **2D.** <u>critical</u> <u>attitudes</u> about the things of God; and **2E.** thoughts that you are not <u>secure</u> in Christ. These thoughts of insecurity include: doubts and fears that you won't make it to heaven; thoughts of condemnation that you have sinned too much and are beyond forgiveness; thoughts of leaving God and giving up your Christian walk to return to your former sinful lifestyle; and thoughts that you have committed the unpardonable sin. With the help of the Holy Spirit, you can overcome these blows to your mind.

The Helmet of Salvation is your absolute confidence in the fact that you have been saved from the guilt and penalty of sin and are safe from condemnation. One of the main aspects of what it means to put on the Helmet is to know and believe God's love for you and His desire to have you in His family; and also all that He has done on the cross to atone for your sins and make you His child. Allow nothing to detract from the hope God has given you in His Word so you remain very sure of your position and security in Christ. This will prevent any demonic force from convincing you to the contrary.

Lesson 12
THE CONCLUSION OF THE HELMET AND THE BREASTPLATE

☑ Before starting the DVD:

This lesson contains a mix of three things. First, we will complete our study of Battlefield #3—the battle for our mind. We'll deal with the fight against believing erroneous thoughts, and learn how to put on the Helmet so we can achieve victory in our thought life. Secondly, we will complete our study on the Breastplate by dealing with two more of the enemy's tactics: creating apathy and indifference, and unforgiveness. Thirdly, we will conclude by pointing out the key elements of how to recapture spiritual territory given over to the enemy. This lesson is divided into two sessions. Please note that the video will give a visual recap of the last section of Lesson 11 before proceeding into this one. Pray that God will illuminate these truths to your heart and meet the needs in your life and in your group.

☑ **DVD Users:** Watch Lesson 12, Session 1 for an overview before proceeding further (10 min.).
☑ When you're through, pick up again at this point. Fill in the blanks from the Summary.

PUTTING ON THE HELMET OF SALVATION:
HOW TO GET VICTORY IN YOUR THOUGHT LIFE

1. To get victory, our minds need to be "R_____."

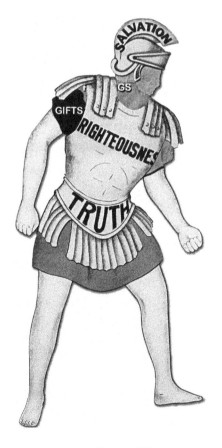

   † **Romans 12:2**—*Do not conform any longer to the pattern of this world, but be transformed by the renewing of your mind. Then you will be able to test and approve what God's will is—his good, pleasing and perfect will.*

📖 **DEFINITION—TRANSFORMED**

Metamorphoō is the Greek word used in **Romans 12:2** and means "to change into another form" much like when Jesus Christ was "transfigured" **(Matthew 17:2)**. It means to "...undergo a complete change which, under the power of God, will find expression in character and conduct." It also indicates a process.[1]

📖 **DEFINITION—RENEWING**

The Greek word used here, *anakainōsis* means the "...adjustment of the moral and spiritual vision and thinking to the mind of God, which is designed to have a transforming effect upon the life;" "a renewal."[2]

   † **Ephesians 4:23** (KJV)—*And be renewed in the spirit of your mind.*

▶**CONSIDER THIS:** Bible teacher Morris Proctor taught this about **Ephesians 4:23:** "The word *'spirit'* means 'wind or breath' and carries the connotation of that which empowers something. God wants our minds to be renewed by changing that which empowers how and what we think. God wants us to be renewed at the source of our thoughts. Before Adam and Eve fell, they received their thoughts from God. The cause of their fall into sin was when Eve and Adam began to decide for themselves what was right and wrong for them, and from what other sources they would obtain information. As Adam and Eve hid from God in the garden, God asked them, *'Who told you...?'* Things have not changed. We, their unregenerate descendents, are getting most of our thoughts on how to order our lives from sources other than God—from our self-centered nature, the world, and the devil. Renewing our minds means we now get our instructions on how to live and think from God who has set up residence within us, and we begin to unlearn erroneous thoughts that we were programmed with before our conversion to Christ."

A. Once we are *"born-again,"* our mind must now come under the rule of the Holy Spirit— a life-long process of aligning our carnal thinking to the mind and will of God. If the content of our brain doesn't line up with the Word of God, we must reject it and begin a re-learning process. Our entire thought processes need to be renewed through reprogramming. Our behavior cannot change without first changing what we believe.

2. To get victory, our mind needs to be D_____.

† **2 Corinthians 10:3-5**—*For though we live in the world, we do not wage war as the world does. **4.** The weapons we fight with are not the weapons of the world. On the contrary, they have divine power to demolish strongholds. **5.** We demolish arguments and every pretension that sets itself up against the knowledge of God, and we take captive every thought to make it obedient to Christ.*

Note: We'll be referring to this Scripture in the points below.

3. To get victory, we must "D_____" (demolish, cast down) strongholds **(2 Corinthians 10:5)**.

📖 **DEFINITION—DESTROY**

kathaireō is the Greek word used in **2 Corinthians 10:5** (*"demolish"*) together with the corresponding noun *kathairesis* used in **10:4** (*"demolish"*) means "to pull down by force."[3]

A. Morris Proctor went on to say: "Usually an emotion is attached to a thought. You also have a predetermined action on how you are going to react in response to it. Also sounds, smells, and tastes can trigger thoughts and experiences in our subconscious mind. Subconscious thoughts affect us just as much as conscious thoughts. All these things we've stored away are determining how we are feeling and acting. So when we get a thought, it produces a feeling, which usually moves the will to action. **Q:** Have you ever wondered why you reacted the way you did in a situation? **Ask the Holy Spirit to reveal the thought that produced the feeling that triggered your reaction.** Identify its source and change the way you think. Allow the Holy Spirit to reprogram your thoughts by exposing all the error and putting His truth in its place." (Visit Morris' website for more outstanding teaching: www.mpseminars.com.)

B. **What is a *"stronghold?"*** It is a fortress or prison. It's anything that robs you of the life and power of the Holy Spirit operating fully in your life. As it relates to our minds, it's an ingrained pattern of erroneous thinking that controls our decisions and dictates our behavior. It distorts our view of reality and truth, and misconstrues how we interpret and react to situations. Simply put, it starts as a toehold, then a foothold, and then it becomes a stronghold.

C. A *"stronghold"* begins with a deceptive, false idea that is believed and accepted as truth (a toehold), which becomes words and action (a foothold). Once a repeated pattern of sin is formed in our thought processes, it becomes an enslaving habit—like a rut we keep slipping back into. A spiritual *"stronghold"* has now been gradually built within us that keeps us in its power. Ironically, we have become its prisoner by our own choosing.

(1) You can recognize a *"stronghold"* by the way it controls you and how you cannot seem to get victory over it. Many times we are not able to recognize one because we are blinded to it. We need God to point it out, and sometimes He uses people to do it. This fortress has given the enemy a foothold where he entrenches himself and from which he can invade into other areas. You can expect to come under demonic influence (see **Demonization** in index).

(2) What are some examples of mindsets that become strongholds?

(a) **Pride**—an attitude of superiority which is expressed by an arrogant insensitivity to others whereby we view them as inferior to us. It is an enemy to us because it will deceive us and lead us to destruction **(Proverbs 16:18)**. Ask yourself these basic questions: How do I react when I am corrected? Am I teachable or do I think I know everything? How do I esteem others? What do your answers reveal about the place of pride in you? (Also see "pride of life" in index.)

† **Obadiah 1:3** (NASB)—*The arrogance of your heart has deceived you...*

† **Philippians 2:3-8**—Our attitude is to be changed to that of Christ Jesus—we are to esteem others more highly than ourselves, and to love our neighbor as we love ourselves. We are called to be humble like Jesus. Humility enables us to be free of the need to defend or prove ourselves to others and it willingly accepts whatever God sends our way—no matter how menial.

▶**CONSIDER THIS:** We are cautioned in Scripture to avoid placing a spiritually immature or inexperienced person in a position of leadership prematurely. Pride could lead to their downfall.

† **1 Timothy 3:6-7** (GNT)—*He* [an elder] *must not be a man who has been recently converted; else he will swell up with pride and be condemned, as the Devil was. 7. He should be a man who is respected by the people outside the church, so that he will not be disgraced and fall into the devil's trap.*

(b) **Prejudice**—Another stronghold is when we form an erroneous belief before seeking out the truth. We make up our minds and stubbornly refuse to be open to change. That preconceived impression becomes truth to us, and our intellectual arrogance keeps us in ignorance, causing us to misunderstand.

(c) **False Views of God's Creation**—The stronghold that causes one to view and value life differently than God does. It's like the doctor who, though having children of his own, believes that an unborn child is merely tissue instead of a living person and deliberately participates in the murder of a child by performing abortions. Or like the scientist or astronomer who beholds the marvels of nature and the universe, but will not believe and acknowledge that a God with intelligent design created it.

(d) **Sexual Impurity**—Misinformation about sex that we absorb from the world and accept as truth, and that we use to justify our sexual behavior, which is in direct opposition to the Bible.

(e) **False Doctrinal Beliefs**—These produce barriers of resistance to accepting the truth of God's Word and entering into all that God has for us. People say, "My parents were (a particular denomination), I was raised that way and I'll die that way." Or, for example, those who believe divine healing or the Baptism in the Holy Spirit are **not** for today.

(f) **Hopelessness**—Believing the lie, "I am what I am. I cannot change."

(g) **Negative Thinking**—Negativity is detrimental to optimism and faith, and impairs confidence in oneself and in others. Refuse to let your mind dwell on the negative—especially thoughts that limit God's ability to work in your life.

(h) **Self-preservation**—Strongholds that lead us to draw wrong conclusions like misinterpreting situations and people's actions toward us. This happened tragically to King Saul to the point of his attempting to murder David (see **1 Samuel 22:9-23**).

D. By an act of our will, empowered by the Holy Spirit, we are enabled "to pull down by force" and destroy every stronghold that raises itself up like a barrier against the knowledge of God, and keeps us from receiving God's truth and help.

E. These fortresses were not built in a day; therefore, they take time to dismantle. They are the product of sinful habits and misinformation that we learned early in our lives. We are encouraged by the Scriptures that our weapons for demolishing them are supernatural. We must choose to demolish them on a daily basis until they are utterly destroyed. Do not believe the lie that your situation is hopeless and cannot be changed.

F. What are some parts of the stronghold that keep us under its power and control?

(1) *"Arguments"* (**2 Corinthians 10:5**)—These are reasonings we use to rationalize and justify our actions and keep us from humbling ourselves and calling on the Holy Spirit for deliverance. *"Arguments"* are wrong sympathetic attitudes that we use to protect and defend the stronghold and thereby make us content to be enslaved. They act as a barrier to keep us from obtaining the knowledge of God and deliverance. We delude ourselves into believing that God has overlooked our fault. We justify our sin by saying, "God understands." Rationalizing and justifying are part of the brick and mortar that build our strongholds.

(2) *"Pretension"* **(2 Corinthians 10:5)**—This part of the fortress seeks to keep us blinded to our sin by encouraging us to deny that we even have the problem. Or it can make us think more highly of ourselves than we should, or trick us into believing we have control of a situation when we don't. These things prevent the knowledge of God from penetrating our blindness so we can bring the disobedient thought into submission to Christ.

G. Similar to strongholds, **defense mechanisms** are unhealthy patterns of living we use to cope with life or defend ourselves. They consist of things like refusal to face the truth (denial); escaping from the real world (fantasy); withdrawing to avoid rejection (emotional insulation); taking our frustrations out on others (displacement); blaming others (projection); and making excuses for poor behavior (rationalization). These and other "...fleshly thought patterns were programmed into your mind when you lived independently of God." They, too, have to be unlearned.[4]

4. To get victory, we must "T_____ C_____" every thought **(2 Corinthians 10:5).**

📖 **DEFINITION—CAPTIVE**

Aichmalōtizō is the Greek word used here signifying "to bring under control" like a prisoner of war.[5]

A. We have to inspect every thought. It takes a disciplined effort to consciously take hold of a thought and then judge it to see if it is pleasing to God, or if it violates His Word. Is the thought selfish or selfless? Does it glorify God? Will we respond like a robot without thinking, or will we preside as a judge over our thoughts? Interestingly, the Greek word used for *"thought"* (*noēma*) here is the same word used for the *"schemes"* devised against us by the enemy in **2 Corinthians 2:11.**

† **Titus 2:12-13**—*...say "No" to ungodliness and worldly passions, and to live self-controlled, upright and godly lives in this present age,* **13.** *while we wait for the blessed hope...*

B. In order to bring every contrary thought under control, we must be watchful and on guard. The thought must not rule us, we must rule it. Take it as a "prisoner of war" and bring it under the rule of our spirit. Our spirit should control our mind, and our mind should control our emotions. All compartments of our life must be given to the Holy Spirit to control and to be in subjection to His Word.

C. Protect your mind as you would your home by using a security system. Think of it like this: Set the alarm by keeping watch over your thought life. When the alarm goes off within you and an intruding thought is detected, shine God's light (His Word) on the ungodly thought to expose the trespasser and use your weapon of God's Word against it to ward it off.

5. To get victory, we must bring every thought into "O_____" to Christ and His Word **(2 Corinthians 10:5).**

A. Submission to God's Word must take preference over what we think and believe. We should always ask, "What does the Bible say about this?" or, "Does this line up with God's Word?"

B. You can protect your mind by not allowing thoughts contrary to Scripture to go unchallenged. Combat these erroneous thoughts **immediately** with the truth of God's Word:

(1) <u>Example</u>: This thought comes to you: "You're not good enough to go to heaven." Now you can entertain the thought and begin to believe it, or you can take the thought captive and bring it into subjection to the Word of God and profess what the Scriptures say concerning it. A proper response to this thought would be, "The Bible says that Christ has put His righteousness to my account and I will enter heaven based on His righteousness—not mine" (also quote related Bible verses). In the same manner, respond to other lies and negative thoughts by declaring outloud the promises of God, or the character of God, or what God states in His word about who you are in Christ.

(2) <u>Example</u>: God gives you an assignment. The thought comes: "You don't have the ability to do that!" Your response should be, "Yes, I can because God's Word says, '*I can do all things through Christ who strengthens me.*'" **(Philippians 4:13).** Bring the thought into subjection to the Word of God. Perhaps the task seems to be beyond your capability, but God will give you wisdom to accomplish it in some way. Declare what God says concerning the situation. Speak the promises of God, but be sure to use the Scripture correctly in context. God is waiting to hear you declare them and to see how much you believe them.

(3) <u>Example</u>: You have just lost your job. The thought comes: "I will never be able to meet all my financial obligations." That is how your situation appears in the natural, but we serve a supernatural God. Don't limit Him. You take hold of that thought by saying, "Father, you are bigger than this situation. I have placed myself in the position to be blessed by aligning to Your commands of tithing and giving offerings. Therefore, You promised, '*...I will open the windows of heaven for you. I will pour out a blessing so great you won't have room enough to take it in!...*' **(Malachi 3:10** NLT**),** and '*...seek first his kingdom and his righteousness, and all these things will be given to you as well.*' **(Matthew 6:32, 33),** and '*My God shall supply all your needs according to His riches in glory in Christ Jesus.*' **(Philippians 4:19).** Therefore, I put my trust in you to provide all of my needs. "

(4) <u>Example</u>: The thought comes: "Lie about this." Your response should be, "The Bible says that lying is the devil's character **(John 8:44).** I choose to reflect my Father's character and tell the truth."

C. We need to guard our thought life and be aware of our ability to absorb subconscious bits of information. Our minds are not to be garbage cans. Sinful thoughts arouse our sinful nature.

† **Philippians 4:8**—*Finally, brothers, whatever is true, whatever is noble, whatever is right, whatever is pure, whatever is lovely, whatever is admirable—if anything is excellent or praiseworthy—think about such things.*

 TACTIC: Procrastination—The enemy will try to persuade you to put off obeying that which you know to be God's will, thereby causing you to sin. ◎ *Main Targets:* Your Love and Will.

D. Let us remember Solomon. We can have all the head knowledge about these things, but they are useless if we don't obey God and put His commands into daily practice.

> † **James 4:17**—*Anyone, then, who knows the good he ought to do and doesn't do it, sins.*

> † **Luke 12:47-48** (NLT)—Jesus taught: *48. "...Much is required from those to whom much is given..."*

6. To get victory, we must R_____ / D_____ O_____ the thoughts.

> † **Numbers 33:55-56**—God said to Israel, *"But if you do not drive out the inhabitants of the land, those you allow to remain will become barbs in your eyes and thorns in your sides. They will give you trouble in the land where you will live. 56. And then I will do to you what I plan to do to them."*

A. God gave the Israelites the "Promised Land" of Canaan, but there were demonic strongholds of false religions and "giants" among the inhabitants of this land. God declared that the land was already theirs, but that they would have to drive out and ruthlessly destroy these enemies of God and possess it. God, alone, was not going to drive them out. His power would only be activated as the Israelites, at His direction, raised their swords and weapons and began to fight. Then God's miraculous deliverance occurred and gave them a tremendous victory. The city of Jericho was conquered and became the beachhead from which the Israelites advanced further into enemy territory. God commanded them to take the entire land by putting the inhabitants to death.

B. This is how God works today in the life of a New Testament believer. The Holy Spirit establishes a beachhead in our spirit when we receive Christ through the new birth. He gives us divine direction concerning areas of our life that we must surrender to His control—until the "whole land" is taken. As we begin to resist by word of faith (our profession), and the obedience of faith (our behavior), we release God's divine power into our situation and the "giants" and "fortresses" of sin will fall.

C. It requires a daily resistance of these enemies to completely drive them out. Otherwise, like Israel, those that remain will eventually ensnare us and *"...will become snares and traps for you, whips on your back and thorns in your eyes..."* (See **Joshua 23:9-13**).

Also read these important related Scriptures: **Exodus 23:20-33; 34:11-17; Deuteronomy 7:1-6; Judges 1:1-11, 19-22, 27; 2:5, 11-15.**

▶**CONSIDER THIS:** Like the ancient inhabitants in the land of Canaan, demonic forces are unwilling to give up territory they have conquered and believe they own. They will seek to influence and control the way you think about these areas. You must retract the permission that gives them legal access, and in the authority of Christ, close the door to any further access.

You might be saying to yourself, "I just don't have enough willpower to do the things God is requiring me to do." We must learn how to motivate and train ourselves to please God as well as control sinful impulses. Love for God must motivate us to obey His Word so we do not give in to actions that displease Him. Another motivating key is to weigh the consequences of our decisions. What will it mean for the cause of Christ?; for our witness for Christ?; for us and our family? As we decide to obey, God will empower us to resist and do the things He is asking us to do.

7. To get victory, we must daily meditate on G_____ W_____ and profess it as the means of renewing our mind.

   A. Feed your mind and spirit with the spiritual food of the Bible, God's Word, and you will have renewed and reprogrammed your thinking, resulting in a harvest of spiritual blessings in your life.

      † **Joshua 1:8**—God commanded, *"Do not let this Book of the Law depart from your mouth; meditate on it day and night, so that you may be careful to do everything written in it. Then you will be prosperous and successful."*

      † **Isaiah 26:3** (NLT)—*You will keep in perfect peace all who trust in you, whose thoughts are fixed on you!*

   B. Your confession of what God's Word has to say about your situation is a powerful weapon.

      † **2 Corinthians 10:4**—*The weapons we fight with are not the weapons of the world. On the contrary, they have divine power to demolish strongholds.*

►**CONSIDER THIS:** One of the powerful spiritual *"weapons"* that **2 Corinthians 10:4** refers to is the profession of our belief in God's Word. Bishop Joseph L. Garlington teaches, "Nothing happens in the Kingdom of God until something is said." As you take *"every thought captive"* and evaluate it in the light of the Scriptures, you should respond to contrary thoughts by declaring outloud what God says about it. Why outloud? One reason is if you say it silently to yourself, demonic spirits cannot know what you are thinking. Saying it aloud enables them to hear it along with the determination in the way you say it. There is power in our declaration of God's Word, but we must know His Word before we can affirm it.

   C. Besides knowing and using the Bible, other mighty spiritual weapons God has given to us so far include: light (truth) to fight darkness; using Christ's name and believing in the power of His sacrificial blood; and also the *"weapons of righteousness"* (**2 Corinthians 6:7**) such as love to conquer hate, goodness to overcome evil, and sanctification to prevent giving a foothold and maintaining protection. Other mighty spiritual weapons that God has given to us will be summarized at the end of Lesson 16 (see "Weapons, spiritual" in index). Remember, fighting a spiritual battle using natural, worldly methods will guarantee our being defeated by the enemy every time.

☑ This ends our treatment of putting on the Helmet of Salvation. Continue on with the Study Questions and Application.

STUDY QUESTIONS AND APPLICATION

1. Name at least two sinful thoughts that are most problematic in controlling your thought life:

   A. _____   B. _____

   Now take each one through the seven steps of How to Get Victory in Your Thought Life.

2. Begin to dismantle spiritual strongholds in your life by answering the following questions (we will complete this exercise by referring back to it at the end of the next session). First identify at least two spiritual strongholds in your life that rob you and keep you in their power. You may find the chart in Lesson 7's SQ&A [#]1 helpful in identifying specific strongholds. Review what *"arguments"* and *"pretensions"* are in **2 Corinthians 10:5** that help keep the stronghold alive, and then ask the Holy Spirit to reveal them to you. Also think of any defense mechanisms you may use.

Name of Stronghold	*"Arguments"* You Use	*"Pretensions"* That Blind You

3. Identify at least two ways you negatively react either to a person or a situation. Ask the Holy Spirit to reveal the source of the thought that produces the feeling that triggers each reaction. Then deal with that thought and ask God to help you change your reaction.

Negative Reaction	The Thought That Produces the Feeling That Triggers Your Reaction

4. How much of a role does the **TACTIC: Procrastination** play in your life? Identify one thing you can do to break its hold on you and then make a decision to begin doing it today.

☑ The next session will wrap up Battlefield [#]1—The Breastplate of Righteousness: Our Sinful Nature vs. Our Spirit.

   Note: I strongly suggest that the remainder of this lesson be done as a separate session.

☑ **DVD Users:** When you are ready, begin the last session by watching Lesson 12, Session 2 (16 min.). When you're through, pick up again at this point. Fill in the blanks from the Summary.

Session 2

WRAP-UP OF THE BREASTPLATE OF RIGHTEOUSNESS
Apathy and Indifference

🐴 **TACTIC: Apathy and Indifference**—The enemy will try to extinguish the fire for God in a believer's spirit and breed indifference, apathy, and lukewarmness in its place. His goal is to deplete God's army of laborers, thus reducing effective opposition against his kingdom.
◎ *Main Targets:* Your Love and Will.

1. If you are on fire for God in your relationship and work for Him, demonic forces will especially oppose you. They see you as a threat to the interests of satan's kingdom. You will draw fire so be prepared.

2. Here are some of the ways the enemy tries to breed apathy and complacency:

   A. He first seeks to cause you to neglect feeding your spiritual life. He knows you are "fueled" by reading the Word of God, worship, and prayer. A fire needs fuel to keep burning. If he can keep you too busy or distract you from maintaining your devotional life, he is sure that lukewarmness will be the result.

   B. He will also try to hinder you from gathering together with other believers for spiritual enrichment (i.e. church, Christian fellowship, etc.). An early church father once said, "If you take a coal away from the fire, it grows cold."

🐴 **TACTIC: Isolate the Prey**—Like a lion stalking its victim, the enemy will try to isolate you by giving you reasons why you should withdraw yourself from going to church and seeking out the support and fellowship of other Christians. This will weaken your spiritual life and make you more vulnerable to his attack. ◎ *Main Target:* Your Mind.

   C. Another breeding ground for apathy is when our Christian walk becomes a mechanical, "dutiful" routine minus the love and passion for God and the things of His Kingdom. Our Heavenly Father may have to orchestrate events in our lives to shake us free of rote habits.

   D. Satan will also seek to get us to focus inward on our own needs and desires so we live for self-centered interests and "the blessings of God," in order to get our focus off the things close to God's heart. We can lose sight of the fact that we are being blessed to be a blessing to those around us—both believers and non-believers alike. Remember, living for ourselves is the same as living for satan's interests.

      † **1 Corinthians 6:19-20**—*...You are not your own; 20. you were bought at a price...*

   E. He will seek to desensitize us so we lack the compassion and desire to meet human need and to rescue unbelievers that are headed to a Christless grave.

   F. Looking for the "rapture" can become an excuse for not being active in God's service.

   G. By convincing us that God's will and work are going to be done without our involvement.

† **2 Corinthians 5:15**—*And he died for all, that those who live should no longer live for themselves but for him who died for them and was raised again.*

† **Revelation 3:15-16** (NLT)—Jesus said to the church at Laodicea: *"I know all the things you do, that you are neither hot nor cold. I wish you were one or the other! 16. But since you are like lukewarm water, I will spit you out of my mouth!"*

UNFORGIVENESS

🐎 **TACTIC: Unforgiveness**—The enemy will try to entrap you by enticing you to have an unforgiving spirit toward someone who has hurt or offended you, cunningly putting you into a position where you will have to forgive that person before God can forgive you. He anticipates that unforgiveness will sever your relationship with God, that person, and/or your church.
◎ *Main Target:* Your Emotions and Pride.

1. In this tactic, the emotions in our soul are under attack. The enemy may even be the instigator and source of this wound or offense we receive. His expectation is that we will react in unforgiveness.

   † **2 Corinthians 2:11** (TLB)—*A further reason for forgiveness is to keep from being outsmarted by Satan; for we know what he is trying to do.*

▶**CONSIDER THIS:** We learned that our emotions cannot always be trusted to give us a correct perspective of things. However, the statement, "Don't go by your feelings" needs to be qualified. We established in Lesson 11 that we know things in two places—in our mind (soul) and in our spirit. Likewise, we feel things in two places—in our emotions (soul) and the Holy Spirit's impressions in our spirit. We must learn to differentiate between the often unreliable feelings in our soul and the Holy Spirit's direction within our spirit (i.e. peace or lack of it, a check or restraint, joy, a burden for intercession, a resounding sense that "You know that you know that you know," or "It's just the right thing to do," etc.).

2. Unforgiveness is intended to bring **separation,** a wedge driven between yourself and others, and yourself and God. Our egocentric nature tends to get easily offended over the most insignificant things—especially in the church. We didn't get to sing in the choir, the pastor didn't shake our hand, someone took our seat, we didn't like the color of the carpet selected, etc. Some of us never return to attending church because of hurt feelings like these that eat in us and taint our ongoing view. There are also family members and friends that haven't talked to each other in years due to some offense. In many cases, it is over petty things, and the devil has us right where he wants us.

3. What does the Bible say about giving and receiving forgiveness?

   † **Matthew 6:14-15**—Jesus taught: *"For if you forgive men when they sin against you, your heavenly Father will also forgive you. 15. But if you do not forgive men their sins, your Father will not forgive your sins."*

   † **John 13:34-35** (NLT)—Jesus said: *"So now I am giving you a new commandment: Love each other. Just as I have loved you, you should love each other. 35. Your love for one another will prove to the world that you are my disciples."*

A. Please read **Matthew 18:21-35.** These verses show that the debt of sin we owed God was impossible for us to pay back, but God forgave our debt to Him. Jesus illustrated this truth by the man who owed a king millions of dollars by today's standards—whose debt the king forgave. But later this same man could not forgive someone else who owed him 100 denarii ($20 in comparison). When we think of the enormous debt for which we have been forgiven, which we could never repay, how then can we **NOT** forgive another's insignificant transgression?? Jesus said that if we don't forgive, He won't forgive us!! This is more apt to be the "unforgivable sin" we Christians commit rather than blaspheming the Holy Spirit.

B. When we forgive someone, we are not condoning the offense. Rather, we break the chains that keep us bound to the hurt that they have inflicted. God wants us to give total, unconditional love and forgiveness just like He gave us. Though we may never forget the incident, evidences that we have truly forgiven someone are when we no longer have a desire to retaliate and get even; we no longer talk about them or the details to others or make them feel guilty later for what they have done; we no longer feel the deep hurt when it surfaces in our memory; we maintain communication with them; and we sincerely pray for their well-being. God will give wisdom for each situation.

4. Watch the chain reaction of unforgiveness:

A. **Temptation**—When we are hurt, a strong emotional response follows (anger and bitterness) that produces thoughts of unforgiveness and retaliation. These emotions in our soul exert great pressure on our will demanding that it give into this attitude. Demonic forces whisper "Don't forgive them!" Our will should be receiving greater pressure from our spirit saying, "Obey the Word of God." It is at this point that we need to quickly make the right decision and forgive that person and thereby escape the trap of entering into the rest of the steps. Also, keep a special watch over tender, sore areas in your life. The devil delights to reopen old wounds. Simply remind him, "I forgave (name of person)" and ignore his taunting.

† **Hebrews 12:15** (NLT)—*Look out after each other so that none of you will miss out on the special favor of God. Watch out that no bitter root...rises up among you, for whenever it springs up, many are corrupted by its poison.*

† **Ephesians 4:26-32**—*...Do not let the sun go down while you are still angry, 27. and do not give the devil a foothold... 30. And do not grieve the Holy Spirit of God, with whom you were sealed for the day of redemption. 31. Get rid of all bitterness, rage and anger, brawling and slander, along with every form of malice. 32. Be kind and compassionate to one another, forgiving each other, just as in Christ God forgave you.*

B. **The Will Concedes**—If we allow our emotions to win by choosing not to forgive, we are held accountable before God for this sin, and we put God in a position where He cannot forgive us. From this point on, the sooner we repent and forgive that person the better. Otherwise, we are headed down a disastrous road. It is more important to forgive than to be right about the matter, and don't wait for the one who offended you to first ask for forgiveness. There is also a danger of waiting until we "feel like it" to forgive somebody because it just won't happen. Our emotions are incapable of correct reasoning. The responsibility rests on our will. Forgiveness is a **decision** to obey God's Word—emotions should eventually follow.

C. It results in **Darkness and Blindness**.

> ✝ **1 John 2:9-11**—*11. But whoever hates his brother is in the darkness and walks around in the darkness; he does not know where he is going, because the darkness has blinded him.*

(1) The initial hurt feelings lead to bitterness which leads to anger and resentment, hatred and revenge. Seething within, it eats you up like a cancer. These negative emotions poison your whole being and affect your spiritual life. Like other negative emotions, it can even cause ailments in your body. You also begin to do and say things that you never thought you would ever say or do. We injure ourselves by walking in darkness and blindness, and we have just given the devil a giant foothold in controlling our lives.

▶**CONSIDER THIS:** What is the correct way to deal with anger? Should we vent to "get it off our chest?" Or should we suppress it and keep it under control within? Researchers tell us that outbursts of anger actually make us more angry, not less.

> ✝ **1 John 3:14-16**—*We know that we have passed from death to life, because we love our brothers. Anyone who does not love remains in death. 15. Anyone who hates his brother is a murderer, and you know that no murderer has eternal life in him. 16. This is how we know what love is: Jesus Christ laid down his life for us. And we ought to lay down our lives for our brothers.*

(2) Think of it! We choose to put ourselves into the position where God looks at us as a murderer. This deals a great blow to our spiritual life.

> ✝ **Matthew 6:22-23**—Jesus said, *"The eye is the lamp of the body. If your eyes are good, your whole body will be full of light. 23. But if your eyes are bad, your whole body will be full of darkness. If then the light within you is darkness, how great is that darkness!"*

(3) Bitterness and unforgiveness can cause us to do extremely unreasonable things. I know of a woman who was so consumed with bitterness and unforgiveness toward certain members of her family. When her mother died, she actually secured a restraining order from the police to prevent certain people from attending her mother's funeral, including her own son and brother! Amazing—our enemy within!

D. It breaks our **Relationship with God**—We grieve the Holy Spirit within us and He withdraws. We place ourselves in a position where God cannot forgive us. Jesus said He won't forgive us unless we first forgive.

> ✝ **Mark 11:25-26**—Jesus said, *"And when you stand praying, if you hold anything against anyone, forgive him, so that your Father in heaven may forgive you your sins. 26. But if you do not forgive, neither will your Father who is in heaven forgive your sins."*

> ✝ **1 John 3:21-22**—*Dear friends, if our hearts do not condemn us, we have confidence before God 22. and receive from him anything we ask, because we obey his commands and do what pleases him.*

(1) Unforgiveness (and refusal to repent) robs us of faith and erodes our confidence in our approach to God that is necessary for a truly effective prayer life.

(2) The Holy Spirit will continue His faithful work of convicting us and challenging us to bring our will more fully under His lordship.

(3) Remember, the enemy wants our fellowship with God severed as well as our relationships with people. Don't let him be successful by allowing a wedge to be driven between you and others.

E. It brings the **Chastisement of God**—If we ignore the promptings of the Holy Spirit to have His rightful rule, then we force a loving God to use more severe measures in order to bring us to repentance. The consequences that follow will have been unnecessarily brought upon ourselves. God, our Father, loves us too much not to rescue us from this dangerous situation. In His love, He will seek to root this sin out of us. A continued state of unrepentance and hardness of heart could keep us out of heaven.

> † **1 Corinthians 11:31-32**—*But if we judged ourselves, we would not come under judgment. 32. When we are judged by the Lord, we are being disciplined so that we will not be condemned with the world.*

F. It can ultimately bring the **Judgment of God**—This is the stage where satan desires to lead us—through unforgiveness or any other sin. If we are foolish enough to harden our hearts and continue to reject the Holy Spirit's conviction and His relentless efforts to bring us to repentance, God in His infinite love will give us up to our own desires! If you are harboring unforgiveness toward someone, I urge you to waste no time in repenting and then releasing forgiveness towards that person. Ask the Lord to forgive you right NOW. He will abundantly pardon. Be willing to humble yourself in going to the person asking for their forgiveness and making restitution, where necessary. **Don't put it off! Do it TODAY!** The next section will show you how to recapture this area of unforgiveness as well as other sins.

HOW TO RECAPTURE TERRITORY LOST TO THE ENEMY

If you have given up ground to the enemy, you can take it back! The effort and difficulty will be in proportion to how deep the roots are or how massive the stronghold. Here are some key elements that God has prescribed for reclaiming lost territory. It is usually in this order, but may differ from person to person; however, they are all necessary ingredients.

1. R_____—It all starts with a determination of the will. What was lost by disobedience must now be regained through obedience to God's Word. Your soul and your mind will try to weaken your resolve by giving you reasons for not obeying. Simply put, you must come to the point where you make the decision to cancel the permission that you gave to the enemy that allowed him to establish footholds in your life, by now making the choice to obey God. This decision is the declaration that begins the reclaiming process.

2. R_____—This means turning away from the sin you were walking in and begin walking in obedience to God. This involves confessing your sin to God and asking for His forgiveness. Doing this tears down the barrier of sin and enables God to forgive and restore your fellowship with Him. Repentance takes away the right of the devil to continue having control over your life.

† **1 John 1:9**—*If we confess our sins, he is faithful and just and will forgive us our sins and purify us from all unrighteousness.*

A. True repentance is evidenced by a change in behavior. We are to *"produce fruit in keeping with repentance"* **(Luke 3:8; Acts 26:20).**

B. Confessing our sins to one another is a source of power and healing. In doing so, we can be miraculously delivered from bondages and sicknesses. Sins should be confessed as openly as they were committed.

† **James 5:15-16** (NASB)—*16. Therefore, confess your sins to one another, and pray for one another so that you may be healed....*

C. Repentance involves renunciation—a clean break with the sin by a formal declaration.

D. What are the types of things that need to be repented of and renounced? (There are specific prayers for each of these areas at the end of this section.)

(1) **Our Sinful Nature**—When we allow the evil character in our sinful nature to sprout, grow, and become dominant (see list in SQ&A [#]1 in Lesson 7).

(a) Hidden or unconfessed sin allows demonic powers to remain in control. As soon as we shine the light of God's Word on the sins—expose them and close the doors, we will experience deliverance by the power of the Holy Spirit. So don't delay!

(2) **Idols in Our Hearts**—Idols are those things we place above God that become our main priority, receiving more importance, love, and devotion from us than He does. They can be people, possessions, or vocations **(Ezekiel 14:3).**

(3) **Generational Sins**—Sins inherited from our ancestors.

(a) God visits ancestral sins upon their descendents to the third and fourth generation **(Exodus 20:5-6; 34:6-7).** Ask God to help you ascertain the type of sin(s) that keeps reoccurring and is being passed down through family bloodlines (i.e., occult involvement, sexual impurity, addictions, profanity, mental or physical illness).

(b) Confess aloud the specific sin(s) of your ancestors. Note that this is one main way the things in the occult are passed on and kept alive.

(4) **Occult Involvement or False Teachings**

(a) In order to adequately ascertain if you have had any occult involvement, knowingly or unknowingly, review the table of contents for Appendix A (which then gives an overview of the topic). This table of contents can be found either on the last page of Lesson 2 or the second page of Appendix A in back of this workbook.

(b) Whenever we unwittingly bring things that belong to the occult and satan's religious systems into our Christian homes, we attract demonic spirits and give them the legal right to work through them. God will not co-exist with them.

▶**CONSIDER THIS:** You may innocently have brought things into your home that you purchased, such as souvenirs, which could be the cause of evil disturbances there. Or perhaps it is an heirloom, or even items in your attic, basement, or in the walls that were there from previous owners. These include idols or figurines from false religions; objects related to secret societies such as Freemasonry, the Shriners, or Eastern Star; anything used in the occult like books, amulets, crystals, religious symbols, etc. These recurring disturbances can take the form of depression, nightmares, physical ailments, family conflict, oppression, accidents, strange sounds or smells, and other abnormal occurrences. The problem usually ceases when the object is destroyed and there is prayer for deliverance.

The disturbances can also result from evil acts done in the home or on the property that produced a stronghold. For example: the performance of occult practices and rituals; a home built on an ancient burial ground; violence and murder (see **Genesis 4:8-12**); sexual impurity; victimization and abuse; the making or selling of drugs; and even a breach of contract (see **Joshua 9:1-27; 2 Samuel 21:1**). At times the type of disturbance manifesting itself may be a clue to identifying the root of the problem. It may be necessary to learn more about the history of the property. The entrenched demonic forces can be driven out through confessing sins against the land, etc., intercession, the application of the Blood of Christ, and the rededicating of the premises to God—anointing it with oil in the name of Christ.[6]

We all need to provide a safe haven for our family. Go through each room and ask the Holy Spirit to reveal the source of any problems that may have entered your home. Be ruthless in cleaning out your house. Rid it of demonic footholds by burning or destroying any object or material that the Spirit shows you. This will change the spiritual atmosphere in your home and deliver you from ailments. Also, don't overlook an unexpected source—tithing. If you don't tithe, you are placing yourself and your household under God's curse (see **Malachi 3:8-11; Matthew 23:23**).

(c) Don't allow sentimentality or the value of the object to cause you to be reluctant to part with it. Neither should you sell it lest the one who buys it then inherits the problem. Follow the Scriptural way of disposing of it. Burn or destroy it.

† **Acts 19:19-20** (GNT)—*Many of those who had practiced magic brought their books together and burned them in the presence of everyone. They added up the price of the books and the total came to fifty thousand dollars. **20.** In this powerful way the Word of the Lord kept spreading and growing stronger.*

† **Deuteronomy 7:25-26** (NLT)—*You must burn their idols in fire, and do not desire the silver or gold with which they are made. Do not take it or it will become a snare to you, for it is detestable to the Lord your God. **26.** Do not bring any detestable objects into your home, for then you will be set apart for destruction just like them. You must utterly detest such things…*

(d) What are some compelling reasons for renouncing and destroying this material?

- You are making an open declaration to God, the devil, and yourself that you mean business.

- You cut off the lifeline that feeds and nourishes the sin.

- Certain objects carry with them a demonic presence and activity that, if allowed to remain, give legal permission for satanic forces to continue to linger and establish their presence in your home. These objects are not just those connected with the occult. They can be drugs, alcohol, tobacco products, pornography, videos and soundtracks or even some toys or games like the Ouija board, Dungeons and Dragons, or video games.

E. One of the gifts that God has given to His church is deliverance from our enemies. The following prayers will assist you in the first step of retaking possession of that lost ground. Be aware that repentance does not guarantee that we will not suffer some future consequences of our past sins, even though we have obtained forgiveness from our Heavenly Father.

(1) **Pray this prayer out loud to repossess an area overrun by your Sinful Nature:** "Heavenly Father, I admit that I have given the enemy a foothold and/or stronghold in my life by committing the sin of (name of sin). I humbly ask Your forgiveness and I now retract the permission I gave to the enemy and with your help, I retake possession of this territory for Your glory. Conform this area of my life to the character of Your Son. I take this step of obedience to allow Your character to be seen instead of it. I say to my soul and body that we will keep a watch over this area and not allow this sinful characteristic to once again gain access through the door of our will. I thank You for being my Father and for showing to me Your love, faithfulness, mercy, forgiveness, and patience. Amen."

(2) **Pray this prayer out loud to tear down an Idol in your life:** "Heavenly Father, forgive me for making (name of idol) an idol in my life by giving it more love, allegiance, and priority than I have given to you. Restore my first love for You and empower me to not return to this sin. I now retract the permission I gave to the enemy. With your help I retake possession of this territory for Your glory. I will continue to take the steps of obedience to counteract this sin. I say to my soul and body that we will begin to only love God with all of our heart, mind, and strength. Thank You for being my Father and for showing to me Your love, faithfulness, mercy, forgiveness, and patience. Amen."

(3) **Pray this prayer out loud to cancel Generational Sins:** "Heavenly Father, I confess the sin of _____ that has been passed down genetically to my generation. I renounce this sin in my life and in my children's lives. I cut these ties to us and declare that they will stop with me and will not be passed down any further. I declare that I and my children and their children will no longer be affected by this sin. I also shut down any perceived right of any "familial spirits" to remain within our family. Through the blood of Christ, I break the power of this sin and any curse passed onto

me or my family as a result of this sin. And I forgive my ancestors of this sin. I now retract the permission my forefathers and I gave to the enemy. With your help I retake possession of this territory for Your glory. I will continue to take the steps of obedience to counteract this sin. I thank You for being my Father and for showing to me Your love, faithfulness, mercy, forgiveness, and patience. Amen."

(4) **Pray this prayer out loud to renounce Occult Involvement or False Teachings:** "Heavenly Father, I regretfully confess that I have exposed myself to this area of the occult: _____. I humbly ask Your forgiveness, knowing now that it is an abomination to You. I renounce all past and present involvement in this practice. I renounce anything I ever did or said that identified me with, and indebted me to, the forces of darkness. Father, also forgive me of anything I have believed that was erroneous regarding teachings or practices that do not align to the Bible. Satan, I command you and every evil spirit in the name of Jesus Christ, to depart from me, my family, and our house and property immediately. You no longer have my permission to be here. Devil, I renounce you and all of your works. I declare that I belong to the one and only true God and, as His child, I will serve only Him. I give my life entirely over to Jesus Christ and claim protection by His blood that He shed on the cross that defeated you. Father, I now retract the permission I gave to the enemy and with your help I retake possession of this territory for Your glory. I will destroy any occult object associated with this sin, and I will continue to take the steps of obedience to counteract this transgression. Thank You for being my Father and for showing to me Your love, faithfulness, mercy, forgiveness, and patience. Amen."

▶**CONSIDER THIS:** Research shows that moral failure among spiritual leaders is mostly the result of sexual lust, inappropriate relationships, mid-life frustrations, and abuse of power. **Q:** What should be done when a leader in ministry falls into a moral failure or commits public sinful misconduct? First, we should always revert to Jesus' instructions in **Matthew 18:15-20** by confronting them with their sin and exposing it so it can be dealt with. Our goal should always be one of forgiveness and restoration, being motivated by a heart of compassion and grieved over the fall of a brother, while demonstrating that the sin will not be tolerated and allowed to infect the church. The fallen, repentant leader should humbly submit to the discipline and restoration process of those in authority over him who should also determine the length of the process. This usually lasts for at least one year, depending on the extent of any addictions and how diligent their commitment has been. Suspension and probation are the disciplines designed for restoration.

† **Galatians 6:1** (NLT)—*...if another Christian is overcome by some sin, you who are godly should gently and humbly help that person back onto the right path. And be careful not to fall into the same temptation yourself.*

Q: When should a leader be permitted to resume ministry? It depends on their wholehearted commitment to the discipline and restoration process. It is one thing to forgive someone, but quite another to place them back into the place of leadership. After all, there has been damage done to the cause of Christ, a betrayal of the public trust, and their loss of credibility has, in all probability, been extended to the church making it guilty by association. If a banker was extorting money from his bank, he could be forgiven but would not be restored to his position. We disqualify ourselves, at least for a time, from holding a leadership position or from participating in a ministry in the church (i.e. teacher, choir member, etc.). In cases where the leader has not genuinely repented and is not in submission to their covering of authority, a Christian organization must be careful to not let their loyalty to the leader blind them to the leader's rebellion and continue to follow and support them, not holding them accountable for their actions.

> † **1 Timothy 5:19-20** (NASB)—*Do not receive an accusation against an elder except on the basis of two or three witnesses.* **20.** *Those who continue in sin, rebuke in the presence of all, so that the rest also will be fearful of sinning.*

3. R_____—Once we are in submission to God, we can resist the devil and he will flee from us **(James 4:7)**. In this step you shut the door on any further thinking of and acting out of this sin. Resist and refuse to entertain any more of these thoughts or listen to the appeals of your sinful nature. Battle them and deny them control. Resisting will maintain your deliverance.

A. When we resist, we activate the power of the Holy Spirit and, together, push that sin off the ground it occupies. Depending on how deep the roots of this habit are, and the degree of deliverance we allowed the Holy Spirit to give, this step of resisting can last quite a while. You will gain new strength and confidence with each victorious refusal. **These are some of the ways we can resist:**

(1) By thoroughly putting on the piece of armor that corresponds to your situation

(2) By keeping a special watch on that sin for, let's say, one month. When you focus particular attention on it, you can immediately deal with it when it begins to raise its ugly head

(3) By declaring your stand by speaking it outloud to your fallen nature and to the devil

(4) By forgetting past failures and resolutely focus in on putting this sin to death

▶ **CONSIDER THIS:** In your struggle to overcome a bad habit, be cautious of relaxing your guard when making progress and risk losing all the gains you have made. Overconfidence can lead to a relapse especially when you are feeling depressed, angry, bored, or lonely. If failure occurs, don't give up. Ask God for a plan to implement for when the temptation returns. Avoid situations that will set you up to fail. Seek the support of friends. Set specific, realistic goals. Focus on one day at a time. Each day's victory will accumulate into a series of triumphs that will strengthen you.

4. R_____—This step brings restoration to relationships.

> † **Matthew 5:23-24**—Jesus commanded, *"Therefore, if you are offering your gift at the altar and there remember that your brother has something against you,* **24.** *leave your gift there in front of the altar. First go and be reconciled to your brother; then come and offer your gift.*

This step involves "clearing the air" with the offended person. Communicate by getting the problem out into the open. Do not keep your feelings bottled up inside. Pray that the Lord would show you how to approach the person and exactly what you should say and when you should say it. When you go to the offended person, approach them with a humble, loving spirit and a pure heart. Reconcile the rift by talking it out, asking for their forgiveness, and making any restitution. Doing this should restore your relationship with them, and remove the foothold given to the devil. Keep in mind that you are not responsible for the person's refusal to accept your attempt to reconcile. (See the last SQ&A in this session for what to do if the person does not respond.)

✝ **Numbers 5:5-7**—*The LORD said to Moses,* **6.** *"Say to the Israelites: 'When a man or woman wrongs another in any way and so is unfaithful to the Lord, that person is guilty* **7.** *and must confess the sin he has committed. He must make full restitution for his wrong, add one fifth to it and give it all to the person he has wronged.'"*

A. Release that person into God's care and pray for His very best in their lives.

B. Once you truly forgive that person, also forgive yourself—**and get over it and move on!**

✝ **Philippians 3:13-14** (NLT)—*...I am focusing all my energies on this one thing: Forgetting the past and looking forward to what lies ahead,* **14.** *I strain to reach the end of the race and receive the prize for which God...is calling us up to heaven.*

C. Do not entertain any further negative feelings that may come. Avoid dwelling on them and just release them to God. Stay free of its hold on you!

D. If you have been victimized in any way, especially as a youth, then this step also includes releasing the burden and any shame that you may be experiencing. Keeping it bottled up within you gives place to the enemy to torment you. It may be necessary to seek out a spiritually mature Christian whom you completely trust, such as your pastor, and share it with them. They can help you release it to the Lord, and pray with you so you can be healed.

5. R_____—Consecrate the recaptured territory to God by praying a prayer of rededication. Thank Him for His forgiveness and for giving you another chance to start anew. If you are ridding your home, property, etc. from evil influences, reconsecrate it by invoking God's presence and protection for each area. Determine that from now on the Holy Spirit will have control.

> ☑ This ends the second session and the DVD content for Lesson 12.
> ☑ Continue on with the Study Questions and Application and the Summary.

STUDY QUESTIONS AND APPLICATION

1. On the scale below, write in the current month and year below the number that represents the zeal you have for serving God.

I Don't Have Any Desire										I Am Fully On Fire For God
0	1	2	3	4	5	6	7	8	9	10

A. Try to identify what may be the cause of any apathy, indifference, and lukewarmness that you may have in fully selling out in love and service to God.

2. Do you have any ill feelings toward someone when you see them or think of them? Search your heart, and ask the Holy Spirit to reveal if you have unforgiveness toward someone (including yourself). If so, name the person(s):

A. _____   C. _____

B. _____   D. _____

Now with each person named, walk through the five-step process given under the heading, **How to Recapture Territory Lost to the Enemy.** In the Repentance step, pray this prayer aloud for each one:

> "Heavenly Father, in obedience to your Word, I forgive (<u>name of person</u>) for what he/she did that caused me such hurt (be specific). I release my anger, resentment, and the desire for retaliation against (<u>name of person</u>). Forgive me for not reflecting Your character of forgiveness sooner. Restore my relationship with you. I pray your richest blessings upon (<u>name of person</u>). Continue to mold me into Your character likeness. Father, I now retract the permission I gave to the enemy and with your help I retake possession of this territory for Your glory. Thank You for being my Father and for showing to me Your love, mercy, forgiveness, and patience. Amen."

3. Refer back to the two strongholds you identified in SQ&A #2 at the end of the <u>first</u> <u>session</u> of this lesson that you need to recover back from the enemy. Then take each one through the five-step process given under the heading, **How to Recapture Territory Lost to the Enemy,** to complete the dismantling of these strongholds.

4. In **Matthew 18:15-20,** Jesus gave us a four-step procedure to use when we see a believer sin, or when someone sins against us. Write in these steps below:

A. **18:15**_____   C. **18:17a** _____

B. **18:16**_____   D. **18:17b**_____

SUMMARY

This lesson dealt with three areas: (1) the conclusion of the study of the Helmet of Salvation and Battlefield [#]3—the battle for our mind, with the objective of learning how to get victory in our thought life; (2) three tactics dealing with the Breastplate of Righteousness, thereby completing the study on this piece of armor; and (3) how to recapture spiritual territory we have given over to the enemy.

First, we sought a practical meaning of how we should put on the Helmet in order to obtain and maintain victory in our thought life. We learned that once we are *"born-again,"* our mind must now come under the rule of the Holy Spirit and be **1.** "<u>renewed</u>" by aligning its carnal thinking to the mind and will of God. To do this, our minds must be **2.** <u>disciplined</u> as commanded in Scripture in the following ways: we must **3.** "<u>destroy</u>" every stronghold, which is an ingrained pattern of erroneous thinking that controls our decisions and dictates our behavior. It consists of *"pretensions"* that blind us to the truth; and *"arguments,"* or the rationalizations that we use to justify our disobedience that keep us in its power. Defense mechanisms are another. Some examples of mindsets that become strongholds were given.

To get to the heart of it, we must ask God to reveal the thought that produced the feeling that triggered our reaction; we also must be watchful and **4.** "take captive" every thought as a "prisoner of war" so it doesn't rule us, and bring every thought in **5.** "obedience" to Christ in order to renew and reprogram our thinking, not allowing thoughts contrary to Scripture to go unchallenged; to **6.** resist/drive out these thoughts (just like Israel did the heathen nations) which will activate the Holy Spirit's power; and finally to meditate on **7.** God's Word every day and maintain the profession of our belief in it. The enemy uses the **TACTIC: Procrastination** to persuade us to put off obeying God's will and that which we know we should do—to a future time. Let's remember Solomon. We can have all the head knowledge about these things, but they are useless if we choose not to obey God and put His commands into daily practice. We must not only deal with the sins that we commit but also repent of those things we know we should do but don't.

We concluded the study on the Breastplate of Righteousness by giving three more tactics of the enemy. Since believers on fire for God are a threat to the interests of satan's kingdom, demonic forces will try to extinguish the flame by using **TACTIC: Apathy and Indifference,** thereby depleting God's army of laborers and reducing our opposition. It also robs us of potential rewards. Another trap the devil uses is **TACTIC: Isolate the Prey** in an attempt to persuade us to withdraw ourselves from support and fellowship with other Christians, therefore growing cold spiritually.

Still another, **TACTIC: Unforgiveness,** is successfully used time and again to get us to put ourselves in a position where God can't forgive us until we forgive someone. Through a detailed explanation of the devil's intended outcome of this strategy, we carefully noted each step of the chain reaction of unforgiveness and the awesome damage it can do to one's life and one's relationship with God.

We concluded by giving a general blueprint of five key steps on how to recapture spiritual territory we have given up to the enemy. These steps usually flow in order but may differ from person to person. God wants us to live in victory and has made a way for us to reclaim lost ground. The first step is to **1.** resolve. It all starts with a determination of our will. A decision must be made to cancel the permission that we gave to the enemy. What was lost by disobedience must now be regained through obedience to God's Word. This decision is the declaration that begins the reclaiming process.

Then we must **2.** repent of the sin and make a clean break with it confessing the sin to God and renouncing it. God will forgive us and restore our relationship with Him. Repentance takes away the right of the devil to continue having control. Be aware that repentance may not prevent future consequences from occurring due to our sin. Next we must **3.** resist. Now that we have submitted to God's will, we can resist the devil and he will flee. In this step we shut the door on any further thinking about and acting out of this sin. As we battle to resist, we activate the power of the Holy Spirit in our life. This ongoing step helps maintain our deliverance. Then we **4.** release our feelings, "clear the air" by making amends and restitution with the offended person—restoring the relationship. This removes the foothold we gave to the devil. Finally, **5.** rededicate to God the recaptured territory and begin anew.

Lesson 13

SHOES FOR COMBAT: Our Christian Walk and Witness
(Battlefield #4)

☑ Before starting the DVD:

Both God and satan use human instrumentality to accomplish their purposes. The goal of this lesson (divided into two sessions) is to show the critical importance of God's high call upon us in representing Him before our fellow man. This involves both being an effective witness in rescuing those who don't know our Lord, as well as being a true brother and sister in Christ to God's people. We will also learn seven tactics the enemy effectively uses on this battlefront.

There are three aspects that God does in the life of a believer according to **Ephesians 2:8-10:**

1. SALVATION—the work God does **for** us
2. SANCTIFICATION—the work God does **in** us
3. SERVICE—the work God does **through** us *"...Christ Jesus has created us for a life of good works, which He has already prepared for us to do"* **(Ephesians 10**–GNT). (Also see **Mark 16:19-20.**) And our service will be judged according to our **works (2 Corinthians 5:10; Romans 14:10-12; 1 Corinthians 3:10-15);** and our **words (Matthew 12:36-37).**

There are four basic categories of our service to God:

A. Walk pleasing to our Commander in Chief.
B. Walk in love—serving one another.
C. Free the captives (evangelism).
D. Transform the culture.

We are all called to advance the kingdom of God in our sphere of influence here in satan's domain. God has a specific work for us to do and a wonderful plan for each of our lives. As we seek Him, He will reveal His assignments to us. We find fulfillment when we accept His call and carry out His will. The enemy of our soul will do all in his power to hinder us from choosing to cooperate with the plan God has selected us to do. And if he is successful, he will cause us to miss out on God's best. One of the hardest things for us to deal with is knowing we are out of God's will and that we have failed Him. Many people heard Kathryn Kuhlman, whose healing ministry was known worldwide, say that the Lord told her that she was not the first one He called to that ministry. The others before her did not respond, but she surrendered and said "Yes." The rest is history!

As you develop the ability to win this invisible war by serving God in these four areas, allow God to show you how to walk in victory and avoid the pitfalls and land mines in Battlefield #4. **Q:** What legacy would you like to leave behind? Do you know the first thoughts people have whenever they hear your name or think of you?

☑ **DVD Users:** Watch Lesson 13, Session 1 for an overview before proceeding further (18 min.).
☑ When you're through, pick up again at this point. Fill in the blanks from the Summary.

REPRESENTING GOD TO THE WORLD

† **Ephesians 6:15** (NLT)—*For shoes, put on the readiness to preach the Good News of peace with God* (*"the gospel of peace"* KJV).

1. The footgear of the Roman soldier consisted of two parts: the armor from below the knee to the ankle called the greave, and the shoe or sandal.[1] Just as the Roman soldier used these combat shoes for firm footing and protection, so the Holy Spirit relates these aspects to a Christian's spiritual walk.

   A. The shoes speak to us of how our testimony and propagation of the Gospel G_____ us spiritually, keeping us from stumbling and slipping and protecting our walk with the Lord.

   B. The shoes also speak to us of our S_____ to God, which reflects our Christian walk before Him—especially in the field of evangelism.

2. God has commissioned us to be His A_____, and has entrusted to us, and has sent us forth, with the ministry of R_____.

   † **2 Corinthians 5:18-20**—*All this is from God, who reconciled us to himself through Christ and gave us the ministry of reconciliation:* **19.** *that God was reconciling the world to himself in Christ, not counting men's sins against them. And he has committed to us the message of reconciliation.* **20.** *We are therefore Christ's ambassadors, as though God were making his appeal through us. We implore you on Christ's behalf: Be reconciled to God.*

📖 DEFINITION—AMBASSADOR

An ambassador is an authorized spokesman or messenger commissioned by a dignitary to a foreign country as the resident representative of his own intentions and government. *Presbeuō* is the Greek word and it also carries the added dimension of spiritual maturity.

The church, the Body of Christ, is the hand of Jesus extended to a lost world. Do **not** believe that you should wait to tell others about Jesus until you are spiritually mature. Just be sure that your "talk" is backed up by your "walk."

   A. In contrast to the Old Testament animal sacrifices, we must present our body and life as a *"living sacrifice"*—an act of worship to God. We put ourselves, as it were, on the altar—bringing death to self in order to carry out God's will. When we die, a sweet smelling fragrance ascends to Him, and the fragrance of life and the knowledge of God impact the person **(2 Corinthians 2:14-16)**. Sacrificial, loving service seeks to benefit others at the expense of self. Nothing will defeat a self-centered lifestyle more than ministering to others.

   † **Romans 12:1**—*...offer your bodies as living sacrifices, holy and pleasing to God—this is your spiritual act of worship.*

(1) In **John 10:10,** Jesus said that He would lay down his self-life (*psuchē*) so we could have God's life (*zōē*). In the Garden of Gethsemane, His spirit struggled with His soul (self-life) over whether He would choose to preserve His sinless life or accept His Father's will by being made sin for us on the cross. His willingness to die that horrible death in our place has given life to all who have accepted His sacrifice.

►**CONSIDER THIS:** The word "Gethsemane" means "oil press." One cannot obtain olive oil until the outer skin has been ruptured. Just as Jesus underwent crushing and brokenness in the garden, so God brings a Gethsemane experience into our lives in order that His life and fragrance can ooze out from us so that many can be ministered to. Oftentimes when we are squeezed, the ugliness of our selfish nature erupts instead. This prevents the beauty and fragrance of God's character from coming forth, and our effectiveness in ministry to hurting people is diminished. Brokenness is used by God to put the sinful nature to death in order that His life can freely flow, unhindered, through our spirit. Let us learn God's way of releasing His life (*zōē*) within us to others and responding in a Christ-like manner.

    B. Proper P_____ is essential in this most critical of assignments, and note again that it involves something that is spoken.

        † **1 Peter 3:15—***...Always be prepared to give an answer to everyone who asks you to give the reason for the hope that you have. But do this with gentleness and respect...*

        † **Ephesians 6:15** (NIrV)—*Wear on your feet what will prepare you to tell the good news of peace.*

        (1) How do we prepare ourselves to take the gospel of peace?

            (a) Study the Bible and learn the basics of personal evangelism **(2 Timothy 2:15).**

            (b) Ask God to help you plan a presentation that fits you—one you're comfortable with.

            (c) Communicate it with love and compassion—simply, accurately, and clearly. Be real.

            (d) Leave something with them that they can read at a later time (literature, etc.).

            (e) Get contact information so you can follow up.

3. These "Boots" provide P_____ and E_____ to our spiritual lives.

    A. God has provided spiritual power to our inner man through *"the word of our testimony"* to others. It is our declaration of the great things that God has done for us and evidence that God is alive and real today. It reinforces faith in our hearts and inspires it in others. Our testimony is a necessary ingredient that gives us power to overcome satan and his dark forces.

        † **Revelation 12:11—***They overcame him* [the devil] *by the blood of the Lamb and by the word of their testimony; they did not love their lives so much as to shrink from death.*

    B. Proclaiming our testimony is essential. Scripture tells us that failure to do so draws both a corresponding positive and negative **response** from God:

† **Romans 10:9-10** (NLT)—*For if you confess with your mouth that Jesus is Lord and believe in your heart that God raised him from the dead, you will be saved. **10.** For it is by believing in your heart that you are made right with God, and it is by confessing with your mouth that you are saved.*

† **Matthew 10:32-33** (NLT)—Jesus said, *"If anyone acknowledges me publicly here on earth, I will openly acknowledge that person before my Father in heaven. **33.** But if anyone denies me here on earth, I will deny that person before my Father in heaven."*

▶ **CONSIDER THIS:** I believe what Jesus meant here is a repeated public denial of Him in word and deed as a basic way of life—not just intermittent failures. God does not condemn us for a few mistakes and shortcomings. His heart is *always* to forgive, restore, and use us. If you have publicly denied Him—repent and don't allow yourself to come under condemnation. Satan would like to use your failures to convince you that you are not worthy to continue walking with Christ. Be encouraged with Christ's restoration of Peter after his denial (see **John 21:15-19; Acts 2:14-42).**

C. Not only will we deprive ourselves of power to overcome and draw a negative response from God, but failure to *"put on"* this armor will also invite the enemy to gain another foothold:

(1) I_____—It causes us to waste our time and become unfruitful for the Kingdom of God. It's an unhealthy state and it can easily develop into the devil's playground.

(a) It contributed to David's sin with Bathsheba—with horrific consequences **(2 Samuel 11:1-5).** If David would have gone into battle with his men rather than remaining behind in Jerusalem, perhaps the incident with Bathsheba would never have occurred.

(b) *"Abundance of idleness"* was one of the causes for the downfall of Sodom and Gomorrah **(Ezekiel 16:49** KJV**).**

(c) We must be active in God's service for both the Kingdom's sake and our own! Furthermore, our work for God will not only be rewarded, but there also seems to be an indication in Scripture that to some extent they will provide our covering.

† **Revelation 19:7-8**—*"Let us rejoice and be glad and give him glory! For the wedding of the Lamb has come, and his bride has made herself ready. 8. Fine linen, bright and clean, was given her to wear." (Fine linen stands for the righteous acts of the saints.)*

(d) Evangelist Steve Hill once asked, "When Jesus calls out your name on Coronation Day...what will all of heaven see?...I want Jesus to give me a crown that causes all of heaven to fall into a holy hush because it will represent the way I lived and what I did for the cause of Christ."[2] Picture yourself before Christ on that Day! How devastating would it be to receive little or no rewards, tragically indicating that you did little or nothing for Christ worth rewarding? Imagine the magnitude of your regret! What will you do about it now while you still have time?

▶ **CONSIDER THIS:** Both God and satan use **human instrumentality** to accomplish their purposes. Christ has chosen to be dependent upon us to rescue captives out of satan's kingdom. God has given His children the responsibility of representing Him to an unbelieving world, and to win those souls for His kingdom. What trust He has placed in us! **Q:** If we fail to reach people within our sphere of influence and our corner of the world, is it possible that they could die and go to hell if God is unable to raise up another to reach them? As His representatives in this ministry of reconciliation, God wants to make His salvation appeal through us, compelling them to make their peace with Him. Christ is counting on us even though He knows at times that we will misrepresent Him, resulting in some rejecting Christ and Christianity perhaps for the rest of their lives.

4. Christ's appeal to the unbeliever is mainly accomplished by the working of the Holy Spirit through human vessels as we witness and proclaim His Word. We are the conduit God works through, as water passes through a pipe, using all of our human faculties.

    ✝ **Matthew 5:14-16**—Jesus taught, *"You are the light of the world. A city on a hill cannot be hidden. **15.** Neither do people light a lamp and put it under a bowl. Instead they put it on its stand, and it gives light to everyone in the house. **16.** In the same way, let your light shine before men, that they may see your good deeds and praise your Father in heaven."*

    ✝ **John 17:20** (NLT)—Jesus said, *"I am praying not only for these disciples but also for all who will ever believe in me because of their testimony."*

    ✝ **Luke 10:1-2** (Phillips)—*...the Lord commissioned seventy other disciples and sent them off in twos as advance-parties into every town and district where He intended to go Himself. "There is a great harvest," he told them, "but only a few are working in it—which means you must pray to the Lord of the harvest that He will send out more reapers to bring in his harvest."*

    ✝ **John 20:21**—*Again Jesus said, "Peace be with you! As the Father has sent me, I am sending you."*

    ✝ **Matthew 28:18-20**—*Then Jesus came to them and said, "All authority in heaven and on earth has been given to me. **19.** Therefore go and make disciples of all nations, baptizing them in the name of the Father and of the Son and of the Holy Spirit, **20.** and teaching them to obey everything I have commanded you. And surely I am with you always, to the very end of the age."*

God has chosen to **rely** on us, as He did with the apostle Paul: *"...to open their eyes and turn them from darkness to light, and from the power of Satan to God, so that they may receive forgiveness of sins and a place among those who are sanctified by faith in me."* **(Acts 26:18).** Proclaim to them God's love and forgiveness. Warn them about the judgment to come. Rescue them out of satan's kingdom. Both God and they are counting on us! I heard the late Dr. Bill Bright once say, **"If not me, who? If not now, when?"** Satan will try to stop us. He uses fear of failure, rejection, and embarrassment, etc. Don't allow those tactics to cause you to quit! Press on and work through them.

    ✝ **Ezekiel 3:18-21**—God said: *"When I say to a wicked man, 'You will surely die,' and you do not warn him or speak out to dissuade him from his evil ways in order to save his life, that wicked man will die for his sin, and I will hold you accountable for his blood. **19.** But if you do warn the wicked man and he does not turn from his wickedness or from his evil ways, he will die for his sin; but you will have saved yourself."*

📖 DEFINITION—GOSPEL OF PEACE

The Greek word for gospel is *euangelion* meaning "good news" or "good message." The **gospel of peace** then is the announcement of the good news that Christ's death on the cross appeased the righteous anger of God toward sin and removed the obstacle of sin which stood between God and man. Christ has reconciled these two opposing parties so that now they can be in a state of peace and friendship. God now waits with outstretched arms—entreating the unbeliever through His children to be reconciled to Him.

    A. The "preaching" or declaration of this message of reconciliation is an offensive weapon used to penetrate satan's evil empire of darkness. More will be said about this in Lesson 15.

    B. A Christian is to be a walking temple—a carrier of the holy presence, power, message, and character of God to other people. Rid yourself of the things that cover up His beauty and prevent it from shining forth from your life. **Live daily in the awareness that you carry within you a Divine Person!!**

    C. When we are instrumental in snatching someone out of satan's kingdom and reconciling them to God, our "feet" can be so beautiful to them.

        † **Romans 10:11-15** (NLT)—*As the Scriptures tell us, "Anyone who believes in him will not be disappointed."... 13. For "Anyone who calls on the name of the Lord will be saved." 14. But how can they call on him to save them unless they believe in him? And how can they believe in him if they have never heard about him? And how can they hear about him unless someone tells them? 15. And how will anyone go and tell them without being sent? That is what the Scriptures mean when they say, "How beautiful are the feet of those who bring good news!"*

> ☑ This ends our first session of Battlefield #4—Shoes for Combat: Our Christian Walk and Witness. Now please answer these SQ&A.

STUDY QUESTIONS AND APPLICATION

1. How would you rate your **overall** quality as an ambassador for Christ?

    ☐ Excellent   ☐ Above average   ☐ Average   ☐ Fair   ☐ Poor

    A. Identify at least two things that hinder your progress and take steps at once to correct them.

        (1)   (2)

2. Do you have a well thought out presentation for witnessing and leading someone to Christ? If not, seek God and ask your pastor how to go about creating one that you'll be comfortable using. Resources can also be obtained at the online bookstore at www.cslovettbooks.com.

3. When was the last time you witnessed to someone about Jesus? _____ (date) When was the last time you led somebody to Christ? _____ (date). Ask God to reveal what is hindering you from doing more.

> ☑ **DVD Users:** When you are ready, begin the last session of Shoes for Combat by watching Lesson 13, Session 2, (14 min.). When you're through, pick up again at this point. Fill in the blanks from the Summary. The 3rd Qtr. Exam can be taken after this session.
>
> Note: I suggest that the remainder of this lesson be treated as a separate session.

Session 2
TACTICS THE ENEMY USES ON BATTLEFIELD #4

There are tactics that the enemy uses on this battlefield that are like pitfalls and landmines to trip us up and eliminate us from being an effective witness for Christ. Among them are: hypocrisy, infiltration, divide and conquer, character assassination, and being used as a stumbling block.

Hypocrisy

 TACTIC: Hypocrisy—The enemy will attempt to ruin your testimony and witness for Christ by enticing you to disobey God's Word and walk in a way contrary to your words and actions, thereby making you an ineffective witness and a reproach to the cause of Christ.
◎ *Main Target:* Your Witness.

1. The main reason for the success of this tactic is disobedience to God. One of the most important possessions we have is our Christian witness, reputation, and integrity. They take years to build, but it only takes one bad decision to lose them and undo all the good that has been done.

►**CONSIDER THIS:** The nation of Israel was raised up by God and planted in the midst of the heathen nations to be a witness to them of the one true God—a light in all the spiritual darkness round about them. For the most part, they miserably failed and caused God's Holy name to be profaned among those nations **(Ezekiel 36:17-23).** Someone once said that you may be the only "Jesus" some people will ever see. There's a dark and spiritually hungry world out there that is wondering if God really exists, and if so, what is He like? We cannot bear the character of the devil and win people to Jesus. Don't cause someone to say, "If this is what being a Christian is, I want no part of it." May God help us to never be the cause of someone rejecting Christ because of our hypocritical actions!!

> † **2 Samuel 12:13-14** (NLT)—The prophet Nathan said to David after his sin with Bathsheba: *14. "But you have given the enemies of the Lord great opportunity to despise and blaspheme him, so your child will die."*

> † **Romans 2:21-(24)**—*...God's name is blasphemed among the Gentiles because of you.*

A. Our "old man" or carnal nature must come under total control of the Holy Spirit in order for our lives to emanate God's character. When it doesn't, it becomes the main reason our witness for Christ is tarnished **(1 Corinthians 3:1-4).**

> † **Titus 2:3-5**—Our behavior must not cause one to find fault with our God or His Word.

> † **Proverbs 11:9** (NKJV)—*The hypocrite with his mouth destroys his neighbor...*

2. God will always honor what He said in the Bible—even if people proclaim it with wrong motives and while walking in sin. His Word will not return to Him empty and unfruitful even though the vessels God once used may have backslidden **(Isaiah 55:11)**.

> † **Philippians 1:15-18**—*It is true that some preach Christ out of envy and rivalry, but others out of goodwill... 17. The former preach Christ out of selfish ambition... 18. But what does it matter? The important thing is that in every way, whether from false motives or true, Christ is preached...*

> † **Matthew 7:21-23** (NASB)—Jesus said: *"Not everyone who says to Me, 'Lord, Lord,' will enter the kingdom of heaven, but he who does the will of My Father who is in heaven will enter. 22. Many will say to Me on that day, 'Lord, Lord, did we not prophesy in Your name, and in Your name cast out demons, and in Your name perform many miracles?' 23. And then I will declare to them, 'I never knew you; DEPART FROM ME, YOU WHO PRACTICE LAWLESSNESS.'"*

Infiltration and Divide and Conquer

🐎 **TACTIC: Infiltration**—The enemy will secretly plant his own among God's people to infiltrate God's church, etc. and cause it harm from within. ◎ *Main Targets*: Local Church or Christian Organization.

> † **Matthew 13:24-30, 36-43**—*Jesus told them another parable: "The kingdom of heaven is like a man who sowed good seed in his field. 25. But while everyone was sleeping, his enemy came and sowed weeds among the wheat, and went away... 37. The one who sowed the good seed is the Son of Man. 38. The field is the world, and the good seed stands for the sons of the kingdom. The weeds are the sons of the evil one, 39. and the enemy who sows them is the devil..."*

1. This tactic is successful because many times the spiritual leader over a group is not on guard and watchful. Note that it was *"while everyone was sleeping"* **(13:25)** that the enemy was able to infiltrate.

2. The goals of this tactic are:

   A. On an <u>individual</u> <u>level</u>: to turn one away from receiving Christ and becoming His disciple—thereby cutting them off from the only Source who has the truth that will set them free.

   B. On a <u>community</u> <u>level</u>: to bring reproach on a local church or Christian organization thereby dimming or extinguishing that organization's light in the very community that it was called to reach.

3. Another purpose of infiltration is to bring **division.**

🐎 **TACTIC: Divide and Conquer**—The enemy will try to get you to be the source of fighting, strife, and dissension within your group so that you become the cause of division—knowing full well that any nation, city, church, or family divided against itself will become weak, ineffective, and eventually break up and collapse **(Matthew 12:25)**. ◎ *Main Targets:* Unity and Pride.

A. Divisiveness comes from the sinful nature and is soulish activity. It is an enemy to peace, unity, and harmony.

† **1 Corinthians 3:3** (NKJV)—*for you are still carnal. For where there are envy, strife, and divisions among you, are you not carnal...*

B. The enemy uses division to try to move us out of God's will thus weakening God's work.

(1) Example: The split between Paul and Barnabas **(Acts 13:2-3; 15:36-40).**

(2) Example: Using people to cause division in order to split church congregations, etc. thereby marring their reputation and witness in the community and weakening their effectiveness. This often results in others being reluctant to become involved with any church ever again. When our selfish, petty interests come before preserving the integrity and reputation of Christ's blood-bought church, we are truly blinded and to be pitied. We're called to *"Make every effort to keep the unity of the Spirit through the bond of peace."* **(Ephesians 4:3).**

4. There are two fronts on which this takes place.

A. **From "members" INSIDE the group**—The enemy works on existing "members" within a group who are serving the Lord. Seeking an opportune time, he works through whoever gives him an opening to cause dissension and bring harm from within. We all are vulnerable and most of the time, we are unaware that we are being used for this diabolical purpose. Even the walls of your church do not provide a safe haven from the enemy of your soul.

(1) Example: Discord within the church at Ephesus

† **Acts 20:28-31**—*Keep watch over yourselves and all the flock of which the Holy Spirit has made you overseers. Be shepherds of the church of God, which he bought with his own blood. 29. I know that after I leave, savage wolves will come in among you and will not spare the flock. 30. Even from your own number men will arise and distort the truth in order to draw away disciples after them. 31. So be on your guard! Remember that for three years I never stopped warning each of you night and day with tears.*

(2) Example: The comment to Job by his wife

† **Job 2:4-9**—Satan challenged God about Job: *5. "But stretch out your hand and strike his flesh and bones, and he will surely curse you to your face."... 9. His wife said to him* [Job], *"Are you still holding on to your integrity? Curse God and die!"*

Note: Once satan got permission from God to touch Job's body he hoped Job would "curse God to His face." It was a close family member he was able to use in trying to get Job to do just that.

(3) Dr. Jay Passavant teaches that "...internal conflict derails many more healthy churches than does any external obstacle." and "...the single most destructive force affecting a congregation is usually unleashed from within. And it usually has to do with one simple thing: the tongue."[3] (See SQ&A #3 for Dr. Passavant's prevention plan.)

(a) Hurt feelings and differences, selfishness, poor communication, immaturity, petty childish behavior, and vocalizing critical opinions and complaints lead to mounting tension and conflict, the dissolution of trust, and relational disarray. These all give the enemy the ammunition needed for an open door to destroy.

(b) Jesus said that *"...the words I speak unto you...are life."* **(John 6:63** KJV**)**. The words that we speak either build up or tear down—releasing life or death to those who hear them. Careless, unfruitful, and worthless words have a negative impact that is released and dumped upon others. These comments may reflect a momentary anger, irritability, insecurity, jealousy, depression, or fatigue that can cut deeply and be remembered for decades. But loving, affirming, encouraging, and truthful words have a positive influence that refresh and bring vitality.

† **Proverbs 18:21** (NLT)—*Those who love to talk will experience the consequences, for the tongue can kill or nourish life.*

† **Proverbs 12:18**—*Reckless words pierce like a sword, but the tongue of the wise brings healing.*

† **James 1:26** (GNT)—*Does anyone think he is a religious man? If he does not control his tongue his religion is worthless and he deceives himself.*

† **James 3:6-9**—*The tongue also is a fire, a world of evil among the parts of the body. It corrupts the whole person, sets the whole course of his life on fire, and is itself set on fire by hell. 7. All kinds of animals, birds, reptiles and creatures of the sea are being tamed and have been tamed by man, 8. but no man can tame the tongue. It is a restless evil, full of deadly poison. 9. With the tongue we praise our Lord and Father, and with it we curse men...*

† **Matthew 12:34-37** (GNT)—Jesus said, *"...For the mouth speaks what the heart is full of...I tell you this: on the Judgment Day everyone will have to give account of every useless word he has ever spoken. 37. For your words will be used to judge you, either to declare you innocent or to declare you guilty."*

B. **From people OUTSIDE the group**—The enemy infiltrates by raising up those from without.

(1) Example: Judas Iscariot

† **Psalm 41:9**—*Even my close friend, whom I trusted, he who shared my bread, has lifted up his heel against me* (see **John 13:18**).

† **John 6:70-71**—*Then Jesus replied, "Have I not chosen you, the Twelve? Yet one of you is a devil!" 71. (He meant Judas, the son of Simon Iscariot, who, though one of the Twelve, was later to betray him.)*

Note: Jesus' decision to include Judas Iscariot as one of the twelve apostles was made carefully with much prayer and direction from His Father **(Luke 6:12-16)**. Christ probably knew early on that Judas would betray Him. And yet our Heavenly Father allowed His Son to experience betrayal by a close friend and associate, therefore adding to His human experience.

(2) Example: Those in the Galatian church who were being drawn back into the false teaching of Jewish legalism to do things to earn their salvation.

† **Galatians 2:4-5** (NASB)—*But it was because of the false brethren secretly brought in, who had sneaked in to spy out our liberty which we have in Christ Jesus, in order to bring us into bondage. **5.** But we did not yield in subjection to them for even an hour, so that the truth of the gospel would remain with you.*

(3) Example: Some of the infiltration of Christian organizations is deliberate with well-conceived strategies inspired by the devil with people fully aware of what they are doing.

† **1 John 2:19** (KJV)—*They went out from us, but they were not of us.*

5. Leaders must boldly bring correction or they will suffer the consequences of their neglect.
Q: What should be done when one of the devil's "weeds" (tares) is detected within the church?

A. Jesus said that there was a danger of uprooting God's people if we pull up the tares—somewhat due to the intermingling relationship of their roots with the wheat **(Matthew 13:29).** Certainly we should identify them and not cultivate them. Seek God for wisdom and use these guidelines:

(1) Follow the procedure Christ gave us in **Matthew 18:15-20** concerning church discipline.

(2) Warn those who cause division and then enforce it as directed by the following Scripture:

† **Titus 3:9-11**—*But avoid foolish controversies and genealogies and arguments and quarrels about the law, because these are unprofitable and useless. **10.** Warn a divisive person once, and then warn him a second time. After that, have nothing to do with him. **11.** You may be sure that such a man is warped and sinful; he is self-condemned.*

Character Assassination

♞ **TACTIC: Character Assassination**—The enemy will try to use you to maliciously slander and defame someone's character by intentionally (or unintentionally) speaking evil about them, falsely accusing and misrepresenting them, in order to destroy their reputation and witness for Christ.
◎ *Main Targets:* Someone's Reputation and/or Witness for Christ.

📖 DEFINITION—SLANDER

The Greek word used in the New Testament is *diabolos*, "an accuser." It is the same word used for the name *"devil."* It is the spreading of false charges or misrepresentations intended to defame and damage another's character and reputation.

1. It is one thing when our testimony is ruined by our own hypocrisy, but quite another when we are falsely accused, having done nothing wrong.

2. Satan attempts to use people to destroy the credibility of true, effective servants of God in order to neutralize the effectiveness of their work for Him. The goal is to discredit them in the public eye so that the truth they speak will be rendered powerless and not be received. When we are involved in slander, we are acting like, and are being used by, the devil.

3. Some ways the enemy is successful in this tactic are by using (or causing) the hurt feelings we receive to motivate us to lash back in retaliation against those who have offended us; and by using people (especially those who like to talk a lot) in gossip and backbiting.

4. Slander can be wordless—a gesture, a wink, a smirk, or other body language can destroy, too. It is caused by hatred **(Psalm 109:3),** idleness **(1 Timothy 5:13),** and pride.

5. **Q:** How should we respond when we are slandered?

    A. By an unbeliever?—*"answer kindly"* **(1 Corinthians 4:13).**

       † **1 Peter 3:16**—*...keeping a clear conscience, so that those who speak maliciously against your good behavior in Christ may be ashamed of their slander.*

    B. By a Christian?—Follow the procedure Christ outlined for us in **Matthew 18:15-20.**

▶ **CONSIDER THIS:** We must realize how very much we need each other in this invisible war. God's people need to look after one another and cover each other's back. If we can't trust a fellow believer to not wound us or "stab us in the back," who can we trust? We must be careful to not become an enemy to them like this and betray their trust, and to not fall into the trap of thinking ill of another based upon what we **heard** about them. *"...Every fact is to be confirmed by the testimony of two or three witnesses."* **(2 Corinthians 13:1** NASB) It is imperative that we always seek the truth in a matter.

6. A variation of this tactic is when people try to subtly set a trap for you (see **Daniel 6:1-24**).

♞ **TACTIC: Distort Their Words**—The enemy will prepare a trap for you, baiting you with a question in order to distort your answer and then cause it to be used against you in the court of public opinion. ◎ *Main Target:* Your Christian Reputation.

       † **Luke 20:20-26**—*...They hoped to catch Jesus in something he said so that they might hand him over to the power and authority of the governor... 26. They were unable to trap him in what he had said there in public. And astonished by his answer, they became silent.*

Be a Stumbling Block

♞ **TACTIC: Be a Stumbling Block**—The devil will try to use you to entrap another Christian so you will be the cause of offending them, or hindering them from doing God's will and leading them into error and sin—thereby tripping up their walk with God so they will eventually fall away from serving Him. ◎ *Main Target:* One's Relationship with God.

1. What are some ways we can be an offense and a stumbling block to a fellow believer?

    A. Through a well-meaning friend: Peter, clearly a child of God, was unwittingly used by satan to lay a trap for Jesus. The enemy's intention was to weaken Christ's resolve about doing His Father's will—dying a horrible death for sin on the cross in order to redeem mankind. This is a graphic example of how, if not on guard, we can be so right and mightily used of God one moment and be so wrong and used by the enemy the next. Pray for discernment.

✝ **Matthew 16:13-23**—*16. Simon Peter answered, "You are the Christ, the Son of the living God." 17. Jesus replied, "Blessed are you, Simon son of Jonah, for this was not revealed to you by man, but by my Father in heaven... 21. From that time on Jesus began to explain to his disciples that he must go to Jerusalem and suffer many things at the hands of the elders, chief priests and teachers of the law, and that he must be killed and on the third day be raised to life. 22. Peter took him aside and began to rebuke him. "Never, Lord!" he said. "This shall never happen to you!" 23. Jesus turned and said to Peter, "Out of my sight, Satan! You are a stumbling block to me; you do not have in mind the things of God, but the things of men."*

B. Through a selfish use of our own liberty in Christ: We are called to be very careful to not do anything (intentionally or unintentionally) that might be a source of harm in the spiritual growth of a fellow believer, especially a new Christian. Even if we feel the Scriptural freedom to do so in our own walk with God, we are to forego that liberty if it might cause our brother or sister in Christ to stumble. Think of it! We could end up destroying the awesome work God has done in their lives and for whom Christ died. Be cautious, for we usually are unaware of being used in this way.

✝ **1 Corinthians 8:9,11**—*Be careful...that the exercise of your freedom does not become a stumbling block to the weak... 11. So this weak brother, for whom Christ died, is destroyed by your knowledge.* (Also see verses **9-13; 10:23-33;** and **Romans 14:12-23.**)

(1) This can happen through a poor Christian example, leaving a bad taste in one's mouth **(Matthew 17:24-27; 2 Corinthians 6:3);** or by the criticism or pressure we exert that causes one to do something that conflicts with following their conscience—thereby inducing that person to sin. A Christian who believes the Bible gives them the liberty to drink alcoholic beverages is one example.

C. Through intentional or unintentional words and actions towards others that cause them to be offended.

D. Through erroneous teachings that contradict the Word of God.

✝ **Romans 16:17-18** (NLT)—*Watch out for people who cause divisions and upset people's faith by teaching things that are contrary to what you have been taught. Stay away from them. Such people are not serving Christ our Lord; they are serving their own personal interests. By smooth talk and glowing words they deceive innocent people.*

✝ **Romans 14:13**—*...make up your mind not to put any stumbling block or obstacle in your brother's way.*

✝ **Luke 17:1-3**—*Jesus said to his disciples: "Things that cause people to sin are bound to come, but woe to that person through whom they come... 3. So watch yourselves..."*

WHOSE INSTRUMENT WILL YOU BE—GOD'S or SATAN'S?

1. We can be a source of blessing to others or we can be used by the enemy to unleash evil into our world. The objectives of God and demons (as well as their character) can be clearly seen through the actions of human instruments that they inspire and use. Here are some examples:

A. The Sabeans and Chaldeans

† **Job 1:12-15, 17**—After God gave satan permission to touch Job's possessions, we see satan waiting for the right time to launch a successive series of calamities upon Job and his family. Satan was able to inspire the Sabeans and Chaldeans to target Job's oxen, donkeys, and camels and steal them—killing all of Job's servants that were tending them except for the four who just happened to escape to tell Job the tragic news.

B. King Herod

† **Matthew 2:1-20** (esp. verse 16)—Through self-preservation, satan tried to use King Herod to kill Jesus, a threat to his kingdom. This resulted in the tragic slaughter of many innocent children two years and younger. Behind most murders there is demonic activity.

C. King Saul threw his javelin at David under the inspiration of an evil spirit **(1 Samuel 19:9-10).**

D. The Antichrist will be the ultimate instrument in the hands of satan at the end of this age. The Bible states that he will rule the entire world. Even now people are being used to bring about a one world government that will culminate in his reign **(Revelation 13:4-8).**

E. Other examples of satan's character portrayed through people's actions are: Hitler in the extermination of three million Jews in the 1940s (as Satan tried to stop the nation of Israel from being formed); the Mafia and organized crime; those who work to take away our religious freedoms; terrorist activity; those who molest, abuse, and kidnap children; those who perform death culture practices such as abortions and euthanasia; serial killers and rapists; those in the entertainment industry who are used to promote the devil's messages and agenda; and those who produce products that are addictive and enslaving to our body. People can do these things from just their own sinful nature; however, much of the time demonic forces are energizing them without their being aware of it.

2. Unfortunately, Christians are also used at times by the enemy to injure their fellow believers with "friendly fire." But true love for one another *"...covers a multitude of sins."* **(1 Peter 4:8).**

TRANSFORMING THE CULTURE

1. What does the Bible teach about God using His children to influence and transform their culture?

▶**CONSIDER THIS:** Do you think God's people should infiltrate and influence the world system controlled by satan and establish God's principles in all of its culture-shaping institutions such as school districts; the local, state, and national government; the media; and the workplace? (See *World, its institutions* in index.) Or should Christians keep to themselves and have little or nothing to do with society—not even to voting in an election? Isn't the church either influencing the culture or it is being shaped by the culture it is called to reach? Consider the following commands that God has given to His church regarding this:

A. Be L_____—We are called to reflect Christ, as beacons of light shining in a dark world attracting those who do not know Him, that they may be drawn to His light. This is primarily for salvation purposes, but also to bring His principles to every phase of life.

† **Matthew 5:14-16** (NASB)—Jesus taught: *"You are the light of the world. A city set on a hill cannot be hidden; 15. nor does anyone light a lamp and put it under a basket, but on the lampstand, and it gives light to all who are in the house. 16. Let your light shine before men in such a way that they may see your good works, and glorify your Father who is in heaven."*

B. P_____—Jesus said that His children have a responsibility to submit to secular government (*"Caesar"*) for His sake—like paying taxes **(Mark 12:17)** and upholding the law.

† **1 Peter 2:13-15**—*Submit yourselves for the Lord's sake to every authority instituted among men...*

C. P_____—God commands us to pray for our nation and its leaders, regardless of their views or their political party.

† **1 Timothy 2:1-2**—*I urge, then, first of all, that requests, prayers, intercession and thanksgiving be made for everyone—2. for kings and all those in authority, that we may live peaceful and quiet lives in all godliness and holiness.*

D. Work for P_____—God intends for us to work to establish His peace in our world.

† **Matthew 5:9** (NLT)—*God blesses those who work for peace, for they will be called the children of God.*

(1) This involves being God's instrument of reconciliation: by using our efforts and influence to bring harmony to each other; by reconciling (or constraining) those who are walking in hate, strife, and contention; by bringing peace to hearts that are troubled; and ultimately, by helping others find Christ as Savior and making their peace with Him.

(2) However, we must be wise enough to realize that not everything in our world that is called "peace" is intended as God's Word defines it.

🐎 **TACTIC: Through Peace, Destroy!**—The enemy will inspire things done in the name of "peace," "peaceful coexistence," and "peace movements" and use them as a disguise to conquer. ◎ *Main Target:* Your Faith, Trust, and Naiveté.

▶**CONSIDER THIS:** For example, in recent times the Marxists/Communists have been successfully using this tactic for decades. When they say "peace," they mean total Communist rule and dictatorship no matter how it is obtained. It is designed to present the illusion of their desire for world peace in order to give them more time to build up their arms, subversively work within countries, and persuade nations to disarm. Since the desire for peace is so strong among us, we want to believe them. So we join and support organizations that profess to work for peace, but are actually working to further the insurgent's cause. Throughout history, many have failed to see beyond a group's lip service to peace. The antichrist will also effectively use this weapon in his future conquest of the world: *"...and by peace shall destroy many..."* **(Daniel 8:25** KJV**).**

Similarly, the devil also tries to get the church to peacefully coexist with false religions and false doctrines in order to water down the truth and mix it with error. Beware of ecumenism that seeks to achieve worldwide unity among all religions, which will lead to the formation of the apostate one world church in the endtimes.

E. R_____ E_____—For the most part, the Holy Spirit has chosen to use His children (the worldwide Body of Christ) to restrain evil in the world.

> † **2 Thessalonians 2:6-10**—*And now you know what is holding him back* [the antichrist], *so that he may be revealed at the proper time.* **7.** *For the secret power of lawlessness is already at work; but the one who now holds it back will continue to do so till he is taken out of the way.* **8.** *And then the lawless one will be revealed...*

(1) *"You are the salt of the earth..."* Jesus inferred that He wants us to not only give the world a taste of the reality of the true God and create in them a thirst for Him, but also like salt, to retard corruption and decay in our society: If we don't affect our culture for Christ, we will be overrun by evil and incur judgment upon ourselves: *"...but if the salt loses its saltiness...It is no longer good for anything, except to be thrown out and trampled under foot by men."* (**Matthew 5:13** NASB). Jesus also added in **Luke 14:34-35**: *"Salt is good, but if it loses its saltiness... 35. It is fit neither for the soil nor for the manure pile; it is thrown out. He who has ears to hear, let him hear."*

▶**CONSIDER THIS:** Tragically, America has begun to enter the post-Christian era and is fast becoming anti-Christian largely due to the church abdicating its responsibility in society. Unless Christians intercede in prayer, get involved in the political process, and become salt and light in our culture-shaping institutions, we will be living under someone else's worldview—with persecution!

(2) **Q:** When the devil motivates his people to plant porn shops, occult stores, areas of prostitution, gambling places, abortion clinics, and unleashes drug dealers and gangs into our community, or infiltrates harmful curriculum into our schools, should the church do nothing and allow its evil to corrupt and harm—especially to our youth**?** Or, should we come out from our comfort zones and rising up with a righteous anger, resist it through prayer, intercession, and action, confronting and challenging its presence and driving it out of our community in a lawful manner? How do you view it?

(3) We could reason that the struggle to restrain evil is a hopeless task, but God intends for us to bring about change in our culture! We can be instrumental to help create conditions in society that will bring the blessings of God instead of His judgment!

▶**CONSIDER THIS:** Our Founding Fathers integrated God's Word and principles into the fabric of our nation's laws and constitutions and it was reflected in our culture-shaping institutions. In the mid-1800s, the Protestant Church handed over the educating of our nation's children to the Government and today our kids are being indoctrinated by the secular humanist religion. Then in the 1960s, the church ceased to influence the entertainment industry by abandoning the Motion Picture Code based on the Ten Commandments that basically regulated every movie script. The result: moral decay. Due to the withdrawal of Christians from secular life during the last 40 years, we have abandoned our culture to unbelievers who have taken over the media, government, education, and the courts. Consequently, one day we and our children may be ruled by those who will impose their godless worldviews upon us by their election of leaders, court decisions, and enacting legislation (i.e. abortion).

Today, the Judeo-Christian ethic remains in only two institutions—the church and the family, with marriage and our children targeted for relentless attack. These two institutions are holding back an onslaught of evil upon our world. If these should fail, the ideological struggle will be over and moral and political chaos will ensue. satan will have captured this jewel of liberty called America, stripping her of every vestige of the true God and her Judeo-Christian heritage.

(4) Incredibly, many Christians do not even realize that a war is going on, or else we are unwilling to show up to engage the battle (even to vote) compared to our opponents who are deeply committed, work tirelessly, and are well-funded. What a shameful legacy for the church to lose by default—even with having the most powerful spiritual weapons at our disposal, and an omnipotent God to work on our behalf. As British statesman, Edmund Burke said, "All that is necessary for the triumph of evil is that good men do nothing."[4] **We must not lack the will! Q:** What will it take to motivate you to rise up to defend biblical values and restrain evil by praying and letting your voice be heard?

† **Obadiah 1:11** (NIrV)—God said to Edom, Israel's neighboring country: *"Strangers entered the gates of Jerusalem. They cast lots to see what each one would get. They carried off its wealth. When that happened, you just stood there and did nothing. You were like one of them."*

(Note: In all of this, I am **not** advocating the kingdom-dominion view that believes Christians will subdue and purify this ungodly world system and bring King Jesus back to a conquered earth.)

F. **Rescue Souls**—Above all, we must put forth our efforts and time engaging the battle for the eternal destiny of our fellow human beings by rescuing and winning them to Christ. Jesus prayed to His Father: *"As you sent me into the world, I am sending them into the world."* (**John 17:18** NLT).

(1) We often focus on the havoc the devil is wreaking on our world and fail to see how God's kingdom is mightily growing and progressing in the earth. The Holy Spirit continues to woo people, calling them out of satan's kingdom into His Kingdom to become a part of the worldwide church—the Bride being prepared for God's Son. We have the greatest power working with us. All we need to do is be available, yielded instruments in His hand.

† **Mark 16:19-20**—*After the Lord Jesus had spoken to them, he was taken up into heaven and he sat at the right hand of God.* ***20.*** *Then the disciples went out and preached everywhere, and the Lord worked with them and confirmed his word by the signs that accompanied it.*

> ☑ This ends the second session and the DVD content for Lesson 13.
> ☑ Continue on with the Study Questions and Application and the Summary.

STUDY QUESTIONS AND APPLICATION

1. Regarding the four basic categories of our service to God, think about your efforts and effectiveness in each area and how well-rounded you are overall. Then evaluate yourself in each area on a scale from 1 to 10 (ten being the highest).

_____ A. Walking pleasing to your Commander-in-Chief

_____ C. Freeing the captives (evangelism)

_____ B. Walking in love—serving one another

_____ D. Transforming the culture

2. Ask God if you have a tendency to be used by the enemy in any of these tactics. If so, how? Is your church or Christian organization experiencing any of these tactics?

   A. Hypocrisy: _____

   B. Infiltration: _____

   C. Divide and Conquer: _____

   D. Character Assassination: _____

   E. Distort Their Words: _____

   F. Be a Stumbling Block: _____

3. In response to the destructive forces of strife and other sinful behavior being unleashed in his church, Dr. Jay Passavant, Senior Pastor of North Way Christian Community in Pittsburgh, PA, felt compelled by God to do something. He and his team crafted a leadership covenant to which each staff member committed. Established in the early 1990s, it has averted many attempts of the enemy to get a foothold in his church to cause a split or fatal blow. With permission, here are the points of the covenant you may want to use in your church as a weapon of spiritual warfare. For more information visit www.northway.org.

   • We will pursue honesty, openness, and grace in our relationships.
   • We will see that hurts, offenses, and differences are reconciled quickly.
   • We will honor and cover one another in word and action.
   • We will not entertain accusations against one another.
   • We will hear one another's opinions, honor one another's differences, hold love supreme and wholeheartedly embrace our collective decisions.
   • We will meet together monthly to pray, share, worship, support, and pursue accountability.
   • We will remain faithful to intentional, personal evangelism (to avoid having an inward focus).[4]

4. How have you been influencing the institutions of the world system for God's kingdom (please refer to Lesson 2's **Institutions of the World System**)? Are you seeing a difference? Could you be doing more? Ask God to show you the hindrance, if you sense you lack the will do more.

5. What kind of legacy do you want to leave behind after you die?

   A. To your family: _____

   B. To the Church: _____

   C. To your community: _____

6. Thus far, what damage do you believe the Holy Spirit has inflicted on satan's kingdom through you?

7. Can you think of a person, group, or nation in the politico-religious arena that is subtly experiencing the **TACTIC: Through Peace, Destroy?**

SUMMARY

The fourth piece of armor is shoes for combat. God has provided them for our protection and for the advancement of His kingdom in satan's domain. There are three aspects that God does in the life of a believer according to **Ephesians 2:8-10.** SALVATION: the work God does **for** us; SANCTIFICATION: the work God does **in** us; and SERVICE: the work God does **through** us. God has a specific work for each of us to do, which He has been preparing us for—impressing it on our hearts. As we seek Him, God will reveal His specific assignments to us. Herein we enter Battlefield #4—Our Christian Walk and Witness. God instructed us how to walk in victory, avoiding the pitfalls and landmines laid for us in this combat zone.

Just as the Roman soldier put on these armored boots for his protection and firm footing, the spiritual application speaks to us about how our testimony and propagation of the Gospel **1A.** grounds us spiritually, giving us solid footing and protecting our walk with God. It also speaks to us about the quality of our **1B.** service to Him. There are four basic categories of our service to God: 1. Walk pleasing to our Commander-in-Chief, 2. Walk in love—serving one another, 3. Free the captives (evangelism), and 4. Transform the culture. God, in His wisdom, has chosen to give us the awesome responsibility of representing Him to an unbelieving world, and to snatch souls out of satan's kingdom and bring them into God's kingdom. To this end, Christ has commissioned us to be His **2.** ambassadors sending us forth with the ministry of reconciliation. Christ desires to make His appeal to the unbeliever through us. In order to effectively proclaim this gospel of peace, proper **2B.** preparation is essential. We must present our bodies as a *"living sacrifice"* and proclaim this glorious message and walk our talk with an impeccable witness for Christ. This will prevent our feet from taking a smelly testimony to those who don't know Him. The last thing any of us want to do is to misrepresent Christ to others and cause them to reject Him.

These "Boots" provide **3.** protection and empowerment to our spiritual lives. In **Revelation 12:11,** one of three essential ingredients that enable us to overcome satan and his dark forces is the *"word of our testimony."* However, failure to witness and walk in obedience leaves us unprotected and without firm footing in our spiritual life. This can produce the unhealthy state of **3C(1).** idleness—causing us to waste time and be unfruitful for God—giving a foothold to the enemy. It can also put us in a dangerous place with God. If we don't confess Christ but instead deny Him, Jesus said that He will deny us before His Father in heaven.

Naturally, the enemy will try to oppose us. He uses at least six strategies, like landmines, to trip us up and eliminate us on this battlefront. The first is **TACTIC: Hypocrisy.** This occurs when we are enticed to disobey the Bible and walk in a way that is contrary to our words and actions. When we choose to walk in hypocrisy, it ruins our testimony and makes us an ineffective witness and a reproach to the cause of Christ. The carnal "old man" must come under the control of our spirit in order for us to emanate God's character in our lives. Satan also uses the **TACTIC: Infiltration** where he secretly plants his own among God's people to cause Christ's church, etc. harm from within.

In tandem with this, he will use the **TACTIC: Divide and Conquer** where the enemy will try to get us to be the source of strife and dissension within our group so that we become the cause of division. This eventually causes the collapse of the group, extinguishing their light to the people in the community that they are called to reach and causing them not to want to have anything to do with the church or Christianity. Infiltration is like a cancer eating from within. Often while the leadership *"sleeps"* and is unwatchful, the enemy will either try to raise up and use existing "members," or bring someone in from outside the group. Most are unaware that they are being used for this destructive, diabolical purpose. Others infiltrate with deliberate, well-conceived strategies fully aware of what they are doing. Within a church congregation, usually the single most destructive, divisive force is our words to each other. The words we speak either build up or tear down—releasing life or death to the hearer.

Another strategy to weaken our witness is **TACTIC: Character Assassination.** Here the enemy will try to use us to slander and defame someone's character in order to destroy their reputation and witness for Christ. By destroying the credibility of true, effective servants of God, this scheme neutralizes their impact and destroys the work they are doing for God. The goal is to discredit them in the public eye so that the truth they speak will be rendered powerless and not be received. A variation of this scheme is **TACTIC: Distort Their Words** where the enemy will bait you with a question in order to distort your answer and then cause it to be used against you in the court of public opinion. When we are involved in slander, we are acting like, and are being used by, the devil.

He uses still another **TACTIC: Be a Stumbling Block** to attempt to use you to lay a trap for another Christian so we will be the cause of hindering their walk with God so they will eventually quit serving Jesus. We can destroy the wonderful work God has accomplished in their lives and for whom Christ died. Many times, we are unaware that we are being used in this way. We can do this through a selfish use of our liberty in Christ as we attempt to work out our salvation, as well as through erroneous teachings that contradict God's Word.

The believer has a responsibility to influence and transform their society by establishing God's principles in every culture-shaping institution. This will ensure God's blessings and avert His judgment as well as enable the Gospel to be proclaimed. Part of the church's duty is to shine as **1A.** light—to dispel the darkness; **1B.** participate in and submit to government (as long as its laws don't violate God's); **1C.** pray for its leaders; work for **1D.** peace; and **1E.** restrain evil. When the devil uses people to plant porn shops, abortion clinics, drug dealers, etc. in our community, we are not to stand by idly and allow its evil to corrupt and harm. Arising from our comfort zone through prayer, fasting, and deed, we are to confront and challenge its presence, driving it out of our community in a lawful manner. We must not lack the will. As British statesman Edmund Burke once said, "All that is necessary for the triumph of evil is that good men do nothing."[5]

Both God and satan use human instruments to accomplish their purposes. We can choose to be a source of blessing to others or be used by the enemy to unleash sin, evil, and demonic power into our world. Whose instrument will you be? Furthermore, how would you like others to remember you? Do you know how people think of you whenever they hear your name? What are you willing to do now to ensure the kind of legacy you will want to finally leave behind?

Be a great representative for Christ and take the *"gospel of peace"* to those subjects of satan's kingdom from which you were once a part. We will never fully know how beautiful our "feet" can become to the one to whom we have carried the message of the *"Good News"* of reconciliation with God, and have led to peace with Him. Think of how you feel about the one who led you to Christ! We are called to be an effective instrument in the hands of God to further His kingdom here on earth. Let us not fail Christ! Let us not fail our fellow man!

Lesson 14

THE SHIELD OF FAITH: Doubt vs. Our Faith in God
(Battlefield #5)

☑ Before starting the DVD:

God has ordained that in order for us to receive anything from Him, we have to exercise our faith. The Shield of Faith is an extremely important piece of defensive armor because we cannot allow our relationship with God to be injured. There is just too much at stake. In developing the ability to win this invisible war, the objectives of this lesson are first to show the critical role that faith plays in our lives. Because of its value, it becomes an object of cultivation by God and a target to assault by the devil. Through the lives of Eve and Job, we will learn about two tactics and four types of flaming arrows the enemy launches at us to attempt to shatter our faith in God. Finally, we'll learn how to use the Shield of Faith to extinguish these flaming arrows in our time of need. Due to its importance, this is our longest lesson and I recommend that it be done in three separate sessions (note the instructions). Before starting, pray that God will anoint these great truths to you.

☑ **DVD Users:** Watch Lesson 14, Session 1 for a brief overview before proceeding further (6 min.).
☑ When you're through, pick up again at this point. Fill in the blanks from the Summary.

📖 DEFINITION—FAITH

The main Greek word used in the New Testament and here in Ephesians chapter six is *pistis*. It means, "primarily 'firm persuasion,' a conviction based upon hearing..."[1]

Faith is not an end in itself. There must be an object or person into which one places their faith. It then becomes the main significance. Faith is developed by the relationship, frequent acquaintance, and the track record one has with them. In the Bible, we learn that God Himself is that person (His character, His motives, His Words, and His ways), an unchangeable God who cannot fail and is worthy of our faith and trust.

Faith must be accompanied by an active deed to make faith complete (see **James 2:14-26**). **Q:** Can you think of some daily natural examples of this as well as some spiritual ones? Faith comes by hearing a word from an unfailing God (see **Romans 10:17**). And when this occurs, faith is the *"...confident assurance that something we want is going to happen. It is the certainty that what we hoped for is waiting for us, even though we cannot see it up ahead"* (**Hebrews 11:1** TLB). Faith comes from our spirit, but unbelief comes from our soul. A simple working **definition of faith** comes from the example of Abraham in **Romans 4:21** (KJV): *"...being fully persuaded, that what* [God] *had promised, He was able also to perform."*

THE CRITICAL ROLE FAITH PLAYS IN OUR LIVES

1. What are some of the critical roles our faith plays in our lives?

   A. Without faith, we can't believe that G_____ E_____—neither can we please Him. (Note: The Bible takes God's existence for granted and doesn't attempt to prove it.)

      † **Hebrews 11:6**—*And without faith it is impossible to please God, because anyone who comes to him must believe that he exists and that he rewards those who earnestly seek him.*

      † **1 Peter 1:8** (NLT)—*You love him* [God] *even though you have never seen him. Though you do not see him, you trust him…*

      † **2 Corinthians 5: 7**—*We live by faith, not by sight.*

      † **Galatians 2:20**—*I have been crucified with Christ and I no longer live, but Christ lives in me. The life I live in the body, I live by faith in the Son of God, who loved me and gave himself for me.*

      † **Hebrews 11:3** (NLT)—*By faith we understand that the entire universe was formed at God's command, that what we now see did not come from anything that can be seen.*

   B. Without faith, we can't believe the Bible is G____—I_____ and without E_____.

      † **2 Peter 1:21** (NLT)—*…It was the Holy Spirit who moved the prophets to speak from God.*

   C. Without faith, we can't be "B_____ A_____."

      † **Luke 7:48-50**—*Then Jesus said to her, "Your sins are forgiven…your faith has saved you; go in peace."*

      † **Romans 10:9-11**—*…if you confess with your mouth, "Jesus is Lord," and believe in your heart that God raised him from the dead, you will be saved. 10. For it is with your heart that you believe and are justified, and it is with your mouth that you confess and are saved. 11. As the Scripture says, "Everyone who trusts in him will never be put to shame."*

      † **Ephesians 2:8-9** (NASB)—*For by grace you have been saved through faith; and that not of yourselves, it is the gift of God; 9. not as a result of works, so that no one may boast.*

   D. Without faith, H_____ and miracles can't take place.

      † **Mark 5:34**—[Jesus] *said to her, "Daughter, your faith has healed you. Go in peace and be freed from your suffering."*

      † **James 5:14-15** (NLT)—*Are any among you sick? They should call for the elders of the church… 15. And their prayer offered in faith will heal the sick…*

      † **Matthew 13:58** (KJV)—*And he* [Jesus] *did not many mighty works there because of their unbelief.*

▶**CONSIDER THIS:** Bishop Joseph L. Garlington teaches, "The atmosphere of expectancy is the breeding ground for the miraculous."

E. Without faith, receiving answers to P_____ cannot occur.

    † **Mark 11:24**—Jesus taught, *"Therefore I tell you, whatever you ask for in prayer, believe that you have received it, and it will be yours."*

    † **Matthew 9:29** (NASB)—Jesus said, *"It shall be done to you according to your faith."*

    † **Hebrews 10:22**—*Let us draw near to God with a sincere heart in full assurance of faith... 23. Let us hold unswervingly to the hope we profess, for he who promised is faithful.*

F. Without faith, we can't be O_____ over sin, satan, the world, and death.

    † **1 John 5:4-5**—*for everyone born of God has overcome the world. This is the victory that has overcome the world, even our faith. 5. Who is it that overcomes the world? Only he who believes that Jesus is the Son of God.*

    † **2 Corinthians 1:21-24**—*Now it is God who makes both us and you stand firm in Christ...it is by faith you stand firm.*

    † **Hebrews 11:13**—*All these people were still living by faith when they died. They did not receive the things promised; they only saw them and welcomed them from a distance. And they admitted that they were aliens and strangers on earth.*

G. Without faith, we cannot enter H_____.

    † **Hebrews 3:12-19**—Referring to Israel in the Old Testament: *See to it, brothers, that none of you has a sinful, unbelieving heart that turns away from the living God... 14. We have come to share in Christ if we hold firmly till the end the confidence we had at first... 16. Who were they who heard and rebelled? Were they not all those Moses led out of Egypt?... 18. And to whom did God swear that they would never enter his rest if not to those who disobeyed? 19. So we see that they were not able to enter, because of their unbelief.*

    † **Jude 1:5** (GNT)—*...I want to remind you of how the Lord saved the people of Israel from the land of Egypt, but afterward destroyed those who did not believe.*

    † **Hebrews 6:12**—*...imitate those who through faith and patience inherit what has been promised.*

    † **1 Peter 1:9**—*...receiving the goal of your faith, the salvation of your souls.*

▶**CONSIDER THIS:** God continually builds up our faith to ultimately prepare us to take our last breath in faith. Therefore, God calls us to exercise our faith in at least four areas: (1) in His character; (2) in His written Word, the Bible; (3) in a personal "word" God may reveal to us in our spirit or through another, which must align with the Scriptures **(Acts 9:10-18; 11:27-28; 21:11);** and (4) believing God for our needs and those of other's **(Mark 11:24).**

2. Because our faith is so necessary to receiving from God and overcoming our enemies, it becomes one of the main objects of God's attention in our lives as He tests and cultivates it.

▶ **CONSIDER THIS:** God chose one thing that every person could give Him—their faith. God doesn't require wealth, good looks, or giftings because not everyone has these to give; however, everyone has the ability to give Him their faith **(James 2:5).** Yet our faith is such a delicate thing. For some odd reason, we are more apt to place our faith in people and things that can fail us rather than put our trust in a God who can **never** fail us—the One Who **always** has our very best in mind. **Q:** Ask yourself these questions: How big is my God**?** Do I serve a God who is limited in any way?

A. We can have various <u>degrees</u> <u>of</u> <u>faith</u> in God, His promises, and His ability. Our faith is primarily determined by our relationship to Him because faith expresses itself through love **(Galatians 5:6).** Our faith can range from having:

(1) *"no faith"* **(Mark 4:40)**

(2) *"little faith"* **(Matthew 6:30; 16:8)**—produced by anxiety and fear

(3) *"great faith"* **(Matthew 8:10; 15:28)**

(4) Or be *"full of faith"* **(Acts 6:5; 11:24)**

B. Since Christ is *"the author and perfecter of our faith"* **(Hebrews 12:2),** He cultivates our faith in Him by bringing things into our lives to help make it grow. God tries to *"increase our faith"* in Him because like love, faith either grows or dies. Here are some of the ways our faith is fed and perfected:

(1) Through <u>M</u>_____ on God's Word and developing faith in His promises, His unchangeable character, and how He dealt with biblical characters **(Romans 10:17).**

(2) Through <u>R</u>_____ the victories God has given to you. Keeping a detailed journal or photo album will remind you of the times God has intervened in your life. Hearing testimonies of what God has done for fellow believers will also uplift your faith.

(3) Through getting us to <u>E</u>_____ our faith in order to make it stronger. **Q:** How would you go about strengthening your own faith? If we want to build up the strength in our body, we exercise (aerobics, push-ups, sit-ups, weight lifting, jogging, etc.). However, if someone tells us to exercise our faith, how do we begin? One of the main reasons God allows trials to come into our lives is for the purpose of strengthening our faith by causing it to be exercised.

† **1 Peter 1:7** (NLT)—*These trials are only to test your faith, to show that it is strong and pure. It is being tested as fire tests and purifies gold—and your faith is far more precious to God than mere gold. So if your faith remains strong after being tried by fiery trials, it will bring you much praise and glory and honor on the day when Jesus Christ is revealed to the whole world.*

† **James 1:2-4**—*Consider it pure joy, my brothers, whenever you face trials of many kinds, 3. because you know that the testing of your faith develops perseverance. 4. Perseverance must finish its work so that you may be mature and complete, not lacking anything.*

(4) Through P_____ our faith, including the sharing of our testimony with others.

† **2 Corinthians 4:13**—*It is written: "I believed; therefore I have spoken." With that same spirit of faith we also believe and therefore speak...*

   (a) It is so important to verbally declare aloud the portion of the Word of God that applies to your particular situation. For example, if you are in need of healing, profess the Scripture that says, *"...By his wounds you have been healed."* **(1 Peter 2:24** GNT**).** Begin to reach out and, by faith, claim what Christ has **already** done for you on the cross. Or if you are having doubts about how you perceive yourself as God's child, profess aloud what God's Word has to say about you regardless of how you "feel." Resist the temptation to walk in the realm of your senses instead of faith in God's character and Word.

   (b) Another aspect of profession is appropriating God's Word. For example, we might say, "I'll begin to tithe when I see God provide the resources." But God would say, "As you tithe through faith and obedience, you will see Me honor my promise of blessing." Our mindset is: "God, do it and I'll believe it," but God's way is: "Child, first believe and obey Me and then I'll do it." This principle applies to any word God has given to us. God has designed that before He acts, He first waits for us to respond to Him. As we step out in faith through our actions on what God's Word says He will do, we will begin to experience the reality of God moving in our lives.

(5) Through R_____ faith directly from God.

   (a) There are times when God Himself gives us a *"measure of faith"* **(Romans 12:3)**, as well as imparts to us the unique spiritual "gift of faith" for ministry purposes that come not from ourselves **(1 Corinthians 12:9).**

C. Since our faith plays such a crucial role, it also becomes a prime target of satan and demonic forces. Unexpected "land mines" can maim or kill our faith in God. God desires to strengthen our faith for the trials ahead. Our faith in God must grow and mature. If it doesn't, it could result in the following:

(1) Our faith can *"fail"* **(Luke 22:32).**

(2) Our faith can be *"shipwrecked"* **(1 Timothy 1:19).**

(3) Our faith can be *"overthrown"* **(2 Timothy 2:18** KJV**).**

(4) We can *"abandon"* and *"depart"* from the faith we once had (a doctrinal belief system)—with eternal consequences **(1 Timothy 4:1; 6:10,21; Acts 13:8).** Jesus once asked that when He returns, *"...will He find faith on the earth?"* **(Luke 18:8).**

☑ This ends our first session of Battlefield #5—The Shield of Faith: Doubt vs. Our Faith in God. Now please answer these Study Questions and Application.

STUDY QUESTIONS AND APPLICATION

1. Since our faith in God plays such a critical role in maintaining our spiritual lives, read these additional Scriptures regarding faith. Then write in that particular aspect about it.

   A. **Romans 3:28** _____

   B. **Romans 4:3-5** _____

   C. **Hebrews 10:32-38** _____

   D. **James 2:14-26** (esp. verse 26) _____

   E. **Hebrews 11:6** _____

   F. **Romans 14:22-23** _____

2. Recall some events in your life that have forced you to exercise your faith in God and how it made you stronger. This faith-building exercise can either be done through group discussion or when used for personal reflection.

Event	How It Made You Stronger
A._____	_____
B._____	_____
C._____	_____
D._____	_____

3. How would you rate the <u>overall</u> quality of your faith in God?

   ☐ Very strong   ☐ Above average   ☐ Average   ☐ Weak Faith   ☐ No Faith

4. Referring to #3 above, identify any obstacle(s) that hinders your trust in God and ask the Holy Spirit how you can increase the level of your faith.

☑ Continue on for more insights into Battlefield #5—The Shield of Faith.
   Note: I suggest that the next part of this lesson be treated as a separate session.

> ☑ **DVD Users:** Begin by watching Lesson 14, Session 2 (21 min.). Pick up here when through.

Session 2
SATAN'S FLAMING ARROWS

1. A Roman shield (*scutum*) was normally rectangular and semi-curved to fit around the body from the shoulders to the knees. It protected the body of the soldier against any projectiles, particularly arrows tipped with flammable materials. Similarly, for a Christian under satanic attack, it is our unwavering faith in the unimpeachable integrity of God's character and in the trustworthiness of the Word of God, which protects us when satan showers his burning arrows of unholy thoughts, subtle temptations, dark despair, blasphemous suggestions, base accusations, nagging doubts, and clouds of fear. It is this kind of faith that shields our heart from utter despair and our will from revolting against God.

🐎 **TACTIC: Create Doubt in Their Commander-in-Chief**—Since faith in God and His Word play such a crucial role in our Christian lives, the enemy aims his flaming arrows at them so as to plant seeds of doubt within us about God's character, His Word, and His ways thereby pressuring our will to revolt against God. ◉ *Main Targets*: Your Relationship with God and Faith

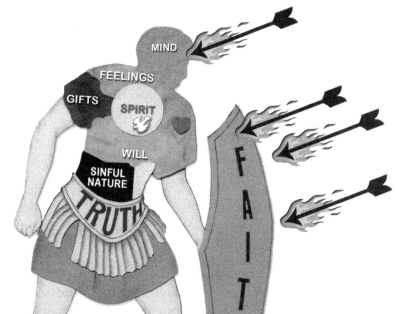

2. The flaming arrows the devil launches at us are the various things designed to create unbelief and doubt in God's character and God's Word. They are intended to cause our faith in God to fail and to produce rebellion, and ultimately the forsaking of God.

3. Over the next two sessions, we will cover four major flaming arrows: **1.** Slander Your Commander-in-Chief; **2.** Tragedies and Misfortunes; **3.** Discouragement; and **4.** Fear.

Flaming Arrow #1

➤——➤ **Flaming Arrow #1: Slander Their Commander-in-Chief**—The enemy will bring subtle or outright false accusations to defame God's Word and character, slandering Him before you, to try to convince you that there are imperfections in His character and ways, in order to damage your faith in His integrity, causing you to disobey Him.

Slander is the spreading of false charges or misrepresentations intended to defame and damage another's character and reputation. (See **Character Assassination** in Lesson 13.) Once a subtle trace of doubt enters our minds about God, we then become susceptible to believing a lie about Him.

Eve Under Attack

1. What follows is an analysis of satan's strategy against Eve—a cleverly contrived method of beguiling an innocent person. To grasp the setting, please read **Genesis 3:1-24** before proceeding.

    A. There are six times in the Bible where satan speaks directly to someone and in five of them he is planting seeds of doubt. Eve was the first person. Each time he opens his "mouth," he declares to all his character.

        †   **Genesis 3:1**—Satan said to Eve, *"Did God really say, 'You must not eat from any tree in the garden'?"*

        (1) Using a talking serpent to arouse curiosity, satan attempts to ensnare Eve, his intended victim, by casting doubt on what God had said to Adam, her husband. This created a climate of uncertainty in her mind. He was trying to destroy her delicate faith.

        (2) The uncertainty has now prepared the way for Eve to entertain a bold lie from satan supported by a rationale questioning the motives and character of God. This placed her in a dangerous defensive position.

        †   **Genesis 3:4-5**—*"You will not surely die," the serpent said to the woman. 5. "For God knows that when you eat of it your eyes will be opened, and you will be like God, knowing good and evil."*

        (3) The devil boldly implied that God was not telling them the truth—in fact, He was lying to them. Satan accused God of having imperfections in His character, implying that He was really withholding something good from them.

        (4) Doubt in God's motives and character came into Eve's spirit as a flaming arrow. Her will was weakening. Her judgment was being impaired not only by the possibility of the truth of his rational explanation, but also by the powerful appeals being made to her body (it was *"good for food"*); to her sight (it was *"pleasing to the eye"*); and to her mind (it was *"desirable for gaining wisdom"*).

        Note: These appeals mirror the three sources of temptation in our fallen nature. **(1 John 2:16** KJV**).** But at this point, Eve had no sinful nature.

        (5) Satan tried to convince Eve of all that she would gain but hide all that she would lose. He promised Eve that she would gain knowledge and power *"just like God"*—but <u>without</u> God! It is the same appeal with which he continually entices mankind, especially in the occult.

        (6) Her weakened will now succumbs to these powerful stimuli. Giving consent, she responds to the deception by reaching out, taking and eating the forbidden fruit. The consequences of disobedience must now be faced. Doubt produced disobedience and rebellion—just as the devil had intended.

        Note: Eve became the first human being to rebel against God. She persuaded Adam to join her in her act of rebellion. He complied and satan was successful in manipulating our first parents to unwittingly join him in his own rebellion against God. They would then reproduce this rebellion through their offspring.

(7) As a result of her will conceding to the deception, a darkness and blindness came over Eve. Her relationship with God was broken. This brought her, then Adam, and ultimately us as their descendents, under the chastisement and judgment of God!

▶ **CONSIDER THIS:** Adam was confronted with a painful decision: As he beheld his beloved but now sinful wife, either he could adamantly refuse to eat the forbidden fruit and obey God, or listen to her and also eat of it and disobey God. In every testing situation in our lives, allegiance to God must take precedence over allegiance to family and friends (see **1 Timothy 2:13-14**).

　† **2 Corinthians 11:3**—*But I am afraid that just as Eve was deceived by the serpent's cunning, your minds may somehow be led astray from your sincere and pure devotion to Christ.*

B. It is highly unlikely that we will ever experience the devil audibly speaking to us like he did to Eve. Nonetheless, we <u>will</u> hear him speak through the **thoughts** and impressions we receive, as well as through **people** whom he uses to plant doubts about God in our minds and hearts.

(1) Example: The enemy used religious unbelievers to discredit God's messengers (Paul and Barnabas) thereby causing doubt about God and His message among their audience. This resulted in division.

　† **Acts 14:1-4**—*At Iconium Paul and Barnabas went as usual into the Jewish synagogue. There they spoke so effectively that a great number of Jews and Gentiles believed. **2.** But the Jews who refused to believe stirred up the Gentiles and poisoned their minds against the brothers. **3.** So Paul and Barnabas spent considerable time there, speaking boldly for the Lord, who confirmed the message of his grace by enabling them to do miraculous signs and wonders. **4.** The people of the city were divided; some sided with the Jews, others with the apostles.*

(2) Example: King Sennacherib of Assyria sent officials to King Hezekiah and Jerusalem to present a plausible rationale (with a satanic "anointing") for doubting the motives, power, and reality of the true God. (Read **2 Chronicles 32:9-23**; also see **Isaiah 36:1** thru **37:38**.)

(3) Example: Concerning the delay in the fulfillment of the promise God gave to Abraham about the birth of his son, Abraham's **spirit** would say, "Keep waiting for God; He will be true to His promise." His and his wife's **soul** would say, "You're getting past the time to have children. God's promise will never happen. Take matters into your own hands and have a child by Hagar." Acting independently of God, they listened to their soul (or perhaps satan) and birthed Ishmael **(Galatians 4:23)**. Our minds can reason away what we are to keep believing by faith. Before God fulfills His promise, He will test us. Beware of birthing an "Ishmael." Keep your soul subservient to your spirit.

C. The devil tries to get us to judge God and conclude that there are imperfections in His character and motives. For example, he does this by suggesting we question Him when answers to prayer are delayed. The following are some typical thoughts he plants that we are prone to throw back into God's face: "When is God going to...?"; "Where was God when...?"; "God, why did you allow...?" "How can a good God permit suffering and evil to continue?" **Let your faith rest in this: God's character and ways are perfect—He can do no wrong. He makes no mistakes.** Remember, to question God is to find fault with Him!!

Flaming Arrow #2

Flaming Arrow #2: Tragedies and Misfortunes—The enemy will either use, or seek permission to cause, tragedies and misfortunes in your life so as to pressure your will to find fault with God so that you will no longer desire to serve Him.

Job's First Attack

1. What follows is an analysis of satan's strategy against Job—a maliciously designed plan to overwhelm a child of God.

2. Job was a chieftain of the land of Uz in Mesopotamia of high rank and great wealth. In fact, he was the greatest man of all the people in the East **(Job 1:3).** He was also noted for his consistent, conscientious relationship with God and his deep concern for the spiritual welfare of his family.

    A. In Eve's case we saw the devil falsely accusing God before man. In Job's case we see the devil falsely accusing man before God.

    B. The angels of God presented themselves before the Lord to give a report on their activities. Either satan intruded himself upon this meeting to maliciously accuse Job or he was required to present himself to also render an account of his activities.

    † **Job 1:6-12**—*One day the angels came to present themselves before the Lord, and Satan also came with them. 7. The Lord said to Satan, "Where have you come from?" Satan answered the Lord, "From roaming through the earth and going back and forth in it." 8. Then the Lord said to Satan, "Have you considered my servant Job? There is no one on earth like him; he is blameless and upright, a man who fears God and shuns evil." 9. "Does Job fear God for nothing?" Satan replied. 10. "Have you not put a hedge around him and his household and everything he has? You have blessed the work of his hands, so that his flocks and herds are spread throughout the land. 11. But stretch out your hand and strike everything he has, and he will surely curse you to your face." 12. The Lord said to Satan, "Very well, then, everything he has is in your hands, but on the man himself do not lay a finger." Then Satan went out from the presence of the Lord.*

    TACTIC: Accuse Them—The enemy will attempt to incriminate you before God, presenting your faults (true or contrived) and misrepresenting your motives for serving Him. His strategy is to persuade God to temporarily lift His hedge of protection from you (as he did with Job), so that as a result of the suffering and guilt you experience in the testing, you will eventually quit serving Him. ◉ *Main Targets:* Your Character, Motives, Shortcomings, and Will

    C. The devil has access to the presence of God, which he uses as the *"accuser of the brethren"* (KJV) to try to move God to get permission to harm us, without cause. This Scripture infers that Job is not an exception but an example of what often occurs to God's people.

    † **Revelation 12:9-11**—*...that ancient serpent called the devil, or Satan...the accuser of our brothers, who accuses them before our God day and night...*

† **Zechariah 3:1-2** (NASB)—*Then he showed me Joshua the high priest standing before the angel of the Lord, and Satan standing at his right hand to accuse him.*

D. The armor of God is intended to prepare us for *"...when the day of evil comes,* [that] *you may be able to stand your ground..."* **(Ephesians 6:13).** With incessant activity and unwearied vigilance the enemy, like a lion, searches with restless spirit for someone he can accuse before God. This bodes no good for any soul much less to a faithful servant of God.

E. Once more we see that we are caught in the middle of satan's war against God. One of the most effective ways the devil can hurt God is to hurt His children. His diabolical plan is to select one of God's children, with cunning discrimination, for his special target— well knowing that their fall could occasion the fall of many others.

▶**CONSIDER THIS:** Contrary to what we may think, the more we try to draw closer to the Lord, to obediently live a Christ-like life, and/or to penetrate satan's kingdom and cause it damage, the more we will draw fire and become a prime target on the devil's "hit list." We should not allow this truth to discourage us or cause us to "let up" in our pursuit of these goals. If so eminent a child of God as Job did not escape satan's accusations, it should not seem strange to us that we should also come under his indictment—whether the accusation is true or false.

F. Satan was not only reluctant to admit to Job's godly life, but he insinuated that Job's motive for serving God was due to His abundance of blessings—for what Job could get out of it. In essence, satan said, "Remove your blessings and hedge of protection from him and his possessions, and he will curse you to your face." Satan also insinuated to God that He had "purchased" Job's worship by bestowing these material blessings, and that God wasn't worthy of Job's worship apart from His benevolent gifts.

▶**CONSIDER THIS:** Satan did not possess foreknowledge of Job's response or he would probably never have asked to test him. Neither does he know how we will respond. He takes a calculated risk based on his thousands of years of experience in dealing with human weakness. He plays the odds and hopes for a specific anticipated outcome. The question is, "Will we prove him correct?"

G. Satan seeks to vent his anger and hatred of God in an attempt to embarrass God before the angels by means of subjecting a faithful child of His to the most vicious and undeserved calamities. He audaciously challenges God regarding His appraisal of Job's character by questioning the influence that God's blessings have to do with why Job worships Him. God accepts the challenge, allowing it to prove that a son of Adam can and will worship and serve God for who He is without the motivation of self-interest **(Job 1: 9-11).**

H. By using the most cunning and diabolical wisdom, satan succeeds in obtaining God's consent **but with limitations (Job 1:12).**

▶**CONSIDER THIS: Job 1:12** and **2:6** should be of great comfort and consolation to us in times of adversity: satan cannot touch God's children without God's permission. Even when God gives the devil permission, He mercifully places limitations on him and his malicious strategies. Our Heavenly Father is mindful of the limits of His children and promises that He will not send into our lives more than we can handle **(1 Corinthians 10:13)**. We established in Lesson 5 that God is involved in everything that affects our life as a child of God. They are either:

(1) Sent by God   (2) Permitted by God   or   (3) Used by God

Sometimes God permits His hedge of protection around us to be lifted for testing purposes. During these times, we can become confused over whether or not we might have done something to step outside that umbrella of protection, when actually it may be something that has been sent or allowed by God to prove us. There are other times when God protects His people against satan's efforts to overthrow them without their being aware of it. Furthermore, the Bible also seems to indicate that one who is not a child of God is without protection from the assaults of their father, the devil, who does not need permission from God to attack them. (**Hebrews 1:14** needs to be factored in here.)

I. In relation to this, reflect for a moment on how satan had to get permission to touch the 11 apostles, especially **Peter.** Perhaps he knew of God's plan for Peter to open the door of the Kingdom to both the Jews **(Acts 2:14-41)** and to the Gentiles **(Acts 10:1-11:18).**

    † **Luke 22:31-32**—Jesus said, *"Simon, Simon, Satan has asked to sift you as wheat. 32. But I have prayed for you, Simon, that your faith may not fail. And when you have turned back, strengthen your brothers."*

    (1) Note that *"you"* in **22:31** is in the plural referring to **all** the disciples. Other translations read:

        (a) *"Satan has received permission to test all of you..."* (GNT)
        (b) *"Satan has asked to have all of you..."* (NLT)
        (c) *"Satan hath desired to have you..."* (KJV)
        (d) *"Satan has demanded permission..."* (NASB)

    (2) Satan seeks to put a believer through the sieve of the pressure of circumstances and temptation with the hope of bringing to light any inherent propensities to failure.

J. Satan leaves God's presence, finalizes his plans, and bides his time to await the most opportune moment. Cunningly, he takes Job by surprise—on a day of festivity when all his family are gathered together and when he least expected trouble. Verse **12** in the KJV reads: *"And the Lord said unto Satan, Behold, all that he hath is in thy power; only upon himself put not forth thine hand. So Satan went forth from the presence of the Lord."* (For more about satan's *"power,"* see "satan: his capabilities" in the index.)

K. The devil's plan was to try to overwhelm his victim by successive calamities of increasing severity in rapid succession. It would appear that he not only has power to employ man's wicked hearts to accomplish his purpose, but is also able to use the elements of nature to some degree.

    † **Job 1:13-19**—*One day when Job's sons and daughters were feasting and drinking wine at the oldest brother's house, 14. a messenger came to Job and said, "The oxen were plowing and the donkeys were grazing nearby, 15. and the Sabeans attacked and carried them off. They put the servants to the sword, and I am the only one who has escaped to tell you!" 16. While he was still speaking, another messenger came and said, "The fire of God fell from the sky and burned up the sheep and the servants, and I am the only one who has escaped to tell you!" 17. While he was still speaking, another messenger came and said, "The Chaldeans*

formed three raiding parties and swept down on your camels and carried them off. They put the servants to the sword, and I am the only one who has escaped to tell you!" **18.** *While he was still speaking, yet another messenger came and said, "Your sons and daughters were feasting and drinking wine at the oldest brother's house,* **19.** *when suddenly a mighty wind swept in from the desert and struck the four corners of the house. It collapsed on them and they are dead, and I am the only one who has escaped to tell you!"*

L. Satan is fully cognizant of the fact that the character of man is generally revealed in the hour of sudden crisis. With no time to think, what is in the heart will suddenly erupt and come forth—especially under the pressure of great anguish and pain.

M. Satan chose a time when Job enjoyed the security of material prosperity, which the adversary would suddenly turn into unprecedented calamity.

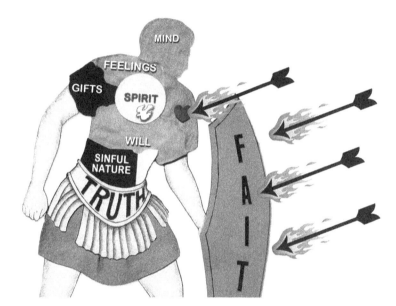

N. The suddenness of satan's blow was calculated to trigger Job into an impulsive denunciation of God, saying in haste what he could later regret—after the damage was done **(Job 1:14-15).**

O. The rapid succession of diverse blows from diverse directions was intended to deprive Job of time for reflection and the preparation of a defensive posture to ward off the attack **(Job 1:16).**

P. The mounting pressure from increasing losses, not only in number but also in value, would tend to undermine Job's faith, questioning his God and breaking down his resistance **(Job 1:17).**

Q. The last blow was the worst of all—the death of his children. Satan confidently expected to overwhelm Job with unbearable personal grief. He was sure this would compel him to renounce his faith and vehemently denounce his God **(Job 1:18-19).**

R. Satan's hand is discernible in the rapid succession of totally unrelated events orchestrated upon one individual, and the escape of a single messenger from each disaster arriving while each previous messenger was still speaking.

S. Satan's avalanche of disaster by which he attacked the citadel of Job's integrity was most cunning in its contrivance. It had all the appearance of the work of an angry God employing natural means.

T. Satan's onslaught was without any pity as stroke fell upon stroke by a merciless adversary solely bent on his victim's destruction.

▶**CONSIDER THIS:** Tragedies and misfortunes can enter our lives at any moment. The loss of a loved one; the loss of property, perhaps confiscated, that we worked so hard to obtain; accidents; unexpected calamities; contracting some physical disease; and other misfortunes will put the pressure on us to question "Why, God?" Sometimes things happen which God allows that we just can't understand, nor are we able to reconcile these circumstances with who we know God to be. It will be faith in God's unchangeable, perfect character that shields our heart from utter despair and our will from giving up and revolting against God.

U. Note Job's reaction to the messenger's reports in **Job 1:20-22.**

(1) Instead of rising up against God in rebellion as satan had wanted, Job fell to the ground in submission to the sovereignty of God.

(2) Instead of turning from God in his sorrow and grief as satan had anticipated, Job turned to God in worship.

(3) Instead of charging God with injustice as satan had expected, Job kept faith in God's righteousness.

(4) Instead of rejecting the hand of Providence as satan had hoped, Job accepted what it brought.

(5) Instead of cursing God as satan had predicted, Job blessed the name of the Lord.

(6) Instead of defeating Job as satan had planned, Job defeated satan and vindicated God.

V. What was the secret of Job's strength in withstanding satan's vicious onslaughts?

† **Job 1:20-22**—*At this, Job got up and tore his robe and shaved his head. Then he fell to the ground in worship 21. and said: "Naked I came from my mother's womb, and naked I will depart. The Lord gave and the Lord has taken away; may the name of the Lord be praised." 22. In all this, Job did not sin by charging God with wrongdoing.*

(1) Job acknowledged God's rights of ownership of all that he had and, therefore, His right to take away as well as to give. Job possessed great riches, but his riches did not possess him. Whether God gave or took away, Job retained an unwavering confidence in the wisdom and righteousness of the absolute sovereignty of God.

(2) Job's relationship with God was such that he had an unshakeable confidence in the unimpeachable integrity of the name of the Lord. In the final analysis, the name of the Lord is what He is.

† **Proverbs 18:10** (NKJV)—*The name of the Lord is a strong tower; the righteous run to it and are safe.*

(3) Job's confidence in the name of the Lord was mingled with the worship of that name. This worship was Job's best and, perhaps, his only defense against the deadly temptation of bringing God's character into question. Worship of the name of the

Lord in the hour of deep distress thwarts satan's attempt to discredit God by bringing Him to trial. Especially during such times one should:

(a) Remember His name **(Jeremiah 23:27)**   (c) Contemplate His name **(Psalm 52:9)**

(b) Call upon His name **(Psalm 99:6)**   (d) Trust in His name **(Isaiah 50:10)**

▶ **CONSIDER THIS: Q:** How should we react towards God when we encounter circumstances that appear to be the very negation of His promises and what we know His character to be? If we bring God into question, and it is pursued to its logical conclusion according to the natural mind, it will inevitably place God in the position of a defendant with satan as the prosecutor, and ourselves as judge and jury. This will have disastrous results. At the extreme end of that trial is the rejection of God, with damning consequences—and the triumph of satan. Guard against allowing any bitterness, anger, or self-pity in your life. There is no fault in God—EVER!—no matter what the circumstances may look like.

(4) Satan wanted Job to interpret his calamity by reaching conclusions that would assail the integrity of God and thereby curse God to His face. Instead, Job proved greater than his calamity. Job's will did not allow his sinful nature to utter a word that would accuse God of injustice or in any way reflect negatively on the character of God. Instead, Job "embarrasses" satan by blessing the name of the Lord openly and resolutely. *"In all this, Job did not sin by charging God with wrongdoing."* **(Job 1:22).**

> ☑ This ends our second session and the DVD content for Lesson 14.
> ☑ Please do the following Study Questions and Application.

STUDY QUESTIONS AND APPLICATION

1. Make an honest examination of the main reason you serve God. Choose <u>one</u> of the following:

   ☐ For His blessings and provisions   ☐ Because I'd be afraid not to   ☐ Because of who He is

   ☐ Out of love for what He's done   ☐ Tradition   ☐ Other: _____

2. Our soul will be prone to act presumptuously and independently of God by using its own natural reasonings or intuition. It can cause us to run ahead of Him and make mistakes. In addition to the example of Abraham and Ishmael given earlier in this session, read these Scriptures and ask God if your soul is trying to act independently of Him in some area of your life due to a lack of faith, etc.

Genesis 25:20-34; 27:1-35	**Psalm 106:9-13**
Numbers 14:40-44	**1 Samuel 13:5-14**
Acts 1:15-26; 26:12-18; 1 Corinthians 15:8-9	**Exodus 40:36-38; Psalm 37:7**

3. One of the Seven Views of God given in Lesson 2 is the belief in finite godism. This belief views God as being limited in some way in His attributes. Examine your belief in the God of the Bible. Ask yourself these questions: Does the God you believe in and serve have any flaws in His character? Any limits to His knowledge or foreknowledge? Are there any restrictions to His power? Any limitations to His omnipresence? Does He have any imperfection that would cause you to find fault with or lose faith in Him? If you answer yes to any of these questions, you have a false view of the true God that the enemy will exploit. As you ponder your answers, try to identify any limitation you may place on God. Seek out your pastor or a mature, godly leader to help you work through these hindrances in your perception of God. Help is also available by writing to the author at info@discoverministries.com.

4. Go to the list of God's unchangeable character given in Lesson 3. Review and study His character until it is rooted in your heart. The better we know Him, the stronger our foundation.

☑ When you are ready to begin the third and last session, continue on in this workbook for additional material about Battlefield #5 **not** on the DVD. We will cover Flaming Arrows #3 and #4 and learn how to extinguish them.

Note: I suggest that the remainder of this lesson be treated as a separate session.

Session 3

Flaming Arrow #3

Job's Second Attack

1. What follows is an analysis of the strategy of satan's second assault against Job. This will set up **Flaming Arrow #3: Discouragement.**

   A. Since his first attempt had failed, satan bides his time awaiting another opportunity to attack Job.

   † **Job 2:1-6**—*On another day the angels came to present themselves before the Lord, and Satan also came with them to present himself before him. 2. And the LORD said to Satan, "Where have you come from?" Satan answered the Lord, "From roaming through the earth and going back and forth in it." 3. Then the Lord said to Satan, "Have you considered my servant Job? There is no one on earth like him; he is blameless and upright, a man who fears God and shuns evil. And he still maintains his integrity, though you incited me against him to ruin him without any reason." 4. "Skin for skin!" Satan replied. "A man will give all he has for his own life. 5. But stretch out your hand and strike his flesh and bones, and he will surely curse you to your face." 6. The Lord said to Satan, "Very well, then, he is in your hands; but you must spare his life."*

   B. Satan tries again by repeating his challenge and seemingly manipulates God to consent to a much more severe onslaught on Job. As long as we live in satan's domain, his attack on us is not a matter of "if" but "when." The more we resist him and pass our tests and overcome temptation, there's a chance that, barring any footholds we may give him, he will give us less attention and use his time and energy on someone else. In Job's case, after this second victory over satan, the devil leaves the scene and is no more heard from again in the life of Job. (Also see **Luke 4:13.**)

C. Satan's argument this time is that the limitation previously set by God was an insufficient means of testing Job, and that an adequate test would have to include an attack on Job's body **(Job 2:4-5).**

D. We again get a glimpse of the kind of depraved enemy we're dealing with. The devil's accusations and assaults on people are done *"without any reason"* or cause **(Job 2:3).**

> † **Job 2:7-10**—*So Satan went out from the presence of the Lord and afflicted Job with painful sores from the soles of his feet to the top of his head. 8. Then Job took a piece of broken pottery and scraped himself with it as he sat among the ashes. 9. His wife said to him, "Are you still holding on to your integrity? Curse God and die!" 10. He replied, "You are talking like a foolish woman. Shall we accept good from God, and not trouble?" In all this, Job did not sin in what he said.*

E. Satan selects and employs against Job a most painful and obnoxious disease by divine permission **(Job 2:7).** The devil has the power to inflict physical disease and sickness and he uses it as a means to turn men and women away from God. However, not every sickness and disease is caused by demonic power and should not be attributed to as such.

F. It is more than coincidence that the very thing that satan wanted Job to do (curse God to His face) was one of the very first words that came out of his wife's mouth as counsel when he contracted the boils **(Job 2:9).** Just as satan had the ability to plant the thought and raise up the raiding parties of the Sabeans and the Chaldeans to attack Job's property, so he was also successful with Job's closest acquaintance, his wife, as she unwittingly lent her voice as satan's instrument. What affect her words must have had on him! Surely it added more inward conflicts to his well nigh unbearable outward sufferings. It was satan's calculated overpowering blow to push Job over the edge and to hopefully hear him utter those fateful words. Don't be surprised when the devil inspires your closest relationships, without them realizing it, to speak hurtful things to you or to lead you in the wrong direction. Be on guard and discern the source. (See "Mind: thoughts from spirit world" in index.)

G. Both God and satan were listening! Each one watching in expectation of the vindication of their position—their "bet" if you will. Would Job "embarrass" and disappoint his God before all of heaven's assembly? No way! When Job spoke, it was to the chagrin and defeat of satan and to the delight and triumph of God.

H. God allowed satan to take away Job's possessions, his family, and his health. Job's reply to his wife indicated his unshakeable conviction that present miseries do not obliterate nor cancel past mercies. He had an invincible faith in the flawless exercise of divine providence whether good or evil came his way.

I. Up to this point, Job did not sin with his lips. This indicated that under such pressures, his spirit was in total control of his being as he was being sustained by God. If it wasn't, the ugly character in his sinful nature would have been manifested outwardly.

➤━━➔ **Flaming Arrow #3: Discouragement**—The enemy will try to bring upon you discouragement, oppression, and despair to cause you to make decisions about God and His will while in this depressed state that are faulty and absurd. His hope is that you will step outside His will or choose to quit serving Him.

2. Even when you get some victories under your belt, so to speak, more trials still await you. Seemingly unending periods of trial, like lengthy illnesses, can wear down a person and their caregivers. When your body is afflicted, it affects the condition of your soul and spirit. It is during times like these, when you are at your lowest point, that another of satan's flaming arrows arrives—gloomy discouragement and a sense of hopelessness. But our great God is always faithful to sustain us.

3. The following quotations from Job give us an insight into his incredible suffering and how he was thinking and feeling during his excruciating trial. As you read these verses, try to understand his plight, feel his passion, grasp his pain, and learn from his experience. Then apply it to your situation, if applicable, and also to one you may know who is going through a similar dark place.

    ✝ **Job 3:1-26**—*After this, Job opened his mouth and cursed the day of his birth... 10. "for it did not shut the doors of the womb on me to hide trouble from my eyes. 11. Why did I not perish at birth, and die as I came from the womb?... 16. Or why was I not hidden in the ground like a stillborn child, like an infant who never saw the light of day?... 20. Why is light given to those in misery, and life to the bitter of soul, 21. to those who long for death that does not come, who search for it more than for hidden treasure... 24. For sighing comes to me instead of food; my groans pour out like water... 26. I have no peace, no quietness; I have no rest, but only turmoil."*

    ✝ **Job 6:1-9**—*Then Job replied: 2. "If only my anguish could be weighed and all my misery be placed on the scales! 3. It would surely outweigh the sand of the seas... 4. The arrows of the Almighty are in me, my spirit drinks in their poison; God's terrors are marshaled against me... 8. Oh, that I might have my request, that God would grant what I hope for, 9. that God would be willing to crush me, to let loose his hand and cut me off!"*

    ✝ **Job 7:2-21**—*"Like a slave longing for the evening shadows, or a hired man waiting eagerly for his wages, 3. so I have been allotted months of futility, and nights of misery have been assigned to me. 4. When I lie down I think, 'How long before I get up?' The night drags on, and I toss till dawn. 5. My body is clothed with worms and scabs, my skin is broken and festering. 6. My days are swifter than a weaver's shuttle, and they come to an end without hope. 7. Remember, O God, that my life is but a breath; my eyes will never see happiness again... 11. Therefore I will not keep silent; I will speak out in the anguish of my spirit, I will complain in the bitterness of my soul... 13. When I think my bed will comfort me and my couch will ease my complaint, 14. even then you frighten me with dreams and terrify me with visions, 15. so that I prefer strangling and death, rather than this body of mine. 16. I despise my life; I would not live forever. Let me alone; my days have no meaning... 20. If I have sinned, what have I done to you, O watcher of men? Why have you made me your target? Have I become a burden to you? 21. Why do you not pardon my offenses and forgive my sins?..."*

    ✝ **Job 10:1-3, 18-21**—*"I loathe my very life; therefore I will give free rein to my complaint and speak out in the bitterness of my soul. 2. I will say to God: Do not condemn me, but tell me what charges you have against me. 3. Does it please you to oppress me, to spurn the work of your* *hands, while you smile on the schemes of the wicked?... 18. Why then did you bring me out of the womb? I wish I had died before any eye saw me. 19. If only I had never come into being..."*

† **Job 16:7-12**—*"Surely, O God, you have worn me out; you have devastated my entire household... 9. God assails me and tears me in his anger and gnashes his teeth at me... 10. Men open their mouths to jeer at me; they strike my cheek in scorn and unite together against me. 11. God has turned me over to evil men and thrown me into the clutches of the wicked. 12. All was well with me, but he shattered me; he seized me by the neck and crushed me. He has made me his target..."*

† **Job 17:1, 6-7**—*"My spirit is broken, my days are cut short, the grave awaits me. 6. God has made me a byword to everyone, a man in whose face people spit. 7. My eyes have grown dim with grief; my whole frame is but a shadow."*

▶ **CONSIDER THIS:** As stated earlier, all that Job was experiencing had the appearance of the work of an angry God. But that was not the case at all. When you are going through a trial, consider the possibility that you may have been accused by the enemy before God's presence just like Job was. An indication of this is when the things that happen to you are out of character with what you know God's nature to be. If so, then realize that what you are experiencing is permitted by God but coming from satan. Focus on passing your test by reacting the way God wants you to. By doing this, you may shorten the length of your trial. Let's read on:

† **Job 19:9-21**—*"He has stripped me of my honor and removed the crown from my head... 13. He has alienated my brothers from me; my acquaintances are completely estranged from me. 14. My kinsmen have gone away; my friends have forgotten me. 15. My guests and my maidservants count me a stranger; they look upon me as an alien. 16. I summon my servant, but he does not answer, though I beg him with my own mouth. 17. My breath is offensive to my wife; I am loathsome to my own brothers. 18. Even the little boys scorn me; when I appear, they ridicule me. 19. All my intimate friends detest me; those I love have turned against me. 20. I am nothing but skin and bones; I have escaped with only the skin of my teeth. 21. Have pity on me, my friends, have pity, for the hand of God has struck me."*

▶ **CONSIDER THIS:** Determine that you will not abandon one that is under attack, and that you will not become a source of any additional emotional pain in their lives. Be the hand of God's comfort extended to them and try to ease their pain. People undergoing physical or emotional debilitation have said that one of their greatest sufferings was enduring sheer loneliness. Let's read on:

† **Job 23:1-10**—*Then Job replied: 2. "Even today my complaint is bitter; his hand is heavy in spite of my groaning. 3. If only I knew where to find him; if only I could go to his dwelling! 4. I would state my case before him and fill my mouth with arguments. 5. I would find out what he would answer me, and consider what he would say... 8. But if I go to the east, he is not there; if I go to the west, I do not find him. 9. When he is at work in the north, I do not see him; when he turns to the south, I catch no glimpse of him. 10. But he knows the way that I take; when he has tested me, I will come forth as gold."*

† **Job 19:25-26**—*"I know that my Redeemer lives, and that in the end he will stand upon the earth. 26. And after my skin has been destroyed, yet in my flesh I will see God..."*

▶**CONSIDER THIS:** When you find yourself in a place where you can't sense God's presence and that He seems to be a million miles away, do what Job did. Let your faith in God arise from within and declare aloud God's Word regarding His promises, what you know to be true of His unchangeable character, and who you are in Christ—even though you can't "see" it in your circumstances.

4. Outside circumstances, or physical and emotional deficiencies, can bring on depression and despair. Or a spiritual "veil" or dark cloud can drop over your spirit and remain upon you accompanied by an awful sense of hopelessness. Or you may be experiencing an abnormal state of grieving. However it may occur, ask God to remove it. Press into Him further by seeking Him with worship and singing—even if you don't feel like it. The *"garment of praise"* is the best weapon against depression and a *"spirit of heaviness."* Force yourself to put it on (see **Why Should We Praise and Worship?** in Lesson 16). At one point in my life I had experienced a brief time of depression and heaviness that came over me. But during a worship service, the Holy Spirit lifted it completely off me and replaced it with His sweet presence!

5. When gloomy discouragement and despair hit us, we are unable to see things in a proper perspective. As a result, conclusions are drawn in these states that are faulty and absurd. It is then that doubts about God can enter our mind and spirit. We should be careful to refrain from forming permanent beliefs or making critical decisions while in this "valley" experience.

 A. Example: John the Baptist found himself in prison. Discouragement affected his faith so much that he began to doubt whether Jesus was truly the Messiah—even after experiencing all the supernatural encounters with Him.

  † **Luke 7:20**—*When the men came to Jesus, they said, "John the Baptist sent us to you to ask, 'Are you the one who was to come, or should we expect someone else?'"*

 B. Example: The nation of Israel saw all of God's miraculous judgments upon Pharaoh and Egypt. They saw the waters of the Red Sea part and walked over on dry ground. They experienced a miraculous daily provision of food—manna in the morning and quail in the evening. They saw God's visible presence—a cloud by day and fire by night. But when the Israelites again encountered a lack of water at Rephidim, they became discouraged and grumbled against God and Moses and formed beliefs about them that were false and absurd.

  † **Exodus 17:5-15** (NASB)—*...But the people thirsted there for water; and they 6. grumbled against Moses and said, "Why, now, have you brought us up from Egypt, to kill us and our children and 7. our livestock with thirst?...they 15. tested the Lord, saying, "Is the Lord among us, or not?"*

  (1) Satan's hope is that a wrong decision or conclusion will be made in this negative state of mind. Let faith in God arise in your heart and declare aloud, "There is no fault in God or His promises. Remember how my Heavenly Father came through for me in the past?"

  (2) Once our faith in God's character, motives, ways, promises, and ability are damaged, it affects our love for Him, which in turn affects our trust and hope.

 C. Keep in mind what the devil's intended outcome is for you, and where discouragement and depression can lead. Press into God, enlist friends to pray and intercede for you, and resist the temptation to find fault with God's character, purposes, motives, and ways as you endure the trial. As Pastor E.V. Hill once said regarding Jesus' painful crucifixion and the seeming hopelessness of the situation, "Friday may be here, but Sunday's a comin'!"

6. If Job was sustained by God when passing through his fiery trials, likewise, you can expect to be undergirded by Him in the day when you find yourself in the crucible of divine testing.

7. In the end, we like Job will reach a height of triumph commensurate with the depth of our trial.

Q: Is there anything that is causing you to be discouraged? If so, identify it so you can take it through the extinguishing process in the next SQ&A section.

Flaming Arrow #4

Flaming Arrow #4: Fear—Like a lion when it roars, the enemy will attempt to intimidate and immobilize you with fear, terrorizing you in combination with discouragement, in order to drive you to make wrong decisions you would never make in your right mind.

1. Fear is a powerful tool used to intimidate and manipulate people to get them to do what a person wants; from secular or religious rulers to your boss and family members. But satan is the ultimate terrorist. What are some of the ways the enemy uses fear to accomplish his malicious goals?

   A. He uses fear to increase the torment of one who is already suffering. Job's pain also included experiencing fear and he thought it was coming directly from God.

   † **Job 30:15**—Job said, *"Terrors overwhelm me..."*

   † **Job 6:4** (NLT)—Job said: *"For the Almighty has struck me down with his arrows. He has sent his poisoned arrows deep within my spirit. All God's terrors are arrayed against me."*

   B. Through fear and discouragement, the enemy can try to coerce you to leave the assignment that God has called you to do as in the case of Israel rebuilding Jerusalem in Ezra's day.

   † **Ezra 4:4-5**—*Then the peoples around them set out to discourage the people of Judah and make them afraid to go on building. 5. They hired counselors to work against them and frustrate their plans during the entire reign of Cyrus king of Persia and down to the reign of Darius king of Persia.*

   C. The prophet Elijah beheld the fire of God coming out of heaven and consuming the water soaked sacrifice, winning a great spiritual victory over the priests and prophets of the false god Baal. Yet when counterattacked by the enemy, fear made him flee into the desert. With faith almost gone, he came to the point where he wanted to end his life.

   † **1 Kings 19:1-4**—*3. Elijah was afraid and ran for his life. When he came to Beersheba in Judah, he left his servant there, 4. while he himself went a day's journey into the desert. He came to a broom tree, sat down under it and prayed that he might die. "I have had enough, Lord," he said. "Take my life; I am no better than my ancestors."*

D. Through fear, Peter denied the Lord and all the other disciples fled and <u>deserted</u> <u>Christ</u> when He was apprehended for trial. There was intense satanic activity during the final hours leading up to Jesus' death. This demonic activity played a role in Peter's denial of Jesus and the other apostles fleeing and deserting Him. Satan's aim was to shake their faith in Jesus that they might abandon Him in His hour of greatest need and ultimately give up serving Him altogether. **(Luke 22:53; Matthew 26:56).**

E. Through fear, <u>unbelief</u> was produced in the hearts of ten of the twelve men that were sent to spy out the land God had promised to Israel. Upon their return they *"...spread among the Israelites a bad report about the land they explored."* **(Numbers 13:32).** It opened a floodgate for the enemy to enter into the whole congregation:

> † **Numbers 14:1-4**—*That night all the people of the community raised their voices and wept aloud. **2.** All the Israelites grumbled against Moses and Aaron, and the whole assembly said to them, "If only we had died in Egypt! Or in this desert! **3.** Why is the Lord bringing us to this land only to let us fall by the sword? Our wives and children will be taken as plunder. Wouldn't it be better for us to go back to Egypt?" **4.** And they said to each other, "We should choose a leader and go back to Egypt."*

> † **Deuteronomy 1:27-28**—*You grumbled in your tents and said, "The Lord hates us; so he brought us out of Egypt to deliver us into the hands of the Amorites to destroy us. **28.** Where can we go? Our brothers have made us lose heart. They say, 'The people are stronger and taller than we are; the cities are large, with walls up to the sky. We even saw the Anakites there.'"*

> (1) The outcome was pandemonium in the camp and their view of God's character got really blown out of proportion. Fear can produce unbelief, which can keep us out of our Promised Land, heaven, just like it kept that generation of the children of Israel out of theirs **(Hebrews 4:1-11).**

F. The fear of confrontation, failure, and what others will think of us <u>holds</u> <u>us</u> <u>back</u> <u>from</u> <u>witnessing</u> to others about Christ, sharing our testimony, and being involved in God's work.

G. The enemy also uses natural fears such as fear of being rejected, the fear of failure, and other phobias in order to drive us into destructive behaviors.

2. Fear can so consume us that serious physical and mental illnesses can result.

3. Fear and worry flourish when we take our focus off God's unchangeable character, His promises, and who we are in Christ.

> † **Isaiah 26:3** (NLT)—*You will keep in perfect peace all who trust in you, whose thoughts are fixed on you!*

4. Fear and worry thrive when there are no consistent times spent worshiping and seeking God. Feed your faith in God and your fear will starve to death.

> † **Psalm 34:4** (NLT)—*I prayed to the Lord, and he answered me, freeing me from all my fears.*

5. The fear of death and future judgment can also be a huge weight hanging over us. We must focus on Jesus' victory on the cross, repent of our sins, and walk in His perfect love.

† **Hebrews 2:14-15** (NLT)—*...only by dying could he* [Jesus] *break the power of the devil, who had the power of death.* **15.** *Only in this way could he deliver those who have lived all their lives as slaves to the fear of dying.*

† **1 John 4:18** (NKJV)—*There is no fear in love; but perfect love casts out fear, because fear involves torment. But he who fears has not been made perfect in love.*

6. Fears can be eradicated by a person used by God to bring uplifting news. Let us be that kind of encourager instead of one of Job's "comforters."

† **2 Corinthians 7:5-6**—*For when we came into Macedonia, this body of ours had no rest, but we were harassed at every turn—conflicts on the outside, fears within.* **6.** *But God, who comforts the downcast, comforted us by the coming of Titus...*

▶**CONSIDER THIS:** A soldier of the Lord is not to retreat or flee from conflict with the enemy out of fear and unbelief. We find no mention of God providing armor for our backs. God intends for us to confront the enemy head on. Also, He has not given us a spirit of cowardice and timidity, but *"...a spirit of power, of love and of self-discipline"* (**2 Timothy 1:7**). Be courageous and stand in the victory Christ purchased for you on the cross. You are not alone in this invisible war!

† **Deuteronomy 1:29-30**—*"Do not be terrified; do not be afraid...* **30.** *The Lord your God, who is going before you, will fight for you..."*

Q: Is there anything that is causing you to be fearful? Have you given fear access by participating in activities that produce fear: like watching scary movies, visiting a haunted house, etc.? If so, try to identify it and its source so you can take it through the extinguishing process in the next SQ&A section. Ask the Holy Spirit to reveal the thought that produces the fear that triggers your reaction.

HOW TO EXTINGUISH THESE FLAMING ARROWS

† **Ephesians 6:16**—*In addition to all this, take up the shield of faith, with which you can extinguish all the flaming arrows of the evil one.*

1. This Scripture tells us to *"take up the shield of faith."* But how do we go about doing that? This section will provide you with some practical applications that will help you guard your faith and give you victory in this invisible war.

2. Regarding the Shield, there are three things needed in order to extinguish the devil's flaming arrows: Recognition, Timeliness, and Utilization.

A. R_____—Be spiritually alert so you might detect the arrows coming so that they do not take you by surprise. Sometimes you will have no warning or time to practice. Pay attention to the signs that can tip you off in identifying the type of arrow that is being launched at you. They all have a common goal. Each is intended to injure your faith in God and in one another. The bottom line is this: satan wants you to find fault with God and rebel against Him thereby robbing Him of His right to receive your love, faith, obedience, and worship. To recap, some of these flaming arrows take the form of:

(1) **Flaming Arrow #1: Slander Their Commander-in-Chief**

    (a) Any circumstance that pressures you to entertain doubt about God's character, God's Word and promises, or God's motives and ways. Be very careful not to place yourself as judge and jury and God as the defendant. Learn from Eve's experience.

(2) **Flaming Arrow #2: Tragedies and Misfortunes**

    (a) Any event that may tempt you to become bitter and angry against God.

    Q: Are you distancing yourself from God because of some trial? Learn from Job's experience.

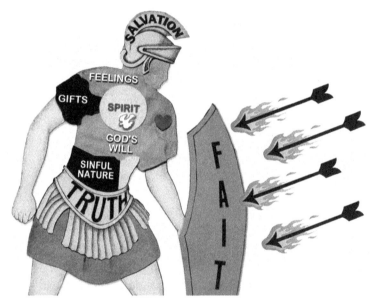

(3) **Flaming Arrow #3: Discouragement**

    (a) Any situation that tends to produce feelings of depression, despair, or hopelessness. It can either drop over you like a veil or come as a result of your perception of the circumstances you are experiencing.

    (b) In this state, you are tempted to entertain erroneous thoughts or draw wrong conclusions about God or His ways that you wouldn't believe or say if conditions were normal. Learn from the experiences of Job, John the Baptist, and Israel.

(4) **Flaming Arrow #4: Fear**

    (a) Any onslaught that causes unnatural fear to arise within you that prompts you to believe and say things that aren't true, make a bad decision, or otherwise rob you of the ability to function normally. Learn from the experiences of Elijah and Peter.

B. T_____—Next, the Shield of Faith has to be raised in time before it hits a vital "organ"—damaging your love, trust, and hope in God. The sooner you recognize that you are under attack the better. Deal with it and guard your heart before doubt, bitterness, and anger have a chance to take root. Pray for discernment to understand the enemy's strategy and purpose, and for an awareness of what is happening to you. Knowledge of satan's strategies is essential because many times we don't have enough time to think, just react.

C. U_____—Through use of the Shield of Faith, the flaming arrows aimed at you can be extinguished, but it must be lifted up and used or it is of no help. A soldier **never** goes into battle and lays his shield on the ground.

How Do We "Use" the Shield of Faith?

1. **By Exercising Faith**—If you place unwavering faith in God's infallible, unchangeable character and wisdom, it will shield your heart from utter despair and your will from giving up and revolting against God **(Proverbs 18:10).** Refer to the list of God's character in Lesson 3. **Let your faith be anchored in who God is, not in what He permits to come your way.**

2. **By Affirming Your Sonship**—Speak aloud what God says in His Word about who you are in Christ. When you become God's child, He jealously watches over you and lovingly always has your best interests in mind, even if outward circumstances seem to be a contradiction. If we don't understand who we are in Christ, we will live our lives beneath the privileges of our sonship.

3. **By Recognizing God as the Potter**—Anticipate that God will exercise His role as the potter, and accept your role as the clay **(Isaiah 64:8).**

   A. Throughout our lifelong sanctification process, God is continually molding us into the image of Christ's character. This process may be painful at times as God applies pressure and heat in forming us into His vessel. Trials and suffering are not necessarily divine retribution for personal sins. Also remember that trials are like the sun—the same sun that melts the wax, hardens the clay. We must maintain a contrite, humble, and pliable spirit and attitude, trusting Him in the shaping process. Allow the trial to draw you closer to Him rather than drive you away from Him. God uses our sufferings to make us ready for His kingdom **(2 Thessalonians 1:5).** Jesus learned obedience through the things that He suffered so how can we expect to be exempt **(Hebrews 5:8)?** Remember, your Father's hand not only molds you but guides, provides, protects, and disciplines.

4. **By Trusting in the Potter's Wisdom and Compassion**—Clay gets "tired" when being worked on. God knows our limitations and gives us "rest" when we need it.

   † **1 Corinthians 10:13** (Phillips)—*God can be trusted not to allow you to suffer any temptation beyond your powers of endurance. He will see to it that every temptation has its way out, so that it will be possible for you to bear it.*

5. **By Believing God Is in Control**—God is involved in everything that affects your life as a child of God (even when you bring it on yourself). They are either:

   A. S_____ by God—These are the things that come directly from the hand of God—His divine will. During such times, *"those who suffer according to God's will should commit themselves to their faithful Creator and continue to do good."* **(1 Peter 4:19).** Examples are the trials of Joseph **(Genesis 37:12-36; 39:1-50:20),** and the apostle Paul's *"thorn"* in the flesh:

   † **2 Corinthians 12:7-9** (NLT)—*...I have received wonderful revelations from God. But to keep me from getting puffed up, I was given a thorn in my flesh, a messenger from Satan to torment me and keep me from getting proud. 8. Three different times I begged the Lord to take it away. 9. Each time he said, "My gracious favor is all you need. My power works best*

in your weakness." So now I am glad to boast about my weaknesses, so that the power of Christ may work through me.

B. P_____ by God—These are the things that come indirectly from God—His permissive will. He allows His hedge of protection around us to be lifted for a season and gives the devil permission to touch us—with limitations. Example: Job **(1:10-12; 2:4-6).**

C. U____ by God—These include the things we "bring on ourselves" through the law of planting and harvesting. They can also be sins from our ancestors passed down to the third and fourth generation **(Exodus 20:4).** And even in these cases, *"...God causes all things to work together for good to those who love God, to those who are called according to His purpose."* **(Romans 8:28** NASB**).** God also promises to convert what the enemy meant for evil into God's higher purposes for us—advancing our walk with Him **(Genesis 50:20).** Notwithstanding, examine yourself to see if something you are doing or have done is the cause for your present trial, that when rectified, will release you from it.

6. **By Resting in God**—The truth is that God is always working on our behalf even though we may not be seeing any immediate results. Never forget that our circumstances are related to *"the end of the Lord"* **(James 5:11** KJV**),** and are but the scaffolding of God to work out His design for our future.

   † **James 5:11**—*...You have heard of Job's perseverance and have seen what the Lord finally brought about. The Lord is full of compassion and mercy.*

Note: Once Job came through his trial by praying for his "comforters," God greatly blessed his latter end more than his beginning (read **Job 42:10-17**). We can also expect God's blessings to be uniquely fashioned for our individual situation and different than that of Job's.

7. **By Persevering Through the Opposition**—Realize that even though you can't control the source of your suffering and trial, you can control how you will respond to it and have some control over the outcome. The more we cooperate with the Holy Spirit by responding in the way He wants us to; we increase the likelihood of the trial being shortened.

A. Another way you can have some <u>control</u> <u>over</u> <u>your</u> <u>outcome</u> is to, by faith, plant seeds of obedience that is in keeping with your situation.

▶**CONSIDER THIS:** Mary Taylor Previte, daughter of the great missionary to China, Hudson Taylor, once told this true story: One day a boy came upon an older man digging holes in a barren hillside and placing something in them. "What are you doing?" asked the boy. "I'm planting acorns," the man replied. "But what for?" the boy responded. The old man was quick to answer: "I'm changing the face of my mountain." But the boy just walked away in bewilderment, muttering as he left, "Sure seems like a lot of fruitless effort to me." The boy grew up, went to high school, and then left the barren, infertile area to pursue a career. Many years later he returned to his childhood home. When he got there, he was shocked! He couldn't believe what he was seeing! Instead of the arid climate, barren mountainsides, and infertile fields, he saw a bustling city with streams of water, fruitful crops, and massive lush, green, oak-tree-covered mountains. Then he remembered the old man—he wasn't crazy after all! That man's vision and labor had transformed the boy's hometown. The man actually did change the face of his mountain![2] You can too! **You don't have to live with the way things are!** Ask God for wisdom on how to change the face of your mountain.

(1) One main way of changing your circumstances is to be proactive and give out of your particular need. For example, let's say you had a financial misfortune. Rebuild by obeying the principles of God's Word and begin to work within God's economic system. Tithe and plant seeds by giving out of your poverty and pray that God will help you eventually come out of it—even in better shape than you were before! The same principle applies to other needs. If you are lonely, then reach out to others. If you need love, begin giving love. If you need a friend, be a friend. And we already know that prayer itself changes things. Also, keep in mind that the seeds you plant today can take many years before a harvest is seen. And remember, we can't keep doing the same thing over again and expect different results—try doing something new but within the confines of God's Word and guidance from the Holy Spirit.

8. **By Keeping in Perspective the Bigger Picture**—God and the angels are watching to see whom you will vindicate—God or satan. This is much bigger than just you and your circumstances.

9. **By Expecting Assaults from the devil**—This is especially true when your lifestyle is one of doing good and/or being effective for the kingdom of God. When attacks come, they shouldn't take you by surprise **(1 Peter 4:12-14).** If God permitted Job to be put into the devil's power and Peter allowed to be put into satan's sieve, you can also expect to be tried.

   † **Job 30:25-26**—Job said: *"Have I not wept for those in trouble? Has not my soul grieved for the poor? 26. Yet when I hoped for good, evil came; when I looked for light, then came darkness."*

10. **By Examining Your Motive for Serving God**—Are you serving Him out of love and for who He is, or for what you can get from Him?

11. **By Waiting Patiently for God**—Waiting is very difficult for us to do. Refrain from murmuring and complaining. God will bring you out of your trial (or kiln) with a new reliance upon Him.

   † **Psalm 37:7** (NASB)—*Rest in the Lord and wait patiently for Him...*

   † **Song of Songs 8:5** (NKJV)—*"Who is this coming up from the wilderness, leaning upon her beloved?"*

...I do not always understand His ways; but this I need not know.
I only know He holds my hand, and where He leads me, I will go.

Grace Opperman

12. **By Realizing the Battle Is the Lord's**—God almighty promises to fight for you! Rely on His power.

   † **Deuteronomy 20:3-4** (NIrV)—*"...Today you are going into battle against your enemies. Don't be scared. Don't be afraid. Don't panic. Don't be terrified by them. 4. The Lord your God is going with you. He'll fight for you. He'll help you win the battle over your enemies."*

13. **By Refusing to Give Up**—Ask yourself the questions: "Where else can I go?" "Who else can I turn to who will give eternal life, truth, and love?" In the overall picture, experiencing a defeat is only a temporary state. Only quitting makes it permanent. Stand to your feet again and press on. God will be there to help and strengthen you.

† **John 6:53, 54, 60, 61, 66-69**—*Jesus said to them, "I tell you the truth, unless you eat the flesh of the Son of Man and drink his blood, you have no life in you.* **54.** *Whoever eats my flesh and drinks my blood has eternal life, and I will raise him up at the last day.* **60.** *On hearing it, many of his disciples said, "This is a hard teaching. Who can accept it?"* **61.** *Aware that his disciples were grumbling about this, Jesus said to them, "Does this offend you?"* **66.** *From this time many of his disciples turned back and no longer followed him.* **67.** *"You do not want to leave too, do you?" Jesus asked the Twelve.* **68.** *Simon Peter answered him, "Lord, to whom shall we go? You have the words of eternal life.* **69.** *We believe and know that you are the Holy One of God."*

For every hill I've had to climb, for every stone that bruised my feet,

For all the blood and sweat and grime, for blinding storms and burning heat

My heart sings but a grateful song—These were the things that made me strong!...

Author Unknown

> ☑ Continue on with the Study Questions and Application and the Summary.

STUDY QUESTIONS AND APPLICATION

1. Are you currently being assaulted by one of these four flaming arrows? If so, which one(s) and how?

   ☐ A. Slander your Commander-in-Chief   ☐ C. Discouragement

   ☐ B. Tragedies and misfortunes   ☐ D. Fear

2. Take each flaming arrow you checked in question #1 and put it through the extinguishing process given in the section above: Recognition, Timeliness, and Utilization.

3. To bolster your faith, recall the last five victories that God has given to you and write them below.

   A. _____

   B. _____

   C. _____

   D. _____

   E. _____

4. Find ways to enlarge your view of the greatness of God like doing a study in astronomy or of the different facets of His name, or maintaining a journal or photo album of the times you experienced God's hand in your life. Ask the Holy Spirit to show you other ways.

SUMMARY

God has ordained that in order for us to receive anything from Him, we have to exercise our faith. The Shield of Faith is a critically important piece of defensive armor because we can't allow our faith in God to be injured—there's just too much at stake. The objectives of this lesson were first to show the critical role faith plays in our lives. Because of its extreme importance, it becomes an object of cultivation by God, and a target to assault by the devil. The Bible calls us to have faith in an unchangeable, unfailing God—His character, His motives, His words, and His ways. Simply put, faith is *"...being fully persuaded that what* [God] *had promised, he was able also to perform"* **(Romans 4:21** KJV**).** Yet many times we place our faith in people and things that can fail us, but we hesitate to place our trust in an Almighty God who will never let us down.

We identified some of the critical roles our delicate faith plays in our spiritual lives. Without it we cannot: believe that **1A.** God exists, or that the Bible is **1B.** God-inspired and without error; or be **1C.** *"born-again"*; receive **1D.** healing or see the miraculous take place; receive answers to **1E.** prayer; be **1F.** overcomers; or enter **1G.** heaven. Because our faith is so essential to receiving from God and overcoming our enemies, it becomes one of the main objects of God's attention in our lives. This is why He is so dedicated to testing and strengthening it. After all, Christ is *"...the author and perfecter of our faith"* **(Hebrews 12:2).**

Therefore, God tries to *"increase our faith"* by helping it to grow through **2B(1)** meditating on His Word (the Bible); through **2B(2)** rehearsing the victories God has given you as well as hearing the testimony of others; through getting us to **2B(3)** exercise our faith by bringing trials and circumstances into our lives that compel us to place our faith in Him—drawing faith out of us and making it grow; through **2B(4)** professing our faith aloud; and through **2B(5)** receiving faith directly from God. Normally, faith in an object or person is developed by frequent acquaintance and building a trust, which gets stronger by the successful "track record" one has with it. The same is true of our relationship with God. Our faith can vary from having *"no faith"* to being *"full of faith"* like Stephen. If our faith doesn't grow and mature, it could *"fail,"* be *"shipwrecked,"* be *"overthrown,"* and we can even *"abandon"* and *"depart"* from the faith we once had.

The shield protected the entire body of the Roman soldier against any projectiles, particularly arrows tipped with flammable materials. Similarly, for Christians under satanic attack, it is our unwavering faith in the unimpeachable integrity of the character of God and in the trustworthiness of the Bible, which protects us when satan showers his burning arrows of unholy thoughts, subtle temptations, dark despair, blasphemous suggestions, base accusations, nagging doubts, and clouds of fear. It is this kind of faith that shields our heart from utter despair and our will from revolting against God. The devil's basic strategy is to use **TACTIC: Create Doubt in Their Commander-in-Chief** in which the enemy aims his flaming arrows at our faith so as to plant seeds of doubt within us about God's character, thereby pressuring our will to rebel against Him. This tactic creates a climate of doubt necessary for the success of the arrows.

The flaming arrows the devil launches at us are the various things that injure our faith in God and cause unbelief and doubt in God's character and God's Word. We covered four main types of flaming arrows satan uses. **Flaming Arrow #1: Slander Their Commander-in-Chief**—The enemy will bring subtle or outright false accusations to defame God's Word and character, slandering Him before man, to try to convince you that there are imperfections in God's character and His ways, thereby damaging your faith in His integrity. Eve was a prime example.

Next is **Flaming Arrow #2: Tragedies and Misfortunes**—The enemy will either use, or try to get permission to cause, tragedies and misfortunes in your life so as to pressure your will to find fault with God to the point where you no longer serve Him. Satan uses the **TACTIC: Accuse Them** to present your faults and shortcomings before God, true or contrived, in order to persuade God to temporarily lift His hedge of protection from you to test you with the intent of turning you away from serving Him. It is comforting to know that our Heavenly Father will not allow satan to touch His children without His permission and with limitations. Job was an example.

Another is **Flaming Arrow #3: Discouragement**—The enemy will try to bring upon you discouragement, oppression, and despair to cause you to make decisions about God and His will while in this depressed state that are faulty and absurd. His hope is that you will step outside His will or choose to quit serving Him. Job, John the Baptist, and the nation of Israel were examples.

Finally, **Flaming Arrow #4: Fear**—Like a lion when it roars, the enemy will attempt to intimidate and immobilize you with fear—terrorizing you in combination with discouragement—in order to drive you to make wrong decisions you would never make in your right mind. Fear is a powerful tool used to intimidate and manipulate people to get them to do what a person wants. Satan is the ultimate terrorist. Some of the ways the enemy uses fear to accomplish his malicious goals are: to increase the torment of one who is already suffering; to pressure you to leave the assignment that God has called you to do; to produce unbelief and prevent you from entering the Promised Land; and to hold you back from witnessing to others about Christ. A soldier of the Lord is not to retreat or flee from conflict with the enemy out of fear and unbelief. He wants us to confront the enemy head on. Also, God has not given us a spirit of cowardice and timidity, but *"...a spirit of power, of love and of self-discipline"* **(2 Timothy 1:7)**.

By using the Shield of Faith, thank God these flaming arrows can be extinguished. There are three things needed in order to extinguish the devil's flaming arrows: **2A.** recognition—being spiritually alert so you can detect the arrows coming before they overtake you by surprise, and identifying the type of arrow that's being launched at you; **2B.** timeliness—the shield has to be raised in time before it hits a vital "organ"—damaging your love, trust, and hope in God; and **2C.** utilization—it must be lifted up and used or it is of no help.

Some of the ways we "use" the Shield of Faith are: by placing unwavering faith in God's infallible, unchangeable character and wisdom; by affirming outloud who you are in Christ; by recognizing God's role as the potter, and accepting your role as the clay and by trusting in His wisdom and compassion; by believing that God is involved in everything that affects your life as a child of God (even when you bring it on yourself) that is, they are either **5A.** sent by God, **5B.** permitted by God, or **5C.** used by God to mold you into the image of Christ; by resting in the truth that God is working even though you don't see it; by realizing you can control how you will respond to the trial and have some control over the outcome; by keeping in perspective the bigger picture that God and the angels are watching to see whom you will vindicate—God or satan; by expecting assaults from the devil; by examining your motive for serving God; by waiting patiently for God to bring you out of your trial without murmuring and complaining; by believing that it is His battle and He will fight for you; and by persevering and refusing to quit—knowing that there is no one else you can turn to who can give you eternal life, truth, and love.

Lesson 15
THE SWORD OF THE SPIRIT

☑ Before starting the DVD:

The Roman soldier used a light, short sword (*gladius*) with a double-edged blade for hand-to-hand combat. It was designed for thrusting into the enemy's body. Spiritually, this is the first of two powerful offensive weapons God has given to us. The Sword of the Spirit enables us to fight against Satan's kingdom of darkness—piercing it with the light of God's absolute truth. It is also a defensive weapon. In developing the ability to win this invisible war, the objectives of this lesson are to present an overview of God's Word, define its two "edges," and then learn from the practical example Jesus gave us how to use this sword in our own daily lives. We will learn nine more of the enemy's tactics including the ways the enemy attacks the Bible. We'll also help you to identify, and give a brief overview, of groups that claim to be Christian but do not hold to the essential doctrines of biblical orthodox Christianity. This lesson is divided into two sessions. Please follow the instructions given. Are you ready? First pray! (Note: If you want to learn more about the basics of how the Bible originated as well as for a general overview, consider taking my course, **An Introduction to the Bible,** at www.DiscoverMinistries.com. Click on the link, "Discover the Bible".)

☑ **DVD Users:** Watch Lesson 15 for an overview before proceeding further (25 min.).
☑ When you're through, pick up again at this point. Fill in the blanks from the Summary.

OVERVIEW OF THE WORD OF GOD

† **Ephesians 6:17** (KJV)—*And take...the sword of the Spirit, which is the word of God.*

What is meant by the Word of God? It consists of the 39 books of the Old Testament and the 27 books of the New Testament. They don't just "contain" the Word of God—they ARE the Word of God. These books were written over a period of about fifteen hundred years (approximately from 1500 B.C. to A.D. 100). The Bible is the complete and final message and revelation of God to mankind. No new revelation or book can be added to it, and everything dealing with life issues, faith, and morals must align and be judged by its contents.

The Bible is relevant for every person, generation, and culture since Adam and Eve because mankind's spiritual condition and needs are the same. Here are some important aspects you need to know about the Word of God:

1. The Bible is I_____. It contains no errors in the original texts.

    A. The Holy Spirit is its author—writing through about 40 human instruments from all walks of life. Most of them never knew one another, and in some cases, had not read each other's writings. What is phenomenal is that collectively, their writings all blend together in theme, continuity, and message, without contradiction.

    B. The Bible is God's gift of absolute truth to the human race—all that we need to know about Him, our adversaries, how to live with our fellow man, what the future end times will bring, and how to get to heaven. In both the Old and New Testaments, men spoke and wrote under the inspiration and revelation of the Holy Spirit.

        † **2 Timothy 3:16-17** (GNT)—*All Scripture is inspired by God and is useful for teaching the truth, rebuking error, correcting faults, and giving instruction for right living **17.** so that the man who serves God may be fully qualified and equipped to do every kind of good work.*

        † **2 Peter 1:20-21**—*Above all, you must understand that no prophecy of Scripture came about by the prophet's own interpretation. **21.** For prophecy never had its origin in the will of man, but men spoke from God as they were carried along by the Holy Spirit.*

        † **1 Peter 1:10-12** (NLT)—*This salvation was something the prophets wanted to know more about. They prophesied about this gracious salvation prepared for you, even though they had many questions as to what it all could mean. **11.** They wondered what the Spirit of Christ within them was talking about when he told them in advance about Christ's suffering and his great glory afterward. They wondered when and to whom all this would happen. **12.** They were told that these things would not happen during their lifetime, but many years later, during yours...*

        † **Matthew 22:41-46** (NLT)—*...Jesus asked them a question: **42.** "What do you think about the Messiah? Whose son is he?" They replied, "He is the son of David." **43.** Jesus responded, "Then why does David, speaking under the inspiration of the Holy Spirit, call him Lord? For David said, **44.** 'The Lord said to my Lord, Sit in honor at my right hand until I humble your enemies beneath your feet?'..."* **(Psalm 110:1).** Also see **Acts 1:15-20; 4:25,26.**

        † **Matthew 5:18**—Jesus said: *"I tell you the truth, until heaven and earth disappear, not the smallest letter, not the least stroke of a pen, will by any means disappear from the Law until everything is accomplished."*

        † **Matthew 24:35** (Phillips)—Jesus said: *"Heaven and earth will pass away, but my words will never pass away!"* (Also see **Isaiah 40:8.**)

2. The Word of God is "L_____."—The Holy Spirit, the greatest power in the universe, energizes it and gives it its life and power.

        † **Hebrews 4:12**—*The word of God is living and active. Sharper than any double-edged sword, it penetrates even to dividing soul and spirit, joints and marrow; it judges the thoughts and attitudes of the heart.*

† **Isaiah 55:10-11**—*As the rain and the snow come down from heaven, and do not return to it without watering the earth and making it bud and flourish, so that it yields seed for the sower and bread for the eater, so is my word that goes out from my mouth: It will not return to me empty, but will accomplish what I desire and achieve the purpose for which I sent it.*

3. The Word of God is "A_____" **(Hebrews 4:12).** Here are some of the ways:

   A. It is P_____ (and authoritative) because the Holy Spirits anoints it.

      † **Luke 4:32**—*They were amazed at his* [Christ's] *teaching, because his message had authority.*

▶**CONSIDER THIS:** We, the church, need to be reminded that what it takes to be successful is not more finances, new programs, or copying the world's ways, but rather to simply proclaim the Word of God under the anointing of the Holy Spirit and allow Him to produce awesome results.

   B. It E_____ in these ways:

      (1) It uncovers doctrinal and philosophical error.

      (2) It reveals satan's existence, character, and the tactics he uses against us.

      (3) It shines its spotlight on the darkness of our hidden evil character, motives, and deeds.

      † **John 3:19-21**—Jesus said, *"This is the verdict: Light has come into the world, but men loved darkness instead of light because their deeds were evil. 20. Everyone who does evil hates the light, and will not come into the light for fear that his deeds will be exposed. 21. But whoever lives by the truth comes into the light, so that it may be seen plainly that what he has done has been done through God."*

      † **Ephesians 5:11-13**—*Have nothing to do with the fruitless deeds of darkness, but rather expose them. 12. For it is shameful even to mention what the disobedient do in secret. 13. But everything exposed by the light becomes visible...*

      † **Hebrews 4:13**—*Nothing in all creation is hidden from God's sight. Everything is uncovered and laid bare before the eyes of him to whom we must give account.*

      Note: Our enemies, satan and our sinful nature, depend on secrecy for their success. Turning on the light by proclaiming God's Word exposes them.

▶**CONSIDER THIS:** In the final analysis, it is our rejection of God's rule over our lives that will keep us out of heaven. When our evil deeds are exposed by the light of His Holy Spirit and His Word, we must respond by embracing the truth, and repenting by changing our direction and behavior. In so doing, we demonstrate that we love light more than darkness.

   C. The Bible "J_____."

      (1) It sets the standard of truth by which everything else must align to. Truth is not determined by what "works" for each individual, by legislation, the situation, or by consensus of opinion.

(2) The Bible judges the thoughts, attitudes, motives, and desires of our heart **(Hebrews 4:12b).** It judges us, we don't judge it!

(3) It will judge every person on Judgment Day in the life hereafter.

† **John 12:48**—Jesus taught, *"There is a judge for the one who rejects me and does not accept my words; that very word which I spoke will condemn him at the last day."*

Note: In my opinion, one of the "books" that will be opened at the Great White Throne judgment in **Revelation 20:11** and **12** will be the Bible.

TACTIC: Make Them Feel Ashamed—The enemy will try to shame you into thinking that if you believe the Bible to be the only divinely inspired, infallible standard of absolute truth that judges everything else, you are an unscholarly, intolerant, hard-hearted, narrow-minded bigot. ◎ *Main Targets:* Your Pride and Confidence.

D. The Word of God "C_____" to the heart, and produces two kinds of responses—submissiveness or anger and rebellion.

† **Acts 2:37**—*When the people heard this* [Peter's sermon], *they were cut to the heart and said to Peter and the other apostles, "Brothers, what shall we do?"*

† **Acts 7:54-58** (KJV)—*When they heard these things* [Stephen's message], *they were cut to the heart, and they gnashed on him with their teeth.*

►**CONSIDER THIS:** The Holy Spirit uses God's Word to convict us of sin **(John 16:8-13).** Once "cut" by the Sword of the Spirit, we will never again be the same because light has penetrated an area of our darkness enabling us to see sin and truth clearly. We are now responsible to deal with it. It also inflicts wounds that produce death in our sinful nature.

E. The Word of God S_____.

(1) It *"divides,"* or makes a distinction, between our *"soul"* and our *"spirit"* revealing the complex nature of humanity within **(Hebrews 4:12b).**

(2) It divides the closest relationships. When you allow the Word to change you and begin to live for God, that decision may cause wounds of division and ostracism from unbelieving members of our family or friends. In such cases, your allegiance to Christ may result in the pain of rejection and the loss of these relationships for a season or even longer **(Matthew 10:32-39).**

4. There are two different Greek words the Holy Spirit used for the Word of God. They can represent the two "edges" of the Sword of the Spirit, if you will.

A. L_____ (the written Word)—It denotes "the expression of thought." It is the Greek word used in **Hebrews 4:12.** It refers to the written Word. It is also used as a name for Jesus denoting His "personal manifestation" of the Godhead **(John 1:1, 14).**[1]

B. R_____ (the spoken Word)—It denotes that which is spoken. This is the word used in **Ephesians 6:17.** In referring to the Sword of the Spirit, W.E. Vine says, "...here the reference is not to the whole Bible as such, but to the individual scripture which the Spirit brings to our remembrance for use in time of need, a prerequisite being the regular storing of the mind with Scripture."[2] The *rhēma* can occur in three ways:

(1) **From God to you**—The Holy Spirit can "speak" or impress upon your spirit a Scripture for personal guidance or encouragement, or through someone used in the Gifts of the Spirit in **1 Corinthians 12:7-11.**

(2) **From God (through you) to another**—The Holy Spirit can use you as an instrument to convey His personal message to the Body of Christ via one of the Gifts of the Spirit **(1 Corinthians 12:7-11; Acts 9:10-18; 21:10-11).**

(3) **From you to the devil and demonic forces**—When you are attacked by the enemy, like with temptation, quote aloud a relevant verse from the Bible as directed by the Spirit for your specific situation. The Truth will expose the lie and deception that demonic forces are tempting you with. The Holy Spirit will use this as an offensive or defensive weapon in resisting the enemy. This is what Jesus did when He was tempted by the devil in the wilderness. Let's see how He did it.

HOW TO USE THE S(WORD) OF THE SPIRIT

The Temptation of Jesus

† **Luke 4:1-2**—*Jesus, full of the Holy Spirit, returned from the Jordan and was led by the Spirit in the desert, 2. where for forty days he was tempted by the devil. He ate nothing during those days, and at the end of them he was hungry.*

1. The background setting of the temptation of Jesus:

A. After having just heard the audible voice of His Father at His baptism, Jesus was *"full of the Holy Spirit"* as He entered the wilderness having been given the Spirit *"without limit"* **(John 1:32-34; 3:34).** Christ was at the highest spiritual level of His life thus far.

B. He entered the wilderness by the direct leading of the Holy Spirit (see **Mark 1:12**) and was in the center of His Father's will. He had to share in the experience of our humanity and be *"tempted in every way, just as we are"* **(Hebrews 4:15).**

▶**CONSIDER THIS:** If Jesus, God's Son, was not exempt from experiencing suffering and temptation by the devil, how can you and I expect to be?

C. His Father called Him to a forty-day fast. The devil knows how to wait until his chances for success are the greatest. This usually involves attacking us when we are at our weakest point. He waited until Jesus' resistance and strength was at its lowest, and His hunger was the keenest, having been weakened by long abstinence from food. Then he attacked!

D. Please note that Jesus did not use His divine power to defeat the devil. He used the same weapons that God still makes available to we humans today—the Bible and the Holy Spirit.

2. **Jesus' first temptation**—The sphere of <u>need</u>: Make a stone become bread.

† **Luke 4:3**—*The devil said to him, "If you are the Son of God, tell this stone to become bread."*

A. First of all, the devil uses his strategy of creating doubt by saying, *"If you are the Son of God..."* He tries to put Jesus in a position to defend His deity. Note that the last thing Jesus heard His Father say to Him at His baptism was the first thing the enemy attacked in the wilderness. Satan still uses this ploy to have us question whether we really are a child of God.

B. Satan was tempting Jesus to use His divine power to satisfy His physical hunger. If He gives into the temptation, He will depart from the place of perfect obedience to His Father's will by ending the fast prematurely. Satan employed a deceptive rationale for satisfying Christ's hunger. It would abuse Jesus' relationship with His Father by taking undue advantage and misusing His power by exercising it independently beyond the boundaries of the will and purpose of God—and thereby sin.

♞ **TACTIC: Eliminate the Competition**—The enemy will try to seduce you to choose to leave God's will, or he will try to prevent you from entering God's will because he knows the resulting damage God will cause to his kingdom of darkness through you.
◎ *Main Targets:* Your Mind, Will, and Service for God.

C. Jesus modeled how we are to respond and counterattack temptation using God's Sword. Since Christ made the Old Testament Scriptures such a part of His being, the Holy Spirit brought **Deuteronomy 8:3** to His remembrance and He quoted it aloud to the devil:

† **Luke 4:4**—*Jesus answered, "It is written: 'Man does not live on bread alone.'"*

(1) Jesus used this *rhēma* word both offensively and defensively to expose the deception and defeat the enemy. That truth silenced the devil and forced him to take another approach.

▶**CONSIDER THIS:** We must know the Bible well enough to be able to use it skillfully so the Holy Spirit can bring Scripture to our remembrance that fit our circumstances **(John 14:26)**. Also use the Sword to proclaim truth into adverse situations. For example, when you encounter circumstances that seem to indicate God's absence or unfaithfulness, declare aloud Scriptures about God's unchanging, perfect character and His promises instead of entertaining negative thoughts. His truth will put things into right perspective. Note that it is very important that you speak out loud the Scriptures with resolve because demonic beings do not know what you are thinking.

3. **Jesus' second temptation**—The sphere of <u>success</u>: Power over the kingdoms of the world.

> † **Luke 4:5-7**—*The devil led him up to a high place and showed him in an instant all the kingdoms of the world.* **6.** *And he said to him, "I will give you all their authority and splendor, for it has been given to me, and I can give it to anyone I want to.* **7.** *So if you worship me, it will all be yours."*

A. The devil offered Jesus power over the kingdoms of the world in exchange for His worship. The subtle trap is that the one who has the right to be worshiped also has the right to be obeyed.

🜚 **TACTIC: Deprive God of Worship**—The devil will attempt to rob God from receiving your love, worship, and obedience by diverting your devotion that rightfully belongs to Him, to himself through false religions or by setting up an idol in your heart. (See also **Malachi 3:8-9.**) ◎ *Main Targets:* Your Love, Worship, and Obedience.

B. Jesus did not argue with the adversary. He simply quoted aloud **Deuteronomy 6:13**—*"It is written: 'Worship the Lord your God and serve Him only.'"* This truth put everything into perspective and left the enemy with nothing else to say about this topic.

C. This strategy was also an appeal calculated to seduce the Lord into a presumed short-cut to the fulfillment of God's promises to Him—namely the rule over all the kingdoms that were to be obtained via the cross. The devil tempted Christ to by-pass the cross, avoiding a degrading, horrible death, and obtain the promised glory without pain. All Christ would need to do is submit to the usurped sovereignty of satan and ascribe to his presumed deity the worship due only to God. Satan tried this tactic on Jesus at least twice. The other time occurred in **Matthew 16:21-23,** when he tried to deter Christ through the influence of a well-meaning friend.

🜚 **TACTIC: Pry Them Away From God's Will**—The enemy will try to get you to miss God's will, or deceive you with the mirage of an easy short cut in obtaining God's will—apart from God's sacrificial ways. By failing to carry out God's plan, God's work suffers a setback and you are robbed of a crown of reward. ◎ *Main Targets:* Your Mind and Will.

> † **Revelation 3:11** (Phillips)—*"...hold fast to what you have—let no one deprive you of your crown."*

> † **2 John 1:8** (NASB)—*Watch yourselves, that you do not lose what we have accomplished, but that you may receive a full reward.*

▶**CONSIDER THIS:** Imagine what it would be like to have your name called on "rewards day" at the Judgment Seat of Christ and to experience the regret of "if only," as you see the reward God intended for you to have, be given to another whom God had to raise up in your place. Don't be tricked into quitting and leaving God's will for your life. Look beyond your hardships and suffering to the bigger picture for *"These little troubles (which are really so transitory) are winning for us a permanent, glorious and solid reward out of all proportion to our pain."* (**2 Corinthians 4:17** Phillips)**.**

D. Caution must also be taken when God gives you initial direction, and then the enemy tries to take you down another path—away from what God intended through other human ideas that are not of God. This happens when we fail to wait on God to get His full plan.

4. Jesus' third temptation—The sphere of <u>religion</u>: Test your Father's Word.

> † **Luke 4:9-11**—*The devil led him to Jerusalem and had him stand on the highest point of the temple. "If you are the Son of God," he said, "throw yourself down from here. **10.** For it is written: 'He will command his angels concerning you to guard you carefully; **11.** they will lift you up in their hands, so that you will not strike your foot against a stone.'"*

A. The devil tried another strategy. Since Jesus knew the Scriptures so well, satan would also use Scripture, but taken out of context, as the basis of trying to get Jesus to jump from the 400-foot pinnacle of the temple in Jerusalem.

▶**CONSIDER THIS:** Satan knows the Bible and can quote it. He uses his knowledge of the Bible with diabolical cunning, masterfully manipulating the intended meaning of Scripture and mixing truth with error. He is the source of all false doctrine, false religions, and churches that claim to be Christian but do not adhere to the inerrancy of the Word of God.

🐎 **TACTIC: Counterfeit the Bible's Teachings**—We'll cover this tactic in the next session.

B. In effect, the devil said this to Jesus: "Let me remind you of this promise from your Father in **Psalm 91,** verses **11** and **12.** Now *if* you believe God's Word as you say you do (note the doubt again), and *if* you really are the Son of God, then jump and prove how great your faith is in what your Father said He would do. Challenge Him and put Him to the test and see if He can be trusted." (Also note his hint of slander.)

C. The devil tried to trick Jesus into proving that His Father would protect Him if He jumped as promised in Psalm 91. Yes, this passage promises protection to those who love God and who are earnestly seeking Him (for which Christ qualified), but does not include presumptuously putting God to the test. By tempting Him to jump, the devil also gave Jesus the opportunity to sensationally display God's power for personal glory.

🐎 **TACTIC: Tempting God**—The enemy will try to get you to test God about keeping His Word by taking Scripture out of context in order to cause you to question God's character and Word when He doesn't respond to being put to the test. ◎ *Main Targets:* Your Faith and Relationship with God.

D. The subtlety in this temptation is that if we take the bait and test God wrongly, God is not obligated to fulfill His promise. Consequently, when He does not respond in the way we thought He should, we find fault with Him, doubting His character and other portions of His Word.

E. Also, beware when you are tempted to "prove how great your faith is" in what God said He would do. One example is people who use **Mark 16:18** as a basis for handling poisonous snakes and drinking poison which God never intended with this verse.

F. Ananias and Sapphira serve as another example of how we can be tricked by the devil to tempt God by putting Him to the test. (See **Acts 5:1-11**—especially **verse 9.**)

G. The intended outcome of these three temptations was to invalidate Christ's messianic claims and negate His work of redemption. Ultimately, what the devil was after in this last temptation was to have Jesus kill Himself so He couldn't die for sin on the cross and save the world. Then there would have been no threat left to satan's kingdom.

H. Jesus did not take the devil's bait, but counterattacked by wielding His "Sword." He quoted aloud a *rhēma* Word from **Deuteronomy 6:16** saying, *"The scripture says, 'You must not put the Lord your God to the test'"* **(Luke 4:12** GNT).

I. Jesus decisively defeated the devil by resisting him with the Old Testament Scriptures. When the devil is resisted by one submitted to God, he will flee **(James 4:7)**—for now.

† **Luke 4:13**—*When the devil had finished all this tempting, he left him until an opportune time.*

▶**CONSIDER THIS:** Our spiritual victories should not cause us to be overconfident or boastful. You have won a battle by the power of the Holy Spirit. Other battles will come in this invisible war. The enemy will wait and visit again when another opportunity presents itself. Be watchful! Remember, Jesus was under satanic attack from His birth until His death. The more one is used effectively by God to bring damage to satan's kingdom, the more attacks one can expect from him.

J. This spiritual experience took a strenuous toll on Jesus. The combination of Jesus' physical weakness from the fast, the spiritually draining temptation experience, and a powerful satanic presence all necessitated *"angels"* to minister to Him **(Matthew 4:11)**. It is noteworthy that the only other mention of direct angelic aid in the life of Jesus was at Gethsemane when just **one** angel strengthened Him **(Luke 22:43-44)**.

5. After His victory over these temptations and wilderness experience, Christ emerged equipped for ministry in the power of the Holy Spirit **(Luke 4:14,18,32)**.

▶**CONSIDER THIS:** There is a price to be paid to go to the next level in God. You will be tested and attacked prior to every plateau that God wants to take you to. Jesus gave us the model. First, the satanic attack comes. Then as you obtain victory, the breakthrough to the next level in your spiritual walk in God and ministry occurs. In fact, the degree of anointing and ministry released through us by the Spirit will probably be in direct proportion to the severity of the attack and our victory over it. You could be on the very threshold of your breakthrough right now. Keep on fighting. Remain obedient and faithful to God. Wait out the storm. It is said that the night is the darkest just before dawn. When satan fights the hardest, it is an indication that God is about to do some great thing. Keep pressing on!

A. A story is told about an old prospector who was mining for gold in an old abandoned mine. He and his small team had backbreakingly chiseled rock for some period of time. Finally, exhausted, low morale, and finances dwindling, he decided to call it quits. The mine lay idle for years. Then another company bought it and resumed where the old man left off. They didn't go three feet further into the dig when they uncovered one of the largest veins of gold in that part of the country. Don't ever give up! Your breakthrough could be just around the corner. Don't allow the devil or anything to rob you of it.

B. There was another way Jesus wielded the *"sword of the Spirit."* He used it in His ministry as an offensive weapon to attack demonic forces by rescuing people being held under satan's power—thereby making an inroad into his evil empire. As the Word of God (*logos*) is "preached" and proclaimed by human vessels through speech, print, audio, and video, the Holy Spirit uses the Word of God to penetrate satan's kingdom of darkness—piercing it with the brilliant light of absolute truth.

C. The Sword breaks the power and grip demonic forces have over a person or region especially when accompanied by fasting and prayer. As the *"children of the devil"* hear that Word and by faith believe it, a light goes on in their minds and spirits and the truth of God's Word dispels their darkness. Christ commissions us to rescue them: *"I am sending you to open their eyes and turn them from darkness to light, and from the power of Satan to God..."* **(Acts 26:17,18).**

D. Through the *"foolishness of preaching"* **(1 Corinthians 1:21** KJV**)** and *"the word of our testimony,"* **(Revelation 12:11)** we invade satan's domain. Victory is achieved each time the spiritually blind begin to see *"the truth"* and are set free from the devil's bondage and power over their lives. Satan's kingdom is dealt a blow each time one of his subjects is birthed into God's kingdom.

▶ **CONSIDER THIS:** We are called to go forth and attack the forces of hell by God's direction and power. Each time portions of the world system's institutions are "recaptured" for God (by incorporating biblical truth and principles), God's rule is extended in those places. As godly men and women rule in the fear of God and allow His Word to be incorporated into their sphere of influence, satan's rule through people is diminished.

Yet this Sword can lie inactive in our hand. To be effective, it must be picked up and used so its power can be released. Then we need to develop skill in using it in combat-tested situations. It is critical that we be familiar with God's Word. We must know it, memorize it, and believe that it is divinely inspired and without error. If we don't, then its power cannot be activated and we have no sword to use at all! (See **Hebrews 5:13-14.**)

☑ This ends our first session and the DVD content for Lesson 15. Now please answer these SQ&A.

STUDY QUESTIONS AND APPLICATION

1. Are you in the will of God in the following areas of your life?

   A. Your marriage?   ☐ Yes ☐ No

   B. Your calling/job?   ☐ Yes ☐ No

   C. Your church?   ☐ Yes ☐ No

2. Referring to #1 above, to the right of every "no" answer write in what the Holy Spirit has been impressing upon you to do so you can choose to enter His will?

3. On a scale from 1 to 10 rate your consistency in the following Bible activities. Write the letters A, B, and C <u>above</u> the appropriate numbers on the scale and the current month and year <u>below</u> that number.

   A. Daily Bible reading and meditation **B**. Weekly Bible study **C**. Weekly memorization of Scripture

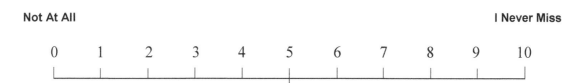

4. Referring to #3 above, identify one thing you can do that would enable you to be more consistent in these three areas—and then begin doing it!

   Daily Bible reading and meditation: _____

   Weekly Bible study: _____

   Weekly memorization of Scripture: _____

5. Is the **TACTIC: Tempting God** being used on you? How? What can you begin to do to stop it?

6. In the **Parable of the Sower,** Jesus taught that when we hear or read God's Word, its effectiveness in our lives is in direct proportion to the condition of the "soil" of our heart. Examine your heart's "soil" by reading the following Scriptures and answering the questions (estimated time: 30 min.). You will learn principles to ensure that your heart is properly prepared to receive His Word.
   (Note: Keep a marker in Matthew 13, Mark 4, and Luke 8 as you will be referring to these chapters often.)

   A. **Hard soil**—please read **Mark 4:2-4.** What happens when the seed falls onto this type of soil? How does it affect the hearer?

      (1) **Matthew 13:18-19** _____

      (2) **Luke 8:11-12** _____

   B. **Shallow soil**—please read **Mark 4:5-6.** What happens when the seed falls onto this type of soil? How does it affect the hearer?

      (1) **Mark 4:16-17** _____

   C. **Competitive soil**—please read **Mark 4:7.**

      (1) What happens when the seed falls onto this type of soil? How does it affect the hearer?

         (a) **Mark 4:18-19** _____

         (b) **Luke 8:14** _____

(2) To what did Jesus liken these "thorns" in **Mark 4:19?** (List them in the order given.)

(a) _____

(b) _____

(c) _____ (also see **Luke 8:14**)

(3) How may we remedy (2) (a), (b), and (c) above?

(a) **Matthew 6:33** _____

    1 John 3:21-24; 5:14-15 _____

    1 Peter 5:7 _____

    Philippians 4:6-7 _____

(b) **Matthew 6:19-21, 24** _____

    Jeremiah 9:23-24 _____

(c) **Ecclesiastes 2:1-11** _____

    Psalm 16:11 _____

D. **Fertile soil**—please read **Mark 4:8.**

(1) What happens when the seed falls onto this type of soil? How does it affect the hearer?

(a) **Mark 4:20** _____

(b) **Matthew 13:23** _____

(c) **Luke 8:15** _____

(2) What is God's process in preparing our heart's soil to receive His Word and produce fruit?

(a) **Hosea 10:12** _____

(b) **Luke 8:6; 1 Corinthians 3:6** _____

(3) What are other "nutrients" that cause the soil of our heart to be fertile?

(a) **Isaiah 66:2** _____

(b) **Job 23:12; Proverbs 2:1-5** _____

(c) **Jeremiah 15:16** _____

(d) **Acts 17:11**_____

Note: Fertile soil will produce fruit without further effort by the sower, and the fruit grows and matures over the process of time (Mark 4:26-28).

† **Luke 8:18**—*Therefore consider carefully how you listen. Whoever has will be given more; whoever does not have, even what he thinks he has will be taken from him.*

> ☑ When you are ready to begin the last session, continue on in this workbook for additional material about the Sword of the Spirit **not** on the video.
>
> Note: I strongly suggest that the remainder of this lesson be done as a separate session.

Session 2
FALSE TEACHINGS AND DOCTRINAL ERRORS

1. God is very concerned that what we believe about Him and His Word are true. There is always the danger of believing a lie (that resembles the truth). This is why the Scriptures exhort us to walk in the truth and maintain sound doctrine **(Titus 2:1).**

   A. To this end, God has given gifts to His church: apostles, prophets, evangelists, pastors, and teachers to help us acquire knowledge of His Word, maturity, and unity so that we will not be *"...blown here and there by every wind of teaching and by the cunning and craftiness of men..."* **(Ephesians 4:11-16).**

2. Throughout history, some verses of the Bible have been interpreted differently. This has caused division not only between church denominations but also within Christendom itself, which resulted in its three major branches: Roman Catholicism, the Eastern Orthodox Church, and Protestantism. This is why it is so critical to apply the proper rules of biblical interpretation to ensure the accuracy of what God intended.

3. In Protestantism, there is a systematic doctrine of fundamental truths based solely on the Bible. They are the foundational beliefs of orthodox Christianity (not to be confused with the Eastern Orthodox Church), and are considered authoritative and are accepted by all true Protestant Christian denominations.[3]

   A. These Bible doctrines can be classified into one of two categories: those that are (1) **Essential** to salvation, and those that are (2) **Non-essential** to salvation.

   B. The Body of Christ needs to **stand firm** on "essential" doctrine while maintaining **unity** over "non-essential" doctrine. The more fragmented Christianity becomes, the more our effectiveness is diluted and crippled in representing God and reaching the people Christ died for.

C. For example, if an individual or denomination does not believe that divine healing, or the Baptism of the Holy Spirit with the initial evidence of speaking in another language, is for today but was only for the early church, then these beliefs (as important as they are) would fall into the second category of "non-essential." The reason it is called, "non-essential," is that holding to these beliefs won't keep a person out of heaven—not that they are in any way inferior to those in the "essential" category. Furthermore, the unfortunate thing is that if these doctrines are true, then that person's misinterpretation of the Scripture and their unbelief would prevent them from receiving and benefiting from these life-changing gifts God desires them to have today.

D. The Bible instructs us to confront error and not allow it to go unchallenged. Therefore, it behooves each of us to thoroughly search the Scriptures so that we are convinced of what the Bible teaches on a given topic. Then we will be prepared to reason with those who hold an erroneous belief, and through prayer, love, patience, and gentleness share what we have found to be truth by directing them to the relevant Scriptures pertaining to that topic.

4. On the other hand, if a teaching has an errant view of God, takes away or adds to the redemptive work of Christ and/or the authority and inspiration of the Bible, or any other belief that could affect one's eternal destiny, then it falls into the "essential" category and should be treated as heresy. God holds each generation responsible to ensure that the integrity of the truth of His Word is maintained. He wants us to be a defender of His Word and *"...contend for the faith that was once for all entrusted to the saints."* **(Jude 1:3).**

📖 DEFINITION—HERESY

The Greek word used in the New Testament is *hairesis*. According to W.E. Vine it is "...a self-willed opinion which is substituted for...truth, and leads to division and the formation of sects...generally with the expectation of personal advantage...in contrast to the uniting power of the 'truth'."[4] In short, it is a work of the flesh where one is quick to disagree rather than find points of agreement. This results in divisions and can have huge destructive, eternal consequences **(2 Peter 2:1-3).**

🔥 TACTIC: Counterfeit the Bible's Teachings—The devil will try to deceive you into believing things the Bible does not teach. These false teachings imitate the real truth in order to keep you from the truth. He will then try to use you to either cause division within the Body of Christ, draw you away to join a counterfeit "Christian" group, or use you to start one in order to lead others astray and into satan's camp. ◎ *Main Targets:* Your Faith in the Bible and God, and your Salvation

5. Through their ability to plan and implant thoughts, the evil one and his minions can convey to us erroneous religious "truth" (*"...doctrines of devils"*) through *"...the spirit of error."* **1 John 4:6** (KJV). See also **Revelation 2:20,24.** God has forewarned us of erroneous teachings and heretical sects: *"Now the Spirit speaketh expressly, that in the latter times some shall depart from the faith, giving heed to seducing spirits, and doctrines of devils..."* **(1 Timothy 4:1-5** KJV).

▶ **CONSIDER THIS:** Outside on a clear, moonlit night, a group of college students are asked by their instructor to point their finger in the direction of where they believe "true north" is. When all had so indicated, the teacher pulled out a compass from his pocket and showed them where it truly lies. It didn't matter how sure the students were about where they **thought** true north was, the standard exists. Likewise, it does not matter what we believe truth to be, God has established an absolute universal standard of truth. If we don't align to it, we wander aimlessly—lost without a moral compass.[5]

SATAN'S "MINISTERS"

1. Satan disseminates these false teachings through his *"ministers"* whom he recruits.

    † **2 Corinthians 11:13-15**—*For such men are false apostles, deceitful workmen, masquerading as apostles of Christ. **14.** And no wonder, for Satan himself masquerades as an angel of light. **15.** It is not surprising, then, if his servants ("ministers" KJV) masquerade as servants of righteousness. Their end will be what their actions deserve.*

▶**CONSIDER THIS:** Just because a group calls itself a "church" or has the word "Christian" in their name, does not mean that they are genuine. We should not be surprised then to learn that there are ministers in Christian churches who are not *"born again"*, who do not know God, and who teach things to people that are not true. Furthermore, just because a "Reverend" or a "church" display "miraculous" phenomenon does not prove or mean that their power is coming from the God of the Bible. The real test is "Are they aligning to the teachings of the Bible?" **(Mark 13:22).**

A. There are times when churches, etc. fall into the devil's hands and become "fronts" for the enemy's operation. Also, satan not only has places of heathen "worship," but also controls some places that claim to represent and worship the God of the Bible.

    † **Revelation 2:9**—Jesus said, *"...I know the slander of those who say they are Jews and are not, but are a synagogue of satan."*

♞ **TACTIC: Recruitment**—The enemy seeks to raise up people who will promote his false teachings and sends them forth to imitate the true ministers of the Gospel. False religions and the occult are presented as harmless and attractive, especially to the young, luring them with the promise of supernatural power and knowledge. Using deceptive means through humor, cartoons, the martial arts, etc., he disarms their fears so they let their guard down and try it—thus ensnaring them not only as victims but as recruiters who will teach others.
◎ *Main Targets:* Your Pride, Naiveté and your Children.

    † **Galatians 2:3-5**—*Yet not even Titus, who was with me, was compelled to be circumcised, even though he was a Greek. **4.** This matter arose because some false brothers had infiltrated our ranks to spy on the freedom we have in Christ Jesus and to make us slaves. **5.** We did not give in to them for a moment, so that the truth of the gospel might remain with you.*

B. Jesus warned us about satan's "ministers."

    † **Matthew 24:4,5,11**—*Jesus answered: "Watch out that no one deceives you. **5.** For many will come in my name, claiming, 'I am the Christ,' and will deceive many... **11.** and many false prophets will appear and deceive many people."*

    † **Matthew 7:15-17**—Jesus warned: *"Watch out for false prophets. They come to you in sheep's clothing, but inwardly they are ferocious wolves. **16.** By their fruit you will recognize them... **17.** every good tree bears good fruit, but a bad tree bears bad fruit."*

C. The enemy works on those within the church so as to use them undercover.

† **Acts 20:28-31**—*Keep watch over yourselves and all the flock of which the Holy Spirit has made you overseers. Be shepherds of the church of God, which he bought with his own blood.* ***29.*** *I know that after I leave, savage wolves will come in among you and will not spare the flock.* ***30.*** *Even from your own number men will arise and distort the truth in order to draw away disciples after them.* ***31.*** *So be on your guard! Remember that for three years I never stopped warning each of you night and day with tears.*

† **1 John 2:18-19**—*Dear children, this is the last hour; and as you have heard that the antichrist is coming, even now many antichrists have come. This is how we know it is the last hour.* ***19.*** *They went out from us, but they did not really belong to us...*

† **Acts 15:24** (NLT)—*"We understand that some men from here have troubled you and upset you with their teaching, but they had no such instructions from us."*

HOW SATAN ATTACKS THE BIBLE

♞ **TACTIC: Attack the Bible**—Since the enemy hates the Bible, he relentlessly attacks it by trying to outlaw and physically stamp it out. When that fails, he then either tries to discredit it, take it out of context, mix it with half-truths, add to it, replace it, or detract from it in order to deprive us of its truth or to cause us to lose faith in it. ◎ *Main Targets:* The Bible and your Faith in it.

Satan detests the Bible because it is the only book that reveals his existence, exposes his tactics, and seals his doom, and teaches us about the true God.

1. What are some of the ways the devil assaults the Word of God and tries to make it ineffective?

A. Satan attacks the Bible by O_____ it. Here are some examples:

(1) **Confiscation**—Through kings and emperors who both confiscated and destroyed copies of the Bible, or through an edict deprived their citizenry of it so as to better control them.

(2) **Legislation**—By efforts of government to legislate a ban on the Bible as "hate speech" when it clashes with the culture.

(3) **Deprivation**—Through religious groups who insist that only the clergy can correctly interpret the Bible and, therefore, discourage or forbid the laity from reading it.

(4) **Obstruction**—By hindering the work of Bible translation for unreached people groups who have yet to hear or read it in their own language, or by preventing its publication.

B. Satan attacks the Bible by D_____ it. Here are some examples:

(1) **Slander**—By propagating that those who wrote the Bible did so without having been under the inspiration of the Holy Spirit; or that the Bible **contains error** thereby creating uncertainty as to which parts of the Bible are true and which parts are false; or the claim of newly discovered "gospels" that cast doubt on the Bible's authenticity.

(2) **Revision**—Through "Higher Criticism's" rationalistic approach to the Bible. Instead of accepting the account of Jesus given in the Bible, these liberal theologians revolted against the supernatural and produced a new Jesus that they were more comfortable with, and in the process tore the beliefs of Christianity apart beyond recognition. They have influenced many pastor and laymen alike to deny the basic fundamental beliefs about God and Jesus Christ.

▶**CONSIDER THIS:** Largely through rationalization, the enemy has been successful in moving New England from the biblical values of the Pilgrims to a hotbed for liberalism. Likewise, the Ivy League universities from being founded as a training ground for ministers to a platform for radicalism, liberalism, and the politically correct.

(3) **Irrelevance**—By promoting that the Bible's message, morality, etc. is outmoded and irrelevant for today.

(4) **False Worldviews**—Through ideologies like Secular Humanism, Postmodernism, and evolution, which teach there is no God, no sin, and therefore, no need of a Savior.

C. Satan also attacks the Bible by taking Scripture out of C_____ or mixing it with H_____—T_____. Here are some examples:

(1) **Perversion**—By twisting the meaning of **Psalm 91** to include putting God to the test as was done in the temptation of Jesus in **Luke 4:9-11.** (See Jesus' third temptation given earlier in this lesson.)

(2) **Distortion**—By distorting the words that God commanded Adam, which he repeated to Eve that enticed her to eat the fruit of the forbidden tree. Satan said to her: *"...God knows that in the day you eat from it your eyes will be opened, and you will be like God, knowing good and evil."* (**Genesis 3:5** NASB—also see verse **22.**)

(3) **Asceticism**—By teaching that to be holier and to find special favor with God is directly linked to doing things like not getting married, the eating (or not eating) of certain foods, or other self-imposed man-made abstinences (**1 Timothy 4:1-5).**

(4) **Misinterpretation**—By teachings such as: God supernaturally created the universe, but does not supernaturally interact with it or with mankind (Deism). Or since God fills heaven and earth; therefore, everything must be God (Pantheism). Or that one must be "born-again," but reincarnation is what is really meant.

Note: These methods are used in all religions that falsely claim to be Christian, as well as in Christian denominations that hold false essential beliefs.

▶**CONSIDER THIS:** An erroneous teaching usually originates by someone being "inspired" by a new "truth." Their inspiration may have come from their own rationale or from demonic spirits. The person then seeks to justify their viewpoint with Scripture—even if they have to take it out of context or mix it with a half-truth. This happens because of their failure to apply the proper rules of biblical interpretation even if it proves their belief wrong. Those who promote false doctrine are usually blinded to their error, but are convinced of its truth. They become what Jesus termed, *"...blind leaders of the blind..."* **(Matthew 15:14).** Note that the increasing trend of eliminating the traditional Sunday school as a vehicle in laying a foundation of God's Word in our hearts is not only an attack by satan but also contributes to the development of erroneous teachings.

D. Satan attacks the Bible by <u>A</u>   to it or <u>S</u>   something else for it. Here are some examples:

(1) **Extra-biblical sources**—Some false teachings come as a result of accepting and forming beliefs from "sacred writings" other than the Bible. People esteem them to be equal to, or greater in authority and inspiration than the Old and New Testaments. A person then believes in the Bible <u>plus</u> something else.

Examples are: *The Book of Mormon*; Christian Science's *Science and Health with Key to the Scriptures*; the Jehovah's Witness' version of the Bible—*The New World Translation,* etc.; "lost" books of the Bible; the Apocryphal books; and tradition.

Note: Notwithstanding the good points of Roman Catholicism, the core problem in the Catholic Church is its unwillingness to accept biblical authority alone as the sole and final determiner of Christian doctrine and practice. By adding extra-biblical sources to the Bible, the church has gradually departed from the truth in many essential doctrinal areas.

(2) **Ecumenism**—By propagating the belief of religious tolerance and ecumenism such as, "All religions lead to God." This aids in the formation and acceptance of a one-world church. How tragic to have our minds so open that we cannot tell truth from error.

(3) **Erroneous Beliefs**—By inspiring false beliefs that have no biblical basis. Some examples: that there is an intermediate place where one goes to be purified from their sins before they can enter heaven (purgatory); or that one must perform good works to help earn their salvation, which leads one to believe in Jesus' work on the cross **plus** something else—as though His work wasn't sufficient in itself; or that we can pray to godly people who have died (who are presumed to be in heaven) and they are able to answer our prayers.

(4) **Rationalization**—By persuading us to substitute human wisdom and psychology in its place. Examples include: creating our own standard of what is right and what is wrong (such as truth being based on moral relativism), or formulating a standard of truth that "works" for us, or applying "tolerance" where everyone's definition of truth is respected and held on an equal plane.

▶ **CONSIDER THIS:** The only absolute truth these days seems to be tolerance, and the greatest "sin" is intolerance—a very clever maneuver by the enemy. This is how the scheme works: Expand the concept of tolerance beyond its normal meaning of just everyone being entitled to their own opinion or respecting another's belief. Enlarge it to mean that they are expected to accept every person's values and "truth" as equally valid. Promote open-mindedness and make people feel ashamed or obligated if they aren't.

Further entrench tolerance in society by persuading them to buy into the notion that in order for Christians, Hindus, Muslims, Buddhists, and Atheists to live together harmoniously, they must all commit themselves to tolerance of what everyone else believes so that no one's beliefs are wrong. Next, create a pressure in society that will compel the masses to refrain from imposing their views on others. The result will limit freedom to proclaim their beliefs.

This ploy especially targets Christians and coerces them to be silent about their convictions. If Christians run the risk of being labeled "intolerant," then their freedom of speech will be repressed and their views ridiculed. This places Christians in a position where their "intolerance" is not tolerated and further contributes to building a climate conducive to persecution. The devil's goal is to make it increasingly difficult to proclaim biblical truth in today's cultural climate.

E. Satan attacks the Bible by D_____ from it through erroneous teachings. Examples are:

(1) By teaching that **Jesus is not God** and He did not come to earth in a body of human flesh.

† **1 John 4:2-3**—*This is how you can recognize the Spirit of God: Every spirit that acknowledges that Jesus Christ has come in the flesh is from God, 3. but every spirit that does not acknowledge Jesus is not from God. This is the spirit of the antichrist, which you have heard is coming and even now is already in the world.*

(2) By teaching that the resurrection and the Second Coming of Christ have **already taken place.**

(3) By leading us to believe that certain doctrines in the Bible were only for the early church period and **not for us today.**

(4) By teaching erroneous beliefs about **the afterlife:** like soul sleep, purgatory, reincarnation, or that we just cease to exist when we die.

(5) By promoting the concept that **people are born inherently good.** This calls into question the need of having religious laws to guide us to right conduct. The rationale is if goodness is the norm and evil is abnormal, then evil must be caused by something beyond a person's control like poverty, society, racism, etc. This relieves one of their responsibility and need for Christ.

† **Warning! Warning! Revelation 22:18-19**—Jesus said: *"I warn everyone who hears the words of the prophecy of this book: If anyone adds anything to them, God will add to him the plagues described in this book. 19. And if anyone takes words away from this book of prophecy, God will take away from him his share in the tree of life and in the holy city, which are described in this book."* (Also see **Deuteronomy 4:2; 12:32.**)

WHAT DOES SATAN ACCOMPLISH THROUGH HIS ATTACK ON THE BIBLE?

1. He D_____ the Word of God of its rightful A_____.

> † **Matthew 15:1-9**—*Then some Pharisees and teachers of the law came to Jesus from Jerusalem and asked, **2.** "Why do your disciples break the tradition of the elders?"... **3.** Jesus replied, "And why do you break the command of God for the sake of your tradition? **4.** For God said... **5.** But you say...Thus you nullify the word of God for the sake of your tradition. **7.** You hypocrites! Isaiah was right when he prophesied about you: **8.** 'These people honor me with their lips, but their hearts are far from me.'"* [NIV] ***9.** "But in vain they do worship me, teaching for doctrines the commandments of men."* [KJV]

> † **Colossians 2:16-23**—*Therefore do not let anyone judge you by what you eat or drink, or with regard to a religious festival, a New Moon celebration or a Sabbath day. **17.** These are a shadow of the things that were to come; the reality, however, is found in Christ. **21.** "Do not handle! Do not taste! Do not touch!"? **22.** These are all destined to perish with use, because they are based on human commands and teachings.*

▶**CONSIDER THIS:** Religious tradition can be good and it can be bad. If it is founded on biblically-based truth, then tradition and customs can strengthen our faith and beliefs **(2 Thessalonians 2:15).** However, if they are not biblically-based, then we pass down traditions to the next generation that are not true. Our descendants usually blindly accept them as truth without questioning their veracity, and then pass them on to the next generation—and the cycle continues. One often hears, "I was born a (denomination), and I'll die that way." It is critical that we first examine our beliefs to ensure they are Bible-based so we do not pass error onto our children.

2. He R_____ the Bible of its C_____. (Note: If the enemy can not discredit the message, he will discredit the messenger.)

> † **2 Peter 2:1-2**—*But there were also false prophets among the people, just as there will be false teachers among you. They will secretly introduce destructive heresies, even denying the sovereign Lord who bought them—bringing swift destruction on themselves. **2.** Many will follow their shameful ways and will bring the way of truth into disrepute.*

3. He P_____ the truth of the Gospel by presenting an attractive I_____ (*"a different Jesus,"* or *"a different kind of gospel,"* with *"a different Spirit"*) offering another way of salvation than through the sacrificial work of Jesus on the cross.

> † **2 Corinthians 11:3-4** (NLT)—The apostle Paul wrote to the Corinthian Church: *But I fear that somehow you will be led away from your pure and simple devotion to Christ, just as Eve was deceived by the serpent. **4.** You seem to believe whatever anyone tells you, even if they preach about a different Jesus than the one we preach, or a different Spirit than the one you received, or a different kind of gospel than the one you believed.*

A. An example of *"a different gospel"* is the one the Galatian church mistakenly accepted that taught that one had to earn their salvation by obeying the tenets of the Old Testament law.

† **Galatians 1:6-7**—*I am astonished that you are so quickly deserting the one who called you by the grace of Christ and are turning to a different gospel — 7. which is really no gospel at all. Evidently some people are throwing you into confusion and are trying to pervert the gospel of Christ.*

B. Contemporary examples of *"a different Jesus"* are: the watered down "Jesus" of Higher Criticism and liberal theologians; the revolutionary "Jesus" of Liberation Theology; the Eastern guru "Jesus" of the New Age; the "social gospel" Jesus; and the different "Jesus" of the various false religions.

C. Satan disguises himself as an *"angel of light"* **(2 Corinthians 11:13-14).** There have been false religions started through angelic visitations or revelations. Examples are: the angel "Moroni" who revealed himself to Joseph Smith, the founder of Mormonism, and through whose instrumentality the *Book of Mormon* was given; early Muslim records say that in A.D. 610, the angel Jibreel (Gabriel) appeared to Muhammad (the founder of Islam) and gave him the verses that became the Koran.[6]

🐎 **TACTIC: Pervert the Truth**—The enemy will try to distort the truth that God has universally established by inverting it and changing it from its intended meaning (whether morally, philosophically, or doctrinally) in order to lead us away from the truth.
◎ *Main Target*: Your Faith.

† **Acts 13:9-10** (NLT)—*Then Saul, also known as Paul, filled with the Holy Spirit, looked the sorcerer in the eye and said, 10. "You son of the Devil, full of every sort of trickery and villainy, enemy of all that is good, will you never stop perverting the true ways of the Lord?"*

D. On another front, social engineers, revolutionaries, and subversive groups use this strategy to pervert God's universal moral standard of right and wrong by redefining the language of a culture in order to remold and subvert that culture. It is the art of reeducating people to think and talk the way you want them to without their being aware of it. They pervert a language by giving different meanings to words than what people normally understand those words to mean, thereby subtly instilling their view in the minds of those people.

▶**CONSIDER THIS:** Let us be wise and learn from the following examples of the enemy's inversions and perversions: "Truth is relative;" "anti-abortion" instead of "pro-life" and "pro-choice" instead of "pro-abortion;" a baby is a "fetus," not a person, just a blob of protoplasm; "love" means having sex; redefine the institution of "marriage" to include same sex and multiple partners; "gay" means homosexuality; and "the separation of church and state" really means the removal of God from public life. Another ploy is to publicly cast the things that pertain to the true God in a negative light, like whenever someone upholds biblical truth; they are portrayed as bigoted, hard-hearted, and intolerant. Another way is by creating a negative connotation to a word like for "Christian," "church," or "minister." "Politically correct" speech is another example. Similarly, the Communists deceptively used fronts, which they called "liberation movements," to inflame and exploit the legitimate grievances of the people in order to overthrow the established "anti-liberation" government in power. And whenever they called for "peace," they really meant war.

† **Isaiah 5:20** (NASB)—*Woe to those who call evil good, and good evil; Who substitute darkness for light and light for darkness; Who substitute bitter for sweet and sweet for bitter!*

† **Isaiah 19:11-15** (NKJV)—*Pharaoh's wise counselors give foolish counsel...13. They have also deluded Egypt...14. a perverse spirit* [is] *in her midst; And they have caused Egypt to err...*

† **Amos 5:7** (NLT)—*You wicked people! You twist justice, making it a bitter pill for the poor and oppressed. Righteousness and fair play are meaningless fictions to you.*

4. He destroys the U_____ and effectiveness of the Christian church by causing divisions and splits. This has occurred countless times throughout church history and continues today.

5. He tries to nurture dead religious ritualistic F_____ like that of the Pharisees and Sadducees of Jesus' day. This is an empty adherence to the legalistic letter of the law without the life-giving power of the Holy Spirit—*"...a form of godliness but denying its power."* **(2 Timothy 3:5).**

▶**CONSIDER THIS:** Some people have so much religion that they do not believe they need to be "born-again." Trusting in an outer veneer of religiosity without inner spiritual regeneration is a bondage that will damn one's soul. It gives a person a deceptive illusion that he or she is earning good favor with God. Nothing provoked the anger of Jesus more than this type of hypocrisy. Churches that promote this type of ritualistic formalism do a great disservice to Christ's church by depriving people of the reality and life-giving power of the Holy Spirit. This can result in driving them away to religions that seem to have real power—demonic power.

6. These attacks are intended to cause one to *"wander from the faith"* with the expectation that the person will eventually *"depart from the faith"* **(1 Timothy 4:1; 6:10, 20-21).** Ultimately, his objective is to *"destroy"* one's faith **(2 Timothy 2:17-18).**

MARKS OF A COUNTERFEIT CHRISTIAN RELIGION

1. In Lesson 2, an overview of predominately **non-Christian religions** was presented (see "God, seven views of" in index). These religions do not worship and serve the God of the Bible and are considered by Christians to be false religions. We will now give a brief treatment of religions that **claim to be Christian,** but whose doctrines contradict those of historic biblical Christianity and, specifically, do not hold to the essential doctrine of salvation.

2. A counterfeit Christian religion teaches its adherents information contrary to the biblical beliefs of orthodox Christianity. These erroneous teachings undermine essential Christian doctrine while maintaining an outward Christian "look and feel." Generally, a group is considered to be a counterfeit Christian religion if one or more of the following signs are present. The following has been adapted from the teachings of Christian apologist Bob Anderson (www.watchman.org/pa):

A. **A Faulty View of the Trinity** (especially about Christ)—Find out their answer to the question: "Is Jesus Christ God?" Almost all non-orthodox Christian groups deny the deity of Christ. They teach that Jesus Christ was not 100% God and 100% man, and that He did **not** rise from the dead—but was merely a great prophet or teacher, etc. (see **1 John 4:1-6).** They deny the doctrine of the Trinity—that the Father, Son, and the Holy Spirit are three distinct, separate persons comprising one God (not three gods).

B. **Salvation Based on Works**—They will teach the heresy that there is another way to atone for one's sins and get to heaven other than by grace alone, through faith alone, in Christ alone—in the work He accomplished for mankind on the cross. They will falsely teach that one must earn their salvation by performing good deeds which are either added to, or take the place of, Christ's redemptive work as a condition to salvation. It becomes Jesus **plus** the works as if Christ's sacrificial death and resurrection were not good enough. These meritorious "works" may include: keeping the Old Testament Law and being circumcised (as encountered by the early church); water baptism; church membership; and legalistic obedience to the teachings of a founder or to an ecclesiastical body.

C. **Bible References Taken out of Context**—When they do use Scripture, it is generally taken out of context or twisted to fit their preconceived theology. They tend to redefine Christian terminology—mixing truth with error. This is why **it is imperative that you seek to understand their definition of the term and do not assume it is the same meaning as yours.** True Bible study is not encouraged, but the study of the group's literature takes preference. It becomes the Bible plus another writing or tradition, elevating the latter to be equal with or greater than the Bible.

D. **An Exalted, Dynamic Leader**—This person usually has a genius for attracting new followers and inspiring their confidence. They claim to have received a "new revelation" or a "progressive revelation" directly from God and declare they are God's spokesman on earth.

E. **Exclusiveness**—The group will commonly claim that they alone possess the "right" interpretation of Scripture—a "higher" understanding than anyone else has. They teach their adherents to view "outsiders" with suspicion and antagonism; therefore, close association with persons outside their group (except for proselytizing) is often discouraged, if not forbidden.

F. **Fear and Control**—In some groups, disciples may be admonished to "forsake all" and to turn over all personal property or personal information to the organization. Absolute submission to the leader or the hierarchy is required which entraps members into bondage to the leadership. Those who challenge doctrines or question authority can be severely disciplined and held in the fear of being excommunicated or disfellowshipped. In addition, the person can become emotionally and spiritually dependent upon the group. Any thoughts of leaving them may be accompanied by fear of losing their approval, acceptance, and attention. They also battle feelings of guilt about leaving the group because it would be equal to deserting God and risking His displeasure.

3. If you presently belong to a group that has any of the above characteristics, you should break with them immediately and seek out and join a Bible-believing church. Ask God to give you courage, wisdom, and guidance.

   † **Romans 16:17-18**—*I urge you, brothers, to watch out for* ["*mark*" KJV] *those who cause divisions and put obstacles in your way that are contrary to the teaching you have learned. Keep away from them.* ["*avoid them*" KJV] *18. For such people are not serving our Lord Christ...By smooth talk and flattery they deceive the minds of naive people.*

4. The following are the main religions that claim to be Christian (there are hundreds of smaller groups). I have given each one a condensed overview of their errors in **Appendix B** regarding their departure from the essential doctrines of: (1) belief in God, (2) the way of obtaining salvation, and (3) the divine inspiration of the Bible. The websites for other Christian apologists who are expert in these fields are also provided.

   • Mormonism   • Jehovah's Witness   • Christian Science   • Unity School of Christianity

5. The following Christian denominations hold many of the essential beliefs of orthodox Christianity, but have added man-made conditions for salvation to Christ's work on the cross. I have given each one a condensed overview on the same three areas in **Appendix C.**

   A. Groups that teach that water baptism is necessary for salvation.
   B. The United Pentecostal Church (Oneness Pentecostal)
   C. Roman Catholicism

   † **Galatians 1:8**—*But even if we or an angel from heaven should preach a gospel other than the one we preached to you, let him be eternally condemned!*

►**CONSIDER THIS:** While visiting a financial institution, Lorraine saw a teller with a large stack of $100 bills. The teller was going through them quickly, one by one, as if he was looking for something. Occasionally, he would set one bill aside and continue on. Turning to her husband Chuck, the bank manager, Lorraine inquired as to what the teller was doing. Her husband replied, "Oh, he's looking for counterfeit bills. When he finds one, he takes it out of circulation." Lorraine responded, "But how can he tell the difference between what is phony and what is real?" Chuck said, "He is so familiar with the genuine that when he encounters an imitation, he can spot it immediately."

How much more should we Christians be so familiar with what the Bible teaches that we can detect doctrinal error as easily as this bank teller detected "funny money?" In order to do so, our emphasis should be on learning biblical truth and not on studying why something is counterfeit.

   † **2 Timothy 2:15** (KJV)—*Study to shew thyself approved unto God, a workman that needeth not to be ashamed, rightly dividing the word of truth.*

   † **1 John 4:1**—*Dear friends, do not believe every spirit, but test the spirits to see whether they are from God, because many false prophets have gone out into the world.*

   † **Jude 1:3-4**—*Dear friends...I felt I had to write and urge you to contend for the faith that was once for all entrusted to the saints. 4. For certain men...have secretly slipped in among you.*

(Note: If you want to learn more about how the Bible originated as well as a general overview, consider taking my non-accredited online course, **An Introduction to the Bible,** at www.DiscoverMinistries.com. Click on the link, "Discover the Bible".)

☑ Now please go to **Appendix B** and **Appendix C** and read them. When you're through, continue on with the Study Questions and Application and the Summary.

STUDY QUESTIONS AND APPLICATION

1. To what extent do you believe that the 66 books of the Old and New Testaments are the inspired Word of God and without error in the original texts?

Not At All   **I Believe They Are**
100% God-Inspired

```
0     1     2     3     4     5     6     7     8     9     10
|_____|_____|_____|_____|_____|_____|_____|_____|_____|_____|
                              |
```

Note: If you scored 9 or under, identify what is keeping you from a 10 rating.

2. Are you aware of any teaching in your church that falls into the false <u>essential</u> doctrine category? Does it adhere to any false <u>non-essential</u> doctrine?

3. The Bible teaches us how to deal with those who teach false doctrine and cause divisions. Look up the following scriptures and write in those aspects. We are to:

   A. **Jude 1:3-4** (see last Scripture above) _____

   B. **Titus 1:9-14** _____

   C. **Titus 3:9-10** _____

   D. **Ephesians 5:11** _____

   E. **Romans 16:17-18** _____

   F. **2 John 1:7-11** _____

4. How are you presently penetrating satan's kingdom of darkness with the Sword of the Spirit?

   A. Referring to #4 above, identify one or more steps that you can start taking that would increase your effectiveness in this area—and then begin doing it!

5. Besides the sword, God uses other symbols to describe His Word. Look up the following references and write them in. For example, in **Luke 8:11** the answer would be <u>Seed</u>.

   A. **Matthew 7:24-27** _____   E. **Proverbs 2:1,4** _____

   B. **Deuteronomy 8:3** _____   F. **Ephesians 5:26** _____

   C. **Psalm 119:105** _____   G. **Jeremiah 23:29** (1) _____

   D. **James 1:23,24** _____   (2) _____

SUMMARY

The Sword of the Spirit, symbolic of the Word of God, is one of two powerful offensive weapons that God has given us to use in this invisible war. It is also a defensive weapon. The Bible consists of the 39 books of the Old Testament and the 27 books of the New Testament. They don't just "contain" the Word of God, they ARE the Word of God—God's final message and revelation to mankind. These books were written over a period of about 1500 years by 40 different people from all walks of life. Collectively, their writings all blend together into one theme, continuity, and message, without contradiction. The Bible is God's gift of absolute truth to the human race—all that we need to know about Him, our adversaries, how to live with our fellow man, what the future end times will bring, and how to get to heaven. The Bible is relevant for every generation and culture since Adam because mankind's spiritual condition and needs are the same.

God asks us to believe the following about the Bible: It is **1.** inerrant—meaning it is absolute truth and contains no errors in the original texts. The Holy Spirit is its author who selected and inspired men to write it. It is **2.** living because the Holy Spirit also uses it and gives it its life. The Word of God is **3.** active, being energized by the Spirit of God in the following ways: it is **3A.** powerful as it is anointed by the greatest power in the universe. It **3B.** exposes as it shines its penetrating light on all darkness, exposing every form of error, piercing through all disguises of deception, and revealing the devil's traps and strategies.

The Word of God **3C.** judges our thoughts, motives, attitudes, and sets the standard by which everything else is measured. The enemy uses the **TACTIC: Make Them Feel Ashamed** to shame you into thinking that if you believe the Bible to be the only divinely inspired, infallible standard of absolute truth that judges everything else, you are an unscholarly, intolerant, narrow-minded bigot. It **3D.** cuts to the heart as the Holy Spirit uses it to convict us of sin. It also **3E.** severs the closest relationships and makes a distinction between our soul and spirit.

The two "edges" of the Sword are represented by the two Greek words used for the Word of God. They are **4A.** _logos_ which means the "written Word" and **4B.** _rhēma_ is the "spoken Word." It is this _rhēma_ word that is used for the Sword of the Spirit. The _rhēma_ can occur in three ways: from God to you, from God through you to another, and like Jesus we can quote aloud the _logos_ to the devil and demonic forces. The _rhēma_ is normally an individual Scripture used in time of need to expose the lies and deception of the enemy. It becomes both a defensive and offensive weapon that is used to resist demonic forces, especially in the times of temptation.

The tactics the devil used against Jesus in the wilderness are also those he tries to use on us. In Jesus' first temptation to make a stone into bread, the enemy used **TACTIC: Eliminate the Competition** where he attempts to seduce us, like Jesus, to choose to leave God's will, or he will try to prevent us from choosing to do God's will because he knows the resulting damage God will cause to his kingdom of darkness through us.

Then in Christ's second temptation when he offered Him the kingdoms of the world, the devil tried two more tactics. The first was **TACTIC: Deprive God of Worship** where the devil attempts to use us to rob God from receiving our love, worship, and obedience that rightly belongs to Him, by diverting them to himself. He also used **TACTIC: Pry Them Away From God's Will** where he'll try to get us to miss God's will, or deceive us with the mirage of an easy short cut in obtaining God's will—apart from God's sacrificial ways. By failing to carry out God's plan, God's work suffers a setback and we are robbed of a crown of reward. In Christ's third temptation to jump from the pinnacle of the temple, the enemy struck with still two more schemes. One was **TACTIC: Tempting God** where our adversary tries to get us, like Jesus, to put God to the test about keeping His Word by taking Scripture out of context in order to cause us to question God's character and Word when He doesn't respond.

The last strategy he used in Christ's third temptation was the **TACTIC: Counterfeit the Bible's Teachings** where the devil attempts to deceive us into believing things the Bible does not teach by imitating the real truth in order to keep us away from the truth. He will then try to use you to either cause division within the Body of Christ, draw you away to join a counterfeit "Christian" group, or use you to start one in order to lead others astray and into satan's camp. He and his minions originate false religious teachings, *"...doctrines of devils"* through *"...the spirit of error"* which are heretical and cause division. Satan disseminates these erroneous teachings through his *"ministers"* whom he recruits and establishes both within and outside of the church.

Some of the ways satan attacks the Bible in order to make it ineffective are: by **1A.** outlawing it; by **1B.** discrediting it; by taking it out of **1C.** context or mixing it with half-truths; by **1D.** adding to it or substituting something else for it; or by **1E.** detracting from it. Through these attacks, satan: **1.** deprives the Word of God of its rightful authority; he **2.** robs the Bible of its credibility; he **3.** perverts the truth of the Gospel by offering an attractive imitation like *"a different Jesus,"* or *"a different kind of gospel,"* with *"a different Spirit"* **(2 Corinthians 11:4);** he destroys the **4.** unity and effectiveness of the Christian church by causing divisions and splits; he nurtures dead religious ritualistic **5.** formalism; and his goal is to cause us to *"depart from the faith"* and ultimately to *"destroy"* our faith.

We also covered marks of a counterfeit Christian religion and exposed essential doctrinal error in Appendices B and C. Christians should be so familiar with what the Bible teaches that they can detect doctrinal error as easily as a bank teller can detect counterfeit money. At what point will you draw the line and rise to defend your belief in biblical truth? God has called His people to be contenders for the faith **(Jude 1:3).**

Another way Jesus wielded the *"sword of the Spirit"* was by using it as an offensive weapon to attack demonic forces through rescuing people being held under satan's power, thereby making an inroad into his evil empire. As the Word of God (*logos*) is proclaimed, the Holy Spirit uses that sword to penetrate satan's kingdom of darkness, piercing it with the great spotlight of God's absolute truth. As satan's children hear that Word and by faith believe and respond to it, the light of God's truth enters their hearts and minds, dispelling their darkness.

Through the *"foolishness of preaching"* and *"the word of our testimony"* we invade satan's domain. The power of that Sword breaks the grip demonic forces have over the lives of satan's subjects. The devil's kingdom is damaged each time the *"truth"* sets one of his prisoners free from bondage and is birthed into God's kingdom. Christ commissions us to rescue them: *"I am sending you to open their eyes and turn them from darkness to light, and from the power of Satan to God..."* **(Acts 26:17-18).** The devil's kingdom is also dealt a blow each time portions of the institutions of the world system are "recaptured" for God by Christians incorporating biblical truth and principles into their sphere of influence, thereby extending God's rule into those areas.

Yet this Sword can lie inactive in our hand. To be effective, it must be picked up and used so its power can be released. Moreover, we need to develop skill in using it in combat-tested situations. It is critical that we be familiar with God's Word. We must know it, memorize it, and believe that it is divinely inspired and without error. If we don't, then its power cannot be activated and we have no sword to use at all!

Lesson 16
PRAYER AND PRAISE

☑ Before starting the DVD:

God has given to us another powerful offensive weapon—the awesome two-pronged weapon of prayer and praise. In keeping with God's ways, He designed that His soldiers would fight best on their knees. Prayer and praise move the very heart and hand of God—releasing Divine power that advances the Kingdom of God against satan's kingdom. It is one of the main weapons that the devil fears the most. Although mentioned last after the armor in the Ephesians six text, obviously it is by no means least. But now that this study is over, it is a fitting way to help you to continue your momentum gained from these lessons and launch your prayer time to a new level.

In this invisible war, it is not enough for us to defend ourselves with armor. God wants His church to be on the offensive to attack and penetrate satan's kingdom. In unevangelized areas of the earth, missionaries testify that prayer pushed back the forces of darkness that impeded their progress, and areas once resistant to the Gospel have now embraced Christ. As Evangelist Steve Hill once said, "A price must be paid in order to break through the enemy's lines and plunder his camp."[1]

Unlike the Sword of the Spirit, prayer has no limitations of distance or time. As our petitions ascend to our Heavenly Father, like an interplanetary missile God launches answers to prayer that penetrate demonic opposition and strike the forces of satan wherever they are at work. The travail of prayer births answers from our God, and He even answers prayers prayed in **this life** long after the intercessor has gone home to be with the Lord.

But, on the other hand, as the late missionary Mark Buntain once wrote, "Prayer is the most neglected and unused weapon of spiritual warfare in the church."[2] Can you imagine a soldier not using the most powerful weapons at his disposal?

In this final lesson, we will delve into how intercessory prayer and the power of worship can effectively be used in our spiritual warfare. In developing the ability to win this invisible war, we will learn one last tactic the enemy uses on this front. We'll also see the necessity of being an overcomer over our sinful nature, the devil, and the world; summarize our weaponry; provide an illustrative summary of this study, and learn to pray effectively by using The Lord's Prayer as our model. I highly recommend that this lesson be done in two separate sessions. Please follow the instructions given. Before you begin, pray and ask Jesus with the disciples of old, *"Lord, teach us to pray."*

☑ **DVD Users:** Watch Lesson 16 for an overview before proceeding further (24 min.).
☑ When you're through, pick up again at this point. Fill in the blanks from the Summary.

INTERCESSORY PRAYER

✝ **Ephesians 6:18**—*And pray in the Spirit on all occasions with all kinds of prayers and requests. With this in mind, be alert and always keep on praying for all the saints.*

✝ **Ephesians 6:18** (NLT)—*Pray at all times and on every occasion in the power of the Holy Spirit...*

1. Prayer is our second O_____ weapon; however, it is not directed at demonic forces as the Sword is, but to our Heavenly Father.

2. Prayer has **two** aspects:

    A. The G_____ of thanksgiving, worship, and praise to God for who He is, what He has done, and what He will do.

    B. P_____ is supplications and requests for our Heavenly Father's help and provision—on behalf of others as well as for ourselves.

📖 **DEFINITION—PRAYER**

It is heartfelt communication with our Heavenly Father, through His Son, where there is a blending of His Spirit with our spirit, and we emerge stronger from that time spent together with an afterglow of His presence—having touched the very heart of God with our thanksgiving, worship, and petitions.

3. Prayer originates and emanates primarily from our S_____.

    ✝ **1 Corinthians 14:14-16**—*...my spirit prays...*

    ✝ **John 4:24**—Jesus said: *"God is spirit, and his worshipers must worship in spirit and in truth."*

    ✝ **Matthew 26:41**—Jesus said, *"Watch and pray...The spirit is willing, but the body is weak."*

▶**CONSIDER THIS:** One of the reasons it is hard for us to cultivate the habit of prayer is due to our body and soul. Our spirit within us is willing but sickness, tiredness, laziness, lack of discipline, etc., affect our spirit. The body and soul must come under the rule of our spirit and be disciplined to spend consistent, daily communication with God. Distractions by other interests of the soul must be brought under control and eliminated by entering the prayer closet or secret place. Unless this happens, we will not grow in this critical area of our spiritual lives.

4. While it is necessary to make an appointment to see an important person in public office or be placed on hold for a prolonged period while on the phone, through Jesus, we have immediate access to the awesome God of the universe, any time of the day or night, through prayer!

WHY SHOULD WE PRAY?

Q: If God already knows our needs before we ask Him, then why must we pray **(Matthew 6:8)**?

1. We pray to keep ourselves D_____ upon God. If God gave us everything we needed without our asking Him for them, we would quickly take both He and His blessings for granted and it would result in an unhealthy relationship.

2. We pray because Christ C_____ us to pray. God desires regular fellowship with us.

   A. Almighty God has given us the awesome responsibility and privilege of involving us in accomplishing His purposes on this planet and has promised to intervene in our human affairs to the degree that we pray.

      † **Matthew 6:5-7**—Jesus said: *"When you pray,"* not "If you pray." We must have consistent, daily communication—not just in times of need.

      † **Luke 18:1**—*Then Jesus told his disciples...they should always pray and not give up.*

3. We pray because it is our spiritual L_____—our umbilical cord to God's life and power. Communication should be a natural outgrowth of a love relationship with someone. Think of the honor of having this relationship with Almighty God Himself!

4. We pray because we live in S_____ D_____.

   A. Demonic opposition is determined to hold back God's answers to our prayers. This kind of opposition needs to be "prayed through." We should intercede until we receive a peace and an assurance in our spirit that our prayer has reached the throne of grace.

      † **Daniel 10:2-20** (NLT)—*When this vision came to me, I, Daniel, had been in mourning for three weeks... 3. All that time I had eaten no rich food or meat, had drunk no wine, and had used no fragrant oils... 12. Then he* [the angel] *said, "Don't be afraid, Daniel. Since the first day you began to pray for understanding and to humble yourself before your God, your request has been heard in heaven. I have come in answer to your prayer. 13. But for twenty-one days the spirit prince of the kingdom of Persia blocked my way. Then Michael, one of the archangels, came to help me, and I left him there with the spirit prince of the kingdom of Persia."*

      (1) Think of it! Our prayers can stir God to action and aid the angels as they fight through enemy territory in the heavenlies to bring us the answers. What power our prayers can have!

   B. Jesus specifically taught us to include these elements in our daily prayers: that God would help us detect temptation and deceit; for protection against exposure to satan's temptations beyond our ability to endure; and for God to deliver us from the overwhelming power and wiles of the evil one. Being on guard in prayer is directly proportionate to whether we fall into temptation.

      † **Matthew 6:13**—*And lead us not into temptation, but deliver us from the evil one.*

      † **Matthew 26:41**—Jesus said, *"Watch and pray so that you will not fall into temptation..."*

C. Some types of demonic oppression and possession in people's lives cannot be broken through to deliverance except by prayer and fasting. Another weapon God has given to His church is the ministry of deliverance which we many times also fail to use as we should.

> † **Matthew 17:19-21** (NLT)—*Afterward the disciples asked Jesus privately, "Why couldn't we cast out that demon?"* **20.** *"You didn't have enough faith," Jesus told them...* **21.** *"But this kind of demon won't leave unless you have prayed and fasted."*

(1) Engaging in fasting and prayer is one way we can **serve** God.

> † **Luke 2:36-37** (NKJV)—*...Anna... **37.** was a widow...who did not depart from the temple, but served God with fastings and prayers night and day.*

▶**CONSIDER THIS:** The New Testament does not give us any "rules" for fasting; but Jesus must have clearly expected us to fast when He said, *"When you fast..."* not "if" **(Matthew 6:16).** Both Jesus and the apostles gave the example of fasting to encourage us to also use this "weapon" with our intercession. It is the most effective when, like prayer, it is God-initiated. There are different kinds of fasts one can undertake. It normally involves going without food (which also has built-in health benefits). It can be done on a regular basis, or occasionally as the need arises—both privately and corporately.

When we are willing to abstain from normal appetites of the body to concentrate on things near to God's heart, we show Him our concern for His interests in this world—and God takes notice! Fasting also brings a note of urgency to our prayers giving them added power. It is also a way to bring our body into submission to our spirit, and it aids us in building a sacrificial attitude that makes us ready to relinquish greater things for the Kingdom of God. You will discover that fasting makes one more attuned to the spirit realm. It has a way of detaching us from material things so we can focus better on spiritual things. Scripture tells us that our prayers are more effective accompanied by fasting. For more about fasting see the SQ&A at the end of this session.

5. We pray because we do not know H_____ or W_____ to pray. The Holy Spirit who lives within our spirit prompts us to pray. As we cultivate awareness and obey that leading, the Holy Spirit places the burden on us and births intercession through us. Intensity in prayer also plays a part in releasing God's power. When we intercede until the Holy Spirit lifts the burden, we can be sure that the breakthrough has occurred in the heavenly realm. We have just "prayed through" the opposition. The answer is on the way! Now we should begin to thank and praise God even before we see it!!

> † **Romans 8:26-27**—*In the same way, the Spirit helps us in our weakness. We do not know what we ought to pray, but the Spirit himself intercedes for us with groans that words cannot express.* **27.** *And he who searches our hearts knows the mind of the Spirit, because the Spirit intercedes for the saints in accordance with God's will.*

A. When Israel fought the Amalekites, two battles were raging: the combat taking place on the battlefield, and Moses' intercession with uplifted arms on the hill overlooking the conflict. The intercession battle determined the outcome of the physical battle **(Exodus 17:8-13).**

B. God searches for people who will allow their hearts to be broken with the things that break His heart, and are willing to stand between Him and sin, interceding to turn away His judgment. But sadly, many times God is grieved that no one is concerned. However, when He does find someone, you can be sure He takes special note of them.

Q: Will you make yourself available to be that intercessor for whom God is searching?

   † **Ezekiel 22:29-30**—*"The people of the land practice extortion and commit robbery; they oppress the poor and needy and mistreat the alien, denying them justice. **30.** I looked for a man among them who would build up the wall and stand before me in the gap on behalf of the land so I would not have to destroy it, but I found none."*

   † **Psalm 106:23** (NASB)—*...He* [God] *said that He would destroy them* [Israel], *Had not Moses His chosen one stood in the breach before Him, To turn away His wrath from destroying them.*

   † **Ezekiel 9:3-4**—*Now the glory of the God of Israel went up from above the cherubim, where it had been, and moved to the threshold of the temple. Then the Lord called to the man clothed in linen who had the writing kit at his side **4.** and said to him, "Go throughout the city of Jerusalem and put a mark on the foreheads of those who grieve and lament over all the detestable things that are done in it."*

▶**CONSIDER THIS:** When we see breakthroughs in situations here on our earthly plane, it means that the breakthrough first occurred in the heavenlies through people *"praying in the Spirit"* (also see **Jude 1:20**). Victories are first established in the invisible spirit realm before they are visibly seen in the natural realm. Having the Baptism in the Holy Spirit is essential in this invisible war.

🐎 **TACTIC: Cut Their Supply Line**—The enemy will try to get you to choose to either neglect your prayer, worship, and Bible time so as to cut off the source of God's spiritual life supply to your spirit, or get you to tolerate sin in your life so that your prayers will be hindered, which in turn will bring defeat. ◎ *Main Targets:* Your Prayer Life, Worship, and Relationship with God.

1. This tactic applies to this invisible war just as it does in an earthly war. Armies attack and dry up their enemy's supply line consisting of food, water, ammunition, communication, and finances. It's the most logical thing to do to defeat your adversary. So does it not make sense that the devil would attack our spiritual lifeline as well?

   A. **Q:** What happens when we neglect our consistent time of prayer?

     (1) An undernourished spirit is in no shape to rule a soul and body. This spiritual inactivity becomes a fertile time for the fallen nature to rise up and take control and thus invite the devil into this spiritual vacuum giving him a foothold in our lives.

     (2) We lose critical power from God to overcome temptation, deal with problems, stress, etc.

     † **Isaiah 40:31** (KJV)—*But they that wait upon the Lord shall renew their strength; they shall mount up with wings as eagles; they shall run, and not be weary; and they shall walk, and not faint.*

(3) Our affections become vulnerable to the things of the world. In any relationship love either grows or dies. Our relationship with God must be nourished with obedience, communication, and expressions of praise and thankfulness.

▶ **CONSIDER THIS:** Again we become our own worst enemy. By neglecting to cultivate a consistent, daily, quality prayer and worship time, **WE** cut the umbilical cord of God's life supply to our spirit. We actually assist the devil in accomplishing this goal in our lives. All he has to do is to induce us to be too busy, too tired, be undisciplined, be distracted by interruptions, or just provoke laziness and disobedience so we don't pray. Church services are often dead, dry, and powerless because well-meaning pastors and laymen have become so preoccupied with other things that they have no time to pray, spend time with the Lord, or get a fresh word from heaven. It seems so easy for the enemy to do—and we sit back and allow it to happen!! Change your mind. Make a resolution right now that you will discipline yourself to spend time in prayer every day, without fail, and adamantly refuse to be disconnected from your Power Source.

B. Answers to prayers are hindered by tolerating sin in our lives.

† **Psalm 66:18** (KJV)—*If I regard iniquity in my heart, the Lord will not hear me.*

† **Proverbs 28:9**—*If anyone turns a deaf ear to the law, even his prayers are detestable.*

† **1 Peter 3:7**—*Husbands, in the same way be considerate as you live with your wives, and treat them with respect as the weaker partner and as heirs with you of the gracious gift of life, so that nothing will hinder your prayers.*

Somebody prayed, and my burden was lighter;
Somebody prayed, and my path became clear;
Clouds rolled away, and the sunshine was brighter;
Jesus my wonderful Saviour was near...

Faith flickered low in my pain-tortured body,
Jesus, the mighty Physician, was there—
Healing me, bringing me joy in His presence,
Answering somebody's unfailing prayer.

Gems for the Master afar I may gather,
Trophies at last at His feet to be laid;
"Well done," He'll say; but methinks I shall answer:
"Thanks to Thy grace, Lord, for somebody prayed."

Louise Walker

WHY SHOULD WE PRAISE AND WORSHIP?

1. It is a way to G_____ B_____ to your Heavenly Father in appreciation for all He is and does—a gift from your heart. You, a created being, have the honor of ministering to Almighty God! Think of it!

   † **Acts 13:2** (NASB)—*...they were ministering to the Lord and fasting...*

2. Our Father S_____ for our genuine worship, and He takes great pleasure in it.

   † **John 4:23**—Jesus said, *"Yet a time is coming and has now come when the true worshipers will worship the Father in spirit and truth, for they are the kind of worshipers the Father seeks."*

   † **Psalm 22:3** (KJV)—*But thou art holy, O thou that inhabitest the praises of Israel.*

3. Worship comes B_____ petition.

   † **Psalm 100:4**—*Enter his gates with thanksgiving and his courts with praise; give thanks to him and praise his name.*

   † **Matthew 6:9,11**—Jesus taught, *"This, then, is how you should pray: 'Our Father in heaven, hallowed be your name... 11. Give us today our daily bread.'"*

4. It is a devastating offensive W_____. It is repulsive to demonic forces to hear God's children give praise to Him. Moreover, let us assume that they cannot stand to be in an atmosphere charged with the Presence of God. So if it is uncomfortable for evil to be in the presence of holiness, do the things that will bring God's presence.

5. Worship produces the A_____ in which God's divine presence resides.

   † **2 Chronicles 5:13-14**—*The trumpeters and singers joined in unison, as with one voice, to give praise and thanks to the Lord. Accompanied by trumpets, cymbals and other instruments, they raised their voices in praise to the Lord and sang: "He is good; his love endures forever." Then the temple of the Lord was filled with a cloud, 14. and the priests could not perform their service because of the cloud, for the glory of the Lord filled the temple of God.*

▶**CONSIDER THIS:** Since worship and praise is so powerful a weapon against the enemy (as is prayer), it should not surprise us that it is a target of the devil's attack on us. **Q:** How much time are you spending daily in worship and praise? Is there a major emphasis on prayer and praise in the church you attend? Each moment throughout the earth, a collective bouquet of worship is ascending to God from the Body of Christ. **Q:** Are you depriving God of your portion of the fragrance?

6. It B_____ the spiritual B_____ of demonic power in people's lives.

   † **1 Samuel 16:23** (NASB)—*So it came about whenever the evil spirit from God came to Saul, David would take the harp and play it with his hand; and Saul would be refreshed and be well, and the evil spirit would depart from him.*

7. Anointed worship music Q_____ God's P_____ word to man.

    † **2 Kings 3:15-16**—The prophet Elisha said, *"But now bring me a harpist." While the harpist was playing, the hand of the Lord came upon Elisha.* **16.** *and he said, "This is what the Lord says:..."*

    † **Acts 13:2** (NASB)—*While they were ministering to the Lord and fasting, the Holy Spirit said...*

8. Worship P_____ our H_____ in times of misfortune and disaster. As we saw in the case of Job, he responded to his horrible tragedies with worship of God's name. It became Job's best and, perhaps, his only defense against the deadly temptation of bringing God's character into question and thwarting satan's attempt to discredit God **(Job 1:20-22).**

▶ **CONSIDER THIS:** Worship should not be based on emotions or on outward circumstances. Whether God blesses or takes away, whether we have good health or poor health, God is worthy to be worshiped. Our worship should be based not on what God does, but on who He is. While our circumstances may not change, worship changes how we look at and respond to them.

It is in these adverse conditions where the *"sacrifice of praise"* should be utilized—to worship Him when we don't "feel" like it. In these uninspired times, learn the secret of just waiting on God and disciplining ourselves to begin singing His praises, and very often our prayer time will begin to flow. Similarly, convert the energy you spend dwelling on your problem into prayer, praise, and giving it over to the Lord.

    † **Hebrews 13:15** (KJV)—*By him [Jesus] therefore let us offer the sacrifice of praise to God continually, that is, the fruit of our lips giving thanks to his name.*

9. Anointed music U_____ the defeated spirit.

    A. Referring to **Isaiah 61:3,** author Dr. David K. Blomgren points out: "Isaiah here speaks of our exchanging a 'spirit of heaviness' for a 'garment of praise.' The Hebrew word for heaviness means literally 'failing.' There are times when a believer has a 'spirit of failing' and accepts defeat. This person must clothe himself with the Song of Praise as a garment. In the Orient the apparel expressed the mood of the mind. As one fills his mind and mouth with Songs of Praise, the spirit of failing will be stripped off him as a worn-out garment."[3]

THE WAR CRY

1. Throughout this section, I will be quoting from Dr. David K. Blomgren's book, *The Song of the Lord.* He gave us an insight into how our song of praise and worship can be used as a war cry against the forces of darkness. Dr. Blomgren writes, "The Hebrew word which is used to describe the singing of worship unto the Lord in the Book of Psalms is the same Hebrew word used elsewhere to describe the battle cry of the soldiers when they went into battle against the enemy."[4]

📖 **DEFINITION—*TEROU'A* (ter-oo-aw)**

According to the Theological Wordbook of the Old Testament, the word's "primary meaning is 'to raise a noise' by shouting or with an instrument, especially a horn..." There are four distinct senses in which this Hebrew word is used:[5]

1. A "signal" **(Leviticus 25:9)**—the "sound of the trumpet" (Shofar) on the Day of Atonement.

2. An "alarm" **(Joshua 6:5; Jeremiah 4:19)**—as in the case of attack.

3. The trumpet in the tumult of the battle **(Amos 1:14; 2:2).**

4. The exultation of Praise to God **(Psalm 150:3,5).**

The most common usage of its root word, *ru'a*, is in: signals for war **(Numbers 10:5-6);** and war cries **(Joshua 6:10)**—like the shout of victory over an enemy **(Jeremiah 50:15).**

A. King David, being the unique blend of psalmist and soldier, shares with us the link between worship of God and victory in battle by combining these two elements.

   † **Psalm 89:15** (NASB)—*How blessed are the people who know the joyful sound* [terou'a]*! O Lord, they walk in the light of thy countenance.*

   † **Psalm 89:15**—*Blessed are those who have learned to acclaim you, who walk in the light of your presence, O Lord.*

   Note: "As we sing forth a Song of Praise unto God, it comes forth as praise unto Him, but it comes to the enemy as a war cry against him."[6]

B. David learned that if he consistently sought after God **(Psalm 27:4)** and "...sang praises unto the Lord as an offering of 'joy' [terou'a], that he would be lifted up above his enemies."[7]

   † **Psalm 27:1-6**—*The Lord is my light and my salvation—whom shall I fear? The Lord is the stronghold of my life—of whom shall I be afraid? 2. When evil men advance against me to devour my flesh, when my enemies and my foes attack me, they will stumble and fall. 3. Though an army besiege me, my heart will not fear; though war break out against me, even then will I be confident...5. For in the day of trouble he will keep me safe in his dwelling; he will hide me in the shelter of his tabernacle and set me high upon a rock. 6. Then my head will be exalted above the enemies who surround me; at his tabernacle will I sacrifice with shouts of joy* [terou'a]*; I will sing and make music to the Lord.*

C. "When the soldiers would go into battle, they would give a war cry which by its nature would be loud and intended to fill the enemy with terror..." This same Hebrew word terou'a is the word used for this battle cry.[8]

   (1) **Example: The Walls of Jericho**—Dr. Blomgren continues: "In Joshua 6:5 and 20 the 'shout' given by the people which flattened the walls of Jericho was the same word 'terou'a,' the word descriptive of the singing of praise in the House of the Lord as an instrument of warfare."[9] (See **Joshua 6:1-21.**) Let's take a closer look:

(a) **God's Promise** —As Israel began to conquer the nations in the Promised Land that God had given them, the Word of the Lord came to Joshua, their commander in-chief: *"See, I have delivered Jericho into your hands, along with its king and its fighting men."* **(Joshua 6:2).**

(b) **Divine Instructions**—After giving him this assurance, in Joshua chapter six, God then gave Joshua specific instructions: *3. "March around the city once with all the armed men. Do this for six days. 4. Have seven priests carry trumpets of ram's horns in front of the ark. On the seventh day, march around the city seven times, with the priests blowing the trumpets. 5. When you hear them sound a long blast on the trumpets, have all the people give a loud shout* [terou'a]; *then the wall of the city will collapse..."*

(c) **The Procession**—First went the "armed guard;" followed by the seven priests blowing the trumpets of ram's horns; then the ark of the Covenant—the symbol of God's presence in their midst; the "rear guard" followed the ark **(Joshua 6:8-9).**

(d) **Divine Intervention**—With faith and obedience they acted on God's Word, and God came on the scene with power and gave them the victory: *"10. But Joshua had commanded the people, "Do not give a war cry, do not raise your voices, do not say a word until the day I tell you to shout. Then shout!" 11. So he had the ark of the Lord carried around the city, circling it once. Then the people returned to camp and spent the night there... 14. So on the second day they marched around the city once and returned to the camp. They did this for six days. 15. On the seventh day, they got up at daybreak and marched around the city seven times in the same manner, except that on that day they circled the city seven times. 16. The seventh time around, when the priests sounded the trumpet blast, Joshua commanded the people, "Shout! For the Lord has given you the city!..." 20. When the trumpets sounded, the people shouted, and at the sound of the trumpet, when the people gave a loud shout* [terou'a], *the wall collapsed; so every man charged straight in, and they took the city. 21. They devoted the city to the Lord and destroyed with the sword every living thing in it—men and women, young and old, cattle, sheep and donkeys."* **(Joshua 6:10-21).**

▶ **CONSIDER THIS:** The Ark of the Covenant was a piece of sacred "furniture" that resided in the Holy of Holies in both the tabernacle and later in the temple in Jerusalem. It was the symbol of the presence of God who dwelt in the midst of His people, Israel. There were at least three occasions when it was taken into battle to ensure Divine intervention **(Joshua 6:6,8, 11-13; 1 Samuel 4:3-5, 11; 2 Samuel 11:11).** Today, as the Holy Spirit resides within us as His temple, we must realize that we never enter into our battles alone. The Holy Spirit, the most powerful force in the universe, is with us. It is His battle in this invisible war. However, just like Joshua we must believe God's promises and by faith act upon them in obedience. Then God will give us the victory as we carry His presence within us into the battle.

On one of those three occasions when the ark was taken into battle, Israel was defeated **(1 Samuel 4:1-11).** Thirty thousand Israelites were killed and the Ark of the Covenant was captured by the Philistines. This was the scenario: *"When the ark of the Lord's Covenant came into the camp, all Israel raised such a great shout* [terou'a] *that the ground shook. 6. Hearing the uproar, the Philistines asked, 'What's all the shouting in the Hebrew camp?' When they had learned that the ark of the Lord had come into the camp, 7. the Philistines were afraid. 'A god has come into the camp,' they said. 'We're in* *trouble!...* **8.** *Woe to us! Who will deliver us from the hands of these mighty gods?'... 10. So the Philistines fought, and the Israelites were defeated."*

We learn from this that God cannot fight for us and win our battles if we are doing something that obstructs Him from bringing victory. We can give what seems like a confident war cry in battle that even makes the ground shake, but we will find to our dismay that God is not with us when we are in sin and are disobedient (also see **Joshua 6:17-8:2**). We must strive to keep ourselves in a position where God can work on our behalf and give us power to overcome.

     (2) **Example: The battle between Israel and Judah.**

        † **2 Chronicles 13:12-20**—*"God is with us; he is our leader. His priests with their trumpets will sound the battle cry* [terou'a] *against you. Men of Israel, do not fight against the Lord, the God of your fathers, for you will not succeed." 13. Now Jeroboam had sent troops around to the rear, so that while he was in front of Judah, the ambush was behind them. 14. Judah turned and saw that they were being attacked at both front and rear. Then they cried out to the Lord. The priests blew their trumpets 15. and the men of Judah raised the battle cry. At the sound of their battle cry, God routed Jeroboam and all Israel before Abijah and Judah. 16. The Israelites fled before Judah, and God delivered them into their hands.*

   D. David Blomgren: "This same war cry against the enemy in music may be the anointed playing on an instrument, *'...play skillfully with a loud noise'* (terou'a; **Psalm 33:3** KJV) ...As we sing forth a Song of Praise unto God, it comes forth as praise unto Him, but it comes to the enemy as a war cry against him...the war cry against the enemy causes him to retreat and spiritual victory is won."[10]

        † **Numbers 10:9**—*When you go into battle in your own land against an enemy who is oppressing you, sound a blast on the trumpets. Then you will be remembered by the Lord your God and rescued from your enemies.*

        † **Deuteronomy 20:1-4**—*When you go to war against your enemies and see horses and chariots and an army greater than yours, do not be afraid of them, because the Lord your God, who brought you up out of Egypt, will be with you. 2. When you are about to go into battle, the priest shall come forward and address the army. 3. He shall say: "Hear, O Israel, today you are going into battle against your enemies. Do not be fainthearted or afraid; do not be terrified or give way to panic before them. 4. For the Lord your God is the one who goes with you to fight for you against your enemies to give you victory."*

        † **Psalm 98:1, 4**—*Sing to the Lord a new song, for he has done marvelous things; his right hand and his holy arm have worked salvation for him. 4. Shout for joy to the Lord, all the earth, burst into jubilant song with music...*

   E. **Example: The battle between Judah and the three nations.**

     (1) **The Promise Came From God**—In **2 Chronicles 20:1-30,** King Jehoshaphat reacted to the news of the three nations preparing to attack him by seeking the Lord and proclaiming a fast. The Spirit of the Lord came upon Jahaziel and assured the people that God was going to give Judah victory as they confronted this great multitude *"for the battle is not yours, but God's"* **(20:15).**

(2) **The Procession**—Having received a genuine Word from God, he acted on it in **faith.** After consulting with the people, he appointed men who would sing to the Lord with thanksgiving, worshiping Him by affirming His attributes, and sent them out before the Hebrew army into battle against their severely outnumbered foe.

(3) **Divine Intervention**—As they began to sing and to praise God by faith, the Lord turned the three enemy nations against one another and they destroyed each other—fulfilling the prophetic word spoken by Jahaziel: *"You will not have to fight this battle. Take up your positions; stand firm and see the deliverance the Lord will give you."* **(20:17).** As they saw the dead bodies of their enemies lying on the ground, none having escaped, Jehoshaphat and his men began carrying off the spoil. It took them three days to do it. As they returned to Jerusalem, they came praising and rejoicing in their God *"with harp and lutes and trumpets"* **(20:28).** As a result *"the fear of God came upon all the kingdoms of the countries when they heard how the Lord had fought against the enemies of Israel. 30. And the kingdom of Jehoshaphat was at peace, for his God had given him rest on every side."* **(20:29-30).**

►**CONSIDER THIS:** God rarely does the same thing in the same way twice. Therefore, we should be careful not to try to duplicate a "formula" but get the mind of God for each situation. In the above example, the Israelites responded to a prophetic word by Jahaziel for their specific predicament—not to be repeated in the exact same way later. Also keep in mind that this war cry was done under the direction of the Holy Spirit.

☑ This ends our first session and the DVD content for Lesson 16. Now please answer these SQ&A.

STUDY QUESTIONS AND APPLICATION

1. How many times a month do you incorporate the weapon of fasting with your prayers? _____

2. Read the following Scriptures about **fasting** and briefly list each aspect. For health reasons, you should be knowledgeable about fasting before you begin. A used copy of one of the best books on the subject, *God's Chosen Fast*, by Arthur Wallis—ISBN: 0875085555, can be located through a search engine on the internet. Dr. C.S. Lovett also has written one on the topic (www.cslovettbooks.com).

   A. What are some key elements that will make your fast successful?

      (1) **Matthew 6:16-18** _____

      (2) **Luke 4:1-2** _____

      (3) **Zechariah 7:4-5** _____

      (4) **Isaiah 58:3-9** _____

B. What are some biblical reasons for fasting?

    (1) **Joel 2:12-14**; **Jonah 3:1-10** _____

    (2) **Deuteronomy 9:18-19** _____

    (3) **2 Chronicles 20:1-4** _____

    (4) **Ezra 8:21-23** _____

    (5) **Esther 3:8-15; 4:15-5:3** _____

    (6) **Isaiah 58:5-9** _____

    (7) **Psalm 35:13a** _____

    (8) **Acts 13:2** _____

    (9) **Acts 13:3; 14:23** _____

    (10) **Mark 9:25-29** _____

C. What are some biblical lengths of fasts?

    (1) **Judges 20:26** _____

    (2) **Esther 4:15-16** _____

    (3) **Daniel 10:2-3** _____

    (4) **Exodus 34:28**; **Matthew 4:2** _____

> ☑ When you are ready to begin the last session, continue on in this workbook for additional material **not** on the DVD. The 4th Qtr. Exam can be taken after this session from our website.
>
> Note: I suggest that the remainder of this lesson be treated as a separate session.

Session 2

THE NECESSITY OF BEING AN OVERCOMER

1. Pertaining to the armor, the words *"to stand"* in **Ephesians 6:13** convey the idea of prevailing or overcoming—especially *"when the day of evil comes."* God clearly wants us to live victoriously over our enemies. If we believe and trust in the work Christ did for us on the cross, we will share in the victory Christ got over sin, satan, the world, and death. Our victory is dependent upon our faith and obedience—keeping our part of the New Testament through overcoming.

   A. **Our part of the New Testament involves a continuing faith in God and in Christ's atonement, dependence upon the Holy Spirit, and a life-long process of sanctification whereby we separate ourselves to God from sin and evil.** Like a bride who keeps herself pure, awaiting the marriage to her bridegroom, we do those things that nurture and maintain our relationship with Christ so we don't disqualify ourselves. These things in **no way merit** forgiveness of our sins **or earn** us an entrance into heaven. (See Figure 7-3 in Lesson 7.)

      † **1 John 5:3-5**—*This is love for God: to obey his commands. And his commands are not burdensome,* **4.** *for everyone born of God has overcome the world. This is the victory that has overcome the world, even our faith.* **5.** *Who is it that overcomes the world? Only he who believes that Jesus is the Son of God.*

      † **Hebrews 12:14-15** (NKJV)—*Pursue peace with all people, and holiness* [sanctification]*, without which no one will see the Lord:* **15.** *looking carefully lest anyone fall short of the grace of God...*

   B. **Q:** If we had automatic victory through Christ over sin, satan, the world, and death, and nothing could prevent us from inheriting the Kingdom of God, then why would God command us to *"put on"* these pieces of armor, pray, and live a life of sanctification?

   C. If we are automatically made overcomers, then there would be no reason for Christ to give the seven churches in the book of Revelation the following **conditional promises** for overcoming:

      † **Revelation 2:4-5,7**—Jesus said: *"Yet I hold this against you: You have forsaken your first love.* **5.** *Remember the height from which you have fallen! Repent and do the things you did at first. If you do not repent, I will come to you and remove your lampstand from its place...* **7.** *He who has an ear, let him hear what the Spirit says to the churches. To him who overcomes, I will give the right to eat from the tree of life, which is in the paradise of God."*

      † **Revelation 2:11**—*...He who overcomes will not be hurt at all by the second death.*

      † **Revelation 2:17**—*...To him who overcomes, I will give some of the hidden manna. I will also give him a white stone with a new name written on it, known only to him who receives it.*

† **Revelation 2:26-28**—*To him who overcomes and does my will to the end, I will give authority over the nations—**27.** 'He will rule them with an iron scepter; he will dash them to pieces like pottery'—just as I have received authority from my Father. **28.** I will also give him the morning star.*

† **Revelation 3:5**—*He who overcomes will, like them, be dressed in white. I will never erase his name from the book of life, but will acknowledge his name before my Father and his angels.*

† **Revelation 3:12**—*Him who overcomes I will make a pillar in the temple of my God. Never again will he leave it. I will write on him the name of my God and the name of the city of my God, the new Jerusalem, which is coming down out of heaven from my God; and I will also write on him my new name.*

† **Revelation 3:15,16,19,21,22**—*I know your deeds, that you are neither cold nor hot. I wish you were either one or the other! **16**. So, because you are lukewarm—neither hot nor cold—I am about to spit you out of my mouth... **19**. Those whom I love I rebuke and discipline. So be earnest, and repent... **21**. To him who overcomes, I will give the right to sit with me on my throne, just as I overcame and sat down with my Father on his throne. **22**. He who has an ear, let him hear what the Spirit says to the churches.*

† **Revelation 21:7-8**—*He who overcomes will inherit all this, and I will be his God and he will be my son. **8.** But the cowardly, the unbelieving, the vile, the murderers, the sexually immoral, those who practice magic arts, the idolaters and all liars—their place will be in the fiery lake of burning sulfur. This is the second death.*

CLOSING COMMENTS

This video series and workbook is intended to be a practical, comprehensive guide to spiritual warfare that you can refer to for the rest of your life. Whenever you encounter a future attack from any of your spiritual enemies: your sinful nature, demonic forces, or the world, I am confident that as you refresh yourself with this material, the Holy Spirit will give you insight and help you to develop the ability to win each conflict. He will help you to identify the type of attack coming against you and how He would have you to respond to it (Note: For a complete listing of the tactics of the devil, see **Index and Summary of Satan's Tactics.**)

We bring this study to a close by summarizing the weapons God has given to us and providing an illustrative overview of the lessons. You may be thinking about what you are going to do now that this study is over. It is not by coincidence that we conclude with prayer and praise. Guidelines for effective prayer are provided so that you can begin improving on your prayer life and continue the momentum that you have gained from this study.

Always keep in mind that we are caught in the midst of satan's war against God's kingdom and we have the most to lose in this invisible war. God will always be God. Satan's future doom is sealed, but the outcome of our lives is still being determined. We have become the targets. We are the prize. The battle is for our very souls! We either win big or lose big. Victory means heaven! Defeat means hell! If you are not yet involved in a Bible believing church, I urge you to seek God to lead you to one. Select five churches and visit one each week until you sense the Lord's direction as to the church family he wants you to join. Isolating yourself from the Body of Christ is dangerous. We need each other and the ministry gifts God has provided!

A SUMMARY OF GOD'S WEAPONRY

Walk in the victory Christ gave you over sin, satan, the world, and death! To ensure being an overcomer in Christ, use the spiritual weapons that God has provided for us to fight with in this invisible war. Let us summarize:

> † **2 Corinthians 10:3-4**—*For though we live in the world, we do not wage war as the world does. **4.** The weapons we fight with are not the weapons of the world. On the contrary, they have divine power to demolish strongholds.*

1. The **Name of Jesus**—*"...at the name of Jesus every knee will bow, in heaven and on earth and under the earth, **11.** and every tongue will confess that Jesus Christ is Lord..."* **(Philippians 2:10** NLT**)**

2. The **Blood of Christ** (i.e. faith in His sacrificial, efficacious, and mediatory work on the cross): *"And they overcame him by the blood of the Lamb..."* **(Revelation 12:11** KJV**)**

3. The **Holy Spirit**—The greatest power in and beyond the universe is available to us to help us and to work for us in an added dimension beyond ourselves! **(John 14:16-18; 16:7-14; Acts 2:1-4)**

4. The **Word of God** (the Sword of the Spirit and the Belt of Truth): **Light** to fight the darkness; **Truth** to combat lies **(John 3:20).**

5. **Love** to conquer hate—Jesus said, *"...love your enemies. Do good to those who hate you."* **(Luke 6:27** NLT**). Goodness** to overcome evil: *"...overcome evil with good"* **(Romans 12:21).**

6. Your **Sonship,** together with who you are in Christ: *"...those who have become part of God's family...God's Son holds them securely, and the evil one cannot get his hands on them."* **(1 John 5:18** NLT**)**

7. The **Breastplate of Righteousness** and **Sanctification** to keep our part of the New Testament by separating ourselves to God, and putting to death our sinful nature by saying "Yes" to God in obedience (which at the same time says "No" to the *"flesh"*) and prevents the devil from gaining a foothold: *"And they overcame him* [Satan] *because...they did not love their life even to death."* **(Revelation 12:11** NASB**; Romans 8:13; Hebrews 12:14)**

8. *"Weapons of righteousness"* **(2 Corinthians 6:7)** to give us an outreach focus to overcome selfishness and help others, and enable us to stay under the umbrella of God's protection. These include submission to God and spiritual disciplines such as giving and serving: *"Submit yourselves, then, to God. Resist the devil, and he will flee from you"* **(James 4:7).**

9. The **Helmet of Salvation** to protect our minds. **Discernment** to distinguish what is of God and satan.

10. **Our Testimony** (Shoes for Combat)—*"And they overcame him* [satan] *by...the word of their testimony..."* **(Revelation 12:11** KJV**). Perseverance** to outlast the opposition.

11. The **Shield of Faith** to quench the fiery arrows of doubts about God's character, tragedies and misfortunes, discouragement, and fears **(1 John 5:3-5).**

12. **Prayer, Praise,** and **Fasting** to provide breakthroughs in the heavenlies, rout the enemy, and bring **deliverance.** And also by calling in the reinforcements—your spouse, pastor, and trusted friends, for spiritual prayer support. The **War Cry** is another spiritual weapon as well.

AN ILLUSTRATIVE SUMMARY OF THIS STUDY

"Who am I?" "Where did I come from?" and **"Where am I going?"** Throughout history, surely every man, woman, and child has wrestled with these questions. God has placed a deep desire in each of us to know our origin, our identity, and our destiny. When we become Christians, God gives us the following biblical answers to these major questions of life: As descendants of Adam and Eve, who fell into sin, every one of us is born into satan's kingdom with a sinful nature and is a child of the devil headed for hell. But when we commit our lives to Christ, we leave the devil's domain and become God's adopted children; now, as part of His kingdom we are headed for Heaven!

We begin our journey as a Christian up a steep road, as it were, that will eventually take us to the "Celestial City" of Heaven. The road to this heavenly kingdom will be long, rough, winding, narrow, and full of obstacles to overcome as we order our lives by the Biblical Christian worldview. At the end of our life's road, we will have to cross the vast sea of death before we can finally enter that heavenly kingdom. When we reach the shoreline of the end of life, Jesus promises to be there to take us over its waters to heaven's shore so we can live with Him forever in that glorious land. We now do everything by faith in that promise, God's character, and the Bible.

As we travel this road, another question will arise: **"Why am I here?"** You are here to enjoy God and glorify Him in your life. You are here to discover and fulfill the special assignments He has chosen you to do. And you are here to impact the lives of those you meet for Christ, to make a contribution to mankind, and to pass down a Godly heritage to your children—preparing them for their own life's journey.

As you make your pilgrimage, you will meet needy people whom God will want you to stop and help. You will also meet many from satan's camp. You are called to help rescue them, persuading them to join you in following Jesus in this Christian walk. Our call is to take as many people to the "Celestial City" with us as possible. Through our testimony and the Word, we are to communicate to those around us the way, the **only way,** to reach heaven.

Another thing you will eventually discover is that you have been drawn into an invisible war, caught in the midst of a conflict between satanic forces and the One True God. You also learn that you have three main spiritual enemies: the enemy *within you* (your own **sinful nature),** the **devil,** and the **world system.** With this insight, you must now arm yourself with the proper attitudes for battle; utilize the spiritual weapons that God has provided; and obtain knowledge of your enemy's character and tactics. You may feel discouraged and alone at times as you walk down this path, but remember, the Holy Spirit will be with you to empower you, give you wisdom, meet your needs, and guide you safely through this world. You are never alone!

As you journey on in this hostile, foreign land, you will encounter many temptations, traps, and pitfalls. These are meant to take you off course and lead you onto the broad road of sin, where the masses are traveling, that will result in destruction. You must fight these attempts to allure your love and obedience away from Christ. You will be enticed to take shortcuts and side streets that will lead you away from God's will. Watch out for enemy ambushes. With distractions like these, staying on the right path is not always easy. You must be careful not to let down your guard!

As you travel through "cities and towns," your enemies will beckon to you from the sidewalks, trying to impede your progress by distracting your focus and getting you sidetracked from your mission. From the windows of buildings along the streets, you will hear them call, "Come up here! We've got something that is a whole lot more fun and exciting than your boring Christian walk." Ignore these voices and keep walking, for those things will only cater to your sinful nature. Remember, being in God's will and in His Presence is *"fullness of joy,"* and the things He has prepared for you in this life and the next cannot compare with what the world has to offer.

Ultimately, *all* of your spiritual enemies are going to try to keep you from reaching your destination. But the only one that can prevent you from reaching that "Celestial City" is YOU! Others along the way will attempt to oppose you, intimidate you, hurt you, discourage you, make you fearful, and cause you to lose heart and quit. Some will try to stop your witness for Christ or force you to renounce Him through persecution. Others may slander your character. But the person who remains faithful to God and endures to the end will make it to that Heavenly City. So don't give up, God will be with you.

You will face other challenges, too, besides people. Setbacks, misfortunes, and other things beyond your control (like "weather" and "terrain") will make your trip difficult—but you can't allow them to stop you. Just keep walking, whether in sunshine or storms, blizzards, and the darkest of nights; or through wilderness, valley, or mountaintop experiences—you must not lose faith. Everything that now affects your life as a Christian is either sent by God, permitted by God, or used by God. Jesus promised never to leave you so you can count on Him being there—right by your side!

When you do stumble along the way, ask God for His help. Each time, get up on your feet, keep walking, and follow Christ's example. Through weariness, neediness, trials, and tribulations you must press on with your eyes focused on Jesus and not lose sight of the goal. If you love Him, He will cause *"...all things to work together for good."* For *"He who overcomes will inherit all this, and I will be his God and he will be my son"* **(Revelation 21:7)**.

Christ has called us to go forth to win souls, reform the culture, restrain evil, represent the true God, continue what was begun in the Book of Acts, and further establish God's kingdom here on earth through spiritual warfare. As you go, be encouraged with these promises of God:

> † **1 John 4:4** (GNT)—*...the Spirit who is in you is more powerful than the spirit in those who belong to the world.*

> † **Matthew 16:16-19**—*Simon Peter answered, "You are the Christ, the Son of the living God." 17. Jesus replied... 18. "...on this rock I will build my church, and the gates of Hades will not overcome it."*

▶ **CONSIDER THIS:** The "gate" of a city was a place where its leaders met to transact business, to plan and advise. Jesus was saying that no plan devised at the gates of satan's citadels to overpower and destroy His church will ever succeed. The enemy may inflict damage, but he will not overcome Christ's church. Neither will death prevent His church from existing in the afterlife! We already know the outcome of this invisible war—WE WIN!! *"But in all these things we overwhelmingly conquer through Him who loved us"* **(Romans 8:35-39** NASB**)**.

> † **Luke 10:17-20**—*The seventy-two returned with joy and said, "Lord, even the demons submit to us in your name." 18. He replied, "I saw Satan fall like lightning from heaven. 19. I have given you authority to trample on snakes and scorpions and to overcome all the power of the enemy; nothing will harm you. 20. However, do not rejoice that the spirits submit to you, but rejoice that your names are written in heaven."*

GUIDELINES FOR EFFECTIVE PRAYER

1. We close this lesson with an in-depth study of Christ's model prayer we know as "The Lord's Prayer." Now that this study is over, the following material on prayer can equip and motivate you to improve on the quality of your prayer time and launch you into a closer relationship with your Heavenly Father. The following material is taken from the teachings of the late Professor Walter H. Beuttler to whom this book is dedicated, and without his influence this book would not have been written.

   A. In order to pray effectively, our approach to God must be biblically based. In response to His disciple's request, *"Lord, teach us to pray."* Jesus taught us "The Lord's Prayer." Perhaps a more appropriate title would be "The Disciples Prayer" since the part of the prayer that asks God to *"forgive us"* would not have applied to Christ.

   B. This model prayer was not intended to be recited mechanically over and over again, or to be one form superseding all other prayers. Jesus designed it to embody principles that should be incorporated into all prayers—for all true prayer is crystallized in this prayer.

2. What are the elements of effective prayer?

   A. **Right motive**—Pray genuinely to God, not just to be seen by people or to seek their praise as the hypocrites do (See **Matthew 6:5.**)

      † **Matthew 15:8-9** (NASB)—Jesus quoted the prophet Isaiah who wrote: *"This people honors Me with their lips, but their heart is far away from Me. 9. But in vain do they worship me..."*

   B. **Be real**—Express to God what is in your heart in your own words. Don't rely on the vain repetition of prayers and requests as a meritorious means of being heard by God. Put yourself in your Heavenly Father's place. Would you want to hear the same prayers recited over and over again without them being heartfelt and sincere? True prayer is not a matter of words but of meaning; not of form, but of heart; not of outward beauty, but of inward reality. The Father seeks those who will worship Him in spirit and in truth. At times there may be more effective prayer in a few words of earnest supplication (with groaning or even total silence) than in lengthy, wordy prayers **(Matthew 6:7-8; 23:14).**

   C. **Be consistent**—Notice Jesus did not say "If you pray" but *"When you pray"* **(Matthew 6:6).** Our Heavenly Father expects His children to pray each day—not just in times of need. Establish your prayer life before the battle begins instead of waiting until after defeat. A realistic goal would be to work your way toward eventually spending one tenth of your day (2½ hrs) in worship and prayer. Note that all this time does not have to be spent on your knees.

   D. **Find a secret place**—The location where you pray is important. Jesus often resorted to a *"solitary place"* **(Mark 1:35).** He taught us to *"...go into your room and close the door..."* **(Matthew 6:6)** to escape from distractions. On a similar note, if you are distracted by other thoughts or images while praying, try picturing each word of your prayer as you say or sing them.

E. **Pray with faith and confidence**—Because God is omnipresent, He sees and hears you no matter where you are **(Jeremiah 23:24)**. And He is kindly disposed towards you for *"He who did not spare His own Son...how will he not also, along with Him, graciously give us all things?"* **(Romans 8:32)**. Expect to receive! As Bishop Joseph L. Garlington teaches, "The atmosphere of expectancy is the breeding ground for the miraculous."

F. **Pray to your Father**—We are instructed to approach our Heavenly Father through His Son, Jesus Christ, in conscious reality of our "sonship" **(Matthew 6:6, John 14:13-14; 15:16; 16:23)**. The Bible does not give us an option to pray to anyone else other than the Trinity.

(1) **Prayer Postures**—No particular posture is prescribed in the Bible. Our posture in prayer is determined by a variety of factors, such as individual personality, emotional state, physical condition, and environmental circumstances—all which tend to diversity rather than uniformity. In short, your posture in prayer should match your attitude:

(a) Standing in worship **(1 Chronicles 23:30; Job 1:20)**

(b) Sitting in prayer **(2 Samuel 7:18-29; Judges 20:26)**

(c) Kneeling in supplication **(2 Chronicles 6:13)**

(d) Prostrate in distress **(2 Samuel 12:16; 1 Kings 18:42)**

G. **Purify your heart**—We cannot pray effectively with malice in our hearts toward others **(Matthew 6:14-15)**.

H. **Put God first**—Obtaining the necessities of life and other answers to prayer will follow when we put God and His kingdom first—over our own needs and interests.

† **Matthew 6:33** (NLT)—Jesus taught: *"...and he will give you all you need from day to day if you live for him and make the Kingdom of God your primary concern."*

PRINCIPLES OF THE LORD'S PRAYER

† **Matthew 6:9-13**—Jesus said: *"This, then, is how you should pray: 'Our Father in heaven, hallowed be your name, 10. your kingdom come, your will be done on earth as it is in heaven. 11. Give us today our daily bread. 12. Forgive us our debts, as we also have forgiven our debtors. 13. And lead us not into temptation, but deliver us from the evil one'"* for yours is the kingdom and the power and the glory forever. Amen.

The Domestic Scene

1. *"Our Father in heaven"* **(6:9)**—The prayer begins with a domestic scene—namely, the Father, the family, and the home.

A. It is significant that all personal pronouns in this prayer are in the plural, none in the singular. This suggests that there is absolutely no room for selfishness by ignoring the needs of others and attending only to our own. The bond of love unites the family of God in mutual interest *"that the members should have the same care one for another"* **(1 Corinthians 12:25** KJV).

B. Recognition of the fatherhood of God—Having been adopted as God's children by the new birth **(John 1:12-13; 3:3; Ephesians 1:5),** Christ places our new relationship to God at the very entrance of our approach to our Heavenly Father. We are now to make use of our rightful claims as His children and thereby give our Father opportunity to demonstrate His benevolent care.

2. *"Hallowed be your name"* **(Matthew 6:9)**

   A. Next the prayer introduces worship indicating that worship comes **before** petition and that prayer is rendered most effective in an atmosphere of praise. Therefore *"with thanksgiving let your requests be made known to God"* **(Philippians 4:6** KJV; also see **Psalm 95:1-3).**

   B. The "name" of God represents the manifold aspects of His nature and embraces all that He really is. God's name is the disclosure and expression of what He is—the unchangeable character of God. His name can be trusted even when we experience times that seem to be contrary to His character and seemingly the very negation of His promises. We are instructed to worship Him by giving Him *"the glory due His name"* **(Psalm 29:2** KJV**).**

   † **Proverbs 18:10** (KJV)—*The name of the Lord is a strong tower: the righteous runneth into it, and is safe.*

   C. This also includes praying for the sanctity of the name of God—that it will be held sacred and esteemed among men. The familiarity of love must not neglect the reverence due to His name.

The Royal Scene

3. *"Your kingdom come"* **(6:10)**—The prayer proceeds to a royal scene—namely, the kingdom, the king, and His subjects. It passes from the revelation of God as Father to the revelation of God as sovereign.

   A. We are to pray for the interests of the kingdom of God on earth. It is a petition for the establishment of God's undisputed and absolute universal reign—one that should take priority over our personal interests **(James 4:3).**

4. *"Your will be done on earth as it is in heaven"* **(6:10)**

   A. The burden of this prayer is that the revelation of God through His name might bring about a universal recognition of the sovereignty of God among men. This is a necessary prerequisite if God's kingdom is to be established in their hearts.

   B. True recognition of the supremacy of God must inevitably involve submission of the human will to the rule of God and be demonstrated by actual obedience to the laws of His kingdom.

   C. *"But seek first His kingdom and His righteousness..."* **(6:33)** refers to compliance with the laws of His kingdom within our hearts **(Luke 17:21)** which are a prerequisite for the abundant supply of our material needs. Examples: planting precedes harvest (**2 Corinthians 9:6**); giving precedes receiving (**Luke 6:38**).

The Earthly Scene

5. *"Give us today our daily bread"* (**Matthew 6:11**)—The prayer now moves to an earthly scene with its material needs, sinful states, and spiritual conflicts.

   A. Now we are instructed to pray for our personal needs and interests as well as those of others. The word *"bread"* represents all the necessities of life.

   B. This prayer is meant to be a *"daily"* prayer for "this day"—entirely content with the provisions for the needs of the present without any anxiety about the needs of the future.

      † **Proverbs 30:8-9** (NLT)—*O God...give me neither poverty nor riches! Give me just enough to satisfy my needs. **9**. For if I grow rich, I may deny you and say, "Who is the Lord?" And if I am too poor, I may steal and thus insult God's holy name.*

   C. *"Give us"* is an acknowledgment of our dependence upon God. Laying aside independent self-sufficiency, we are to be content to rely on our Father's care with humble childlike faith and simplicity.

6. *"Forgive us our debts as we also have forgiven our debtors"* (**6:12**)

   A. All sins are *"debts"* because of our unfulfilled obligations both to God and man, whether by omission or commission. Forgiveness is the only way to liquidate our indebtedness—especially when there is no unforgiving spirit on our part to form an obstacle to our being forgiven (**Matthew 5:23-24; Luke 11:4**).

7. *"Lead us not into temptation"* (**6:13**)

   A. This is an acknowledgment of our moral weakness. Due to our inherent propensity to evil and consequent susceptibility to sin, this is a petition for protection against exposure to satan's temptation beyond our ability to endure (**Matthew 26:41**).

8. *"But deliver us from the evil one."* (**6:13**)

   A. This is an acknowledgment of our weakness. This is an entreaty to God for deliverance from the overwhelming power and wiles of the devil. This prayer presupposes that we are not giving the enemy a foothold in our lives.

9. *"For yours is the kingdom and the power and the glory forever"* (**6:13**). The prayer ends with a triumphant scene in the form of a doxology.

   A. This is an affirmation of God's right to the kingdom and of God's sovereign power. Satan's rule will be terminated so that *"The kingdom of the world has become the kingdom of our Lord and of His Christ and He will reign forever and ever"* (**Revelation 11:15**).

B. This is also an affirmation of the glory of God, for it is the object of not only all true prayer but our very existence. *"So whether you eat or drink or whatever you do, do it all for the glory of God"* **(1 Corinthians 10:31).**

C. Finally, this affirms the ultimate triumph of God over sin and evil, our sinful nature, the devil, the world, and death. God's kingdom has come and we have been delivered from them all—forever! Amen.

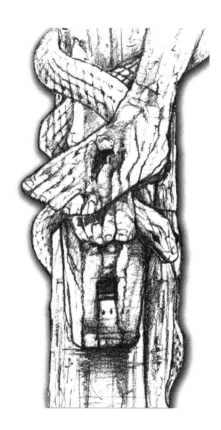

† **Matthew 28:18-20**—Jesus said, *"...All authority in heaven and on earth has been given to me. 19. Therefore go and make disciples of all nations, baptizing them in the name of the Father and of the Son and of the Holy Spirit, 20. and teaching them to obey everything I have commanded you. And surely I am with you always, to the very end of the age."*

† **Genesis 3:15**—God addressed satan through the serpent, *"And I will put enmity between you and the woman, and between your offspring and hers; he will crush your head, and you will strike his heel."*

Note: This Scripture was fulfilled on the cross. Satan played a part in Jesus' crucifixion depicted by the nail piercing His feet and heel. But by His death and resurrection, Jesus crushed the head of the serpent, satan, and defeated him and all his forces.[11]

† **Romans 16:20** (NLT)—*The God of peace will soon crush Satan under your feet. May the grace of our Lord Jesus Christ be with you.*

Crowns and thorns will perish, kingdoms rise and wane,
But the Church of Jesus constant will remain;
Gates of hell can never, against that Church prevail;
We have Christ's own promise, which can never fail.
Onward, Christian soldiers! Marching as to war,
With the cross of Jesus going on before.

Sabine Baring-Gould

☑ Would you like to learn more about prayer as well as other topics about God and His Word? If so, visit our website at www.DiscoverTheBible.net. We are offering non-accredited online Bible courses for the Beginner, Intermediate, and Advanced student. **Consider taking the FREE sample.**

☑ Continue on with the Study Questions and Application and the Summary.

STUDY QUESTIONS AND APPLICATION

1. If you did this study in a group, conclude this last session by sharing with each other how these lessons have changed or impacted your life and how you plan to order your life differently (or any other way the Holy Spirit leads you).

2. On the scale below indicate the amount of time you consistently spend in prayer each day—individually and corporately combined. Write the current month and year below the length.

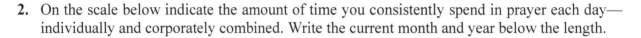

| Not At All | Under 5 Min. | Between 5-20 Min. | Between 20-40 Min. | Between 40-60 Min. | Over 1 Hr. |

3. Referring to #1 above, identify one or more things that you can start doing to increase the quality and length of your prayer time—and then *"just do it!"*

4. List the ways you can incorporate more praise, worship, and music into your personal prayer time (i.e. speaking out loud, singing, playing an instrument, etc.).

    A._____

    B._____

    C._____

5. Take the principles of the Lord's Prayer and begin to integrate them into your prayers.

6. Referring to the section above entitled, **A Summary of God's Weaponry,** give practical "hands on" examples of how you would use these weapons in your everyday life.

SUMMARY

God has given to us the awesome two-pronged weapon of prayer and praise that move the very heart and hand of God—releasing His divine power. In this invisible war, it is not enough for us to defend ourselves. God wants His church to attack and penetrate satan's kingdom and advance the Kingdom of God! Through prayer, we push back the forces of darkness that impede the spread of the Gospel. Prayer has no limitations of distance or time. As our petitions ascend to our Heavenly Father, like an interplanetary missile God launches answers to prayer that penetrate demonic opposition and strike the forces of satan wherever they are at work. It is one of the main weapons that the devil fears the most. But many times it is a weapon that we neglect and fail to use.

Our prayer life is crucial to obtaining victory. Intercessory prayer is the first prong of this second **1.** offensive weapon, and is part of the complete armor God has provided for us. For the most part, this weapon is not directed at demonic forces like the Sword, but is directed to our Heavenly Father. Prayer has two aspects: the **2A.** giving of thanksgiving, worship, and praise to God for who He is and what He has done, and **2B.** petition to our Heavenly Father for our needs and for others.

We defined prayer as heartfelt communication with your Heavenly Father, through His Son, where there is a blending of your spirit with His Spirit, and you emerge stronger from that time spent together with an afterglow of His presence—having touched the very heart of God with your thanksgiving, worship, and petitions. Prayer originates and emanates primarily from our **3.** spirit which is affected by the condition of our body and soul. These must be disciplined in order for our prayer life to be successful.

Why do we have to pray if God already knows our needs before we ask Him? The reasons are: we pray to keep ourselves **1.** dependent upon God; because Christ **2.** commanded us to pray; it is our spiritual **3.** lifeline (our umbilical cord) to God's life and power; because we live in **4.** satan's domain where demonic opposition holds back God's answers to our prayers so that they need to be "prayed through" with intercessory prayer and fasting; and because we don't know **5.** how or what to pray. The Holy Spirit prompts us to pray and as we cooperate and obey His leading, the Spirit places the burden in our spirits and births intercession through us. When we intercede until the Spirit lifts the burden, breakthroughs occur in the heavenly realm. Victories are first established in the spirit realm before they are manifested in the natural realm. Having the Baptism in the Holy Spirit is essential in this area. God also searches for people who will allow their hearts to be broken with the things that break His heart—those who will stand between God and sin and intercede to turn away His judgment. Many times, He is grieved to find no one that is interested or available.

Naturally, our prayer life becomes a target of the enemy. So he uses **TACTIC: Cut Their Supply Line**—where the enemy will try to get you to choose to either neglect your prayer, worship, and Bible time so as to cut off the source of God's spiritual life supply to your spirit, or get you to tolerate sin in your life so that your prayers will be hindered, which in turn will bring defeat. Again, we actually become our own worst enemy. Think of it! Through our neglect and lack of discipline, **WE** cut the umbilical cord of God's life-supply to our spirit.

Praise and worship is the other prong of this offensive weapon. We must praise and worship God for these reasons: It is a way to **1.** give back to our Heavenly Father in appreciation for all He is and does; our Father **2.** <u>searches</u> for our genuine worship and takes great pleasure in it; because worship comes **3.** <u>before</u> petition; it is a devastating offensive **4.** <u>weapon</u>; it produces the **5.** <u>atmosphere</u> in which God's presence resides; it **6.** <u>breaks</u> the spiritual <u>bondages</u> of demonic power in people's lives; it **7.** <u>quickens</u> God's <u>prophetic</u> word to man; it **8.** <u>protects</u> our <u>heart</u> in times of disaster from finding fault with God; and it **9.** <u>uplifts</u> the defeated spirit.

Dr. David K. Blomgren in his book, *The Song of the Lord*, gave us an insight into how our praise and worship can be used by the Holy Spirit as a **war cry** against the forces of darkness—much like a soldier uses one against his enemy during battle. When done in obedience to the prompting of the Holy Spirit, it ascends as praise to God but it comes to the enemy as a war cry against him causing the enemy to retreat and spiritual victory to be won! Some Old Testament examples were given.

Through the victory Jesus obtained for us on the cross, we can now overwhelmingly conquer all our foes. However, we do not have automatic victory imparted to us. The conditional promises of **Revelation 2:4-3:22** and God's command to put on the armor clearly indicate to the contrary. If we believe and trust in Christ's redemptive work and keep our part of the New Testament by overcoming and maintaining our gift of salvation, we will share in the victory Christ got over sin, satan, the world, and death. Keeping our part of the New Testament involves a continuing faith in God, dependence upon the Holy Spirit, and a life-long process of sanctification whereby we separate ourselves from sin and evil. Like a bride who keeps herself pure, awaiting the marriage to her bridegroom, we strive to do those things that nurture and maintain our relationship with Christ so we don't disqualify ourselves. These things **in no way merit** forgiveness of our sins **or earn** us an entrance into heaven.

To ensure being an overcomer in Christ, we are called to use the weaponry God has provided. We summarized the spiritual weapons that God has given to us to fight with in this invisible war. They are: the Name of Jesus; the Blood of Christ; the Holy Spirit; the Word of God (the Sword of the Spirit and the Belt of Truth); Love to conquer hate; Goodness to overcome evil; Sanctification; the Breastplate of Righteousness (*"weapons of righteousness"*); our Testimony (Shoes for Combat); the Shield of Faith; Prayer, praise, and fasting; and the Helmet of Salvation.

Our prayer time, which establishes our relationship with God, plays a critical role in our being an overcomer. In order to pray effectively, Christ gave us guidelines and taught us a model prayer (known as "The Lord's Prayer"), which embodies principles that should be incorporated into all prayers and was not intended to be recited mechanically over and over again as a meritorious means of being heard. We covered the elements of effective prayer which are: Right motive; Be real; Be consistent; Find a secret place; Pray with faith and confidence; Pray to your Father; Purify your heart; and Put God first. Fittingly, this Prayer and Praise lesson was dealt with last in order to equip and motivate you to improve the quality of your prayer time and launch you into a closer relationship with your Heavenly Father now that this study is over.

Christ has empowered us and has given us authority to overcome all the power of the enemy. He has promised us that *"...the gates of Hades will not overcome..."* His church. But even as tremendous as this is, remember that Jesus emphasized, *"...do not rejoice that the spirits submit to you, but rejoice that your names are written in heaven"* **(Luke 10:19-20)**. God has called us to go forth to win souls, reform the culture, write more of the Book of Acts, and further establish God's kingdom here on earth through spiritual warfare. *"But in all these things we overwhelmingly conquer through Him who loved us"* **(Romans 8:35-39** NASB). *"The God of peace will soon crush Satan under your feet"* **(Romans 16:20** NLT).

APPENDIX A

The Occult: An Overview of Satan's Religious Systems

Introduction—In Lesson 2, an overview of the Seven Views of God was provided as well as an outline overview of the very bizarre but very real world of the **occult**. In order to get the full impact of the overall picture of the practices of satan's religious systems, please read this entire appendix in consecutive order.

WARNING! These areas are extremely dangerous. The author does not recommend that his readers expose themselves to occult material. This treatment should be sufficient in most cases. There is no such thing as "harmless involvement" in any aspect of the occult. Just one exposure is all it can take to give the devil a foothold in your life resulting in **demonization.** God forbids us to dabble in any occult practice or false religion!

Satan incorporates these occult practices either within a false religious system or independently of them. His goals are to receive mankind's obedience and worship indirectly through them, and to provide a philosophy that feeds man's ego and fallen nature and encourages his rebellion against God. Whenever an evil spirit observes a person placing their faith in any area of the occult, or even stepping foot on their territory, the demon will take advantage of the invitation given to him and claim the right to be involved in that person's life. An example of this is when people believe that if they don't follow their horoscope reading, that something bad will happen to them. The devil looks for ways to gain access to one's life in order to further destroy it. Always bear in mind that when accurate information is received or demonstrations of power are seen that these alone should never be accepted as "proof" that the experience is genuinely "of God."

While part of the Christian church is still deliberating whether God is doing miracles today, satan through the occult is offering his own version of the supernatural. We see the influence of satan's religious systems all around us as his tentacles reach into every part of our world. For example, six of our calendar months and all seven days of our week are named in honor of pagan gods who ruled them. Many of us mindlessly parrot superstitions like: saying "God bless you" after someone sneezes (originally meant to prevent an evil spirit from entering that person); or we wish someone "good luck;" we cross our fingers; knock on wood; and participate in Halloween. We have fears about Friday the 13th, walking under a ladder, a black cat crossing our path, or breaking a mirror and receiving bad luck. We attempt to prevent evil spirits from bothering us by carrying a rabbit's foot, birthstones, wearing various medals, as well as other amulets and good luck charms.

For the most part, the false religious worldviews that have dominated mankind throughout history have been **polytheism** and **pantheism.** False gods and the occult with their secret rites have been revived in the past few generations with the same demonic influence and disastrous social consequences that they had on previous civilizations. These gods and occult practices have been passed down to us from ancient Egypt, Babylon, Assyria, Phoenicia, Persia, Greece, Rome, the Celts, etc., as well as from the pantheistic Eastern religions of Hinduism, Buddhism, etc. Furthermore, man believes that these gods are capable of being contacted and influenced by some religious activity in which he engages. However, occult practices are strictly forbidden by the God of the Bible.

> † **Deuteronomy 18:10-12**—*Let no one be found among you who sacrifices his son or daughter in the fire, who practices divination or sorcery, interprets omens, engages in witchcraft, **11.** or casts spells, or who is a medium or spiritist or who consults the dead. **12.** Anyone who does these things is detestable to the Lord…*

Generally speaking, devotees of false religions and the occult attempt to do three things: they **APPEASE** their gods, **INQUIRE** of them, and **INVOKE** them to do something. Practically all of the elements of satan's religious systems can be categorized under these headings. The table of contents follow:

TABLE OF CONTENTS FOR APPENDIX A

HOW PEOPLE APPEASE THEIR FALSE GODS

Tragically, sinful man, blinded and separated from the true God, fell victim to satan's lies and began to deify and worship God's creation instead of God Himself. Mankind personified the elements of nature that he beheld and believed them to be living entities—the sun, moon, stars, day and night, planting and harvesting, earth and sky, rain, lightning, thunder, wind, etc., including the creative power of sexuality. In this view of the world, invisible spirits (gods) reside in these elements and govern every aspect of our lives. They are all a potential source of good or evil that need to be pacified and placated.

Some believe that the elements of nature like animals, insects, rocks, streams and rivers, trees and other vegetation, possess conscious life as living souls. This is called **animism.** These "souls" could be people who had died who now are reincarnated and paying off their debt of **karma.** Jainism is an example of a religion that teaches all life is sacred and prohibits the killing of certain kinds of life for this and other reasons. Others see nature as the abodes of unknown imprisoned spirits. Then there are those who believe the earth is divine— revering it as a goddess, like the Greek Mother-goddess, Gaea, or holding the pantheistic belief that everything is god. Whatever the belief, man has feared, revered, and worshiped nature, and it's one reason why some today fanatically overprotect the environment. See **Deuteronomy 4:15-20; Romans 1:19-25.**

Then there are those who worship their ancestors. Some do this through totem poles which represent their family or clan. Man also created gods in his own sinful likeness and also worshiped their king or emperor as divine such as the Egyptian pharaohs, Roman emperors, and Japanese emperors (Shintoism).

Satan has always controlled his children through deceit, fear, and intimidation. Religion is also used as a means of manipulating and controlling people. He attempts to enslave them with superstitious beliefs and induces them to live under the shadow of terror of the unknown. He fosters the fear that their god(s) are upset with them and will cause bad things to happen to them and their families, their possessions, and their livelihood. They are terrorized by being forced to nervously live each day with the possibility that, at any moment, they can come under a spell of a sorcerer. Or they fear spirits who lay in wait ready to assault anyone coming by who is unprotected by the magical arts. They are also controlled through fear of **fate**—the belief that events in one's life are unalterably destined and decreed, usually by the god(s). Then there is the fear that they haven't done enough to atone for their sins. Therefore, the frightened devotee has no other option than to try to appease his gods. Some type of "spiritual leader" such as a priest or priestess, normally conducts the proceedings. Satan craves worship and demands complete submission from his worshippers.

ACTS OF WORSHIP

Depending upon the false religion or occult practice, the following acts of worship are examples of what people give to false gods to try to appease them and gain their favor. This worship goes indirectly to satan and his demons.

1. Obedience to "sacred" writings and traditions (other than God's inspired Word, the Bible).

2. The commemoration of pagan festivals and "holy days."

3. The reciting of prayers and incantations and singing of hymns such as the first few lines of this prayer to the Babylonian goddess Ishtar, and a hymn to the Egyptian sun god, which were taken from texts discovered from archaeological excavations:

    > "…Mother of the gods…begetress of all, who makest all offspring thrive, Mother Ishtar, whose might no god approaches, majestic lady, whose commands are powerful, a request will I proffer, which—may it bring good to me!…"[1]

"Hail to thee, beautiful god of every day! Rising in the morning without ceasing…Hail to thee! O disc of day, Creator of all and giver of their sustenance…The primordial being, who himself made himself; Who beholds that which he has made…"[2]

4. Acts of obeisance (devotion) such as bowing down to the idol with their face to the ground and kissing and burning incense to it, etc.

5. The performance of rituals and ceremonies—including dancing, purification rites, and the taking of solemn oaths.

6. Acts of self-mutilation and other severe forms of asceticism to earn atonement for sins as in Jainism or what occurred in the following account of the ancient Mystery Religions:[3]

   A. The Mystery Religions existed in the Graeco-Roman era from the 6th century B.C. to the 5th century A.D. (most notable were the Eleusinian, Orphic, Phrygian, and Mithric mysteries). They offered secret knowledge of the deity (and the means of union with them) to only those who qualified and underwent a strict process of initiation. These initiates were expected to make vows of silence that forbade them to divulge details of the mysteries under penalty of great harm or death. These oaths were so feared that very little is known even today of what actually occurred in these ceremonies.

   B. A Mystery Religion was a portrayal of the story of a deity—their struggle, sufferings, and victory and even their death and resurrection as in the case of Dionysus, Osiris, and Attis, whose Passion Plays were publicly acted out. These deities were all primarily Savior-gods who offered redemption and a hope of life hereafter through human effort. Ironically, the mysteries mixed opposites like gross sensuality with asceticism and abstinence, magic and astrology with prayer. Their appeal was not primarily to one's intellect, but to stir one's emotions and to bring a person into an ecstatic religious experience with their god(s).

   C. The "initiate" began with purification and introductory rites leading to initiation into the brotherhood. It was followed by illumination of its secrets, and then identification and union with their god. Purification rites included: baptism—especially in the blood of bulls and other animals—a sacrament that was believed to remove their sins (i.e. "baptismal regeneration"); sacramental meals which made a person one with their god by ingesting the life of the deity through holy food or drink; and various kinds of asceticism were practiced such as prolonged fasts, pilgrimages for penitential purposes, and severe mutilations and flagellations of one's body. Practically every form of self-abasement and renunciation was practiced for remission of sins and to appease their deity. They also did this to enter into fellowship with their deities' sufferings so they could partake of their victories.

   D. Eventually the person was initiated into the revelation of its mysteries and, being purged from all sin, was brought into an experience of mystical communion with the deity. A main way was through "marriage" to the god that at times involved copulation with the deity through the priests or priestesses (see Sex, integrated in worship in index). They would go into trance-like states and be possessed by their god—the deity speaking through them and giving them other types of supernatural revelation and power. Man, himself, had now become "like God" **(Genesis 3:5)**.

   E. Today's mystery religions include secret societies like the Mormon temple rituals (its founder, Joseph Smith, was a 32nd degree Mason). Another, Freemasonry, is one of the most secretive of all with its divisions of the Shriners, Eastern Star, Daughters of Job, Rainbow Girls, and Demolay. Here we have the modern counterpart of the ancient mystery religions that contain much of the same elements of old: revelation of secretive knowledge about their deities obtained through initiation rites, taking solemn oaths (some with curses upon themselves for disclosure), secret passwords, and the worship of ancient deities such as: Egypt's sun god, Osiris, and Isis the moon goddess; the Great Architect of the Universe; and phallic worship. The Shriner's god is Allah, Islam's deity. Though it may deny that it is a religion, Freemasonry has all the tenets of one.

7. Sacrifices

A. The giving of <u>non</u>-<u>blood</u> gifts and offerings—the dearest and best that a person had

B. Sacrificial blood offerings (also used in some practices in the **Inquiring** and **Invoking** sections)

(1) Animals

(2) Human beings—including babies and children who were sacrificed to gods and goddesses like the Ammonite's Molech **(Leviticus 20:2; Ezekiel 16:20-21),** the Phoenician's Tanit, Hinduism's Kali, some Eastern tantric sects, the Aztecs, Mayans and Incas, satanism, and others throughout history and today. (Note: the sacrifice of children was also used in **divination.)**

▶**CONSIDER THIS:** The thought of humans being sacrificed to satan is utterly appalling. It still occurs today throughout the world. Tragically, however, is the little concern we have for the holocaust going on around us each day—America's annual sacrifice of 1.5 million babies, through abortion, to the god of **hedonism.** Currently, in America, a total of over 46 million unborn babies have been murdered through abortion since 1973, and over 1 billion killed worldwide, which represents 1/6th of our planet's population!!

Many in the occult believe that a living being is energy encased in a body of flesh. It is also believed that the "gods" are especially moved to action on behalf of the petitioner at the moment blood is shed, or during sexual orgasm, as these powerful energies and life forces are released into the spirit world. To them, the murder of a human being is undoubtedly the most powerful sacrifice they could make to their god(s).

A terrible example of this is the Aztecs. Each day, an unblemished human being was taken usually to the top of a pyramid. They were laid on an altar and their still-beating heart was torn out of their chest and offered as a sacrifice to their god, Huitzilopochtl, to ensure the rising of the sun that day. Later their bodies were cooked and eaten. It is estimated that approximately 20,000 people were sacrificed each year.[4] The Aztecs also sacrificed their babies and children to their god Tlaloc to ensure rain and these were then cannibalized.[5] The Mayans and Incas did similar things.

8. **The integration of sex in worship**—From antiquity down through today, sex has played a key role in many of satan's religions. Every conceivable type of sexual perversion has been, and is being done, under the guise of religious duty. The use of sex not only gave legitimacy for sexual promiscuity to occur under a "religious" banner, but it also bonded the people to their false god and religion and corrupted their nation's moral fabric. When one considers the sexual influence of demonic spirits with men and women in these religious practices, it is extremely sobering. Imagine the children born from such unions who are demonized or demon-possessed (many from birth), and through heredity pass it onto their children—keeping the religion alive.

A. **Sex in Polytheistic Religions**—The mysterious reproductive life force observed in nature was thought to have miraculous powers; therefore, it was worshiped. Once the populace was seduced (or coerced) into believing that sexual indulgence was a divinely ordained duty, the concept of sex integrated into worship became an acceptable practice. Through the blindness of his heart and demonic influence, man created gods and goddesses that represented this creative principle. So among the pantheon of gods of a religion or nation, there was usually some type of fertility cult that involved appeasing the deity to ensure a successful planting and harvest, having children, obtaining the love of someone through spells or potions, or simply to achieve union with the divine through sexual ecstasy.

(1) Some of the notable cults were: Isis and Osiris in ancient Egypt; Ishtar, the Babylonian goddess of love and war who was called the "Mother of Harlots"—being herself a courtesan to the other gods. Her counterparts that spread to other nations were the Canaanites' Anath and Ashtoreth (snares to the Israelites); the Phoenician's Astarte and Tanit; the Greek's Aphrodite; the Syrian Mylitta (a counterpart of Aphrodite); and the Roman goddess Venus. These goddesses required

"sacred prostitutes" to serve them in their temples. In fact, history tells us that Ishtar's holy city, Erech, was called the "town of the sacred courtesans."[6] Religious sexual intercourse with the populace in the temples of deities also occurred in some or all of the Mystery Religions. After the fall of Rome, some of the religions that came on the scene also had their equivalents of sex in worship—even right down to this very day.

Warning! Some readers may find the following material on sex in worship offensive (Up through the section on Satanism)

(2) In general, religious festivals were held in honor of the goddess or phallic deity. Some would have processions carrying replicas of the male and/or female genitals through the streets as religious symbols—as in the festivals of Egypt's Isis and the Greek's Dionysus—culminating in sexual orgies. Also in other nations religious festivals were known for their unbridled sex as were the Roman Bacchanalia, Liberalia, Saturnalia, Lupercalia, the Floralia (like Ishtar, the goddess Flora was basically a deified prostitute; her Greek counterpart was Chloris). Alcohol and drugs were usually used to help lower inhibitions and produce ecstatic dancing. The sexual act is also a part of the ritual of most forms of witchcraft and satanism today (see below).

(3) Male and female prostitutes were essential to these cults and were normally called priests and priestesses. Some religions would reenact the sexual union of their gods like the Sumerian custom of the "sacred marriage." It took the form of the ceremonial mating of the high priestess, (believed to be an incarnation of the goddess) with the high priest (the embodiment of the earth) to ensure that nation's fertility in every area of life (or with the king to confer upon him divine power). Interestingly, the original meaning of the word "prostitute" was "to stand on behalf of," that is, to represent the power of the goddess. Those having sexual relations with these harlot priestesses and priests viewed the encounter as experiencing direct union with the goddess, and being recipients of divine energy and ecstasy. The "sacred courtesans" viewed the sexual act as their offering of worship and as being a channel of divine energy for the goddess.[7]

(4) Hundreds of girls and women served the fertility goddess as "sacred prostitutes." Some of the goddesses required girls, prior to marriage, to sacrifice their virginity to them via a priest, on an actual stone or a wooden idol (like Greece's Priapus), or by any stranger on demand. Sometimes it was mandatory for every woman to give herself for the goddess once in her lifetime, some children were given to the goddess as an offering by their parents, and some girls served in the temple until their first period. The money they received for their services was made sacred by the act, and was given to the coffers of that goddess. Some women voluntarily spent their lives in this lifestyle. Esteeming their selection as the highest honor and privilege, they would give up everything in life and live only on daily allowances to meet their basic needs. These sacrifices to the deity of a woman's most personal and valued possession was done in hope of bringing the blessing of fertility upon the land as well as to secure their god's divine favor. God forbade this despicable practice (See **Deuteronomy 23:17-18**).

† **Exodus 34:15-16**—*Be careful not to make a treaty with those who live in the land; for when they prostitute themselves to their gods and sacrifice to them, they will invite you and you will eat their sacrifices. 16. And when you choose some of their daughters as wives for your sons and those daughters prostitute themselves to their gods, they will lead your sons to do the same.*

B. **Satanism**—A modern example of sex used in worship is satanism's "black mass"—a blasphemous parody of the Roman Catholic mass. The cult was once a secretive, closed order emerging in the seventeenth century. In 1966, Anton LaVey opened the doors to the First Church of satan in San Francisco. Since then, some satanists have come to Christ and more is known about it. I include it here to give you a glimpse of the intensity of satan's true contempt and hatred for the true God.

(1) The cross is inverted on the wall or worn upside down by the high priest or priestess. The black robed coven of usually 12 in number recites the Lord's Prayer backwards. Bible verses referring to Jesus Christ are directed at satan, and Christ is addressed with words of blasphemy. In place of the communion table is a "living altar"—usually an unclothed woman upon a table that is covered by a dark velvet cloth. Sometimes a corpse is used.

(2) The holy ordinance of communion is blasphemed as a chalice is filled with wine, liquor (even urine), and can be laced with drugs to induce an altered state of consciousness. Instead of the wafer, a black turnip or the like is used. The high priest burns incense, bows before the "altar" and proclaims honor and praise to satan. He invokes him to look favorably on this "sacrifice" which is prepared in his name, and calls upon him for blessings, protection, and answers to their petitions. Other demons are also invoked. Among other things, these requests may include killing, injuring, or the destruction of the property of their enemies.

(3) To put "power" into these petitions, the blood of an animal, and at times even a human baby, is shed as their blood drips down into the chalice on the table next to the naked woman. Some experts believe that a number of children who are kidnapped yearly are used as sacrifices in these types of satanic rituals. The priest makes obscene gestures with the "wafer" with the "living altar," derogatorily addresses Christ, and then tramples it on the floor. Then all drink of the chalice. The ceremony ends with an orgy of sexual relations beginning with the high priest— symbolically "sacrificing" her to satan. In this type of ceremony, children are initiated into the "faith" by their parents, and couples are married. Yet amazingly, despite all of the above, it is said that most satanists do not believe that satan is a literal person!!

(4) The ultimate power for a petition is the "sacrificing" of a virgin as the "living altar" by the coven, especially when done on grounds sacred and dedicated to Christ—such as desecrating a church by using their communion table, etc. Sometimes an animal is used. Remember, satan delights in corrupting that which is pure and holy and set apart for the true God.

C. **Sex in Pantheistic Religions**—An example of sex in worship in this worldview is tantrism. It is of Hindu origin but also practiced by other religions including the New Age Movement. Devotees of some sects use the sexual act for spiritual enlightenment by achieving mystical ecstasy and union with the universal divine consciousness. In tantra, any type of sexual perversion is considered "holy" and is a means of spiritual advancement.[8] Through this union, it is believed that a man obtains an exchange of energy (ch'i) absorbed from the female during intercourse. Some of these Hindu and Buddhist sects also had their temples of sacred harlots. Some yogis, like Yoyogi-San, can bring women to orgasm without touching them through meditation and channeling sexual energy from one person to another.[9]

CAN DEMONS INFLUENCE HUMAN SEXUALITY?

Incubus and succubus are terms used to describe evil spirits (fallen angels) who attempt to have sexual relations with human beings—as preposterous as this may sound. There are some Scriptural grounds for this belief as well. There is also significant historical and modern day personal attestation to this phenomenon— supported by the testimonies of people that recur worldwide who report having experienced seductive sexual advances by spirit beings. Allow me to take you deeper into this subject to establish the possible biblical basis for demonic influence in human sexuality.

Incubus is the term used when these spirits assume a male form; succubus when in a female form. Interestingly, the Latin word *incubo* means nightmare, which is commonly defined as an evil spirit who oppresses people during sleep. Both of these experiences can be characterized by feelings of fear, suffocation, and helplessness, and can be caused by spells and hexes put on people by witches and other sorcerers. In connection with this, people have reportedly experienced things like: an invisible presence in their room, something sitting down next to them on the bed, the sense of being touched on parts of their body, or a weight lying on top of them. However, if the person resists and commands them to leave, they should depart. But if one should participate, one opens a dangerous door for more **demonization** to occur (and even **demon possession**) as the spirit will likely return. Also see **Potions** in index.

There are those like Thomas Aquinas, the Roman Catholic theologian, who believed that it was possible for a demon to appear to a man as a female and then appear to a woman as a male—depositing the male's sperm within her. True or not, people testify that these types of sexual advances occur, and others claim to have ongoing relations with spirit lovers. Some say evil spirits deceptively present themselves as a deceased husband or wife and may carry on the "relationship" for years.

I realize that all this may sound very far out and incredible. But before dismissing this abnormality as a very real possibility, consider the following Scriptures, and if need be, research documented experiences that exist. Many times living here in satan's kingdom, truth is stranger than fiction. Let's begin in the Old Testament book of Genesis prior to the flood:

> † **Genesis 6:1,2,4** (NLT)—*When the human population began to grow rapidly on the earth, **2.** the sons of God saw the beautiful women of the human race and took any they wanted as their wives... **4.** In those days, and even afterward, giants lived on the earth, for whenever the sons of God had intercourse with human women, they gave birth to children who became the heroes mentioned in legends of old.*

> The James Moffatt translation of the Bible renders **Genesis 6:2** and **4** this way: *2. "...the angels noticed that the daughters of men were beautiful... **4.** It was in these days that the Nephilim giants arose on earth, as well as afterwards whenever angels had intercourse with the daughters of men and had children born to them..."*

The term *"sons of God"* here in verses **2** and **4**, is only mentioned three other times in the Old Testament. Each time the term refers to the good angels whom God created **(Job 1:6; 2:1; 38:7)**. These particular angels became fallen angels either at the time of lucifer's original rebellion or sometime during the time period from Adam to the Great Flood. It is believed by some theologians that it was for this sin that they were imprisoned by God in Tartarus **(2 Peter 2:4-5)**; however, satan and other fallen angels were not.

> † **Jude 1:6-7** (GNT)—*Remember the angels who did not stay within the limits of their proper authority, but abandoned their own dwelling place: they are bound with eternal chains in the darkness below, where God is keeping them for that great Day on which they will be condemned. 7. Remember Sodom and Gomorrah, and the nearby towns, whose people acted as those angels did and committed sexual immorality and perversion...*

Among those who held the belief that the *"sons of God"* were fallen angels were the translators of the Septuagint; the Jewish historian Josephus; Philo; some of the earliest Church Fathers such as Justyn Martyr, Tertullian, Cyprian, and Ambrose; Roman Catholics such as Pope Benedict XIV and Pope Innocent VIII, Thomas Aquinas, Bonaventura, Martin Luther, and many others.[10]

If the *"sons of God"* were fallen angels, these questions arise: Did fallen angels have sexual relations with human beings **after** the flood? If so, can it happen in our day? If understood correctly, this is what we know from the Holy Scriptures:

1. That some fallen angels can have sexual relations with the human female. This occurred *"In those days..."* that preceded the great flood **(Genesis 6:4)**.

2. Demons can commit sexual immorality and perversion **(Jude 1:7)**. Evil spirits may somehow arouse sexual cravings in a human being (perhaps when we sense the sexual lust of that demon). Also, the unusual passage in **1 Corinthians 11:10** makes more sense if it applies to this topic.

3. That it is possible for human children to be born from this union **(6:4)** who seem to have monstrous type features (i.e. the Nephilim who became legendary heroes). This union did **not** procreate other evil spirits.

4. That because of this sin, God imprisoned these fallen angels from Noah's day in a compartment in the underworld, called Tartarus, until Judgment Day **(2 Peter 2:4-5; Jude 1:6).** It is uncertain whether this is a second "fall" of good angels from heaven or whether they were demons that fell with lucifer. There also seem to be fallen angels imprisoned in the abyss to be let loosed during the reign of the antichrist in the end times **(Luke 8:31; Revelation 9:1,2,10).**

5. That after the Flood (*"...and also afterward..."* **6:4**) the Nephilum were once again on the earth including the Anakims and the Rephaims **(Numbers 33:31-33; Deuteronomy 9:1-3).** If the Nephilim are the product of evil spirits cohabiting with women, then perhaps the giants Israel found in the Promised Land were once again a result of this union after the flood. If so, this raises the possibility that this type of phenomena could have reoccurred to some degree throughout history up to and including today.

6. In **Luke 20:35-36** and **Mark 12:24-25** Jesus taught that angels cannot die and neither do they marry. Angels also do not have to procreate to perpetuate themselves as humans do, but does this mean that they are sexless? Possibly not. There is no mention of female angels in the Bible.

7. That there is such a thing as a *"spirit of prostitution"* **(Hosea 4:12; 5:4).** This term was used to indicate the source that tempted Israel to commit spiritual adultery by abandoning the true God to serve false gods. This term can also include acts of sexual perversion which were involved in the worship of some of Israel's gods like Baal and Ashtoreth.

HOW PEOPLE INQUIRE OF THEIR GODS

Devotees of false religions or the occult believe in the existence of supernatural beings who can be contacted, and who are willing to respond if petitioned in the proper way. Tragically, people unwittingly contact evil spirits while all along assuming they were contacting the god they had in mind. Thus they were inviting demonic spirits to control their lives and were unaware of the danger. One reason for contacting their god(s) was to acquire future or secret knowledge from them, and mankind has tried every conceivable way. The term for this is *"divination"* or fortune-telling.

📖 DEFINITION—DIVINATION

It is the art of acquiring knowledge of a future or secret nature by forbidden occultic means. Divination is satan's imitation of the true God's gifts of prophetic revelation. It brought the reality of the supernatural to their otherwise empty religious rituals. Here are some ways satan is deceiving his children into trying to obtain guidance and to control their future apart from the true God.

1. **Astrology** (astromancy)—It is the ancient art of divining by the movements of the stars and planets. It teaches that the personality traits, conduct, and events of a person's life are predetermined, and can be known, by the configurations of the sun, moon, and planets as they pass through the 12 constellations of the Zodiac. It is based upon the belief that the deities, who are thought to reside in these heavenly bodies and "houses" among the stars, influence our lives from birth to death—somewhat like the moon influences the earth's tides, or like the gravitational pull of the planets on each other. This notion of the planets and stars having influence over a person's life is consistent in principle with the occult belief in a universal energy that has an interrelationship with all things. Its system is also based upon **reincarnation** and the terribly oppressive belief in **fatalism.**

    Astrologers claim to be able to "read" these astronomical alignments and tell how they relate to every aspect of a person's life. Their task is to interpret the signs and omens in these alignments (called *horoscopes*). It is a complex system consisting of many variables with few standards, and there is disagreement among astrologers about the principles of interpreting the information. When it is accurate, it isn't because it is scientific, etc.—it works because deceptive, evil spirit beings make it work. Astrology is not to be confused with the legitimate science of astronomy which studies the celestial bodies. In fact, the field of science has repudiated the scientific claims of astrology.

Astrology's influence in our world is huge. It has become so mainstream in many cultures. Millions consult their daily horoscope—placing their faith and trust in a religious worldview that often controls them with fear, and compels them to live their lives in obedience to its predictions. In addition, courses on astrology are offered in our schools, it is used within the health professions, and even some governments and corporations employ an astrologer on staff to give guidance. It also provides a foundation upon which other occult practices are built. Astrology has given us the popular term, "New Age," which refers to the coming "Age of Aquarius." This is allegedly the arrival of a new era of spirituality, enlightenment, and humanitarianism—as the mystical Age of Pisces (the fish, or Christianity as some take it to mean), passes off the heavenly scene and history. A new age supposedly happens every 2000 years.

Its <u>dangers</u> <u>include</u>: It is a hook to draw and entrap people into accepting occult philosophy; it acts as a gateway to other occult activities such as the development of psychic powers, and the contacting of "spirit guides," etc. (inviting **demonization**); it relieves one of responsibility for their decisions and undermines one's initiative and planning for the future; it creates fear of the future and causes people to do things that they ordinarily would never do to fulfill or avert what they believe is his or her destiny—even to committing crimes and murder. The Bible denounces its practice in **Deuteronomy 4:19; 17:2-5; 18:10-12; Isaiah 47:13-15.**

2. **Ouija Boards**—Promoted as a harmless entertaining game, it deceptively lures naive people into the occult by giving them a small taste of the supernatural. This "game" arouses their curiosity about the spirit world and draws them into a deeper search after unknown powers. The board contains the words "Yes," "No," the alphabet, and numbers. One consults the Ouija with a question, and then places their fingers on a small heart-shaped stool that rests on the board. The evil spirit has now been invited to guide one's hand so that the pointed end of the stool spells out the answer to their questions. (See **Automatic Writing**.)

3. **Reading Omens** (augury)—The art of interpreting an incident and predicting good or bad fortune from it (like a prophetic sign). An omen can be read into practically anything such as: the way a candle flame flickers (<u>pyromancy</u>) or the way wax melts (<u>ceromancy</u>), the way birds fly (<u>ornithomancy</u>), or the way trees move in the wind. An augur was a religious official in ancient Rome that foretold events in this manner.

4. **Interpreting Numbers** (numerology)—Its basis is the mystical belief that numbers have magical powers and meanings due to their interconnectedness to all things. This universal harmonic relationship theory led to the belief that everything has a numerical relationship. It is expressed by the single numbers of 1-9 which have been assigned certain characteristics and definitions. Alphabetical letters were given one of these numbers. When added up (i.e. one's name, birthday) and reduced to a single number, it would allegedly reveal its influence upon one's life. This system is believed to have originated with Pythagoras in the sixth century B.C.

5. **Palm Reading** (chiromancy)—It is the art of examining the shape, lines, and marks on the human hand for divination purposes. It is also known as <u>palmistry</u>. It claims to be able to reveal one's personality traits and how one's character will evolve over time. It also alleges to disclose one's fate (good and bad) in relationships, traumatic events, sickness, and length of life. Astrological concepts have also been integrated into it.

6. **Reading Cards** (cartomancy)—It is the art of foretelling one's future by interpreting the meaning of symbols, colors, and shapes of playing cards—especially <u>tarot</u> <u>cards</u>. Of obscure origin, tarot cards usually consist of a 78-card deck with each card representing a human life experience or behavior. It is believed that magical powers influence the arrangement of the cards as one shuffles and cuts the deck. Then allegedly, the reader's intuitive skills are needed to interpret the overall meaning of one's cards. A person is then either warned or presented with the probable outcomes of a certain series of events or behaviors— which could be altered by other courses of action.

7. **Dowsing** (rhabdomancy or radiesthesia)—An ancient divinatory art used to locate things by use of a divining rod, a pendulum, a map—almost anything can be used. A person who has this ability is usually consulted to do the locating. These people normally enter a light trance state and after inquiring of the unknown power, these instruments supernaturally react and move their hands to indicate the location of the object being sought. Dowsing for water ("water witching") by using a rod made from specific trees is the most familiar to us. Other things include finding mines, precious metals and stones, oil, natural gas, and underground lines. In fact, utility and other companies employ dowsers. It is also used for locating objects and people, as well as for medical diagnosis. It is said that when this external force reacts to the object, it can be felt so powerfully in the diviner's hands that it can be beyond his ability to control it.

This power is believed by some to have a rational scientific basis (i.e. the detection of energies and magnetic force fields in the earth). Others see it as a learned aptitude or as a natural or psychic ability (i.e. bioenergy or mind power). Pantheists view it as a universal energy or intelligence (the "god within you"). But this power is not impersonal. It is personal and intelligent and desires to be contacted. The possibility that it could be demonic is scoffed at. The fact that "it works" usually overshadows any concern for what the source is that makes it work. Most dowsers and onlookers may consider it a divine gift. However, it has failed the scrutiny of scientific testing. As it gains more favor within the New Age Movement, attempts are being made to remove its occult stigma and make it more socially acceptable.

Its <u>dangers</u> <u>include</u>: development of occult powers; conversion to the occult; and the general spiritual, mental, and physical oppression and ailments that come with occult involvement. Make no mistake, this power and the ability to dowse comes from demonic spirits—not the person, the instrument, energy fields, or anything else for that matter. God has denounced this practice under the general prohibition of divination as well as in **Hosea 4:12:** *"My people consult their wooden idol, and their diviner's wand informs them; For a spirit of harlotry has led them astray and they have played the harlot, departing from their God."* Also related to dowsing are radionics, **psychometry,** and the ancient practice of divination by arrows known as <u>belomancy</u>. (See **Ezekiel 21:21-22.**)

8. **Psychometry**—Related to dowsing, this is the superhuman ability to divine information about someone through contact with an object that a person used or had in their possession. It is based, in part, upon the belief that events impress themselves upon inanimate objects at hand. For example, the "picture" of a murder that takes place in a room is captured (witnessed) by that room and the objects within it. This allegedly leaves an indelible trace of itself in history, which can be tapped into for information. This occult practice is also used at times to solve crimes and diagnose illnesses.

9. **Reading Tea Leaves** (tasseomancy)—It is the art of foretelling one's future by interpreting the shapes of the residue of tea leaves at the bottom of a cup. Some see a resemblance between the oval shape of the cup and the tea leaves with the dome of the heavens and the stars. The tasseomancer will usually involve their client in the process of making and drinking the tea. It is believed that one's contact with the cup influences the pattern of the leaves and is critical to the personalization and accuracy of the reading.

10. **Reading Internal Organs** (haruspicy)—It is the art of inspecting the internal organs of animals in order to interpret messages from their gods for courses of action. It was derived from an earlier form of fortune-telling popular among the Babylonians called <u>hepatoscopy</u>, which was the inspection of the liver of animals (see **Ezekiel 21:21-22**). It was believed that the god to whom the animal was sacrificed revealed his will through the way the liver was molded. A haruspex (one who reads the entrails) was included on military staffs so he could consult the gods on military strategies as well as in the midst of battle (like the Roman augers). The entrails of human beings were also inspected (<u>anthropomancy</u>).

11. **Lots** (sortilege)—It was a means to obtain guidance for decisions. In the occult, it was used to obtain guidance by blind chance—believing that a higher power would ensure that the right answer comes forth. Lots were objects that took different forms and were used in various ways such as: words formed from pouring out contents of a container on a surface of alphabetical letters; or drawing out of a container; or the casting of dice. Divination by lot was a method used in the Sibylline oracles in Roman times.

Perhaps to our surprise, the God of the Bible permitted the use of lots under the Mosaic Law. It was to be used exclusively by the priests (not by the lay people) to obtain divine guidance. God commanded its use in: the selection of the sin offering to make atonement for the priest and his family **(Leviticus 16:7-10)**; the dividing up of the land of Canaan for the 12 tribes **(Numbers 26:52-56; Joshua 18:1-19:51)**; God permitted its use in the detection of a party at fault **(1 Samuel 14:41;** see also **Jonah 1:7)**; and the selection of an apostle to replace Judas Iscariot **(Acts 1:26)**—though the apostle Paul was really God's choice. Also see **Proverbs 16:33.**

God also instituted the Urim and Thummim for divine guidance for the priests in the Old Testament **(Numbers 27:21; Ezra 2:63)**; however, its use is little understood. One view was that one or more of the 12 stones in the High Priests' breastpiece (representing the 12 tribes of Israel) were supernaturally illuminated in some way **(Exodus 28:15-28)**. It was called the *"breastpiece of decision"* **(Exodus 28:29-30; Leviticus 8:8)**. The generally held view was that they were two sacred lots—one a positive indicator and one a negative (i.e. "yes" and "no"). You may ask what made these legitimate and the occultic form wrong? Simply that the former was instituted and permitted by God under specific instructions, and the answers were sought from the true God. The latter sought another source—demonic power.

However, since the Holy Spirit was given on the Day of Pentecost, divine guidance by lot has become obsolete. No longer just the prerogative of a few priests, Christ has made it possible for all His children to be guided by the Holy Spirit. This occurs through his Word, His witness within our spirit (i.e. a peace or lack of it), and through some of the nine gifts of the Spirit in **1 Corinthians 12:7-11. Dreams** and **visions** round out the God-ordained guidance that He has provided in the New Testament **(Acts 2:16-18).**

12. **By Consulting a Book** (stichomancy)—This is one of the oldest forms of divination. It is when a person opens up a randomly selected book to a randomly selected page to find an answer to their question or problem. A well-known example of this is I Ching in which the ancient Chinese *Book of Changes* is consulted. Related to this is the opening of certain books (especially "holy books" including the Bible) and embracing the first passage one sees as the answer (bibliomancy). The I Ching is one of the *Five Classics*, the fundamental books of Confucianism, and based on the Taoist philosophy of Yin (the passive or feminine force) and Yang (the active or masculine force). It is believed to be the oldest intuitive decision-making system. It allegedly gives a snapshot of what is presently happening in one's life and also reveals probable options that can affect one's future—which are not predetermined. When "casting" the I Ching, six lines are formed (called a "hexagram") which represents a particular kind of human characteristic or situation. It is then looked up in the *Book of Changes* which describes the meaning of the lines. The way the lines are cast is believed to reflect the state of a person's mind at the moment they cast the reading, and is based upon the pantheistic belief that all things are interconnected.

13. **Clairvoyance**—Reemerging in the late 1700s, it is the superhuman ability to know or see things apart from the use of our normal human senses. These visual perceptions can occur spontaneously and unexpectedly, or be induced via altered states of consciousness. This experience normally takes place in the waking state in the form of a vision. Clairvoyants have amazed others by "reading" the contents within a sealed envelope, relating personal details of one's life and character, and even diagnosing sickness in one's body. Some have predicted certain events before they occurred. Others have allegedly received their "sacred scriptures" thinking they were supernatural revelations from "God". Clairaudience is a similar experience. People allegedly hear things inaudible to the human ear such as voices from the spirit world, including messages from departed loved ones. Beware of consulting a psychic! The source of this activity is demonic spirits, not a "gift" from the true God.

Clairvoyance and clairaudience are one of satan's counterfeits of the true God's gift of **prophecy** and **visions**. The God of the Bible calls them false prophets for two reasons. First the source is false (it is not originating from the true God) even though the information given may be accurate and may have actually come to pass. Second, some claim to speak for the true God. However, God did not send them nor give them the authority to do so; therefore, the content of their message was false. Throughout history, this prophetic "office" has had its counterpart in practically all false religions and the occult.

A. **Prophecy**—Prophecy and visions are legitimate ways in which the true God speaks to His people today. In both Old and New Testaments, the God of the Bible has chosen to give messages to His children through the mouth of a prophet (or seer). The word, prophecy, not only means to foretell but to "forth tell"—or to speak forth a message from God. At least four of the nine gifts of the Holy Spirit in **1 Corinthians 12** incorporate this principle. This prophetic word is communicated to a person's spirit under the divine inspiration of the Holy Spirit. The content of the message is imparted into their mind and spirit supernaturally, which cannot be known or learned through human effort or experience **(1 Kings 6:12)**. The message is then delivered to God's people either in written form or orally. For example, the writers of the books of the Bible received God's words in this manner (not through **automatic writing** as in the occult). Its words were God-breathed as *"holy men of God spake as they were moved by the Holy Ghost"* **(2 Peter 1:21)**—using each person's own vocabulary, styles, etc. In **1 Chronicles 28:11-19**, David received detailed plans of the temple from the Holy Spirit. When given orally, it is a spontaneous, divinely inspired, ecstatic utterance by the Holy Spirit using that person's vocabulary and voice.

B. **Visions**—These are messages received from the true God while in the waking state but through an altered state of consciousness. In the Old Testament, God gave His messages to His people Israel through prophets who sometimes received them by a vision (i.e. **Ezekiel 1:1; Zechariah 1:7-8)**. This was also a way God said that He would use to speak to His people during the church age **(Acts 2:14-18)**. The following people received visions from God in the New Testament—usually at critical times in the plan of God: Ananias **(Acts 9:10-16)**; Cornelius **(Acts 10:1-6)**; Peter **(Acts 10:9-20; 11:4-5)**; the apostle Paul **(Acts 16:9-10; 18:9-11; 22:17-18)**, and the Apostle John **(Revelation 1:10-11)**.

DIVINATION BY ALTERED STATES OF CONSCIOUSNESS

† **Acts 16:16-23**—*Once when we were going to the place of prayer, we were met by a slave girl who had a spirit by which she predicted the future. She earned a great deal of money for her owners by fortunetelling.*

This subsection will cover areas of the occult where altered states of consciousness (ASC) are induced in order to acquire forbidden knowledge or power from sources on the "other side." It normally involves some degree of **demon possession**. One purpose for ASCs is to remove out of the way the "hindrance" of the conscious mind in order to make one more susceptible to the spirit world. These altered or trance-like mental states can be induced by hypnosis, drugs, alcohol, incense, music or dancing, natural gases, fumes, etc., and even voluntarily at will. Here are some of the ways:

14. **Hypnotism**—It is a term used for an abnormal state of consciousness that, when artificially induced, manifests various degrees of the sleep state. In this state, one's subconscious becomes very susceptible to the power of suggestion which directs the body in a physical or mental action. There are three levels— from light (mental relaxation) to the deepest (hypnotic trance). During the third level, one is said to be insensible to pain and there is no remembrance of what took place in the trance when the person returns to the waking state. No one knows how hypnosis works, and the general population varies in their degree of susceptibility to it.

Though an integral part of the occult from antiquity, the 16th century resurgence of hypnotic phenomenon was studied by science and they attributed to it a type of magnetism. They theorized that the celestial bodies radiate a magnetic influence, or fluid, on the earth; therefore, it must affect human health. In the 1770s, Franz Anton Mesmer named it *"animal magnetism,"* hence the term *"mesmerize."* He and other "magnetists" were successful in applying this "medical breakthrough" to their patients. They healed bodily diseases through their belief in the laws of magnetic attraction. This led to the "discovery" of *somnambulism*—the conscious state we now know and call the hypnotic trance.

This laid the foundation for the spiritualist movement that began in 1848. It enabled the medium at a séance to go into a trance-like state and allegedly call up "spirits of the dead" to speak through them. In fact, much of the strange phenomenon that occurs when a medium goes into a trance state can also occur in a hypnotic state (see **Spiritualism**). Somnambulism and spiritualism were identified with each other until the 1840s when Dr. James Braid declared that the healing force was not magnetic, but psychic. He was instrumental in establishing "hypnotism" as a new "science" where it gained medical and psychological status. Eventually it was no longer associated with the occult.

Today, hypnotism has become increasingly accepted and hailed by the medical and educational community as a legitimate tool in treating disorders such as weight loss, addictions, learning disorders, relieving pain, and curing sickness. The use of hypnotherapy, including hypnotic regression, is being used to find the causes for: a person's phobias, bad habits, childhood problems, multiple personality disorders, past-life therapy, repressed memory therapy, alleged UFO abductions, etc. in order to resolve their present problems. It also deceptively lures people to gain information by getting in touch with that wiser, deeper part of themselves (sometimes through self-hypnosis). It can also be used for divination purposes like medical diagnosis, finding lost items, or solving crimes.

The enemy has also infiltrated the medical profession in the disguise of hypnotism—luring unsuspecting people by claiming to cure or help their problems. How can the use of hypnosis be acceptable in the medical profession when its use is clearly wrong when used in occult circles? Who is determining the boundary between medicine and the occult? Other dangers include: problems associated with returning to the waking state; one permits their mind to be controlled by the suggestions of another—giving the hypnotist great power over them, even abuse; one can be manipulated to do something against one's will; it can be a gateway to becoming a medium or psychic; you invite, and leave yourself vulnerably exposed to, **demonization** and/or **demon possession**. Hypnosis may fall into the category of *"enchanters"* or *"charmers"* in the Bible—a forbidden practice. **Never agree to allow anyone or anything to put you into a passive state of mind—especially hypnosis!**

15. **Necromancy**—It is divination by consulting people who have died. (See **Leviticus 19:31; 20:6; Deuteronomy 18:11; Isaiah 19:3; 8:19.**) This ancient practice is done through a "medium" who becomes the link between the departed person and the living. Through the medium, messages from the spirit world are given to those consulting them (see **Spiritualism** and **Demon Possession** in index). The modern term for this is **channeling** (see below) which also includes contacting spirit entities who have not been human.

📖 DEFINITION—Familiar Spirit

It is called *"familiar"* because this spirit was familiar to the person or family when it was called up from the spirit world by a medium to be consulted. When this demonic spirit possesses the body of the medium, both the medium and the family believe that he or she is the deceased person when, in reality, it is an evil spirit deceiving them. The spirit would continue to be the *"familiar"* of this "divinely bestowed gift" to the next generation of that family.

📖 DEFINITION—Wizard

This is the biblical term that is more often associated with a medium who consults the dead. It means a "knowing or wise one." The medium received this extraordinary intelligence from the evil spirit who spoke through them—impersonating the spirits of the departed. Today, a wizard is thought of as a sorcerer having magical powers.

A. **Spiritualism**—The revival of necromancy in modern times began around the 1800s with what is known as spiritualism (spiritism is similar). It was based on the belief that there is life after death and that it is possible to communicate with the dead through a "medium." This person acts as a mouthpiece to relay information from the "deceased." The information they give supposedly reveals the knowledge that the deceased has acquired since their death, and also of the future. This normally takes place in a <u>séance</u> which is a sitting held for this purpose; These disembodied spirits claim to be departed ancestors; loved ones; famous people; spirit guides, and other types of imposters impersonated by evil spirits. During the séance, these spirits can also produce certain superhuman phenomena that defy known physical laws. Obviously, the phony exists as well. But when it is real, these phenomena can manifest themselves in the following ways:

(1) **Telekinetic Events** occur such as: levitation of furniture and human beings; movement of draperies, etc. and objects about the room; auditory phenomenon such as rapping, music (with or without instruments), voices, and general noises.

(2) **Apports** is the name given to objects that materialize during the séance. Tangible items like flowers, fruit, jewelry, perfume, and even animals are said to magically appear and disappear and even seem to pass through closed doors and windows, etc. Physiological wonders such as: breezes blowing in a closed-up room; the feeling of someone touching, hitting, or caressing you; written messages or answers to questions by spirits; healing of sicknesses; immunity from being burned by fire. <u>Stigmatic</u> <u>wounds</u> can appear on the medium. These are bleeding marks resembling the wounds suffered by Christ when He was crucified (religious statues have also been known to ooze blood). There are also <u>ectoplasmic</u> phenomena that come out of the medium's body that have been photographed.

(3) **Xenoglossy** is a term meaning to speak in a language that a person had never learned or spoken before. There have been reports of recognizable foreign languages being spoken fluently by the medium. Even sitters from other countries would converse with a spirit through a medium in their native tongue. These languages also come forth in a different voice other than the medium's (some with accents).

Note: This is satan's counterfeit of the true God's genuine Gift of Languages as given by the Holy Spirit **(1 Corinthians 12:10)**. It's the ability given by the Holy Spirit to speak in a language unknown to the person for ministry purposes as on the Day of Pentecost **(Acts 2:1-11)**. It also includes the interpretation of those "tongues" in the language of the hearers.

(4) **Materialization**—This is the ultimate phenomenon that can occur in a séance. It is the appearance of the "person" (either parts of their body or full materialization). The spirit can be visibly seen and even touched and conversed with. These demonic spirits inhabit "<u>haunted houses</u>" under the guise of a person who was reportedly killed there, etc. and are also known as apparitions, specters, and ghosts. Those who make loud sounds such as rapping, knocking, scratching, etc., are called <u>poltergeists</u> (German for "noisy ghosts") and phenomena, like that at a séance, accompany them. There are hundreds of haunted houses throughout the world. Two of America's well-known are Winchester Mystery House in San Jose, California and Myrtles Plantation in St. Francisville, Louisiana (see **Psychokinesis** in index).

▶**CONSIDER THIS:** All of the above phenomena, when not done fraudulently, are done by the power of evil spirits. And if these types of manifestations can take place in a séance, they can also be reproduced at other times and places. These lying spirits who have observed deceased loved ones and friends now impersonate them as they are called up during a séance. These spirits exploit and play on the sympathy and heartache of those who lost dear ones in order to deceive them.

A person should not be amazed, for example, that a medium is able to tell them their mother's name and describe her perfectly to them. Accurate information or demonstrations of power should never be accepted as "proof" that the experience is genuinely "of God." The Bible condemns necromancy and teaches that when we leave our bodies at death, our soul and spirit go directly to heaven or hell **(Luke 16:22-23; 2 Corinthians 5:6-8).** They do not roam the earth or appear to former loved ones and friends. Neither do evil spirits have the power to bring them forth as in a séance. Beware of this insidious deception and trap.

God has, however, made some exceptions to this in history such as: the appearance of Moses and Elijah on the Mount of Transfiguration who talked to Jesus about His death in Jerusalem **(Luke 9:28-36)**; the resurrected Old Testament believers who appeared to many as proof of Christ's resurrection **(Matthew 27:52-53)**; and Samuel whom God sent to Saul when he consulted the medium at Endor **(1 Samuel 28:3-21)**. In Samuel's case, God Himself (not the medium or an impersonating evil spirit) brought Samuel back to pronounce judgment on Saul. One should not take these isolated incidents as a license to contact the dead. They do not override God's prohibition of necromancy which was punishable by death and the rejection of that soul by God **(Leviticus 20:6, 27)**. The incident of King Saul resorting to the occult for guidance instead of waiting and pressing into the true God should be a solemn warning to us all **(1 Chronicles 10:13-14)**.

B. **Channeling**—Like a medium in a séance, the channeler allows a spirit entity to use their body's faculties to communicate superhuman knowledge through them (see **Necromancy, Spiritualism,** and **Demon Possession** in index). Allegedly, this information can consist of counsel, lectures, diagnosis, or other knowledge obtained from a "higher intelligence." They also perform demonstrations of power like "healings" (see **Healing, in the Occult** in index). While in a state of possession, the channeler can communicate these messages to others through handwriting, discourses, singing, etc. (see **Automatic Writing** in index). Sometimes advice is given via the channeler to kill themselves or someone. Whatever the message these spirits give, you can be sure it will contradict the Bible's teachings.

At times possession occurs when the spirit wants to—not just when the channeler is prepared for it and invites him. The degree of their trance state can range from full to partial. Usually while in full possession, the medium normally remembers nothing of what took place when they return to normal consciousness, whereas in a partial, some things are retained.

These "spirit guides" often reappear to the person and become a companion (see **Familiar Spirit** in index). Spirit guides claim to be anyone from deceased human beings, doctors, and ascended masters, to nature spirits, ancient deities, extraterrestrials, angels, and anything else one could imagine. What is absolutely incredible is that the channeler gives total blind faith and trust to these guides. In fact, it seems that the possibility of these spirits being malevolent is unthinkable to some and is totally dismissed by most. Evil spirits will do anything to gain one's trust in order to deceive them and to destroy them in the end. As with other kinds of occult involvement, many experience tragic endings to their lives. Amazingly, it has become socially acceptable to be "possessed" by these spirits today. Imagine the deceptive power satan has to dupe us into <u>wanting</u> to be possessed and making it a <u>popular</u> thing to do in society![11] (For more information visit www.johnankerberg.com.)

† **Isaiah 8:19-20**—*When men tell you to consult mediums and spiritists, who whisper and mutter, should not a people inquire of their God? Why consult the dead on behalf of the living? 20. To the law and to the testimony! If they do not speak according to this word, they have no light...*

(1) **Contacting Angels**—This is an outgrowth of channeling and is also popular in the New Age Movement. The Bible teaches the existence of good angels—that they are created, spirit beings that serve and worship the true God. They supernaturally intervene in the affairs of mankind only <u>under</u> <u>God's</u> <u>directive</u>. In the Bible, angels have appeared to humans and have even conversed with them. The Scriptures also teach that people are assigned guardian angels (especially God's children and those who will become Christians **Psalm 91:11; Hebrews 1:14; Matthew 18:10**).

Satan has masterfully taken these truths one step further by cunningly prodding us to communicate with angels, which is forbidden. Some Christian churches encourage its people to pray to their guardian angel for guidance and answers to prayer. If so, then the next logical steps one may take are to try to converse with him, and even dispatch angels to do something, which is reserved for God alone. It's all very subtle. At some point, demonic spirits can enter the scene and actually be the source of the thoughts or the voices. Ultimately, it can lead to worshiping angels which is also forbidden. The devil also propagates the belief that human beings become angels after they die.

† **Colossians 2:18** (NLT)—*...And don't let anyone say you must worship angels, even though they say they have had visions about this...*

The Bible tells us that satan *"...disguises himself as an angel of light"* (**2 Corinthians 11:14** NASB). There have been many false religions started through angelic visitations or revelations. Examples are: the angel "Moroni" who revealed himself to Joseph Smith, the founder of Mormonism, and through whose instrumentality the *Book of Mormon* was given; Mohammed, the founder of Islam; and Swedenborgianism to name a few.

† **Galatians 1:8** (NLT)—*...Even if an angel comes from heaven and preaches any other message, let him be forever cursed.*

16. **Parapsychology**—This is the "scientific" study of occult phenomena—though not necessarily divinatory. It originated in the mid-1800s in the attempt to investigate and record spiritistic and psychic phenomena occurring within Spiritualism. Since then it has tried to make the study of the occult appear respectable under the guise of a psychic science. It has even infiltrated the church and taken on a Christian facade. Parapsychology has played a significant role in preparing the world for the revival of the occult that we see in our day. It strongly advocates that mankind has a latent, untapped power residing within him. Its worldview is generally pantheistic. Parapsychology holds to the belief that an impersonal universal divine energy unites nature and humanity to the cosmos—similar to other Eastern religious beliefs like **reincarnation.**

Others hold the view that since man has already observed and measured invisible "energies" in the vast cosmos (i.e. radio waves, electricity, magnetism, etc); therefore, it is assumed that there surely exists the possibility of yet many undiscovered natural energies that mankind could harness and use. Proponents raise this question: "Why must everything we don't have an explanation for have to be attributed to the Christian devil?"

Whether one adheres to the universal energy theory or the possibility of new natural energies, the belief is held that this power is either an innate part of man's nature or separate and distinct from him. Regardless of the viewpoint, people attempt to develop and direct this energy from both within and outside of themselves. After all, they reason, aren't we an electromagnetic being combined with matter that is linked to the earth and universe? Doesn't our mind emit "brain waves," and couldn't they penetrate things outside of our bodies? Couldn't our thoughts be magnetic emanations? Surely, they reason, these innate natural abilities are a gift from God waiting to be discovered and cultivated.

Through various techniques, we are encouraged to get in touch with this invisible force. We are taught to tap into it, contact it, and direct and release its power to another person or thing (like from doctor to patient, etc.)—or to receive the same from others (telepathic messages, etc.). This energy can even come into them from an outside source. It is referred to by many names such as: one's "higher Self," psychic abilities, mental powers, one's "inner or divine potential," Psi energy, ESP, intuition, soul power, odic force, bioenergy, animal magnetism, orgone, psychotronic energy, the kundalini, and others (see **Pantheism**).

Still others hold to the belief in the existence of spirit entities such as: deceased human beings who have evolved to a higher level through **reincarnation,** etc.; nature spirits; aliens from outer space; angels; and practically anything else one can imagine. These allegedly desire to contact us from the "other side," or we wish to contact them. Connection is normally made through spirit possession (see **Channeling** in index) which is very popular in the New Age Movement.

Together with **evolution,** the beliefs in **pantheism** (universal energy) and **reincarnation** are three of the greatest deceptions ever to come from the "pit of hell." Satan is truly the master of deceit. These beliefs are unsupported by Scripture. According to the Bible, mankind has no latent superhuman power residing in him. Any supernatural power that interacts with man comes either from the God of the Bible or angels (good or fallen). Neither are we born with a divine nature. What some religions call divinity within, God calls depravity. The devil's appeal to man is to *"be like God"* and we take that bait much of the time.

A. **Telepathy**—It's the psychic ability to send one's thoughts to someone and receive or read the thoughts of another (living or dead)—irrespective of distance (even from outer space). Its common term is ESP (extra sensory perception) or the ability to know things beyond our five senses. There have been many theories given as to how this phenomenon occurs (i.e. an astral influence, brain waves, etc). This is a playground for evil spirits. Because telepathy can, in part, seem to be satisfactorily explained by scientific means, it becomes attractive to those who do not believe in the supernatural. Telepathic communication does not usually involve telling the future. Telepathy is not to be confused with the intuitive discernment God created us with—like the times when our human spirit comes in close contact with another human spirit and we intuitively sense their mood or disposition. Or when we can sense the presence of evil in a particular place or while a person speaks. This also does not apply to any gift or sovereign act of the Holy Spirit.

B. **Psychokinesis** (telekinesis)—It's the psychic ability to move inanimate objects apart from any human strength or intervention or known natural laws—presumably through mind power alone. Examples are: bending spoons and forks, moving objects, levitating objects or a human body, etc. These can be real "demon-strations" (not illusions) done through people who have this "gift." In its wider sense, it includes other telekinetic phenomena that occur with or without a person being involved and are more associated with séances and poltergeist activity in haunted houses. These include: the lifting of heavy furniture and pianos off the ground and moved throughout the room as if under the control of an intelligent force; the shaking and vibrating of walls, floors, etc; candle flames being extinguished; the electricity going out; musical instruments being played; objects (solid and liquid) that vanish and reappear; unexplained noises; and more. Many theories exist as to how these phenomena occur, but in the final analysis, demonic spirits cause it and give it its reality.

17. **Automatic Writing**—This is when spiritual forces write messages through a person without their conscious self in control. AW can occur in both a trance state and in a waking state. It's a common feature that happens to a medium during a séance, but not limited to that. The end product ranges from: unintelligible and meaningless babble to highly intellectual content. This includes words written in mirrored effect or in reverse order, in different languages, and the whereabouts of lost articles. Whole books and poems have been written by people while in a semi-trance state and under control of an evil spirit. They are then published for the public to read. Even religious teachings with biblical themes have been written—some being accepted as divinely inspired (see **Clairvoyance** in index). The Ouija Board and planchette can be forms of automatic writing. This automatic phenomenon can also extend to artistic expression such as drawing, painting, and sketching (also with biblical themes). Some were done in total darkness or even when blindfolded. Finally, dictations, singing, and even the playing of musical instruments during a trance have reportedly occurred. Once again, this is another example of demonic activity.

Note: A comment is in order regarding the type of inspiration that an artist, writer, musician, etc. receives. It could come naturally from within themselves, from God, or an evil spirit. However, the automatism outlined above involves some degree of demonic possession and is different from just receiving impressions and thoughts from the spirit world. The Holy Spirit used the faculties of man to write the Bible, but not with automatism. (See **Prophecy** in index.)

18. **Oracles**—This is a religious site dedicated to the worship of a god who gives oral, prophetic messages through a human channel to people who consult him or her for guidance. These oracles existed in civilizations as far back as ancient Egypt, Babylon, and right up through today like in Africa and Tibet. The oracles in ancient Greece and Rome were especially well known such as Apollo's oracles at Delphi, Colophon, Clarus, and Didyma; Zeus' at Dodona, and the oracle of Jupiter at Trophonius, to name a few. The Greek and Roman oracles lasted until the third or fourth century A.D. At the oracle, the medium receives inspired messages from their god through: a trancelike state induced by hypnosis, drugs, natural gases, incense, etc.; through dreams; clairvoyantly; by some type of divination they performed; or by outright demon possession. Devotees received a mixture of real and false responses to questions pertaining to their religious, public, and private lives. Government officials would inquire about political and military affairs. A person believed that by obeying the god's message, they would ensure success and avoid misfortune.

19. **Dreams** (oneiromancy)—Dreams are a legitimate way that the God of the Bible uses to communicate to mankind—both those in right relationship with Him and those who are not. In the Bible, whenever an interpretation was needed, it was given to someone by the Holy Spirit (**Genesis 20:1-9; 37:5-11; 42:1-9; 40:1-22; 41:1-57; Daniel 2:1-47; 4:1-37; 7:1ff; Matthew 1:18-20; 2:11-13, 19, 22**). When God gave the dream, no one in satan's camp could provide the interpretation. Since the outpouring of the Holy Spirit on the Day of Pentecost and throughout this church age, God has promised that one of the ways he would communicate with His people was through dreams (received in the sleep state) and **visions** (received in the waking state). See **Acts 2:14-18.**

Satan has once again imitated another gift of God and he uses it in his religious systems with convincing results, mainly because he is the giver of the information. In the occult, there are those who are "gifted" with interpreting dreams in order to reveal information, guidance, or foretell someone's future. People claim to have received from dreams: solutions to problems, musical pieces, and revelations of the location of dead bodies and lost objects. Information received from a dream has even started new false religions. Some induce sleep through the use of drugs. According to the ancient historian Herodotus, in Babylon's temple of Bel, a priestess would deliberately induce sleep in order to receive a dream that would divine the future.[12] Today the use of dreams for occult purposes are a popular New Age practice.

20. **Crystal Gazing** (crystalomancy)—It's obtaining secret knowledge with the aid of transparent objects such as a crystal ball, a pool of water, or other types of shiny surfaces. It is a form of clairvoyance. Scrying is another term for it, and hydromancy is related. This is one of the main ways Nostradamus received his visions that are still being published today. Normally, the goal is for the "reader" to be induced into a hypnotic state so they may see visions in the object. Sometimes a milky clouding of the surface signals its start. There are reported cases of this type of divination having been successfully used in solving crimes and recovering lost or stolen property. It should not be looked upon as harmless, amusing psychic entertainment. It is a dangerous trap to hook one into the occult.

21. **Occult Healing**—Can healing occur from a source other than from the true God? First, nowhere does the Bible indicate that man has the innate power within himself to heal someone's sickness and disease or to perform other supernatural feats. This power must come from an outside source. The Bible contains many instances where the true God healed people in the Old and New Testaments. Due to Jesus' death on the cross and His resurrection, the price for our healing has been purchased and is available to all people through Him. Jesus said that greater miracles would be done by His followers after Him during this church age because of the outpouring of the Holy Spirit (**John 14:12**). Now all true followers of Christ can, through the power of His Holy Spirit, *"...lay hands on the sick, and they shall recover"* (**Mark 16:18** KJV). Perhaps angels can also heal by God's directive.

There is also a Scriptural basis for satan using his power and deception to heal. In Revelation chapter thirteen, the Bible foretells a future day when satan will empower the Antichrist (*"the beast"*). At that time, one of the *"heads"* of the beast which *"seemed to have a fatal wound...the fatal wound had been healed"*—through satanic power or simulation (**Revelation 13:1-4, 11-14**).

The God of the Bible desires that His power would be made manifest among His people. However, due to a lack of faith and appropriation of God's gifts, an often lifeless, powerless church has driven away many into the waiting hands of the devil where he is eager to demonstrate his power and meet their needs. His goal is to make people unbelievers in the true God, and believers in his counterfeits. Satan imitates the true God's *"gifts of healings"* (**1 Corinthians 12:9**) through occult healing, and has deceived countless people with his healing power in every primitive and modern culture.

The following is a brief overview of the phenomena of occult healing: Generally, this healing can occur within the framework of any occult practice. In fact, some kind of occult belief and practice will accompany it and this should tip you off as to its demonic source. Also keep in mind that the Scriptures tell us that satan can be the cause of some illnesses (**Job 2:6-7; Luke 13:11**). Perhaps in some cases he heals by releasing the cause of the illness to simulate healing. Regardless, these cures defy explanation by the medical community. We should not be concerned with the details of how it occurs but that it occurs. Let us be concerned with discerning the source of the healing (God or satan), and not allowing occult cures to take place in our bodies.

Like the true God, satan and his evil spirits search the masses to find a suitable person that he can select and prepare for any occult practice. Recruitment starts at an early age. This is especially true of children whose parents are involved in the occult. Regardless of age, the person chosen may begin seeing pictures clairvoyantly like scenes of hurting people pleading for help. Some may experience visitations from "deceased doctors," etc. Some children may see an invisible playmate. Whatever the means, they are being targeted and called into the devil's service. The devil will even resort to coercive means to force them into service until the person acquiesces. Such was the case, I believe, with Arigo, the famous Brazilian peasant turned psychic healer in the mid-1900s. He experienced disturbing, reoccurring dreams and voices. They were accompanied by terrible headaches, blackouts, and hallucinations which stopped when Arigo accepted his "calling" (and reoccurred when he quit for a brief time).[13]

There have been psychic healers and surgeons whose strange, incredible "medical practice" have been observed, confirmed, and documented by the modern medical community. Arigo was one of them, and he was one of the most thoroughly researched. It has been estimated that he treated an average of 300 people a day for nearly 20 years (1950-1970). Out of total desperation, people from all walks of life and from all over the world flocked to him for help—having been given up as hopeless by leading physicians etc.[14]

Generally speaking, these phenomena can occur while the healer is under the spirit's influence:

A. The healer enters a trance-like state as the spirit of the alleged deceased doctor, surgeon, medicine man, psychiatrist, etc. (from various countries and languages), takes possession of his body. There may even be a "team of medical specialists" present. These often claim to have obtained a higher knowledge and skill since their death that they now want to "share" with humanity. The spirit(s) performs surgery through the healer, reveals things to him, and speaks through him in a voice not his own.

B. For some healers, the length of time it takes for surgery is up to a few minutes per person (as in the case of Arigo).[15] When "performing surgery," the healer usually takes a non-sterilized instrument, like a knife, and cuts or plunges it into the problem area of a person's body while they are awake. Or their hand becomes the instrument used that seems to disappear into the patient's body. No anesthesia is used, there is no pain, no blood loss (or it's minimal), no sutures, no scars, and no post-operative effects. These phenomena have been seen by eyewitnesses and even photographed and filmed. Tumors and growths have even been extracted from a person's body and sent to labs for evaluation.[16]

C. Generally, psychic healers claim to "operate" on a person's etheric body (or aura) instead of directly on their physical body. Why doesn't the patient feel pain? Some believe that this is an unknown life energy that acts as a repelling force, like magnets, between the cutting instrument and the tissues which prevents it from touching them—and may actually do the cutting.[17]

D. There are also various methods of healing used by the healer: by moving their hand over a person's body; by the laying on of hands; through various pendulum or pyramidal practices; through stones or plants, etc. How permanent are these healings? It varies. For some it is temporary, and others may eventually get the illness back or end up in a worse state. Don't expect compassion from the devil.

E. There can be a high percentage of accuracy in the psychic healer's ability to diagnose ailments (while in a trance). This has been confirmed by medical doctors. Another example is Edgar Cayce. He would routinely go into a trance and, speaking in a voice not his own, would give detailed medical diagnosis. He gave over 15,000 readings. Prescriptions were also written out with great speed that had no rational medical basis to them—and patients "miraculously" recovered (see **Automatic Writing** in index). It is also alleged by some that illness affects the color of one's aura and that the illness can be diagnosed by this color change. When the healer comes out of his trance (i.e. when the demon leaves them), they normally don't remember anything that had taken place.

F.   They also claim to be able to heal or diagnose illnesses over great distances (via radio, television, or telephone). A healer's "magnetism" has also been known to be transferred to an object like a piece of cloth and taken to a sick person and they are healed—imitating a method God used in the Bible (**Acts 19:11-12**). See **Psychometry** in index.

It is not uncommon for these healers to view themselves as God's chosen instrument, to channel his healing power as a gift to those in need. For various reasons, most healers never charge for their services. Some even believe it is Jesus working through them; however, none are sure what this power is or where it comes from. But it is very real! As with others in the occult, some healers call it a higher intelligence, a cosmic force, a divine energy, a life force, a magnetic current, etc. Most healers can feel this power come into them and work through them.

It is also not unusual for the healer (like Arigo) to have Christian religious symbols in their "operating room" such as: a picture of Christ or the Virgin Mary, a crucifix on the wall, an open Bible on a table, and even the reciting of prayers before or after treatment.[18] They even endure long periods of fasting.

There are churches and organizations whose business name sounds like the entity is Christian, but in fact are not. They may use the right Christian lingo, but blindly they perform healing through occultic means and claim it is from the true God. In America, it is illegal to prescribe medication without a license; therefore, many healers obtain a clergy license and establish themselves under the protective covering of a church and thereby escape legal entanglements. As a result, many Christians become deceived. Ministers, priests, and nuns are also known to visit psychic healers for help. In fact, in some countries with large Catholic or Protestant populations, churchgoers will resort to consulting a medium, or someone else in the occult, when they are really in need.

Besides psychic healers and surgeons, occult healing is practiced worldwide by witchdoctors, shamans, medicine men, witches, and other sorcerers. It is prevalent in New Age medicine like Therapeutic Touch (a form of psychic healing where one passes their hand over the patient's body). Whatever the person or method, the results come from the same source—the power of evil spirits performing or simulating healing.

When demons heal, they imitate the omnipotence of the true God, draw people away from Him, and lure them into the occult. The result is that many of those who receive healing are more open to spiritualism and consult a medium. Even some doctors and surgeons consult mediums to obtain diagnostic skills and knowledge from "deceased physicians" that they can not learn anywhere else.

22. **New Age Medicine**—In an attempt to extend his reach and entrap a greater number of people, satan has subtly infiltrated the medical field under the guise of medicine and psychiatry in order to promote his occult religions and practices and to increase followers. Unwittingly, government and medical authorities are cooperating by facilitating the merger. This, along with parapsychology and other practices of the New Age Movement, is a clever, subtle invasion of the occult upon unsuspecting humanity on a scale perhaps unlike anything in the history of mankind. This is yet another case where an ancient pagan religion has been repackaged into a modern day setting in the West. The enemy will exploit any of our legitimate needs in order to enslave us. So health concerns have always been high on his "list" in every culture (see **Healing, in the Occult** and **Tactics of Satan, control and enslave** in index).

The New Age Movement has its own alternative to conventional health and medicine. This movement's worldview is steeped in Eastern mysticism and the occult so it shouldn't surprise us if its health approach and methods are too. New Age medicine is also known as "holistic" or "alternative medicine" and claims to treat the "whole" person—mind, body, and spirit. This should not be confused with the legitimate field of natural and nutritional remedies (vitamins, etc.) that have been proven to be authentic, effective, and based on nature.

Increasingly, both qualified and unqualified medical practitioners are also prescribing occult activities, masqueraded as "therapies," to help their patients get well. These New Age treatment and diagnostic practices include: aikido; autogenics; ayurvedic medicine; bioenergetics; biofeedback; chromotherapy; homeopathy; **hypnotism;** iridology (diagnosis via the iris in one's eye); kinesiology (both applied and behavioral); **meditation;** mind control therapies; past life therapy (reincarnation); polarity therapy; radionics; reflexology (muscle testing); rolfing; shiatsu; therapeutic touch; visualization; **yoga;** and the list goes on. Many of the body "therapies" supposedly work on one's body to influence and unite one's mind and spirit.

Many New Age medical personnel do not have adequate training, and their practices and diagnoses are not based upon proven clinically tested facts and approval by an official medical body. They will often base their approach of the treatment of one's symptoms on a pantheistic religious worldview—the common denominator that unites New Age medicine. It's the belief that an impersonal universal divine energy unites nature and humanity to the cosmos (as well as other Eastern religious beliefs including **reincarnation**). Consequently, our health is said to be directly related to the condition of this energy within us; therefore, our "energy fields" must be "properly adjusted" by various energy-based "therapies." These are believed to unite us with God and the universe in order to bring our misaligned, unbalanced, or blocked energies (i.e. illness) into health and wholeness. They believe that if we recognize God and ourselves as energy, then cures will come by the manipulation of this energy (see **Pantheism** in index).

As with other forms of the occult, the fact that something "works" usually overrides the concern there should be for what it is that makes it work. This "blind faith" and irrational trust should concern us because the reasons given for its success do not align with the known laws of medical science. Just because people report that they have been cured through New Age medicine doesn't prove that the source of the cure was a good or genuine source. So what exactly is this "energy"? Demonic spirits are the main reason for why it works, but we should be careful to not attribute every successful recovery to them (i.e. the body may heal itself, etc.). Psychotherapies can also lead to psychic experiences. These patients then often embrace New Age occult beliefs and practices when these treatments seem to work for them.

The dangers of New Age medicine include: misdiagnosis and its consequences; acceptance of occult beliefs and practices; physical, mental, emotional, and spiritual damage; and **demonization** through the physician or therapy. It is critically important that one learn about the background and beliefs of one's physician or therapist because he or she could be treating their patients on the basis of their personal occult religious beliefs rather than by sound medical principles. Ask them what their worldview and belief in God is (see Lesson 2). Do they use New Age medical practices? Does he or she have "spirit guides"? Has the treatment been scientifically proven and approved by conventional medicine? Does he or she use altered states of consciousness for themselves or for treating their patients? Are the treatments based on their psychic or intuitive abilities? **Caution! Don't allow anyone to pass their hands over you for healing purposes or to hypnotize you.**[19] (For more information visit www.johnankerberg.com.)

23. **Meditation**—This is one of the most widespread and popular of all the modern religious practices. "Meditation techniques have assumed a prominent place in large numbers of physical, spiritual, and health therapies where relaxation is a primary goal."[20] It is also a pillar of New Age education and medicine and is permeating the mainstream community, especially in our universities and public schools (where it is disguised by various names like "centering exercises"). It deviously fosters in our children the desire to develop psychically and to be open to the occult. It lures unsuspecting people in by claiming many mental and physical health benefits (especially stress reduction) and is widely perceived as a harmless form of relaxation. This therapeutic feature is a hook to introduce millions of people to the occult (also see **Yoga** and **Mantras**).

A. Many religions (especially Eastern) require meditation in conjunction with their religious practices. A key element in meditation is the repetitious chanting of a word or phrase called a **Mantra** which puts a person in a kind of hypnotic state where they are open to suggestions from demonic spirits. Basically, all meditation uses the mind in an abnormal manner to radically restructure a person's perception of self and the world. This is done by altering one's consciousness whether one is a short or long-term practitioner. Most all of the meditation systems lead to the same end—a psychic merging either into union with God (i.e. the Hindu Brahman) or emptiness (the Buddhist Nirvana). They also involve three similar occult phenomena: cultivation of altered states of consciousness (trance, hypnotic state, etc.); eventual development of psychic powers (and occult abilities); and the possibility of spirit possession.

B. The goals of Eastern and occult meditation are some form of cosmic consciousness, enlightenment, or the development of the "higher self." Here is an attempt to briefly explain it: The religious worldview of Eastern and New Age religions is normally pantheistic—the belief that everything is God. It logically follows then that this impersonal universal cosmic energy also permeates our beings/bodies and that therefore, we too, are divine. It is believed that this "divine power" residing potentially within us all can be tapped, and that through meditation these "psychic energies" can be discovered and developed. The problem, it is said, is that most people don't realize this "truth," so they need to achieve "spiritual enlightenment" to be able to perceive the "true" reality of their divine nature.

C. Through pantheistic beliefs, a person is led to believe that the material universe is an illusion. So if our body and personality are an illusion, then we must escape from or "transcend" them. This is necessary in order to comprehend "self-realization" or our "true" inner nature which is supposedly one essence with "God" or "ultimate reality"—however it is defined. Therefore, the "false" perception of things (which we commonly view as normal) that limit and hinder our understanding of this must be overcome through controlling and regulating the mind. It has as its final goal union with ultimate reality and the resulting dissolution of the individual personality. "The goal of enlightenment is not only to alter one's perspective but to destroy one's basic identity so that it may be replaced with a new, alien consciousness."[21]

D. However, this "enlightenment" turns out not to be an advanced or "higher" state as claimed but just the opposite. The altered states of consciousness that one experiences are wrongly interpreted as "higher" states of consciousness, presumably divine states, and the meditation-developed psychic powers are likewise wrongly viewed as the awakening and developing latent "god-nature" of the individual. It opens one up for demonic manipulation and bondage. It is also used, as in Transcendental Meditation for example, as the means for allegedly releasing the soul from the physical body and projecting it into the astral realm.

E. The potential dangers of meditation are: "...philosophical conversion to the occult, demon possession, and various forms of physical, spiritual, and psychological damage"[22]—including mental illness, insanity, and suicide.[23] (For more information visit www.johnankerberg.com.)

24. **Yoga**—A religious philosophy and discipline most likely originating within Hinduism, but also practiced in other Eastern religions like Buddhism, Taoism, and by sects in the New Age Movement. There are various schools and methods within these religions, but overall each teaches much the same religious worldview and goals. The basic premise of their pantheistic worldview is the belief that mankind and nature are all part of God who is an impersonal Being. The ultimate aim of yoga is to bring the individual (the yogi) into an awareness of their inner impersonal divine nature and to experience oneness with this impersonal God. Hence, the name yoga means "union." This is achieved through meditation (also see **Meditation** and **Mantras** in index), and cultivation of occult energies which are designed to induce altered states of consciousness in their quest for union with God. This state of being one with God is also referred to as cosmic or universal consciousness, or *prana*—a universal energy (in reality demonic power).

A. Adherents believe that mankind is only considered divine in his inner spirit. So man's body and personality are viewed as an illusion (or *maya*) which interferes with his becoming aware of his true inner divinity. "Thus another purpose of yoga must be to slowly dismantle the outer personality—man's illusory part—so that the supposed impersonal divinity can progressively 'emerge' from within his hidden divine consciousness."[24] (i.e. his "higher self") "Yoga is, after all, a *religious* practice seeking to produce 'union' with an impersonal ultimate reality, such as Brahman or Nirvana. If ultimate reality is impersonal, of what final value is one's own personality? ...his 'false' self must be destroyed and replaced with awareness of his true divine nature."[25] Yoga claims to "transcend" or "liberate" one from that which hinders him or her from realizing their true "godhood."

B. There are normally eight (8) interdependent stages, or "limbs," one must progress through to obtain God consciousness. These stages include physical exercises and postures for training and purification purposes (stages 1-3); followed by controlled breathing techniques to strengthen and control the mind and direct the divine energy within called *pranayama* (stages 4-6); then meditation and chanting of mantras to transcend the limitations of the body (7th stage). All this is designed to prepare one's being for the ultimate experience found in the 8th and last stage (Samadhi)—oneness with the impersonal universal spirit.

C. In order to achieve this eighth stage of oneness, yogis attempt to awaken the Kundalini—the serpent goddess of Hindu mythology believed to reside dormant at the base of one's spine. She is said to be separated from her divine lover Shiva who resides in the brain. Through a long period of mastering the stages (meditation, chanting, and breathing), she slowly travels up one's spine toward the brain opening the *chakras* (specific points along the way that supposedly connect the astral body to the physical). When she reaches the brain and is united with Shiva, one's soul is said to be freed from all bondages of the body and limitations of time and space. One has finally experienced cosmic consciousness or divine enlightenment. Gaining perfect control of *prana* brings the person into union with this supreme universal Being—Brahman, and makes the person God (Self-Realization = God realization). In this state of bliss, all knowledge and powers are at his or her command. The yogi is now able to perform the miraculous and even claim to travel outside of their physical body in their astral body to other places (astral projection). "Kundalini arousal" also has its counterpart in other religions, occult practices, and even in New Age medicine.

D. The dangers of yoga involvement are the same as for **meditation** (see above). By their own admission, yoga authorities state that lack of proper instruction in performing the physical and breathing exercises can be harmful and even lead to death. The mere act of doing the seemingly harmless and allegedly "beneficial" physical or breathing exercises can attract demonic activity in one's life. This is because these exercises are designed to invoke and awaken "occult energies" which are a disguise for demonic power. Having entered the devil's territory, one will invite serious danger to their physical, mental, and spiritual well-being. Yoga has marketed itself to be a neutral, non-religious practice that is therapeutically beneficial to mind and body. This has caused millions of people to let down their guard and embrace this dangerous deception. Endorsements by health professionals notwithstanding, little do people realize that instead of obtaining health benefits, or contacting an impersonal energy, they are exposing themselves to a personal devil.

25. **The Martial Arts**—These are another unsuspected entry ways into the occult. One may be surprised to learn that the MA have always had a religious aspect to them. Originating in the Far East, these ancient forms of self-defense are based on the religious beliefs of that region—Taoism, Buddhism (Zen), Shintoism, and Confucianism (much like Oriental medicine). These philosophies are pantheistic in nature and teach the normal religious objectives of **meditation** and **yoga**—the attuning of oneself to the universal energy and to gain enlightenment (see **Pantheism** in index). The goals of the MA go beyond the learning of the various skills of self-defense or physical disciplines. They have to do with harnessing the divine power within us all (i.e. *ch'i, ki*). Through meditation etc., one is to arouse the power and direct it inwardly to parts of one's body and unleash it outwardly to one's opponent.

This "cosmic energy" is the force believed to be behind some of the MA's incredible, powerful feats that defy natural explanations like "repelling energy," "telepathic hypnosis," and the "death touch." It's all about who is able to best combine the physical movements and the energy within them. This is done through a regimen of Eastern forms of meditation and physical discipline—unifying the mind, spirit, and body. Its appeal is mainly to our youth who are recruited through compelling videos that portray its mystique, instill a high respect for the art, and depict a way of acquiring power. Like the physicians of **New Age medicine**, MA instructors incorporate their religious beliefs into their teachings. **Those who want to escape the religious aspects of the MA must select an instructor they know and trust.** The dangers include: conversion to Eastern religious philosophies; physical harm; and the normal perils resulting from exposure to occult involvement.[26] (For more information visit www.johnankerberg.com.)

HOW PEOPLE INVOKE THEIR GODS TO DO SOMETHING

The third thing devotees of false religions and the occult attempt to do is petition and summon their god(s) to work on their behalf. Satan willfully persists in pursuing his foolish, self-delusive quest *"to be like God"* and continually entices mankind with this same evil desire. The promise of God-like power and control over people, nature, and sickness feeds the sinful cravings in our lower nature. It is the same age-old deception that has been offered to mankind since Adam and Eve.

Those who were skilled in the art of persuading their god(s) to do something were highly respected and feared in a society. The Bible calls them *"sorcerers," "magicians," "enchanters,"* and *"charmers."* These practice the magical arts by using incantations, rituals, ceremonies, etc., (*"enchantments"*) to bring someone under demonic influence and control—with "good" or bad results. We know them as priests and priestesses, witches and warlocks, medicine men, shamans, and witch doctors. All of mankind has, and is being dominated by the oppression of occult magic and sorcery, especially before the time of Christ. Just as **divination** was satan's imitation of the revelatory gifts of the Holy Spirit, so <u>magic</u> and <u>sorcery</u> are his counterfeits of the true God's *"miracles."* Its practice is forbidden in Scripture **(Deuteronomy 18:10-12)**.

📖 DEFINITION—SORCERY

In the Old Testament, the word *"sorcery"* encompasses a broader scope of occultism than the connotation and limited aspects of the modern word "witch" used by some Bible translators. The word included divination and necromancy. *"Sorcerers"* conjure up the supernatural power of evil spirits. Their earliest mention in the Bible is during the plagues God sent on Egypt through Moses in **Exodus 7:11.** Later in the Mosaic Law, God placed a death sentence upon those who practiced sorcery **(Exodus 22:18).** Besides Egypt, Assyria **(Nahum 3:4);** Babylonia **(Daniel 2:2);** and sadly, His chosen people Israel, practiced sorcery to their own destruction **(Micah 5:12).** Practically every nation had a sorcerer-type office as part of their false religion that was consulted by their leaders.

In the New Testament, there are two Greek words translated sorcery. One is *pharmakia* from which we get our English word pharmacy. Interestingly, it signifies the use of drugs and magical potions in the muttering of incantations and the subsequent casting of spells. Sorcery (*"witchcraft"*) is listed as one of the *"works of the flesh"* in **Galatians 5:20.** It will play a significant part in the end-time tribulation period **(Revelation 9:21; 18:23).** The sorcerer's role in society is to contact their gods and other spirits through ceremonial magical rites and attempt to influence or compel these evil spirits to obey them. On behalf of the people who enlist their services, they exert power over the weather, bring fertility, impart supernatural knowledge, cast spells over others, and cure sickness through their healing arts. They can become the religious and medical figures in the community. Some even accompany soldiers into battle to aid them with their secret arts.

The other Greek word is *magia* from which we get our English word **MAGIC,** which is the skillful practice of the magical arts of occultism. It is used in connection with the two sorcerers Elymas **(Acts 13:6-12),** and Simon, whose demonic power amazed the common people who had a hard time distinguishing the demonic supernatural from the miracles done by the true God.

> † **Acts 8:9-11**—*Now for some time a man named Simon had practiced sorcery in the city and amazed all the people of Samaria. He boasted that he was someone great,* **10.** *and all the people, both high and low, gave him their attention and exclaimed, "This man is the divine power known as the Great Power."* **11.** *They followed him because he had amazed them for a long time with his magic.*

📖 DEFINITION—MAGICIAN

The magician referred to in the Bible is a person who performs supernatural phenomena through demonic power (knowingly or unknowingly). The magical arts were usually passed down from previous nations and cultures as well as through heredity. The first mentions of magicians in Scripture are those of ancient Egypt in **Genesis 41:8,24.** Later in Egypt's history, they duplicated three of the ten miraculous plagues that God did through Moses by transforming their staffs into snakes **(Exodus 7:11-12);** turning water into blood **(7:22),** and bringing frogs upon the land with their secret arts **(8:7)**. The nation of Babylon also had them **(Daniel 2:2,27)**. Like sorcerers, almost every false religion had the counterpart of those skilled in the magical arts and it was normal to have this official religious office consulted by its governmental leader(s). Today, the term magician usually refers to an illusionist. However, not all illusions are sleight-of-hand. Some are what I call a demon-stration of demonic powers. To stay undetected, satan blends his real power among sleight-of-hand illusions and acts of outright fakery. As in all aspects of the occult, the phony must exist because it is needed to explain away the real thing. Practicing the magical arts will prevent someone from entering heaven **(Revelation 21:8; 22:15)**.

📖 DEFINITION—WITCHCRAFT

Modern witchcraft ("the Craft") in America was imported from Britain (Wicca) whose roots were in Druidism. It is comprised of various sects whose beliefs may vary somewhat from coven to coven. Once persecuted and outlawed, today it operates freely in America, Great Britain, and Europe. It is a polytheistic fertility cult whose chief deities usually include a mother goddess (moon goddess) and a horned god (goat) as well as other nature spirits. Its lure is to obtain power—to have spirits at one's disposal to "Do all that I command thee!" People from all walks of life are attracted to it.

Each coven is headed by a high priestess or high priest though the female role is predominant. The primary goal of the coven's rites and ceremonies is to "raise the power" of their gods (idiom: "raise hell"), and dispatch this "energy" toward a specific person or object that it's intended to help or hurt. Derived from this is the concept of the "white witch" who does "good" and the "black witch" who harms (see **Spells** in index). The main way the "power" is generated is usually through rites done within the protective area of a magic circle and/or pentagram. These rites include: casting spells from grimoires, which are textbooks on the proper way to invoke and dismiss spirits; creating a "cone of power" through chanting and dancing to form the collective energies of the coven; performing rites without clothing; and culminating at least the most important festivals with sexual intercourse—referred to by some as the Great Rite. This sexual energy is believed to release the life force in nature (see Sex, integrated in worship). Sacrifices also "raise the power."

In some sects, the goddess is called upon by the High Priestess to inhabit her body for the duration of the ceremony. Trance and meditation are part of their paths to fulfillment. Divination and astral projection are also practiced. Their main seasonal festivals, or sabbats, occur on February 2, March 21, April 30, June 22, July 31, September 21, October 31, and December 22. An increase in demonic activity can be expected in connection with these dates. It is up to the coven how often it meets. Witches believe they serve the well-being of mankind. Today, satan is using those in the media and entertainment industry to make this forbidden occult practice appear fashionable to our youth. And our higher places of learning offer it as an accredited course.

MAGICAL ARTS USED TO INVOKE EVIL SPIRITS

1. **Incantations**—These are a repetitive, ritualistic recitation or chanting of "prayers" and special magical formulas to petition one's god(s) to carry out their will and desires. If performed in the correct tone of voice, and repeated often enough, it is believed to produce meritorious, magical results in the casting of spells. The names of evil spirits and/or false gods of ancient civilizations are called upon and summoned. Especially potent are incantations said in an ancient language and/or from a "sacred book" or "magical text."

    A. **Mantras and Mandalas**—These incantations are used in worship and meditation within most Eastern religions (i.e. Transcendental Meditation, Yoga, Mahayana Buddhism, etc.) as well as in the New Age Movement. A **mantra** is a sacred utterance or sound that is repeatedly said aloud or hummed and used to invoke a god. Far from being meaningless words or a mere prayer, the mantra is often the name of the god being called upon. For example, the mantra *"om"* evokes the three greatest Hindu gods—rahma, Visnu, and Siva. In part, its power is believed to lie in the number of times the deity's name is repeated. This will then bring one into contact with the god and even imbibe the nature of that deity. Many who innocently experiment with this are unwittingly invoking evil spirits. Reciting a mantra incorrectly or without proper spiritual preparation is said to be very dangerous. Its other alleged functions include: use as a magical incantation; its mindless repetition aids one in developing altered states of consciousness; power is developed that is concentrated and then projected within or without; and the development of psychic powers. A **mandala** is a "sacred" picture or diagram at whose center the deity is depicted. It is similar in function to the mantra. Both "...are held to invoke, represent, or contain the essence of the gods..."[27,28] See **Meditation** and **Yoga** in index. (For more information visit www.johnankerberg.com.)

2. **The Casting of Spells**—These are words believed to have magical powers. To place a person, animal, or object under a spell is to target them for a bad or "good" purpose. This is an offensive weapon for occultists. Spells can either be those passed down from ancient times or ones a person creates. An ancient, familiar one is the word ABRACADABRA. The Bible states that the nation of Babylon regularly cast spells **(Isaiah 47:9-12)**. God forbade it to His people: *"Let no one be found among you who...engages in witchcraft, or casts spells..."* **(Deuteronomy 18:10-12)**.

   A. **Black Magic (a curse or a hex)**—It is when someone with malicious intent summons an evil spirit to harass, vex, or harm a specific person, animal, or thing—especially for revenge. Some curses like the "evil eye" can even bring death. Some historic examples of a curse put on a family would be: their crops would be harmed; members of their family or their animals would become sick or not produce, develop mental disorders, be barren or have miscarriages, or even die; or their homes, barns, etc. would mysteriously catch on fire. It occurs in similar ways today. In some occult religions (as in voodoo, witchcraft, etc.), a doll is made into an effigy representing the person targeted. This replica is made out of clay, wood, cloth, wax, etc., and is stabbed, buried, bound, burned, or pricked with pins. Basically, it's treated the way the petitioner wants the person to be harmed. For a spell to be most effective, one must obtain a "relic" from the targeted person. Things like a piece of clothing or parts from their body (hair, nails, blood, saliva, etc.) are used because it is believed that they are forever mysteriously linked to that person. Curses can also come from some ancient occult figurines and religious sites which are still a residence for evil spirits and are considered taboo. When one invades their "sacred territory," the curse that was made long ago in connection with it now comes on the intruding person—even centuries later. The tombs of the Pharaohs are believed to be protected by powerful curses even today.

      (1) Are spells or curses put on Christians? Yes! It probably happens every day somewhere in the world. Can the spell be effectively carried out on that Christian by the evil spirit? No and yes. **Proverbs 26:2** (NLT) says, *"Like a fluttering sparrow or a darting swallow, an unfair curse will not land on its intended victim."* For example, when Goliath, the Philistine, cursed David by his gods with an oath, it had no effect on David **(1 Samuel 17:43)**. *"Christ redeemed us from the curse of the* (Old Testament) *law by becoming a curse for us..."* **(Galatians 3:13)**. He is our protection from all curses. Evil spirits have to get past the "blood of Christ" that covers a believer's life—and that's one awesome shield and an extremely difficult feat for the enemy (see "Security, in Christ" in index). If you have any reason to believe that you may be under a curse, appropriate the work Jesus did on the cross in His victory over satan in your life, and get trusted Christians to join you in prayer for your deliverance.

      (2) On the other hand, the apostle Paul asked the church in Galatia who had *"bewitched"* them into accepting false doctrine **(Galatians 3:1-3)**. They had been duped into believing the lie that by adding "works" to their faith in Christ's work on the cross, it would bring them salvation from sin. They were in gross error. For demonic power to effectively touch a born-again Christian through a spell, it seems from Scripture that the believer would have had to step out from under the umbrella of God's protection by giving the enemy a foothold. Or God would have to lift His protective hedge and allow it to happen. Another aspect that may appear as a curse, but may not be, is a spiritual attack resulting from effective ministry. Jesus taught us that the proper Christian response to someone who curses or persecutes us is to bless that person and pray for them **(Luke 6:28; Romans 12:14)**.

(3) The "curse" we should most be concerned about falling under is God's. If a person is not *"born-again,"* he or she is already under God's judgment **(Ephesians 2:1-3; John 3:3,36; Matthew 25:41).** However, once we come into covenant with God through Christ and the new birth, and should quit serving Him, we then bring upon ourselves God's curses for breaking the covenant **(Deuteronomy 27:15 through 28:68; Daniel 9:10-13; Hebrews 6:4-8; 10:26-31).** Failing to pay God our tithes will also bring a curse from God upon us **(Malachi 3:8-12).**

B. **White Magic**—The name given to those who claim to help people in a beneficial way and have only good intentions. However, no spell is "good" if evil spirits are involved. Most importantly, it is forbidden by the God of the Bible. These spells are cast to obtain for people things like: riches, power, fame, love, beauty, success, healing, protection, and to reverse a spell. Love spells are especially popular. These are used to attract a particular person, keep a lover, or take someone away from another. The use of love potions are also used (see **Potions** in index). The sorcerer may even call on the name of the God of the Bible or use Christian symbols, etc. White magic is a lure to draw in a broader range of people into the trap of the occult.

3. **Magical Brews and Potions**—These consist of a mixture of herbs, drugs, and other bizarre ingredients that claim to produce magical powers. Perhaps the most well known is the love potion or philter. Potions and brews can contain such obnoxious ingredients as wine, drugs, blood (human or animal), urine, various types of herbs and plants (some toxic), and even reptile venom. The concoction has no power in itself, but when the person exercises faith and obedience in making it and drinking it, this activates demonic power. This is another indication of the ability of evil spirits to have influence over human sexuality (see **Sex, Influenced by Demons?** in index). One of the purposes for potions and brews is that they produce an altered state of consciousness by which one is vulnerable to demon possession and control. As noted above, one of the Greek words used for sorcery in the Bible is *pharmakia* from which we get our English word pharmacy. It signifies the use of drugs and magical potions in the muttering of incantations and the subsequent casting of spells.

4. **Amulets, Talismans, and Charms**—One of the ways satan controls his children is through superstition and fear of receiving curses. Out of this dread and insecurity, people resort to defensive measures called amulets and talismans, which are also known as a fetish. These are believed to protect them from evil powers, and to ward off evil forces and sickness. All three are generally worn on one's body. They are made of metal, stone, gems, etc. and are worn as rings, pendants, etc. Some are inscribed with a magical incantation or symbol that magically activates it with protective powers to counteract any curse. Some believe a spirit resides in these inanimate objects. While both amulets and talismans passively protect a person from evil, a talisman is also considered a positive active force that ensures good fortune (like a good luck charm). To activate a talisman one is told to rub it, touch it, kiss it, wave it, etc. Examples of both are: the cross (i.e. crossing one's fingers), saint medallions, birthstones, the 12 signs of the zodiac, hex signs on the homes and barns of the Amish, the Jewish mezuzah on doorway entrances, the Egyptian Ankh, the horseshoe, and rabbit's foot, etc. and practically anything else behind which spirits can work (except faith in the true God). The use of crystals is similar. They are believed to have an energy that connects a person to the earth's energy field. This power can be directed to other people and objects for occult purposes like healing or developing psychic abilities.

5. **Sacrifices**—The offering of both animals and humans is also an integral part of invoking demons. This has been covered briefly in our first section (see **Sacrifices** under How People Appease Their False Gods).

WARNING

If you have ever had any involvement with the practices outlined in this appendix, it is critical that you renounce your past or present involvement immediately by walking through the five steps in How to Recapture Territory Lost to the Enemy in Lesson 12 (look up in index: "Recapturing lost territory, five steps to"). The current problems you may be experiencing may very well be due to exposing yourself to demonic powers through these doorways to the occult!

Appendix B - Counterfeit Christian Religions

Religious Group	Their View of God	Their Belief in God/Trinity	Their Way of Obtaining Salvation	Authoritative Source(s)
Mormonism (The Church of Jesus Christ of Latter-day Saints and its splinter group - Reorganized Church of Jesus Christ of Latter-day Saints) **Founder:** Joseph Smith in approx. 1820 **Headquarters:** Salt Lake City, Utah, and Independence, Missouri respectively **Membership:** 11 million and 240,000 respectively	Polytheism Note that the Mormon group - the Reorganized Church (a.k.a. Community of Christ) claims **not** to believe in polytheism	The Mormon doctrine of God rivals anything pagan mythology ever produced. Their core belief is the theory of eternal progression. They believe in a main finite god named Elohim, or God the Father, who was once a human being and still has a human body, and who evolved into a god through good works. He and his wives continually produce a great number of spirit children (their 1st birth), who wait for Mormons to produce human bodies for them to inhabit (their 2nd birth). Through performing specific good works given by the Mormon Church (including celestial marriages and proxy baptisms), they strive to become a god themselves so they may rule over one of innumerable planets and continue begetting offspring throughout eternity (thus their emphasis on large families and their rationale for polygamy). Besides Elohim, they say they believe in Jesus and the Holy Spirit who rule our planet. They are 3 separate and distinct gods (tritheism). However, there are other countless gods who were once human on countless other planets. They believe Jesus was the first one created by Elohim and one of his celestial wives, and that he was later conceived as a human being through sexual union between Elohim and Mary – **not** by a true virgin birth. Jesus was imperfect before he came to earth and sinless while on earth. He had to earn his own salvation and the right to become god – just like any other Mormon does. Christ is considered just a god among many. For more information visit www.johnankerberg.com (click on "Search").	Jesus' atonement on the cross provided only two limited things: 1. A universal salvation from hell and eternal punishment by making it possible for all mankind to be raised from the dead – unconditionally – a salvation by grace. 2. The starting point for mankind to have the **opportunity** to earn their own salvation by performing good works. Christ's death did not provide forgiveness of sins, but only made forgiveness possible through zealous and impeccable obedience to Mormon teachings. There are works attached to every aspect of Mormon salvation. To some degree, there is spiritual progression beyond the grave, for it can take ages before one can evolve to godhood – like Elohim did No Mormon knows for certain which of the 3 heavens or kingdoms they will go to until all the stringent requirements are met. These 3 heavens are: • Telestial – For the wicked heathen. • Terrestrial – For non-Mormons who lived good lives. • Celestial – This heavenly kingdom has 3 levels: The highest level is where Mormons experience eternal life: forgiveness of sin, endless marriage, and sexual right to produce spirit children, and rule planets. To a Mormon, eternal "damnation" is going to a lesser heaven and forever remaining single in a servant status, with limits on their eternal progression, and without the possibility of achieving godhood. Mormonism claims to be the only true church offering true salvation to the world.	**"The Four Standard Works":** 1. Doctrine and Covenants 2. The Pearl of Great Price 3. The Book of Mormon 4. The Bible
Jehovah's Witnesses **Founder:** Charles Taze Russell in 1879 **Headquarters:** Brooklyn, NY **Membership:** 6.5 million	Unitarian Monotheism	There is one God named Jehovah. The very first being he created was his only begotten son, Jesus, who is "a god" and also known as Michael the Archangel. They believe that Jesus began his existence as sort of a super-angelic deity both inferior to and subordinate to Jehovah, and did not preexist from all eternity. Michael's life force was transferred to the womb of Mary and the perfect and sinless human being, Jesus, was born – but not as an incarnation. Jesus completed his ministry and died as a ransom for mankind, but only provided a limited atonement – not fully covering all human sin. His body was not resurrected, but Jehovah disintegrated it while he was in the tomb. God then recreated him and he soon ascended back to heaven to become Michael once more. Christ then returned invisibly to earth in 1914. They believe the Holy Spirit is an active force, not a person, thereby denying that both Jesus and the Holy spirit are part of the trinity.	JWs believe a person's soul dies when their body dies, and they remain in an unconscious state until the resurrection. Therefore, there is no hell or fear of eternal punishment. However, since they believe that only 144,000 will go to heaven, the remainder of these Witnesses have no hope of going there. These must earn favor with Jehovah by performing works specified by the Watchtower Society, allegedly God's true and only delegated authority and visible representative on earth. These good works (like door-to-door recruitment) enable them to be among those who remain on the earth in the end times to live in the new paradise. For more information visit www.goodnewsdefenders.com.	**The New World Translation** (their translation of the Bible)

Appendix B - Counterfeit Christian Religions

Religious Group	Their View of God	Their Belief in God/Trinity	Their Way of Obtaining Salvation	Authoritative Source(s)
Christian Science (Church of Christ, Scientist) **Founder:** Mary Baker Eddy in 1870. **Headquarters:** Boston, MA **Membership:** 200,000	Pantheism	Their religious beliefs defy the principles of sound logic and experience. The reason for this is that they base everything on a pantheistic worldview that all is God. To them, God is not a person. It is a divine Principle, an infinite Mind that consists as spirit; therefore, much emphasis is placed on things being thoughts and ideas. Their reasoning goes something like this: if everything is God and God is spiritual benevolent Mind, then everything else that is not spirit (God) must not exist. Therefore, since matter is not spirit, then things like the physical universe, our human bodies, and sickness, disease, and even death are illusions. And because God is good and all is God, then evil, sin, and satan also cannot exist. They view Jesus as the spiritual idea of God. Mary conceived and gave birth to God's idea. Due to their view on matter, Jesus did not exist as a physical man so He could not have died; consequently, He could not have been resurrected. It follows then that His blood didn't exist to provide atonement. The Christ spirit is infallible but no different than other humans because we are all part of God. They reject the Trinity because they view them as three separate Gods. The Holy Spirit is called Divine Science. Their religion was established by its founder as a pursuit of physical healing (she, herself being sickly), a discovery of the power of healing through mind over matter.	They view man as spirit, an idea, a part of God, and therefore, not a physical being in need of salvation. Sin is an illusion. Heaven and hell are states of thought and not real places. They claim to be Christian, but bear no likeness whatsoever to the teachings of the Bible. For more information visit www.watchman.org.	1. **Science and Health with Key to the Scriptures** 2. **The Bible:** (as interpreted by Science and Health)
Unity School of Christianity (Unity Church) **Founder:** Charles & Myrtle Fillmore in 1889 **Headquarters:** Lee's Summit, MO **Membership:** Over one million	Pantheism	USC, like Christian Science and the Church of Religious Science, belong to the Mind Science religions which have a pantheistic view of God. They, too, confuse God with the things He has created – making Him an impersonal force – a type of energy that permeates the universe and that manifests itself in everything. Therefore, they reject the Trinity. To them, Jesus was only a man, but Christ is divine consciousness – the God part that resides in each of us and makes us all divine. They strive to tap into, and become united with, the Divine Mind. When one is successful, then spiritual, physical, and mental problems are healed (see **Occult Healing**). They believe this is much like when Jesus and other Biblical characters used their "spiritual energy" and "power of thought" to release this force which produced their supernatural feats. The USC's beliefs about God differ from that of their sister church, Christian Science (see above), in that they disagree with them over the nonexistence of matter. USC's beliefs also contain traces of teachings taken from Eastern religions – like reincarnation. This is another religion that got its start due to the founder's (Myrtle) quest for the physical healing of their body.	Since mankind exists as part of God (pantheism), man's duty (or salvation) is to discover and to raise the level of the Christ consciousness potential within them, regardless of their religious beliefs, and to realize their oneness with this impersonal force also called the "universal principle of love." The USC believes that heaven and hell are not real places but are states of consciousness. They define sin as "our separation from God in consciousness." They believe in a modified Hindu view of reincarnation. This belief enables everyone to have the opportunity to evolve into immortality and then reincarnation ceases. This nullifies the Biblical definition of sin, hell, the resurrection, and heaven and makes it nonexistent in their view. Therefore, there is no need for the atonement of Jesus Christ for sin. The USC's unique approach of encouraging their followers to continue attending their regular church enables them to infiltrate that body with the "light" of their teachings. For more information visit www.watchman.org/pa.	**The Bible** But it is just one book among many other sacred writings that also teach truth, and it is interpreted from a symbolic, metaphysical viewpoint

Appendix C - Christian Denominations That Hold False Essential Beliefs

Denomination	Their Belief in God/Trinity	Their Way of Obtaining Salvation	Authoritative Source(s)
Groups that teach Water Baptism is necessary for Salvation Proponents: **Roman Catholics** **Eastern Orthodox** Protestants: **The Churches of Christ** (*NOT* the United Church of Christ) Most **Lutherans**	Overall, these denominations have a Biblically correct view of God and the trinity. However, some of the liberal elements within these groups hold to erroneous views of Jesus – denying that He is the Son of God and was bodily resurrected. Roman Catholics, Eastern Orthodox, and in Protestantism many Lutherans, believe that water baptism is a sacrament through which one's are saved – an essential element that secures the forgiveness of one's sins. This is known as "baptismal regeneration" – the belief that the rite of water baptism is **conditional** for salvation and marks the moment one is placed into the true Church. This includes infant baptism. The Churches of Christ is the main group that espouses the teachings of what is called "Campbellism" – named after its founders, Thomas and Alexander Campbell. They, and a few others, began the "Restoration Movement" in the early 1800s to restore to the world the "true Gospel" and "true church" that was "lost" since the first century church. Their teachings also promote baptismal regeneration. The churches that teach Campbellism state that there are four steps necessary in order to be saved. They are: faith, repentance, confession of Christ, and water baptism which is necessary for the forgiveness (continued in next column)	of one's sins and the placement of one into their true church. Some even go as far as denying the salvation of those Christians baptized in another Christian denomination. According to Dr. Robert Morey, one of the notable Christian apologists of our day, Campbellism had a significant influence in the origination of the Mormon and Jehovah Witnesses religions.[1] Note: The Bible teaches that water baptism is extremely important and not optional. However, it is meant to be a public profession of one's faith that reflects one's inner "born again" experience. It means identifying with Christ in His death (being lowered into the water), His burial (being submerged), and His resurrection (up out of the water) – into newness of life. The act, in itself, has no power to save or to forgive sin. Only Christ's work on the cross can do that. Also note that both Jesus and the apostle Paul refrained from water baptizing converts – leaving that up to their disciples (**John 4:1 & 2; 1 Corinthians 1:14 & 17**). If it really was essential to salvation, they would have placed more emphasis on it. For more information visit www.watchman.org/pa For a thorough analysis of this subject visit: www.middletownbiblechurch.org/salvatio/baptsave.htm.	**The Bible**
Oneness Pentecostal Churches Notably **The United Pentecostal Church** Founder: Frank Ewert in 1913 Headquarters: Hazelwood, MO Membership: 4 million	The UPC was formed in 1945 and is the major group among Oneness Pentecostals. This movement believes it was birthed in order to restore two original truths to our generation - hidden from us since the days of the early church. The first "divine revelation" is that the Godhead does not consist of three distinct persons – only one. The second is the correct way that one is to be water baptized. They say the titles of Father, Son, and Holy Spirit are different roles, functions, or "manifestations" of the one God. For example, when God acts as the Creator and has the type of relationship He had with Israel in the Old Testament, He is the Father. When He provides redemption for mankind, He is Jesus, and when He works within the hearts of New Testament believers, He is the Holy Spirit. It's like a man who performs three roles in life (i.e. father, provider, and counselor), and yet being one person. This belief denies the triune nature of God – that three persons comprise one God. In reality, this view of God is an old heresy called Modalism or Sabellianism that was encountered by the early church and is being revived again in our day through this movement. Note: The devil successfully attacked the great Azusa Street Revival in the early 1900s by using this erroneous doctrine to cause division. It came through a so-called "divine revelation." For more information visit www.watchman.org.	Though most of the Oneness beliefs align with orthodox Christianity, their error lies in adding conditions to the work of Christ in order to be saved. Most Oneness churches adhere to these beliefs: They believe that one's salvation is dependent upon certain words said at the time of water baptism. In their view, one must be baptized by orally invoking the name of "Jesus only" – not the trinity – as one is being immersed into the water. They base this on **Acts 2:38; 4:12** while ignoring **Matthew 28:18 & 19**. The UPC does not recognize a person's water baptism that was done in another church. Therefore, a person is required to be re-baptized when he or she joins their denomination. They believe the Scriptures teach that "speaking in other languages" is the evidence of not only receiving the Baptism in the Holy Spirit, but is also the evidence that one has met one of the conditions of salvation. In other words, they believe that just as works are an evidence of genuine faith, tongues are the evidence that one has received the Holy Spirit and is saved. They err by confusing the first indwelling of the Holy Spirit when one receives Christ and is "born again", with the other distinct experience of the Baptism in the Holy Spirit which is an enduement of power to witness and to live the Christian life – not a condition to salvation. An abnormal amount of legalistic "Do's and Don'ts" are also required in order to remain in a state of grace.	**The Bible**

Appendix C - Christian Denominations That Hold False Essential Beliefs

Denomination	Their Way of Obtaining Salvation	Authoritative Source(s)
The Roman Catholic Church **Headquarters:** Rome, Italy **Membership:** 1 billion (estimate) Note: **The Eastern Orthodox Church**, which split from the RCC in 1054, holds similar views of God, and water baptism for salvation. **Headquarters:** Istanbul, Turkey **Membership:** 300 million **The RCC's Belief in God/Trinity** The RCC adheres to Biblical Christianity's belief of one God in three Persons: Father, Son, and Holy Spirit as well as the doctrine of Christ	The RCC affirms many of the central doctrines of Christianity; however, they have also **added** traditions and Papal and Council decrees that are viewed as equal to the authority of the Bible. There are also differences about the way some Scriptures have been interpreted that do not seem to align to sound principles of Biblical interpretation. Here we will only deal with the essential doctrine of salvation. Allegedly, the RCC says it officially teaches that our salvation is based on grace through faith in Christ's work on the cross. However, by their own admission, the RCC has not been successful in transmitting this truth to their priests and laity. Consequently, many of their members tend to confuse the difference between living out their faith through the lifelong sanctification process with the erroneous belief that they must earn their salvation through performing good works to finish what was begun by faith. The issue is further complicated by the official RCC statement: "The expiation of sins continues...by joining our human acts of atonement to the redemptive action of Christ, both in this life and in Purgatory."[2] Renewal efforts within the RCC have been attempting to correct this ignorance. Therefore, the following is presented for those who mistakenly believe that Christ's work alone on the cross was not fully adequate in dealing with our sins, but rather that one's salvation must be further obtained by doing additional things to complete the process He started. The RCC allegedly teaches that the 7 Sacraments are an unmeritorious means of connecting to the power and sufficiency of Christ's death and resurrection. However, if one misconstrues this to mean that these are meritorious "human acts of atonement" added to Christ's work on the cross in order to receive justification and forgiveness of sins, then they are believing something that isn't true. These "works" include: 1. **Water Baptism** – This is the gateway to the other sacraments. It involves the one-time event of the immersing or sprinkling of an infant or adult in water (and exorcism). Baptism is claimed to forgive both Original Sin (the sin we inherit from Adam) and personal sin as well as their punishment, and provides "sanctifying grace" through justification. This act of "conversion" is said to reconcile the person to God, unite them with Christ, and initiate them into the RCC. These gifts received at Baptism are believed to be a grace from Christ which cannot be earned. They base this sacrament on **Mark 16:15 & 16**. However, the Bible requires that a deliberate, personal choice must be made to receive Christ **(John 1:12)**. In the case of infant baptism, this can not occur. The RCC expects that decision will be made as the baptized infant grows older. But in no way should the rite of water baptism **itself** be viewed as a means of obtaining or guaranteeing forgiveness of sins (just as one can not be saved only through the Roman Catholic Church). God intended water baptism to be a public confession of a work already done in one's heart as one identifies with the death, burial, and resurrection of Christ **(Romans 6:3,4)**. 2. **Eucharist** – It is also called Holy Communion, the Mass, and the Holy Sacrifice. It dates back to the second century A.D. and was made an official dogma by Pope Pius III in 1215. It is derived from the literal interpretation of **John 6:53-68** and is at the very heart of the Roman Catholic faith. The RCC allegedly believes that Christ died only once for our sins and claims that the Eucharist does not endlessly and repeatedly "sacrifice" Him afresh daily across the world (without shedding blood), but is a memorial being invoked for present blessings and a means to avail themselves of its power. Extreme care must be taken not to view the Mass and the Eucharist as another sacrifice of Christ on the cross in continuing, and applying, the work of our redemption – as if His sacrifice 2000 years ago was insufficient to take away all sin. The Bible declares that Christ died once for all. He did **not** have to be repeatedly offered up like the Old Testament sacrifices which only indicated their inadequacy **(Hebrews 9:25-10:2,10-18)**. Also, the Mass itself should not be viewed as a means of forgiveness of sins for either the living or for those who have died and hope to be released early from Purgatory. They also believe that through the "miracle" of transubstantiation, the priests have the power to transform the wafer or bread into a mysterious "sacramental" form where Christ becomes substantially present. 3. **Penance & Reconciliation** – The RCC believes that Christ's authority to "bind and loose" and "to retain or remit" sin was apostolically passed down to them to exercise in His Name **(Matthew 16:19; 18:18; 28:16-20)**. Thus in this sacrament, one must confess their sin to a priest **(i.e. James 5:16)** instead of directly to Christ, our only mediator and High Priest **(1 Timothy 2:5)**. The priest, in turn, offers a prayer of absolution that forgives one's sins and metes out penance (meritorious works) that shortens one's time in Purgatory. Penance consists of: saying rote prayers (i.e. the Rosary), fasting, an offering, almsgiving, self-denial, visiting shrines, etc. The Bible says that a "born again" experience is essential in order to live with power over sin – instead of after confession, committing the same sins the next day. Closely associated with this are indulgences – a major reason Protestantism was birthed. The RCC believes every sin must be purified either in this life or in Purgatory – a place of final, temporal purification where a person who died "in God's friendship" awaits release prior to entering heaven. Catholicism enables a person to have Masses, say prayers for the dead, etc. in order to shorten the time loved ones have to spend in Purgatory. This is another interpretation and "works" problem. The doctrine of Purgatory was established by Pope Gregory I in the year 593, and is based on the Apocryphal book, **2 Maccabees 12:46** (which Jews and Protestants do not believe is divinely inspired), and **1 Corinthians 3:12-15** (interpreted by many as taking place after the resurrection of the believer). The Bible teaches us that Christ's atonement does not need our help and we can't help the dead. 4. **Anointing of the Sick** – Formerly called Extreme Unction, among other things it provides for the forgiveness of sins (by a priest) of a sick or dying person. We can't forgive someone's sins if they haven't truly repented, and like the RCC's water baptism, neither can one be saved by someone else's faith. Catholic lay evangelist Ralph Martin wrote about the #1 reason he hears for those leaving the RCC: "How could it be that I spent 22 years in the Catholic Church and never heard the Gospel?...We left because we met Jesus Christ, and He changed our lives in a way that we never knew in the Catholic Church..."[3]	1. **The Bible** (This includes the Apocryphal books decreed divinely inspired by the Council of Trent in 1546. They also believe that the way the Bible is interpreted should conform to what the RCC teaches.) 2. **Sacred Tradition** (Allegedly passed down from the Apostles and Church Fathers and was declared having equal authority with the Bible by the Council of Trent in 1546.) 3. **The Roman Catholic Church itself** (Through infallible decrees of the Pope and Councils in matters of faith and morals. This was decreed by the Vatican Council in 1870.)

SOURCE NOTES

Lesson 1

[1] R. Laird Harris et al., eds., *Theological Wordbook of the Old Testament*, (Chicago: Moody Press, 1980), II, 653.
[2] W.E. Vine, *Vine's Complete Expository Dictionary of Old and New Testament Words*, ed. Merrill F. Unger and William White, Jr., (Nashville: Thomas Nelson, 1984, 1996) p. 576.
[3] Ibid., p. 157.
[4] Source: www.Barna.org. (Click on: "Barna by Topic", then "Beliefs: Trinity, Satan").

Lesson 2

[1] Vine, p. 685.
[2] Source: www.Barna.org. (enter under search: Only Half Of Protestant Pastors Have A Biblical Worldview.)
[3] Michael Ramsden, adapted from the video "Disillusionment, Postmodernism, and Re-Birth," Ravi Zacharias Ministries. For more information visit www.rzim.org.
[4] Adapted from the *Understanding the Times* video, "Understanding Postmodernism," J.P. Moreland, Summit Ministries. For more information visit www.summit.org.
[5] Michael Ramsden.
[6] Fred Schwarz, Christian Anti-Communist Crusade Newsletter, October 15, 1982, p. 1.
[7] George Grant, *Trial and Error: The American Civil Liberties Union, and Its Impact on Your Family*, (Brentwood, TN: Wolgemuth and Hyatt, 1989), p. 38-39.
[8] Taken from Dr. D. James Kennedy's television program, The Coral Ridge Hour, 7/13/03.
[9] David Noebel and Chuck Edwards, *Countering Culture*, (Nashville, TN: Broadman and Holman Publishers, 2004), p. 96.

Lesson 3

[1] Vine, p. 158.

Lesson 4

[1] Ibid., p. 468.
[2] R. Russell Bixler, *Faith Works*, (Shippensburg, PA: Treasure House, 1999), p. 14.
[3] Alan Sears and Craig Osten, *The ACLU vs. America*, (Nashville, Broadman, and Holman Publishers, 2005), p. 7, 10, 17.
[4] Ibid., p. 16.
[5] Ibid., p. 84.
[6] Ibid., p. 2, 6.
[7] Ibid., p. 21.
[8] Ibid., p. 4, 5, 125, 158, 161.
[9] Ibid., p. 2, 3, 79, 110, 187.
[10] Ibid., p. 2, 29.
[11] Ibid., p. 174-177, 183-187.

Lesson 5

[1] Vine, p. 583.
[2] Ibid., p. 667.
[3] Ibid., p. 606.
[4] Ibid., p. 166.

Lesson 5 (continued)

[5] Ibid., p. 676.
[6] Michael Youssef, *Know Your Real Enemy*, (Nashville: Thomas Nelson, 1997), p. 170.

Lesson 6

[1] Harris et al, II, 767.

Lesson 7

[1] Vine, p. 136.
[2] Vine, p. 303.
[3] Vine, p. 204.

Lesson 8

[1] J. Dwight Pentecost, *Your Adversary the Devil*, (Grand Rapids, Zondervan, 1969), p. 157.
[2] Vine, p. 13.
[3] Martin R. DeHaan II, *Our Daily Bread*, (Grand Rapids, RBC Ministries, 2003), March 3rd.

Lesson 9

[1] Kathryn Kuhlman, *Great Pilots Are Made in Rough Seas*, The Kathryn Kuhlman Foundation, p. 75.
[2] Vine, p. 622.
[3] Vine, p. 14.
[4] Vine, p.252.
[5] From the 2003 National Survey on Drug Use and Health, Department of Health and Human Services, Substance Abuse and Mental Health Services, Administration Office of Applied Studies (http://oas.samhsa.gov/nhsda/2k3nsduh/2k3Overview.htm#ch1).
[6] NAADAC's Position Statement: Nicotine Dependence (http://naadac.org/documents/display.php?DocumentID=36).
[7] Taken from the video, "Battle Lines in the Drug War," Speaker: Dr. Joseph D. Douglass, Jr. (author of *Red Cocaine: The Drugging of America* ISBN 0-9626646-0-X), John Birch Society, 2001.
[8] Fred Schwarz, Christian Anti-Communist Crusade Newsletter, October 15, 1982, p. 1.
[9] Adapted from Henry J. Rogers, *The Silent War*, (Green Forest, AR, New Leaf Press, 1999).
[10] Ibid., p. 188.
[11] Ibid., p. 86.
[12] "Sexually Oriented Business," National Coalition for the Protection of Children and Families.
[13] Taken from Dr. Jack Hayford's television program, "The Living Way," Program # SC-179.
[14] The video, *A Drug Called Pornography*, United Broadcast Group (from 12:46—21:06 into the program).
[15] Victor B. Cline, *Pornography Effects in Adults and Children*, (New York, Morality in Media, 2002) p. 3-5. To contact Dr. Victor B. Cline: (801) 278-6838; victor1723@comcast.net.
[16] *A Drug Called Pornography*, 50:23 into the video.
[17] Rogers, p. 20.
[18] Hayford.
[19] Hayford.
[20] Hayford.

Lesson 10

[1] Taken from the video of Evangelist Steve Hill's Cincinnati, Ohio crusade (9:51:04—9:54:20 into the video), 9/14/99.

Lesson 11

[1] Taken from Dr. D. James Kennedy's television program, "The Coral Ridge Hour", 7/13/03.
[2] C.S. Lovett, *Dealing with the Devil*, (Baldwin Park, CA, Personal Christianity, 1967).
[3] Vine p. 54.
[4] Vine p. 142.

Lesson 12

[1] Vine, p. 639.
[2] Vine, p. 524.
[3] Vine, p. 164.
[4] Neil T. Anderson, *The Bondage Breaker*, (Eugene, OR: Harvest House, 2000), p. 60.
[5] Vine, p. 88
[6] Adapted from Chuck D. Pierce and Rebecca Wagner Systema, *Ridding Your Home of Spiritual Darkness*, (Colorado Springs: Wagner Publications, 2000), pp. 20-22, 33-41.

Lesson 13

[1] James Orr et al, *International Standard Bible Encyclopeadia*, (1939; rpt. Grand Rapids: Wm. B. Eerdmans, 1974), I, 254.
[2] Stephen L. Hill, *Together in the Harvest Newsletter*, March 2, 1998, p.1.
[3] Jay Passavant, "Stop Strife Before It Starts," *Ministries Today*, January/February 2002, p. 56.
[4] Ibid., pp. 57-60.
[5] Source: www.thinkexist.com (enter under "search": All that is necessary for the triumph of evil).

Lesson 14

[1] Vine, p. 222.
[2] Mary Taylor Previte, *Hungry Ghosts*, (Grand Rapids, Zondervan, 1994).

Lesson 15

[1] Vine, p. 683.
[2] Vine, p. 683.
[3] For beliefs of Orthodox Christianity go to:
www.greatcom.org/resources/handbook_of_todays_religions/01chap03/default.htm.
[4] Vine, p. 303.
[5] Adapted from the video, *My Truth, Your Truth, Whose Truth*, (Colorado Springs, Focus on the Family, 2000).
[6] Dimitra Kessenides, "Angels, Why We Believe," Reader's Digest April, 2006: p. 145.

Lesson 16

[1] John Kilpatrick, *When the Heavens are Brass*, (Shippensburg, PA: Revival Press, 1997), p. vii.
[2] Mark Buntain, *Waging Spiritual Warfare*, (Springfield, MO: Gospel Publishing House, 1996), p.19.
[3] David K. Blomgren, *The Song of the Lord*, (Portland, OR: Bible Temple, 1978), p. 46. (Note: The book, *The Song of the Lord*, will be reprinted and available through Christian Life Publishing, a division of Christian Life Heritage Foundation—bdaehn@hotmail.com.)
[4] Ibid., p. 41.
[5] Harris et al, II, 839.
[6] Blomgren, p. 42.
[7] Ibid.
[8] Ibid.
[9] Ibid.
[10] Ibid.
[11] Line drawing entitled, "Genesis 3:15: The Promise Fulfilled" courtesy of Jim Kessler (www.jimkessler.com).

Appendix A

[1] George A. Barton, *Archaeology and the* Bible, Sixth Edition, (Philadelphia, American Sunday School Union, 1933), p. 496.

[2] Ibid, p. 500.

[3] This section on the Mystery Religions was adapted from S. Angus, *The Mystery Religions*, (New York: Dover Publications Inc., 1975).

[4] "The Enigma of Aztec Sacrifice" by Michael Harner, *Natural History*, April 1977, Vol. 86, No. 4, pp. 46-51.

[5] Ibid.

[6] Sarah Dening, *The Mythology of Sex*, (New York, Macmillan, 1996), p. 54.

[7] Ibid. pp. 49, 54, 56.

[8] John Ankerberg and John Weldon, *Encyclopedia of New Age Beliefs*, (Eugene, OR, Harvest House Publishers, 1996), p. 254; for more information visit www.johnankerberg.com.

[9] "Yoyogi-san, Master of Orgasm" segment within "The Orgasm special: A Real Sex Xtra", HBO (realsex@hbo.com).

[10] Merrill F. Unger, *Biblical Demonology*, (Wheaton, IL, Scripture Press Publications, 1952), p. 46

[11] This section on channeling was adapted from John Ankerberg and John Weldon, *Encyclopedia of New Age Beliefs*, (Harvest House Publishers, Eugene, OR, 1996), pp. 79-112. For more information visit www.johnankerberg.com.

[12] Lewis Spence, *An Encyclopaedia of Occultism*, (Secaucus, NJ, The Citadel Press, 1974), p. 130.

[13] John G. Fuller, *Arigo: Surgeon of the Rusty Knife*, (New York, Thomas Y. Crowell, 1974), pp. 52-62, 121.

[14] Ibid., pp. 5, 6, 76, 128, 157-161.

[15] Ibid., p. 20.

[16] Ibid., pp. 19, 21, 46, 82, 95, 160.

[17] Ibid., pp. 44, 208.

[18] Ibid., pp. 15, 16, 82, 83.

[19] This section on New Age medicine was adapted from John Ankerberg and John Weldon, *Encyclopedia of New Age Beliefs*, (Eugene, OR, Harvest House, 1996), pp. 477-508. For more information, visit www.johnankerberg.com.

[20] John Ankerberg and John Weldon, *Encyclopedia of New Age Beliefs*, (Eugene, OR, Harvest House, 1996), p. 380.

[21] John Ankerberg and John Weldon, *Encyclopedia of New Age Beliefs*, (Eugene, OR, Harvest House, 1996), p. 241; for more information, visit www.johnankerberg.com.

[22] Ibid., p. 380.

[23] This section on meditation was adapted from John Ankerberg and John Weldon, *Encyclopedia of New Age Beliefs*, (Eugene, OR, Harvest House, 1996), pp. 239-241, 379-395. For more information, visit www.johnankerberg.com.

[24] John Ankerberg and John Weldon, *Encyclopedia of New Age Beliefs*, (Eugene, OR, Harvest House, 1996), p. 600; for more information, visit www.johnankerberg.com.

[25] Ibid., 601.

[26] This section on the martial arts was adapted from John Ankerberg and John Weldon, *Encyclopedia of New Age Beliefs*, (Eugene, OR, Harvest House, 1996), pp. 351-368. For more information, visit www.johnankerberg.com.

[27] John Ankerberg and John Weldon, *Encyclopedia of New Age Beliefs*, (Eugene, OR, Harvest House, 1996), p. 343.

[28] This section on mantras and mandalas was adapted from John Ankerberg and John Weldon, *Encyclopedia of New Age Beliefs*, (Eugene, OR, Harvest House, 1996), pp. 341-350. For more information, visit www.johnankerberg.com.

Appendix C

[1] Robert Morey, "Campbellism and 'The Church of Christ,'" *The Truth*, June 1998, pp. 2-3.

[2] Catechism of the Catholic Church, Second Edition, United States Catholic Conference, Inc.—Libreria Editrice Vaticana, 1994, 1997, p. 878.

[3] Ralph Martin, *The Catholic Church at the End of an Age,* (San Francisco: Ignatius Press, 1994), p. 91.

INDEX AND SUMMARY OF SATAN'S TACTICS

(Listed in order as they appear in this book)

The Breastplate of Righteousness: Your Soul and Spirit

The enemy will try to entice you to indulge in something that will give you a "high" for pleasure or as a means of escape from life's problems—knowing we will help him by finding reasons to justify its use. This often results in the chemical addiction of your body, which will enslave your entire trinity, and bring you under the control of evil forces. If you are a Christian, it further defiles the temple of the Holy Spirit, and he succeeds in making you a damaging, ineffective witness for Christ.

◎ *Main Targets:* Your Body, Mind, and Witness.

To divert your love and obedience that should rightfully go to God—to someone or something else via the things of this world, thereby displacing God as the center of your life.

◎ *Main Targets:* Your Love and Affection.

The enemy will attempt to exert peer pressure on you through close acquaintances—intimidating you to conform to the standards of this world system.

◎ *Main Target:* Your Will.

The enemy will visit you in times of spiritual and material prosperity with the hope of catching you with your guard down so as to make conditions right for you to choose to become self-reliant, so eventually you no longer remain dependent on God, thereby forgetting Him and His commandments.

◎ *Main Targets:* Your Dependence on God; Pride; Selfishness.

The enemy will come to you during a time of God's special favor in your life to persuade you to think that you are "above" one of God's laws, and that somehow God will exempt and overlook your disobedience.

◎ *Main Targets:* Your Mind and Pride.

The Helmet of Salvation: Your Mind

The enemy will try to get control of your thought life by delivering blows to your mind. He will do this by offering his suggestions to influence you to think in the soulish realm and live for self-centered interests, causing you to doubt your *"born-again"* experience and your security in Christ.

◎ *Main Target:* Your Mind.

♞ **TACTIC: Procrastination** 178

The enemy will try to persuade you to put off obeying that which you know to be God's will, thereby causing you to sin.

◎ *Main Targets:* Your Love and Will.

♞ **TACTIC: Apathy and Indifference**..182

The enemy will try to extinguish the fire for God in a believer's spirit and breed indifference, apathy, and lukewarmness in its place. His goal is to deplete God's army of laborers, thus reducing effective opposition against his kingdom.

◎ *Main Targets:* Your Love and Will.

♞ **TACTIC: Isolate the Prey** 182

Like a lion stalking its victim, the enemy will try to isolate you by giving you reasons why you should withdraw yourself from going to church and seeking out the support and fellowship of other Christians. This will weaken your spiritual life and make you more vulnerable to his attack.

◎ *Main Target:* Your Mind.

♞ **TACTIC: Unforgiveness**...183

The enemy will try to entrap you by enticing you to have an unforgiving spirit toward someone who has hurt or offended you, cunningly putting you into a position where you will have to forgive that person before God can forgive you. He anticipates that unforgiveness will sever your relationship with God, that person, and/or your church.

◎ *Main Target:* Your Emotions and Pride.

Shoes For Combat: Your Christian Walk and Witness

♞ **TACTIC: Hypocrisy** 201

The enemy will attempt to ruin your testimony and witness for Christ by enticing you to disobey God's Word and walk in a way that is contrary to your words and actions, thereby making you an ineffective witness and a reproach to the cause of Christ.

◎ *Main Target:* Your Witness.

♞ **TACTIC: Infiltration**..202

The enemy will secretly plant his own among God's people to infiltrate God's church, etc. and cause it harm from within.

◎ *Main Targets:* Local Church or Christian Organization.

♞ **TACTIC: Divide and Conquer** 202

The enemy will try to get you to be the source of fighting, strife, and dissension within your group so that you become the cause of division—knowing full well that any nation, city, church, or family divided against itself will become weak, ineffective, and eventually break up and collapse **(Matthew 12:25)**.

◎ *Main Targets:* Unity and Pride.

🐴 **TTACTIC: Accuse Them** 224

The enemy will attempt to incriminate you before God, presenting your faults (true or contrived) and misrepresenting your motives for serving Him. His strategy is to persuade God to temporarily lift His hedge of protection from you (as he did with Job), so that as a result of the suffering and guilt you experience in the testing, you will eventually quit serving Him.

◎ *Main Targets:* Your Character, Motives, Shortcomings, and Will.

➤➤ **Flaming Arrow #3: Discouragement** 232

The enemy will try to bring upon you discouragement, oppression, and despair to cause you to make decisions about God and His will while in this depressed state that are faulty and absurd. His hope is that you will step outside His will or choose to quit serving Him.

➤➤ **Flaming Arrow #4: Fear**..235

Like a lion when it roars, the enemy will attempt to intimidate and immobilize you with fear, terrorizing you in combination with discouragement, in order to drive you to make wrong decisions you would never make in your right mind.

The Sword of the Spirit: The Word of God

🐴 **TACTIC: Make Them Feel Ashamed**...248

The enemy will try to shame you into thinking that if you believe the Bible to be the only divinely inspired, infallible standard of absolute truth that judges everything else, you are an unscholarly, intolerant, hard-hearted, narrow-minded bigot.

◎ *Main Targets:* Your Pride and Confidence.

🐴 **TACTIC: Eliminate the Competition** 250

The enemy will try to seduce you to choose to leave God's will, or he will try to prevent you from entering God's will because he knows the resulting damage God will cause to his kingdom of darkness through you.

◎ *Main Targets:* Your Mind, Will, and Service for God.

🐴 **TACTIC: Deprive God of Worship**...251

The devil will attempt to rob God from receiving your love, worship, and obedience by diverting your devotion that rightfully belongs to Him, to himself through false religions or by setting up an idol in your heart. (See also **Malachi 3:8-9.**)

◎ *Main Targets:* Your Love, Worship, and Obedience.

🐴 **TACTIC: Pry Them Away From God's Will**...251

The enemy will try to get you to miss God's will, or deceive you with the mirage of an easy short cut in obtaining God's will—apart from God's sacrificial ways. By failing to carry out God's plan, God's work suffers a setback and you are robbed of a crown of reward.

◎ *Main Targets:* Your Mind and Will.

TOPICAL INDEX

(See below)

SCRIPTURE INDEX

Other Resources by David Skeba

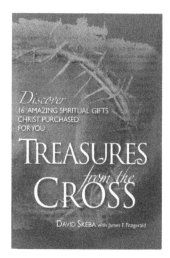

Chapters: 17
Dimensions:
8.5" x 5.5" x .44"
Pages: 166 (Paperback)
ISBN: 978-0-578-02308-3

Treasures from the Cross
By David Skeba with James F. Fitzgerald

What really happened that Friday on a Roman cross 2000 years ago? How does it relate to your life today? Hidden in this mystery are treasures just waiting to be discovered!

Jesus Christ paid the highest price possible to secure for you the greatest treasures of all. *Do you know what these treasures are?* Uncover 16 precious spiritual gifts that are already yours as a believer but may remain hidden from you.

The book reveals **what Jesus accomplished** for us on the cross by **simplifying** theological terms with easy-to-understand language and helpful illustrations. It features **medical insights** into Christ's horrific suffering. And it has broad **cross-denominational appeal**—Protestant, Catholic, and Orthodox.

Of all the vast knowledge that you can obtain in this Information Age, these are the most valuable truths that you could ever know in this life. Discover every treasure Christ has for you, and realize how much God loves you. Your life will never be the same!

Ways to Use It:

For your own personal devotions; or as a Bible study guide for small groups; for Sunday school, or for mid-week church services. The study can be configured by the leader to fit their number of classes.

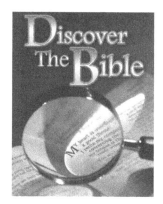

Discover the Bible Online Courses

Have you ever wanted to learn more about the Bible but felt that taking an accredited college course was just not possible—perhaps due to lack of time to devote to it, its high cost, or because it is too scholarly, intimidating, and labor intensive?

Did you ever wish that simplified Bible courses were available to fit your busy schedule? Courses that are brief in duration (from 4 to 6 lessons) and that were about 30 minutes per lesson, as well as minimal in cost? Then Discover the Bible online courses are for you.

In an effort to make it easier for you to learn more about God and the Bible, and meet the critical need of addressing Biblical illiteracy in our day, we are offering **non-accredited** Bible courses on DiscoverMinistries.com within the Discover the Bible section. These online courses will be targeted for Christians at the Beginner, Intermediate, and Advanced levels.

We will launch the site with the School of Prayer, Knowing God, and Bible 101 with much more to be added. Some of the courses will require a textbook to be purchased, but many courses will simply use your Bible. Check it out at www.DiscoverTheBible.net, and try our **free sample**.

Additional copies of this book and other
book titles from DESTINY IMAGE are
available at your local bookstore.

Call toll-free: 1-800-722-6774.

Send a request for a catalog to:

Destiny Image® Publishers, Inc.

P.O. Box 310
Shippensburg, PA 17257-0310

*"Speaking to the Purposes of God for This
Generation and for the Generations to Come."*

**For a complete list of our titles,
visit us at www.destinyimage.com.**